Multiregional Economic Development in China

Rongxing Guo · Hao Gui
Luc Changlei Guo

Multiregional Economic Development in China

Springer

Rongxing Guo
Regional Science Association
Peking University
Beijing
China

Luc Changlei Guo
Xinhua Daxin
Shenzhen
China

Hao Gui
Shenhua Group
Beijing
China

ISBN 978-3-662-46619-3 ISBN 978-3-662-46620-9 (eBook)
DOI 10.1007/978-3-662-46620-9

Library of Congress Control Number: 2015937524

Springer Heidelberg New York Dordrecht London

Printed on acid-free paper

Springer-Verlag GmbH Berlin Heidelberg is part of Springer Science+Business Media
(www.springer.com)

Notes on the Text

Most of China's provinces (autonomous regions and municipalities that are under the direct control of the central government), which are the average size and scale of a European country in population or land area, are considerable political and economic systems in their own right. Indeed, the Chinese economy is far too huge and spatially complicated and diversified to be misinterpreted. The only feasible approach to analyzing it is, therefore, to divide it into smaller geographical elements through which one can have a better insight into the spatial mechanisms and regional characteristics.

This book provides, in an easy-to-use format, a broad collection of data and information on China's 31 provinces and its interprovincial economic linkages. It is a resource book that profiles the geography, demography, and economy for each of these provinces. The materials presented in this book, which are gathered from a variety of sources and some of which (especially those in Chap. 2) are not easily found in English media, will be of great value to students, researchers, business and government agencies, and news media who are interested in either individual provinces or China as a whole.

In this book, the geographical scope of China covers only mainland China, although Hong Kong, Macau, and Taiwan are also mentioned in a few cases. Unless stated otherwise, we will use the term "province" to denote all of the three kinds of administrative divisions (provinces, autonomous regions, and municipalities directly under the central government).

All entries are organized alphabetically in Chaps. 1 and 2. In addition, in Chap. 2 only one entry for the narrative of each pair of provinces will be included, even though actually there are two entries for the pair. For example, when addressing the economic linkages between Anhui and Zhejiang provinces, we have two entries: "Anhui–Zhejiang" and "Zhejiang–Anhui." To save space, we will only include the "Anhui–Zhejiang" entry in the text and the reader who intends to look for the "Zhejiang–Anhui" entry will be stipulated to find the "Anhui–Zhejiang" entry automatically. As a result, Chap. 2's total entries, as shown in the "Table of Contents," are summed to 30 + 29 + 28 + 27 + ··· + 3 + 2 + 1 = 465.[1]

The maps of the administrative divisions of all the 31 provinces in Chap. 1 are created by Luc Guo who has also collected and translated (from Chinese into English) the major portion of Chap. 2. Except the maps of Beijing, Chongqing, Shanghai, and Tianjin, all the other maps are redrawn based on the files from the Wikimedia Commons—a freely licensed media file repository (the copyright holders have either released these maps into the public domain and or agreed to grant anyone the right to use these maps; see http://commons.wikimedia.org/wiki/Main_Page for more information). Of course, our maps have higher resolutions than their original versions.

The data on the natural, geographical, and environmental features of each province, cited in Chap. 1 of this book, are based on China's national online news service network (www.china.org.cn) and other miscellaneous news clippings available at the province's official Web site. The data on the socioeconomic features of each province are based on the province's 2000 and 2010 statistical yearbooks (published in 2001 and 2011, respectively). The monetary values are measured at current prices. The Chinese currency is renminbi (RMB). The exchange rate of the RMB yuan to the US dollar was approximately 8.5:1 and 6.8:1 as of 2000 and 2010, respectively. It was further appreciated to 6.3:1 in 2012 when this book was compiled.

The sources for the data cited in the "Quick facts" of Chap. 2 are described in Chap. 3. The narratives relating to China's interprovincial cooperation and development experiences, reported in Chap. 2, are collected and compiled from various sources: (i) the Web site of and the official documents released by each of China's 31 provinces; (ii) the documents and news briefings released by each province's local governments, chambers of commerce, and major enterprises; and (iii) other miscellaneous news clippings collected by the authors from such channels as local TVs and the Internet. Since the interprovincial entries of all the 31 provinces are summed to as large as 465 entries, it took us about six months (i.e., from June to November 2012) to collect and compile all these narratives. Except for a few cases, most of the materials of these entries cover the time period from January 2000 to June/November 2012 (with those of the first and last entries being as of June and November 2012, respectively).

The methodology for the index of each province's industrial comparative advantages, reported in Tables 1.2, 1.4, 1.6, 1.8, 1.10, 1.12, 1.14, 1.16, 1.18, 1.20, 1.22, 1.24, 1.26, 1.28, 1.30, 1.32, 1.34, 1.36, 1.38, 1.40, 1.42, 1.44, 1.46, 1.48, 1.50, 1.52, 1.54, 1.56, 1.58, 1.60, and 1.62 of Chap. 1, is included in Appendix A. And the measurement of the index of interprovincial ethnic linkages, reported in Chaps. 2 and 3, is described in Appendix B.

February 2015 Rongxing Guo

[1]Mathematically, this can also be formulated as $C_{31}^{2} = \frac{31!}{2!(31-2)!} = \frac{31 \times 30}{2} = 465$.

Contents

Abbreviations

AQTS	Administration of Quality and Technical Supervision
ASEAN	Association of Southeast Asian Nations
CCP	Chinese Communist Party
CCPCC	Chinese Communist Party Central Committee
CNPC	China National Petroleum Corporation
CPPCC	Chinese People's Political Consultative Congress
DRC	Development and Reform Commission
EU	European Union
FDA	Food and Drug Administration
FDI	Foreign direct investment
GRP	Gross regional product
ICBC	Industrial and Commerce Bank of China
IQB	Inspection and Quarantine Bureau
IT	Information technology
MNC	Multi-national Company
PCSC	People's Congress Standing Committee
PPCC	People's Political Consultative Congress
PRC	People's Republic of China
R&D	Research and development
SAR	Special Administrative Region
SASAC	State-owned Assets Supervision and Administration Commission
SOE	State-owned Enterprise
TGPCC	Three Gorges Project Construction Committee of the State Council
UNESCO	United Nations Educational, Scientific, and Cultural Organization
XPCC	Xinjiang Production and Construction Corps

Units of Measurement

°C	Centigrade
¥	Yuan (unit of Chinese currency, renminbi)
m^3	Cubic meter
cm	Centimeter
ha	Hectare
km	Kilometer
km^2	Square kilometer
kW	Kilowatt
kW h	Kilowatt hour
m	Meter
mm	Millimeter
mu	Chinese unit of land area (1 mu equals about 667 m^2)
cm^2	Square centimeter
m^2	Square meter

Key Terms

Chinese Communist Party (CCP): The CCP has been virtually the most important body of power in China and holds real political power in China's de facto one-party state. The name "communist party" originates from the 1848 tract Manifesto of the Communist Party by Karl Marx and Friedrich Engels. A political party described as a communist party includes those that advocate the application of the social principles of communism through a communist form of government. Nevertheless, after over three decades of reform, the CCP is no longer the single representative of poor, working-class people; rather, it has also become the representative of the economic and cultural elites in China.

CCP Central Committee (CCPCC): In China, the CCP's organizations run in parallel with those of the government at all levels. At the bottom of this pyramid are "primary party organizations" in workplaces and villages. The CCP's structure is characterized by "democratic centralism" (minzhu jizhong), a system whereby the individual party member is subordinate to the organization, and where minority groups or opinions are subordinate to the wishes of the majority, embodied by the CCPCC. Seated at Zhongnan Sea in central Beijing, Political Bureau (PB) is the standing organ of the CCPCC. The PB's members and its more powerful standing members can be frequently found in the evening news of China's official media, including the CCTV.

People's Congress Standing Committee (PCSC): The People's Congress is the supreme legislative organ of each province and of China as a whole. The provincial congress representatives, coming from different regions and sectors, meet annually (usually in spring) in the province's capital to discuss provincial affairs, to approve those who are recommended by the provincial CCP committee as provincial government officials, and to issue provincial laws and regulations. During the period of time when the People's Congress is not held, the PCSC represents the People's Congress and the PCSC members convene all meetings.

People's Political Consultative Congress (PPCC): Under the leadership of the CCP, the PPCC—an institution similar to the Senate in the USA—consists of representatives of the CCP, several democratic parties, democrats with no party affiliations, various people's organizations and ethnic groups, and other specially invited individuals. In China, the PPCC is organized via two levels—national and provincial. The primary functions of the provincial PPCC are to conduct political consultations and democratic supervisions, and to discuss and manage provincial affairs. During the period of time when the PPCC is not held, the Standing Committee of the PCSC represents the PPCC and the Standing members of the PPCC convene all meetings.

Gross Regional Product (GRP): It is also called regional gross domestic product (GDP) and refers to the final products at market prices produced by all resident units in a region during a certain period of time. It is expressed from three different perspectives—namely value, income, and products. GRP from its value perspective refers to the total value of all goods and services produced by all resident units during a certain period of time, minus the total value of input of goods and services of the nature of non-fixed assets—in other words, it is the sum of the value-added of all resident units. GRP from the perspective of income includes the primary income created by all resident units and distributed to resident and nonresident units during a given period of time. GRP from the perspective of products refers to the value of all goods and services for final demand by all resident units plus the net export of goods and services during a given period of time. In the practice of national accounting, GRP is calculated from three approaches, namely the production approach, the income approach, and the expenditure approach, which reflect GDP and its composition from different angles.

Map

The provincial administrative divisions of China (*Note* This is the official version published by the Chinese government. Land and waters also include those that are in disputes or claimed by other countries.)

Chapter 1
An Introduction to Provinces A to Z

Anhui

[Quick Facts: Official name: Anhui Province; Capital: Hefei; Land area: 139,400 km^2; Population density: 440/km^2; Major ethnic groups: Han, Hui, Miao, Manchu, Zhuang]

Anhui is a province of the PRC. Its name derives from the names of two cities—Anqing and Huizhou (now Huangshan City)—both of which are located in south Anhui. The abbreviation for the province is "Wan", because in ancient times there was a state called Wan in areas around the mountain called Wan in the province.

Situated in the southeast of China, and across the basins of the Yangtze and the Huai rivers, Anhui Province shares borders with Jiangsu Province to the east, Zhejiang Province to the southeast, Jiangxi Province to the south, Hubei Province to the southwest, Henan Province to the northwest and Shandong Province to the north. It extends about 570 km from north to south, and 450 km from west to east, with an area accounting for 1.45 % of the country.

There are 17 prefecture-level administrative divisions in Anhui, which are subdivided into 105 county-level divisions (44 districts, 5 county-level cities and 56 counties). Those are in turn divided into 1845 township-level divisions (972 towns, 634 townships, 9 ethnic townships and 230 sub-districts).

R. Guo et al., *Multiregional Economic Development in China*,
DOI 10.1007/978-3-662-46620-9_1

Topographically, Anhui Province is quite diverse. The north is part of the North China Plain, while the north-central areas are part of the Huai River watershed. Both of these regions are very flat and densely populated. The land becomes more uneven further south, with the Dabie Mountains occupying much of southwestern Anhui and a series of hills and ranges cutting through the southeast. The Yangtze River finds its way through south Anhui between these two mountainous regions. Major rivers include the Huai in the north and the Yangtze in the south. Lake Chaohu, with an area of about 800 km^2, is the largest lake and is located in the center of the province. The southeastern part of Anhui near the Yangtze River has many lakes as well.

With the Yangtze and Huai rivers running through the province from the west to the east, Anhui is divided into three geographical regions, including Huaibei (north of the Huai), Jianghuai (between the Yangtze and the Huai), and Jiangnan (south of the Yangtze). The north of the Huai, part of the North China Plain, is a vast expanse of flatland. The middle area between the Yangtze and the Huai is a chain of undulating hills. The lands by the two sides of the Yangtze and around Lake Chaohu are low and flat, belonging to the well-known Middle-Lower Yangtze River Plain. The south mainly comprises hills.

Generally, the province can be divided into five topographical zones: the plain north of the Huai River, the hilly land between the Huai and Yangtze rivers, the Dabieshan mountain area of West Anhui, the plains along the Yangtze River and the hilly area in southern Anhui. Located in the transition region of the warm-temperate zone and subtropical zone, the climate is warm and humid with distinct seasons. The province's annual rainfall and weather in general varies greatly, with frequent spring droughts and summer floods.

Anhui differs in climate from north to south. The north is more temperate and has more clear-cut seasons. The average annual temperature of the province is 14–17 °C. January temperatures average −1 to 2 °C north of the Huai, and 0–3 °C south of the Huai. In July, temperatures average 27 °C or above. The average frost-free period lasts 200–250 days. Plum rains (a term used in some Chinese provinces to denote the rainy season) occur in June and July and may cause flooding. The annual average rainfalls are 800–1800 mm. Plum rains occur in June and July and may cause flooding.

Anhui has a variety of natural resources. It has rich mineral reserves and the deposits of iron, copper, pyrite, limestone and alunite are among the top five in the nation. In addition, these resources are concentrated in distribution. Among the 138 discovered minerals, 104 have had their reserves proved. Major production sites of minerals in the province include iron in Ma'anshan, coal in Huainan and copper in Tongling, and there are industries related to these natural resources.

Covering an area of 4.33 million hectare/40,907 km^2 of fertile farmland and benefiting from the mild climate, Anhui province is rich in agricultural resources. Its major crops include rice, wheat and sweet potato. Many of its agricultural products are also famous. These include grapes, pears, pomegranates, tea and crabs. Agriculture varies according to the climate zones that the province crosses. Wheat and sweet potatoes are grown on the northern side of the Huai River, while rice and wheat are on the southern side. The total water reserve of Anhui is about 68 billion cubic meter. The Bishihang Irrigation and the Simashan Diversion and Irrigation are two key irrigation projects of the province. Forested areas amounted to 3.6 million hectare as of the end of 2005.

Anhui is rich in plants and animals. It has 1300 woody plants and 2100 herbaceous plants. Among its more than 500 species of animals, 54 are listed as rare and under state protection, including the Yangtze alligator and the white-fin dolphin.

As of 2005, the province had established 31 nature reserves, including 5 at the national level, 25 at the provincial level and 1 at the county level. Its principal tourism sites include ancient villages in southern Anhui (e.g. Xidi and Hongcun [World Heritage Site]); Mount Huangshan (World Heritage Site); Mount Jiuhua;

Mount Qiyun; Mount Tianzhu; the old town of Tunxi; Mount Langya; Zuiweng Pavilion, named after the poet Ouyang Xiu (AD 1007–1072); Lake Chao; Taiji Cave (the longest karst cave in East China); and the Zhenfeng Pagoda (built in the Ming Dynasty [AD 1368–1644] in Anqing City).

In 2010, Anhui's nominal GRP was ¥1.23 trillion (about US$181.1 billion) and per capita was ¥20,888 (about US$2400). It is considered to be a mid-size province in terms of economic output. Compared with its more successful neighbors to the east, Zhejiang and Jiangsu, Anhui has lagged markedly behind in economic development, with a GRP per capita around one-third of those two provinces. There is great regional disparity as well. Regions such as Hefei, Wuhu and Ma'anshan have benefited from their closeness to the Yangtze River and so are significantly wealthier than the rest of the province due to their industrial and manufacturing industries (Table 1.1).

Anhui's GRP is largely driven by fixed-asset investment. This, coupled with the province's pool of cheap labor and the establishment of an export processing zone

Table 1.1 Demographic and socioeconomic profile: Anhui

Indicator	2000	2010
Population (thousands)	59,860	59,567
Illiteracy rate of population aged 15 or over (%)	10.06	8.34
GRP (¥ billions)	303.82	1235.93
Composition of GRP (%)		
Primary sector	24.1	14.0
Secondary sector	42.7	52.1
Tertiary sector	33.2	33.9
Fixed asset investment (¥ billions)	80.40	1154.29
Status of foreign-funded enterprises		
Number of registered enterprises	2216	5633
Total investment (US$ millions)	9144	30,324
Registered capital (US$ millions)	5868	17,349
Foreign trade (US$ millions)		
Export	2119	10,927
Import	1570	12,453
Sales of consumer goods (¥ billions)	105	420
Per capita annual disposable income of urban residents (¥)	5293.55	15,788.17
Engle's coefficient (%)	45.71	37.96
Per capita annual net income of rural residents (¥)	1934.57	5285.17
Engle's coefficient (%)	37.94	40.69
Number of patent applications granted	1482	16,012
Inventions	104	1111
Utility models	894	8839
Designs	484	6062

Note All monetary values are measured at current prices. *Source* Anhui Statistical Yearbook, 2001 and 2011

Table 1.2 Anhui's comparative (dis)advantage indexes by sector, 2010

Sector	Index
Agriculture, forestry, animal husbandry and fishery	0.57
Mining	2.00
Manufacturing	0.73
Production and distribution of electricity, gas and water	1.08
Construction	1.16
Transport, storage and post	0.84
Information transmission, computer service and software	0.72
Wholesale and retail trades	0.91
Hotels and catering services	0.62
Financial intermediation	1.09
Real estate	0.81
Leasing and business services	0.52
Scientific research, technical services and geological prospecting	0.80
Management of water conservancy, environment and public facilities	1.02
Services to households and other services	0.31
Education	1.34
Health, social security and social welfare	1.22
Culture, sports and entertainment	0.91
Public management and social organization	1.14

Notes All the sectors included in this table are determined according to China's official definitions and for urban areas only. Numerals greater than, equal to and less than one indicate that the province's sectors have advantages, no apparent (dis)advantages and disadvantages, respectively
Source Calculated by the authors based on China Statistical Yearbook, 2011. See Appendix A for a detailed methodological description

in Hefei, which will offer numerous incentives (e.g. tax rebates and exemptions for manufacturers to set up shop) will likely further increase the growth of Anhui's more industrialized regions.

Anhui has several pillar industries—equipment manufacturing, metallurgy, coal exploration and chemicals. Its equipment manufacturing industry focuses on the fabrication of engineering machinery, electrical appliances and automobiles, with Wuhu City being one of the major air-conditioner production bases in China. It is highly concentrated in terms of the industrial group of products and has strongly competitive brands. However, there is a low level of creativity and high energy consumption in the industry. Examples of famous manufacturing firms in the region are Anhui HELI Corp (the nation's top company for forklift manufacturing), Meiling Corp (the leading enterprise in the China's refrigeration industry) and Chery Auto (a major enterprise in the country's automobile industry). The metallurgy industry in Anhui focuses on steel and copper. The output of refined copper products from Ma'anshan, Wuhu and Tongling accounts for one-third of the nation's total. Key enterprises in this industry are Masteel Group Corp and Tongling Nonferrous Metals Group Corp, the country's seventh largest steel producer and the world's eighth copper refiner.

Anhui's major exports include mechanical and electrical products, spinning- and fabric-and related products, and land vehicles. The major imports are metal ore, metal waste material and special industrial machinery. Chile, Japan, Australia, Germany and Brazil are among the major import sources, while the US, Japan, South Korea, Hong Kong and Russia are the key export destinations.

The province receives large amounts of FDI (more than half of the total) from Hong Kong. Other major sources are the US, Taiwan, Singapore and Japan. Manufacturing is the key recipient of FDI in Anhui. Energy supply, real estate, mining and accommodation are other noteworthy recipients.

As of 2010, compared with those of other provinces, "mining", "education" and "health, social security and social welfare" were relatively strong, while "services to households and other services", "leasing and business services" and "agriculture, forestry, animal husbandry and fishery" were relatively weak sectors (see Table 1.2).

Beijing

[Quick Facts: Official name: Beijing Municipality; Capital: Beijing; Land area: 16,807 km^2; Population density: 1167/km^2; Major ethnic groups: Han, Manchu, Hui, Mongol, Korean]

Beijing is a province-level municipality of the PRC and is also the capital of China. It is the country's second largest city by urban population (after Shanghai) and is the country's political and cultural center. It is home to the headquarters of most of China's largest state-owned companies. Beijing is a major transportation hub in the national highway, expressway, railway and high-speed rail network. Its Capital International Airport is the second busiest in the world by passenger traffic.

Over the past 3000 years, Beijing has adopted numerous other names, including Ji, Yanjing, Youzhou, Nanjing, Zhongdu, Dadu, Cambaluc and Beiping. In AD 1421, when Emperor Yongle moved the capital of the Ming Dynasty north from Nanjing in Jiangsu Province, he renamed the city Beijing. From the Chinese characters, Beijing means, literally, the "northern capital". This official English spelling is based on the pinyin romanization of the two characters. In 1928, when the capital of the Republic of China was moved to Nanjing, the city was renamed Beiping, meaning "north peace". In 1949 it became the capital of the PRC. An older English spelling, Peking, was applied worldwide before the 1970s and is still occasionally used today.

Located at 39°56′N and 116°20′E, on the northwest edge of the North China Plain, Beijing adjoins Tianjin Municipality to the east and Hebei Province to the north, west and south. The Bohai Sea lies about 150 km to the southeast. The urban area of Beijing is in the south-central part of the municipality and occupies a small but expanding area. It spreads out in bands of concentric ring roads, of which the fifth and outermost, the Sixth Ring Road, passes through several satellite towns. Tian'anmen Square is at the center of Beijing, directly to the south of the Forbidden City, the former residence of the emperors of China. To the west of Tian'anmen is

Zhongnanhai, home to the paramount leaders of the PRC. Running through central Beijing from east to west is Chang'an Avenue, one of the city's main thoroughfares.

The municipality currently comprises 16 administrative subdivisions, including 14 prefectural-level urban and suburban districts and two rural sub-prefectural-level counties. On July 1, 2010, Chongwen and Xuanwu districts were merged into Dongcheng and Xicheng districts, respectively. The districts and counties are further subdivided into 273 lower third-level administrative units at the township level: 119 towns, 24 townships, 5 ethnic townships and 125 sub-districts. Towns within the municipality but outside the urban area include (but are not limited to) Changping, Huairou, Miyun, Liangxiang, Liulimiao, Tongzhou, Yizhuang, Tiantongyuan, Huilongguan, Beiyuan and Xiaotangshan. Several placenames in Beijing end with mén, meaning "gate", as they were the locations of gates along the former Beijing city wall. Other placenames end in cūn, meaning "village", as they were originally villages outside the city wall.

Beijing Municipality is situated at the northern tip of the roughly triangular North China Plain, which opens to the south and east of the city. Mountains stand in the west, north and northeast, with an average elevation of 1000–1500 m, accounting for the 10,417.5 km^2 of mountain areas (or 62 % of its territory). In the southeast lies the vast North China Plain of 6390.3 km, with an average altitude of 20–60 m above sea level. The 2303 m high Mount Lingshan on the border between the municipality and Hebei Province is the highest peak of the city. The Great Wall of China stretches across the northern part of Beijing.

Five major rivers flow across the city, including the Chaobai River in the east and the Yongding River in the west. Most of Beijing's rivers originate from the city's northern mountain areas and, after winding southeastwards across the plain area, they flow into the Bohai Sea. The 174 km long Yongding River, running through southwest Beijing, is the city's biggest river. It also has several dozen lakes (e.g. the Kunming, the Yuyuantan, the Beihai, the Zhonghai, the Nanhai, the Qianhai, the Houhai, the Xihai, the Longtan, the Taoranting and the Zizhuyuan). Miyun Reservoir, built on the upper reaches of the Chaobai River, is Beijing's largest reservoir and is crucial to its water supply. In addition, the city is also the northern terminus of the Grand Canal, which was built across the North China Plain to Hangzhou.

The municipality has four clear-cut seasons: short spring and autumn and long winter and summer. It has a rather dry, monsoon-influenced humid continental climate characterized by hot, humid summers and cold, windy, dry winters. The average annual temperature is 13 °C (averaging 25.2 °C in July, the hottest month, and −3.7 °C in January, the coldest month). The average annual rainfall is 507.7 mm (with the great majority of it falling in the summer) and the frost-free period lasts 180–200 days.

Beijing's mountain areas produce various minerals (e.g. coal and iron ores) and building materials (e.g. granite and marble). The forest coverage had reached 50.5 % by the end of 2005. There are now 20 nature reserves covering an area of 1342 km^2 and 7 ecological demonstration zones covering an area of 9246 km^2. Human activities began in the Beijing area about 0.5 million years ago. The recorded history of Beijing as a city dates back more than 3000 years, of which Beijing has served as a national capital for more than 700 years, being one of China's seven great ancient capitals. In this famed historical city, cultural heritage sites and scenic spots are found everywhere. Ancient palace groups, temples, parks, ancient pagodas with rock carvings, imperial gardens and tombs, and former residences of historical individuals throng the city side by side with the modern buildings of museums and memorial halls.

Beijing Municipality is not only the cultural and political center of China but also home to over 100 of China's largest companies. Its economy is based on the high-end manufacturing and service sectors, particularly the tourism, media and IT industries. Although it does not have any exchanges for securities or other financial derivatives, the capital is where the country's market watchdogs and regulators are based. Alongside Shanghai, Beijing attracts the Chinese or Asia-Pacific headquarters of many multi-national companies (MNCs).

As Chinese enterprises continue to springboard their businesses onto the global platform, Beijing's economic environment has projected an optimistic outlook over the past decade. In 2010, its GRP reached ¥787.0 billion (about US$100.3 billion). Meanwhile, its per capita GRP amounted to ¥50,467 (about US$6428) in 2010. The service sector contributed the most to the municipal's GRP, accounting for 70.0 % of the overall GRP in 2010. Meanwhile, the agricultural and industry sector made up 0.9 and 24.0 % of the GRP, respectively (see Table 1.3).

As manpower, land costs and environmental pressure have been relatively higher than those of other Chinese cities, Beijing has placed its focus on higher-value-added

Table 1.3 Demographic and socioeconomic profile: Beijing

Indicator	2000	2010
Population (thousands)	13,820	19,619
Illiteracy rate of population aged 15 or over (%)	4.23	1.70
GRP (¥ billions)	247.88	1411.36
Composition of GRP (%)		
Primary sector	3.6	0.9
Secondary sector	38.1	24.0
Tertiary sector	58.3	75.1
Fixed asset investment (¥ billions)	128.05	540.30
Status of foreign-funded enterprises		
Number of registered enterprises	8495	24,853
Total investment (US$ millions)	40,246	119,206
Registered capital (US$ millions)	21,738	71,477
Foreign trade (US$ millions)		
Export	7667	30,717
Import	16,577	79,977
Sales of consumer goods (¥ billions)	144	623
Per capita annual disposable income of urban residents (¥)	10,349.69	29,072.93
Engle's coefficient (%)	36.30	32.07
Per capita annual net income of rural residents (¥)	4604.55	13,262.29
Engle's coefficient (%)	36.47	32.36
Number of patent applications granted	5905	33,511
Inventions	1074	11,209
Utility models	3463	16,579
Designs	1368	5723

Note All monetary values are measured at current prices. *Source* Beijing Statistical Yearbook, 2001 and 2011

manufacturing. Electronics manufacturing, such as that of mobile phones and computers, is the biggest industry in Beijing. Semiconductor Manufacturing International Corporation, the largest semiconductor foundry in China and one of the leading foundries in the world, invested in a 12-in. wafer plant in the Beijing Economic and Technological Development Zone. Beijing Oriental Electronics has also established the largest thin-film transistor liquid-crystal display manufacturer in China within the zone. Other leading electronics manufacturers in the area include Nokia and Lenovo.

Beijing is also one of China's biggest automobile producers. Driven by rising sales of automobiles, its automobile industry has grown rapidly in the past decade. Beijing Hyundai (a joint venture between Beijing Automotive Industry Holding [BAIC] and Hyundai Motor of South Korea) and Beijing Benz-DaimlerChrysler Automotive (a joint venture between BAIC and DaimlerChrysler AG) are two of the major passenger car makers in the municipality.

Within the manufacturing sector, Beijing Shougang Group had a leading role in the iron and steel industry in China. However, in an effort to reduce the pollution levels in the capital for the 2008 Olympic Games, the government imposed sanctions on coal-burning heavy industries, resulting in the relocation of their facilities. All of Shougang's steel production was thus closed in 2010. In the meantime, Beijing's service sector has achieved rapid growth. Within its retail industry, many new shopping and commercial districts have emerged in various districts, including Chaoyang, Haidian, Wangfujing, Xidan and Qianmen.

Beijing has placed more effort into R&D than the other municipalities. The city's investment in this area has contributed to more than 5 % of its GRP. Meanwhile, gross added value from the high-tech industry has accounted for a substantial portion of its overall gross industrial added value.

As part of Beijing's 11th five-year plan, the government also prioritized the development of a cultural and creative industry. This is to function as a pillar of the region's growing economy and reinvent its long-standing industries, which have been facing stronger domestic and overseas competition. Apart from a Beijing Creative Center in the Dongcheng District, five other districts have plans to develop the Shijingshan Digital Amusement Base, Zhongguncun Pioneering Base, the National New Media Base, Deshengyuan Creative Base of Industrial Design and the Dashanzi Arts Center. As the capital of China, Beijing also attracts overseas and local tourists, bringing in substantial revenues for its municipal government.

During recent decades, Beijing's foreign trade has experienced rapid growth. Its largest export market was Hong Kong, followed by the US and Japan, while imports were mainly from (in order of import volume) Japan, Germany and the US.

Nearly half of the world's 500 largest enterprises had placed investments in Beijing. Its foreign investments were mainly channeled into the service industry, where the amount of utilized FDI in the service sector accounted for more than

50 % of its utilized FDI. Within the sector, utilized FDI in leasing and commercial services took the largest share, followed by the real-estate sector. Hong Kong contributed the most to Beijing's overseas investment market. It invested heavily in the area's property sector, with an influx of Hong Kong developers, such as New World Development, Sun Hung Kai, Kerry Group and Cheung Kong, developing shopping centers, commercial complexes and residential buildings.

Furthermore, about 200 MNCs, such as SUN, NEC and Motorola, have developed R&D centers in the city. With the growing affluence of its residents and the development of new shopping and commercial districts in various areas of the capital (e.g. Chaoyang, Haidian, Wangfujing, Xidan and Qianmen), many foreign chain supermarkets have also set foot in its retail market. These include Carrefour, Makro and Ito Yokado.

As of 2010, compared with those of other provinces, "leasing and business services", "information transmission, computer service and software", "scientific research, technical services and geological prospecting", "real estate", "hotels and

Table 1.4 Beijing's comparative (dis)advantage index by sector, 2010

Sector	Index
Agriculture, forestry, animal husbandry and fishery	0.17
Mining	0.16
Manufacturing	0.56
Production and distribution of electricity, gas and water	0.44
Construction	0.63
Transport, storage and post	1.63
Information transmission, computer service and software	4.53
Wholesale and retail trades	2.09
Hotels and catering services	2.70
Financial intermediation	1.17
Real estate	3.01
Leasing and business services	5.06
Scientific research, technical services and geological prospecting	3.16
Management of water conservancy, environment and public facilities	0.81
Services to households and other services	2.50
Education	0.52
Health, social security and social welfare	0.66
Culture, sports and entertainment	2.34
Public management and social organization	0.58

Notes All the sectors included in this table are determined according to China's official definitions and for urban areas only. Numerals greater than, equal to and less than one indicate that the province's sectors have advantages, no apparent (dis)advantages and disadvantages, respectively
Source Calculated by the authors based on China Statistical Yearbook, 2011. See Appendix A for a detailed methodological description

catering services", "services to households and other services", "culture, sports and entertainment" and "wholesale and retail trades" were relatively strong, while "mining", "agriculture, forestry, animal husbandry and fishery" and "production and distribution of electricity, gas and water" were relatively weak sectors (see Table 1.4).

Chongqing

[Quick Facts: Official name: Chongqing Municipality; Capital: Chongqing; Land area: 82,300 km^2; Population density: 350/km^2; Major ethnic groups: Han, Tujia, Miao, Hui, Yi]

Chongqing is a province-level municipality of the PRC. A major city in Southwest China, its provincial status was approved at the Fifth Session of the Eighth National People's Congress on March 14, 1997, succeeding its status as a sub-provincial administration of Sichuan Province. Administratively, it is one of the PRC's four provincial-level municipalities (the other three are Beijing, Shanghai and Tianjin).

Chongqing (which means "double celebration") received its current name in the Song Dynasty (AD 960–1279) when Emperor Guangzong renamed the city Chongqing Fu. "Yu" is the official abbreviation of the name of Chongqing. The shortened version derives from the old name of part of the Jialing River that runs through Chongqing and feeds the Yangtze River.

Chongqing lies in the transitional area between the Qinghai–Tibet Plateau and the plain on the middle and lower reaches of the Yangtze River. Jialing River passes through the city into the Yangtze River, lending Chongqing the name of "a city on rivers". Located at the northern end of the Yunnan-Guizhou Plateau and the eastern limits of the Sichuan Basin, it is intersected by the Jialing River and the upper reaches of the Yangtze. Chongqing is also known as "a city of mountains" as it is surrounded by the Daba Mountains to the north, the Wushan Mountains to the east, the Wuling Mountains to the Southeast and the Dalou Moutains to the south. Geographically, it shares provincial borders with Hubei (in the east), Hunan (in the southeast), Guizhou (in the south), Sichuan (in the west) and Shaanxi (in the north).

The boundaries of Chongqing Municipality reach much farther into the city's hinterland than the boundaries of the other provincial-level municipalities of China, and much of its administrative area is still rural. It is divided into 38 subdivisions consisting of 19 districts, 15 counties and 4 autonomous counties.

The municipality has a monsoon-influenced humid subtropical climate and experiences very humid conditions for most of the year. Its average annual temperature is around 18 °C. Known as one of the "Three Furnaces" of China, along with Wuhan and Nanjing, its summers are long and among the hottest and most humid in China, with highs of 33–34 °C in July and August. However, conditions are cooler in the southeast part of the municipality due to the higher elevations there. Winters are short and somewhat mild, but damp and overcast. Chongqing is also known as the "Fog City", and a thick layer of fog shrouds it during the spring and autumn. The city's location in the Sichuan Basin causes it to have one of the lowest sunshine totals annually in China.

Chongqing is rich in mineral resources. Some 75 types of minerals have been discovered and 40 have yielded reserves. These include coal, natural gas, manganese, mercury, aluminum, marble, limestone and strontium. The region leads China and ranks second in the world in deposits of strontium. It is one of the nine largest iron and steel centers in China and one of the three major aluminum producers.

Important manufacturers include Chongqing Iron and Steel Company and South West Aluminum, which is Asia's largest aluminum plant. The municipality has been selected as the site of a refinery operated by China National Petroleum Corporation (CNPC, the parent company of PetroChina) to process imported crude oil from the Sino-Burma pipeline. The pipeline, after it is finished, will eventually run from Sittwe (in Myanmar's western coast) through Kunming in Yunnan Province before reaching Chongqing and it will provide China with fuels sourced from Myanmar, the Middle East and Africa.

Agriculture remains significant in area. Rice and fruit (especially oranges) are the area's main produce. Biological resources are also plentiful. Specifically, Chongqing has more than 2000 species of vascular plants, 380 animal species and 120 river fish. It has crisscrossing rivers and the water resources can generate 7.5 million kilowatt of power. It has one of the three largest resources of mineral water in China.

With mountains, rivers, forests, springs, waterfalls, gorges and caves, all displaying the majesty, the fantasy, the danger and the seclusion of nature, Chongqing is proud of its popularity among tourists. Its famous tourist attractions include the Three Gorges on the Yangtze River; the night view of the City of Mountains; the rock carvings at Dazu, a World Cultural Heritage Site; the Lotus Cave near the Four-Sided Mountains; and Tiankeng (Heavenly Pit) and Difeng (Earthly Rift Valley), two rare geological spectacles at Fengjie.

Chongqing is one of the most notable cities for history and culture in China, and it serves as the economic center of the upstream Yangtze area. The city enjoys a great cultural and natural heritage. The Three Gorges, the Dazu Stone Sculptures, the Ghost City in Fengdu, the Hot Spring Park, the Red Crag Memorial Museum, Baidicheng City in Fengjie and the Ba people's hanging coffins have attracted many tourists. Chongqing has been selected as one of the Historical and Cultural Cities of China by the State Council.

Chongqing has witnessed an average two-digit growth rate since 1997, when it was approved as the fourth municipality directly under China's central government. However, its overall economic performance is still lagging behind eastern coastal cities such as Shanghai. For instance, its per capita GRP is still below the national average. Nevertheless, there is massive government support to transform Chongqing into the region's economic, trade and financial center and to use it as a platform to open up the country's western interior to further development (Table 1.5).

Chongqing aims to become a financial center; a manufacturing base with a focus on notebooks and IT products; a free trade zone, leveraging its railway access to Europe; and a transport hub leveraging the Yangtze River's waterway capacity and air, rail and road connections. The incorporation of Chongqing as a province-level municipality shows how serious the government is about its development.

Chongqing has increased investments in fixed assets in a bid to accelerate the economic development and living standard of its people. Areas that have attracted the largest share of fixed asset investment include real estate, manufacturing, administration of water conservancy, environment and public facilities, logistics,

Table 1.5 Demographic and socioeconomic profile: Chongqing

Indicator	2000	2010
Population (thousands)	30,900	28,846
Illiteracy rate of population aged 15 or over (%)	6.95	4.30
GRP (¥ billions)	158.93	792.56
Composition of GRP (%)		
Primary sector	17.8	8.6
Secondary sector	41.4	55.0
Tertiary sector	40.8	36.4
Fixed asset investment (¥ billions)	57.26	668.89
Status of foreign-funded enterprises		
Number of registered enterprises	1708	4827
Total investment (US$ millions)	6602	34,885
Registered capital (US$ millions)	4419	20,350
Foreign trade (US$ millions)		
Export	1060	6994
Import	791	4835
Sales of consumer goods (¥ billions)	64	294
Per capita annual disposable income of urban residents (¥)	6275.98	17,532.43
Engle's coefficient (%)	41.45	37.59
Per capita annual net income of rural residents (¥)	1892.44	5276.66
Engle's coefficient (%)	32.34	48.28
Number of patent applications granted	1158	12,080
Inventions	56	1143
Utility models	677	6704
Designs	425	4233

Note All monetary values are measured at current prices. *Source* Chongqing Statistical Yearbook, 2001 and 2011

and electricity, water and gas production and supply. As a traditional industrial base of China, it has made an effort to restrict the high pollution and high energy-consumption industries. As a result, the fixed asset investment in the service sector has increased, accounting for over two-thirds of the total.

Chongqing is China's third largest center for motor vehicle production and the largest for motorcycles. It is the biggest auto and motorcycle production base in western China. By the end of 2006 there were 24 car-makers in the city, including 10 auto assembly firms and 14 special-purpose vehicle manufacturing enterprises. The backbone of its automobile industry is the Chang'an Group, China's fourth largest car-maker. Its joint ventures in Chongqing include Chang'an Suzuki Auto Corp and Chang'an Ford Mazda. Chongqing Lifan is China's second largest motorcycle maker. Other leading motorcycle makers include Loncin Group, Chongqing Jianshe Motorcycles, Jialing Industrial Co. Ltd and Zhongshen Industrial Group. In addition, the growth of the auto and motorcycle industry has accelerated the development of auto parts and accessories.

Recently there has been a drive to move up the value chain by shifting towards high-technology and knowledge-intensive industries resulting in new development zones, such as the Chongqing New North Zone (CNNZ). Chongqing's local government hopes to apply favorable economic policies for the electronics and IT sectors.

The city has also invested heavily in infrastructure to attract investment. The network of roads and railways connecting it to the rest of China has been expanded and upgraded, thus reducing logistical costs. Furthermore, the nearby Three Gorges Dam, which is the world's largest, not only supplies Chongqing with power but also allows ocean-going ships to reach Chongqing's Yangtze River port. These infrastructure improvements have led to the arrival of numerous foreign investors in industries ranging from auto to finance and retailing, such as Ford, Mazda, HSBC, Standard Chartered Bank, Citibank, Deutsche Bank, ANZ Bank, Scotiabank, Wal-Mart, Metro AG and Carrefour among other MNCs.

Chongqing is diversifying its industries and developing its high-tech sectors. With the government's support, the electronics industry has been developing steadily. To speed up the development of the electronics industry, local government has established the Xiyong Micro-Electronic Park, which focusses on chip production, electronic material production, and solar cell and software development, in a bid to turn the park into the "Silicon Valley" of the city. Hewlett-Packard has agreed to launch China's fourth software base in the park. The founding groups, Kingdee and Huayang, are among the first to have a seat in the park.

There are 207 enterprises producing petrochemicals, raw chemical materials and chemical products. Sinopec Fuling Chongqing Chemical Industry Co and Chongqing Chuandong Chemical Co. Ltd are two large chemical producers in the city.

Chongqing is the wholesale and retail center of southwestern China. With a large population, it is an important consumer market in the region. The retail industry is fairly competitive. Chaotianmen market is a leading wholesale center in the area. Its products include garments, plastic products and textiles. Carrefour from France, Wal-Mart from the US, Metro from Germany, B&Q from Britain and Gome from Beijing have tapped into the market. In addition, Chongqing General Trade Group and Chongqing Department Store Co. Ltd are the two largest local retailers.

Chongqing is the logistics center of western China due to its convenient transportation infrastructure. The Yangtze River and the Jialing River weave through it, making it a large inland port along the upper reaches of the Yangtze. It is also the intersection point for three railways (the Chengdu–Chongqing Railway, the Chengdu–Guiyang Railway and the Xiangfan–Chongqing Railway) and two expressways (the Chongqing–Behai Expressway and the Chongqing–Zhanjiang Expressway). Chongqing Airport Development Zone aims to set up a 48-h logistics center through which goods are able to reach major cities around the world within 48 h.

Table 1.6 Chongqing's comparative (dis)advantage index by sector, 2010

Sector	Index
Agriculture, forestry, animal husbandry and fishery	0.24
Mining	0.82
Manufacturing	0.84
Production and distribution of electricity, gas and water	1.04
Construction	1.85
Transport, storage and post	1.11
Information transmission, computer service and software	0.75
Wholesale and retail trades	1.02
Hotels and catering services	1.00
Financial intermediation	1.11
Real estate	1.29
Leasing and business services	0.84
Scientific research, technical services and geological prospecting	0.92
Management of water conservancy, environment and public facilities	0.83
Services to households and other services	0.74
Education	1.08
Health, social security and social welfare	0.90
Culture, sports and entertainment	0.97
Public management and social organization	0.84

Notes All the sectors included in this table are determined according to China's official definitions and for urban areas only. Numerals greater than, equal to and less than one indicate that the province's sectors have advantages, no apparent (dis)advantages and disadvantages, respectively
Source Calculated by authors based on China Statistical Yearbook, 2011. See Appendix A for a detailed methodological description

Chongqing has maintained steady growth in foreign trade. A breakdown of the top imported goods includes mechanical and electrical equipment, vehicles, aircraft, ships and related transportation equipment, minerals, optical and medical instruments, clocks and musical instruments, and base metals and related products. As it is one the main manufacturing bases in western China, machinery and electrical appliances are important exports. The value of exported machinery and electrical appliances represents more than two-thirds of the total value of exports. Other major exported goods include base metals, chemicals, construction materials and textiles.

Chongqing has attracted a large number of MNCs to set up business, including ABB, Sony Ericsson, Honda and Coca Cola. The manufacturing, real estate and finance sectors received the largest share of FDI. Hong Kong continues to be the top overseas investment source for area. Other major overseas investors are from the US, Japan and Singapore. The Chongqing government currently encourages foreign investment in infrastructure, traditional Chinese medicine, hi-tech industries and modern services.

As of 2010, compared with those of other provinces, "construction" and "real estate" were relatively strong, while "Agriculture, forestry, animal husbandry and fishery", "services to households and other services" and "Information transmission, computer service and software" were relatively weak sectors (see Table 1.6).

Fujian

[Quick Facts: Official name: Fujian Province; Capital: Fuzhou; Land area: 121,400 km^2; Population density: 291/km^2; Major ethnic groups: Han, She, Hui, Tujia, Miao]

Fujian is a province of the PRC. Located on the southeast coast of mainland China, it borders Zhejiang to the north, Jiangxi to the west and Guangdong to the south. Taiwan lies to the east, across the Taiwan Strait. Situated on the coast of the East China Sea, Fujian measures 540 km from east to west and 550 km from north to south. Its coastline stretches 3324 km. Encompassing 1401 islands of different sizes, it is a vital navigation hub between the East China Sea and the South China Sea.

The name comes from the combination of Fuzhou and Jianzhou (a former name for Jian'ou)—two important cities in Fujian during the Tang Dynasty. With a Han majority, it is one of the most culturally and linguistically diverse provinces in China. The province has the abbreviated name "Min" since it was the place for an ancient kingdom called Minyue. The word "Mǐnyuè" was derived by combining "Mǐn" (an ethnic name associated with the Chinese word for barbarians, mán) and "Yue" (after the State of Yue, a kingdom during the Spring and Autumn Period (771–221 BC) in Zhejiang Province to the north). This is because the royal family of Yuè fled to Fujian after their kingdom was annexed by the state of Chu in 306 BC. Mǐn is also the name of the main river in this area.

Currently there are nine administrative divisions—at both prefectural and sub-provincial levels. These are divided into 85 county-level divisions (26 districts, 14 county-level cities and 45 counties). These are in turn divided into 1107 township-level divisions (605 towns, 328 townships, 18 ethnic townships and 156 sub-districts). These are the official PRC numbers. Thus, Quemoy (Jinmen) is included as one of the 45 counties and Matsu (Mazu) as one of the 334 townships. Most of Fujian is administered by the PRC. However, the archipelagos of Quemoy and Matsu are under the control of the Republic of China.

Fujian Province is mostly mountainous and is traditionally described as "eight parts mountain, one part water, and one part farmland". The northwest is higher in altitude, with the Wuyi Mountains forming the border between Fujian and Jiangxi provinces. It is the most forested provincial-level administrative region in China, with 62.96 % forest coverage in 2009. The highest point of Fujian is Huanggang Peak in the Wuyi Mountains with an altitude of 2157 m.

The Min River and its tributaries cut through much of northern and central Fujian. Other rivers include the Jinjiang River and the Jiulong River. Due to its uneven topography, the region has many cliffs and rapids. It is separated from Taiwan by the 180 km wide Taiwan Strait. Some of the small islands in the strait are also part of the province. Small parts of the province, namely the islands of Quemoy and Matsu, are under the administration of the Republic of China.

Fujian Province has a subtropical humid monsoon climate, with annual temperatures averaging between 17 and 21 °C. The average temperatures in the coldest month (January) are 10–13 °C in the southeast coastal parts and 5–8 °C in the inland mountain areas. In the hottest month (July) the temperatures average 26–29 °C. The average annual precipitation is 1000 mm and the frost-free period lasts 240–330 days a year.

Fujian possesses 86 kinds of minerals with verified reserves, including 34 kinds of metallic minerals and 47 non-metallic minerals. Among those with considerable reserves are gold, silver, lead, zinc, manganese, kaolin, limestone, granite, alunite, pyrophyllite and sulfur. Its reserve of quartz-sandstone ranks among the best nationally in both quantity and quality.

Farmland is sparse. Rice is the main crop, supplemented by sweet potatoes, wheat and barley. Cash crops include sugar cane and rapeseed. Fujian leads the provinces of China in longan production, and is also a major producer of lychees and tea. Seafood is another important product, with shellfish production especially prominent.

Mountains and hilly areas constitute over 80 % of Fujian's land area while plains are concentrated in its southeast coastal areas. Forests cover 52.4 % of Fujian's land area. Plant species are abundant. There are 1943 kinds of woody plants, including 400 species of timber tree and 140 varieties of bamboo. Fujian has 400 million cubic meter of timber reserved, its timber production ranking third in China. There are several thousand species of terrestrial wild animals in Fujian. They include 100 species of mammals, 540 species of birds, 115 species of reptiles and 44 species of amphibians. There are also more than 5000 kinds of insects. The Wuyi Mountain Nature Reserve is abundant in wildlife resources. It is also a world-renowned specimen base for new species of vertebrates and insects. The Meihua Mountain Nature Reserve in Longyan City is home to large numbers of animals. Fujian has five big fishing grounds which abound in marine resources. Among the more than 3000 species of marine organisms, 750 are fish, accounting for 50 % of the country's total marine fish species.

Fujian Province is rich in water resources, and its annual rainfall totals 201.1 billion cubic meter. More than 500 rivers in the province each have a drainage area of more than 50 km^2. The volume of river runoff stands at 115 billion cubic meter a year on average. The province's theoretical waterpower reserves total 10.46 million kilowatt, which can generate 91.6 billion kilowatt hour of power annually. There are 1000 places suitable for building a hydropower station with a generating capacity of over 500 kW. Their combined generating capacity can reach 7.05 million kilowatt and their annual power generation 32 billion kilowatt hour, both ranking first in eastern China. The existing generating capacity accounts for only 30 % of the province's total potential, leaving huge room for development. Fujian also has rich underground water resources. More than 100 hot springs have been discovered, with water temperatures of 40–60 °C.

There are many beautiful mountains in the province. Famous resorts include the Wuyi Mountain, the Gushan (Drum Hill) in Fuzhou, the Tailao Mountain in east Fujian and Wanshiyan in Xiamen. The province also has many beautiful beaches, such as the bathing beach on Gulangyu Islet of Xiamen, Luanwan Beach on Dongshan Island, Longwangtou Beach at Pingtan and Meizhou Island at Putian. Its numerous rivers offer many picturesque water spots, including the Jiuqu (nine-bend) Stream in Wuyi Mountain and Jinhu Lake, the largest artificial lake in Fujian. Northwest Fujian is noted for danxia and karst landforms, with countless grotesque rocks and fantastic caves. The Wuyi and Meihua mountain nature reserves preserve vast expanses of virgin forest, with rich fauna and flora resources. These reserves and other scenic resorts are ideal places for enjoying the charms of nature, taking holidays and conducting scientific explorations. In addition, Fujian has a lot of gardens and parks of different types.

Fujian Province is rich in tourist attractions, abounding with places of historical and cultural interest, and beautiful scenic spots. It has preserved many cultural sites from the Qin (221–207 BC), the Han (206 BC–AD 220), the Tang (AD 618–907), the Song (AD 960–1279), the Yuan (AD 1271–1368) and the Ming (AD 1368–1644) dynasties. There are numerous ancient temples, pagodas, bridges and castles, as well as former residences of celebrities. Fujian has a variety of navigation relics and religious legacies thanks to its long history of navigation and frequent contact with the wider world.

Colorful ethnic customs, unique local cultures and rich products also add attraction to the province's tourism resources. Currently, Fujian encompasses two national tourist holiday resorts, nine national scenic spots, four national nature reserves (forest parks), four national-level famous historic and cultural cities, 29 key cultural sites under state protection, 19 provincial-level scenic spots, six provincial tourist economic development areas and 204 cultural sites under provincial protection.

Hakka, a Han Chinese people with their own distinct identity, live in the southwestern parts of the province. Hui'an, also a Han branch with a distinct culture and fashion, populate Fujian's southeast coastline near Chongwu in Hui'an County. The She, scattered over mountainous regions in the north, are the largest minority ethnic group of the province. Many ethnic Chinese around the world, especially in Southeast Asia, trace their ancestry to Fujian. Descendants of the region's emigrants make up the majority ethnic Chinese populations of Taiwan, Singapore, Malaysia, Indonesia and the Philippines. Fujian, especially Fuzhou, is also the major source of Chinese immigrants in the US.

Fujian Province is located on China's southeastern coast and is the closet point in mainland China to Taiwan. Because of this close geographical proximity, Fujian was once considered the battlefield frontline in a potential war between mainland China and Taiwan. Today, although Fujian is one of the wealthier provinces of China, its GRP per capita is the lowest among the country's coastal administrative divisions. In 2010 Fujian's nominal GRP was ¥1.43 trillion (about US$212 billion), representing a rise of 12 % from the previous year. It's GRP per capita was ¥33,051 (about US$4890). The Minnan Golden Triangle, which includes Xiamen, Quanzhou and Zhangzhou, accounts for 40 % of the GRP of Fujian Province (Table 1.7).

Table 1.7 Demographic and socioeconomic profile: Fujian

Indicator	2000	2010
Population (thousands)	34,710	36,930
Illiteracy rate of population aged 15 or over (%)	7.20	2.44
GRP (¥ billions)	392.01	1473.71
Composition of GRP (%)		
Primary sector	16.3	9.3
Secondary sector	43.7	51.0
Tertiary sector	40.0	39.7
Fixed asset investment (¥ billions)	111.22	819.91
Status of foreign-funded enterprises		
Number of registered enterprises	16,013	23,463
Total investment (US$ millions)	47,084	124,831
Registered capital (US$ millions)	27,585	69,358
Foreign trade (US$ millions)		
Export	13,623	66,619
Import	9334	43,931
Sales of consumer goods (¥ billions)	137	531
Per capita annual disposable income of urban residents (¥)	7432.26	21,781.31
Engle's coefficient (%)	44.66	39.26
Per capita annual net income of rural residents (¥)	3230.49	7426.86
Engle's coefficient (%)	41.19	46.14
Number of patent applications granted	3003	18,063
Inventions	93	1224
Utility models	1074	9664
Designs	1836	7175

Note All monetary values are measured at current prices. *Source* Fujian Statistical Yearbook, 2001 and 2011

In terms of spending power, retail sales for the province were roughly equivalent to that of Shanghai or Beijing. Fujian has been a major beneficiary of FDI, especially from overseas Fujianese and Taiwanese, but now that it is no longer the only point of access to Taiwan it is losing out on investment to Jiangsu and Guangdong. Major industries include petrochemicals, machinery and electronics. Its tourism sector has seen very strong growth and continues to be one of the brighter spots in its economy.

Fujian is one of the more affluent provinces with many industries, spanning tea production, clothing and sports equipment manufacturers (such as Anta, 361 Degrees, Xtep, Peak Sport Products and Septwolves). Many foreign firms have operations in Fujian. These include Boeing, Dell, GE, Kodak, Nokia, Siemens, Swire, TDK and Panasonic.

Table 1.8 Fujian's comparative (dis)advantage index by sector, 2010

Sector	Index
Agriculture, forestry, animal husbandry and fishery	0.46
Mining	0.22
Manufacturing	1.71
Production and distribution of electricity, gas and water	0.77
Construction	1.27
Transport, storage and post	0.68
Information transmission, computer service and software	0.64
Wholesale and retail trades	0.67
Hotels and catering services	0.93
Financial intermediation	0.71
Real estate	1.10
Leasing and business services	1.02
Scientific research, technical services and geological prospecting	0.48
Management of water conservancy, environment and public facilities	0.52
Services to households and other services	0.61
Education	0.73
Health, social security and social welfare	0.64
Culture, sports and entertainment	0.72
Public management and social organization	0.55

Notes All the sectors included in this table are determined according to China's official definitions and for urban areas only. Numerals greater than, equal to and less than one indicate that the province's sectors have advantages, no apparent (dis)advantages and disadvantages, respectively
Source Calculated by authors based on China Statistical Yearbook, 2011. See Appendix A for a detailed methodological description

Fujian Province has been the major economic beneficiary of China's direct linkage scheme with Taiwan. Commenced on December 15, 2008, this scheme includes direct flights from Taiwan to major Fujian cities, such as Xiamen and Fuzhou. In addition, ports in Xiamen, Quanzhou and Fuzhou will be upgrading their port infrastructure to allow increased economic trade with Taiwan.

The province is host to the China International Fair for Investment and Trade. This is held annually in Xiamen to promote foreign investment for all of China.

Since 1978, when China opened to the world, Fujian Province has received a significant amount of FDI. The largest share comes from Hong Kong, followed by Singapore, the UK and Canada. Since Taiwan and China had not established direct links before 2008, most of the Taiwanese investments were counted as those from third sources (such as Hong Kong and other overseas sources). Since the late 2000s the region has benefited from China's direct links with Taiwan. Its FDI has been concentrated in Fuzhou, Xiamen, Quanzhou and Zhangzhou. Fujian's major foreign trade partners have been ASEAN, the US and Japan.

As of 2010, compared with those of other provinces, "manufacturing", "construction" and "real estate" were relatively strong, while "mining", "agriculture, forestry, animal husbandry and fishery" and "scientific research, technical services and geological prospecting" were relatively weak sectors (see Table 1.8).

Gansu

[Quick Facts: Official name: Gansu Province; Capital: Lanzhou; Land area: 454,000 km^2; Population density: 73/km^2; Major ethnic groups: Han, Hui, Dongxiang, Tibetan, Tu]

Gansu is a province of the PRC. It lies in northwest China on the upper reaches of the Yellow River in China's western inland area, between the Tibetan Plateau, Inner Mongolia Autonomous Region and the Loess Plateau. It borders Shaanxi Province to the east, Ningxia Hui Autonomous Region to the northeast, Qinghai Province and Xinjiang Uygur Autonomous Region to the west, and Inner Mongolia Autonomous Region and the People's Republic of Mongolia to the north. The Yellow River passes through the southern part of the province. Gansu contains the geographical center of China, marked at 35°50′40.9″N and 103°27′7.5″E. Part of the Gobi Desert is located here, as well as small parts of the Badain Jaran Desert and Tengger Desert. Lanzhou, its capital city, lies in the southeast.

Often abbreviated to "Gan" or "Long", Gansu is situated at the juncture of three highlands: the Qinghai–Tibet Plateau, the Inner Mongolia Plateau and the Huangtu (Loess) Plateau. The landscape is very mountainous in the south and flat in the north. The mountains in the south are part of the Qilian mountain range. At 5547 m above the sea level, Qilian Mountain is Gansu's highest peak and is located at latitude 39°N and longitude 99°E. The Yellow River gets most of its water from the province. It also flows straight through Lanzhou. The area around Wuwei is part of Shiyang River Basin. A natural land passage known as Hexi Corridor, stretching some 1000 km from Lanzhou to the Jade Gate, is situated within Gansu Province. It is bound on the north by the Gobi Desert and on the south by the Qilian Mountains.

With a land area of 455,000 km^2, Gansu has a large concentration of Hui Chinese and, along with Shaanxi, is the historical home to the dialect of the Dungans, who are Hui migrated to Central Asia. The southwestern corner of Gansu is home to a large Tibetan population.

The region is rich in mineral resources and 145 types of minerals have been discovered there. It boasts 94 types of reserves, including nickel, cobalt, platinum, selenium, gold and iridium. It also has large deposits of petroleum, natural gas, chromite and zinc. As a result of the 450 rivers (78 of which each have an annual runoff of over 100 million cubic meter), water resources are abundant in Gansu. It has special advantages in tapping 15 kinds of minerals, such as nickel, zinc, cobalt, platinum, iridium, copper, stibium, barite and baudisserite. Along with its vast deposits of coal and rare earths, it is home to China's largest nickel deposits located around Jinchang City. Proven reserves of the metal there are in the neighborhood of 5.5 million tons, which is 90 % of China's nickel reserves and the third largest in the world.

The water resources in Gansu are mainly distributed across nine river systems in the Yellow River, Yangtze River and inland river drainage basins with an annual discharge of 61.4 billion cubic meter and a combined hydropower potential of 17.24 million kilowatt. Gansu ranks ninth among China's provinces and autonomous regions in terms of hydropower potential. To date, 29 hydropower stations have been constructed in the province with an installed generating capacity of 30 million kilowatt and an annual output of 23.565 billion kilowatt hour. The Liujiaxia, Yanguoxia and Bapanxia hydropower stations on the upper reaches of the Yellow River, and the Bikou Hydropower Station on the Bailong River, have a total installed capacity of 2.125 million kilowatt. The proven reserves of coal are 8.92 billion tons, and those of petroleum are between 600 and 700 million tons. There is also considerable potential for the development of wind and solar energies.

There are 659 species of wild animals (including the giant panda, the snub-nosed monkey, antelope, the snow leopard, musk deer and the bactrian camel), of which 24 first-class rare animals are under state protection. Gansu is home to 441 species of birds; it is a center of endemism and home to many species and subspecies which occur nowhere else in the world. The area holds second place among China's provinces and autonomous regions in terms of the variety of medicinal herbs. There are over 4000 species of wild plants, including 951 of medical value. Among the latter, 450 species, such as angelica root, rhubarb, hairy asiabell root, licorice root, fritillary bulb, mariajuana, the bark of eucommia, glossy ganoderma and Chinese caterpillar fungus have been found.

Gansu has many relics and places of interest. The Yangshao culture can be traced back about 6000 years. The Silk Road, linking China with the western countries in ancient times, was built during the reign of Emperor Wu in the Western Han Dynasty (206 BC–AD 8). The historic Silk Road starts in Chang'an and stretches to Constantinople. On the way, merchants would go to Dunhuang in Gansu. Here they would get fresh camels, food and guards for the journey around the dangerous Taklamakan Desert. Before departing, they would pray to the Mogao Grottoes for a safe journey. These grottoes offer a collection of Buddhist art. There are 492 grottoes and 425 painted clay figures. Treated as the "Art Treasure House of China", the Dunhuang Mogao Grottoes are the largest and best-preserved Buddhist art museum. Each temple has a large statue of a buddha or bodhisattva and paintings of religious scenes.

Gansu has become a hot spot for tourism. Located about 5 km southwest of the city of Dunhuang, Yueyaquan (crescent lake) is an oasis and popular spot for tourists seeking respite from the heat of the desert. Bingling Temple (or Bingling Grottoes) is a Buddhist cave complex in a canyon along the Yellow River. Established in AD 420 during the Western Jin Dynasty, the site contains dozens of caves and caverns filled with outstanding examples of carvings, sculpture and frescoes. The great Maitreya Buddha is more than 27 m tall and is similar in style to the great Buddha that once lined the cliffs of Bamiyan in Afghanistan. Access to the site is by boat from Yongjing in the summer or fall.

Gansu's economy has been growing at an average rate of about 10 % since 2000. The industrial and service sectors account for the majority of the province's GRP. Agriculture remains the lowest contributing sector. The region's consumption market is also expanding steadily. Despite recent growth in Gansu and the booming

Table 1.9 Demographic and socioeconomic profile: Gansu

Indicator	2000	2010
Population (thousands)	25,620	25,600
Illiteracy rate of population aged 15 or over (%)	14.34	8.69
GRP (¥ billions)	98.34	412.08
Composition of GRP (%)		
Primary sector	19.7	14.5
Secondary sector	44.7	48.2
Tertiary sector	35.6	37.3
Fixed asset investment (¥ billions)	39.54	315.83
Status of foreign-funded enterprises		
Number of registered enterprises	826	2116
Total investment (US$ millions)	2565	6289
Registered capital (US$ millions)	1817	2766
Foreign trade (US$ millions)		
Export	421	1275
Import	271	6113
Sales of consumer goods (¥ billions)	36	139
Per capita annual disposable income of urban residents (¥)	4916.25	13,188.55
Engle's coefficient (%)	37.63	37.41
Per capita annual net income of rural residents (¥)	1428.68	3424.65
Engle's coefficient (%)	28.60	44.71
Number of patent applications granted	493	1868
Inventions	82	349
Utility models	326	1131
Designs	85	388

Note All monetary values are measured at current prices. *Source* Gansu Statistical Yearbook, 2001 and 2011

economy in the rest of China, the province is still considered to be one of the poorest. Tourism has been a bright spot in contributing to its economy. Gansu offers a variety of choices for national and international tourists (Table 1.9).

As stipulated in the country's 12th five-year plan, the local government of Gansu hopes to increase the province's GRP by 10 % annually by focusing investments on five pillar industries: coal and renewable energy, chemicals, non-ferrous metals, and pharmaceuticals and services.

Gansu is located on the western edge of central China. It is one of the country's poorest provinces and has one of the harshest climates. While its climate is not favorable for attracting companies or individuals to work there, it is an optimal place for solar power stations as well as wind farms, and it is rich with mineral resources, including antimony, chromium, coal, cobalt, copper, fluorite, gypsum, iridium, iron and lead.

Most of Gansu's economy is based on mining and the extraction of minerals, especially rare-earth elements. The province has significant deposits of antimony, chromium, coal, cobalt, copper, fluorite, gypsum, iridium, iron, lead, limestone, mercury, mirabilite, nickel, crude oil, platinum, troilite, tungsten and zinc, among others. The oilfields at Yumen and Changqing are considered significant. Nickel production in Jinchang is exclusively controlled by the Jinchuan Group, one of the largest companies in the region.

Industries other than mining include electricity generation, petrochemicals, oil exploration machinery and building materials. In addition, Gansu is a center for China's nuclear industry. Thanks to the rich resources, petrochemicals, non-ferrous metals, electricity, metallurgy, food and equipment have become Gansu's five pillar industries. The province has relatively rich oil reserves. The two most important oilfields are the Yumen Oilfield and the Xifeng Oilfield. The former, located along the Silk Road, was the first found in China. The Xifeng Oilfield has more than 1 billion tons of oil and gas reserves. The Lanzhou Chemical Company, the Yumen Oilfield and the Qingyang Refinery and Petrochemical Co. Ltd—three units under the country's largest oil firm, China National Petroleum Corporation (CNPC)—are the most important players in Gansu's petrochemical industry.

Thanks to ferrous and non-ferrous metals clustered in Lanzhou, Jinchang and Baiyin, state-level non-ferrous metal new material industrial bases have been formed. Major players in this industry include the Jinchuan Group, the Lanzhou Liancheng Aluminum Industrial Co. Ltd, the Lanzhou Aluminum Co. Ltd and the Baiyin Nonferrous Group. The booming non-ferrous metal sector has driven up the development of metallurgy. The Lanzhou Lanshi Group and the Spark Machine Tool Co. Ltd are two major equipment manufacturers in Gansu.

The province generally has a semi-arid to arid, continental climate with warm summers and very cold winters. Most of the precipitation is concentrated in the summers. Gansu was once an important agricultural base in ancient China. However, due to such ecological problems as severe water and soil losses and water shortage, the value-added output of farming, forestry and animal husbandry have been growing at a moderate pace. Agricultural production includes cotton, linseed oil, maize, melons, millet and wheat. Gansu is known as a source for the production of wild medicinal herbs which are used in Chinese medicine.

The turnover of foreign trade has hit a record high year after year over the past decade. The main exported products include equipment, chemicals and base metals, while the main imported goods are minerals, base metals and equipment. Australia is Gansu's largest foreign trade partner, followed by South Korea, Chile, the US and Germany.

Gansu has made various efforts to attract FDI. Foreign investors have chosen to set up ventures in the equipment and energy sectors. Much of the utilized FDI has been channeled into the manufacturing industry. Other industries with high utilized

FDIs are energy, logistics, real estate and mining. Hong Kong remains the major FDI source for Gansu. Netzsch from Germany, Veolia from France, CIC Hightime Resources Limited from Hong Kong and Nuskin from the U.S have made their presence felt in the province.

As of 2010, compared with those of other provinces, "public management and social organization" "production and distribution of electricity, gas and water" and "education" and "Culture, sports and entertainment" were relatively strong, while "services to households and other services", "leasing and business services" and "real estate" were relatively weak sectors (see Table 1.10).

Table 1.10 Gansu's comparative (dis)advantage index by sector, 2010

Sector	Index
Agriculture, forestry, animal husbandry and fishery	0.94
Mining	1.09
Manufacturing	0.65
Production and distribution of electricity, gas and water	1.47
Construction	0.82
Transport, storage and post	1.08
Information transmission, computer service and software	0.64
Wholesale and retail trades	0.71
Hotels and catering services	0.61
Financial intermediation	0.97
Real estate	0.55
Leasing and business services	0.40
Scientific research, technical services and geological prospecting	1.19
Management of water conservancy, environment and public facilities	1.04
Services to households and other services	0.26
Education	1.45
Health, social security and social welfare	1.06
Culture, sports and entertainment	1.45
Public management and social organization	1.73

Notes All the sectors included in this table are determined according to China's official definitions and for urban areas only. Numerals greater than, equal to and less than one indicate that the province's sectors have advantages, no apparent (dis)advantages and disadvantages, respectively
Source Calculated by authors based on China Statistical Yearbook, 2011. See Appendix A for a detailed methodological description

Guangdong

[Quick Facts: Official name: Guangdong Province; Capital: Guangzhou; Land area: 177,900 km^2; Population density: 536/km^2; Major ethnic groups: Han, Zhuang, Yao, Miao, Tujia]

Guangdong is a province of the PRC. It is located on the northern coast of the South China Sea at the south end of mainland China, with a coastline of about 3368 km. Its islands add a further 1600 km^2. The Pearl River, which is 2122 km long—the third largest river in the country—flows through Guangdong and forms a delta region. It is economically comparable to the Yangtze River Delta in eastern China where the region's economic hub is Shanghai.

Guangdong borders Fujian Province to the northeast, Jiangxi and Hunan provinces to the north, Guangxi Autonomous Region to the west, Hainan Province to the southwest, and Hong Kong and Macau SARs to the south. Certain of the Pratas Islands, which are administered by the Republic of China, have traditionally been regarded as part of the province. The modern abbreviation of Guangdong is Yue, which is a shortened form of Baiyue—a collective name for various peoples who lived in southern China in ancient times.

Guangdong is officially China's most populous province. The massive influx of migrants from other areas, dubbed the "floating population", is due to the region's booming economy and high demand for labor. Guangdong is also the ancestral home of large numbers of overseas Chinese. Most of the railroad laborers in Canada, the western US and Panama in the 19th century came from Guangdong. The majority of the province's population is Han Chinese. Within this group, the largest subgroup in Guangdong are the Cantonese people. Two other major groups are the Teochew people in Chaoshan and the Hakka people in Huizhou, Meizhou, Heyuan, Shaoguan and Zhanjiang. There is a small Yao population in the north. Other smaller minority groups include the She, Miao, Li and Zhuang.

Guangdong has a humid subtropical climate, but with a near tropical climate in the far south. Winters are short, mild and relatively dry, while summers are long, hot and very wet. Its average annual temperature is 22 °C. The average daily highs in Guangzhou in January and July are 18 and 33 °C, respectively, although the humidity makes it feel much hotter in summer. Frost is rare on the coast but may occur a few days each winter well inland. Most areas enjoy a subtropical monsoon climate with adequate rainfall, long summers and warm winters. The annual precipitation in 2005 averaged 1770 mm.

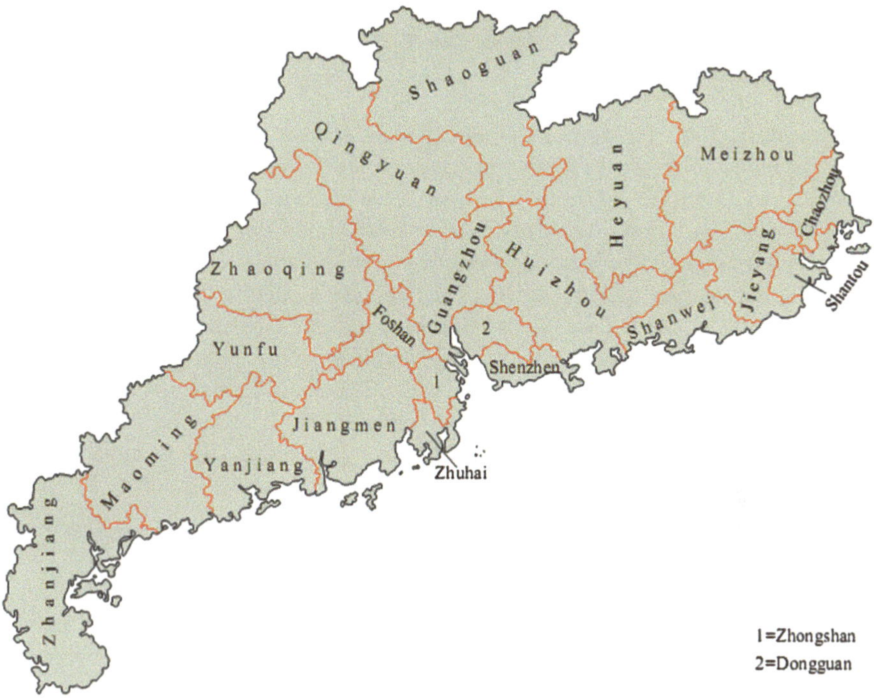

Guangdong boasts rich mineral resources. By the end of 2005 some 129 minerals had been discovered and the reserves of 92 minerals had been proven. The Tropic of Cancer runs through the center of this low-latitude province. The fertile Pearl River Delta is rich in fish and rice. Forests cover 57.5 % of the province with standing timber reserves of 300 million cubic meter. Tree species include pine, Chinese catalpa, fir and eucalyptus. By the end of 2005, 237 forest, wetland and wildlife reserves had been established, covering an area of 1.07 million hectare.

The province has extensive access to the sea together with a network of interconnected waterways with many reservoirs and fish ponds. It is rich in aquatic products. Its marine breeding areas cover 780,000 ha and it has a further 430,000 ha of freshwater breeding areas. The main crops are rice, vegetables and fruit. Zhanjiang is the main center for sisal hemp while fruit production is predominately based around Maoming. Among the 200 varieties of fruit grown in Guangdong are pineapples, bananas and litchi, together with longans and oranges.

Many of Guangdong's cities have been designated as "Excellent Tourist Cities". The province's scenic spots and scenic areas have been graded 4–A. Top-quality tourist areas in China include the Baiyun Hill in Guangzhou, the Xiangjiang Wildlife Park in Guangzhou, the Overseas Chinese Town in Shenzhen, the Guanlan Golf Course in Shenzhen, the Yuanming New Park in Zhuhai, Dr Sun Yat-sen's birthplace in Zhongshan, Lake Star in Zhaoqing, Mount Sijiao in Foshan, Mount Danxia in Shaoguan, the Qingxin Hot Springs in Qingyuan, and Hailing Island's

Dajiao Bay in Yangjiang. Development of the tourism triangle based on Guangdong, Hong Kong and Macau has now taken off. The State Council has approved the introduction of a 144-h visa-endorsement service in the ten above-mentioned cities on the Zhujiang River Delta and Shantou City.

Guangdong Province surpassed Henan and Sichuan provinces to become the most populous province in China in January 2005, with 79 million permanent residents and 31 million migrants who lived there for at least six months of the year. Since 1989 it has topped the total GRP rankings among all provincial-level divisions, with Jiangsu and Shandong being second and third in rank. According to provincial annual preliminary statistics, Guangdong's GRP in 2010 reached ¥4601 billion, or US$689.02 billion. It has the third highest GRP per capita among all provinces of mainland China after Jiangsu and Zhejiang (Table 1.11).

Guangdong Province is home to the production facilities and offices of a wide-ranging set of multinational and Chinese corporations. It hosts the largest import and export fair in China called the Canton Fair in its capital city, Guangzhou. It is not only China's largest exporter of goods but also the largest importer. Its annual

Table 1.11 Demographic and socioeconomic profile: Guangdong

Indicator	2000	2010
Population (thousands)	86,420	104,410
Illiteracy rate of population aged 15 or over (%)	3.84	1.96
GRP (¥ billions)	966.22	4601.31
Composition of GRP (%)		
Primary sector	10.4	5.0
Secondary sector	50.4	50.0
Tertiary sector	39.3	45.0
Fixed asset investment (¥ billions)	314.51	1562.37
Status of foreign-funded enterprises		
Number of registered enterprises	49,865	93,756
Total investment (US$ millions)	216,510	421,260
Registered capital (US$ millions)	128,086	249,493
Foreign trade (US$ millions)		
Export	93,428	467,177
Import	82,060	366,829
Sales of consumer goods (¥ billions)	407	1746
Per capita annual disposable income of urban residents (¥)	9761.57	23,897.80
Engle's coefficient (%)	38.62	36.49
Per capita annual net income of rural residents (¥)	3654.48	7890.25
Engle's coefficient (%)	41.34	47.68
Number of patent applications granted	15,799	119,343
Inventions	261	13,691
Utility models	4797	43,900
Designs	10,741	61,752

Note All monetary values are measured at current prices. *Source* Guangdong Statistical Yearbook, 2001 and 2011

fair is the largest trade fair in China. The region's largely private manufacturing base is one of the main engines which have made its economy so dynamic. Guangdong has also led the way in moving up the manufacturing value chain from light industry production of textiles, toys and shoes to high-end manufacturing of things like IT products and power equipment.

The province is now one of the richest in the nation with the most billionaires in mainland China and the highest GRP per capita among all the provinces. In addition there is an overconcentration of wealth in the Pearl River Delta cities of Guangzhou, Huizhou, Jiangmen and Shenzhen, and there are large swaths of rural Guangdong which still remain relatively poor in comparison.

The region has played a pioneering role in China's economic reforms ever since the country's implementation of opening policies in the late 1970s. Three of China's "special economic zones", namely, Shenzhen, Zhuhai and Shantou, are located in Guangdong. In recent years, the province's leading economic position has been challenged by Shandong and Jiangsu, which are the second and third largest economies in China, respectively. Despite this threat, the industrial output of the area is on the rise. Its robust manufacturing sector has also greatly benefited from foreign investments.

Guangdong is a major export-processing base for Hong Kong and Taiwan investors. Major industrial production bases are clustered in Guangzhou, Shenzhen, Dongguan, Foshan, Huizhou, Jiangmen and Zhuhai. In addition, the province has a robust manufacturing base. The traditionally strong light industries, such as textiles and garments, food and beverages, and toys formerly accounted for more than half of its total industry output. These products still rank near the top of China's export market. The nine pillar industries in Guangdong currently include three new leading industries (electronic information, electric machinery and special purpose equipment, and petroleum chemicals), three traditional industries (textiles and garments, food and beverages, and construction materials) and three potential leading industries (paper making, pharmaceuticals and automobiles).

Guangdong is China's electronics industry base. The electronics enterprises in the province, which are mainly located in Shenzhen and Guangzhou, account for about one-third of China's total. Other important production bases include Zhuhai, Foshan, Dongguan and Shantou. Examples of major products produced in Guangdong are telecommunications equipment, personal computers, video/audio products, consumer electronic products, electronic parts and components, and optical information storage. Currently, the province has quite a large number of successful domestic enterprises whose products are also well known on the global market. Major domestic brands include Huawei, ZTE, TCL, Midea, Konka and Galanz.

A newly developed industry in Guangdong Province is petroleum and chemicals. Major enterprises in this area include Sinopec Maoming Refining and Chemical, Sinopec Guangzhou Petrochemical, CNOOC Shenzhen Ltd, CNOOC and Shell Petrochemicals Company Ltd.

Guangdong is the largest textile and garment production and export base in China. By the end of 2006 it had more than 6000 textile and garment enterprises with major production bases in Dongguan, Foshan, Zhongshan, Guangzhou, Shantou and Zhuhai. Key players in this industry are the Guangdong Yida Textile, Yishion and Foshan Shunde Qianjin Industry Co. As the first area in China to open up to foreign investors, Guangdong has attracted a large number of foreign garment makers and exporters. These companies have facilitated the transfer of technology that helped local enterprises to grow quickly. In recent years, however, Guangdong has faced the problem of rising labor and land costs. Most private enterprises are labor-intensive and they focus on mass production and export of low-end products. All of these challenge the sustainable growth of local enterprises.

Guangdong has a vibrant service sector with enormous growth potential. Its service sector is characterized by the presence of diverse channels, a high level of maturity, a strong clustering and radiation effect, and brisk trading.

The province has one of the most developed retail markets in China. In 2006 the added value of the retail and wholesale sector amounted to ¥254.2 billion, up 11.2 % from the previous year. The sector accounted for 22.7 % of the province's services sector and contributed 9.7 % to the GRP. Large foreign retail enterprises have established a presence there. These include Wal-Mart from the US, Carrefour from France, Jusco from Japan, and Park'N Shop, Watsons and Mannings from Hong Kong.

Guangdong has always been the logistics hub of southern China. Logistics and its related services, such as road transportation, warehousing, loading and unloading, processing, packaging, delivery, and related information and consultancy service for ordinary goods have developed quickly. Demand for large-scale, third-party logistics companies is also expected to increase.

The province is the largest foreign trade center in China. Among the major export products are machinery, and garments and textiles. Foreign-invested enterprises are the largest contributors to the province's exports. Exports from private enterprises have also expanded quickly. Major trading partners of the Guangdong province include Hong Kong, the US, countries in the EU and the ASEAN, and Japan.

The booming Yangtze Delta region has recently threatened the leading position of the Pearl River Delta, with foreign investment momentum in Guangdong being weakened. The largest FDI destination has also shifted to Jiangsu since 2003. Most funds were invested in Guangdong's manufacturing sector. Major industries include computers and accessories, machinery and electrical products, refined chemicals, and some traditional industries, such as toys, garments and textiles. The service sector has also seen rapid growth, with real estate being one of the most attractive industries.

As of 2010, compared with other provinces, "real estate" "manufacturing" and "hotels and catering services" were relatively strong, while "mining", "agriculture, forestry, animal husbandry and fishery" and "construction" were relatively weak sectors (see Table 1.12)

Table 1.12 Guangdong's comparative (dis)advantage index by sector, 2010

Sector	Index
Agriculture, forestry, animal husbandry and fishery	0.27
Mining	0.07
Manufacturing	1.53
Production and distribution of electricity, gas and water	0.70
Construction	0.59
Transport, storage and post	1.04
Information transmission, computer service and software	1.10
Wholesale and retail trades	0.93
Hotels and catering services	1.41
Financial intermediation	1.02
Real estate	1.60
Leasing and business services	1.13
Scientific research, technical services and geological prospecting	0.72
Management of water conservancy, environment and public facilities	0.75
Services to households and other services	1.24
Education	0.83
Health, social security and social welfare	0.93
Culture, sports and entertainment	0.84
Public management and social organization	0.77

Notes All the sectors included in this table are determined according to China's official definitions and for urban areas only. Numerals greater than, equal to and less than one indicate that the province's sectors have advantages, no apparent (dis)advantages and disadvantages, respectively
Source Calculated by authors based on China Statistical Yearbook, 2011. See Appendix A for a detailed methodological description

Guangxi

[Quick Facts: Official name: Guangxi Zhuang Autonomous Region; Capital: Nanning; Land area: 236,700 km^2; Population density: 207/km^2; Major ethnic groups: Han, Zhuang, Yao, Miao, Dong]

Guangxi is an autonomous region (officially called Guangxi Zhuang Autonomous Region) of the PRC, a region with special privileges created specifically for the Zhuang people. Guangxi's location in the far south of China has placed it on the frontier of Chinese civilization throughout much of China's history. The current name "Guang" means "expanse" and has been associated with the regions of Guangdong and Guangxi since the creation of the Guang Prefecture in AD 226.

One of China's five autonomous regions, Guangxi Zhuang Autonomous Region lies on the southeastern part of the Yunnan-Guizhou Plateau, with a mountain area in its north. It is bordered by Yunnan Province to the west, Guizhou Province to the north, Hunan Province to the northeast and Guangdong Province to the east and southeast. It is also bounded by Vietnam in the southwest and the Gulf of Tonkin in the south. The abbreviated name for Guangxi Zhuang Autonomous Region is Gui, which derives from Guilin, the former capital of, and currently a major city in, the autonomous region.

Guangxi is a mountainous region. The Nanling Mountains form the northeast border, with the Yuecheng and Haiyang mountains branching from them. Also in the north are the Duyao and Fenghuang mountains. Near the center of the region are the Dayao and Daming mountains. On the southeastern border are the Yunkai Mountains. The highest point is Mount Mao'er in the Yuecheng, at 2141 m. Many rivers cut valleys through the mountains. Most form the tributary basin of the West River. Guangxi has a short coastline on the Gulf of Tonkin (Beibu Wan). Important seaports include Beihai, Qinzhou and Fangchenggang. Along the border with Vietnam is Detian Waterfall.

Situated in a low-latitude region, Guangxi borders the tropic sea to the south and has mountain ranges in the north. The Yunnan-Guizhou Plateau extends into the western part of the province. Under the joint action of the sun's radiation and atmospheric circulation, the climate is characterized as having short winters and long summers with an annual average temperature of 16–23 °C. The annual rainfall is between 1000 and 2800 mm, with the level growing gradually southward from the north. The rainfall from April through September makes up 75 % of the annual rainfall. The rainy season just coincides with the hot season. The sub-tropical monsoon climate with plenty of rainfall brings with it an abundance of plant species. About 8000 tree species, including the Cathay silver fir, have been found in this province. It is also rich in mineral resources, such as silver, aluminum, antimony and vanadium.

The southern section of Guangxi is ringed by seacoast. The Beibu (Tonkin) Bay, a natural semi-enclosed bay in the northwest of the South China Sea, covers an area of 129,300 km^2, with the depth of water averaging 38 m, the deepest point being at 100 m. Due to the abnormal advances and retreats of monsoon, the area often sees changes in precipitation and temperature. Drought, floods, typhoons and hailstorms frequently hit the area. Crossed by a number of rivers, Guangxi is rich in water resources. Because of the abundance of water, it has the potential to generate significant hydropower.

Guangxi is known for having various mineral deposits, and it serves as one of the ten most important production bases of non-ferrous metals in the country. The number of proven mineral resources is 96, including 53 for which the deposits rank 10th or above among the provinces. The region has especially abundant reserves of manganese and tin, which account for one-third of the national reserves of each. In addition, Guangxi has sizeable reserves of vanadium, tungsten, antimony, silver, aluminum, talcum and others. What makes the province a favorite place for mineral development and production is the fact that the mineral resources are relatively concentrated.

Located in the tropic zone, the Beibu Bay provides a favorable environment for breeding various fish species. It is home to over 500 types of fish and shellfish. Among them more than 50 are of economic value. These include red snapper, grouper, Spanish mackerel, butterfish and red coat. The fish resources amount to 750,000 tons. By now, 929 kinds of land-based vertebrates are found in Guangxi, accounting for 43.3 % of those found in China. Among these, 149 are rare species.

Guangxi ranks first among the Chinese provinces and autonomous regions in terms of its rare species of plants. About 8354 wild plants have been found in the region, including 122 that are close to extinction and need special protection. Among the 670 species of fruits growing in China, 110 are found there. As the tropical or sub-tropical fruits account for 80 % of the total growing there, Guangxi is regarded as a leading province in China for the production and export of these delicacies. The region is well known for high-quality shaddock, banana, pineapple and orange.

The favorable climate and geographical location enable Guangxi to have as many as 8000 tree species, including more than 1000 kinds of arbor. Most of the precious forest resources are concentrated in the northeastern and Baise areas. By the end of 2005, 72 nature reserves had been established across the region, covering an area of 1.515 million hectare. The picturesque scenic spots in Guangxi are famous worldwide, symbolized by Guilin, a natural beauty spot produced by unique karst geology. The province has established several tourist attractions, including 3 state-level natural scenic spots, 11 state-level forest parks, 30 regional natural scenic spots, 15 state-level cultural and historical relics, 221 regional cultural and historical relics and 1 state-level tourist resort in Beihai City.

The Han Chinese are the largest ethnic group in the province. Of these the main sub-groups are those that speak the Southwestern Mandarin and Cantonese varieties of Chinese. The region has over 14 million Zhuang, the largest minority ethnicity of China. More than 90 % of Zhuang in China live in Guangxi, especially in the central and western regions. There are also a significant number of both Dong and Miao minority peoples. Other ethnic groups include Yao, Hui, Yi (Lolo), Shui and Gin (Vietnamese). There is a minor Christian population, which is subject to rigorous official regulations. Given its large population of ethnic minorities and beautiful scenery, cultural tourism is Guangxi's major industry.

With picturesque scenery, Guangxi is a hot tourism spot in China. Guilin and Yangsuo along the Li River, Hezhou Stone Forest and Behai Silver Bay attract a large number of domestic and overseas tourists. The major tourist attraction of Guangxi is Guilin, a town famed across China and the world for its spectacular setting by the Li Jiang (Li River) among striking karst peaks. It also used to be the capital of Guangxi, and Jingjiang Princes' City, the old princes' residence, is open to the public. South of Guilin down the river is the town of Yangshuo, which has become another favorite destination for foreign tourists. Ethnic minorities in Guangxi, such as the Zhuang and Dong, are also interesting for tourists. The northern part of the province, bordering with Guizhou, is home to the Longsheng Rice Terraces, some of the steepest in the world. Nearby is Sanjiang Dong Autonomous County.

During the past decade, Guangxi Zhuang Autonomous Region has achieved a fast economic growth. Its industrial and service sectors have attracted a large proportion of fixed asset investments. Manufacturing and real estate represent the largest portion of fixed asset investments, followed by energy, logistics, water conservancy, and environmental and public facility management. The economy has languished behind that of its wealthy neighbor and twin, Guangdong. Due to its lack of major manufacturing industry in comparison with other provinces, despite its proximity to Guangdong and low wages, Guangxi is the fourth most energy-efficient province in China, helping to boost its green image further (Table 1.13).

Local government has embarked on a major infrastructure upgrade in the hope of bringing more business and industry into the province. In particular, the Beibu Gulf Economic Zone has been a major priority for development because of its land and water access to Southeast Asia. Growth in exports from this region has helped to boost confidence in the economy and as a result increase real-estate investment.

Liuzhou is the main industrial center and is a major motor vehicle manufacturing area. General Motors has a manufacturing base here in a joint venture as SAIC-GM-Wuling Automobile. The city also has a large steel factory and several related industries. Local government hopes to expand the province's manufacturing sector, and during the drafting of China's five-year plan in 2011 it earmarked ¥2.6 trillion for investment in the province's Beibu Gulf Economic Zone.

With its suitable weather and geographic location, Guangxi is one of China's most important sugarcane, vegetable and fruit bases. The increasing production of vegetables, fruit and crops has brought about the large growth in its food-processing industry. As a large production base for sugarcane in China, it has also gained two-thirds of the value-added output from the food-processing sector. Nanning Sugar Industry Co. Ltd, Guangxi Guitang Group and Guangxi Funan East Asia Sugar Co. Ltd are the top-three sugar makers in the province. In the automobile industry,

Table 1.13 Demographic and socioeconomic profile: Guangxi

Indicator	2000	2010
Population (thousands)	44,890	46,100
Illiteracy rate of population aged 15 or over (%)	3.79	2.71
GRP (¥ billions)	205.01	956.99
Composition of GRP (%)		
Primary sector	26.3	17.5
Secondary sector	36.5	47.1
Tertiary sector	37.2	35.4
Fixed asset investment (¥ billions)	58.33	705.76
Status of foreign-funded enterprises		
Number of registered enterprises	2705	5327
Total investment (US$ millions)	10,850	27,973
Registered capital (US$ millions)	6268	15,478
Foreign trade (US$ millions)		
Export	1640	6525
Import	644	13,024
Sales of consumer goods (¥ billions)	86	331
Per capita annual disposable income of urban residents (¥)	5834.43	17,063.89
Engle's coefficient (%)	39.90	38.06
Per capita annual net income of rural residents (¥)	1864.51	4543.41
Engle's coefficient (%)	40.20	48.49
Number of patent applications granted	1191	3647
Inventions	99	426
Utility models	730	2167
Designs	362	1054

Note All monetary values are measured at current prices. *Source* Guangxi Statistical Yearbook, 2001 and 2011

major players include Liuzhou Wuling Motors Co. Ltd, SAIC-GM-Wuling Automobile Co. Ltd, Dongfeng Liuzhou Motor Co. Ltd and Yucai Group.

Equipment manufacturing, metallurgy, food processing, electrical power and automobile manufacturing form the major industries in the industrial sector. Guangxi Liugong Machinery Co. Ltd, set up in 1958, is China's top construction equipment manufacturer and the first listed company in the domestic industry. Rich resources in the province have aided the strong development of its metallurgy industry. Guangxi Liuzhou Steel Corp, with annual production capacity of steel and iron both surpassing 5 million tons, is a major player in Guangxi.

Due to the many scenic locations in Guangxi, tourism contributes significantly to the development of the service sector. The finance sector, though not as strong as others in China's coastal regions, has been emerging as another important industry.

Major imported products include soybeans, mechanical and electrical products, spinning fibers, coal, and high-tech products. Mechanical and electrical products remain the most important export products for the province. Other important export products include travel goods, boxes and bags, rolled steel, porcelain and pottery wares, and high-tech products. Guangxi's largest foreign trade partner is Vietnam (for both export and import). The other major trade partners are the US, Hong Kong, Japan and Taiwan (for export) and Australian Japan, the US and Germany (for import).

Guangxi has also strengthened its effort to attract foreign investors. Hong Kong was the largest foreign investment source, followed by the British Virgin Islands, Singapore, Japan and the US. The industrial sector has received the largest proportion of foreign investment, followed by the real-estate and public service sectors, which are followed by the agricultural sector and logistics.

As of 2010, compared with those of other provinces, "education" "health, social security and social welfare" and "management of water conservancy, environment and public facilities" were relatively strong, while "mining", "services to households and other services" and "manufacturing" were relatively weak sectors (see Table 1.14).

Table 1.14 Guangxi's comparative (dis)advantage index by sector, 2010

Sector	Index
Agriculture, forestry, animal husbandry and fishery	1.18
Mining	0.32
Manufacturing	0.71
Production and distribution of electricity, gas and water	1.19
Construction	0.99
Transport, storage and post	1.18
Information transmission, computer service and software	0.79
Wholesale and retail trades	0.92
Hotels and catering services	0.85
Financial intermediation	0.86
Real estate	0.83
Leasing and business services	1.18
Scientific research, technical services and geological prospecting	0.98
Management of water conservancy, environment and public facilities	1.40
Services to households and other services	0.57
Education	1.51
Health, social security and social welfare	1.49
Culture, sports and entertainment	1.00
Public management and social organization	1.14

Notes All the sectors included in this table are determined according to China's official definitions and for urban areas only. Numerals greater than, equal to and less than one indicate that the province's sectors have advantages, no apparent (dis)advantages and disadvantages, respectively
Source Calculated by authors based on China Statistical Yearbook, 2011. See Appendix A for a detailed methodological description

Guizhou

[Quick Facts: Official name: Guizhou Province; Capital: Guiyang; Land area: 176,100 km^2; Population density: 222/km^2; Major ethnic groups: Han, Miao, Buyi, Tujia, Dong]

Guizhou is a province of the PRC located in the southwestern part of the country. Its provincial capital city is Guiyang. Guizhou (often abbreviated to "Gui" or "Qian") is located on the eastern slope of the Yunnan-Guizhou Plateau in the southeastern part of China. It borders Hunan Province to the east, Guangxi Autonomous Region to the south, Yunnan Province to the west and Sichuan Province and Chongqing Municipality to the north.

Overall Guizhou is a mountainous province. However, it is more hilly in the west while the eastern and southern portions are relatively flat. About 92.5 % of the province's area is blanketed by mountains and hills and 61.9 % of this land is dominated by karst landforms. Its average altitude is 1100 m. Unique natural landscapes, such as Huangguoshu (yellow fruit tree) Waterfall, the Limestone Cave and the Stone Woods are major tourist attractions.

In the province there are over 300 basins which are wide in the middle and narrow at both ends, and each covers over 160 ha. The average annual temperature is 14–16 °C. High in the east and low in the west, Guizhou lies over 1000 m above sea level. It enjoys ample precipitation. Rivers flow through steep terrain, resulting in a hydropower generating resource of 18.74 million kilowatt, placing the province at sixth place in the country. It is also rich in gas stored in coal reserves. The abundant water and coal reserves allow the province to have a strategy of developing water and coal energy at the same time.

As one of the resource-rich provinces, Guizhou boasts more than 110 kinds of minerals, of which the amount of reserves of 76 of them is already known. It is among the top-ten sites in the nation in terms of reserves of 42 kinds of minerals and the top three for 22 of these. The province is particularly strong in reserves of coal, phosphorus, mercury, aluminum, manganese, antimony, gold, barite, raw materials for cement and bricks, dolomite, sandstone and limestone.

The province also has the largest bauxite reserves in China, accounting for 28.1 % of the country's total. With a reserve of 241.9 billion tons of coal, it has the largest reserves in south China. Guizhou has been known as the "home of coal in south China". Its phosphorus reserve accounts for 44 % of the national total while the mercury reserve, after long years of tapping, still makes up 38 % of the total amount in the country. The newly discovered gold reserve of 150 tons offers the country another gold production base.

Guizhou has a subtropical humid climate with few seasonal changes. Its annual average temperature is roughly 10–20 °C, with January temperatures of 1–10 °C and July temperatures of 17–28 °C. The climate and abundant rainfall mean that the province is home to over 3800 species of wild animals. Out of this figure, over 1000 are rare species under state protection. More than 3700 kinds of medicinal herbs (80 % of the total in China) are found in Guizhou. There are 130 nature reserves covering an area of 961,000 ha and accounting for 5.5 % of the province's territory.

Guizhou is a newly flourishing tourist destination. Unique natural scenery, rich ethnic traditions, splendid culture and history, and a pleasant climate draw tourists to the province. Now over 120 tourist sites have been opened up, including national scenic areas of Huangguoshu Waterfalls, the Dragon Palace, the Golden Brocade Cave, the Red Maple Lake, the Maling River Valley, the Shizhang Cave on the Chishui River, four national nature reserves (the Fanjing Mountain Botanic Garden, the Maolan Karst Primeval Forest, the Chishui Primeval Forest and the bird reserve at Caohai), eight national cultural relic sites and many villages with distinctive ethnic minority customs and ways of life.

Demographically, Guizhou is one of China's most diverse provinces. Minority groups comprise 37.8 % of the total population. These groups, such as the Miao, Bouyei, Dong, Yi, Shui, Hui, Gelao, Zhuang, Yao, Bai and Tujia, have brought rich and varied folk customs, culture, architecture and festivals to the province, offering another important tourism resource. The rich population of minorities in Guizhou allows for a great number of ethnic festivals throughout the calendar. During the first lunar month (usually February), the early festival in Kaili (in the east of Guiyang) celebrates local culture with acts of bullfighting, horse racing, pipe playing and comedy works. The southeastern corner of the province is known for its unique Dong minority culture. Towns such as Rongjiang, Liping, Diping and Zhaoxing are scattered amongst the hills along the border with Guangxi.

Guizhou is a relatively poor and economically undeveloped province but is rich in natural, cultural and environmental resources. Its nominal GRP for 2010 was ¥460.22 billion. Its per capita GRP of ¥10,258 (US$1502) ranks last in all provinces of the PRC (Table 1.15).

Table 1.15 Demographic and socioeconomic profile: Guizhou

Indicator	2000	2010
Population (thousands)	35,250	34,789
Illiteracy rate of population aged 15 or over (%)	13.89	8.74
GRP (¥ billions)	99.35	460.22
Composition of GRP (%)		
Primary sector	27.3	13.6
Secondary sector	39.0	39.1
Tertiary sector	33.7	47.3
Fixed asset investment (¥ billions)	39.70	310.49
Status of foreign-funded enterprises		
Number of registered enterprises	715	1936
Total investment (US$ millions)	1493	4132
Registered capital (US$ millions)	1166	2510
Foreign trade (US$ millions)		
Export	482	2016
Import	375	1443
Sales of consumer goods (¥ billions)	34	148
Per capita annual disposable income of urban residents (¥)	5122.21	14,142.74
Engle's coefficient (%)	42.95	39.90
Per capita annual net income of rural residents (¥)	1374.16	3471.93
Engle's coefficient (%)	36.13	46.26
Number of patent applications granted	710	3086
Inventions	65	441
Utility models	377	1936
Designs	268	709

Note All monetary values are measured at current prices. *Source* Guizhou Statistical Yearbook, 2001 and 2011

Guizhou relies heavily on agriculture and tourism to prop up its economy. It is China's third largest grower of tobacco and home to the Guizhou Tobacco, a well-known consumer brand. Its natural industry includes timber and forestry. Other important industries in the province include energy (especially electricity) and mining (especially in coal, limestone, arsenic, gypsum and oil shale). A target of investments, the province's significant coal reserves and power generation industry allow the export of a large amount of produced energy to Guangdong and other provinces.

Poor infrastructure has limited the development of a manufacturing industry and hinders tourism. A high-speed rail line from Guiyang to Guangzhou and other projects meant to expand the province's transportation links with neighboring provinces are planned in the hope of spurring on economic growth.

The structure of the region's industrial output reflects the province's natural resources. The production and distribution of electricity, gas and water, metallurgy, tobacco manufacturing, coal, raw chemical materials and chemical products, beverage manufacturing, coal, and medical and pharmaceutical products form the pillar industries of the province. Guizhou is known as "coal home of South China". Guizhou Shuicheng Coal Mining Co. Ltd is the largest coal miner in the province.

Guizhou has high altitudes in the east and low altitudes in the west. The dramatic downward flow of water offers vast hydropower generating resources, making the region a major base for supplying electricity from the western part of China to the eastern regions. Guizhou Power Grid is the largest state-owned electricity power operator in the province. During the past decade, smelting and pressing of non-ferrous metal has yielded a sharp increase in industrial value-added output. Shuicheng Steel Group and Guizhou Branch of Aluminum Corp of China (Chalco) are the two largest companies in Guizhou's metallurgical sector.

In 2006 the province produced 297,300 tons of tobacco, 13.7 % less than 2005, due to the government's control over land use for the tobacco industry. It produced 10.6 billion cigarettes, accounting for over 5.2 % of the country's total. The industrial value-added output from tobacco manufacturing amounted to ¥7.9 billion by the end of 2006, up 5.8 % year on year. Guizhou Huangguoshu Tobacco Group is the largest tobacco maker in the province. The industrial value-added output from the beverage-manufacturing industry surpassed ¥5 billion, representing an increase of 23.5 % year on year, while the industrial value-added output from alcohol production jumped 23.1 % year on year to ¥4.9 billion, making up 98 % of the total generated by the province's beverage manufacturing sector. The China Kweichow Moutai Distillery Group is one of China's largest and most ancient alcohol makers.

The ample number of medicinal herbs have favored the development of the medical and pharmaceutical industry there. In 2006 this sector generated ¥3.7 billion of industrial value-added output, up 9.9 % compared with the previous year. Large pharmaceutical producers include Guizhou Yibai Pharmaceutical Corp, Guizhou Eakan Pharma Group and Guizhou Baixiang Pharmaceutical Group.

Table 1.16 Guizhou's comparative (dis)advantage index by sector, 2010

Sector	Index
Agriculture, forestry, animal husbandry and fishery	0.32
Mining	1.22
Manufacturing	0.59
Production and distribution of electricity, gas and water	1.31
Construction	1.07
Transport, storage and post	0.88
Information transmission, computer service and software	0.85
Wholesale and retail trades	1.12
Hotels and catering services	0.71
Financial intermediation	0.80
Real estate	1.06
Leasing and business services	0.62
Scientific research, technical services and geological prospecting	0.86
Management of water conservancy, environment and public facilities	0.89
Services to households and other services	0.98
Education	1.54
Health, social security and social welfare	1.09
Culture, sports and entertainment	0.81
Public management and social organization	1.64

Notes All the sectors included in this table are determined according to China's official definitions and for urban areas only. Numerals greater than, equal to and less than one indicate that the province's sectors have advantages, no apparent (dis)advantages and disadvantages, respectively
Source Calculated by authors based on China Statistical Yearbook, 2011. See Appendix A for a detailed methodological description

Wholesale and retail trade, and tourism are the two most important industries in Guizhou's service sector. By the end of 2006 there were 1801 wholesale marts, 23 of which had annual transaction volumes of more than ¥100 million. Hualian from Beijing and Wal-Mart from the US have made their presence felt. As a popular tourist destination, Guizhou attracted 321,400 foreign tourists and 47 million domestic tourists in 2006, which brought in US$115 million and ¥38 billion revenue.

The top export products include chemicals and related products, followed by base metal and related products, mechanical and electrical products, rubber and related products, and metal and related products. Major import products are iron ore, sulfur, rubber, ribbed smoke sheets and manganese. Major export destinations are the US, Vietnam, Hong Kong, Japan and South Korea, while key import sources are India, Australia, Canada, Thailand and Brazil.

Among the foreign-funded projects approved by provincial government, manufacturing and real estate received the greatest amount of FDI. A substantial portion of this has also been channeled into other industries, such as logistics, accommodation and catering, research, and technical service. Foreign investors are encouraged to invest in auto parts, tourism, textiles, food processing, medicines, health products and other high-tech industries.

As of 2010, compared with those of other provinces, "public management and social organization" "education" and "production and distribution of electricity, gas and water" were relatively strong, while "agriculture, forestry, animal husbandry and fishery", "manufacturing" and "leasing and business services" were relatively weak sectors (see Table 1.16).

Hainan

[Quick Facts: Official name: Hainan Province; Capital: Haikou; Land area: 33,920 km^2; Population density: 241/km^2; Major ethnic groups: Han, Li, Miao, Zhuang, Hui]

Hainan is a province of the PRC. The name also refers to Hainan Island, the main island of the province, which measures 155 km long and 169 km wide. The province lies at the southernmost tip of China, facing Guangdong in the north across the shallow and narrow Qiongzhou Strait, Vietnam in the west across the Beibu Gulf (Gulf of Tonkin), and Taiwan in the east across the South China Sea. To the south and southeast it is bounded in the South China Sea by the Philippines, Brunei and Malaysia.

For centuries Hainan Island was part of Guangdong Province. In 1988 this resource-rich tropical island became part of the newly created Hainan Province, which has an area of 33,920 km^2 and is China's southernmost province. Although it comprises some 200 islands scattered among three archipelagos off the southern coast, 32,900 km^2 (97 %) of its land mass is Hainan Island.

There are 8 major cities and 10 counties in Hainan Province. Haikou on the northern coast of Hainan Island is the capital, whilst Sanya is a well-known tourist destination on the south coast. The other major cities are Wenchang, Qionghai, Wanning, Wuzhishan, Dongfang and Danzhou.

Hainan Province uses a slightly different administrative system than the other provinces. Most others are divided into prefecture-level divisions, while county-level divisions generally do not come directly under the province. In Hainan, however, nearly all county-level divisions (the four districts are the only exceptions) come directly under the province. The Paracel Islands and Spratly Islands, south of Sanya, are claimed by the PRC and are thus considered to form an administrative division of Hainan Province by them. Sovereignty of the islands is disputed, however.

With Mount Wuzhi (five fingers) and Mount Yingge (parrot) standing at its very heart, Hainan Island has a staircase-like topography descending step by step from towering mountains to flat tablelands and plains at its periphery. Most mountains on the island are 500–800 m high. Among those rising 1500 m or higher above sea level are Mount Wuzhi, Mount Yingge, Mount Ezong, Mount Houmi, Yajiada Ridge and Mount Diaoluo. The inland has 154 streams flowing directly into the sea. Most rivers on the island originate from the central mountain area, forming a radiating river system. The drainage area covered by the three major rivers of Nandu, Changhua and Wanquan accounts for 47 % of the island's territory.

Hainan is rich in mineral resources. Among the 148 minerals with verified workable reserves nationwide, 57 (or 65 if classified based on their potential industrial purposes) are of certain mining value in Hainan. In addition, 126 mineral deposits (including six large groundwater sources) have had their reserves verified. More than ten varieties of superior minerals produced here hold a very important position in China's mining industry, including glass-quality quartz sand, natural gas, titanium, zircon, sapphire, crystal, gibbsite, oil shale and zeolite. The reserves of iron ore accounts for roughly 70 % of the country's high-grade iron ore. Those of titanium and zircon make up 70 and 60 % those of China as a whole, respectively. In addition, gold, granite and mineral water are of significant developmental value in the region.

Hainan abounds with oil and natural gas. General survey and exploration have targeted three large sedimentation basins—the Beibu Gulf, Yingge Sea and southeast Hainan—with a total area of around 120,000 km^2, of which 60,000 km^2 prospect well with oil-gas mines. The potential reserves of hydroelectricity on the island amount to 1 million kilowatt, of which 650,000 kW are expected to generate 2.6 billion kilowatt hour of electricity annually. The volume of groundwater is about 7.5 billion cubic meter, making up about 20 % of Hainan's water reserves, of which approximately 2.53 billion cubic meter is potentially exploitable. Its untapped energy sources with great potential include ocean energy, solar energy and bioelectricity. In addition, Hainan Island is one of China's ideal natural saltworks. Salt can be made by evaporating brine in the sun along its coast, which stretches for hundreds of miles from Sanya to Dongfang. At present, several large saltworks, including Yinggehai, Dongfang and Yuya, have been developed.

A tropical maritime climate prevails in Hainan, bringing it all-year-round windy but warm days, abundant rainfall, clearly divided dry and wet seasons, frequent tropical storms and typhoons, and diverse climatic resources. Winterless Hainan Island has annual sunshine of 1750–2650 h, a yearly average temperature of 23–25 °C and an average annual rainfall of more than 1600 mm. The wet central part and east coast receive more rainfall than the semi-dry southwest coast and other semi-wet areas. Winter and spring are usually dry while summer and autumn produce the wettest seasons.

Hainan Island makes up 42.5 % of the nation's tropical land, with an average per capita possession of 0.48 ha of land used for agriculture, forestry, animal husbandry and fishery. As a result of such excellent conditions of sunlight, heat and water, the farmlands here can be cultivated anytime of the year, and many plants can yield two or three crops annually. Based on tits suitability the land on Hainan Island can be assigned to seven major categories: that suitable for farming, rubber planting, tropical crop growing, forestation, livestock breeding, aquaculture and other purposes. Currently, 3.152 million hectare of land on the island have been cultivated, while 260,000 ha remain virgin soil, around 90 % of which is potential farmland.

Grain crops, which have the widest distribution and highest yield in Hainan, mainly comprise rice, upland rice, shanlanpo rice, wheat, sweet potato, cassava, taro, maize, Chinese sorghum, millet and beans. Among the industrial crops are sugarcane, hemp, peanuts, sesame and tea. There also exist a great variety of both cultivated and wild fruits that fall into 29 families and 53 genera. Cultivated commodity fruits consist of pineapple, litchi, longan, banana, plantain, citrus, mango, watermelon, parambola, jackfruit and others. In addition, over 120 kinds of vegetables are grown here. Hainan Island is rich in tropical crop resources. Major tropical crops with a large growing area and of high economic value include rubber plant, coconut palm, oil palm, betel palm, pepper, sisal hemp, lemongrass, cashew and cocoa.

More than 4000 kinds of plants have been found in Hainan—roughly one-seventh of the nation's total. Hainan's tropical forests, characterized by conspicuous vertical zoning and mixed growth of trees of different species and ages, and with high trunks and broad crowns, are mainly distributed over the mountains of Wuzhi, Jianfeng, Bawang, Diaoluo and Limu, with those on Wuzhi Mountain belonging to rainforests. Hainan is home to over 500 species of terrestrial vertebrates, including 37 kinds of amphibians (of which 11 are only found in Hainan, and 8 are listed as unique to China), 104 kinds of reptiles, 344 kinds of birds and 82 varieties of mammals (21 of which are peculiar to Hainan). In addition to black-crested gibbon —one of the four anthropoid apes living on earth—and slope deer, which are among the rarest species in the world, there are such treasured animals as sambar, macaque and cloud-leopard. By the end of 2005, 15 kinds of wild animals were under first-class state protection and 87 under second-class state protection.

Farms of tropical crops on the island also present charming pictures of unique rural scenery. As a result of Hainan's tropical climate, the province is an important source of paddy rice, coconuts, palm oil, tropical fruit and fish. Tourist-related services and agriculture are the main economic drivers. Secondary industries, such as automobile equipment, constitute a small portion. Hainan is rich in medicinal herbs. Of the 4000 or so kinds of plants growing there, about 2500 can be used as medicinal herbs. About 50 kinds of animals and marine products can be used to serve medicinal purposes too.

Vast offshore fishing grounds with an area of nearly 300,000 km^2, great variety of aquatic products with a short growth period, and a long fishing season form the characteristics of Hainan's aquatic and marine resources. This makes Hainan an ideal place to develop tropical marine fishing. There are more than 800 kinds of aquatic products, including over 600 fish, of which over 40 are cash fish. The province's coastal beaches that can be used for sea farming totals 25,700 ha.

As Hainan Island is not heavily industrialized, its greenery, together with its beautiful beaches, hot springs, clean air and other attractions, make it popular with tourists. In 2000 the province initiated a visa-upon-arrival policy for foreign tourist groups. This is available to citizens of 26 different countries and was established to attract visitors. The top scenic sites include the Yalong Bay National Resort, the Dadonghai Tourist Resort, the Qizhi Shan (Seven Finger Mountain), the Nuilin Mountain Tropical Botanical Reserve in Lingshui County, the Guantang Hot Spring Resort, the Shishan Volcanic Garden, the Wanquan River, the Baishi Ridge Scenic Zone and the Baihua Ridge.

Hainan Island is densely crossed by rivers. Winding streams, deep pools, fantastic waterfalls and mirror-like reservoirs dotted through the mountains and virgin forests add beauty to the landscapes and attract tourists. Hainan is noted for its singularly shaped mountains, of which many are summer resorts. Densely spread tropical primeval forests are characteristic of Hainan's lofty mountains, such as the four most well-known virgin forest regions of Mount Jianfeng in Ledong County, Mount Bawang in Changjiang County, Mount Diaoluo in Lingshui County and Mount Wuzhi in Qiongzhong County.

To protect rare birds and animals, several wildlife reserves and have been established in Hainan, including the Bawangling Black-Crested Gibbon Reserve in Changjiang County, the Datian Slope Deer Reserve in Dongfang County, the Dazhou Isle Esculent Swift Reserve in Wanning City and the Macaque Reserve on the Nanwan Peninsula in Lingshui County.

Hainan is the home of the Li as well as many other ethnic groups who still hold to their unsophisticated folk customs and unique living habits, which have made the island even more valuable to tourism.

Its province's GRP for 2010 was ¥206.45 billion (about US$30 billion), making it the fourth smallest in the PRC, and it contributes just 0.5 % to the country's economy. In December 2009 the government of China announced that it plans to establish Hainan as an "international tourist destination" by 2020. This announcement contributed to a surge in the province's economy (Table 1.17).

Table 1.17 Demographic and socioeconomic profile: Hainan

Indicator	2000	2010
Population (thousands)	7870	8686
Illiteracy rate of population aged 15 or over (%)	6.98	4.08
GRP (¥ billions)	51.85	206.45
Composition of GRP (%)		
Primary sector	37.9	26.1
Secondary sector	19.8	27.7
Tertiary sector	42.3	46.2
Fixed asset investment (¥ billions)	19.89	131.70
Status of foreign-funded enterprises		
Number of registered enterprises	7248	4171
Total investment (US$ millions)	23,436	25,886
Registered capital (US$ millions)	13,926	14,545
Foreign trade (US$ millions)		
Export	609	2162
Import	486	8209
Sales of consumer goods (¥ billions)	17	64
Per capita annual disposable income of urban residents (¥)	5358.32	15,581.05
Engle's coefficient (%)	49.31	44.81
Per capita annual net income of rural residents (¥)	2182.26	5275.37
Engle's coefficient (%)	45.75	50.04
Number of patent applications granted	320	714
Inventions	15	190
Utility models	90	305
Designs	215	219

Note All monetary values are measured at current prices. *Source* Hainan Statistical Yearbook, 2001 and 2011

Table 1.18 Hainan's comparative (dis)advantage index by sector, 2010

Sector	Index
Agriculture, forestry, animal husbandry and fishery	5.24
Mining	0.26
Manufacturing	0.36
Production and distribution of electricity, gas and water	1.01
Construction	0.86
Transport, storage and post	1.09
Information transmission, computer service and software	0.63
Wholesale and retail trades	1.06
Hotels and catering services	3.35
Financial intermediation	0.72
Real estate	2.41
Leasing and business services	1.13
Scientific research, technical services and geological prospecting	0.92
Management of water conservancy, environment and public facilities	1.63
Services to households and other services	0.83
Education	1.19
Health, social security and social welfare	1.05
Culture, sports and entertainment	1.45
Public management and social organization	1.09

Notes All the sectors included in this table are determined according to China's official definitions and for urban areas only. Numerals greater than, equal to and less than one indicate that the province's sectors have advantages, no apparent (dis)advantages and disadvantages, respectively
Source Calculated by authors based on China Statistical Yearbook, 2011. See Appendix A for a detailed methodological description

Hainan's economy is predominantly agricultural, and more than a half of the island's exports are agricultural products. Its elevation to province-level status in 1988, however, was accompanied by its designation as China's largest special economic zone, the intent being to hasten the development of the island's plentiful resources. Prior to this, the province had a reputation for being a "Wild West" area. Even today there are relatively few factories in the province. Tourism plays an important part in Hainan's economy, thanks largely to its tropical beaches and lush forests.

Central government has encouraged foreign investment in Hainan and has allowed the island to rely to a large extent on market forces. Hainan's industrial development has been limited largely to the processing of its mineral and agricultural products, particularly rubber and iron ore. Since the 1950s, machinery, farm equipment and textiles have been manufactured in the Haikou area for local consumption. A major constraint on industrial expansion has been an inadequate supply of electricity. Much of the island's generating capacity is hydroelectric, and this is subject to seasonal fluctuations in stream and river flows.

The largest share of Hainan's FDI is Hong Kong, which concentrates mainly on Haikou, Sanya and Wanning. The EU is now Hainan's largest export partner, while Oman, Angola, the US, Russia, Malaysia and Japan are the major import partners.

As of 2010, compared with those of other provinces, "agriculture, forestry, animal husbandry and fishery" "hotels and catering services" and "real estate" were relatively strong, while "mining", "manufacturing" and "information transmission, computer service and software" were relatively weak sectors (see Table 1.18).

Hebei

[Quick Facts: Official name: Hebei Province; Capital: Shijiazhuang; Land area: 187,700 km^2; Population density: 372/km^2; Major ethnic groups: Han, Manchu, Hui, Mongol, Zhuang]

Hebei is a province of the PRC in north China. The name means "north of the river", referring to its location completely above the Yellow River. Its abbreviated name is Ji after the ancient prefecture "Ji" (Jizhou), which included the southern part of present-day Hebei. A common (unofficial) alternate name is "Yanzhao," which is after the Yan and the Zhao—two kingdoms that existed during the Eastern Zhou Dynasty (771–221 BC). In 1928, Hebei was formed after central government dissolved the province of Zhili (which means "directly ruled by the Imperial Court").

Hebei Province is located in the northern part of the North China Plain extending into the Inner Mongolian Plateau. The Bohai Bay of the Yellow Sea lies to the east of Hebei, which represents a 487 km coastline. Beijing, the capital of China, and Tianjin, an important trading port in north China, are situated at the center of the province but are not part of it. It adjoins Liaoning and Inner Mongolia to the north, Shanxi to the west, Shandong to the southeast and Henan to the south. A small part of Hebei, an exclave disjointed from the rest of the province, is wedged between the municipalities of Beijing and Tianjin.

Most of central and southern Hebei lies within the North China Plain. The western part rises into the Taihang Mountains (Taihang Shan), while the Yan Mountains (Yan Shan) run through northern Hebei, beyond which lie the grasslands of Inner Mongolia. The Great Wall of China cuts through northern Hebei from east to west as well, briefly entering the border of Beijing Municipality, and terminates at the seacoast of Shanhaiguan in northeastern Hebei. The highest peak is Mount Xiaowutai in northwestern Hebei, with an altitude of 2882 m above sea level.

Hebei borders Bohai Sea to the east. The Hai He watershed covers most of the province's central and southern parts, and the Luan He watershed covers the northeast. Among the numerous reservoirs found in the hills and mountains, the largest lake is Baiyangdian, located mostly in Anxin County.

Ancient Hebei has been ruled by a multitude of dynasties. Situated in the north of China, it sits at the mouth of the Yellow River at the Bohai Sea and spans a land area of 187,700 km^2, completely surrounding the Beijing and Tianjin municipalities. Made up of 11 cities, it houses a population of 69 million. The major ethnic group within the province is the Han, and the minority ethnic groups are the Manchus, the Hui and the Mongols. These are subdivided into 172 county-level divisions (22 county-level cities, 108 counties, 6 autonomous counties and 36 districts). These are, in turn, divided into 2207 township-level divisions (1 district public office, 937 towns, 979 townships, 55 ethnic townships and 235 sub-districts).

The topography of Hebei Province is composed of three major geomorphic features, of which the average height of the Bashang highland is 1200–1500 m above sea level, making up 8.5 % of the total area. Meanwhile, Mount Yanshan and Mount Taihangshan, including hilly land and basins, mostly lie within an elevation below 2000 m, accounting for 48.1 % of the total area. The Hebei Plain is part of the North China Plain, with an elevation mostly below 50 m, accounting for 43.4 % of the provincial area.

Hebei has a continental monsoon climate, with cold, dry winters and hot, humid summers. In most areas the change of season is distinct, with yearly sunshine averaging 2500–3100 h. The annual frost-free period lasts about 120–200 days. The annual rainfall averages 300–800 mm, concentrated heavily in summer. The monthly mean temperature is 3 °C or below. The mean temperature in July is 18–27 °C.

The province has a coastline of 487.3 km, covering an area of 1 million hectare. As a result the province can develop such industries as offshore petroleum oil drilling, marine chemicals, marine transportation and marine tourism. Qinhuangdao is a well-known ice-free port in north China. The Yellow River, the Haihe River and the Luanhe River run across the province where an offshore aquatic breeding industry could easily be developed.

So far 116 varieties of mineral ores have been discovered, the deposits of 74 of which have been surveyed. There are 45 mines whose reserves are among the nation's top 10. The province boasts two large coalmines at Kailuan and Fengfeng, in addition to the North China oilfield.

In the province there are more than 3000 species of plants, of which more than 140 are fiber plants, more than 1000 are medicinal herbs and plants, and more than 100 are sources of timber. There are 300 or more kinds of forage grass, 140 kinds of oily plants and more than 450 varieties of cultivated plants. Of these, the output of cotton makes up one-seventh of the nation's total and that of maize and fruits each makes up one-tenth. There are 215 varieties of farming products in 12 major categories that can be listed as brand name and best products, or native or rare products. There are more than 20 varieties of medicinal herbs and materials for export.

The province is the only one in the country that boasts highlands, mountainous and hilly areas, plains, lakes and a coastline. Across the region there are 304 ancient ruins and groups of ancient buildings, including 58 key relics under state protection. The number of historical and cultural relics in the province ranks first in the country along with Shaanxi Province. The number of natural and human cultural scenic sites ranks second nationally. These include the Chengde Summer Resort, Shanhaiguan Pass at the head of the Great Wall of China, Beidaihe Holiday Resort and the Eastern and Western Tombs of the emperors of the Qing Dynasty (AD 1644–1911).

The Great Wall of China crosses the northern part of Hebei. The eastern end is located on the coast at Shanhaiguan (Shanhai Pass) near Qinhuangdao. The Shanhaiguan is known as the "First Pass of The World". Beidaihe, near Shanhaiguan, is a popular beach resort well known as a former meeting place for top governmental officials.

The Qing Dynasty's imperial tombs are located in Zunhua and Yi counties, which are called the Eastern Qing Tombs and the West Qing Tombs, respectively. The Eastern Qing Tombs are the resting place of 161 Qing emperors, empresses and other members of the Qing imperial family, while the West Qing Tombs number 76. They are also part of a World Heritage Site. The Zhaozhou, or Anji Bridge, built by Li Chun during the Sui Dynasty (AD 581–618), is the oldest stone arch bridge in China and one of the most significant examples of pre-modern Chinese civil engineering.

The Chengde Mountain Resort and its outlying temples are a UNESCO World Heritage Site. Also known as the Rehe Palace, this was the summer resort of the Manchu Qing Dynasty emperors. The Chengde Resort was built between 1703 and 1792. It consists of a palace complex, a large park area consisting of lakes, pavilions, causeways, bridges and so on, and a number of Tibetan Buddhist and Han Chinese temples in the surrounding area.

Thanks to its favorable geographical location, Hebei's GRP reached ¥2.04 trillion (about US$303 billion) in 2010, an increase of 10.1 % over the previous year, and ranked 6th in all the Chinese provinces. Meanwhile, its per capita GRP reached ¥24,428. More than half of its GRP comes from the industry sector and approximately a third from the service sector (Table 1.19).

Table 1.19 Demographic and socioeconomic profile: Hebei

Indicator	2000	2010
Population (thousands)	67,440	71,936
Illiteracy rate of population aged 15 or over (%)	6.65	2.61
GRP (¥ billions)	508.90	2039.43
Composition of GRP (%)		
Primary sector	16.2	12.6
Secondary sector	50.3	52.5
Tertiary sector	33.5	34.9
Fixed asset investment (¥ billions)	181.68	1508.34
Status of foreign-funded enterprises		
Number of registered enterprises	3812	9531
Total investment (US$ millions)	14,010	40,348
Registered capital (US$ millions)	8290	21,663
Foreign trade (US$ millions)		
Export	3278	27,974
Import	2209	34,079
Sales of consumer goods (¥ billion)	161	682
Per capita annual disposable income of urban residents (¥)	5661.16	16,263.43
Engle's coefficient (%)	34.91	32.32
Per capita annual net income of rural residents (¥)	2478.86	5957.98
Engle's coefficient (%)	28.62	35.15
Number of patent applications granted	2812	10,061
Inventions	221	954
Utility models	1917	6838
Designs	674	2269

Note All monetary values are measured at current prices. *Source* Hebei Statistical Yearbook, 2001 and 2011

Hebei's economy is largely dominated by iron and steel manufacturing, as consolidation of the province's steel industry continues.

Going forward, tighter integration of Beijing, Tianjin and 13 municipalities from Hebei into an economic zone will help to promote growth in Hebei, particularly in the areas of high-tech manufacturing, logistics and tourism. Currently, a large amount of transportation infrastructure construction is underway to make this a reality. Along with helping to promote the province's economy, this is also likely to create strong growth in the region's real-estate market.

Hebei's industries include textiles, coal, steel, iron, engineering, chemical production, petroleum, power, ceramics and food. Kailuan, with a history of over 100 years, is one of China's first modern coal mines and remains a major operation with annual production of over 20 million metric tons. Much of the North China Oilfield is situated in Hebei, and there are also major iron mines at Handan and Qian'an.

With a large area of cultivated land, Hebei is a major agricultural base in China. Some 40 % of the labor force work in the agriculture, forestry and animal husbandry sectors, with the majority of production from these industries going to Beijing and Tianjin. Hebei's main agricultural products are cereal crops, including wheat, maize, millet and sorghum. Cash crops like cotton, peanuts, soya beans and sesame are also produced.

Rich in resources, Hebei's iron and steel industry is one of the key industries within the province. In 2006 it was the largest producer of iron and steel in China. Tangshan Iron and Steel Group and the Handan Iron and Steel Group are amongst the largest enterprises within the national industry. Meanwhile, Shougang Iron and Steel Group closed its plants, which were responsible for much pollution in Beijing. It relocated to a new facility in Hebei, built with an annual capacity of 9.7 million tons. In addition to iron and steel, Hebei is also the largest producer of cement among all the other municipalities and provinces.

Boasting a large quantity of mineral reserves, Hebei offers rich energy resources, such as coal, natural gas and petroleum. Within the province, the supply of petroleum and natural gases comes mainly from the Jidong, Jizong and Dagang oilfields. Other leading industries within the sector are the pharmaceutical and electronics industries. Two established pharmaceutical enterprises within the province are North China Pharmaceutical Group and Shijiazhuang Pharmaceutical Group.

Thanks to its strategic location, Hebei serves as a convenient distribution center for northern China. The major retail and commercial centers are the cities of Shijiazhuang, Tangshan, Handan and Cangzhou. Besides Chinese departmental chains, many foreign supermarkets, such as Carrefour and Trust-Mart, have penetrated the growing retail market. The US, Australia, Japan, South Korea and Taiwan serve as Hebei's major export destinations. Primary exports include iron and steel, crude oil, fabrics and food. Meanwhile, the major import markets are Australia, Brazil, the US, Germany and India.

Most of Hebei's FDI has been channeled into the manufacturing industry, followed by real estate, transport, storage and postal services, farming, forestry, animal husbandry and fishery, and rental and business services. Within its overall foreign investment climate, Hong Kong was Hebei's largest source of FDI. Cities such as Shijiazhuang, Tangshan, Qinhuangdao and Langfang continue to receive large amount of foreign investments, while a growing number of investments are pouring into Handan and Chengde. Foreign investments that have established their presence within the provinces include Microsoft, GM and Siemens.

As of 2010, compared with those of other provinces, "production and distribution of electricity, gas and water", "education" and "public management and social organization" were relatively strong, while "leasing and business services", "agriculture, forestry, animal husbandry and fishery" and "real estate" were relatively weak sectors (see Table 1.20).

Table 1.20 Hebei's comparative (dis)advantage index by sector, 2010

Sector	Index
Agriculture, forestry, animal husbandry and fishery	0.44
Mining	1.24
Manufacturing	0.83
Production and distribution of electricity, gas and water	1.61
Construction	0.72
Transport, storage and post	1.00
Information transmission, computer service and software	0.85
Wholesale and retail trades	1.06
Hotels and catering services	0.54
Financial intermediation	1.30
Real estate	0.49
Leasing and business services	0.40
Scientific research, technical services and geological prospecting	0.76
Management of water conservancy, environment and public facilities	1.16
Services to households and other services	0.85
Education	1.37
Health, social security and social welfare	1.10
Culture, sports and entertainment	0.95
Public management and social organization	1.36

Notes All the sectors included in this table are determined according to China's official definitions and for urban areas only. Numerals greater than, equal to and less than one indicate that the province's sectors have advantages, no apparent (dis)advantages and disadvantages, respectively
Source Calculated by authors based on China Statistical Yearbook, 2011. See Appendix A for a detailed methodological description

Heilongjiang

[Quick Facts: Official name: Heilongjiang Province; Capital: Harbin; Land area: 460,000 km^2; Population density: 83/km^2; Major ethnic groups: Han, Manchu, Korean, Mongol, Hui]

Heilongjiang is a province of the PRC, located in the northeastern part of the country. The name literally means "black dragon river," the Chinese name for the Amur. The province is located at the highest latitudes. It neighbors Russia across the Amur and Wusuli rivers running in its north and east, respectively. In the west it adjoins Inner Mongolia Autonomous Region and to its south is Jilin Province. The one-character abbreviation of Heilongjiang Province is "Hei".

Much of province is dominated by mountain ranges, such as the Greater Khingan Range, the Lesser Khingan Range, the Zhangguangcai Mountains, the Laoye Mountains and the Wanda Mountains. The highest peak is Mount Datudingzi at 1690 m, located on the border with Jilin Province. The Greater Khingan Range contains China's largest remaining virgin forest and is an important area for China's forestry industry. The interior of the province, which is relatively flat and low in altitude, contains the Muling River, the Naoli River, the Songhua River, the Nen River and the Mudan River, all of which are tributaries of the Amur's basin, while the northern border forms part of the Amur Valley. Xingkai Lake (or Khanka Lake) is found on the border with Russia's Primorsky Krai. It covers an area of 454,000 km^2, accounting for 4.7 % of the nation's total. Under its jurisdiction are 13 prefectures and cities, 66 counties (cities), 1211 townships (towns) and 14,488 villages.

Heilongjiang Province has a sub-arctic climate. The winters are long and cold with an average temperature of −31 to −15 °C in January, while summers are short and cool with an average temperature of 18–23 °C in July. The annual average rainfall is 500–600 mm and is concentrated in summer. Clear weather is prevalent throughout the year. In the spring the Songnen Plain and the Sanpingjiang Plain provide abundant sources of wind energy. The warm summer with plentiful rainfall and sun is good for crops.

The province's topography is higher in the northwest, the north and the southeast, and lower in the northeast and the southwest. In the northwest are the Greater Hinggan Mountains and in the north the Lesser Hinggan Mountains. In the southeast there are the ridges of Zhangguangcai, Laoye and Taiping, in addition to Wanda Mountain. The Nenjiang River and Songhua River run across the province from south to north, forming the Sanjiang (three-river) Plain in the northeast and the Songnen Plain in the southwest. Also in the southeast is Xingkai Lake. Hilly land and mountain areas account for 70 % of the province's land, with heights ranging from 300–1780 m above sea level. Plains, 50–250 m above sea level, make up about 30 % of the province's total area.

The province has 44.37 million ha of soiled land with rich organics, of which 40 % is suitable for farming. Heilongjiang is one of the world's three major black soil zones, with 67.6 % of its farmland being cultivated on black soiled land, marshland or black calcium soil. Furthermore, the province ranks first in terms of farmland and forest area, seventh in area of pasture, fourth in land to be developed; and second in land reserved for farming. Both its farmland area and the reserved land resources account for one-tenth or more of the nation's total. The average per head area of farmland operated by individual farmers is three times the nation's average.

The province has the largest forestry industry in the country, occupying an important position in China's forest ecology. The area involved is 68.9 % of the province's total land area. Its forests cover 19.19 million hectarea of land, with a reserve of 1.5 billion cubic meter of live timber. With 41.9 % of its land covered with forest, Heilongjiang ranks first among all China's provinces in afforested area, reserve of forest resources and timber output. It is the most important state-owned forest area and the largest timber center in the country. In its forests are more than 100 species of trees, including 30 of high use-value. Natural forests, which constitute the principal part of its forest resources, are mainly distributed in the Greater Hinggan Mountains, the Lesser Hinggan Mountains and the Changbai Mountains.

Some 131 minerals have been discovered in the province and reserves of 74 of them have been surveyed. The deposits of ten minerals lead the country: petroleum, graphite, sillimanite, cast basalt, asbestos-use basalt, cement-use marble, colorant loess, lava ash, glass-use marble and orthoclase. Its coal deposit is the largest among the three northeast China provinces. Some 39 minerals have been mined and the annual output value of various minerals ranks second in the country.

Heilongjiang is one of China's water-rich provinces. Its numerous rivers form five water systems: those of the Amur River, the Wusuli River, the Songhua River, the Nenjiang River and the Suifeng River. There are about 6000 lakes and reservoirs covering a surface area of more than 800,000 ha. About 70 % of the area's rainfall is concentrated in the warm season, providing an ideal environment for plants and crops to grow.

The province also has a rich resource of wildlife. There are 86 species of vertebrates in 20 families of six orders, accounting for 21.6 % of the nation's total species. Of them, five are under first-class state protection, including sable, glutton, leopard, tiger and sika deer. There are 343 bird species in 57 families of 19 orders, making up 29 % of the nation's total, of which 12 species are under first-class state protection, including white cranes, Chinese goosanders, stocks and golden eagles. There are 2100 species of wild plants, 17 of which are gymnosperms in 8 genera of 4 families, 1747 species of angiosperms of 636 genera in 107 families; and 1764 species of seed plants in 644 genera of 111 families. There are 2.5 million tons of reserved wild plants of economic value, including more than 250,000 tons of edible plants, over 1 million tons of wild grasses for paper making and 1.25 million tons of medicinal herbs. The province's major agricultural products include soybeans, wheat, maize, potato, rice, beet, flax and tobacco. At the end of 2005 the province had 170 nature reserves covering an area of 4.689 million ha.

The majority of Heilongjiang's population is Han Chinese, while the major ethnic minorities include the Manchus, Koreans, Mongols, Hui, Daur, Xibe, Oroqin, Hezhen and Russians. Harbin, the provincial capital, is a city of contrasts, with Chinese, Russian and eclectic worldwide influences clearly apparent. Bukui Mosque, a national heritage site, is the largest glazed tile building in the province. Eastern Orthodox, Roman Catholic and Protestant churches dot the city.

Heilongjiang has abundant tourism resources. Its resorts for ice and snow activities are the best in China. The snow-skiing period in the province lasts 120–140 days a year. In the mountain area, snow on the ground can be 100–300 cm deep and it's of good quality. Among its smooth mountain slopes, 100 have been chosen for building large-scale skiing grounds. The area's beautiful landscape, forests, grasslands, wetlands, rivers and lakes provide rich resources for developing eco-tourism.

The province's unique history has also left it a rich cultural legacy and colorful customs. In addition, there are the Zoo of Northeast China Tigers, the Reserve of Red-Crowned Cranes, a site for admiring the northern lights, and a number of large-scale enterprises relating to mining, farming and oilfields open to tourists. The province has set up 84 nature reserves (including 7 at state-level and 17 at provincial level), which cover an area of 2.30 million ha, or 5.05 % of the province's land area.

In 2010, Heilongjiang's nominal GRP was ¥1036.86 billion (about US$140 billion). The industry and service sectors take up more than 40 % of the overall GRP each. Agriculture contributes significantly less to the economy, comprising only one-tenth of the GRP (Table 1.21).

The agriculture of Heilongjiang, heavily defined by the region's cold climate, is based on crops such as soybeans, maize and wheat. As one of the country's most important commodity grain production bases, it occupies first place in terms of both the volume and storage of commodity grains. Commercial crops grown include beets, flax and sunflowers. Heilongjiang is also an important source of lumber for China. Pine, especially Korean pine and larch, are the most important forms of lumber produced there. Forests are mostly to be found in the Daxingan Mountains

Table 1.21 Demographic and socioeconomic profile: Heilongjiang

Indicator	2000	2010
Population (thousands)	36,890	38,334
Illiteracy rate of population aged 15 or over (%)	5.10	2.06
GRP (¥ billions)	325.30	1036.86
Composition of GRP (%)		
Primary sector	11.0	12.6
Secondary sector	57.4	50.2
Tertiary sector	31.6	37.2
Fixed asset investment (¥ billion)	83.26	681.26
Status of foreign-funded enterprises		
Number of registered enterprises	3318	5814
Total investment (US$ millions)	8344	19,617
Registered capital (US$ millions)	5606	12,046
Foreign trade (US$ millions)		
Export	2424	8506
Import	1569	9833
Sales of consumer goods (¥ billion)	109	404
Per capita annual disposable income of urban residents (¥)	4912.88	13,856.51
Engle's coefficient (%)	38.42	35.42
Per capita annual net income of rural residents (¥)	2148.22	6210.72
Engle's coefficient (%)	38.30	33.79
Number of patent applications granted	2252	6780
Inventions	208	1512
Utility models	1663	4391
Designs	381	877

Note All monetary values are measured at current prices. *Source* Heilongjiang Statistical Yearbook, 2001 and 2011

and Xiaoxingan Mountains, which are also home to protected animal species, such as the Siberian Tiger, the red-crowned crane and the lynx. Herding in Heilongjiang is centered upon horses and cattle. The area has the greatest number of milking cows and the highest production of milk among all the provinces of China.

Heilongjiang is the traditional base of industry for the PRC. Industry is focused on coal, petroleum, lumber, machinery and food. Petroleum is of great importance there and the Daqing oilfields are a key source of petroleum for the country. Coal, gold, and graphite are other important minerals to be found there. Heilongjiang also has great potential for wind power, with an average wind energy density of 200 W/m^2. In line with central government's policy to revitalize the northeast, it is now restructuring its six pillar industries, namely equipment manufacturing, petrochemicals, food processing, energy, pharmaceuticals, and forestry and timber processing.

Heilongjiang has rich energy resources. The Daqing Oilfield is not only the biggest in the nation but also in the world. The region also has the fifth-largest gas field and the seventh-largest coal mine in the country. However, like the other two provinces with energy resources in northeast China, it is facing a major resource depletion problem after decades of energy production. Oil production has dropped in recent decades. As a result, the province has moved down the industrial chain to producing petrochemicals.

Heilongjiang has become one of China's most important equipment manufacturing bases. Large-scale enterprises have been set up there. Examples of these are Qiqihar Heavy CNC Equipment Corp., Qier Machine Tool Group Corp., Harbin Power Equipment Corp. and China First Heavy Industries. The province is the nation's largest organic food processing base. It has the largest organic food production output as well as the largest crop area. Harbin Beer, Wandashan and Red Star are among the better-known brands.

The service sector in Heilongjiang contributes more than 40 % to the region's overall GRP. However, it still contributes less in GRP than the service industry in other developed areas in China. Traditional service industries are still the focus and the newly emerging service industries are in need of development. To improve this situation, Heilongjiang has been encouraging the development of the computer, software, exhibition, sports and entertainment industries, while at the same time continuing the development of traditional service industries, such as real estate, transportation, warehousing and resident services.

Large foreign investors in Heilongjiang include Lane Crawford and New World from Hong Kong, Wal-Mart and Coca-Cola from the US, and Mitsubishi and Kirin from Japan. Mechanical and electrical products comprise the major portion of imports. Given its geographical location, the province is an important gateway for trade with Russia, so Russia is the main trading partner, with trade between the two areas amounting to more than half of Heilongjiang's overall trade. Other major trading partners include Hong Kong, the US, Japan and Saudi Arabia.

In terms of FDI, the Virgin Islands and Hong Kong have injected the most into Heilongjiang. The Cayman Islands is also a key source of FDI. Of all the various sectors, manufacturing has received the most. Other noteworthy sectors are real estate and energy.

Table 1.22 Heilongjiang's comparative (dis)advantage index by sector, 2010

Sector	Index
Agriculture, forestry, animal husbandry and fishery	7.02
Mining	2.13
Manufacturing	0.52
Production and distribution of electricity, gas and water	1.31
Construction	0.60
Transport, storage and post	1.13
Information transmission, computer service and software	0.85
Wholesale and retail trades	0.94
Hotels and catering services	0.50
Financial intermediation	0.86
Real estate	0.66
Leasing and business services	0.54
Scientific research, technical services and geological prospecting	1.17
Management of water conservancy, environment and public facilities	1.26
Services to households and other services	3.06
Education	0.83
Health, social security and social welfare	0.88
Culture, sports and entertainment	0.85
Public management and social organization	0.83

Notes All the sectors included in this table are determined according to China's official definitions and for urban areas only. Numerals greater than, equal to and less than one indicate that the province's sectors have advantages, no apparent (dis)advantages and disadvantages, respectively
Source Calculated by authors based on China Statistical Yearbook, 2011. See Appendix A for a detailed methodological description

As of 2010, compared with those of other provinces, "agriculture, forestry, animal husbandry and fishery", "services to households and other services" and "mining" were relatively strong, while "hotels and catering services", "manufacturing" and "leasing and business services" were relatively weak sectors (see Table 1.22).

Henan

[Quick Facts: Official name: Henan Province; Capital: Zhengzhou; Land area: 167,100 km^2; Population density: 591/km^2; Major ethnic groups: Han, Hui, Mongol, Manchu, Buyi]

Henan is a province of the PRC located in the center of the country. Henan means "south of the river" in Chinese, and it received this name due to its location to the south of the Yellow River, which runs more than 700 km across the region. At present, however, approximately one-quarter of the province lies north of the

Yellow River. The name is abbreviated to "Yu," after Yuzhou, an ancient prefecture that used to include parts of present-day Henan. The Chinese character "Yu" is closely related to that for "elephant," probably indicating that Henan had a tropical climate in ancient times.

Situated on the plain between the Yellow River and the Huai River, Henan is often referred to as Zhongyuan, which literally means "central plain" or "mid-land", although the name is also applied to the entirety of China proper. The province shares borders with six other provinces, including Shaanxi to the west, Hubei to the south, Shanxi to the northwest, Hebei to the northeast, Shandong to the northeast and Anhui to the southeast. The 17 prefecture-level divisions and 1 directly administered county-level city of Henan are subdivided into 159 county-level divisions (50 districts, 21 county-level cities and 88 counties; Jiyuan is counted as a county-level city here). These are in turn divided into 2440 township-level divisions (866 towns, 1234 townships, 12 ethnic townships and 328 sub-districts).

Henan Province is in the transitional area between the second and third steps of China's four-step terrain rising from east to west, with rolling mountains over 1000 m above sea level in its western part and a plain area of 100 m or lower in its east. Laoyacha in Lingbao City, 2413.8 m above sea level, is the highest peak. The lowest point, at 23.2 m, is found at the place where the Huaihe River leaves the province. High in the west and low in the east, even in the north and concave in the south, Henan is surrounded by four mountain ranges (Taihang in the north, Funiu in the west, and Tongbai and Dabie in the south), leaving subsidence basins here and there. In its middle and eastern parts there is a vast fluvial plain created by the Yellow, Huaihe and Haihe rivers. Mountainous regions comprise 44.3 % of its area and the plains 55.7 %.

Four rivers run across Henan, the Yellow River, the Huaihe River, the Weihe River and the Hanshui River. The Yellow River passes through central Henan. It enters from the northwest via the Sanmenxia Reservoir. After it passes Luoyang, the mountains give way to plains. Excessive amounts of sediments are formed due to the silt it picks up from the Loess Plateau, raising the riverbed and causing frequent floods, which have shaped the region. More recently however, the construction of dams and levees, as well as the depletion of water resources, has ended the floods. The Huai River in southern Henan is also important and has been recognized as part of the boundary dividing the northern and southern Chinese climate and culture.

Henan has a temperate climate that is humid subtropical to the south of the Yellow River and bordering on humid continental to the north. Located between the northern sub-tropical zone and warm temperate zone, it has four distinctive seasons with complicated weather conditions characterized with a hot and rainy summer and generally cool to cold, windy, dry winter. Southern Henan is in the northern sub-tropical zone. The province's average temperature of the year is 13–15 °C, with around freezing in January and 27–28 °C in July. The average annual rainfall is 807 mm, the great majority of which occurs during the summer. The frost-free period lasts 275–308 days.

Henan is also rich in minerals and natural resources. Some 126 kinds of minerals are found, of which the reserves of 74 have been confirmed. Some 61 have been mined and utilized. With considerable reserves of petroleum and natural gas, the region includes Zhongyuan Oilfields and Henan Oilfields and it is the fifth largest petroleum and natural gas producer in China. Some 121 of the 150 kinds of minerals found on earth are available in the province. It is also home to over 3800 species of plants and more than 400 kinds of animals. This territory is an important production base for wheat, corn, cotton, tobacco and oil plants. Some 32 nature reserves have been established in the province covering an area of 748,400 ha.

Henan has water reserves of 40.6 billion cubic meter or about 410 m^3 per capita. The average annual precipitation stands at 797.7 mm. The key water-conservation project at Xiaolangdi on the Yellow River, supported by a loan from the World Bank, has a total installed capacity of 1.8 million kilowatt.

With a population of approximately 93.6 million, Henan is the second most populous Chinese province after Guangdong. Although the population is highly homogeneous with 98.8 % being Han, Henan has the largest Muslim Hui population in eastern China, which constitute approximately 1 % and lives mostly in Muslim enclaves in the Guancheng District (in Zhengzhou), the Chanhe District (in Luoyang) and the Shunhe District (in Kaifeng). Small populations of Mongols and Manchus exist in scattered rural communities as well as major urban centers. Kaifeng is also known for its historical Jewish communities, although, after centuries of integration, few are aware of their ancestry and Jews are not an officially recognized ethnic minority in China.

Henan has a diverse landscape with floodplains in the east and mountains in the west. Much of the province forms part of the densely populated North China Plain, an area known as the "breadbasket" of China. The Taihang Mountains intrude partially into Henan's northwestern borders from Shanxi, forming the eastern edge of Loess Plateau. To the west the Xionger and Funiu mountains form an extensive network of mountain ranges and plateaus, supporting one of the few remaining temperate deciduous forests which once covered all of Henan. The famous Mount Song and its Shaolin Temple is located in the far east of the region, near the capital city of Zhengzhou. To the far south the Dabie Mountains divide Hubei from Henan. The Nanyang Basin, separated from the North China Plain by these mountains, is another important agricultural and population center, with culture and history distinct from the rest of Henan and closer to that of Hubei. Unlike the rest of northern China, desertification is not a problem in Henan, though sand storms are common in cities near the Yellow River due to the large amount of sand present there.

Henan plays an important role in China's history, including as it does four of the country's ancient capitals (Anyang, Kaifeng, Luoyang and Zhengzhou). More than ten ancient dynasties have established their capitals in Henan. This has contributed to the vast number of ruins and relics found throughout the province. As one of the major birthplaces of Chinese civilization, the area offers several epoch-making archeological discoveries, including the Peiligang Culture Site dating back 7000 years, Yanshao Culture Site of some 6000 years ago and Dahe Culture Site of more than 5000 years ago. In ancient China, more than 20 dynasties established their capitals there. Three of China's seven great ancient capitals are located in Henan: Anyang of the Shang Dynasty, Luoyang of nine dynasties and Kaifeng of seven dynasties. Three of ancient China's four great inventions—the compass, paper making and gunpowder—were made in Henan. The province comes first place in the country in terms of underground cultural relics, and second with regard to existing cultural relics on the ground. The Yellow River, with numerous ancient relics and scenic attractions, also provides a rich tourist trap. There are 16 key national units of protected historical relics and 267 provincial units. The overground historical relics of the provice take second place. Historical relics in museums represent one-eighth of those in China, and the underground historical relics are the greatest in number in the country. In Henan Museum there are 120,000 historical relics, including more than 40,000 classified as rare.

The province has seen rapid development in its economy over the past two decades, and this has expanded at an even faster rate than the national average. This rapid growth has transformed Henan from one of the poorest provinces to one that matches other central provinces, though it is still relatively impoverished on a national scale. In 2010 its nominal GRP was ¥2.31 trillion (about US$339 billion), making it the fifth largest economy in China, although it ranks 19th in terms of GRP per capita (Table 1.23).

Henan is the fifth largest provincial economy of China and the largest among inland provinces. However, the per capita GRP is low compared with other eastern and central provinces, and Henan is considered to be one of the more backward areas in China. The economy continues to depend on its dwindling aluminum and coal reserves, as well as agriculture, heavy industry, tourism and retail. High-tech industry and the service sector are underdeveloped and are concentrated around Zhengzhou and Luoyang.

Table 1.23 Demographic and socioeconomic profile: Henan

Indicator	2000	2010
Population (thousands)	92,560	94,055
Illiteracy rate of population aged 15 or over (%)	5.87	4.25
GRP (¥ billions)	513.77	2309.24
Composition of GRP (%)		
Primary sector	22.6	14.1
Secondary sector	47.0	57.3
Tertiary sector	30.4	28.6
Fixed asset investment (¥ billion)	137.77	1658.59
Status of foreign-funded enterprises		
Number of registered enterprises	3004	10,254
Total investment (US$ millions)	11,359	37,866
Registered capital (US$ millions)	7337	20,535
Foreign trade (US$ millions)		
Export	1587	12,194
Import	1537	7821
Sales of consumer goods (¥ billions)	179	800
Per capita annual disposable income of urban residents (¥)	4766.26	15,930.26
Engle's coefficient (%)	36.20	32.99
Per capita annual net income of rural residents (¥)	1985.82	5523.73
Engle's coefficient (%)	32.21	37.24
Number of patent applications granted	2766	16,539
Inventions	209	1498
Utility models	2113	11,048
Designs	444	3993

Note All monetary values are measured at current prices. *Source* Henan Statistical Yearbook, 2001 and 2011

Agriculture has traditionally been a pillar of the region's economy, with the nation's highest wheat and sesame output and second highest rice output, earning its reputation as the breadbasket of China. Henan is also an important producer of beef, cotton, maize, pork, animal oil and corn. Food production and processing make up more than 14 % of the output from the province's secondary industry, and it is said that 90 % of Chinese McDonald's and KFC ingredients come from Henan.

Although Henan's industry has traditionally been based on light textiles and food processing, recent developments have diversified the industry sector to metallurgy, petrol, cement, chemical industry, machinery and electronics. It has the second largest molybdenum reserves in the world. Coal, aluminum, alkaline metals and tungsten are also present in large amounts in the west of the province. Export and processing of these materials is one of the main sources of revenues.

Henan is actively trying to build its economy around the provincial capital of Zhengzhou, and it is hoped that it may become an important transportation and manufacturing hub in the future. Foreign exchanges are increasing continuously. Friendly provincial relationships have been established with 16 states (districts) in the US, Japan, Russia, France, Germany and other countries. Some cities of Henan have established friendly relationships (sister city) with 32 foreign cities.

The service sector is rather small and underdeveloped. Finance and commerce are largely concentrated in urban centers, such as Zhengzhou and Luoyang, where the economy is fueled by a large and relatively affluent consumer base. In order to make the economy more knowledge and technology based, government established a number of development zones in all of the major cities, promoting industries such as software, information technologies, new materials, bio-pharmaceuticals and photo-machinery-electronics. Henan is a major destination for tourists, with places such as Shaolin Temple and Longmen Grottoes attracting millions each year.

With the vast amount of cultivated land and sown area, Henan is a large and well-known agricultural region in China. It is the largest production base for grain, oil-bearing crops and fruits. Rich agricultural products (such as wheat, corn, oil-bearing crops, fruit and vegetables) and a large number of livestock ensure sufficient supply for its food-processing industries. As a result, the region has developed into a major food-processing base, producing foodstuffs such as meat, frozen food, instant noodles, biscuits and seasoning. Henan is the second largest food-processing base in China, after Shandong. Sanquan Corp, the country's largest frozen food-processing firm, is located in Henan. It is also home to Shineway Group, China's biggest meat-processing enterprise. Zhengzhou Commodity Exchange, set up in 1990, is one of three commodity futures markets in the country. The trading items of futures contracts include wheat, cotton, white sugar, pure terephthalic acid, rapeseed oil and green beans.

With the advantages of cheap labor and low land prices, Henan's prospects appear to be found in its development as a major transportation hub, which may benefit other industries and pave the way for Henan to become a manufacturing hub as well.

Table 1.24 Henan's comparative (dis)advantage index by sector, 2010

Sector	Index
Agriculture, forestry, animal husbandry and fishery	0.33
Mining	1.63
Manufacturing	0.76
Production and distribution of electricity, gas and water	1.18
Construction	1.28
Transport, storage and post	0.80
Information transmission, computer service and software	0.45
Wholesale and retail trades	1.24
Hotels and catering services	0.83
Financial intermediation	0.83
Real estate	0.74
Leasing and business services	0.63
Scientific research, technical services and geological prospecting	0.68
Management of water conservancy, environment and public facilities	0.97
Services to households and other services	0.56
Education	1.25
Health, social security and social welfare	1.12
Culture, sports and entertainment	0.92
Public management and social organization	1.29

Notes All the sectors included in this table are determined according to China's official definitions and for urban areas only. Numerals greater than, equal to and less than one indicate that the province's sectors have advantages, no apparent (dis)advantages and disadvantages, respectively
Source Calculated by authors based on China Statistical Yearbook, 2011. See Appendix A for a detailed methodological description

The province's pillar industries include food processing, equipment manufacturing, metallurgy, coal and textiles. Equipment manufacturing is the second largest industry in terms of value-added industrial output in the area. A key player in this industry is CITIC Heavy Machine Inc, located in Luoyang. It is one of China's largest mining equipment manufacturers.

Henan is China's third largest coal production base, after Shanxi and Inner Mongolia. The main coal producers include Pingdingshan Coal Group, Yima Coal Industry Group and Yongmei Group. Thanks to the abundance of mineral resources, the metallurgy industry plays an important role in the province's industrial sector. Anyang Iron&Steel Group and the Henan branch of China Aluminum Corp are the two major players in the metallurgy sector.

Tourism plays an important role in Henan's service sector, thanks to its great number of historical ruins and relics.

The province conducts international trade with various countries. Major export destinations are the US, South Korea, Hong Kong, Taiwan and India, while key import sources are Japan, the US, India, Germany and Brazil. Henan's main import products are minerals, including vanadium ore, unsintered iron ore, cathodes and alumina. All these account for more than half of the imported products. In terms of exports, Henan mainly exports wigs, unwrought and non-alloyed aluminum, and unwrought and refined lead. The province has also seen an increase in the export of machinery and electrical appliances.

The primary sources of foreign investment are from Hong Kong and Latin American countries. Henan attracts many foreign investors, such as Coca-cola, GE, Metro and Toshiba. The manufacturing sector receives the highest amount of FDI among all the sectors. Other noteworthy recipients are the production and distribution of electricity, gas and water, real estate, mining, and tenancy and business services.

As of 2010, compared with those of other provinces, "mining", "public management and social organization" and "construction" were relatively strong, while "agriculture, forestry, animal husbandry and fishery", "information transmission, computer service and software" and "services to households and other services" were relatively weak sectors (see Table 1.24).

Hubei

[Quick Facts: Official name: Hubei Province; Capital: Wuhan; Land area: 185,900 km^2; Population density: 324/km^2; Major ethnic groups: Han, Tujia, Miao, Hui, Dong]

Hubei is a province of the PRC, situated in central China. Extending across two major river systems—the Yangtze and its largest tributary, the Han—the region adjoins Henan Province to the north, Anhui Province to the east, Jiangxi Province to the southeast, Hunan Province to the south, Chongqing Municipality to the west and Shaanxi Province to the northwest. Hubei means "north of the lake" in Chinese, referring to its position north of Lake Dongting. It is officially abbreviated to "È", an ancient name associated with the eastern part of the province since the Qin Dynasty (221–206 BC), while a popular, though unofficial, name for it is "Chu" after the powerful state of Chu that existed there during the Eastern Zhou Dynasty (771–221 BC).

About 10 % of the province consists of lakes, lending it the nickname "province of a thousand lakes." The 13 prefecture-level divisions and 4 directly administered county-level divisions of Hubei are subdivided into 102 county-level divisions (38 districts, 24 county-level cities, 37 counties, 2 autonomous counties, 1 forestry area; the directly administered county-level divisions are included here). These are in turn divided into 1234 township-level divisions (737 towns, 215 townships, 9 ethnic townships and 273 sub-districts).

The major rivers of Hubei are the Yangtze (Chang-jiang) and its tributary Han-shui, which give their names to the Jianghan Plain. The Yangtze River enters Hubei from the west via the Three Gorges. The eastern half of the Three Gorges (the Xiling Gorge and part of the Wu Gorge) lies in western Hubei, while the western half is in neighboring Chongqing Municipality. The Han-shui enters the province from the northwest. After crossing most of the province, the two rivers meet at Wuhan, the provincial capital. The Jianghan Plain takes up most of central and eastern Hubei, while the west and the peripheries are more mountainous, with ranges such as the Wudang Mountains, the Jingshan Mountains, the Daba Mountains and the Wu Mountains (in rough north-to-south order). The Dabie Mountains lie to the northeast of the Janghan Plain, on the border with Henan and Anhui; the Tongbai Mountains lie to the north on the border with Henan; and to the southeast, the Mufu Mountains form the border with Jiangxi. The highest point in Hubei is Shennong Peak.

Hubei is located in the transitional region from the second to the third terrace in the terrain of China, thus having a variety of landforms. It is surrounded by the mountains of Wuling, Wushan, Daba, Wudang, Tongbai, Dabie and Mufu on the west, north and east. Lying in the central and southern parts is the Jianghan Plain, which extends to Hunan Province to link with Lake Dongting Plain. Except for the hills on the fringes of the plain, the altitude there is 35 m or less above sea level. The various geographical features of the province include 55.5 % of mountains, 24.5 % of hills and hillocks, and 20 % of plain and lake areas. The elevation of different parts varies greatly. The Shennong Summit, the highest peak of Shennongjia in west Hubei, which is known as the "Roof of Central China", is 3105 m above sea level, while the Tanjiayuan of Jianli County on the eastern plain has an elevation of zero.

Hubei has a subtropical monsoon climate. It enjoys abundant sunlight, with the annual amount of solar radiation totaling 85–114 kilocalories/cm^2 and the annual duration averaging 1200–2200 h. The temperature is on the high side, with the annual temperature averaging 13–18 °C. It can reach 41 °C at its highest, while the lowest can be −14.9 °C. The short frost period and abundant precipitation are favorable for agriculture. There are 230–300 days free of frost in a year and the annual rainfall has stood at 1180 mm for many years. The rainfall is unevenly distributed. The amount of precipitation in the Wuling Mountain area is as high as 1600–1700 mm, while that in west Hubei is as low as 700–800 mm.

To date 138 kinds of minerals have been discovered, 89 of which have had their reserves verified. The reserves of phosphorus ore, hongshiite, wollastonite, garnet and marlstone rank fifth in China, and several others, including iron, phosphorus, copper, gypsum, rock salt, gold amalgam, manganese and vanadium, rank seventh. However, the province lacks energy resources, with limited verified reserves of coal, petroleum and natural gas. Its proven reserves of coal stand at 548 million tons.

Hubei is rich in underground water resources. Of its estimated 265 billion cubic meter of underground water reserves, 35.57 billion cubic meter are ready for annual extraction, amounting to approximately 36 % of the province's average annual surface runoff. There are 58 large reservoirs in the province with water storage of 43.75 billion cubic meter. The area boasts a number of large and medium-sized hydropower stations—the Gezhouba, Danjiangkou, Geheyan, Hanjiang, Duhe, Huanglongtan, Bailianhe, Lushui and Fushui. In addition, some thermal power stations have been built in Wuhan, Jingmen, Huangshi and at other sites in recent years.

There are 570 species of terrestrial vertebrates in Hubei. Dozens of them have been listed as rare animals under state protection. These include the golden-haired monkey, serow, leopard, white bear, white musk, white deer, white snake, white-crowned king pheasant and red-bellied tragopan. There are also 175 kinds of fish, accounting for about one-quarter of the country's freshwater fish species. Rare species under key state protection include the Chinese sturgeon, Chinese paddlefish, mullet and giant salamander.

Hubei boasts both large numbers of broad-leaved deciduous species, which are typical of northern China, and many broad-leaved evergreen species, which are well known in southern China. There are more than 2000 species of wild plants, including some 1300 kinds of medicinal plants and over 30 species that are either rare in the world or peculiar to China. The well-preserved Shennongjia virgin forest is a natural park of subtropical fauna and flora. By the end of 2005 the number of nature reserves in the province had reached 62, covering an area of 1.086 million hectare.

Thanks to its geographic location, the province enjoys favorable environmental conditions and diversified natural resources suitable for different crops. It is a main production base for rice, cotton, tea and oil crops, and as such it has long been known as "the land of rice and fish" in China. Some potential problems include the long-term effects of the Three Gorges Dam: while the project provides power and significantly reduces the risk of potential losses from Yangtze River floods, environmental impacts of the project are becoming apparent. Additionally, Hubei has yet to show that its large economy can maintain growth without depending on influxes of fixed asset investment.

Hubei has rich tourism resources that feature both beautiful landscapes and abundant places of historic and cultural interest. It was once the capital for the Chu Kingdom during the Warring States Period (475–221 BC). It also played an important strategic role in the Three Kingdoms Period (AD 190–280). There are 6 national-level scenic spots, 13 national forest parks and 3 national nature reserves. Shennongjia has been listed in UNESCO's program of Man and Biosphere and Wudang Mountain is on the list of World Cultural and Natural Heritage Sites. The Three Gorges of the Yangtze River, the Yellow Crane Tower and the Gezhouba Dam have been listed among China's top-40 tourist scenic spots. Hubei encompasses five famous historical and cultural cites designated by the state, 20 cultural sites under state protection, 365 cultural sites under provincial protection, 5 sites of Chu City ruins, 73 Chu cultural sites and over 140 sites relating to the Three Kingdoms.

The province's most famous natural attraction (shared with the adjacent Chongqing Municipality) is the scenic area of the Three Gorges of the Yangtze. Located in the far west, the gorges can be conveniently visited by one of the numerous tourist boats (or regular passenger boats) that travel up the Yangtze from Yichang through the Three Gorges and into the neighboring Chongqing municipality.

The mountains of western Hubei, in particular in Shennongjia District, offer a welcome respite from Wuhan's and Yichang's summer heat, as well as skiing opportunities in winter. The tourist facilities in that area are concentrated around Muyu in the southern part of Shennongjia, the gateway to Shennongjia National Nature Reserve. Closer to the provincial capital, Wuhan, is Mount Jiugong (Jiugongshan) National Park in Tongshan County near the border with Jiangxi.

Hubei's economy ranks 11th in the country and its nominal GRP for 2010 was ¥1.60 trillion (about 233.4 billion US$) with a per capita of 21,566 ¥ (about US $2863) (Table 1.25).

Hubei has witnessed rapid economic development since the opening up of the Yangtze Economic Belt and the construction of the Three Gorges Dam project. The soaring investment, consumption and exports have helped the regional economy to grow. Industry and service lead the economy, while agriculture remains a moderately significant contributor.

The province has developed into an important industrial production base in central China with major industries including automobiles, iron and steel

Table 1.25 Demographic and socioeconomic profile: Hubei

Indicator	2000	2010
Population (thousands)	60,280	57,279
Illiteracy rate of population aged 15 or over (%)	7.15	4.58
GRP (¥ billions)	427.63	1596.76
Composition of GRP (%)		
Primary sector	15.5	13.4
Secondary sector	49.7	48.6
Tertiary sector	34.9	37.9
Fixed asset investment (¥ billions)	133.92	1026.27
Status of foreign-funded enterprises		
Number of registered enterprises	5123	7486
Total investment (US$ millions)	16,670	42,864
Registered capital (US$ millions)	10,348	24,314
Foreign trade (US$ millions)		
Export	1900	13,910
Import	1993	12,119
Sales of consumer goods (¥ billions)	179	701
Per capita annual disposable income of urban residents (¥)	5524.54	16,058.37
Engle's coefficient (%)	38.31	38.68
Per capita annual net income of rural residents (¥)	2268.59	5832.27
Engle's coefficient (%)	33.86	43.10
Number of patent applications granted	2198	17,362
Inventions	156	2025
Utility models	1573	10,431
Designs	469	4906

Note All monetary values are measured at current prices. *Source* Hubei Statistical Yearbook, 2001 and 2011

production, machinery, power generation, textiles, food and beverage, electronics, shipbuilding, and chemical raw materials and Hubei is one of the major automobile production centers in China. The concentration of the automobile industry there has resulted in the rapid growth of the auto accessories industry. The Dongfeng Motor Corporation, which was launched in 1969, is one of the Big Three Auto Groups in China. Its subsidiaries in the area include the Dongfeng Peugeot Citroen Automobile, a joint venture with French car maker Peugeot, and the Dongfeng Honda Automobile Co. Ltd, a joint venture with Japanese car giant Honda.

Since the launch of China's first iron plant (Hanyang Iron Plant) in Wuhan in 1891, Hubei has developed into a comprehensive iron and steel production base in China. A key player in this industry is Wuhan Iron and Steel Group. It has an annual production capacity of 20 million tons and is ranked the third largest iron and steel consortium in China after nearly 50 years of development. Steel products

Table 1.26 Hubei's comparative (dis)advantage index by sector, 2010

Sector	Index
Agriculture, forestry, animal husbandry and fishery	0.94
Mining	0.45
Manufacturing	0.97
Production and distribution of electricity, gas and water	0.98
Construction	1.46
Transport, storage and post	1.03
Information transmission, computer service and software	0.62
Wholesale and retail trades	1.03
Hotels and catering services	0.94
Financial intermediation	0.88
Real estate	0.80
Leasing and business services	0.42
Scientific research, technical services and geological prospecting	0.95
Management of water conservancy, environment and public facilities	1.04
Services to households and other services	0.51
Education	1.06
Health, social security and social welfare	1.22
Culture, sports and entertainment	0.99
Public management and social organization	0.98

Notes All the sectors included in this table are determined according to China's official definitions and for urban areas only. Numerals greater than, equal to and less than one indicate that the province's sectors have advantages, no apparent (dis)advantages and disadvantages, respectively
Source Calculated by authors based on China Statistical Yearbook, 2011. See Appendix A for a detailed methodological description

are the key export of Hubei. Wuhan Steel&Iron Group and the Hubei Xinyegang Co. Ltd are the two major exporters in the province.

Hubei's service sector is developing rapidly and steadily. Retail and tourism are the key industries that have helped the sector's growth. Many overseas retail enterprises, such as the New World Development Group, the Tak Shun Group, Carrefour, Wal-Mart and Metro, have invested in the region.

Like other provinces in China, Hubei conducts a great deal of trade with many other countries. The main export destinations (in terms of trade volume) include the US, Hong Kong, South Korea, Japan and Germany. Major import sources are Japan, France, Germany, Australia and Taiwan. Among all the exports, those of machinery and electrical appliances have expanded the most. Major imports include iron ore, auto accessories, copper ore and piston engine components.

FDI sources include Hong Kong, Japan, the Virgin Islands, the UK and France. The manufacturing sector accounts for the majority of the total actualized FDI, followed by the service sector, with a focus on the hotel, retail, logistics and real-estate industries.

As of 2010, compared with those of other provinces, "construction", and "health, social security and social welfare" were relatively strong, while "leasing and business services", "mining" and "services to households and other services" were relatively weak sectors (see Table 1.26).

Hunan

[Quick Facts: Official name: Hunan Province; Capital: Changsha; Land area: 211,800 km^2; Population density: 316/km^2; Major ethnic groups: Han, Tujia, Miao, Dong, Yao]

Hunan is a province of the PRC. It is located to the south of the middle reaches of the Yangtze River and south of Lake Dongting. Its name means "south of the lake". The province borders Hubei Province to the north, Jiangxi Province to the east, Guangdong Province to the south, Guangxi Zhuang Autonomous Region to the southwest, Guizhou Province to the west and Chongqing Municipality to the northwest. It is sometimes called and officially abbreviated to "Xiang", after the Xiang River, which runs through the area.

Hunan is located on the south bank of the Yangtze River, about midway along its length. Shanghai lies 1000 km away, Beijing 1200 km away and Guangzhou 500 km away. It is situated between 109°–114°E longitude and 20°–30°N latitude. The east, south and west sides of the province are surrounded by mountains and hills, with the Wuling Mountains to the northwest, the Xuefeng Mountains to the west, the Nanling Mountains to the south and the Luoxiao Mountains to the east. The mountains and hills occupy more than 80 % of the area and the plains comprise less than 20 %. The land in the province generally slopes from the east, south and west towards the north in the shape of a horse's hoof. The majority of Hunan Province lies at altitudes between 100 m and 800 m.

Hunan is 667 km wide and 774 km long. As an inland province adjacent to coastal areas, it has an area of 211,800 km^2, 2.2 % of the national total, ranking as the 11th largest in China. The 14 prefecture-level divisions of Hunan are subdivided into 122 county-level divisions (34 districts, 16 county-level cities, 65 counties and 7 autonomous counties). These are in turn divided into 2587 township-level divisions (1098 towns, 1158 townships, 98 ethnic townships, 225 sub-districts and 8 district public offices).

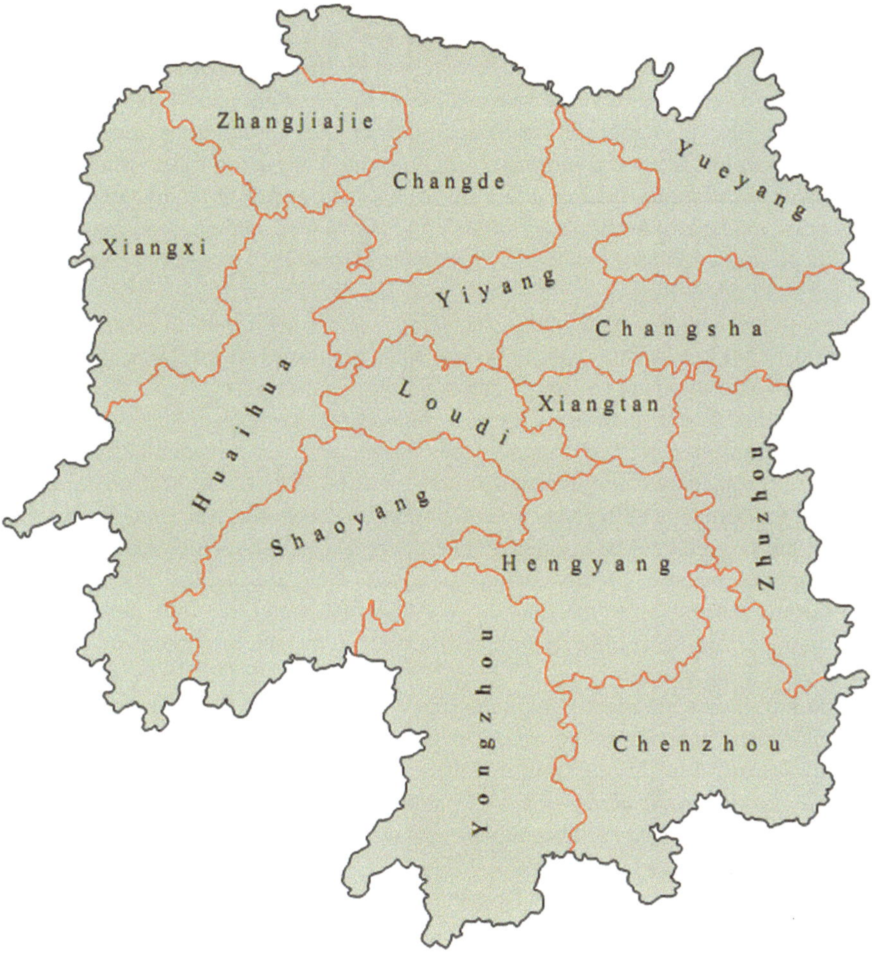

The Xiangjiang, Zijiang, Yuanjiang and Lishui rivers converge on the Yangtze River at Lake Dongting in the north of Hunan. The center and northern parts are somewhat low and form a U-shaped basin, open in the north and with Lake Dongting as its center. Most of Hunan Province lies in the basins of four major tributaries of the Yangtze River. Lake Dongting is the largest lake in the province and the second largest freshwater lake of China. Due to the reclamation of land for agriculture, the lake has been subdivided into many smaller lakes, though there is now a trend to reverse some of the reclamation, which has damaged wetland habitats surrounding the lake.

Hunan Province has a humid continental and subtropical monsoon climate with average annual sunshine of 1300–1800 h. The annual average temperature is 16–18 °C (average 3–8 °C in January and 27–30 °C in July), with a frost-free period of 260–310 days and mean annual precipitation of 1200–1700 mm. Its climate has three characteristics. First, it has abundant sunshine, heat and water resources, and they reach their peak synchronously. During the period from April to October, the total radiation is 70–76 % of the whole year, and rainfall accounts for 68–84 % of the total. Second, there are distinct seasons, with cold winters and hot summers. The temperature always changes in spring and then declines abruptly in autumn. There is much rainfall in spring and summer, with drought every autumn and winter. Third, areas with an abruptly changeable climate are surrounded by mountains in three directions, especially in the mountainous regions in west and south Hunan.

The province has an extensive water system. Dongting Lake in northern Hunan, the second largest freshwater lake in China, has an area of 2691 km^2. It takes the waters of the Xiangjiang, Zishui, Yuanjiang and Lishui rivers (a total waterway length of 2200 km in Hunan, with nearly 5000 tributaries) from the southwest and then flows into the Yangtze River at Chenglingji.

The region has rich mineral reserves. A land and geological survey conducted within the province in 2005 found 11 new mines with six minerals having proven reserves. The lead and zinc deposits amounted to 64,100 tons and the coal deposits to 6.54 million tons. The reserves of tungsten, antimony, zinc and bauxite are among the largest in China. Other major mineral deposits include lead, tin, barite and graphite. Because of this the province has often been called "the country of non-ferrous metals" and "the country of non-metal minerals". The Lengshuijiang area is noted for its stibnite mines and is one of the major centers of antimony extraction in the country.

The province's traditional crops are rice and cotton. The Lake Dongting area is an important center of ramie production, and Hunan is also an important center for tea cultivation. Aside from agricultural products, in recent years it has grown to become an important center for steel, machinery and electronics, especially as China's manufacturing sector moves away from coastal areas such as the Guangdong and Zhejiang provinces.

Incomplete statistics show that Hunan has 70 kinds of mammals, 310 kinds of birds, and over 160 kinds of fish. It has 44 rare and state-protected species, of which 18 are under Class A protection, such as the white-flag dolphin and the south China tiger, and 19 are under Class B protection, such as the macaque and the short-tail monkey. By the end of 2005 the province had set up 92 nature reserves to ensure protection for 1.1 million hectare.

The region offers many beautiful landscapes and numerous historic sites. It now has over 20,000 cultural remains, including 22 national-level key protection units and 211 provincial-level key protection units. There are 4 state-class natural reserves, 22 provincial-class natural reserves and 21 national forest parks. The total area of nature reserves is 7260 km^2, which is 3.43 % of the province's total area.

Hunan Province has developed 43 scenic areas. There are 3 national-level key scenic areas covering Mount Hengshan, WulingYuan, Yueyang Tower, Dongting Lake and Shaoshan, and 27 provincial-class scenic areas. WulingYuan tourist area (including Zhangjiajie, Suoxi Valley, Tianzi Mountain and Mengdong River), with its unique limestone caves, brooks, hot springs, ancient trees and rare animals, has been placed by UNESCO on the World Natural Heritage Site list. Mount Hengshan is the famous sacred mountain of Buddhism and a summer resort. Yueyang Tower is also well known at home and abroad for its long history, folklore and grand architecture. Changsha, the provincial capital, is a historic and cultural city. Tourist sites there include Han Dynasty Tombs at Mawangdui, Yuelu Hill, Loving Youth Pavilion (Aiwanting), Orange Isle (Juzizhou) and Yuelu Academy of Classical Learning.

Located in southern China, the province is traditionally a rice and cotton grower in China but machinery, steel, tobacco, food processing and electronics are now also major contributors to its economy. As manufacturing industries begin moving from coastal provinces like Guangdong and Zhejiang to inland China, Hunan is a desirable destination due to its low wages, low-real estate costs and one of the largest populations of migrant workers.

Hunan Province had a nominal GRP of ¥1.60 trillion (about US$234.9 billion) in 2010. Its per capita GRP is ¥20,226 (about US$2961). Thanks to its fertile soil, the output of major farm and sideline products occupies a leading position in China. It has the highest output of rice and the second highest output of ramie in China. The output of rapeseed, cured tobacco and freshwater fish is also among the top five in the country (Table 1.27).

Table 1.27 Demographic and socioeconomic profile: Hunan

Indicator	2000	2010
Population (thousands)	64,400	65,701
Illiteracy rate of population aged 15 or over (%)	4.65	2.67
GRP (¥ billions)	369.19	1603.80
Composition of GRP (%)		
Primary sector	21.3	14.5
Secondary sector	39.6	45.8
Tertiary sector	39.1	39.7
Fixed asset investment (¥ billions)	101.22	966.36
Status of foreign-funded enterprises		
Number of registered enterprises	2316	5410
Total investment (US$ millions)	7306	32,406
Registered capital (US$ millions)	4338	16,111
Foreign trade (US$ millions)		
Export	1632	8578
Import	1360	7031
Sales of consumer goods (¥ billions)	136	584
Per capita annual disposable income of urban residents (¥)	6218.73	16,565.70
Engle's coefficient (%)	37.24	36.55
Per capita annual net income of rural residents (¥)	2197.16	5621.96
Engle's coefficient (%)	40.21	48.44
Number of patent applications granted	2555	13,873
Inventions	197	1920
Utility models	1759	7861
Designs	599	4092

Note All monetary values are measured at current prices. *Source* Hunan Statistical Yearbook, 2001 and 2011

Table 1.28 Hunan's comparative (dis)advantage index by sector, 2010

Sector	Index
Agriculture, forestry, animal husbandry and fishery	0.36
Mining	0.70
Manufacturing	0.75
Production and distribution of electricity, gas and water	1.01
Construction	1.54
Transport, storage and post	0.86
Information transmission, computer service and software	0.79
Wholesale and retail trades	0.78
Hotels and catering services	1.12
Financial intermediation	1.02
Real estate	1.18
Leasing and business services	0.70
Scientific research, technical services and geological prospecting	0.74
Management of water conservancy, environment and public facilities	1.02
Services to households and other services	0.64
Education	1.14
Health, social security and social welfare	1.27
Culture, sports and entertainment	0.90
Public management and social organization	1.41

Notes All the sectors included in this table are determined according to China's official definitions and for urban areas only. Numerals greater than, equal to and less than one indicate that the province's sectors have advantages, no apparent (dis)advantages and disadvantages, respectively
Source Calculated by authors based on China Statistical Yearbook, 2011. See Appendix A for a detailed methodological description

Metallurgy, equipment manufacturing and tobacco manufacturing are the three pillar industries of the region. After many years of development, metallurgy is the top industry. This has an optimized structure and is strongly competitive. At present, fine products with high value-add and high technology are the focus of the industry. Major companies include the Valin Steel Group Corp, the Lengshuijiang Steel Group Corp and the Hunan Nonferrous Metals Holding Group Corp.

In recent years the region has also focused on several categories of products in the equipment manufacturing industry. These are primarily engineering machinery (the province has the second largest base in China), electrical appliances, automobiles and rail transportation equipment. The Sany Group Corp, the Tebian Electric Apparatus Stock Company, the Chang Feng Group Corp and the CSR Zhuzhou Electric Locomotive Works are the top players in these fields. Hunan's tobacco industry ranks second in the nation and its brand competitiveness ranks first.

The province's major import sources are Japan, Australia, Germany, the US and South Korea while key export destinations include Hong Kong, the US, Japan, South Korea and the Netherlands. Its major export products are rolled steel, textiles, manganese, clothing and fireworks, and major import products are iron ore, rolled steel, machine tool, paper pulp and liquid pumps.

Several dozens of the world's top 500 enterprises have invested in Hunan, including Pepsi, NEC, Hutchison Whampoa, Mitsubishi and Time Warner. Hong Kong is the largest investor, making up half of the province's FDI sources. Its investment has further accelerated since the Closer Economic Partnership Arrangement was implemented in 2004. Other noteworthy FDI sources are Taiwan, the US and the Virgin Islands. In terms of sectors, industry has received the most FDI at 61.0 %, while agriculture accounts for only 2.8 %. The service sector has also received a fairly substantial portion of FDI, making up 36.2 % of the total.

As of 2010, compared with those of other provinces, "construction", "public management and social organization" and "health, social security and social welfare" were relatively strong, while "agriculture, forestry, animal husbandry and fishery", "services to households and other services" "mining" and "leasing and business services" were relatively weak sectors (see Table 1.28).

Inner Mongolia

[Quick Facts: Official name: Inner Mongolia Autonomous Region; Capital: Hohhot; Land area: 1,183,000 km^2; Population density: 20/km^2; Major ethnic groups: Han, Mongol, Manchu, Hui, Daur]

Inner Mongolia (also officially called Nei Mongol) is an autonomous region of the PRC, located in the northern frontier of the country. It lies along the northern border of China, neighboring Heilongjiang, Liaoning, Jilin, Hebei, Shanxi, Shaanxi and Gansu provinces and Ningxia Hui Autonomous Region to the east, south and west, as well as Russia and Mongolia to the north. The region is a long, narrow strip of land sloping from north to south, spanning 2400 km from west to east and 1700 km from north to south.

The region was established in 1947 on the area of the former provinces of Suiyuan, Chahar, Rehe, Liaobei and Xing'an, all of which were established during the period of the Republic of China. It is the third-largest subdivision of China and covers about 12 % of the country's total land area. The majority of its population are Han Chinese, with a substantial Mongol minority. The official languages are Chinese and Mongolian, the latter written in Mongolian script as opposed to the Mongolian Cyrillic alphabet used in the state of Mongolia.

The region is divided into 12 prefecture-level divisions. Until the late 1990s, most of these were known as leagues (meng in Chinese), a usage retained from Mongol divisions of the Qing Dynasty (AD 1644–1911). Similarly, county-level divisions are often known as banners (qi in Chinese). The prefecture-level divisions are further subdivided into 101 county-level divisions, including 21 districts, 11 county-level cities, 17 counties, 49 banners and 3 autonomous banners. These are in turn divided into 1425 township-level divisions, including 532 towns, 407 townships, 277 sumu, 18 ethnic townships, 1 ethnic sumu and 190 sub-districts.

Due to its elongated shape, Inner Mongolia experiences a variety of climates. Officially, most of the region is classified as either a cold arid or steppe regime. A small portion is classified as humid continental in the northeast, or subartic in the far north near Hulunbuir. Spring is warm and windy; summer is short and hot with many rainy days; autumn usually sees an early frost and plummeting temperature; and winter is long and bitter cold with frequent polar outbreaks and blizzards. Dangerous sand storms can occur between spring and autumn. The region has an annual precipitation of 100–500 mm, 80–150 frost-free days and around 2700 h of sunshine. The Greater Xing'an and the Yinshan mountains divide the regions into areas with different climates. That east of the Greater Xing'an Mountains and north of the Yinshan Mountains has a lower temperature and less precipitation than the area to the west.

More than 120 kinds of minerals of the world's 140 have been found in the region, 5 of which have the largest deposits in China and 65 of which rank among the top ten in the country. The reserves of rare-earth metals amount to 84.59 million tons, or 80 % of the world's total and over 90 % of the country's total. The proven deposits of coal are 224.75 billion tons, the second largest in the country. The region has large reserves of ferrous metals, non-ferrous metals, precious metals, industrial chemicals and non-metal minerals. It also has abundant oil and natural gas—13 large oil and gas fields have been discovered with expected oil reserves of

2–3 billion tons and gas reserves of 1000 billion cubic meter. The minerals (excluding oil and natural gas) in the region have a potential value of ¥13,000 billion (about US$1570 billion), accounting for 10 % of the country's total volume and ranking as the third largest in the country.

Inner Mongolia has an abundance of resources, especially coal, cashmere, natural gas and rare-earth elements, and it has greater deposits of niobium, zirconium and beryllium than any other province-level region in China. It boasts almost one-quarter of the world's total coal reserves. However, due to its reliance on coal and energy resources, the province is susceptible to economic slowdowns and sluggish demand; additionally, its major industries are environmentally harmful and energy intensive. With the largest usable wind power capacity in China, there is potential for the development of new energy industries based on natural resources.

The region has 7.22 million ha of cultivated land (6.11 % of the country's total), 86.67 million ha of grasslands (73.3 % of the total) and 18.67 million ha of forests (15.8 % of the total). With a continental monsoon climate, vast grassland plateaus with a flat surface and mountains along its fringe, the region is home to 362 species of birds, 117 species of animals and 2351 species of plants.

The region is also rich in water, especially mineral water and springs with medicinal value. It has a total water area of 984,300 ha including 655,000 ha of freshwater, which accounts for 10.68 % of the country's total freshwater area. Nearly 1000 rivers flow through the area, 107 averaging a valley area of more than 1000 km^2 each. Moreover, 1000 lakes dot the region, eight of them with an area of over 100 km^2 each. Inner Mongolia has water resources of 90.3 billion cubic meter, of which 67.5 billion is surface water.

Mongols are the second largest ethnic group. They include many diverse Mongolian-speaking groups, such as the Buryats and the Oirats. Many of the traditional nomadic Mongols have settled in permanent homes as their pastoral economy was collectivized during the Maoist Era. Other ethnic groups include the Daur, the Evenks, the Oroqen, the Hui, the Manchus and the Koreans.

Besides hills, plains, deserts, rivers and lakes, Inner Mongolia has plateau landforms, mostly over 1000 m above sea level, including the Inner Mongolia Plateau, the second largest among the four major plateaus in the country. The region is rich in tourist attractions, including colorful ethnic culture, grassland scenery, the virgin forests in the Greater Xing'an Mountains, grand views along the Yellow River, the majestic Xiangsha Gulf, rivers, lakes, and springs. It is home to the Mausoleum of Genghis Khan, the Zhaojun Tomb, the ancient Great Wall of China, Wudang Monastery at the bottom of the Yinshan Mountains, Wuta Monastery, Bailing Temple and tomb murals dating back to the Eastern Han Dynasty (AD 25–220).

The nominal GRP of Inner Mongolia in 2010 was ¥1.16 trillion (about US $172.1 billion), with an average annual increase of 20 % from the year 2003 onwards. Its per capita GRP reached ¥47,347 in 2010. The industrial sector contributes more than 50 % of the total GRP, while the service and agricultural sectors contribute 36.1 and 9.4 %, respectively. As with much of China, economic growth has led to a boom in construction, including new commercial development and large apartment complexes (Table 1.29).

Table 1.29 Demographic and socioeconomic profile: Inner Mongolia

Indicator	2000	2010
Population (thousands)	23,760	24,722
Illiteracy rate of population aged 15 or over (%)	9.12	4.07
GRP (¥ billions)	140.10	1167.20
Composition of GRP (%)		
Primary sector	25.0	9.4
Secondary sector	39.7	54.6
Tertiary sector	35.3	36.1
Fixed asset investment (¥ billions)	42.36	892.65
Status of foreign-funded enterprises		
Number of registered enterprises	874	3693
Total investment (US$ millions)	2536	23,243
Registered capital (US$ millions)	1718	12,240
Foreign trade (US$ millions)		
Export	1114	4357
Import	1272	7325
Sales of consumer goods (¥ billions)	48	338
Per capita annual disposable income of urban residents (¥)	5129.05	17,698.15
Engle's coefficient (%)	41.14	36.52
Per capita annual net income of rural residents (¥)	2038.21	5529.59
Engle's coefficient (%)	28.85	37.55
Number of patent applications granted	775	2096
Inventions	60	262
Utility models	530	1276
Designs	185	558

Note All monetary values are measured at current prices. *Source* Inner Mongolia Statistical Yearbook, 2001 and 2011

Inner Mongolia has a strong agricultural industry. It is China's largest livestock producer, including cashmere, milk, and meat. Farming of crops, such as wheat, takes precedence along the river valleys. In the more arid grasslands, herding of goats, sheep and other animals is a traditional method of subsistence. Forestry and hunting are important in the Greater Khingan ranges in the east. Reindeer herding is carried out in the Evenk Autonomous Banner. More recently, growing grapes and winemaking have become an economic factor in the Wuhai area.

The province's economic growth has surged as a result of coal and huge discoveries of other energy and metal resources. In the past, the exploitation and utilization of resources were rather inefficient, which resulted in poor returns from rich resources. Inner Mongolia is also an important coal production base. Industry in Inner Mongolia has grown up mainly around coal, power generation, forestry-related industries, and related industries. Well-known Inner Mongolian enterprises include ERDOS, Yili and Mengniu.

In addition to its large reserves of natural resources, Inner Mongolia has the largest usable wind power capacity in China (thanks to strong winds which develop in the province's grasslands). Some private companies have set up wind parks in areas such as Bailingmiao, Hutengliang and Zhouzi.

The pillar industries include metallurgy, coal mining and processing, food processing, equipment manufacturing, petrochemicals and chemicals, and energy, which make up more than 80 % of the region's total gross output. The region has rich chromite ore and zinc reserves, both ranking the second largest in China. It is also rich in iron ore, with its reserves ranking the fourth largest in the country. The rich mineral resources contribute to the steady development of the region's metallurgy industry, which includes the production of steel and steel products, pig iron and ten major non-ferrous metals. Baotou Iron&Steel (Group) Co. Ltd, with total assets amounting to ¥29.5 billion, is the largest industrial enterprise in Inner Mongolia. Other major players in this sector include Inner Mongolia Baotou Steel Union Co. Ltd, Baotou Aluminum Industry Group, HongJun Aluminum and Power Co. Ltd, and East Hope Baotou Rare-Earth and Al Industry Co. Ltd.

Rich solar power and wind power resources, together with large coal reserves, make the region one of the key power suppliers for China's Northeast Power Grid, the Beijing–Tianjin–Tangshan Power Grid and China's neighbor, Mongolia. Many solar power plants, wind power plants and coal power plants are clustered in the region. The key players include Datang Tuoketuo Power Generation Company, Shenhua Group Zhungeer Energy Industry Co. Ltd and Yimin Huaneng Coal and Electricity Co. Ltd. Its coal reserves are the second largest in the country.

Similarly, the great variety of farming products and large amount of livestock contribute to the development of the food processing industry in the region. Inner Mongolia is thus known as China's largest dairy product manufacturing base. In 2006 nearly 3.5 million tons of dairy products were produced in the region, 12.4 % more than the previous year. Mengniu Milk Industry Group and Inner Mongolia Yili Industrial Group Co. Ltd, China's two leading milk product manufacturers, have established their headquarters there.

There have been hundreds of enterprises specializing in petrochemical and chemical products in Inner Mongolia. The most profitable industries include petroleum processing, raw chemical and chemical products, coke products and nuclear fuel processing. Leading enterprises in this sector include the Tianye Chemical Industry (Group) Co. Ltd, the Inner Mongolia Jinhe Industry Group and the Lan Tai Industrial Co. Ltd.

Major import goods include minerals, wood and wooden products, charcoal, cork and related products, straws, plaited products, baskets and wickerwork, chemicals and related products, and electronics. The main export goods include base metals and related products, textile materials and related products, chemicals and related products, electronic products, and vegetables, fruit and cereals. Major export destinations are Japan, the US, South Korea, Italy and Mongolia.

Most of the FDI has been channeled into manufacturing, energy, real estate and resident services, and other services. The investments have mainly come from Hong Kong, Taiwan, Japan, the US and Australia.

As of 2010, compared with those of other provinces, "agriculture, forestry, animal husbandry and fishery", "services to households and other services"

Table 1.30 Inner Mongolia's comparative (dis)advantage index by sector, 2010

Sector	Index
Agriculture, forestry, animal husbandry and fishery	3.72
Mining	1.72
Manufacturing	0.54
Production and distribution of electricity, gas and water	1.71
Construction	0.56
Transport, storage and post	1.35
Information transmission, computer service and software	1.10
Wholesale and retail trades	0.66
Hotels and catering services	0.59
Financial intermediation	1.13
Real estate	0.38
Leasing and business services	0.48
Scientific research, technical services and geological prospecting	0.78
Management of water conservancy, environment and public facilities	1.74
Services to households and other services	1.78
Education	1.15
Health, social security and social welfare	1.02
Culture, sports and entertainment	1.33
Public management and social organization	1.29

Notes All the sectors included in this table are determined according to China's official definitions and for urban areas only. Numerals greater than, equal to and less than one indicate that the province's sectors have advantages, no apparent (dis)advantages and disadvantages, respectively
Source Calculated by authors based on China Statistical Yearbook, 2011. See Appendix A for a detailed methodological description

"management of water conservancy, environment and public facilities" and "mining" were relatively strong, while "real estate", "leasing and business services", "manufacturing" and "construction" were relatively weak sectors (see Table 1.30).

Jiangsu

[Quick Facts: Official name: Jiangsu Province; Capital: Nanjing; Land area: 102,600 km^2; Population density: 767/km^2; Major ethnic groups: Han, Hui, Miao, Tujia, Zhuang]

Jiangsu is a province of the PRC, located along the east coast of the country. It lies at the center of China's east coast. It borders Shandong Province to the north, Anhui Province to the west, and Zhejiang Province and Shanghai Municipality to the south. It has a coastline of over 1000 km along the Yellow Sea, and the Yangtze River passes through its southern parts. The name "Jiangsu" comes from Jiang, which is short for the city of Jiangning (now called Nanjing), and Su, short for the city of Suzhou. The abbreviation for this province is "Su", the second character of its name.

Although there is no official definition of the boundary, the province is divided into Su Nan (or southern Jiangsu) and Su Bei (or northern Jiangsu). The Yangtze River lies along the line that roughly divides the two regions. The cities of Nanjing, Zhenjiang, Suzhou, Wuxi, Changzhou, Yangzhou, Taizhou and Nantong (the province's economic hub) lie within the Su Nan region and the cities of Xuzhou, Lianyungang, Huaiyin, Xiancheng and Shuqian lie within Su Bei.

The region comprises mainly plains, abundant rivers and numerous lakes., The Yangtze River cuts through the province in the south before flowing into the East China Sea. The 13 prefecture-level divisions of Jiangsu are subdivided into 106 county-level divisions (54 districts, 27 county-level cities and 25 counties). These are in turn divided into 1488 township-level divisions (1078 towns, 122 townships, 1 ethnic township and 287 sub-districts).

Located in a transit belt from the sub-tropics to a warm temperate zone, Jiangsu features a distinctive monsoon climate. Generally speaking, the area south of the Huaihe River and the Northern Jiangsu General Irrigation Canal enjoys a subtropical humid monsoon climate, while the area to the north enjoys a warm temperate humid monsoon climate. It is warm with moderate rainfall and clear-cut seasons in the province. The annual average temperature is 13–16 °C, with temperatures at an average of −2 to 4 °C in January and 26–30 °C in July. The annual rainfall is 724–1210 mm. The rainfall in summer accounts for 50 % of the annual rainfall. The province has clear-cut seasonals.

Jiangsu is very flat and low-lying, with plains covering 68 % of its area and waters another 18 %. It is located in the fertile land of the Yangtze River Delta. Most of its land is flat. On its southwestern and northern borders are hilly lands. Jiangsu also borders the Yellow Sea. The main cash crops are cotton, soybeans, peanuts, rape, sesame, ambary hemp and tea. Other products include peppermint, spearmint, bamboo, medicinal herbs, apples, pears, peaches, loquats and ginkgo. Silkworms also form an important part of Jiangsu's agriculture, with the Lake Taihu region to the south a major base of silk production.

Jiangsu Province boasts a network of rivers and lakes. The Yangtze River, China's longest river, runs over 400 km through the province from west to east while the Beijing–Hangzhou Grand Canal runs 690 km from north to south, traversing all the east–west river systems. There is the Qinhuai River in its southwest and the Northern Jiangsu General Irrigation Canal, Xinmu River and Nantong–Yanzhou Canal in the north. The province also boasts more than 290 lakes, including the third and fourth largest freshwater lakes in China, Lake Taihu and Lake Hongze. Jiangsu has abundant aquatic resources. The area of fish farms in the east coast reaches 154,000 km^2. The four most notable farms, including Lusi and Haizhou Bay, teem with yellow croaker, cutlass fish, butterfish, shrimps, crabs, shellfish and algae. The province is also the major producer of freshwater crabs and eel fry. The inland waters within the province cover a total area of 1.73 million hectare.

Jiangsu has a wide distribution and rich variety of mineral resources. The number discovered so far is 120. Major energy resources include coal, petroleum and natural gas. Non-metallic resources include sulfur, phosphorus, sodium salt, crystal, cyanite, sapphire, diamond, kaolin, limestone, quartz sand, marble and pottery clay. The metallic resources include copper, lead, zinc, silver, gold, strontium and manganese. The province is particularly rich in clay, building materials, chemical raw materials, metallurgic auxiliary materials, minerals for special uses and non-ferrous metals.

The province originated in the 17th century with the splitting of the defunct and erroneously named Jiangnan Province ("south of the river") into Jiangsu and Anhui. Before then the northern and southern parts of Jiangsu had less connection with each other than they later did. Traditionally, South Jiangsu is referred to as the three more prosperous southern cities: Suzhou, Wuxi and Changzhou. Their culture (the

"Jiangnan" culture shared with Shanghai and Zhejiang) is often referred to as the Wu. All the other parts of the province are dominated by the so-called Jianghuai culture, which means the culture in the area between the Yangtse River (Jiang) and the Huaihe River (Huai), though not all of them lie within the district defined by the term.

Jiangsu has a long history of a relatively developed economy and culture. Rich in landscape gardens, scenic attractions and historical sites, it is noted for having the largest number of historical cities in the country. Such cities include Nanjing, Suzhou, Yangzhou, Zhenjiang, Changshu, Xuzhou and Huai'an. There are 20 scenic spots, 23 forest parks, 6 holiday resorts and 416 cultural heritage sites under state and provincial-level protection. Classical gardens in Suzhou have been added to the World Cultural Heritage Site list by UNESCO.

In 2010, Jiangsu's nominal GRP was ¥4.14 trillion (about US$612 billion), making it the second largest GRP of all the provinces after Guangdong Province. Its per capita GRP was ¥52,448 (about US$7945). Since the inception of economic reforms in 1978, Jiangsu has been a hot spot for economic development and it now has the highest GRP per capita of all Chinese provinces. The wealth divide between the rich southern and the poor northern regions, however, remains a prominent issue there. Cities like Nanjing, Suzhou and Wuxi have GRP per capita around twice the provincial average, making south Jiangsu one of the most prosperous regions in China (Table 1.31).

The agricultural sector is based on rice, wheat, peanuts and cotton. Although the province has some petro-carbon deposits, more significant deposits include rock salt, sulfur, phosphorus and marble.

The region is historically oriented towards light industries, such as textiles and food. Since 1949 it has also developed heavy industries, such as chemicals and construction materials. Its important industries include machinery, electronics, chemicals and automobiles. Recently, government has worked hard to promote the solar industry. Economic reform and the opening-up policies of China have greatly benefited the southern cities, especially Suzhou and Wuxi, which outstrip the provincial capital Nanjing in total output. In the eastern outskirts of Suzhou, Singapore has built the Suzhou Industrial Park, a flagship of Sino-Singapore cooperation and the only industrial park in China that is in its entirety the investment of a single foreign country.

Jiangsu is known for its "Su'nan" (or southern Jiangsu) Model, which developed many booming collective and township enterprises in the 1980s and 1990s. These are government-funded enterprises that were set up by rural farmers and the remaining workforce after the government made appeals for them to do so. They started to prosper as a result of reforms carried out by government. Until the mid-1990s, the township enterprises were a fast-growing sector and were the main contributors to the economy. Today, however they are slowly losing their importance as industrial parks bring in large revenues from Chinese state and foreign investors.

Table 1.31 Demographic and socioeconomic profile: Jiangsu

Indicator	2000	2010
Population (thousands)	74,380	78,693
Illiteracy rate of population aged 15 or over (%)	6.31	3.81
GRP (¥ billions)	858.27	4142.55
Composition of GRP (%)		
Primary sector	12.0	6.1
Secondary sector	51.7	52.5
Tertiary sector	36.3	41.4
Fixed asset investment (¥ billions)	257.00	2318.43
Status of foreign-funded enterprises		
Number of registered enterprises	18,060	51,666
Total investment (US$ millions)	75,004	508,106
Registered capital (US$ millions)	40,657	273,899
Foreign trade (US$ millions)		
Export	26,377	281,449
Import	22,817	217,334
Sales of consumer goods (¥ billions)	260	1,361
Per capita annual disposable income of urban residents (¥)	6800.23	22,944.26
Engle's coefficient (%)	43.04	39.51
Per capita annual net income of rural residents (¥)	3595.09	9118.24
Engle's coefficient (%)	33.09	38.08
Number of patent applications granted	6432	138,382
Inventions	341	7210
Utility models	4095	41,161
Designs	1996	90,011

Note All monetary values are measured at current prices. *Source* Jiangsu Statistical Yearbook, 2001 and 2011

The north lags behind the south of Jiangsu. The three main reasons for this are the underdeveloped transportation system of the north, its immature industries and its immense distance from Shanghai compared with the south. Also, in the past, northern Jiangsu was frequently affected by heavy floods from the Hai River. The uneven development of economies on either side of the Yangtze River poses an issue for the continued sustainability of the province as a whole.

The pillar industries in Jiangsu are electronics, chemicals, textiles, metallurgy, electrical equipment manufacturing and general purpose equipment manufacturing. Electronics is the leading industry. The region also has a well-established industry cluster which has set up various types of production models, such as export-oriented (in Jintan), market-oriented (in Changshu) and brand-oriented (in Ganjiang). Most of the electronic enterprises in Jiangsu are jointly set up by Chinese and foreign companies. Major investors include Philips Semiconductor, Hejian

Table 1.32 Jiangsu's comparative (dis)advantage index by sector, 2010

Sector	Index
Agriculture, forestry, animal husbandry and fishery	0.45
Mining	0.38
Manufacturing	1.58
Production and distribution of electricity, gas and water	0.71
Construction	0.71
Transport, storage and post	0.85
Information transmission, computer service and software	0.80
Wholesale and retail trades	0.93
Hotels and catering services	0.87
Financial intermediation	0.98
Real estate	0.59
Leasing and business services	0.66
Scientific research, technical services and geological prospecting	0.63
Management of water conservancy, environment and public facilities	0.96
Services to households and other services	0.30
Education	0.92
Health, social security and social welfare	0.98
Culture, sports and entertainment	0.74
Public management and social organization	0.75

Notes All the sectors included in this table are determined according to China's official definitions and for urban areas only. Numerals greater than, equal to and less than one indicate that the province's sectors have advantages, no apparent (dis)advantages and disadvantages, respectively
Source Calculated by authors based on China Statistical Yearbook, 2011. See Appendix A for a detailed methodological description

Technology (Suzhou), Infineon, Samsung, Hitachi Display, Sumitomo Bakelite and Seagate. Moreover, Jiangsu has developed a number of famous domestic brands, such as Bosideng Corp, Jiangsu AB Group, Hongdou Group and Jiangsu Sunshine Group.

The chemical industry is another important sector. Major producers include Nanjing Jinling Chemical Plant, Lianyungang Taisheng Chemical, Yancheng City Longgang Perfume Chemical Factory and Yangzhou Aokang Chemical. It should be noted that Nanjing Jinling Chemical is one of the largest PVC plastic stabilizer producers in China. In 2000, BASF, the largest chemical producer in the world, and Sinopec (a Chinese petroleum giant) jointly set up an integrated petrochemical site in Nanjing. The core business is the supply of steam crackers to nine world-scale downstream plants, and the production of chemicals and polymers for the domestic market.

The province is a leading textile and garment production base in China. It is also a major export market for textiles and garments. In recent years the rapid growth of the Yangtze River Delta has gradually threatened Guangdong's leading position in the industry. This growth is partially due to the fact that the delta has more available land and a larger labor supply from less developed neighboring provinces, such as Anhui and Jiangxi.

Jiangsu Province has strong trade ties with more than 200 countries and regions. Its foreign trade ranks second in China (after Guangdong province). Foreign-invested enterprises are the main contributors to the area's exports, followed by private enterprises. Major export destinations include the EU, the US and Japan, while the import regions are Taiwan, Japan and Korea. To a great extent the rapid growth of the economy is the result of surging foreign investment in the province. In 2003, Jiangsu displaced Guangdong as the largest FDI recipient. Since then it has remained at the top position.

As of 2010, compared with those of other provinces, "manufacturing" was relatively strong, while "services to households and other services", "mining", "agriculture, forestry, animal husbandry and fishery" and "real estate" were relatively weak sectors (see Table 1.32).

Jiangxi

[Quick Facts: Official name: Jiangxi Province; Capital: Nanchang; Land area: 166,900 km^2; Population density: 264/km^2; Major ethnic groups: Han, She, Miao, Hui, Zhuang]

Jiangxi is a province of the PRC, situated in the middle and lower reaches of the Yangtze River. Spanning from the banks of the Yangtze River in the north into hillier areas in the south, and locked in on all sides by the neighboring provinces of China, Jiangxi Province shares a border with Anhui Province to the north, Zhejiang Province to the northeast, Fujian Province to the east, Guangdong Province to the south, Hunan Province to the west, and Hubei Province to the northwest.

The name "Jiangxi" derives from the Jiangnan xidao (Western Jiangnan Lu—a provincial administration under the Tang Dynasty in AD 733). Jiangxi is also called "Gan" for short after the Gan River, which runs from the south to the north and flows into the Yangtze River. The 11 prefecture-level divisions of Jiangxi are subdivided into 99 county-level divisions (19 districts, 10 county-level cities and 70 counties). These in turn are divided into 1548 township-level divisions (770 towns, 651 townships, 7 ethnic townships and 120 sub-districts).

Mountains surround Jiangxi on three sides, with the Mufu Mountains, Jiuling Mountains, and Luoxiao Mountains on the west; the Huaiyu Mountains and Wuyi Mountains on the east; and the Jiulian Mountains and Dayu Mountains in the south. The southern half of the province is hilly with ranges and valleys interspersed, while the northern half is flatter and lower in altitude. The highest point in Jiangxi is Mount Huanggang in the Wuyi Mountains, on the border with Fujian Province.

The Gan River dominates the province, flowing the entire length of the region from south to north. It enters Lake Poyang in the north, the largest freshwater lake of China, which in turn empties into the Yangtze River, which forms part of the northern border of Jiangxi. Important reservoirs include the Xiushui Tuolin Reservoir in the northwest on the Xiushui River and the Wan'an Reservoir in the upper section of the Gan River.

The topographies of Jiangxi are dominated by mountainous and hilly land, with mountains covering 36 % of the province's total territory and hills 42 %. The remaining 22 % comprises plains and waters. Most of the mountains lie on the provincial borders. Mount Huaiyu in the northeast has the province's largest copper reserve; Wuyi Mountain, a World Cultural Heritage Site, lies in the east; the Dageng Ridge and Jiulian Mountain in the south are known as the "capital of tungsten"; in the west there is the Luoxiao Mountain; and in the northwest lie the mountains of Mufu and Jiuling.

The climate is subtropical. Jiangxi's annual average temperature is around 18 °C, with temperatures of 3–9 °C in January and 27–31 °C in July. Temperatures in the northeastern and northwestern areas and along the Yangtze River are lower, at 16–17 °C. Other parts of the province are warmer, with temperatures of 18–20 °C. Rainfall is plentiful. The average annual rainfall is 1341–1940 mm. It is greater in the southern, eastern and mountainous regions and less in the northern, western and basin areas. The average annual rainfall in the mountains of Wuyi, Huaiyu and Jiuling can be as high as 1800–2000 mm, while that of the area along the Yangtze River, the Poyang Lake and the Jitai Basin is 1350–1400 mm. Other parts of the province have average annual rainfall of 1500–1700 mm.

Like many other provinces in China, Jiangxi is rich in mineral deposits. In particular, it has huge reserves of copper, tungsten, lead, zinc and rock salt. It is also famous for local traditional products, such as china produced in Jingdezhen. Jiangxi has abundant mineral resources. Of the 150 known minerals, more than 140 have been found in Jiangxi. Among these, the deposits of 89 have been verified, with 33 of them ranking among the top five in the country. Ferrous metals include iron, manganese, titanium and vanadium. Among the 13 non-ferrous and precious metals are copper, lead, zinc, gold and silver. Noted centers of mining include Dexing (copper) and Dayu County (tungsten). There are also 29 rare and rare-earth minerals, such as niobium and tantalum. The province has developed the largest copper mine in Asia and its copper-smelting base is the largest in China.

The mountainous terrain and large forest coverage of Jiangxi has made it one of the wilder areas in central China. South China Tigers have been seen as recently as 15 or 20 years ago and projects are underway to document evidence of any that remain. Several mountain areas along the northern border with Hunan and Hubei are potential sites for "wilderness" preserves, specifically for protecting or even reintroducing tigers. Other wildlife, though not plentiful, are more numerous in Jiangxi than in many other developed areas of China. Numerous species of birds are common, especially around the marshes of Lake Poyang in the north. Though protected, mammals such as muntjak, wild boar, civet cats and pangolins are still common enough that they'll even occasionally be seen in markets for sale as game meat, or possibly even in a forest.

Some 59 % of the territory is covered in forest. Its timber reserve amounts to 250 million cubic meter, in addition to 1 billion plants of bamboo, both figures taking leading positions in the country. Most of the forests are natural secondary forests. Coniferous forests occupy a larger proportion, with pine and masson pine being the major species. Tea-oil tree, tung tree and Chinese tallow tree are the major economic species scattered across the province, which also boasts more than 4000 species of seed plants, some 470 types of pteridophyte and over 100 types of bryophyte. Among the lower plants, the varieties of large fungus alone are as many as 500. There are more than 2000 species of woody plants, including over 400 kinds of arbor. Jiangxi is also home to many ancient trees, such as ginkgo, known as the "living fossil" of plants.

The good ecological environment characterized by a rich water resource, changing topographies and wide coverage of vegetation ensures an abundance of wildlife. The 30 nature reserves cover a total area of 9016 km^2, accounting for 5.4 % of the province. Jiangxi now has over 600 kinds of vertebrates, including more than 170 species of fish, which account for 21.4 % of the national total of freshwater fish. There are more than 40 species of amphibians accounting for 20.4 % of the national total; some 70 species of reptiles, accounting for 23.5 %; 270 species of birds, accounting for 23.2 %; and 50 species of mammals, accounting for 13.3 %.

Jiangxi boasts more than 2400 rivers and streams, some 160 of which, totaling 18,400 km in length, having water running all year round. Ganjiang, Fuhe, Xinjiang, Xiuhe and Raohe are the five largest rivers in the province. Jiangxi's total water reserve is 150.5 billion cubic meter, with the per capita figure standing at 3491 cubic meter, which is 1393 cubic meter more than the national average. Fish and birds have great economic value and therefore take priority for protection. Lake Poyang offers an ideal winter shelter for migratory birds.

Jiangxi has beautiful landscapes with green mountains and clear waters. It has 11 cultural relics under state protection and 2406 of its scenic spots and tourism areas have been registered as major provincial projects. The key scenic spots include Mount Lushan, Jinggang Mountain, Longhu (dragon and tiger) Mountain, Sanqing Mountain, Poyang Lake, and the cities of Nanchang and Jingdezhen. Near the northern port city of Jiujiang lies the well-known resort area of Mount Lushan—one of the 14 major international tourist routes in China. Also near the city are the Donglin (East Wood) Temple and the Tiefo (iron Buddha) Temple, two important Buddhist temples. Mount Lushan has been listed as a World Heritage Site by UNESCO and, together with Jinggang and Sanqing mountains, offers charming peaks and quiet valleys.

Guifeng Peak and Dragon Palace are noted for their precipitous cliffs and deep caves. The landscapes of Poyang Lake and Ganjiang River are attractive, while ancient temples at Longhu Mountain, Qingyuan and Donglin attract visitors with their unique religious architectures. Other attractions include Tengwang Tower, Bajing Terrace, the former residences of historical nobilities in Linchuan and Jiujiang, headquarters of the Red Army on Jinggang Mountain, the Memorial Museum of the Nanchang Uprising, and Ruijin, the first capital of the Communist administration in China.

The province is rather poor area compared with its neighbors. It is located near some of the richest provinces of China (Guangdong, Zhejiang, Fujian), which are sometimes blamed for taking away talents and capital from the area. Jiangxi has the lowest wages and third lowest property prices in China and, as a result of wages and labor, the economy sits at the low end of the value chain. As Guangdong and Zhejiang draw away skilled labor with higher wages, Jiangxi has been victim to a brain drain and finds itself trapped in a combination of low skill, low value-added, low innovation and low energy efficiency. Thus, without meaningful structural changes, its rich mineral resources may be at risk. The province plans to expand railways and develop new energy projects, including nuclear (Table 1.33).

Jiangxi's consumer market lags behind that of other provinces, ranking 21st in terms of retail sales of consumer goods. Most of the goods consumed are food, clothing and household articles. Its major consumer centers are located in Nanchang, Jiujiang and Jingdezhen.

Table 1.33 Demographic and socioeconomic profile: Jiangxi

Indicator	2000	2010
Population (thousands)	41,400	44,622
Illiteracy rate of population aged 15 or over (%)	5.16	3.13
GRP (¥ billion)	200.31	945.13
Composition of GRP (%)		
Primary sector	24.2	12.8
Secondary sector	35.0	54.2
Tertiary sector	40.8	33.0
Fixed asset investment (¥ billion)	51.61	877.23
Status of foreign-funded enterprises		
Number of registered enterprises	2246	7574
Total investment (US$ millions)	6876	43,917
Registered capital (US$ millions)	3301	28,136
Foreign trade (US$ millions)		
Export	1188	11,807
Import	864	9146
Sales of consumer goods (¥ billions)	70	296
Per capita annual disposable income of urban residents (¥)	5103.58	15,481.12
Engle's coefficient (%)	39.36	32.26
Per capita annual net income of rural residents (¥)	2135.30	5788.56
Engle's coefficient (%)	39.82	46.34
Number of patent applications granted	1072	4349
Inventions	67	411
Utility models	690	2588
Designs	315	1350

Note All monetary values are measured at current prices. *Source* Jiangxi Statistical Yearbook, 2001 and 2011

The province is a major producer of rice, freshwater products, timber and bamboo. Rich in minerals, its reserves of copper, gold, silver and rare earths are among the largest in the country. As such, metal-related mining, smelting and pressing dominate its secondary industry. Jiangxi has the lowest average wage and third lowest property prices in China, allowing the province to lure manufacturing from its neighbors, Guangdong and Zhejiang provinces. While agriculture lags behind industry and services, it is one of the third largest rice-producing provinces in China in terms of output. In addition, its output of freshwater fish is amongst the highest. Cash crops commonly grown include cotton and rapeseed. Jiangxi is the leading producer of kumquats in China, particularly in Suichuan County.

The region's pillar industries are in metallurgy, chemicals, food processing, automobiles, electrical appliances and pharmaceuticals. The metallurgy industry has grown rapidly in terms of output volume and revenue. Metals processed include iron, steel and copper. Home to the biggest copper mine in Asia (located in Dexing), the province is a major source of copper for most copper companies. Key players in this industry are Jiangxi Copper Corp and Xinyu Iron & Steel Corp. Starting in the 1960s, automobile manufacturing there is focussed on the development of light and compact cars. Most of the automobile technologies are introduced from outside the province owing to its limited R&D capability. Famous companies in the automobile industry are Jiangling Motors Corp and Jiangxi Changhe Motor Corp.

Another key industry is in electrical appliance manufacturing. Appliances made there are mainly digital audiovisual products and home air-conditioners. AUX (Nanchang) Corp is one of the key manufacturers of air-conditioners. The food-processing industry is also growing in the province.

Jiangxi's pharmaceutical industry concentrates on the development of Chinese medicine. It has a high concentration of industrial groups, such as Huiren Group and Jiangzhong Medical Corp. As for the chemical industry, this focuses on the development of petrochemicals, silicone and dry cement. A major company in this industry is Jiujiang Petrochemical Corp.

Major export products include clothing, mechanical and electrical products, rolled steel, textiles and copper, while major import products include mechanical and electrical products, copper ore, hi-tech products, iron ore and copper. A substantial share of trade has been conducted with the US and Japan. The US is the province's fifth largest import source as well as the top export destination, while Japan is the province's third largest import source and export destination. Other key trading partners are Chile, Taiwan, Australia, Hong Kong, the Netherlands and South Korea. While Hong Kong may not be a key source of imports, it is the main source of FDI for Jiangxi. The US, Taiwan, Singapore and Japan are the other key sources.

As of 2010, compared with those of other provinces, "agriculture, forestry, animal husbandry and fishery", "production and distribution of electricity, gas and water" "public management and social organization" and "education" were relatively strong, while "Hotels and catering services", "services to households and other services" "leasing and business services" and "real estate" were relatively weak sectors (see Table 1.34).

Table 1.34 Jiangxi's comparative (dis)advantage index by sector, 2010

Sector	Index
Agriculture, forestry, animal husbandry and fishery	1.41
Mining	0.70
Manufacturing	0.86
Production and distribution of electricity, gas and water	1.34
Construction	1.02
Transport, storage and post	1.06
Information transmission, computer service and software	0.78
Wholesale and retail trades	0.65
Hotels and catering services	0.34
Financial intermediation	0.98
Real estate	0.44
Leasing and business services	0.41
Scientific research, technical services and geological prospecting	0.76
Management of water conservancy, environment and public facilities	1.12
Services to households and other services	0.37
Education	1.32
Health, social security and social welfare	1.16
Culture, sports and entertainment	1.06
Public management and social organization	1.34

Notes All the sectors included in this table are determined according to China's official definitions and for urban areas only. Numerals greater than, equal to and less than one indicate that the province's sectors have advantages, no apparent (dis)advantages and disadvantages, respectively
Source Calculated by authors based on China Statistical Yearbook, 2011. See Appendix A for a detailed methodological description

Jilin

[Quick Facts: Official name: Jilin Province; Capital: Changchun; Land area: 187,400 km^2; Population density: 145/km^2; Major ethnic groups: Han, Korean, Manchu, Mongol, Hui]

Jilin is a province of the PRC, located in the central area of northeast China. It borders Heilongjiang Province to the north, Liaoning Province to the south, Inner Mongolia Autonomous Region to the west, Russia to the east and North Korea to the southeast across the Tumen and the Yalu—two rivers serving as the boundary between China and North Korea.

The region is drained by various river systems, including the Yalu and Tumen rivers, tributaries of the Liao River along the southern border, and the Songhua and Nen rivers (both of the latter eventually flowing into the Amur). The literal meaning of the Chinese characters for "Jilin" is "auspicious forest". The name "Jilin" probably originates from "Girin Ula", a Manchu term meaning "along the river", which was then shortened to Jilin in Chinese.

The land is high in the southeast and low in the northwest, with a vast plain lying in its mid-west. The eastern part of the province includes the mountain area of the Changbai Mountains with an elevation of over 1000 m and the Jidong hilly land of 500 m above sea level or lower. The western part of the province is the Songliao Plain, whose low and level western section is the grain base of the province.

Jilin is located in the middle latitudes of the northern hemisphere, east of the Euro-Asian continent, the northernmost section of the temperate zone in China, near the sub-frigid zone. The eastern part of the province is close to the Yellow Sea and the Sea of Japan, where the atmosphere is moist and often accompanied by much rain. The climate of its western part, which is far from the sea and approaches the arid Mongolian Plateau, is dry. As a whole, the area has a distinct temperate continental monsoon climate with four clear-cut seasons. The yearly average temperature of most parts is 3–5 °C. The annual precipitation is 550–910 mm and the frost-free period lasts 120–160 days (beginning in the last ten days of September and lasting until the end of April or early May). With hot and rainy days in the same season, it is good for farming.

There is an abundance of minerals, with a total of 136 varieties of ores discovered. The number of surveyed mineral deposits is 93, of which 75 have been explored. The reserves of 22 minerals rank as the top five in the country. The main minerals include coal, with a reserve of nearly 2.1 billion tons; petroleum, with a remaining potential reserve of 113.99 million tons; iron ores, with a reserve of 460 million tons; gold, with a reserve ranking 13th in the country; reserves of ten other minerals, such as oil shale, diatomite and wollastonite, ranking first; veneer gabbro and carbon dioxide gas, ranking second; molybdenum and germanium, ranking third; and the remaining potential reserve of petroleum, ranking sixth. Jilin is favored with non-metallic mineral products and most of its exports are crude non-metallic minerals and their products. The reserves of wollastonite, diatomite, bentonite and refractory clay are rich enough for mining. Those of petroleum, natural gas and coal are also abundant.

The province is one of China's six major forestry areas. The Changbai Mountains stretching about 500 km are known as the "Changbai Sea of Forest." Forests cover 7.98 million hectare, accounting for 82.04 % of the total land used for forestry, ranking eighth in the country. The province's storage of live limber is 840 million cubic meter, ranking sixth in the country. The province's forest coverage is 42.4 %. Timber production by Jilin is ranked sixth in the nation. Trees of quality timber for industrial use include Korean pine, Changbai pine, yeddo spruce, northeast China ash, yellow pineapple, Manchurian walnut catalpa and linden. Chinese grapes, the fruit of Chinese magnolia vine, cowberry and haw are all used for brewing wine. There are 300 varieties of wild plants that provide a rich source for honey-making.

The prairie in western Jilin is situated in the center of the Songhuajiang-Nenjiang Prairie, one of the famous grasslands in China. It is known for its rich forage grasses for sheep, most of which are perennial rootstock and bushy grasses. It is also one of the breeding bases for commercial cattle and fine-wool sheep in northern China. There are 4.379 million ha of grassland available in the province, mainly in its western and eastern parts.

There is a rich wildlife in the area, particularly in the Changbai Mountains. Jilin is the original producer of the world-famous Three Northeast China Treasures—ginseng, marten fur and pilose antler. Its other products, such as glossy ganoderma, the tuber of elevated gastrodia, astragali, pine mushroom, hedgehog fungus and frog fat are all well known at home and abroad.

Jilin has an abundance of traditional Chinese medicinal resources, with approximately 27,000 kinds of wild plants and 9000 kinds of medicinal herbs. Among its 437 species of wild animals, there are precious fur animals and feather fowls, such as sables, otters, lynx, Manchurian tigers, leopards and flowery-tail pheasants. Precious animals that can be used as medicinal materials include red deer, musk deer, brown bears, badgers, frogs and wood frogs. Animals of high economic value include wild boars, roe deer and grouse.

The province's soil is fertile and thus suitable for growing grains, beans, oil crops, beetroot, tobacco, jute, potato, ginseng, traditional Chinese medicinal herbs and fruits. It has 55,760 km^2 of arable land area, accounting for 4.3 % of the nation's total arable land area. The arable land area per capita in Jilin is 134 % higher than the country's average level. The province's sown area is 3.96 million ha. The Song-Liao Plain is an important grain base of the country and a well-known corn-growing zone. It has been called one of the "Golden Corn Belts" of the world. As the largest granary of China, the province's grain output accounts for 5.5 % of the country's total output. It also produces soybeans, rice, maize and sorghum. Rice is mostly cultivated in the eastern parts, such as Yanbian Korean Prefecture. The region's per capita consumption of grain, the commodity rate of grain, the volume of grains shipped to other provinces and the export of corn have been the highest in the country for many years.

The province boasts rich tourism resources. In the provincial capital, Changchun, are the former government office of the Manchurian State, established by Japanese invaders during World War II, the Jingyuetan Forest Park, the Automobile Town and the Changchun Film Studio. The Changbaishan Nature Reserve covers a vast area in the three counties of Changbei, Antu and Fusong and boasts scenic spots such as the Heavenly Pond, waterfalls, and groups of hot springs and grand canyons. The Goguryeo sites and tombs found in Ji'an and Jilin, including Wandu, Gungnae Fortress, and the pyramidal General's Tomb, have been listed as World Heritage Sites by UNESCO. The Baekdu Mountain, especially Heaven Lake on the border with North Korea, is another popular tourist destination.

In 2010 the nominal GRP of Jilin province totaled ¥866.76 billion (about US $120 billion). It has been rising at more than 10 % since 2003 (Table 1.35).

The Changbai Mountains are a key source of lumber. Herding of sheep is an important activity in the western parts, such as Baicheng. Traditionally, Jilin has been known as a major pharmaceutical center, with yields of ginseng and deer antlers among the largest in China, being used extensively in traditional Chinese medicine.

While agriculture still counts as one of Jilin's largest industries, since the reforms of the 1980s, the ever-expanding secondary and tertiary sectors have driven economic growth. A significant automobile industry as well as important petroleum and chemical industries continue to underpin the economy, and future sights are set on nurturing a high-tech industry centered on photoelectron products. Ongoing reforms to modernize traditional heavy industries increase the efficiency of state-owned enterprises and develop foreign trade aim to widen the province's economic achievements.

Industry is the leading contributor making up near a half of the GRP, followed by the service sector and agriculture. Jilin has four pillar industries: automobile manufacturing, petrochemicals, food processing and pharmaceuticals. The province was once the center of the nation's industrial base. First Auto Works, China's second largest carmaker after Shanghai Automotive Industry Corp, is the pioneer of

Table 1.35 Demographic and socioeconomic profile: Jilin

Indicator	2000	2010
Population (thousands)	27,280	27,466
Illiteracy rate of population aged 15 or over (%)	4.57	1.92
GRP (¥ billions)	182.12	866.76
Composition of GRP (%)		
Primary sector	21.9	12.1
Secondary sector	43.9	52.0
Tertiary sector	34.2	35.9
Fixed asset investment (¥ billions)	60.35	787.04
Status of foreign-funded enterprises		
Number of registered enterprises	2747	4309
Total investment (US$ millions)	7661	22,259
Registered capital (US$ millions)	5277	12,299
Foreign trade (US$ millions)		
Export	1487	4507
Import	1498	12,517
Sales of consumer goods (¥ billions)	81	350
Per capita annual disposable income of urban residents (¥)	4810.00	15,411.47
Engle's coefficient (%)	40.68	35.08
Per capita annual net income of rural residents (¥)	2022.50	6237.44
Engle's coefficient (%)	37.05	36.73
Number of patent applications granted	1650	4343
Inventions	154	785
Utility models	1142	2806
Designs	354	752

Note All monetary values are measured at current prices. *Source* Jilin Statistical Yearbook, 2001 and 2011

the country's automobile industry. The petrochemical industry is the second pillar industry of Jilin. Since China's first petrochemical company, Jilin Petrochemical Corp, was founded in 1957, the petrochemical industry in this region has been the strongest in the nation due to its rich mineral resources, such as oil, oil shale and natural gas.

Benefitting from the advantages of rich agricultural resources, Jilin's food processing industry has grown substantially in recent years. Three major categories have been formed: corn processing led by Dacheng Corp, meat processing led by the Aoyue Corp and mineral water processing led by Quanyang Corp. Jilin also has the largest biofuel project in China.

Jilin is China's primary base for modern Chinese traditional medicine. Today there are 317 pharmaceuticals manufacturers there. Tonghua Dongbao, Jilin Aodong and Changchun Haiwang are well-known brands in China.

Table 1.36 Jilin's comparative (dis)advantage index by sector, 2010

Sector	Index
Agriculture, forestry, animal husbandry and fishery	2.17
Mining	1.35
Manufacturing	0.81
Production and distribution of electricity, gas and water	1.29
Construction	0.52
Transport, storage and post	1.12
Information transmission, computer service and software	1.37
Wholesale and retail trades	0.81
Hotels and catering services	0.71
Financial intermediation	1.06
Real estate	0.83
Leasing and business services	0.70
Scientific research, technical services and geological prospecting	1.11
Management of water conservancy, environment and public facilities	1.81
Services to households and other services	0.89
Education	1.13
Health, social security and social welfare	1.18
Culture, sports and entertainment	1.38
Public management and social organization	1.07

Notes All the sectors included in this table are determined according to China's official definitions and for urban areas only. Numerals greater than, equal to and less than one indicate that the province's sectors have advantages, no apparent (dis)advantages and disadvantages, respectively
Source Calculated by authors based on China Statistical Yearbook, 2011. See Appendix A for a detailed methodological description

The logistics industry has also developed very quickly in the region. The province has sped up the construction of infrastructure such as railways and highways to connect the far east of Russia with coastal cities like Dalian and Dandong. In addition, several large-scale logistics enterprises have been set up, such as Jilin Materials Group Corp.

There are more than 150 countries and areas that have trade relationships with Jilin. The province has 12 national open ports and 6 provincial open ports. Jilin has organized different trade fairs in recent years to boost trade. Examples include those held for automobile and auto parts (China Changchun International Automobile Fair), optical goods (China International Optoelectronic Expo), agricultural products and the China Jilin-Northeast Asia Investment and Trade Expo.

The province's FDI comes mainly from the industries of manufacturing of transportation equipment, food processing, computer applications and software, production and supply of gas, and pharmaceutical products. Changchun and Jilin City are the two leading cities in attracting foreign investment. Local government encourages investment in auto parts, pharmaceuticals, agricultural products, optical and electronic products, infrastructure and public utilities. Germany is Jilin's largest foreign investor, followed by the US, Hong Kong, South Korea and Japan. Well-known international enterprises that have invested there include Pepsi-Cola, Ford and Chrysler from the US, Pilkington from the UK, Siemens and Volkswagen AG from Germany, and Nissan from Japan.

The region's major trading partners are Germany, Japan, South Korea, the US and Russia. Its major exports are clothing, corn, steel, plywood and automobiles, while its major imports are auto parts, automobiles, ores, measuring instruments and engine parts.

As of 2010, compared with those of other provinces, "agriculture, forestry, animal husbandry and fishery", "management of water conservancy, environment and public facilities" and "culture, sports and entertainment" were relatively strong, while "construction", "leasing and business services" and "hotels and catering services" were relatively weak sectors (see Table 1.36).

Liaoning

[Quick Facts: Official name: Liaoning Province; Capital: Shenyang; Land area: 145,900 km^2; Population density: 289/km^2; Major ethnic groups: Han, Manchu, Mongol, Hui, Korean]

Liaoning is a province of the PRC, located in the southern part of China's northeast. It adjoins Jilin Province to the northeast, Hebei Province to the west and Inner Mongolia Autonomous Region to the northwest. On the south and southeast sides it is surrounded by the Yellow Sea (Korea Bay) and the Bohai Sea to the south, and is bordered along the Yalu River by the Democratic People's Republic of Korea. The name "Liaoning" is taken from the Liao River that flows through the province; "ning" means "peace". Its one-character abbreviation is "Liao."

The coastline of the province is 2178 km long—nearly 12 % of China's total. The hilly regions in the east are the main areas of forest. Adjoining the long, narrow coastal plains (called the Liaoxi Corridor) is the main road for northeast China, linking with the north of the country. The Liaohe Plain in central Liaoning, as part of the Northeastern China Plain, has sedimentary deposits from the Liaohe River and other tributaries. It has abundant water and fertile soil, and it is the main farming area and commodity grain base in the province.

The modern provincial administration of Liaoning was first established in 1907 as Fengtian Province and the name was changed to Liaoning in 1929. Under the Japanese puppet Manchukuo regime, the province reverted to its 1907 name, but the name Liaoning was restored in 1945. It is split administratively into 100 county-level divisions (17 county-level cities, 19 counties, 8 autonomous counties and 56 districts), which are then further subdivided into 1511 township-level divisions (613 towns, 301 townships, 77 ethnic townships and 520 sub-districts).

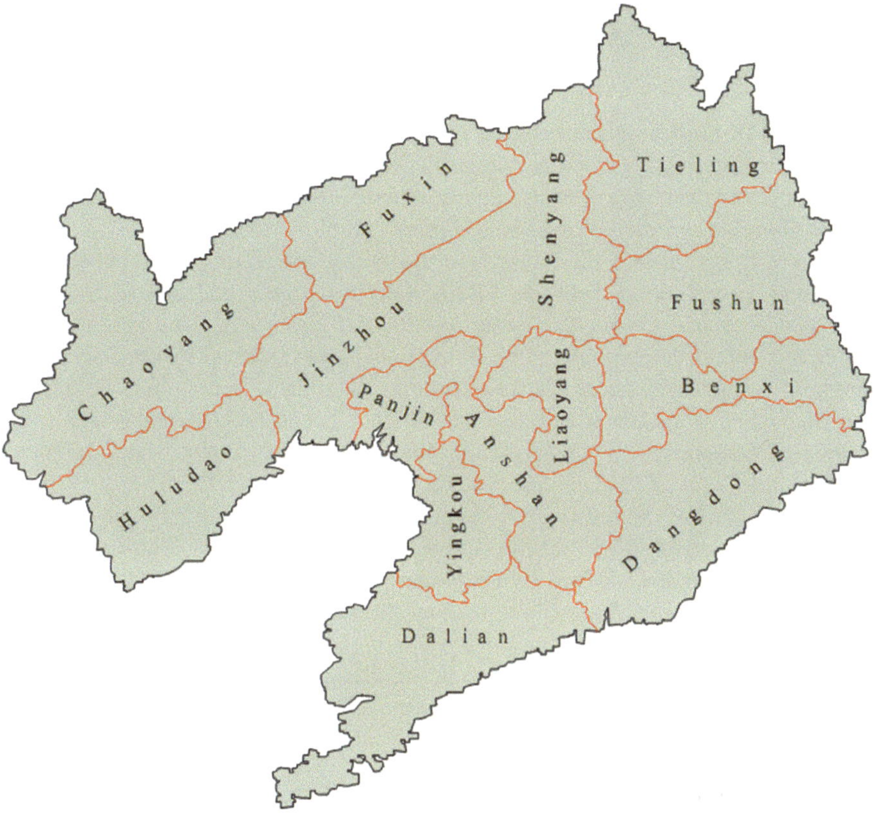

The area can be approximately divided into three geographical regions: the highlands in the west, the plains in the middle and the hills in the east. The highlands are dominated by the Nulu'erhu Mountains, which roughly follow the border between Liaoning and Inner Mongolia. The entire region has many low hills. The central part consists of the watersheds of rivers such as the Liao, the Daliao and their tributaries. This region is mostly flat and low altitude. The eastern part of Liaoning is dominated by the Changbai Shan and Qianshan ranges, which extends into the sea to form the Liaodong Peninsula. The highest point (1336 m above sea level) is Mount Huabozi.

The province has a continental monsoon climate with distinct seasonal variations. It has an annual rainfall of 714.9 mm and an annual average temperature of 4–10 °C with a frost-free period of 140–200 days. Liaoning features a temperate continental monsoon climate with a long winter, a warm summer and a short spring and fall. The summer is rainy while the other seasons are dry.

There are 392 rivers of 160,000 km total length and a drainage area of 145,000 km^2 within the province. Liaohe River, one of the seven longest rivers in China, is 512 km long and has a drainage area of 69,000 km^2 within the province.

The average runoff of rivers there is 32.5 billion cubic meter (or a 223 mm runoff depth). The province has a total water resource of 36.3 billion cubic meter. Liaoning has plentiful fishing resources with its marine life area ranking second in China.

Nearly 115 minerals have been found in Liaoning, including reserves of 64 of these. Its deposits of iron, boron, magnesite, diamonds and talcum are some of the largest in China. The region is also an important source of petroleum (especially in Liaohe Oilfield) and natural gas. Salt is produced along the coast.

The main agricultural products there are maize, sorghum and soybeans. The region also grows a lot of fruit trees. It has the third largest total area of fruit in the defoliated zone and the second largest production in the area. The region around Dalian produces three-quarters of China's exported apples (from Dalian and Yingkou) and peaches (from Dalian). Liaoning also grows pears (from Beizhen of Jinzhou), white pears (from Huludao and Suizhong) and apricots and plums (from Gushan of Dandong). Cotton is also produced. The total forestry area measures 4.185 million ha with 28.7 % forest cover.

The province has more than 11,300 cultural remains, including 19 national-level key protection units and 159 provincial-level key protection units. There are 7 state-class natural reserves and 7 provincial-class natural reserves. Some of the folk festivals attract the attention of both domestic and foreign visitors, such as the Dalian Costume Festival.

The Mukden Palace was the palace of the Qing Dynasty emperors before they conquered the rest of China and moved their capital to Beijing. It is significant for its representation of palace architecture at the time and has recently been included on the UNESCO World Heritage Site as an extension of the Imperial Palace site in Beijing. In addition, three imperial tombs dating from the Qing Dynasty are located in Liaoning. Wunu Mountain City, a Goguryeo site found in Huanren Manchu Autonomous County, is part of a combined UNESCO World Heritage Site. Liaoyang City, one of the oldest continuously inhabited cities in northeast China, has a number of historical sites, including the White Pagoda (Baita), which dates to the Yuan Dynasty (AD 1279–1368). The port city of Dalian, located at the tip of the Liaodong Peninsula, is a tourist destination in its own right, with beaches, resorts, zoos, seafood, shopping, Russian- and Japanese-era architecture, and streetcars—a rare sight in China.

The province has the largest economy of northeast China. Its nominal GRP for 2010 was ¥1.85 trillion (about US$270 billion), making it the seventh largest in China. Its per capita GRP was ¥41,782 (about US$6172). Among the three provinces of northeast China, Liaoning is the largest in terms of GRP (Table 1.37).

Leading industries include petrochemicals, metallurgy, electronics, telecommunications and machinery. On a national level, Liaoning is a major producer of pig iron, steel and metal-cutting machine tools, all of whose production rank among the top three in the nation. The province is one of the most important raw materials production bases in China. Industries such as mining, quarrying, smelting and pressing of ferrous metals, petroleum and natural gas extraction are all of great significance.

Table 1.37 Demographic and socioeconomic profile: Liaoning

Indicator	2000	2010
Population (thousands)	42,380	43,749
Illiteracy rate of population aged 15 or over (%)	4.76	1.93
GRP (¥ billions)	466.91	1845.73
Composition of GRP (%)		
Primary sector	10.8	8.8
Secondary sector	50.2	54.1
Tertiary sector	39.0	37.1
Fixed asset investment (¥ billions)	126.77	1604.30
Status of foreign-funded enterprises		
Number of registered enterprises	13,146	18,377
Total investment (US$ millions)	65,543	147,615
Registered capital (US$ millions)	39,626	97,535
Foreign trade (US$ millions)		
Export	10,589	42,943
Import	9478	52,349
Sales of consumer goods (¥ billions)	185	689
Per capita annual disposable income of urban residents (¥)	5357.79	17,712.58
Engle's coefficient (%)	35.73	33.24
Per capita annual net income of rural residents (¥)	2355.58	6907.93
Engle's coefficient (%)	34.90	38.18
Number of patent applications granted	4842	17,093
Inventions	458	2357
Utility models	3,703	12,067
Designs	681	2669

Note All monetary values are measured at current prices. *Source* Liaoning Statistical Yearbook, 2001 and 2011

Meanwhile, Liaoning is an important production base of equipment and machinery manufacturing, with Shenyang and Dalian being the industrial centers. Enterprises such as Shenyang Jinbei Co. Ltd., Daxian Group Co. Ltd. and Shenyang Machine Tool Co. Ltd. are leaders in their sectors. The province's light industry mainly focuses on textiles and clothing industries, which include cotton and wool spinning, chemical fiber production, knitting, silk production, and the manufacturing of both garments and textile machinery. Meanwhile, the province is concentrating on developing its four pillar industries: petrochemicals, metallurgy, machinery and electronics.

Liaoning is an important transportation hub as it is home to Dalian Port.

Liaoning is one of China's most important industrial bases, covering a wide range of industries, such as machinery, electronics, metal refining, petroleum, chemical industries, construction materials and coal. The sea off Dalian abounds with quality seafood, such as abalones, sea cucumbers, scallops, prawns, crabs and sea urchins. The big fish of Dandong, the jellyfish of Yingkou and the clams of

Panjin are known worldwide for their good taste right from the sea, and seafood products are made in Liaoning for export domestically and internationally. Dependence on heavy industry and the province's energy inefficiency are signs that Liaoning is still at the lower end of the value chain. To stimulate economic growth, the province aims to nurture the private sector and specifically help small and medium-sized enterprises by raising funds from equity and debt markets.

Equipment manufacturing is the top industry in Liaoning. The industry focuses on the manufacture of general equipment, special use equipment and transport equipment. Famous companies include Shenyang Machine Tool Works, Dalian Machine Tool Works, Shenyang SIASUN Robot Corp, Dalian Locomotive and Roll Stock Works, Brilliance Auto (which has a joint venture with BMW to produce 3 and 5 series BMW sedans in Shenyang), Daxian Group Corp, Northeast Electric Transmission and Transformation Equipment Group Corp.

The metallurgy industry is Liaoning's traditional pillar industry. The region has the advantage of having rich mineral resources, a central location and a strong talent pool. The industry mainly focuses on the development of ferrous metallurgy as the province has the biggest iron ore reserve in China. The Anshan and Benxi Iron and Steel Group is the leading steel maker in Liaoning.

The petrochemical industry is the third pillar industry of Liaoning, focusing on the development of fine chemical, rubber products and newly emerging petrochemical technologies. PetroChina (Liaohe) Corp and Jinhua Chemical Group are the leading companies in this industry.

The development of new service industries, such as logistics, IT and commercial services, is currently being encouraged by government. The cities of Dalian, Dandong and Yingkou have been developed as major ports and economic gateways to the rest of northeast China. Liaoning ranks fifth in China and first in the northeast in terms of retail sales of consumer goods. The major consumer centers in the province are located in Shenyang and Dalian.

The major export products are steel, refined oil, water products and tires, while the major import products are machine tools, automobiles, steel, rubber and copper. The major import sources are Japan, South Korea, Germany, the US and Australia. Its major export destinations are Japan, the US, South Korea, Singapore and Hong Kong.

The province has attracted the largest amount of FDI among all the three provinces in northeast China. Dalian and Shenyang are the most popular destinations for FDI. Hong Kong is the largest source of FDI, followed by the US, Singapore, Japan and South Korea.

Apart from Dalian and Shenyang, Anshan, Dandong and Yingkou have become destinations of foreign companies. Leading Hong Kong enterprises such as Cheung Kong, Hang Lung and New World, and MNCs such as General Electric, Siemens, Mitsubishi, Toshiba and Sanyo, have invested in the province. The manufacturing industry has attracted the largest share of FDI, in terms of both contracted amount and utilized amount. Government has placed emphasis on equipment manufacturing, raw materials, new technology and high-tech endeavors, food processing and

Table 1.38 Liaoning's comparative (dis)advantage index by sector, 2010

Sector	Index
Agriculture, forestry, animal husbandry and fishery	1.87
Mining	1.58
Manufacturing	1.00
Production and distribution of electricity, gas and water	1.35
Construction	0.62
Transport, storage and post	1.21
Information transmission, computer service and software	0.95
Wholesale and retail trades	0.80
Hotels and catering services	0.77
Financial intermediation	1.11
Real estate	1.05
Leasing and business services	0.99
Scientific research, technical services and geological prospecting	1.03
Management of water conservancy, environment and public facilities	1.48
Services to households and other services	1.20
Education	0.83
Health, social security and social welfare	1.02
Culture, sports and entertainment	0.98
Public management and social organization	0.87

Notes All the sectors included in this table are determined according to China's official definitions and for urban areas only. Numerals greater than, equal to and less than one indicate that the province's sectors have advantages, no apparent (dis)advantages and disadvantages, respectively
Source Calculated by authors based on China Statistical Yearbook, 2011. See Appendix A for a detailed methodological description

service industries. To re-vitalize the old industrial base, government has begun selling off stakes in state-owned enterprises to foreign acquirers.

As of 2010, compared with those of other provinces, "agriculture, forestry, animal husbandry and fishery", "mining" and "management of water conservancy, environment and public facilities" were relatively strong, while "construction", "hotels and catering services" and "wholesale and retail trades" were relatively weak sectors (see Table 1.38).

Ningxia

[Quick Facts: Official name: Ningxia Hui Autonomous Region; Capital: Yinchuan; Land area: 66,000 km^2; Population density: 89/km^2; Major ethnic groups: Han, Hui, Manchu, Mongol, Tujia]

Ningxia Hui Autonomous Region ("Ning" for short) of the PRC is located in northwest China. As part of the Loess Plateau, it is crossed by the Yellow River. It lies along the western part of the Yellow River and is bordered by Inner Mongolia Autonomous Region to the north and west, Shaanxi Province to the east and Gansu Province to the south. The Great Wall of China runs along its northeastern boundary Home of the Hui people, the region was once a part of the Silk Road that connected China with central Asia and Europe.

Ningxia is one of China's five autonomous regions inhabited by the minority groups. Formerly a province, it was incorporated into Gansu Province in 1954 but was detached and reconstituted as an autonomous region for the Hui people in 1958. This sparsely settled area is a relatively dry, desert-like region. Significant irrigation supports the growing of wolfberries, a commonly consumed fruit throughout the area. Its deserts include the Tengger Desert in Shapotou. Its ecosystem is one of the least studied regions in the world. Some plant genera have been estimated at more than 40,000 years old. Over the years an extensive system of canals has been built. Significant land reclamation and irrigation projects have made increased cultivation possible. The northern section, through which the Yellow River flows, supports the best agricultural land. A railroad linking Lanzhou with Baotou crosses the region and a highway has been built across the Yellow River at Yinchuan, the capital.

The topography of Ningxia slants toward the north with an elevation from 1100 to 2000 m. The highest point is 3556 m above sea level. The region is 1200 km from the sea and has a continental climate with average summer temperatures rising to 17–24 °C in July and average winter temperatures dropping to between −7 and −10 °C in January. Seasonal extreme temperatures can reach 39 °C in summer and −30 °C in winter. The diurnal temperature variation can reach above 17 °C, especially in spring. The average annual rainfall is 190–700 mm, with more rain falling in the south.

Ningxia boasts 0.71 million hectare of wasteland suitable for farming, one of China's eight areas that each have more than 0.63 million hectare of wasteland suitable for agriculture. There are 3 million hectare of exploitable meadows, making the region one of the ten major pastures in China. The Weining Plain, which features 0.37 million hectare of land irrigated with water diverted from the Yellow River, is one of the four principal areas with gravity irrigation in northwest China. For years the annual runoff from the Yellow River there has remained at 32.5 billion cubic meter and the water resources allocated to Ningxia by the state for irrigation are 4 billion cubic meter. Owing to irrigation the region is known as "an oasis in a desert".

The rich land resources, convenient conditions for diverting water from the Yellow River and abundant sunshine offer a solid foundation for the area's the development of agriculture. Its major crops include rice, wheat, maize, beans, sugar beet and Chinese wolfberries. Rice is its most famous produce, giving Ningxia the nickname of "the Pearl of the Northern Frontier" or "the Southern Yangtze of Northern China". Watermelons, apples and grapes from the irrigated area have a 15–20 % higher sugar content than those produced in central China. The per-hectare yield of single-cropping paddy reaches 10,500 kg, placing first among the provinces and autonomous regions in western China and making it one of the nation's 12 grain production bases. The mountain area in the south of Ningxia is suitable for both forestry and animal husbandry. The region has broad prospects for the development of the stock rearing and livestock processing industries. Efforts have been made to build Ningxia into a national agricultural demonstration area with high yield, efficiency and quality.

Livestock breeding makes up 29 % of local agriculture. Of the 82,000 ha water surfaces, 10,000 ha can be used for aquaculture. Ningxia produces various species of carp, river shrimp and river crabs. In recent years, aquatic production has developed rapidly. It leads other provinces and autonomous regions in the northwest in per-capita output of aquatic products.

Ningxia is rich in minerals, with verified deposits of 50 kinds of minerals, including coal, gypsum, oil, natural gas, pottery clay, quartz sandstone and barite. The potential value of these natural resources per capita is 163.5 % of the nation's average, putting the region fifth in the country. There are abundant reserves of various kinds of coal and the area undertakes coal production on a considerable scale. It leads the country in terms of gypsum reserves, with verified deposits of more than 4.5 billion tons. Top-grade gypsum makes up half of these. The Huojiakouzi deposit in Tongxin County features a reserve of 20 tons of gypsum in 20 layers with a total thickness of 100 m. The reserves of oil and natural gas are ideal for the large-scale development of oil, natural gas and chemical industries. There are considerable deposits of quartz sandstone, of which 17 million tons have been confirmed. In addition are phosphorus, firestone, copper, iron and Helan stone (a special clay stone).

Ningxia has the third smallest GRP in China, even though its neighbors, Inner Mongolia and Shaanxi, are among the strongest emerging provincial economies in the country. The region's fundamental resources are weak, lacking the rich natural resources of Inner Mongolia or the talent that drives high value-added industries and services in Shaanxi. It also has to invest heavily to maintain its agricultural production in the face of natural disadvantages, such as a dry climate, shortage of water and sand storms (Table 1.39).

Unlike some poor regions with low labor costs, the average wage in Ningxia is higher than that in two-thirds of other provinces, making it less attractive as a base for manufacturers. At the same time, it does not have the population size to be a consumption hub. Its key industries are chemical manufacturing and metal smelting, both of which consume large amounts of energy. This problem is exacerbated by outdated equipment and technology that make it the least energy-efficient region in China.

The manufacturing sector receives the largest amount of fixed-asset investment. Real estate, production and supply of electricity, gas and water, transportation and storage, and mining rank in the top five in terms of total fixed-asset investment.

Major consumer markets in this region are located in the capital of Yinchuan, and major department stores and shopping centers include Xinghua Shopping Center, Yingchuan Department Store, Ningxia Hualian Commercial Building and Yinchuan Xincheng Department Store. Clothing, household articles, medicine and medical services, transportation and communication, recreation, cultural activities and education, and residential housing account for other significant expenditures.

Industry in Ningxia is developing very rapidly. Many industrial enterprises, such as those in the coal, electric power, metal, petroleum, machinery, chemical, building materials and textile industries, have been established there. The coal industry is the pillar of the industrial sector. Based in the Shizuishan mining area, a complete

Table 1.39 Demographic and socioeconomic profile: Ningxia

Indicator	2000	2010
Population (thousands)	5620	6330
Illiteracy rate of population aged 15 or over (%)	13.40	6.22
GRP (¥ billions)	26.56	168.97
Composition of GRP (%)		
Primary sector	17.3	9.4
Secondary sector	45.2	49.0
Tertiary sector	37.5	41.6
Fixed asset investment (¥ billions)	15.75	144.42
Status of foreign-funded enterprises		
Number of registered enterprises	408	529
Total investment (US$ millions)	940	3964
Registered capital (US$ millions)	696	1785
Foreign trade (US$ millions)		
Export	354	1552
Import	178	1015
Sales of consumer goods (¥ billions)	9	40
Per capita annual disposable income of urban residents (¥)	4912.40	15,344.49
Engle's coefficient (%)	40.88	39.37
Per capita annual net income of rural residents (¥)	1724.30	4674.89
Engle's coefficient (%)	29.76	38.42
Number of patent applications granted	224	1081
Inventions	21	61
Utility models	166	307
Designs	37	713

Note All monetary values are measured at current prices. *Source* Ningxia Statistical Yearbook, 2001 and 2011

system has been set up—from excavating and washing to comprehensive utilization. Much of the coal mined in the area is supplied to the steelworks in Baotou and Jiuquan for steelmaking.

The region offers abundant tourism resources, including desert landscapes and the cultural heritages along the Yellow River. These have attracted both domestic and foreign tourists.

Ningxia has traded with 115 countries. Key trade partners include the US, Japan and Australia. Important export goods include machinery, chemicals, rubber tires, cashmere, anthracite, and farm and sideline products. Import items include rubber, chemicals and light industrial products. Hong Kong is still the largest investor in the region but other major investors include Taiwan, Canada and Japan.

As of 2010, compared with those of other provinces, "production and distribution of electricity, gas and water", "mining" and "management of water conservancy, environment and public facilities" were relatively strong, while "services to households and other services", "hotels and catering services" and "construction" were relatively weak sectors (see Table 1.40).

Table 1.40 Ningxia's comparative (dis)advantage index by sector, 2010

Sector	Index
Agriculture, forestry, animal husbandry and fishery	1.54
Mining	2.26
Manufacturing	0.64
Production and distribution of electricity, gas and water	2.61
Construction	0.52
Transport, storage and post	1.00
Information transmission, computer service and software	0.76
Wholesale and retail trades	0.63
Hotels and catering services	0.44
Financial intermediation	1.25
Real estate	0.84
Leasing and business services	0.99
Scientific research, technical services and geological prospecting	0.90
Management of water conservancy, environment and public facilities	1.79
Services to households and other services	0.00
Education	1.10
Health, social security and social welfare	1.15
Culture, sports and entertainment	1.28
Public management and social organization	1.28

Notes All the sectors included in this table are determined according to China's official definitions and for urban areas only. Numerals greater than, equal to and less than one indicate that the province's sectors have advantages, no apparent (dis)advantages and disadvantages, respectively
Source Calculated by authors based on China Statistical Yearbook, 2011. See Appendix A for a detailed methodological description

Qinghai

[Quick Facts: Official name: Qinghai Province; Capital: Xining; Land area: 721,000 km^2; Population density: 7/km^2; Major ethnic groups: Han, Tibetan, Hui, Tu, Salar]

Qinghai is a province of the PRC, named after Lake Qinghai. It borders Gansu Province to the northeast, Xinjiang Uygur Autonomous Region to the northwest, Sichuan Province to the southeast and Tibet Autonomous Region to the southwest. It is located in northwestern China on the Qinghai–Tibet Plateau. The Yellow River originates in the middle of the province, while the Yangtze and Mekong have their headwaters in the south. More than 42 % of the population is Tibetan, Hui, Tu, Salar, Mongol or of another ethnicity.

The province is rich in cultural history. It is the source of the Chinese Kunlun legend that was spread throughout the country before finally blending into mainstream Chinese culture. The area is attractive not only for its beautiful scenery but also for its colorful local customs.

Qinghai is located on the northeastern part of the Tibetan Plateau. The Yellow River originates in the south while the Yangtze and Mekong have their sources in the southwest. The average elevation is more than 3000 m above sea level, varying from 1650 to 6860 m, while 54 % of the area is between 4000 and 5000 m. The province is divided into the Qilian Mountains, the Qaidam Basin and the Qingnan Plateau. It has a plateau continental climate thanks to its elevation, topography, latitude and atmospheric circulation. The region has a long, warm winter and a short, cool summer. The temperature varies with an annual average of −5.6 to 8.7 ° C. The precipitation also varies noticeably, with the southeast receiving 450–600 mm of rainfall annually and the rest of the region being rather dry. It is also prone to heavy winds as well as sand storms from February to April.

Qinghai is the fourth largest provincial administration in China after Xinjiang, Inner Mongolia and Tibet. Lake It has the largest saltwater lake in China and the second largest in the world. Qaidam basin lies in the northwest. About a third of this resource-rich basin is desert. It is at an altitude of 3000–3500 m. The Sanjiangyuan National Nature Reserve (also referred to as the Sanjiangyuan Nature Reserve or the Three Rivers Nature Reserve) contains the headwaters of the Yellow River, the Yangtze River and the Mekong River. It was established to protect the headwaters of these three rivers. It consists of 18 subareas, each containing three zones which are managed with differing degrees of strictness.

There are deposits of 107 minerals in the province. Of these, 50 are among the top ten in the country and 11, including potassium chloride and magnesium salts, have the largest deposits of their kinds in China. Of the 45 urgently needed minerals in China, 21 have been found in the province, their deposits all ranking among the top ten in the country. In addition, Qinghai has more than 30 salt lakes with proven reserves of 70 billion tons. It is also rich in non-ferrous metals and non-metallic minerals. Its reserve of asbestos leads other provinces and regions in China. The famed Qaidam Basin is abundant in natural gas and oil. The total oil reserve is 1.244 billion tons, of which 200 million tons has been explored. The explored gas reserve is 47.2 billion cubic meter. At present there are 16 oilfields and 6 natural gas fields in the region.

The province has 178 hydropower stations with a total installed generation capacity of 21.66 million kilowatt. The province plans to build seven more medium-sized hydropower stations which, with a total installed generation capacity of 11 million kilowatt, will produce 36.8 billion kilowatt hour each year. The construction cost of each power station in Qinghai is 20–40 % lower than the national average. The province is also rich in solar, wind and geothermal energy.

It is one of the five major pasture lands in China, boasting 31.6 million hectare of grazing land which accounts for 15 % of the country's total. Among the 940 species of grass growing in its grasslands, 190 are of high nutrition with crude protein, crude fat and low coarse fiber. The livestock kept there include sheep, yak, horse, camel and goat, all of which are cold-resistant. Qinghai has the most domestic yaks in the country, accounting for one-third of the world's total.

Of the wild plants discovered in Qinghai, some 1000 have economic value, including over 100 medicinal herbs. Its Chinese caterpillar fungus, in particular, is. There are 290 kinds of birds and 109 species of mammals, of which 21 are under first-class state protection, 53 are under second-class state protection, 36 are under provincial protection and 22 have been listed in the International Trade Convention on Endangered Wild Animals and Plants, appendixes I and II. By the end of 2005 there were 11 nature reserves in the province covering a total area of 21.76 million ha and accounting for 30.12 % of the province's region.

As the origin of the Yangtze, Yellow and Mekong rivers, Qinghai has an area of 720,000 km^2, including 31.6 million hectare of grassland, 589,900 ha of cultivated land and 250,000 ha of forests. The remaining land is mountains, lakes, deserts and glaciers.

The population of is approximately 5.2 million, among which the Han account for 54.5 %. Other groups include the Tibetans (20.87 %), Hui (16 %), Tu (4 %), Salar and Mongols.

Qinghai's economy is amongst the smallest in China. Its nominal GRP for 2010 was just ¥135.04 billion (about US$20 billion) and it contributes to about 0.3 % of the country's economy. The per capita GRP was ¥19,407 (about US$2841), the second lowest in China (Table 1.41).

Table 1.41 Demographic and socioeconomic profile: Qinghai

Indicator	2000	2010
Population (thousands)	5180	5630
Illiteracy rate of population aged 15 or over (%)	18.03	10.23
GRP (¥ billions)	26.36	135.04
Composition of GRP (%)		
Primary sector	14.6	10.0
Secondary sector	43.3	55.1
Tertiary sector	42.1	34.9
Fixed asset investment (¥ billions)	15.11	101.69
Status of foreign-funded enterprises		
Number of registered enterprises	113	499
Total investment (US$ millions)	577	2,349
Registered capital (US$ millions)	332	1389
Foreign trade (US$ millions)		
Export	134	318
Import	93	500
Sales of consumer goods (¥ billions)	8	35
Per capita annual disposable income of urban residents (¥)	5169.96	13,854.99
Engle's coefficient (%)	35.82	37.06
Per capita annual net income of rural residents (¥)	1490.49	3862.68
Engle's coefficient (%)	34.31	38.23
Number of patent applications granted	117	264
Inventions	16	41
Utility models	67	134
Designs	34	89

Note All monetary values are measured at current prices. *Source* Qinghai Statistical Yearbook, 2001 and 2011

The region's economy is based on minerals, hydropower and agro-husbandry. The province also plays an important ecological role as the source of major rivers. Oil and natural gas production at the Chaidamu Basin also contributes to the economy. Outside Xining, most of the province remains underdeveloped. Qinghai ranks second lowest in China in terms of highway length and only with significant infrastructure will the province be able to fully capitalize on its natural resources. Looking forward, Qinghai plans to focus on solar, wind and low-carbon energy projects. The area's heavy industry includes iron and steel production, located near its capital.

The industrial sector leads the economy with a contribution of more than a half of GRP, while the service sector follows relatively close behind with 37.60 %. Agriculture brings up the rear with 10.80 %. The industries with the highest amount of fixed-asset investments are in the areas of production and supply of electricity, gas and water, manufacturing, transportation and storage, mining, and real estate.

The area's livestock include sheep, yaks and horses. Qinghai produces large quantities of meat, sheep's wool, leather and sausage casings for other parts of the country. It is also an important producer of medicinal materials, such as caterpillar fungus, antlers, musk and rhubarb. The province grows spring wheat, highland barley, broad beans, potatoes and rapeseed.

Qinghai is rich in resources, such as hydropower, lead, zinc, minerals, saline and petroleum and gas. The natural resources have had a great influence in shaping the province's industry structure so the pillar industries depend largely on these resources to develop. The four pillar industries include petroleum and natural gas, hydropower, non-ferrous metals and saline chemicals.

Many tourist attractions center on Xining, the provincial seat of Qinghai. During the hot summer months, many tourists from the hot southern and eastern parts of China travel to the city as the climate there in July and August is quite mild and comfortable, making it an ideal summer retreat.

Lake Qinghai is another tourist attraction, albeit further from Xining than Kumbum. It is located on the "Roof of the World", the Tibetan Plateau. The lake lies at an elevation of 3600 m. The surrounding area is made up of rolling grasslands and is populated by ethnic Tibetans. Most pre-arranged tours stop at Birds Island. An international bicycle race takes place annually from Xining to Lake Qinghai.

The province features ethnic custom tours unique to the plateau. It has more than ten scenic spots, including the Birds Islet, the Mengda Natural Reserves, Ta'er Monastery, snow-capped A'Nyemaqen Mountain, Sun-and-Moon Hill, Gold and Silver Meadow, Longyang Gorge Reservoir (the largest artificial reservoir in China) and the Dulan International Game Land. Together these account for the growing tourist industry in the area.

The Qinghai–Tibet Railway is the world's highest railway line and it weaves between Xining and Lhasa. It has a favorable impact on the local logistics industry and on sightseeing. The operation of the railway in 2007 helped boost goods exchanges between the secluded Qinghai–Tibet Plateau and other parts of China.

Major export items included aluminum and rolled aluminum, silicon, yarn, woolen fiber and carpets. Major export markets included Japan, Hong Kong and the US. Key import products are aluminum oxide, semiconductors, parts for auto data-processing equipment, motor vehicles and chassis. Major sources of imports are Australia, India and Bosnia.

Foreign investments in Qinghai are mainly channeled into the manufacturing industries. Hong Kong is an important source of FDI, accounting for 28.4 % of the province's contracted FDI in 2006.

As of 2010, compared with those of other provinces, "scientific research, technical services and geological prospecting", "public management and social organization" and "culture, sports and entertainment" were relatively strong, while "hotels and catering services", "leasing and business services" and "manufacturing" were relatively weak sectors (see Table 1.42).

Table 1.42 Qinghai's comparative (dis)advantage index by sector, 2010

Sector	Index
Agriculture, forestry, animal husbandry and fishery	1.15
Mining	0.88
Manufacturing	0.67
Production and distribution of electricity, gas and water	0.99
Construction	0.79
Transport, storage and post	1.29
Information transmission, computer service and software	1.05
Wholesale and retail trades	0.81
Hotels and catering services	0.56
Financial intermediation	1.04
Real estate	0.74
Leasing and business services	0.66
Scientific research, technical services and geological prospecting	1.96
Management of water conservancy, environment and public facilities	1.28
Services to households and other services	1.26
Education	1.18
Health, social security and social welfare	1.25
Culture, sports and entertainment	1.38
Public management and social organization	1.55

Notes All the sectors included in this table are determined according to China's official definitions and for urban areas only. Numerals greater than, equal to and less than one indicate that the province's sectors have advantages, no apparent (dis)advantages and disadvantages, respectively
Source Calculated by authors based on China Statistical Yearbook, 2011. See Appendix A for a detailed methodological description

Shaanxi

[Quick Facts: Official name: Shaanxi Province; Capital: Xi'an; Land area: 205,800 km^2; Population density: 180/km^2; Major ethnic groups: Han, Hui, Manchu, Mongol, Tibetan]

Shaanxi is a province of the PRC. It includes a portion of the Loess Plateau on the middle reaches of the Yellow River in addition to the Qinling Mountains across the southern part of the region. It borders Ningxia Hui Autonomous Region and Inner Mongolia Autonomous Region to the north, Shanxi Province to the northeast, Henan Province to the east, Hubei Province to the southeast, Sichuan Province and Chongqing Municipality to the south and Gansu Province to the west.

Shaanxi is the official spelling of this province. It is the only name of a Chinese province that is not written according to the Chinese pinyin system. By standard Pinyin rules, both Shaanxi and its neighboring province of Shanxi should be spelled "Shanxi". The difference is in the tone: Shănxī for Shaanxi and Shānxī for Shanxi. The abbreviated name for the region is Shaan (Shăn in Chinese).

The area is composed of several distinct areas. In the north is desert along the border with Inner Mongolia Autonomous Region. The Loess Plateau further south has an elevation of 800–1300 m and accounts for 45 % of the total area of the province. The Central Shaanxi Plain in the middle averages an elevation of 520 m. The Qinling Mountains (elevation 1000–3000 m), Daba Mountains (1500–2000 m) and Hanjiang River Valley account for 36 % of the region. Taibaishan is the highest peak in the Qinling Range. Finally the subtropical area is south of the Qinling Mountains.

An inland province along the middle reaches of the Yellow River and a gateway to northwest China, it links the west to the east and the north to the south. The Eurasia Continental Bridge, an international economic link starting from Lianyungang in the east and ending in Rotterdam in the Netherlands, traverses the region.

The northern part of Shaanxi is cold in winter and very hot in summer, with dry winter and spring seasons. Its southern portion generally receives more rain. The average annual temperature is 8–16 °C, with January temperatures ranging from −11 to 3.5 °C and July of 21–28 °C.

The province produces a large quantity of nature's treasures and is endowed with rich natural resources. With substantial development of the west, Shaanxi will become the nation's important area for the transportation of energy sources, such as gasses, electricity and coal from west to east.

Reserves of 91 kinds of minerals have been identified in Shaanxi, of which 58 rank among the top ten in the country, 18 (including coal, natural gas, molybdenum, mercury and gadolinite) take second or third place and 12 (including strontium, rhenium and cement rock) rank first. The reserves and output of gold rank fifth and fourth in China, respectively. The output of molybdenum amounts to half of the country's total. Proven deposits of coal, the most abundant mineral in the province, amount to 161.8 billion tons. The Shenmu-Fugu Coalfield in northern Shaanxi has reserves of 134 billion tons. It is one of the best fields in the world because of its thick coal layer and its easy access and exploitation. In addition, northern Shaanxi has a gas field with proven reserves of 350 billion cubic meter. The region has an area of 50,000 km^2 that contains coal, the recoverable deposits of which are 161.8 billion tons. Few other coalfields for quality power like this one exist in the world. Northern Shaanxi Natural-Gas Field has proven reserves of 350 billion cubic meter and is a word-class continental self-contained natural gas field.

The northern part of the Qinling Mountains is characterized by the Yellow River system, including the Weihe, the Jinghe, the Luohe and the Wuding rivers. South of the mountains is the Yangtze River system consisting of the Hanjiang, Danjiang and Jialing rivers. The Hanjiang, the largest river in the province, provides more than half of the province's total water runoff. Shaanxi has 583 rivers with an annual runoff of 42.6 billion cubic meter. representing 14,000,000 kw of waterpower storage. Through development over the years, 80,000 irrigation projects of various types have been constructed and 1,410,000 ha of land are irrigated, accounting for 42 % of the cultivated land.

The region has more than 750 species of wild vertebrates, which include 79 rare species. It is also home to 12 species of animal—such as giant pandas, golden-haired monkeys and clouded leopards—which are national treasures under the state's priority protection, and rare ibis. Qinchuan cattle, which are bred in the province, are well known all over the world. The number of improved breeds of milking goats is the highest number in the country and the breeding of boar goats is on a significant scale.

The province has 5.93 million ha of forest in the Qinling, Daba, Guanshan, Huanglong and Qiaoshan mountain areas with 28.8 % forest coverage. It has 3300-plus species of wild plants, 37 of which are rare. Some 800 species of medicinal plants are of great economic value, including sea buckthorn and *Gynostemma pentaphylla*. The region leads the country in the output and quality of raw lacquer. The traditional exports of the province are dates, walnut meat and tung oil. By 2005 the number of nature reserves in the province had reached 45, covering a total area of 995,000 ha.

Shaanxi Province is an important place concerning the origin of ancient Chinese civilization. The Banpo Neolithic village is located near Xi'an. Dispersed across the region are 72 imperial mausoleums, witness to the ancient economy and culture of the area. It is best known for ten scenic spots, including the Mausoleum of Huangdi, the Qin Terra-cotta Warriors and Horses, the Xi'an Forest of Stone Tablets, the Shaanxi Museum of History, and the city gate and wall of Xi'an. The Qin Terra-cotta Warriors and Horses, known as the "eighth wonder of the world", has been included by UNESCO on the list of World Cultural Heritage Sites. In addition, Yan'an was the destination of the Long March of and the center of the Chinese Communist Revolution from 1935 to 1948.

Table 1.43 Demographic and socioeconomic profile: Shaanxi

Indicator	2000	2010
Population (thousands)	36,050	37,352
Illiteracy rate of population aged 15 or over (%)	7.29	3.74
GRP (¥ billions)	166.09	1012.35
Composition of GRP (%)		
Primary sector	16.8	9.8
Secondary sector	44.1	53.8
Tertiary sector	39.1	36.4
Fixed asset investment (¥ billions)	65.37	796.37
Status of foreign-funded enterprises		
Number of registered enterprises	2761	5378
Total investment (US$ millions)	8322	18,044
Registered capital (US$ millions)	5071	11,012
Foreign trade (US$ millions)		
Export	1327	5635
Import	1061	6069
Sales of consumer goods (¥ billions)	61	320
Per capita annual disposable income of urban residents (¥)	5124.24	15,695.21
Engle's coefficient (%)	34.73	32.06
Per capita annual net income of rural residents (¥)	1443.86	4104.98
Engle's coefficient (%)	32.53	34.25
Number of patent applications granted	1462	10,034
Inventions	188	1887
Utility models	1022	6093
Designs	252	2054

Note All monetary values are measured at current prices. *Source* Shaanxi Statistical Yearbook, 2001 and 2011

Shaanxi's nominal GRP for 2010 was ¥1012.35 billion (about US$150 billion) and its GRP per capita was ¥27,133 (about US$3500), ranking 14th in the PRC (Table 1.43).

The fossil fuel and high technology sectors compose the two largest industries in Shaanxi. It is a major producer of fossil fuels. In 2009 it produced 296 million tons of coal, 27 million tons of crude oil and 18,950 million cubic meter of natural gas, all ranked among the top three in China. The reserves of these resources are large and have yet to be fully explored. The capital, Xi'an City, has a high-tech industrial zone that is supported by several of the best universities and research institutions in western China. The focus is on software development, aerospace technology, new materials and aircraft technology, all of which are among China's new priority industries. Transforming Shaanxi's high-tech advantages into actual production will be the main challenge for the future. Some areas, such as space technology, where the province leads the country, may take longer to commercialize.

As of 2010, compared with those of other provinces, "mining", "scientific research, technical services and geological prospecting" and "information transmission, computer service and software" were relatively strong, while "leasing and

Table 1.44 Shaanxi's comparative (dis)advantage index by sector, 2010

Sector	Index
Agriculture, forestry, animal husbandry and fishery	0.42
Mining	1.57
Manufacturing	0.80
Production and distribution of electricity, gas and water	1.27
Construction	0.71
Transport, storage and post	1.08
Information transmission, computer service and software	1.36
Wholesale and retail trades	0.83
Hotels and catering services	1.08
Financial intermediation	1.08
Real estate	0.87
Leasing and business services	0.40
Scientific research, technical services and geological prospecting	1.57
Management of water conservancy, environment and public facilities	1.29
Services to households and other services	1.02
Education	1.25
Health, social security and social welfare	1.09
Culture, sports and entertainment	1.26
Public management and social organization	1.24

Notes All the sectors included in this table are determined according to China's official definitions and for urban areas only. Numerals greater than, equal to and less than one indicate that the province's sectors have advantages, no apparent (dis)advantages and disadvantages, respectively
Source Calculated by authors based on China Statistical Yearbook, 2011. See Appendix A for a detailed methodological description

business services", "agriculture, forestry, animal husbandry and fishery" and "construction" were relatively weak sectors (see Table 1.44).

Shandong

[Quick Facts: Official name: Shandong Province; Capital: Jinan; Land area: 156,700 km^2; Population density: 600/km^2; Major ethnic groups: Han, Hui, Korean, Manchu, Mongol]

Shandong is a province of the PRC and is part of the east China region. Situated in the lower reaches of the Yellow River, its territory consists of the Shandong Peninsular and adjacent inland. It borders the Bohai Sea to the north, Hebei Province to the northwest, Henan Province to the west, Jiangsu Province to the south and the Yellow Sea to the southeast. It also shares a very short border with Anhui Province. The region stretches 420 km from south to north and 700 km from east to west. Its coastline is 3000 km long.

In Chinese "Shandong" means "mountain" (shan) and "east" (dong). The name can thus be translated literally as "east of the mountain" and it refers to the province's location to the east of Mount Taihang. A common nickname for the province is Qilu, after the states of Qi and Lu that existed in the area during the Eastern Zhou Dynasty (771–221 BC). Whereas the state of Qi was a major power of its era, that of Lu became renowned for being the home of Confucius. The cultural dominance of Lu is reflected in the official abbreviation for Shandong, which is "Lu."

The Yellow River passes through Shandong's western areas, entering the sea along the northern coast. The Grand Canal of China enters the province from the northwest and leaves on the southwest. Lake Weishan is the largest lake of the region. Shandong Peninsula has a rocky coastline with cliffs, bays and islands. The large Laizhou Bay, the southernmost of the three bays of the Bohai Sea, is found to the north between Dongying and Penglai; Jiaozhou Bay, which is much smaller, is found to the south, next to Qingdao. The Miaodao Islands extend northwards from the northern coast of the peninsula. The 17 administrative divisions of Shandong Province are subdivided into 140 county-level divisions (49 districts, 31 county-level cities and 60 counties). These are in turn divided into 1941 township-level divisions (1223 towns, 293 townships, 2 ethnic townships and 423 sub-districts).

The area's topography is complicated and interwoven with nine types of landform, including plains, basins, hills, terraces, deltas and mountains. Mountain area and plains account for 15.5 and 55 % of the province's territory, respectively, while hilly areas take up 13.2 %, and rivers and lakes 1.1 %. The centre of the province is mountainous, with the summit of Mount Taishan, 1545 m above sea level, being the highest point. Most hills distributed in the eastern part are at the altitude of 500 m and lower. Plains lying to the west and north are mostly below 50 m in elevation. The lowest area of the province is the Yellow River Delta, which is generally 2–10 m above sea level.

Shandon has a warm temperate monsoon climate with most rainfall concentrated in the hot summer. It has a short spring and autumn but a long winter and summer. The average temperature is 11–14 °C. The annual average rainfall is between 550 and 950 mm. Mainly relying on rainfall, the province's water resources are scarce, with only 520 m^3 available per resident, accounting for 18.8 % of the national average of 2770 m^3 per head. Currently the water supply is 19.224 billion cubic meter, including 7.844 billion cubic meter of surface water, 5.88 billion cubic meter of underground water and 5.5 billion cubic meter diverted from the Yellow River.

Some 128 minerals, 78 % of which are found elsewhere in China, have been discovered in the province, of which 33 have their surveyed deposits listed among the top ten of the nation: gold, natural sulfur and gypsum rank first; petroleum, diamond, magnetite, cobalt, hafnium and granite rank second; and kali salt, graphite, talc, bentonite and limestone rank third. The reserves of many other minerals, such as natural gas, iron, aluminum, barite, diatomite, zircon, bauxite and refractory clay, are also plentiful. Shandong produces approximately 26 % of China's gold, and the country is the world's fourth largest producer. A famous gold producer in Shandong is the Shandong Gold Mining Co. Ltd. It is the second largest China listed gold producer behind Zhongjin Gold.

The province is one of China's important energy bases: the crude oil produced in Shandong makes up one-third of the nation's total. The province has 50,000 km^2 of coalfields and is one of China's ten major coal-production bases. Coal mines are mainly found in the cities of Zibo, Zaozhuang, Yanzhou and Linyi. Intensive petroleum exploration is carried out along the Yellow River Delta. Its Shengli Oilfield is the second largest oil-production base in China, accounting for a large portion of the national total. The Shengli Oilfield extends over an area of 61,000 km^2 in northern Shandong, producing more than 200 million barrels of crude oil annually. The region is also a rich source of electricity. The Shandong power network is one of the country's six major power networks that are operated separately on a provincial basis.

The region has abundant agricultural and marine resources. With provincial rivers like the Yellow River, the Haihe River and the Huaihe River passing through, Shandong comprises mainly low-lying land with some mountainous terrain. There are more than 3100 varieties of plant there. Among the 450 species of wild vertebrates (accounting for 21 % of the nation's total), 55 are mammals, 362 are birds, 8 are amphibians and 25 are reptiles. In addition, there are many species of land invertebrates, insects in particular, making the province rank first in the country.

One of China's major agricultural production bases, Shandong is known as "a warehouse of grains, cotton and oil, and the land of fruits and aquatic products". It's also an important producer of wheat, peanuts, tobacco, hemp, silkworms, and traditional Chinese medicinal herbs and materials. The apples produced in Yantai, pears from Laiyang, peaches from Feicheng and Leling's golden-threaded jujubes are all famous specialties.

The province is rich in marine resources too. Its offshore area makes up 37 % of the total surface area of the Bohai and the Yellow seas, with a shoal area accounting for 15 % of the nation's total. There are about 260 species of fish and prawn in its seas, including more than 40 major cash species of fish and 100 species of shellfish. Shandong leads the country in the production of prawns, shellfish, abalones, sea slugs and urchins. Meanwhile, with many large and medium-sized salt works, it is also one of China's four major salt producers. In its 266,000 ha of freshwater, there are more than 40 species of freshwater plants and more than 70 species of fish.

The region has played a major role in Chinese history from the beginning of Chinese civilization along the lower reaches of the Yellow River, and it served as a pivotal cultural and religious site for Taoism, Chinese Buddhism and Confucianism. Mount Tai is the most revered mountain of Taoism and the site with the longest history of continuous religious worship worldwide. The Buddhist temples in the mountains to the south of the provincial capital of Jinan were once among the foremost Buddhist sites in China. The city of Qufu is the birthplace of Confucius and was later established as the center of Confucianism.

With beautiful natural landscapes and numerous historical and cultural relics, Shandong has rich tourist resources. It offers a string of attractions, such as two World Heritage Sites—Mount Taishan and the Temple, and the Mansion and Cemetery of Confucius; Lingzi, capital of the ancient Qi State; Penglai, the well-known "fairyland on earth"; Mount Laoshan, a sacred land of Taoism; Weifang, the "world capital of kites"; Qingdao, a charming coastal city famous for its annual International Beer Fair; Yantai, known worldwide as a wine producer; Rongcheng, a place considered as "the edge of the world" by the ancient Chinese; Jinan, the provincial capital honored as "the city of springs"; and a site for watching the wonderful scene of the Yellow River running into the sea.

The province is the second largest economy and consumer market in China next to Guangdong. In 2010 its nominal GRP was ¥3.92 trillion (about US$603 billion), ranking third in the country (behind Guangdong and Jiangsu provinces). Its GRP per capita was ¥42,014 (about US$6365), ranking eighth. It is one of the rich regions in China and its economic development focuses on large enterprises with well-known brand names. Shandong is the biggest industrial producer and one of the top manufacturing provinces in the country. The richest part is the Shandong Peninsula. Its growing purchasing power has led to the widespread development of major commercial centers, mainly situated in the cities of Ji'nan, Qingdao, Weifang and Yantai (Table 1.45).

Table 1.45 Demographic and socioeconomic profile: Shandong

Indicator	2000	2010
Population (thousands)	90,790	95,879
Illiteracy rate of population aged 15 or over (%)	8.46	4.97
GRP (¥ billions)	854.24	3916.99
Composition of GRP (%)		
Primary sector	14.9	9.2
Secondary sector	49.7	54.2
Tertiary sector	35.5	36.6
Fixed asset investment (¥ billions)	253.11	2328.05
Status of foreign-funded enterprises		
Number of registered enterprises	12,389	29,486
Total investment (US$ millions)	38,950	124,523
Registered capital (US$ millions)	23,097	72,865
Foreign trade (US$ millions)		
Export	16,093	110,301
Import	12,157	114,860
Sales of consumer goods (¥ billions)	255	1,462
Per capita annual disposable income of urban residents (¥)	6489.97	19,945.83
Engle's coefficient (%)	44.15	33.52
Per capita annual net income of rural residents (¥)	2659.20	6990.28
Engle's coefficient (%)	34.18	37.54
Number of patent applications granted	6962	51,490
Inventions	363	4106
Utility models	4627	36,391
Designs	1972	10,993

Note All monetary values are measured at current prices. *Source* Shandong Statistical Yearbook, 2001 and 2011

Table 1.46 Shandong's comparative (dis)advantage index by sector, 2010

Sector	Index
Agriculture, forestry, animal husbandry and fishery	0.18
Mining	1.62
Manufacturing	1.30
Production and distribution of electricity, gas and water	0.89
Construction	0.86
Transport, storage and post	0.75
Information transmission, computer service and software	0.48
Wholesale and retail trades	0.98
Hotels and catering services	0.72
Financial intermediation	0.97
Real estate	0.73
Leasing and business services	0.52
Scientific research, technical services and geological prospecting	0.51
Management of water conservancy, environment and public facilities	0.72
Services to households and other services	0.80
Education	0.94
Health, social security and social welfare	0.94
Culture, sports and entertainment	0.69
Public management and social organization	1.00

Notes All the sectors included in this table are determined according to China's official definitions and for urban areas only. Numerals greater than, equal to and less than one indicate that the province's sectors have advantages, no apparent (dis)advantages and disadvantages, respectively
Source Calculated by authors based on China Statistical Yearbook, 2011. See Appendix A for a detailed methodological description

Shandong ranks first among the provinces in the production of a variety of products, including cotton and wheat, as well as precious metals (such as gold) and diamonds. It also has one of the biggest sapphire deposits in the world. Other important crops include sorghum and maize. It has extensive petroleum deposits too, especially in the Dongying area in the Yellow River Delta, the location of Shengli Oilfield, one of the country's major oilfields. It also produces bromine from underground wells and salt from seawater.

The region boasts a strong food manufacturing and processing industry, focusing on vegetables and seafood. It also has a strong excavating and energy industry related to coal and oil. Its high-tech industry has been growing quickly and local government will continue to champion this sector, particularly the development of computers and software related to network communications. The province also benefits from a large consumer market, notable South Korean investment and tourism directed at Shandong Peninsula. Among the various sectors, manufacturing accounts for the largest fixed-asset investment.

Other noteworthy industries within the province include the electronics industry, the automobile industry in Ji'nan City, the locomotive industry in Qingdao City and the cotton textile industry in Qingdao and Ji'nan. A renowned company in Shandong's electronics industry is Haier Electronics, which controls about 30 and 20 % of China's refrigerator and air-conditioner market, respectively. Shandong has 93 products that have been awarded "Chinese Famous Brand Names", marginally behind Zhejiang and Guangdong provinces. These include Haier Electronics, Tsingdao Beer, Hisense Electronics and China Qingqi Motorcycles.

Foreign trade in the province continues to display excellent growth. The major import source is South Korea, followed by the US and Japan. The main imports include machinery, steel, equipment and technology. Trailing behind Japan, Korea and the US, the fourth largest trading partner is Hong Kong. The area's manufacturing sector receives the largest amount of utilized FDI, followed by real estate.

As of 2010, compared with those of other provinces, "mining" and "manufacturing" were relatively strong, while "agriculture, forestry, animal husbandry and fishery", "information transmission, computer service and software" and "scientific research, technical services and geological prospecting" were relatively weak sectors (see Table 1.46).

Shanghai

[Quick Facts: Official name: Shanghai Municipality; Land area: 6340.5 km^2; Population density: 3966/km^2; Major ethnic groups: Han, Hui, Tujia, Miao, Manchu]

Shanghai is a province-level municipality of the PRC. It is also the largest city proper by population in the world. Located in the Yangtze River Delta in eastern China, it sits at the mouth of the river in the middle portion of the Chinese coast. The municipality consists of a peninsula between the Yangtze and the Hangzhou Bay, Chongming (mainland China's second-largest island) and a number of smaller islands. It is bordered to the north and west by Jiangsu Province, to the south by Zhejiang Province and to the east by the East China Sea.

The Chinese characters of Shanghai's name mean "upon the sea". The earliest occurrence of this name dates from the 11th-century Song Dynasty, when there was already a river confluence and a town with this name in the area. Shanghai is officially abbreviated to Hu in Chinese. An older name for it is "Shen", from "Chun Shen Jun", a nobleman and locally revered hero of the 3rd-century BC state of Chu. From this it is also called the "City of Shen".

The city is bisected by the Huangpu River, a tributary of the Yangtze. The traditional center, the Puxi area, is on the western side of the Huangpu, while the newly developed Pudong, containing the central financial district Lujiazui, developed on the eastern bank. Shanghai is administratively equal to a province and is divided into 17 county-level divisions (16 districts and 1 county). As of 2009, these county-level divisions were further divided into 210 township-level divisions (109 towns, 2 townships and 99 sub-districts). These were in turn divided into the village-level divisions (3661 neighborhood committees and 1704 village committees).

The average elevation is about 4 m above sea level. Except for a few hills lying in the southwest corner, most parts of the region are flat and belong to the alluvial plain of the Yangtze River Delta. Shanghai is known for its rich water resources, with the water area accounting for 11 % of its total territory. The region includes 122 km^2 of water. It extends 120 km from south to north and 100 km from east to west. The city's location on the flat alluvial plain has meant that new skyscrapers must be built with deep concrete piles to prevent them from sinking into the soft ground. The highest point is at the peak of Dajinshan Island at 103 m. As part of the Taihu drainage area, the city has many rivers, canals, streams and lakes and is known for its rich water resources.

With a pleasant northern subtropical maritime monsoon climate, Shanghai enjoys four distinct seasons, with generous sunshine and abundant rainfall. Its spring and autumn are relatively short compared with the summer and winter. The average annual temperature is about 17.6 °C (averaging 4.2 °C in January and 27.9 °C in July). Winters are chilly and damp, and cold northwesterly winds can cause nighttime temperatures to drop below freezing. Summers are hot and humid, with an average of 8.7 days exceeding 35 °C annually. The city has a frost-free period of some 300 days and it receives an annual rainfall of around 1300 mm. However, nearly 50 % of the precipitation comes during the May–September flooding season, which is divided into three rainy periods: the spring rains, the plum rains and the autumn rains. The most pleasant seasons are spring, although it is changeable and often rainy, and autumn, which is generally sunny and dry. Shanghai experiences on average 1878 h of sunshine per year, with the hottest temperature ever recorded at 40.2 °C, and the lowest at −12.1 °C.

The wide river mouth of the Yangtze is home to 108 species of fish, including 20 that are economically important. Shanghai also boasts a number of natural lakes with abundant bottom living things, such as conch, a fresh-water variety of bivalve and clams. Originating from Taihu Lake, the 113 km Huangpu River winds through the downtown area of the city. It is varies between 300 and 770 m wide with an average width of 360 m. The ice-free river is the main waterway in the Shanghai area. The total water reserve in Shanghai stands at 2.7 billion cubic meter.

Shanghai is a popular tourist destination renowned for its historical landmarks, such as The Bund, City God Temple and Yuyuan Garden, as well as the extensive and growing Pudong skyline. It has been described as the “showpiece” of the booming economy of mainland China. Because of the city’s status as the cultural and economic center of East Asia for the first half of the 20th century, it is popularly seen as the birthplace of everything considered modern in China. It was there, for example, that the first motor car was driven, and (technically) the first train tracks and modern sewers were laid. As a city of long history, it has 13 historical sites under state protection, including characteristic gardens built during the Tang, Song, Yuan, Ming and Qing dynasties. A group of buildings constructed since the 1990s have added something new to the scenic attractions of the city.

Well-known parks in Shanghai include People’s Square Park, Gongqing Forest Park, Fuxing Park, Zhongshan Park, Lu Xun Park, Century Park and Jing’an Park. The Shanghai Disney Resort Project, approved by government in 2009, should be operational by 2016. The city boasts several museums of regional and national importance. The Shanghai Museum of Art and History has one of the best collections of Chinese historical artifacts in the world, including important archaeological finds since 1949. The Shanghai Art Museum, located in the former Shanghai Race Club building in People’s Square, is a major art museum holding both permanent and temporary exhibitions. The Shanghai Natural History Museum also houses a large collection of exhibits. In addition, there are a variety of smaller, specialist museums, some housed in important historical sites such as that of the Provisional Government of the Republic of Korea and the site of the First National Congress of the Chinese Communist Party.

In the last two decades, Shanghai has been one of the fastest-developing cities in the world. Since 1992 it has recorded a double-digit GRP growth rate almost every year. In 2010 its total GRP grew to ¥1.72 trillion (about US$297 billion), with GRP per capita of ¥82,560 (about US$12,784). The three largest service industries are financial services, retail and real estate. The manufacturing and agricultural sectors account for 42.1 and 0.7 % of GRP, respectively (see Table 1.47).

Table 1.47 Demographic and socioeconomic profile: Shanghai

Indicator	2000	2010
Population (thousands)	16,740	23,027
Illiteracy rate of population aged 15 or over (%)	5.40	2.74
GRP (¥ billions)	455.12	1716.60
Composition of GRP (%)		
Primary sector	1.8	0.7
Secondary sector	47.5	42.1
Tertiary sector	50.6	57.3
Fixed asset investment (¥ billions)	186.94	510.89
Status of foreign-funded enterprises		
Number of registered enterprises	15,930	55,666
Total investment (US$ millions)	98,540	339,385
Registered capital (US$ millions)	53,345	200,919
Foreign trade (US$ millions)		
Export	24,640	173,255
Import	30,064	192,189
Sales of consumer goods (¥ billions)	172	607
Per capita annual disposable income of urban residents (¥)	11,718.01	31,838.08
Engle's coefficient (%)	34.91	31.17
Per capita annual net income of rural residents (¥)	5,596.37	13,977.96
Engle's coefficient (%)	38.56	37.28
Number of patent applications granted	4050	48,215
Inventions	304	6867
Utility models	2083	21,821
Designs	1663	19,527

Note All monetary values are measured at current prices. *Source* Shanghai Statistical Yearbook, 2001 and 2011

Once a fishing and textiles town, Shanghai, thanks to its favorable port location, grew in importance in the 19th century. It was one of the cities opened to foreign trade by the 1842 Treaty of Nanking, which allowed the establishment of the Shanghai International Settlement. The city then flourished as a center of commerce and became the undisputed financial hub of Asia Pacific in the 1930s. With the Chinese Communist Party takeover of the mainland in 1949, the city's international influence declined. Since the 1980s, China's economic reform and opening-up policies have resulted in intense re-development, aiding the return of finance and foreign investment to the city.

Shanghai is one of four province-level municipalities of the PRC, with a total population of over 23 million as of 2010. It is a global city, having an influence in commerce, culture, finance, media, fashion, technology and transport. It is a major financial center and the busiest container port in the world. In 2009 the Shanghai Stock Exchange ranked third amongst worldwide stock exchanges in terms of trading volume, and sixth in terms of the total capitalization of listed companies, and the trading volume of six key commodities, including rubber, copper and zinc, on the Shanghai Futures Exchange all ranked first in the world.

The municipality is one of the main industrial centers in China, playing a key role in the country's heavy industry. A large number of industrial zones, including Hongqiao Economic and Technological Development Zone, Jinqiao Export Economic Processing Zone, Minhang Economic and Technological Development Zone and Caohejing High-Tech Development Zone, form the backbone of Shanghai's secondary industry. Heavy industry accounted for 78 % of the gross industrial output in 2009. China's largest steelmaker, Baosteel Group, and Jiangnan Shipyard, one of China's oldest shipbuilders, are both located there. Auto manufacture is another important industry. Shanghai Automotive Industry (Group) Corporation is one of the top-three automotive companies in China. It has a strategic partnership with Volkswagen and General Motors.

Shanghai is the commercial and financial center of mainland China, as exemplified by Pudong district, a pilot area for integrated economic reforms. Major capital markets in the city include the Shanghai Stock Exchange, the Shanghai Futures Exchange and the Shanghai Gold Exchange. It is a clear leader in terms of

Table 1.48 Shanghai's comparative (dis)advantage index by sector, 2010

Sector	Index
Agriculture, forestry, animal husbandry and fishery	0.14
Mining	0.01
Manufacturing	1.29
Production and distribution of electricity, gas and water	0.58
Construction	0.30
Transport, storage and post	1.91
Information transmission, computer service and software	1.20
Wholesale and retail trades	1.64
Hotels and catering services	1.85
Financial intermediation	1.67
Real estate	1.75
Leasing and business services	2.00
Scientific research, technical services and geological prospecting	2.64
Management of water conservancy, environment and public facilities	0.89
Services to households and other services	1.82
Education	0.55
Health, social security and social welfare	0.88
Culture, sports and entertainment	1.19
Public management and social organization	0.43

Notes All the sectors included in this table are determined according to China's official definitions and for urban areas only. Numerals greater than, equal to and less than one indicate that the province's sectors have advantages, no apparent (dis)advantages and disadvantages, respectively
Source Calculated by authors based on China Statistical Yearbook, 2011. See Appendix A for a detailed methodological description

the quality of its growth—60.7 % of GRP comes from the service sector, while the remaining 39.3 % comes from relatively high-end manufacturing of automobiles, electronics, petrochemicals, iron and steel, and equipment. It has the highest average wage and disposable income, and the lowest urban to rural income gap in China. Its GRP was ¥1.68 trillion ($256 billion) in 2010. It still lags far behind global financial centers, such as London, New York and Tokyo, in terms of the "soft" environment, such as financial innovation and products, the rules of law, free capital flows and human capital. The cost of living in Shanghai has increased, catching up with its global peers. The city still faces numerous challenges, such as traffic congestion, affordable housing, pollution control and population.

As of 2010, compared with those of other provinces, "Scientific research, technical services and geological prospecting", "leasing and business services" and "transport, storage and post" were relatively strong, while "mining", "agriculture, forestry, animal husbandry and fishery" and "construction" were relatively weak sectors (see Table 1.48).

Shanxi

[Quick Facts: Official name: Shanxi Province; Land area: 156,800 km^2; Population density: 217/km^2; Major ethnic groups: Han, Hui, Manchu, Mongol, Tujia]

Shanxi is a province of the PRC. The name literally means "mountain's west", which refers to its location west of the Taihang Mountains. Situated in the middle of the Yellow River Valley, it borders Hebei Province to the east, Henan Province to the south, Shaanxi Province to the west and Inner Mongolia Autonomous Region to the north. Its abbreviation is "Jin" in Chinese, after the state of Jin that existed here during the Eastern Zhou Dynasty (771–221 BC).

Shanxi is located on a plateau made up of higher ground to the east (Taihang Mountains) and the west (Lvliang Mountains) and a series of valleys in the center through which the Fen River runs. The highest peak is Mount Wutai in the northeast, which has an altitude of 3058 m. The Great Wall of China forms most of the northern border with Inner Mongolia Autonomous Region. The Zhongtiao Mountains run along part of the southern border and separate Shanxi from the east–west part of the Yellow River. This river forms the western border of Shanxi with Shaanxi. The Fen and the Qin rivers, tributaries of the Yellow River, run north-to-south through the province and drain much of the area. The north of the province is drained by tributaries of the Hai River, such as Sanggan and Hutuo rivers. The largest natural lake is Xiechi Lake, a salt lake near Yuncheng in southwestern Shanxi.

Originating from eastern and western mountain areas, all rivers in the province have their outlets in other regions. The rivers running west and south belong to the Yellow River system, while those flowing east belong to the Haihe River system. The Yellow River drainage area totals 97,503 km^2, accounting for 62.2 % of Shanxi's land area. The Haihe River drainage area covers 59,320 km^2, constituting

37.8 %. The 11 prefecture-level divisions of Shanxi are subdivided into 119 county-level divisions (23 districts, 11 county-level cities and 85 counties). These are in turn divided into 1388 township-level divisions (561 towns, 634 townships and 193 sub-districts).

The area has a continental monsoon climate and is rather arid. Average January temperatures are below 0 °C, while average July temperatures are around 21–26 °C. Winter is long, dry and cold, while summer is warm and humid. Spring is extremely dry and prone to dust storms. Shanxi is one of the sunniest parts of China and early summer heatwaves are common. The average annual precipitation is around 350–700 mm, with 60 % of it concentrated between June and August.

The province abounds in mineral resources. Of more than 120 kinds of underground minerals so far discovered, 53 have proven reserves. Of these, reserves of coal, bauxite, pearlite, gallium and zeolite rank first in the nation. It is especially noted as the "kingdom of coal", with proven reserves amounting to 261.2 billion tons, accounting for one-third of the nation's total. As a result, Shanxi is a leading producer of coal in China and has more coal companies than any other area, with its annual production exceeding 300 million tons. The Datong, Ningwu, Xishan, Hedong, Qinshui, and Huoxi coalfields are the most important there. It also has about 500 million tons of bauxite deposits, about one-third of the country's total Chinese.

Shanxi has 1214.6 billion cubic meter of underground water resources but only 45 % of them are recoverable. These are mainly distributed on the fringe of basins and in provincial border areas. There is a lack of surface water, but the available resources are evenly distributed. There are eight rivers, each over 150 km. The total volume of river water runoff stands at 11.4 billion cubic meter, a figure slightly more than that in Ningxia Hui Autonomous Region and so ranking last but one nationally.

The province has about 1700 species of known seed plants in 134 families, including more than 480 kinds of woody plants. The southern and southeastern parts of the province are richest in diversity of vegetation types and plant species. These include broadleaved deciduous forests, estival (summer) broadleaved forests composed chiefly of secondary deciduous shrubs, and mixed coniferous and broadleaved forests. The central part has vast expanses of forests, mainly composed of coniferous forests, mesophytic deciduous scrub forests and estival broadleaved forests. The north and northwest are rich in temperate bush and semi-arid grassland, but have fewer forests. Dominant plants there include Chinese silver grass, xeric wormwood, Caragana microphylla and sea buckthorn. In general, Shanxi lacks forest resources, being one of China's most deficient provinces. Of the more than 1000 species of wild plants so far discovered, there are over 90 species of wild medicinal plants widely distributed in the hilly areas. Famous ones include Codonopsis pilosola, Astragalus membranaceus, liquorice and weeping golden bell. Major wild fiber plants include nilghiri nettle, splendid achnatherum, Chinese small iris, kudzu vines, chaste trees and Chinese alpine rush.

There are more than 400 species of terrestrial wild animals in the region, including some 70 species of rare animals under state protection. The 14 species under first-class protection include white stork, black stork, golden eagle, sea eagle, vulture, brown pheasant, red-crowned crane, great bustard, leopard, tiger and sika deer. The 56 species under second-class protection comprise 40 kinds of birds, two kinds of amphibians and 14 kinds of mammals. In addition, there are more than 20 species of fur-bearing animals, including otter, Marten foina, raccoon-dog, leopard cat, yellow weasel, badger and fox. Table animals include hare, wild boar, ring-necked pheasant, rock partridge and partridge. There are also more than 70 species of medicine-supplying animals.

Shanxi abounds in tourism resources. It now has 31,401 unmovable cultural relics of different kinds. They comprise 2639 ruins of ancient monuments, 1666 ancient graves, 18,118 old buildings and memorial structures of historic interest, 300 grottoes and temples, 360 sites bearing ancient vertebrate fossils, 6852 sites with stone inscriptions and 1466 memorial buildings. There are 12,345 painted sculptures in these old buildings and memorial structures of historic interest and 26,751 m^2 of murals in old temples. The province therefore has the opportunity to develop tourism based on its rich cultural relics and to make it a pillar sector of the economy. The Ancient City of Pingyao is a World Heritage Site near Taiyuan.

Once a great financial center of China, it is noted for its preservation of many features of northern Han Chinese culture, architecture and the way of life during the Ming and Qing dynasties. The Yungang Grottoes (literal translation "The Cloud Ridge Caves") are shallow caves near Datong. There are over 50,000 carved images and statues of Buddhas and Boddhisatvas within these grottoes, ranging from 4 cm to 7 m tall.

In addition, Mount Wutai (Wutai Shan) is known as the residence of the bodhisattva Manjusri, and as a result is also a major Buddhist pilgrimage destination, with many temples and natural sights. Points of interest include the Tang Dynasty (AD 618–907) era timber halls located at Nanchan Temple and Foguang Temple, as well as a giant white stupa at Tayuan Temple built during the Ming Dynasty (AD 1368–1644). Mount Hengshan in Hunyuan County is one of the "Five Great Peaks" of China and is also a major Taoist site. Not far away is the Hanging Temple, located on the side of a cliff, which has survived for 1400 years despite earthquakes in the area. The Pagoda of Fogong Temple in Ying County was built in AD 1056 during the Liao Dynasty. It is octagonal with nine levels (five are visible from outside), and at 67 m high it is the tallest wooden pagoda in the world. It is also the oldest in China, although many existing stone and brick pagodas predate it by centuries.

The region's nominal GRP in 2010 was ¥920.09 billion (about US$150 billion), ranking 18th in China. The GRP per capita is below the national average. Compared with the provinces in East China, it is less developed for many reasons. Its geographic location limits it participation in international trade, which involves mostly eastern coastal provinces. The local climate and dwindling water resources limits agriculture in Shanxi, but important crops there include wheat, maize, millet, legumes and potatoes (Table 1.49).

Situated in the north of China, Shanxi is an important energy source base with abundant reserves of coal, magnesium, bauxite and fireclay. As a result its economy depends heavily on the mining industry, in particular coal extraction, and it is home to the largest group of coal companies in the country. Huge reserves of coal have drawn investment into railways, power plants, and coal- and chemical-related research and products.

Industry is centered on heavy industries, such as coal and chemical production, power generation and metal refining. There are many military-related industries in the province due to its geographic location and history (it is used to be the base of the People's Liberation Army). Taiyuan Satellite Launch Center, one of three in China, is located in the middle of the province with the country's largest stockpile of nuclear missiles.

Many private corporations have invested in Shanxi's mining industry. Hong Kong billionaire Li Ka-shing made one of his largest investments ever in China in exploiting coal gas there. Foreign investors include mining companies from Canada, the US, Japan, the UK, Germany and Italy. Mining-related companies include Daqin Railway Co. Ltd., which runs one of the busiest and most technologically advanced railways in China, connecting Datong and Qinhuangdao and exclusively used for coal shipping.

Table 1.49 Demographic and socioeconomic profile: Shanxi

Indicator	2000	2010
Population (thousands)	32,970	35,741
Illiteracy rate of population aged 15 or over (%)	4.18	2.13
GRP (¥ billions)	164.38	920.09
Composition of GRP (%)		
Primary sector	10.9	6.0
Secondary sector	50.4	56.9
Tertiary sector	38.7	37.1
Fixed asset investment (¥ billions)	54.82	606.32
Status of foreign-funded enterprises		
Number of registered enterprises	959	3,665
Total investment (US$ millions)	4827	22,929
Registered capital (US$ millions)	2560	11,128
Foreign trade (US$ millions)		
Export	2091	6741
Import	701	7119
Sales of consumer goods (¥ billions)	63	332
Per capita annual disposable income of urban residents (¥)	4724.11	15,647.66
Engle's coefficient (%)	41.48	39.48
Per capita annual net income of rural residents (¥)	1905.61	4736.25
Engle's coefficient (%)	34.78	37.46
Number of patent applications granted	968	4752
Inventions	173	739
Utility models	627	3096
Designs	168	917

Note All monetary values are measured at current prices. *Source* Shanxi Statistical Yearbook, 2001 and 2011

The area's industrial share in total GRP is the highest among all the provinces. The pillar industries in the province are coal mining, metallurgy, chemicals and machinery. The deposit volume and output of coal account for one-third and one-quarter of the country's total, respectively. Major coalfields are located near Taiyuan and Datong, and the Datong Coal Group Corp is one of the most renowned coal enterprises in the nation.

Benefiting from the abundant mineral resources as well as the electricity generated from coal, a large and comprehensive metallurgy system has been set up with ferrous and non-ferrous metallurgy industries. Taiyuan Iron and Steel Group Corp is a large iron and steel company in China and is also a key stainless steel producer. Shanxi Aluminum Plant is one of the nation's biggest aluminum production bases. The chemical industry's current strategy is to utilize coal resources. Besides this resource advantage, Shanxi also has a good industrial base and a high concentration of industrial groups for developing the coal chemical industry. The Shanxi Fertilizer Plant has become the largest compound fertilizer production base that uses coal as raw material in Asia. The development of coal-related industries, however, brings

Table 1.50 Shanxi's comparative (dis)advantage index by sector, 2010

Sector	Index
Agriculture, forestry, animal husbandry and fishery	0.28
Mining	4.69
Manufacturing	0.65
Production and distribution of electricity, gas and water	1.06
Construction	0.59
Transport, storage and post	1.07
Information transmission, computer service and software	0.73
Wholesale and retail trades	1.09
Hotels and catering services	0.67
Financial intermediation	0.97
Real estate	0.40
Leasing and business services	0.68
Scientific research, technical services and geological prospecting	0.68
Management of water conservancy, environment and public facilities	0.96
Services to households and other services	0.40
Education	1.02
Health, social security and social welfare	0.84
Culture, sports and entertainment	1.17
Public management and social organization	1.30

Notes All the sectors included in this table are determined according to China's official definitions and for urban areas only. Numerals greater than, equal to and less than one indicate that the province's sectors have advantages, no apparent (dis)advantages and disadvantages, respectively
Source Calculated by authors based on China Statistical Yearbook, 2011. See Appendix A for a detailed methodological description

with it heavy pollution and serious mining accidents. Many cities in Shanxi are rated as the most polluted cities in China.

As one of the steel and aluminum production bases in China, Shanxi has cheap raw material as well as convenient transportation for machinery manufacturing. Types of machines produced include trucks, coal machines, railway equipment, textile machinery, and auto engines and parts. Taiyuan Heavy and Mining Machinery Works and Taiyuan First Machine Tool Works are among the more well-known companies in this field.

Major export products include minerals, base metals, machinery, chemicals, gypsum and cement, while major import products are minerals, machinery, base metals, chemicals and optical products. The main import sources are Australia, Germany, India, Japan and Cuba, while key export destinations are the US, South Korea, Japan, Belgium and Italy.

During recent years, Shanxi has encouraged foreign investors to participate in the technological improvement of traditionally advantageous industries, such as the coal and coke, metallurgy and electric power industries. As a result, most of the FDI received is channeled into manufacturing and mining. Real estate, energy supply and logistics also receive some FDI. Most of this investment comes from the Virgin Islands, the Bahamas, Hong Kong, the UK, and the US.

As of 2010, compared with those of other provinces, “mining”, “public management and social organization” and “culture, sports and entertainment” were relatively strong, while “agriculture, forestry, animal husbandry and fishery”, “services to households and other services” and “real estate” were relatively weak sectors (see Table 1.50).

Sichuan

[Quick Facts: Official name: Sichuan Province; Capital: Chengdu; Land area: 485,000 km^2; Population density: 180/km^2; Major ethnic groups: Han, Yi, Tibetan, Qiang, Miao]

Sichuan is a province of the PRC. It is located along the upper Yangtze River in the southwest of China and borders Qinghai Province to the northwest, Gansu Province to the north, Shaanxi Province to the northeast, Chongqing Municipality to the east, Guizhou Province to the southeast, Yunnan Province to the south and Tibet Autonomous Region to the west. Its name is abbreviated to “Chuan” in Chinese.

The Yangtze River and its tributaries flow through the mountains of western Sichuan and the Sichuan Basin, thus the province is upstream of the great cities that stand along the Yangtze River in central and eastern China, such as Chongqing, Wuhan, Nanjing and Shanghai. One of the major tributaries of the Yangtze within the province is the Minjiang River of central Sichuan, which joins the Yangtze at Yibin.

The region is high in the west and low in the east in terms of its topography. The western part includes plateaus and mountainous regions, with some 4000 m above sea level; while the eastern part is the basin and hilly land, with an elevation of between 1000 and 3000 m. Western Sichuan consists of the numerous mountain ranges forming the easternmost part of the Tibetan Plateau, which are known generically as Hengduan Mountains. One of these ranges, Daxue Shan, contains the highest point of the province, Gongga Shan, at 7556 m. Lesser mountain ranges surround the basin on the north, east and south. Among them are the Daba Mountains in the province’s northeast. The Longmen Shan fault runs under the north-easterly mountain location of the 2008 earthquake.

Sichuan Province covers most of the Sichuan Basin. The Sichuan Basin, covering an area of 165,000 km^2, is one of the four largest in China. The elevation within the basin is between 200 and 750 m, sloping down from north to south. Surrounded by mountains, it has a mild climate. This provides a favorable environment for plants and animals. The forests cover 7.46 million hectare. Sichuan is home to one-fifth of the country's dawn redwoods and *Cathaya argyrophylla*, two species so old that they are regarded as living fossils. The region is also rich in animal resources. There are over 1000 kinds of vertebrates, accounting for 40 % of those in the whole country. Among them are 55 rare species. The well-known giant panda lives mainly in 36 of the counties and in the natural reserves of four mountain ranges within Sichuan's territory.

Due to the great differences in the terrain, the climate is very variable. The Sichuan Basin (including Chengdu) in the eastern half of the province experiences a subtropical monsoon climate with long, warm to hot, humid summers and short, mild to cool, dry and cloudy winters, with China's lowest sunshine totals. The western areas have a mountainous climate characterized by very cold winters and mild summers with plentiful sunshine. The south, including Panzhihua, has a sunny, subtropical climate with very mild winters and hot summers.

Sichuan is rich in minerals. It has more than 132 kinds of proven underground resources, of which reserves of 11 kinds, including vanadium, mirabilite, fluorite, sulfur iron, titanium and lithium, are the largest in China. The Panxi region alone possesses 13.3 % of the country's reserves of iron, 93 % of titanium, 69 % of vanadium and 83 % of the cobalt. It also possesses China's largest proven natural gas reserves, and large amount of Sichuan's natural gas production is transported to eastern, more developed provinces.

The reserves of hydropower resources in the area amount to 150 million kilowatt, second only to Tibet, and the exploitable potential is over 100 million kilowatt, more than any other area in China. It is also the hometown of the world-famous giant panda.

Sichuan has historically been known as the "Province of Abundance". The crops produced there are those that survive in sub-tropical and cool temperate zones. The region is a leading producer of rice and also a major producer of other crops, such as corn, sweet potatoes, wheat, rapeseed, sorghum, barley, soybeans and millet. It has a long history of silk production and it is famous for hemp and other fiber crops, which normally rank second in China. Sichuan is the only region in which both the oxen of north China and the water buffaloes of south China are found living side by side. It also has the largest output of pork among all the provinces and the second largest output of silkworm cocoons in the country.

The province has one of the most diverse ranges of ethnic groups in China. The majority of the population are Han, who are found scattered throughout the region with the exception of the far west. Thus significant numbers of other minorities, such as the Tibetans, the Yi, the Qiang and the Naxi, reside in the west, forming a traditional transition zone between Central Asian and East Asian cultures. Most of the minority ethnic groups have maintained their traditional lifestyles and practices —often a mixture of agriculture, animal husbandry and hunting.

Sichuan's beautiful landscapes and rich historical relics have made the province a major center for tourism. The UNESCO World Heritage Sites list includes five world heritages—three natural heritages, one cultural heritage and one mixed heritage. These are the Huanglong Scenic, Jiuzhaigou Valley, Emei Mountain, Qingcheng Mountain and Dujiangyan Irrigation System, and the Sichuan Giant Panda Sanctuaries. In addition there are 9 state-class scenic areas, 11 national forest parks, 40 nature reserves and 44 provincial-class scenic areas. Almost every variety of landscape of interest to tourists is available here: plateaus, mountains, ravines, basins, hills, plains, rivers, lakes, hot springs, waterfalls, limestone caves and even danxia formation.

Sichuan's nominal GRP for 2010 was ¥1.72 trillion (about US$250 billion), equivalent to a per capita level of ¥17,380 (about US$2545) (Table 1.51).

The province is one of the most industrialized areas in western China and thrives in such light industries as building materials, wood processing, food processing and silk processing. There are also several world-famous wine breweries in the province, such as Wu Liangye Group, Jian Nanchun Group and Luzhou Laojiao,

Table 1.51 Demographic and socioeconomic profile: Sichuan

Indicator	2000	2010
Population (thousands)	83,290	80,449
Illiteracy rate of population aged 15 or over (%)	7.64	5.44
GRP (¥ billions)	401.03	1718.55
Composition of GRP (%)		
Primary sector	23.6	14.4
Secondary sector	42.4	50.5
Tertiary sector	34.0	35.1
Fixed asset investment (¥ billions)	141.80	1311.67
Status of foreign-funded enterprises		
Number of registered enterprises	3539	12,050
Total investment (US$ millions)	10,107	54,383
Registered capital (US$ millions)	7028	33,457
Foreign trade (US$ millions)		
Export	1434	12,403
Import	1344	13,893
Sales of consumer goods (¥ billions)	152	681
Per capita annual disposable income of urban residents (¥)	5894.27	15,461.16
Engle's coefficient (%)	40.10	35.87
Per capita annual net income of rural residents (¥)	1903.60	5086.89
Engle's coefficient (%)	36.83	48.27
Number of patent applications granted	3218	32,212
Inventions	248	2,204
Utility models	1699	12,724
Designs	1271	17,284

Note All monetary values are measured at current prices. *Source* Sichuan Statistical Yearbook, 2001 and 2011

accounting for about one-fifth of the country's total production. The region's high-tech industry has been developing fast and has attracted a number of internationally renowned IT companies, such as Microsoft, Cisco, Intel, IBM and Motorola, to set up manufacturing centers there.

In addition to heavy industries, such as coal, energy, iron and steel production, the auto industry is a key sector of the machinery industry in Sichuan. Most of the auto manufacturing companies are located in Chengdu, Mianyang, Nanchong and Luzhou. Other important industries there include aerospace and defense (military). A number of China's rockets (Long March rockets) and satellites have been launched from the Xichang Satellite Launch Center, located in the city of Xichang.

Great strides have been made in developing Sichuan into a modern hi-tech industrial base by encouraging both domestic and foreign investments in electronics and IT (such as software), machinery and metallurgy (including automobiles), hydropower, pharmaceuticals, and the food and beverage industries.

As the economy grows the province must focus on growth outside the capital, where cities face inadequate transport infrastructure and an expressway system that

Table 1.52 Sichuan's comparative (dis)advantage index by sector, 2010

Sector	Index
Agriculture, forestry, animal husbandry and fishery	0.31
Mining	0.83
Manufacturing	0.78
Production and distribution of electricity, gas and water	1.12
Construction	1.80
Transport, storage and post	0.84
Information transmission, computer service and software	0.78
Wholesale and retail trades	0.73
Hotels and catering services	0.60
Financial intermediation	1.04
Real estate	0.58
Leasing and business services	0.44
Scientific research, technical services and geological prospecting	1.07
Management of water conservancy, environment and public facilities	1.02
Services to households and other services	0.36
Education	1.19
Health, social security and social welfare	1.19
Culture, sports and entertainment	0.77
Public management and social organization	1.24

Notes All the sectors included in this table are determined according to China's official definitions and for urban areas only. Numerals greater than, equal to and less than one indicate that the province's sectors have advantages, no apparent (dis)advantages and disadvantages, respectively
Source Calculated by authors based on China Statistical Yearbook, 2011. See Appendix A for a detailed methodological description

does not link many cities to each other. Local government plans to improve transportation linkages between cities in the northeast and south. Sichuan is the biggest consumer market in Western China. In recent years the expansion of foreign retail enterprises there has sped up since China fully liberalized the retail and wholesale distribution sectors. Major foreign retail enterprises include Carrefour and Auchan from France, Metro from Germany, Wal-Mart from the US, Ito-yokado from Japan and Parkson from Malaysia.

Thanks to significant improvement in the local business environment, there have been major achievements in foreign trade. Key export markets include the US, Hong Kong, India and Japan. The main exports are machinery and electrical equipment, video and audio appliances, textiles, and base metals and related products. The US and Japan are also key import sources, in addition to Germany and South Korea. Major imports include machinery and electric equipments video and audio appliances, transport equipments and minerals.

Sichuan has attracted the most FDI among all the western provinces. The actual utilized FDI comes from the British Virgin Islands, Hong Kong, Taiwan,

Singapore, the US, Samoa, Cayman Islands and Malaysia. Most of it is channeled into real estate and manufacturing.

As of 2010, compared with those of other provinces, "construction" and "public management and social organization" were relatively strong, while "agriculture, forestry, animal husbandry and fishery", "services to households and other services" and "leasing and business services" were relatively weak sectors (see Table 1.52).

Tianjin

[Quick Facts: Official name: Tianjin Municipality; Capital: Tianjin; Land area: 11,760 km^2; Population density: 1173/km^2; Major ethnic groups: Han, Hui, Manchu, Mongol, Korean]

Tianjin is a province-level municipality of the PRC. It is under the direct administration of Chinese central government. It is located on the northeast side of the North China Plain, facing the Bohai Sea in the east, with a coast stretching about 133 km. It adjoins Beijing Municipality to the north and borders Hebei Province to the east, west and south. Tianjin is officially abbreviated as "Jin" in Chinese.

The municipality is located on both sides of the lower reaches of the Haihe River. Several other rivers run into the sea in the area, such as the New Ziya River, the Duliujian River, the New Yongding River, the New Chaobai River and the Canal Ji. The distance from the city proper to the seacoast is 50 km and that to Beijing is 120 km. It is an important passage by sea to Beijing, having served as fort and gateway to Beijing since ancient times. It is also a communication hub linking north, northeast and northwest China. The city boasts the largest man-made harbor in the north. Tianjin Port is an important passage linking a dozen provinces and cities in the north with the sea. Tianjin's geographical position and strategic importance is unmatchable. With more than 30 navigation routes leading to more than 300 international ports, it serves as a major channel linking the continents of Asia and Europe by sea.

Tianjin's name first appeared in the early years of the Yongle reign of the Ming Dynasty (AD 1368–1644) and it refers to the ferry port used by the emperor. In AD 1404 it became a military position of strategic importance, and construction of city walls and garrison installations began. It was eventually called the Tianjin Fort. It is divided into the old city and the Binhai New Area. The latter is a focus for expansion and has maintained an annual growth rate of nearly 30 % of GRP since its establishment in 2009. As of the end of 2010, 285 Fortune Global 500 companies had established branch offices there. It is a base for advanced industry, financial reform and innovation.

The municipality is generally flat, and swampy near the coast, but hilly in the far north, where the Yan Mountains intrude into northern Tianjin. The highest point is Jiushanding Peak on the northern border with Hebei, at an altitude of 1078 m. The city is located across the River Haihe, the largest river in north China, which has at its upper reaches more than 300 tributaries of more than 10 km long. These converge into North Canal, Yongdin River, Daqing River, Ziya River,and South Canal, which then join in the Haihe River at Sanchakou near the Jin'gang Bridge of Tianjin. The Haihe River, which flows into the Bohai Sea at Dagukou, is 72 km long with an average width of 100 m and a depth of 3–5 m. It used to carry 3000-ton ships. Since the project of diverting water from the Luanhe River to Tianjin was finished in the 1980s, 1 billion cubic meter of water has been sent to the city every year. Tianjin also has a rich deposit of underground water. In the mountain area, quality mineral water with low mineral content oozes from the cracks of rocks at a rate of 7.2–14.6 tons/h, and the flow can reach 720–800 tons/h during the rainy season. There are three large reservoirs there with a total capacity of 340 million cubic meter.

The municipality features a four-season, monsoon-influenced climate, typical of East Asia. In winter the wind often blows from the north because of the cold high pressure from Mongolia. In summer, affected by the subtropical high pressure from the western Pacific, the city sees much southerly wind. The region has a semi-moist warm temperate continental monsoon climate with an apparent feature of transit from continental climate to marine climate. The seasons are distinct but the duration of each is different. Precipitation is not substantial with uneven distribution over the year. The monsoon wind is significant and sunshine is adequate. The annual average temperature is 12.3 °C. The hottest month is July, during which the average temperature can reach 26 °C. January is the coldest month with an average temperature of −4 °C. The yearly average rainfall is 550–680 mm, 80 % of which is concentrated in the summer.

More than 20 varieties of minerals worthy of excavation have been discovered in the area. These include manganese, manganese-boron stone, gold, tungsten, molybdenum, copper, aluminum, zinc, limestone, marble, medical stone, barite and natural oilstone. There are petroleum and natural gas reserves underground in the plain and in the continental framework of the Bohai Sea. Tianjin also has about 1 billion tons of petroleum deposits, with Dagang District (in the Binhai New Area) containing important oilfields. Salt is also important, with Changlu Yanqu being one of China's most important salt-production areas. Geothermal energy is another resource.

Farmland takes up about 40 % of the municipality's total area. Wheat, rice and maize are the key crops. Fishing is important along the coast. Tianjin is also significant industrial base. Major industries include petrochemicals, textiles, car manufacturing, mechanical industries and metalworking.

In the coastal area there are a lot of salt- and alkali-resistant plants. In the wetlands there are reeds, calamus, and cultivated water chestnut and lotus root. In the northern mountain area there are Chinese pine, Chinese walnut, walnut, haw and persimmon. The wild animals are mostly herbivores, such as wild goat, river deer, hedgehog, squirrel and birds. There are about 30 varieties of freshwater fish in ponds and reservoirs, including common carp, snail carp, grass carp, silver carp and mullet. Tianjin cuisine focuses heavily on seafood. It also has several famous snack items.

The majority of Tianjin residents are Han Chinese. There are also 51 of the 55 minor Chinese ethnic groups living there. Major minorities include Hui, Koreans, Manchus and Mongols. Despite its proximity to Beijing, the local dialect sounds quite different but provides the basis for Putonghua, the official spoken language of the PRC.

The main attractions of the region include Luzutang (Boxer Rebellion Museum), Guwenhua Jie, Ancient culture street, Tianjin Wen Miao (an important temple of Confucius), Yuhuangge Taoist Temple, Temple of Great Compassion Zen Buddhist Temple, Tianhou Palace, a temple dedicated to the goddess Mazu and the biggest in the North China region, Tianjin Water Park, the largest urban park and recreation area in the region, Tianjin Zoo, home to approximately 3000 animals and 200 species, Italian Town and a polar marine animals theme park in Tianjin. The city is the respected home base of Beijing opera, one of the most prestigious forms of Chinese opera.

The nominal GRP of Tianjin was approximately ¥922 billion (about US$145 billion) with a per capita GRP of ¥72,994 in 2010. The manufacturing sector is the largest and the fastest-growing sector of Tianjin's economy (see Table 1.53).

Although the output value of primary industry has continued to grow in recent years, its share of GRP has gradually decreased. The agriculture sector is currently undergoing strategic restructuring. Fish breeding, poultry raising and high-quality planting have become the main agriculture industries of the area.

The municipality is an important industrial center in northern China. Its pillar industries include electronics, automobiles, metallurgy and petrochemicals, of which the electronics and telecommunications are the most important and have developed rapidly.

Table 1.53 Demographic and socioeconomic profile: Tianjin

Indicator	2000	2010
Population (thousands)	10,010	12,993
Illiteracy rate of population aged 15 or over (%)	4.93	2.10
GRP (¥ billions)	163.94	922.45
Composition of GRP (%)		
Primary sector	4.5	1.6
Secondary sector	50.0	52.5
Tertiary sector	45.5	46.0
Fixed asset investment (¥ billions)	61.09	627.81
Status of foreign-funded enterprises		
Number of registered enterprises	9942	12,918
Total investment (US$ millions)	33,086	109,624
Registered capital (US$ millions)	18,510	62,044
Foreign trade (US$ millions)		
Export	7674	37,771
Import	9482	53,841
Sales of consumer goods (¥ billions)	74	290
Per capita annual disposable income of urban residents (¥)	8140.50	24,292.60
Engle's coefficient (%)	46.27	50.05
Per capita annual net income of rural residents (¥)	3622.39	10,074.86
Engle's coefficient (%)	35.47	41.74
Number of patent applications granted	1611	11,006
Inventions	163	1930
Utility models	994	6718
Designs	454	2358

Note All monetary values are measured at current prices. *Source* Tianjin Statistical Yearbook, 2001 and 2011

In recent years, more than ten large business establishments, including Gulou Trade Street, have been reconstructed. Currently there are more than 50 shopping centers with an area of more than 10,000 m^2. Modern sales channels and new trade forms have developed quickly. Some internationally famous supermarket companies have established chain stores in Tianjin, including Metro, Makro, Walmart, Osun and Trust-mart. Shanghai Lianhua, Jiangsu Suning, Beijing Gome and other well-known domestic enterprises have also set up supermarkets in Tianjin. Its indigenous retailer, Family World, is also competitive.

The region's industrial development owes much to the rapid growth of hi-tech industries—electronics and IT in particular. Meanwhile, a lot of hi-tech enterprises, such as GMCC, Jinyao Group, Nankai Guard Group and Tasly Group, have become competitive. EADS Airbus is an important manufacturer and has opened an assembly plant in the municipality for its Airbus A320 series airliners, operational since 2009.

In the short term, infrastructure spending will buoy the economy. There are substantial projects underway to extend the metro system (which currently has only one line) and to improve road and rail links with Beijing.

Foreign investments are mainly in manufacturing (including textiles and garments, chemical products, machinery and equipment, electronics and telecommunication), trade, catering, and real estate. Some 95 of the world's top 500 enterprises have invested in Tianjin, such as Motorola, Samsung, BridgeStone, LG, GE, TOYOTA, Honda, Sanyo, 3 M and Kyocera. Foreign-invested enterprises are playing an important role in the economy. Hong Kong is traditionally the biggest investor in Tianjin but US and Japanese investment has increased rapidly in recent years. Other major sources of foreign investment are Korea, Germany and Taiwan.

Tianjin has a highly externally oriented economy. Manufactured goods account for the majority of its exports, of which machinery and electronic products (such as mobile phones, displays and compact disc players) are the most important. The export of hi-tech products has seen rapid growth in recent years. Other export items include textiles and related products, mineral products and metallurgy products. Foreign-, Hong Kong-, Macau- and Taiwan-funded enterprises continue to be the largest players in the city's foreign trade. The major export markets are Japan, the US, South Korea, Hong Kong, the Netherlands and Germany. The key import sources are Japan, the US, South Korea, Hong Kong and Germany. Over the past five years, imports from these countries have grown rapidly—in particular, imports from Korea, Taiwan, Germany and France.

As of 2010, compared with those of other provinces, "services to households and other services", "wholesale and retail trades" and "hotels and catering services" were relatively strong, while "agriculture, forestry, animal husbandry and fishery", "construction" and "public management and social organization" were relatively weak sectors (see Table 1.54).

Table 1.54 Tianjin's comparative (dis)advantage index by sector, 2010

Sector	Index
Agriculture, forestry, animal husbandry and fishery	0.12
Mining	1.01
Manufacturing	1.31
Production and distribution of electricity, gas and water	0.67
Construction	0.51
Transport, storage and post	1.26
Information transmission, computer service and software	0.77
Wholesale and retail trades	1.47
Hotels and catering services	1.47
Financial intermediation	0.94
Real estate	1.08
Leasing and business services	1.42
Scientific research, technical services and geological prospecting	1.40
Management of water conservancy, environment and public facilities	1.03
Services to households and other services	7.24
Education	0.66
Health, social security and social welfare	0.90
Culture, sports and entertainment	0.85
Public management and social organization	0.61

Notes All the sectors included in this table are determined according to China's official definitions and for urban areas only. Numerals greater than, equal to and less than one indicate that the province's sectors have advantages, no apparent (dis)advantages and disadvantages, respectively
Source Calculated by authors based on China Statistical Yearbook, 2011. See Appendix A for a detailed methodological description

Tibet

[Quick Facts: Official name: Tibet Autonomous Region; Capital: Lhasa; Land area: 1,228,400 km^2; Population density: 2/km^2; Major ethnic groups: Tibetan, Han, Hui, Monba, Lhoba]

Tibet Autonomous Region is in the PRC. It is a plateau on the northeast side of the Himalayas. It adjoins Xinjiang Uygur Autonomous Region and Qinghai Province to the north, Sichuan Province to the east and Yunnan Province to the southeast, and it shares international borders with Myanmar, India, Bhutan and Nepal to the south and west. It is the traditional homeland of the Tibetan people as well as of other ethnic groups, such as the Monpas, the Qiang and the Lhobas. Tibet is now also inhabited by considerable numbers of the Han and the Hui people.

The modern Chinese pinyin for "Tibet" is "Xizang", which derives from two Chinese characters, "xi" (west) and "zang". Zang refers to Tibetan people, language and culture, regardless of where they are from. The term "Xizang" was coined during the Qing Dynasty during the reign of Emperor Jiaqing (AD 1796–1820).

Following the collapse of the Qing Dynasty in 1911, Tibet declared its independence. The region maintained its autonomy until 1951, when it was incorporated into the PRC. The previous Tibetan government was abolished in 1959. Today the PRC divides the western and central parts of Tibet to be Tibet Autonomous Region, while the northeastern, eastern and southeast areas are under the administrations of Qinghai, Sichuan and Yunnan provinces, respectively. In addition, Arunachal Pradesh (called Zangnan or Shannan in Chinese), which is currently under Indian administration, is claimed by the PRC as a district of Tibet Autonomous Region.

The region, averaging more than 4000 m above sea level, forms the main part of the Qinghai–Tibet Plateau and is well known as the "Roof of the World". Mount Everest (about 8848 m above sea level), located on the border with Nepal, is the highest mountain on earth. Several major rivers have their source on the Tibetan Plateau (mostly in Qinghai Province). These include the Yangtze, the Yellow, the Indus, the Mekong, the Ganges, the Salween and the Yarlung Tsangpo (Brahmaputra) rivers. The Yarlung Tsangpo Grand Canyon is among the deepest and longest in the world. The Indus and Brahmaputra originate from western Tibet.

The atmosphere is severely dry for nine months each year, and the average annual snowfall is only 460 mm. The Indian monsoon exerts some influence on eastern Tibet. Northern Tibet is subject to high temperatures in summer and intense cold in winter. Western passes receive a small amount of fresh snow each year but remain traversable all year round. Low temperatures are prevalent throughout these western regions, where bleak desolation is unrelieved by any vegetation bigger than a low bush, and where wind sweeps unchecked across vast expanses of arid plain.

There are more than 90 known mineral types in the area, of which 26 have proven reserves and 11 rank among the top five in China. The minerals include chromite, lithium, copper, gypsum, boron, magnesite, barite, arsenic, mica, peat, kaolin, salt, natural soda, mirabilite, sulfur, phosphorus, potassium, diatomaceous earth, iceland spar, corundum, rock quartz and agate. In 2007 Chinese central government issued a report outlining the discovery of a large mineral deposit in Tibet. This may double China's previous reserves of zinc, copper and lead. Government sees this as a way to alleviate the nation's dependence on foreign mineral imports for its growing economy. However, the exploitation of these vast resources could harm Tibet's fragile ecosystem and also undermine its culture.

Tibet is rich in hydro, geothermal, solar and wind energy. It produces approximately 200 million kilowatt of natural hydroenergy annually, about 30 % of the nation's total. It has 354.8 billion cubic meter of surface water resources, about 13.5 % of the nation's total, and 330 billion cubic meter of glacial water resources. The region has 56. 59 million kilowatt exploitable hydroenergy resources, about 15 % of the nation's total. It also leads China in geothermal energy. The Yangbajain geothermal field in Damxung County, Lhasa, is the country's largest high-temperature steam geothermal field and also one of the largest in the world.

Tibet is like a giant plant kingdom with more than 5000 species of high-grade plants. It is also one of China's largest forest areas and includes intact primeval forests. Most plant species from the tropical to the frigid zones of the northern hemisphere are found there. Forestry reserves exceed 2.08 billion cubic meter and the forest coverage rate is 9.84 %. Common species include Himalayan pine, alpine larch, *Pinus yunnanensis*, *Pinus armandis*, Himalayan spruce, Himalayan fir, hard-stemmed long bract fir, hemlock, Monterey *Larix potaniniis*, Tibetan larch, Tibetan cypress and Chinese juniper. There are about 926,000 ha of pine forest in Tibet. Two species, Tibetan longleaf pine and Tibetan lacebark pine, are among those species under state protection. There are more than 1000 wild plants used for medicine, 400 of which are common medicinal herbs. Particularly well known medicinal plants include Chinese caterpillar fungus, *Fritillaria thunbergii*, Rhizoma picrorhizae, rhubarb, Rhizoma gastrodiae, pseudo-ginseng, *Codonopsis pilosula*, Radix gentiane, Macrophyllae, Radix salviae miltiorrhizae, glossy ganoderma and *Caulis spatholobi*. There are over 200 known species of fungi, including famous edible fungi, such as songrong, hedgehog hydnum, zhangzi fungus, mushrooms, black fungi, tremellas and yellow fungi. Fungi for medical use include tuckahoes, songganlan and stone-like omphalias.

There are 142 species of mammals, 473 species of birds, 49 species of reptiles, 44 species of amphibians, 64 species of fish and more than 2300 species of insects. Wild animals include old world monkeys, Assamese macaque, rhesus monkey, muntjak, head-haired deer, wild cattle, red-spotted antelope, serows, leopards, clouded leopards, black bears, wild cats, weasels, little pandas, red deer, river deer, whitelipped deer, wild yaks, Tibetan antelopes, wild donkeys, argalis, Mongolian gazelles, foxes, wolves, Iynxes, brown bears, jackals, blue sheep and snow leopards. The Tibetan antelope, wild yak, wild donkey and argali are all rare species particular to the Qinghai–Tibet Plateau and they are under state protection. The white-lipped deer, found only in China, is particularly rare. The black-necked crane and the Tibetan pheasant are under first-grade state protection.

Historically, the population of the region consisted of primarily ethnic Tibetans and some other ethnic groups. The original ancestors of the Tibetan people, as represented by the six red bands in the old Tibetan flag, are Se, Mu, Dong, Tong, Dru and Ra. Other traditional ethnic groups with a significant population or with the majority of the ethnic group residing in Tibet (excluding the area disputed with India) include the Bai, Blang, Bonan, Dongxiang, Han, Hui people, Lhoba, Lisu people, Miao, Mongols, Monguor (Tu people), Menba (Monpa), Mosuo, Nakhi, Qiang, Nu people, Pumi, Salar and Yi.

The area's cultural influences extend to the neighboring states of Bhutan and Nepal, as well as regions of India (such as Sikkim, Ladakh, Lahaul and Spiti), in addition to the Tibetan autonomous areas that are under the administration of adjacent Chinese provinces (such as Qinghai, Sichuan and Yunnan). Lhasa is the traditional center of Tibetan culture and the capital of Tibet Autonomous Region. It contains two World Heritage Sites—the Potala Palace and Norbulingka, which were the residences of the Dalai Lama. Lhasa contains a number of significant temples and monasteries, including Jokhang and Ramoche Temple.

Tibet is called "rooftop of the world". It draws visitors because of its great religious significance. Many tourists and pilgrims from Nepal and India enter through the Burang port of entry to visit the area's sacred mountains and lakes. The southwest Tibet tourist district is a place for mountaineers, many of whom are Nepalese, who come to Tibet through the Zhamu entry/exit port to enjoy the mountain scenery or do some climbing. In southern Tibet, centered on Nyingchi, one can pass through the four seasons of the year in a single day. There are snow-capped mountains, dense primeval forests, surging rivers and azalea-covered mountainsides. This beautiful scenery is easy to enjoy given the pleasantly humid and mild climate.

The region has continually developed and exploited its unique tourism resources, both human and natural. It currently has four tourist areas of Lhasa, the west, the southwest and the south. The Lhasa tourist area includes Lhasa, Yangbajain, Damxung, Gyangze, Zetang, Xigaze and Yamzhoyum Co Lake. Lhasa is not only Tibet's political, economic, cultural and transportation hub but also the center of Tibetan Buddhism. Major tourist sites include the Jokhang Temple, Ramoche Temple, Potala Palace, Barkhor Bazaar, Norbulingka Palace and three great monasteries of Ganden, Drepung and Sera. The Jokhang Temple, the Potala and Norbulingka palaces and Ganden, Drepung and Sera monasteries are key cultural relics under state-level protection.

New tourist routes and specialty tours have been added in recent years. They are Lhasa–Nyingschi–Shannan–Lhasa (eastern circle line) and Lhasa–Xigaze–Ngari–Xigaze (western circle line). Tours include exploration by automobile, trekking and scientific investigation tours. Other special events include the Shoton Theatrical Festival in Lhasa, the Qangtam Horseracing Festival on the North Tibet Plateau and the Yarlung Culture and Arts Festival in Shannan.

At the westernmost end of China, Tibet is the least urbanized area, with an economy that depends on agriculture, finance from central government and a thriving tourism industry. Economic development in the area is stunted by low

Table 1.55 Demographic and socioeconomic profile: Tibet

Indicator	2000	2010
Population (thousands)	2620	3007
Illiteracy rate of population aged 15 or over (%)	32.50	24.42
GRP (¥ billions)	11.75	50.75
Composition of GRP (%) Primary sector Secondary sector Tertiary sector	30.9 23.2 45.9	13.5 32.3 54.2
Fixed asset investment (¥ billions)	6.41	46.27
Status of foreign-funded enterprises Number of registered enterprises Total investment (US$ millions) Registered capital (US$ millions)	78 335 188	264 534 296
Foreign trade (US$ millions) Export Import	109 40	538 52
Sales of consumer goods (¥ billions)	4	19
Per capita annual disposable income of urban residents (¥) Engle's coefficient (%)	7426.32 36.38	14,980.47 36.23
Per capita annual net income of rural residents (¥) Engle's coefficient (%)	1330.81 53.83	4138.71 49.71
Number of patent applications granted Inventions Utility models Designs	17 4 4 9	124 16 49 59

Note All monetary values are measured at current prices. *Source* Tibet Statistical Yearbook, 2001 and 2011

population density, high transportation costs and high exploration costs. While it could be a large producer of natural resources and raw materials, there have been few advances in these areas. The focus is on expanding secondary industries, in particular energy, mining and new building materials (Table 1.55).

At present, central government exempts Tibet from all taxation and provides most of its government expenditures. Due to limited arable land, the primary occupation on the Tibetan Plateau is raising livestock, such as sheep, cattle, goats, camels, yaks, dzo and horses. The main crops grown are barley, wheat, buckwheat, rye, potatoes, and assorted fruits and vegetables. The development of agriculture and animal husbandry has been given top priority in the Tibetan economy. The major agricultural products, such as broad beans, barley, wheat, rapeseed, garlic and mushrooms, have great competitive advantage in terms of quality due to several unique natural conditions.

In recent years, due to increased interest in Tibetan Buddhism, tourism has become an increasingly important sector and is actively promoted by the authorities.

Table 1.56 Tibet's comparative (dis)advantage index by sector, 2010

Sector	Index
Agriculture, forestry, animal husbandry and fishery	1.38
Mining	0.23
Manufacturing	0.13
Production and distribution of electricity, gas and water	1.45
Construction	0.36
Transport, storage and post	0.64
Information transmission, computer service and software	1.16
Wholesale and retail trades	0.65
Hotels and catering services	0.96
Financial intermediation	1.03
Real estate	0.00
Leasing and business services	0.27
Scientific research, technical services and geological prospecting	1.36
Management of water conservancy, environment and public facilities	0.45
Services to households and other services	0.00
Education	1.47
Health, social security and social welfare	1.41
Culture, sports and entertainment	2.78
Public management and social organization	3.63

Notes All the sectors included in this table are determined according to China's official definitions and for urban areas only. Numerals greater than, equal to and less than one indicate that the province's sectors have advantages, no apparent (dis)advantages and disadvantages, respectively
Source Calculated by authors based on China Statistical Yearbook, 2011. See Appendix A for a detailed methodological description

This brings in most income from the sale of handicrafts. These include Tibetan hats, jewelry (silver and gold), wooden items, clothing, quilts, fabrics, rugs and carpets.

Industry still plays an important role in the economy although its service sectors have developed rapidly over the last few decades. Industrial products such as minerals, medicine, Qingke barley wine, carpets and building materials are renowned globally. Traditional Tibetan medicine, in particular, boasts a history of more than 2000 years.

In 2006 the construction of the 1956 km Qinghai–Tibet Railway was completed. This stretches from Xining, capital of Qinghai Province, to Lhasa, and across the Kunlun Mountains and Tanggulashan. For 960 km it is constructed 4000 m above sea level and is thus the world's highest railway. Its completion makes Tibet more accessible. It is also responsible for 75 % of cargo, which greatly reduces transportation costs.

The economy of the region is dominated by subsistence agriculture, though tourism has been growing in recent decades. Major consumer markets are located in Lhasa and Rikaze. Traditional shopping districts are located around Jokhang Square, Beijing Road and Barkhor Street. In Lhasa, Barkhor Street is a famous market for buying small commodities, such as carpets, ethnic costumes and jewelry. Tibet has consistently developed and exploited its unique tourism resources, both human and natural. The region is home to unique folk customs and stunningly beautiful natural scenery, such as Namtso Lake, the Great Gorges of Yarlung, Tsangpu River, Potala Palace and Jokhang.

Major exports include light industry products, livestock products, traditional Chinese medicine and carpets. The main imports are motor vehicles and machinery products. Tibet's cross-border trade plays an important role in its economy as a result of its special geographic location.

Priority for foreign investments are given in the following areas: infrastructure (such as transportation and communications), education, agriculture (plateau agriculture, water-conservative agriculture and food processing) and Tibetan medicine. Foreign investments come mainly from Nepal, Japan, the US, the UK, South Korea, Denmark, Canada and Australia.

As of 2010, compared with those of other provinces, "public management and social organization" and "culture, sports and entertainment" were relatively strong, while "services to households and other services", "real estate", "manufacturing" and "mining" were relatively weak sectors (see Table 1.56).

Xinjiang

[Quick Facts: Official name: Xinjiang Uyghur Autonomous Region; Capital: Urumqi; Land area: 1,660,000 km^2; Population density: 12/km^2; Major ethnic groups: Uygur, Han, Kazak, Hui, Kirgiz]

Xinjiang Uyghur Autonomous Region is in the PRC. It is a large, sparsely populated area (comparable in size to Iran) which takes up about one-sixth of the country's territory. It borders Tibet Autonomous Region and India's Leh District to the south, and Qinghai and Gansu provinces to the southeast. The region shares a 5000 km land border with eight countries (including Mongolia to the northeast, Russia to the north, and Kazakhstan, Kyrgyzstan, Tajikistan, Afghanistan, Pakistan and India to the west). The name "Xinjiang", which was first given to it during the Qing Dynasty (AD 1644–1911), literally means "new frontier/territory". It has the abbreviated name "Jiang".

In ancient times, Xinjiang was known in China as the Western Territory. It is split by the Tian Shan mountain range. This east–west chain of mountains separate Dzungaria in the north from the Tarim Basin in the south. Dzungaria is dry steppe. The Tarim Basin is desert surrounded by oases. On the east side is the Turpan Depression, while the Tian Shan split in the west forms the Ili River Valley. Much of the Tarim Basin is dominated by the Taklamakan Desert. The lowest point in Xinjiang, and in the entire PRC, is the Turpan Depression, 155 m below sea level. Its highest point is the mountain K2, about 8611 m above sea level, on the border with Pakistan. Other mountain ranges include the Pamir Mountains to the southeast, the Karakoram to the south and the Altai Mountains to the north.

Xinjiang is the largest political subdivision of China. It is divided into 2 prefecture-level cities, 7 prefectures and 5 autonomous prefectures for Mongol, Kirgiz, Kazakh and Hui minorities. These are then divided into 11 districts, 20 county-level cities, 62 counties and 6 autonomous counties, then 5 sub-prefectural level cities (Aral, Beitun, Shihezi, Tumxuk and Wujiaq), which do not belong to any prefecture, are administered by the Xinjiang Production and Construction Corps (XPCC) —a de facto sub-provincial unit directly under Chinese central government. The Tian Shan mountain range marks the Xinjiang–Kyrgyzstan border at the Torugart Pass. The Karakorum Highway links Islamabad in Pakistan with Kashgar over the Khunjerab Pass.

About 68 million ha or 41.2 % of Xinjiang's total area are considered suitable for agriculture, forestry and animal husbandry. Of this there are some 48 million ha of natural grassland for grazing, 9 million hectare available for reclamation, over 4 million ha under cultivation and 666,700 ha of man-made pastures. The region is one of the country's five major grazing areas. In addition there are some 4.8 million hectare of land available for forestry, including 1.5 million hectare in production with reserves of some 250 million cubic meter of timber.

Fruits such as the Yili apple, Korla pear, seedless white grape and Hami melon are famous both locally and abroad. The region is famed for its unique natural environment and resources that nurture the growth of specific fruits which cannot be easily farmed elsewhere. Xinjiang is also China's largest and fastest-growing base for cotton, hops and lavender. Additionally, with the second largest pastureland in the country, the region is one of China's major sheep-farming areas and fine-wool production bases.

Among the 122 minerals that have been discovered in Xinjiang, several are the largest reserves nationwide. These include beryllium, muscovite, natron saltpeter, pottery clay and serpentine. Known reserves of iron ore are put at 730 million tons, while those for salt are 318 million tons, mirabilite 170 million tons and natron saltpeter over 2 million tons. With its deposits of more than 70 non-metallic minerals, the region is well known for its muscovite, gemstones, asbestos and Khotan (Hetian) jade. In addition, estimates put its coal reserves at more than one-third of the national total. Petroleum and natural gas reserves are estimated at 30 billion tons and account for more than 25 % of the national total. Xinjiang is noted for producing salt, soda, borax, gold, jade and coal. It is also known for its fruits and produce, including grapes, melons, pears, cotton, wheat, silk, walnuts and sheep.

Xinjiang has an annual runoff of some 88 billion cubic meter of surface water together with 25 billion cubic meter of exploitable groundwater. Glaciers covering 24,000 km^2 lock away over 2580 billion cubic meter of water.

Xinjiang is home to 699 species of wild fauna, including 85 species of fish, 7 species of amphibians, 45 species of reptiles and 137 species of mammals. More than 4000 species of wild flora have been identified, of which over 1000 varieties, such as bluish dogbane and Russian dandelion, are of significant economic value.

The region is home to a number of different ethnic groups, including the Uyghur, the Han, the Kazakh, the Hui, the Kyrgyz and the Mongol. These follow various religious traditions, with the majority of the population adhering to Islam. Afaq Khoja Mausoleum and Id Kah Mosque in Kashgar are among the most important Islamic sites in Xinjiang. Emin Minaret is another key Islamic site, in Turfan. Bezeklik Thousand Buddha Caves is a major Buddhist site. According to one source, more than 2 % of the population are Christians. Action against Christian activity tends to be stricter than in other parts of China. Home to 47 ethnic groups, a diverse range of religions co-exist there. Lamaism (Tibetan Buddhism), Islam, Buddhism, Taoism, Christianity, Catholicism, Eastern Orthodoxy and Shamanism all thrive side by side in the country's foremost multicultural melting pot.

Xinjiang has an abundance of valuable tourism resources and the region is notably famous for the ancient Silk Road. It is also home to 256 ancient cultural sites, tombs, ruins, Buddhist caves, stone sculptures and numerous contemporary monuments. Approximately 154 of the sites are under state protection. Popular scenic and historical attractions include Heavenly Lake, Bosteng Lake, Gaochang Ancient City and the ruins of Loulan.

The region's nominal GRP was ¥543.75 billion (about US$85 billion) in 2010. Southern Xinjiang, with its 95 % non-Han population, has an average per capita income half that of the area as a whole (Table 1.57).

Table 1.57 Demographic and socioeconomic profile: Xinjiang

Indicator	2000	2010
Population (thousands)	19,250	21,851
Illiteracy rate of population aged 15 or over (%)	5.56	2.36
GRP (¥ billions)	136.44	543.75
Composition of GRP (%)		
Primary sector	21.1	19.8
Secondary sector	43.0	47.7
Tertiary sector	35.9	32.5
Fixed asset investment (¥ billions)	61.04	342.32
Status of foreign-funded enterprises		
Number of registered enterprises	371	1,751
Total investment (US$ millions)	1143	5229
Registered capital (US$ millions)	749	3330
Foreign trade (US$ millions)		
Export	1147	12,555
Import	1439	8809
Sales of consumer goods (¥ billion)	37	138
Per capita annual disposable income of urban residents (¥)	5644.86	13,643.77
Engle's coefficient (%)	40.34	41.48
Per capita annual net income of rural residents (¥)	1618.08	4642.67
Engle's coefficient (%)	31.05	40.32
Number of patent applications granted	717	2562
Inventions	66	189
Utility models	475	2012
Designs	176	361

Note All monetary values are measured at current prices. *Source* Xinjiang Statistical Yearbook, 2001 and 2011

Thanks to its abundant reserves of coal, crude oil and natural gas on the one hand, and China's Western Development Policy introduced by the State Council on the other, Xinjiang has achieved rapid economic development during the past decade. Its GRP doubled between 2004 and 2010. The oil and gas extraction industry in Aksu and Karamay is booming, with the West–East Gas Pipeline connecting to Shanghai. The oil and petrochemical sector accounts for 60 % of the local economy.

The region has recently become one of the most important energy producers in China. While the discovery of natural resources has certainly been a boost for the province, these remain scattered about an uninhabited and undeveloped landscape. Development in the areas of production and transportation will be necessary to maximize the region's economic growth. In 2009 Xinjiang produced more natural gas than any other province, the fourth most crude oil in China and large amount of coal. It also has a thriving agriculture sector.

Ever since the initiation of China's opening-up and reform drive in 1979, the area's economy has been changed dramatically. Industry leads with a contribution

Table 1.58 Xinjiang's comparative (dis)advantage index by sector, 2010

Sector	Index
Agriculture, forestry, animal husbandry and fishery	7.95
Mining	1.60
Manufacturing	0.37
Production and distribution of electricity, gas and water	1.00
Construction	0.61
Transport, storage and post	0.90
Information transmission, computer service and software	0.51
Wholesale and retail trades	0.61
Hotels and catering services	0.56
Financial intermediation	0.78
Real estate	0.56
Leasing and business services	0.80
Scientific research, technical services and geological prospecting	0.84
Management of water conservancy, environment and public facilities	1.19
Services to households and other services	0.49
Education	1.10
Health, social security and social welfare	1.12
Culture, sports and entertainment	1.04
Public management and social organization	1.27

Notes All the sectors included in this table are determined according to China's official definitions and for urban areas only. Numerals greater than, equal to and less than one indicate that the province's sectors have advantages, no apparent (dis)advantages and disadvantages, respectively
Source Calculated by authors based on China Statistical Yearbook, 2011. See Appendix A for a detailed methodological description

of 47.7 % to the GRP. The service sector also makes a substantial contribution at 32.5 %; while agriculture contributes the remaining 19.8 %.

Urumqi, the capital city of Xinjiang, is the region's largest consumer center. Major department stores and shopping centers include Urumqi Tianshan Department Store, Urumqi Pacific Department Store and Urumqi Youhao Department Store. The French international hypermarket chain Carrefour has also established outlets and its northwest headquarters in the city.

Thanks to its wealth of natural resources, Xinjiang's well-developed industrial infrastructure focuses on a variety of industries, such as raw and refined oil, iron and steel, metallurgy, machinery, chemicals and power generation. The region's natural resources include coal, oil, iron, manganese, chromium, lead, molybdenum, zinc, beryllium, lithium, niobium, tantalum, cesium, white mica, asbestos and crystal. Oil and petrochemicals, food and beverages, textiles, metallurgy, building materials and electric power are the region's pillar industries of Xinjiang.

Most of the imports and exports are directed to and from Kazakhstan through the Ala Pass. China's first border free trade zone (Horgos Free Trade Zone) is located in the Xinjiang–Kazakhstan border city of Horgos. This is the largest "land port" in

China's western region and it has easy access to the Central Asian market. Xinjiang also opened its second border trade market to Kazakhstan in 2006, the Jeminay Border Trade Zone.

Major imports in the region include rolled steel, medical equipment, crude oil, oil products and fertilizers. Due to the area's sparse population and underdeveloped transport network, FDI remains relatively low. However, in recent years, growth in FDI has increased dramatically. The top three sectors that utilize the most foreign capital are manufacturing, mining and quarrying, and the production and distribution of electricity, gas and water. Denmark has injected the most FDI into the region. Other key sources are Australia, Hong Kong and Singapore.

As of 2010, compared with those of other provinces, "agriculture, forestry, animal husbandry and fishery", "mining" and "public management and social organization" were relatively strong, while "manufacturing", "services to households and other services" and "information transmission, computer service and software" were relatively weak sectors (see Table 1.58).

Yunnan

[Quick Facts: Official name: Yunnan Province; Capital: Kunming; Land area: 394,100 km^2; Population density: 112/km^2; Major ethnic groups: Han, Yi, Hani, Bai, Dai]

Yunnan is a province of the PRC, located in the far southwest of the country, with the Tropic of Cancer running through its southern part. The north of the province forms part of the Yunnan–Guizhou Plateau. The province borders Guangxi Zhuang Autonomous Region and Guizhou Province to the east, Sichuan Province to the north and Tibet Autonomous Region to the northwest. It shares 4060 km of land borders with Vietnam, Laos and Myanmar, and it is connected to Thailand and Cambodia via waterways. Yunnan has two abbreviated names: "Dian" and "Yun".

The region is situated in a mountainous area with high elevations in the northwest and low elevations in the southeast. Most of the population lives in the east. In the west, the relative height from mountain peaks to river valleys can be as much as 3000 m. There are a relatively large number of ethnic groups living in the province: 25 are found in Yunnan, which include Yi, Bai, Hani, Zhuang, the Dai, Miao, Lisu, Hui, Lahu, Va, Naxi, Yao, Tibetan, Jingpo and Blang. In its 16 prefecture-level divisions, it has 129 county-level divisions and 1455 township-level divisions

The area has a generally mild climate with pleasant weather because its location on south-facing mountain slopes, receiving the influence of both the Pacific and Indian oceans. The January average temperature is 8–17 °C and July is 21–27 °C. Average annual rainfall is 600–2300 mm, with over half falling between June and August. The plateau region has moderate temperatures. The western canyon region is hot and humid at the valley bottoms but freezing winds are common on the mountaintops.

More than 150 kinds of minerals have been discovered in 2700 places in the province. The most valuable proven deposits are of fuel and non-metallic minerals. Some 13 % of the proven deposits of minerals are the largest of their kind in China, and two-thirds are among the largest of their kind in the Yangtze River valley and in south China. Yunnan ranks first in the country with respect to deposits of zinc, lead, tin, cadmium, indium, thallium and crocidolite, and it has large deposits of iron, coal, lead, copper, gold, mercury, silver, antimony and sulfur. Gejiu city is well known as "the Kingdom of Zinc" with its reserves ranked first in the country. In addition, reserves of germanium, zirconium, platinum, rock salt, nickel, phosphate, arsenic and blue asbestos are also substantial.

The area is rich in natural resources and has the largest diversity of plant life in China. It has over 600 rivers and lakes, providing about 200 billion cubic meter of water supply per year, three times that of the Yellow River. The rivers flowing into the province from outside add 160 billion cubic meter. The rich water resources offer abundant hydro-energy.

Yunnan is known as the kingdom of plants and animals. At the end of 2005 there were 198 nature reserves, covering a total area of 3.55 million hectare. The province is China's most diverse, biologically as well as culturally. It contains snow-capped mountains and true tropical environments, thus supporting an unusually full spectrum of species and vegetation types. During the summer the Great Plateau of Tibet acts as a barrier to monsoon winds, trapping moisture in the province. This gives the alpine flora in particular what one source has called a "lushness found nowhere else".

This topographic range combined with tropical moisture sustains extremely high biodiversity and high degrees of endemism, probably the richest botanically in the world's temperate regions. The province not only has more plant species of tropical, subtropical, temperate and frozen zones than any other province in the country but also has many ancient, derivative plants, as well as species introduced from foreign countries. Among the 30,000 species of plants in China, 18,000 can be found in Yunnan. Some 144 species of plants are now under Class I and Class II protection.

Yunnan offers rich tourism resources, including beautiful landscape, colorful ethnic customs and a pleasant climate. Its most popular tourist spots include Kunming, Dali, Lijiang, Xishuangbanna and Shangri-la. Most visitors are Chinese tourists, although trips to Yunnan are organized by an increasing number of foreign travel agencies. Also a new trend is developing: small-scale ecotourism. UNESCO World Heritage Sites include the Old Town of Lijiang (accepted in 1997 as a cultural site), the Three Parallel Rivers of Yunnan Protected Areas (accepted in 2003 as a natural site) and the South China Karst (accepted in 2007 as a natural site).

Yunnan is one of China's relatively undeveloped areas with more poverty-stricken counties than other provinces. Its nominal GRP in 2010 was ¥722.42 billion (about US$110 billion). Its per capita GRP was ¥13,494 (about US$1975). The shares of GRP of Yunnan's primary, secondary and tertiary industries are 15.3, 44.6 and 40.0 %, respectively (see Table 1.59).

A poverty-alleviation plan includes five large projects aimed at improving infrastructure facilities. These include attempts at soil improvement, water conservation, electric power, roads and "green belt" building. The province hopes that this will alleviate the shortages of grain, water, electric power and roads.

Yunnan lags behind the east coast in relation to socioeconomic development. However, because of its geographic location it has comparative advantages in regional and border trade with countries in southeast Asia. The Lancang River (upper reaches of the Mekong River) is the waterway to Southeast Asia. In recent years, land transportation has been improved to strengthen economic and trade co-operation among countries in the Greater Mekong Subregion. Yunnan's abundance of resources means that its pillar industries are agriculture, tobacco, mining, hydroelectric power and tourism.

The main manufacturing industries are iron and steel production and copper smelting, commercial vehicles, chemicals, fertilizers, textiles and optical instruments. Tobacco is the biggest industry in Yunnan. Hongta Group is one of the most important tobacco-production bases and the nation's largest cigarette manufacturer.

Table 1.59 Demographic and socioeconomic profile: Yunnan

Indicator	2000	2010
Population (thousands)	42,880	46,016
Illiteracy rate of population aged 15 or over (%)	11.39	6.03
GRP (¥ billions)	195.51	722.42
Composition of GRP (%)		
Primary sector	22.3	15.3
Secondary sector	43.1	44.6
Tertiary sector	34.6	40.0
Fixed asset investment (¥ billions)	68.40	552.87
Status of foreign-funded enterprises		
Number of registered enterprises	1634	3833
Total investment (US$ millions)	4819	17,949
Registered capital (US$ millions)	3101	10,450
Foreign trade (US$ millions)		
Export	1093	5108
Import	791	5225
Sales of consumer goods (¥ billions)	58	250
Per capita annual disposable income of urban residents (¥)	6324.64	16,064.54
Engle's coefficient (%)	39.20	34.26
Per capita annual net income of rural residents (¥)	1478.60	3952.03
Engle's coefficient (%)	37.83	47.21
Number of patent applications granted	1217	3823
Inventions	140	652
Utility models	606	2026
Designs	471	1145

Note All monetary values are measured at current prices. *Source* Yunnan Statistical Yearbook, 2001 and 2011

With the imposition of tougher smoking regulations, this industry is stalling, as is its GRP growth. As a result there is a need to find a new economic driver.

The electricity industry is another important economic pillar of Yunnan and this plays a key role in the West-East Electricity Transmission Project. The electricity produced in the region is mainly transported to Guangdong Province. Production and supply of electricity, gas and water have the highest amount of fixed-asset investment. The other four industries with substantial investments in fixed assets are transport, storage and post, real estate, manufacturing, and water, environment and public facilities management.

The largest consumer center is in Kunming and a number of foreign retail enterprises have invested there. These include Wal-Mart from the US, Carrefour from France, and Price-Mart and Trust-Mart from Taiwan.

Yunnan is one of China's largest forest zones. Its forest area accounts for 24.2 % of the country's total. The province also yields a large number of plant and animal species, and these provide the foundation for its Chinese medicine and food industries. The flowers, tea leaves, fruits and vegetables of the province are well known.

Tobacco is the main export product and makes up a large part of the provincial GRP. Yunnan also has strong competitive potential in the fruit and vegetable industries, especially in low value-added commodities, such as fresh and dried vegetables and fresh apples.

The region is currently China's most important producer of Arabica coffee. Besides the export of roasted coffee, coffee-related products such as extracts, essences and substitutes may be promising products. Yunnan is the birthplace of tea and ancient tea trees can still be found there. Tea is becoming an important export product and in the US and Japan the demand is growing.

As a result of the country's growing consumption of dairy products (a trend heavily supported by national government), the province's dairy industry is developing rapidly and receiving large subsidies to develop a competitive edge in southwest China. Exports to its ASEAN neighbors are also planned.

A growing sector heavily supported by local government is horticulture. The flower industry in Yunnan started to develop towards the end of the 1980s. Currently it is the most important province nationwide in terms of flower growing. It accounts for 50 % of China's total cut-flower production. The size of the planting area for cut flowers in the province amounts to 4000 ha. Apart from sales on the domestic market, it also exports to a number of foreign countries and regions, such as Japan, Korea, Hong Kong, Thailand and Singapore. Rapid developments in this sector soon attracted the attention of Dutch horticultural companies, and Dutch investments in flower related projects and businesses are steadily growing.

The transport sector has maintained steady development. The area has more than 1700 km of railways (the Guiyang–Kunming, Chengdu–Kunming, Kunming–Hekou and Mengzi–Baoxiu railways) and a highway network of 44,000 km. The Jinsha, Nanpan, Yuanjiang and Lancang rivers are also navigable by boat. Telecommunications and postal services developed rapidly there.

The province has trade contacts with more than 70 countries and regions in the world. It established the Muse border trade zone (located in Ruili) along its border with Burma. It mainly exports tobacco, machinery and electrical equipment, chemical and agricultural products, and non-ferrous metals. ASEAN is the region's largest trading partner. Imports are mainly minerals, machinery and electrical appliances, electronics and telecommunications equipment. Major import sources include Hong Kong, the EU and Myanmar.

The largest investment is in manufacturing. Other areas include production and supply of electricity, gas and water, business services, and mining and quarrying. Hong Kong is the largest source of foreign investment in Yunnan. Hong Kong companies, such as New World, invested in the development of Chinese medicine there. Other major investors are Singapore, the US, the Virgin Islands and Taiwan.

As of 2010, compared with those of other provinces, "agriculture, forestry, animal husbandry and fishery", "education" and "public management and social organization" were relatively strong, while "services to households and other services", "manufacturing" and "information transmission, computer service and software" were relatively weak sectors (see Table 1.60).

Table 1.60 Yunnan's comparative (dis)advantage index by sector, 2010

Sector	Index
Agriculture, forestry, animal husbandry and fishery	1.56
Mining	1.09
Manufacturing	0.65
Production and distribution of electricity, gas and water	1.11
Construction	1.20
Transport, storage and post	0.86
Information transmission, computer service and software	0.76
Wholesale and retail trades	1.18
Hotels and catering services	1.12
Financial intermediation	0.78
Real estate	0.79
Leasing and business services	0.94
Scientific research, technical services and geological prospecting	0.86
Management of water conservancy, environment and public facilities	0.98
Services to households and other services	0.52
Education	1.32
Health, social security and social welfare	1.01
Culture, sports and entertainment	1.09
Public management and social organization	1.31

Notes All the sectors included in this table are determined according to China's official definitions and for urban areas only. Numerals greater than, equal to and less than one indicate that the province's sectors have advantages, no apparent (dis)advantages and disadvantages, respectively
Source Calculated by authors based on China Statistical Yearbook, 2011. See Appendix A for a detailed methodological description

Zhejiang

[Quick Facts: Official name: Zhejiang Province; Capital: Hangzhou; Land area: 101,800 km^2; Population density: 464/km^2; Major ethnic groups: Han, Miao, Tujia, She, Buyi]

Zhejiang is a province of the PRC, situated on China's southeastern coast, on the southern part of the Yangtze River Delta. It borders Jiangsu Province and Shanghai Municipality to the north, Anhui Province to the northwest, Jiangxi Province to the west and Fujian Province to the south. To the east is the East China Sea. The name Zhejiang ("crooked river") derives from the old name of the Qiantang River, which passes through Hangzhou, the provincial capital. The name is often abbreviated to "Zhe".

The territory slopes down from the southwest to the northeast. The former is mountainous with an average height of 800 m above sea level. Most of the province's mountains with a height of over 1500 m are found in this area. Huangmaojian in Longquan County, 1929 m above sea level, is the highest peak. The middle region is hilly and scattered with many large and small basins.

The northeast is a low, flat alluvial plain covered with a thick layer of fertile soil and crisscrossed with waterways. The mountain ranges stretch towards the East China Sea forming many peninsulas and islands.

Of its total land area, the mountainous and hilly regions account for 70.4 % and the plains and basins make up 23.2 %. The coastline stretches for 6486 km. Zhejiang has 3061 islands, the largest number in China. Its 11 administrative divisions are subdivided into 90 county-level divisions (32 districts, 22 county-level cities, 35 counties and 1 autonomous county). These are in turn divided into 1570 township-level divisions (761 towns, 505 townships, 14 ethnic townships and 290 sub-districts).

The region has a sub-tropical monsoon climate with four distinct seasons and abundant sunshine. Spring starts in March and is rainy with changeable weather. Summer, from June to September, is long, hot, rainy and humid. Autumn is generally dry, warm and sunny. Winter is short and cold, except in the far south. The average annual temperature is around 15–19 °C, with January temperatures around 2–8 °C and July temperatures around 27–30 °C. The annual precipitation is about 1000–1900 mm. There is plenty of rainfall in early summer, and by late summer the area is directly threatened by typhoons forming in the Pacific.

More than 100 minerals have been found in Zhejiang, including 12 non-metallic ones, ranking among the top three in China in terms of the size of reserves. Five new mineral reserves were proven in 2004. Its reserves of stone coal, alunite, pyrophyllite, limestone for cement-making and limestone for construction rank first in the country. Fluorite occupies second place in China and diatomite third. The reserves of silica, pearlite, granite, zeolite, silver, zinc, vanadium and cadmium rank among the country's top ten.

The province has a coastline (including island lines) of 6486 km with a domestic sea area of 30,900 km^2. It has the country's largest in-shore fishery, with 400 km^2 of shallow sea and 2886 m^2 of low beach for aquaculture. In addition the continental shelf of the East China Sea is rich in petroleum and natural gas.

Zhejiang is famed as "a treasure house of plants in southeastern China" with substantial forest coverage. It has as many as 3800 species of plants. Among these, gingko and more than 50 others are listed as rare plants under state protection. There are more than 1900 species of wild animals in the province, 120 of which are listed as the first or second grade of wild animals under state protection, making up on-third of China's total protected rare animals.

Zhejiang is a favored tourist destination. It has 11 state-level scenic areas, including West Lake, Fuchun River, Xin'an River, Thousand-islet Lake, Mount Yantang, Nanxi River, Mount Putuo, the Shengsi Islands, Mount Tiantai, Mount Mogan, Mount Xuedou, Twin-Dragon Cave and Mount Xiandu, in addition to 35 province-level scenic spots. The Hangzhou River is a national holiday resort, and ten other resorts, including Lake Xianghu in Xiaoshan, Oujiang River in Wenzhou and Mount Huiji in Shaoxing, are of provincial level. The Surging Qiantang Tides, a unique natural site, attracts numerous visitors from both home and abroad.

Longjing tea (also called "dragon well tea"), originating in Hangzhou, is one of the most famous Chinese teas. Hangzhou is also renowned for its silk umbrellas and hand fans. Zhejiang cuisine (subdivided into many traditions, including Hangzhou cuisine) is one of the eight great traditions of Chinese cuisine.

Zhejiang's nominal GRP for 2010 was ¥2.78 trillion (about US$402 billion) with a per capita GRP of ¥44,335 (about US$6490). After more than 20 years of development since the reforms and opening-up of China, the province now has a strong economy, with industry as its leading sector. It has become one of the most commercial and richest provinces in China. Compared with many other regions, the development of different areas in Zhejiang is more balanced (Table 1.61).

The fourth largest economy and the third largest exporter in China, the region leads all provinces in rankings of GRP per capita in both urban and rural areas. As a result of local government's business-friendly policies, this region witnessed the success of thousands of small and medium-sized enterprises. Compared with the rest of the country, people in Zhejiang are the most entrepreneurial, which has also helped the province to achieve a small urban-to-rural income gap.

Table 1.61 Demographic and socioeconomic profile: Zhejiang

Indicator	2000	2010
Population (thousands)	46,770	54,465
Illiteracy rate of population aged 15 or over (%)	7.06	5.62
GRP (¥ billions)	603.63	2772.23
Composition of GRP (%) Primary sector Secondary sector Tertiary sector	11.0 52.7 36.3	4.9 51.6 43.5
Fixed asset investment (¥ billions)	235.00	1237.60
Status of foreign-funded enterprises Number of registered enterprises Total investment (US$ millions) Registered capital (US$ millions)	10,002 29,313 17,122	28,769 183,233 106,942
Foreign trade (US$ millions) Export Import	20,482 11,040	200,944 86,306
Sales of consumer goods (¥ billions)	230	1025
Per capita annual disposable income of urban residents (¥) Engle's coefficient (%)	9279.16 34.46	27,359.02 30.09
Per capita annual net income of rural residents (¥) Engle's coefficient (%)	4253.67 37.72	11,302.55 34.22
Number of patent applications granted Inventions Utility models Designs	7495 184 3439 3872	114,643 6410 47,617 60,616

Note All monetary values are measured at current prices. *Source* Zhejiang Statistical Yearbook, 2001 and 2011

An important maker of electronics and other equipment, its manufacturers have a significant competitive advantage: a combination of low prices, cheap labor, low resource costs and high volumes. However, as other provinces become cheaper, Zhejiang's growth is shrinking and structural reform is needed. Additionally, high incomes and limited investment choices have resulted in high property costs.

Rice is the area's main crop, followed by wheat. North Zhejiang is also a center of aquaculture, and the Zhoushan fishery is the largest in the country. The main cash crops include jute and cotton, and the region also leads the provinces of China in tea production. (The renowned Longjing tea is a product of Hangzhou.) The region's towns are known for the hand production of goods such as silk, for which it is ranked second among the provinces. Its many market towns connect the cities with the countryside.

Southern Zhejiang was traditionally poor and underdeveloped due to its mountainous geography. Economic reforms of the late 1970s brought huge changes to the region. However, the private sector has seen rapid growth, especially in the cities of Wenzhou, Ningbo and Shaoxing. The region, together with the more developed north Zhejiang, has helped the province to leapfrog over other regions and become one of the richest in China.

The main manufacturing sectors are electromechanical industries, textiles, food and construction materials. In recent years the province has followed its own development model, dubbed the "Zhejiang model", which is based on prioritizing and encouraging entrepreneurship, an emphasis on small businesses responsive to the whims of the market, large public investments in infrastructure, and the production of low-cost goods in bulk for both domestic consumption and export. As a result it has made itself one of the richest provinces, and the "Zhejiang spirit" has become something of a legend within the country. It encourages and gives autonomy to township enterprises. Although being the majority shareholder of many township enterprises, local government normally refrains from intervening in their investment and operation decisions. Completely independent, they are essentially the same as private enterprises.

In the past, light industry played a major role in the economy. However, fuelled by the development of the economy and foreign investment, the industrial structure has changed since 2003. In 2006, heavy industry contributed 56.4 % of the total value-added industrial output in Zhejiang. The four pillar industries are textiles, electrical equipment and machinery, power, and general-purpose equipment manufacturing. The province has always been the leading textile and garment production base in China. It is the second largest producer in the country with about 20 % market share, while its rival, Guangdong Province, took 26 % in 2006. In addition, it is a major export market for textiles and garments.

Compared with Guangdong, Zhejiang has an advantage in terms of labor costs as it is equipped to draw on low-cost labor from neighboring provinces, such as Anhui and Jiangxi. It has a more convenient and cheaper transportation system than Guangdong. The province also has five ports in Ningbo, Zhoushan, Zhapu, Haimen and Wenzhou. Famous garment producers include Younger, Meters Bonwe, Shan Shan, Langsha and Peacebird. Most of the textile and garment enterprises are located in Ningbo, Wenzhou, Shaoxing and Hangzhou.

The electronics industry is a fast-growing sector in the region. Zhejiang has set up a relatively strong industrial base in this. Hangzhou, Ningbo, Jiaxing and Shaoxing are major production bases of electronic products. Geely Group is a major contributor to the auto industry there. It is a private enterprise, located in Hangzhou, with four manufacturing bases in Linhai, Ningbo, Taizhou and Shanghai, specializing in the production of auto parts. The company was among the first batch of automakers that launched self-developed brands. It is one of the fastest-growing automakers in China. While it started out as a refrigerator manufacturer in 1986, the company moved to motorcycle manufacturing in 1994 and commenced auto production in 1998.

Zhejiang has more than 1000 software enterprises with over 50,000 employees. Famous software enterprises include Insigma Technology, Alibaba.com Corporation, Huansun Technology and SUPCON Group. In 2007 the Hangzhou-based e-business provider Alibaba was listed on the Hong Kong Stock Exchange, raising a sum of US$1.7 billion. This is a record high for an internet company from

Table 1.62 Zhejiang's comparative (dis)advantage index by sector, 2010

Sector	Index
Agriculture, forestry, animal husbandry and fishery	0.06
Mining	0.05
Manufacturing	1.43
Production and distribution of electricity, gas and water	0.60
Construction	2.10
Transport, storage and post	0.59
Information transmission, computer service and software	0.89
Wholesale and retail trades	0.86
Hotels and catering services	1.10
Financial intermediation	0.92
Real estate	0.95
Leasing and business services	1.24
Scientific research, technical services and geological prospecting	0.71
Management of water conservancy, environment and public facilities	0.74
Services to households and other services	0.40
Education	0.57
Health, social security and social welfare	0.76
Culture, sports and entertainment	0.70
Public management and social organization	0.60

Notes All the sectors included in this table are determined according to China's official definitions and for urban areas only. Numerals greater than, equal to and less than one indicate that the province's sectors have advantages, no apparent (dis)advantages and disadvantages, respectively
Source Calculated by authors based on China Statistical Yearbook, 2011. See Appendix A for a detailed methodological description

mainland China. Other industries dealing with software, IT service outsourcing and on-line games provided by Zhejiang enterprises have also expanded quickly.

The province has four major ports. Among them, the Ningbo-Zhoushan Port is the largest iron ore and oil transshipment base in China. Together with Shanghai Port, Zhejiang is the gateway to the world for China. Ningbo, Wenzhou, Taizhou and Zhoushan are important commercial ports. The Hangzhou Bay Bridge between Haiyan County and Cixi is the longest bridge over a continuous body of seawater in the world.

Zhejiang is also a major player in China's foreign trade. Exports include machinery and electronic products. Private companies and foreign invested enterprises are the major exporters and the key export destinations include the EU, the US and Japan, while the main import sources are Japan, Korea and Taiwan.

At the same time, a lot of foreign investment has rushed into the area. Most of the investments have been injected into the developed regions of the province, such as Hangzhou, Ningbo, Shaoxing, Jiaxing, Huzhou and Zhoushan. Among the various sectors, manufacturing (specifically textiles, chemicals, mechanical and electronics industries) has attracted the most foreign investment.

As of 2010, compared with those of other provinces, “construction”, “manufacturing” and “leasing and business services” were relatively strong, while “mining”, “agriculture, forestry, animal husbandry and fishery” and “services to households and other services” were relatively weak sectors (see Table 1.62).

Chapter 2
Interprovincial Cooperation and Development

Anhui-Beijing

[Quick Facts] Average distance = 1074 km; Geographical adjacency = 0; Index of ethnic linkages = 0.9636 (2000) and 0.9658 (2010); Freight exchange via national railway = 370 k tons (2000) and 350 k tons (2010). ★ September 4, 2004, the Huayuan Pharmaceutical Co., Ltd. of Anhui Province establishes a marketing branch in the Miyun Industrial Development Zone of Beijing Municipality. April 2, 2006, in order to serve the common development of Anhui-funded enterprises in Beijing, the Anhui Chamber of Commerce in Beijing is established; in the first member congress, the board of supervisors and the leadership of the chamber are elected. May 11, 2007, the government officials of Anhui Province visit Beijing Municipality and hold discussions with members of the Anhui Chamber of Commerce in Beijing, calling for all Anhui business personnel working in Beijing to actively contribute to the social capacity building of and the economic development of Anhui Province. April 26–28, 2009, in order to strengthen the bilateral trade and economic cooperation between Anhui Province and Beijing Municipality, the Anhui provincial government invites Deputy Mayor of Beijing Municipality as a special envoy to attend the "Fourth Central China Investment and Trade Fair" held in Hefei City, Anhui Province. November 3, 2009, the Tongling Nonferrous Metals Holding Company of Anhui and the Beijing Research Institute of Mining and Metallurgy sign an agreement concerning the establishment of a joint venture in Anhui and other issues relating to their bilateral cooperation.

Anhui-Chongqing

[Quick Facts] Average distance = 1562 km; Geographical adjacency = 0; Index of ethnic linkages = 0.9366 (2000) and 0.9343 (2010); Freight exchange via national railway = 140 k tons (2000) and 290 k tons (2010). ★ March 10, 2000, the Three

R. Guo et al., *Multiregional Economic Development in China*,
DOI 10.1007/978-3-662-46620-9_2

Gorges Project Construction Committee (TGPCC) of the State Council approves the notice of the Resettlement and Development Bureau of the TGPCC concerning the "Management Measures of Resettlement Fund for the Rural Migrants in the Reservoir Area of the Three Gorges". The notice includes a working schedule for the resettlement of a portion of Chongqing's rural population in Anhui Province. May 12, 2006, after approved by the Chongqing Municipal Bureau of Civil Affairs, the Anhui Chamber of Commerce in Chongqing is established. The chamber has more than 300 member enterprises, involving elevator, building security intelligence, food, packaging, automotive modification and sales, real estate, architectural design, building materials, medical, logistics, tourism, trade, investment, legal services and other industries, with the total economic value of more than 30 billion yuan. November 27, 2006, Anhui and Chongqing decide to comprehensively upgrade their bilateral cooperative partnerships; Anhui Province has now about 200,000 people working in and more than 2000 enterprises registered at Chongqing Municipality. May 9–17, 2011, Anhui's provincial inspectors visit Chongqing Municipality and exchange experiences in (i) the enforcement and supervision of administrative law; (ii) the management of certification and documentation; (iii) the standardization of execution and the improvement of legislative work; and (iv) others.

Anhui-Fujian

[Quick Facts] Average distance = 1196 km; Geographical adjacency = 0; Index of ethnic linkages = 0.9870 (2000) and 0.9828 (2010); Freight exchange via national railway = 2100 k tons (2000) and 1960 k tons (2010). ★ August 23, 2007, in order to better serve the common development of Anhui-funded enterprises in Fujian, the Anhui Chamber of Commerce in Fujian is established—it is the first chamber of commerce approved by the Federation of Industry and Commerce of Fujian Province; now the Chamber has a total number of 480 enterprise members. May 12, 2008, the Fujian Chamber of Commerce in Anhui is established in Hefei City. There are nearly 50,000 Fujian merchants living in Anhui, mainly engaged in real estate, electronic communications, automotive parts, iron and steel metallurgy, building materials, and chemistry. August 12, 2009, Anhui and Fujian Provinces signs an agreement on the mutual recognition of quality supervision, which aims to establish a mutually recognized system by which to issue the safety certificates on foods and agricultural products, market access and joint action between the two provinces. March 5, 2011, the ICBC Fujian Branch and the Anhui Chamber of Commerce in Fujian sign an agreement on bank-enterprise cooperation. April 2–3, 2012, the Fuyang municipal government of Anhui Province and the Administrative Committee of the Fuyang Development Zone organize, in Quanzhou City of Fujian Province, an investment promotion and an illustration meeting of investment environment in Fuyang City. December 17–18, 2012, Anhui's provincial officials in charge of regional economic coordination attend a conference titled "China Regional Economic Development and Cooperation" held in Fuzhou City and pay a special trip to Xiamen and Quanzhou Cities to meet the government department of Xiamen and visit the Anhui Chambers of Commerce in both Xiamen and Quanzhou Cities.

Anhui-Gansu

[Quick Facts] Average distance = 1832 km; Geographical adjacency = 0; Index of ethnic linkages = 0.9190 (2000) and 0.9119 (2010); Freight exchange via national railway = 380 k tons (2000) and 1080 k tons (2010). ★ August 9, 2010, in order to serve the common development of Anhui-funded enterprises in Gansu, the Anhui Chamber of Commerce in Gansu is established. The Chamber is composed of 210 enterprise members, 500 individual members, 26 standing members, 26 deputy presidents as well as one president. December 26, 2011, the Bank of Lanzhou approves 500 million yuan of credit limits to support the development of the Anhui Chamber of Commerce in Gansu. June 4, 2012, staff of the Anhui Energy Co. (Group) Ltd. and officials of Anhui Province visit Gansu Province, and participate in the "Anhui-Gansu Forum for Economic and Social Development and Cooperation" held in Lanzhou City, Gansu Province. During the meeting, Gansu and Anhui Provinces sign a memorandum of strategic cooperation and announce a number of sister cities between the two provinces. June 2–7, 2012, a large business delegation, with more than 1800 people and led by the Anhui provincial government, visits Lanzhou City and organizes a series of activities on the Anhui-Gansu cooperation. During this period, the "Anhui's Famous Products" fair is held in the Gansu International Convention and Exhibition Center; and the agreements of 16 large joint and cooperative projects, totaling to 20 billion yuan of investment, are reached between Anhui and Gansu Provinces.

Anhui-Guangdong

[Quick Facts] Average distance = 1826 km; Geographical adjacency = 0; Index of ethnic linkages = 0.9864 (2000) and 0.9818 (2010); Freight exchange via national railway = 1420 k tons (2000) and 1170 k tons (2010). ★ March 22, 2004, Anhui and Guangdong Provinces decide to establish cooperative partnerships, with 311 projects being proposed by both sides; in addition, the cities and prefectures of Anhui bring thousands of investment projects to seek cooperation with Guangzhou, Foshan, Dongguan and Shenzhen Cities of Guangdong. December 22, 2008, the Guangdong Chamber of Commerce in Anhui is established in Hefei City. The Chamber has more than 500 member enterprises, involving real estate, electronic industry, auto parts, agricultural products processing, tourism, business, and trade service, with a total investment of 300 billion yuan. August 12, 2009, Anhui and Guangdong Provinces sign an agreement on the mutual recognition of quality supervision, which aims to establish a mutually recognized system by which to issue the safety certificates on foods and agricultural products, market access and joint action between the two provinces. July 30–31, 2011, the "Anhui-Guangdong Trade and Economic Cooperation Achievements Exhibition", the "Guangdong's Famous Products Fair" and the "Anhui-Guangdong Economic Development and Trade Cooperation Conference" open simultaneously in the Anhui International Convention and Exhibition Center, in which 864 joint and cooperative projects (with a total investment of 760 billion yuan) are contracted between Anhui and Guangdong Provinces. July 24, 2012, the Anhui Chamber of Commerce in Guangdong is the established in Guangzhou City. October 29, 2012, Anhui and Guangdong Provinces sign a strategic framework agreement of economic and social cooperation; the government delegation of Anhui Province also conducts inspections to Guangdong's local developments, and discuss with Guangdong Province about a win-win interprovincial cooperation.

Anhui-Guangxi

[Quick Facts] Average distance = 2098 km; Geographical adjacency = 0; Index of ethnic linkages = 0.6179 (2000) and 0.6301 (2010); Freight exchange via national railway = 480 k tons (2000) and 1010 k tons (2010). ★ November 10, 2007, the Anhui Chamber of Commerce in Guangxi, under the Federation of Industry and Commerce of Guangxi Zhuang Autonomous Region, celebrates its inauguration in Nanning City; the chamber aims to build an exchange platform for the governments and enterprises of and to promote economic and trade cooperation between Anhui and Guangxi. August 3, 2010, a delegation of Bengbu City, Anhui Province, after two years of cooperation, pays a field trip to Liuzhou city, Guangxi Autonomous Region, and to the Liugong Group to seek deeper bilateral cooperation. October 21, 2010, a delegation led by the Governor of Anhui Province attends the "China-ASEAN Expo" held in Nanning City of Guangxi and discusses, with the Governor of Guangxi, the potentials of bilateral complementarities and cooperation. May 19, 2011, the Nanshan Enterprise and the Guangxi Liugong Machinery Co., Ltd. successfully reach an agreement on strategic cooperation. September 20, 2011, after many joint efforts, the Anhui Conch Group and the Guangxi Sihe Industrial and Trade Company meet in Anhui Province and sign a cooperation agreement between the two companies. August 2, 2012, a ten-people delegation, led by the Deputy Mayor (also the CCP Standing Member) of Xuancheng City (Anhui Province) and the General Manager of the Land Reclamation (Group) Co. Ltd. of Anhui Province, visits Guangxi and pays an inspection to Guangxi's land reclamation.

Anhui-Guizhou

[Quick Facts] Average distance = 2076 km; Geographical adjacency = 0; Index of ethnic linkages = 0.6274 (2000) and 0.6611 (2010); Freight exchange via national railway = 170 k tons (2000) and 540 k tons (2010). ★ March 27, 2010, in order to serve the common development of Anhui-funded enterprises in Guizhou, the Anhui Chamber of Commerce in Guizhou is established. According to incomplete statistics, the number of the Anhui-funded enterprises registered at and of the Anhui people working in Guizhou have reached 2000 and 100,000, respectively. January 7, 2011, the Anhui Tobacco Industry Company and the Guizhou Tobacco Monopoly Administration (Company) sign a framework agreement in Hefei City of Anhui Province, which is intended to strengthen the tobacco strategic cooperation between the two sides. August 20, 2011, leaders of Anhui Province visit the China (Guizhou) International Wine Fair, and help to reach a number of agreements on the establishment of joint and cooperative ventures between several Anhui-based enterprises and Bijie Prefecture of Guizhou Province. November 24, 2011, the Anhui Huayuan Pharmaceutical Co., Ltd. and the Guizhou Jiean Pharmaceutical Group signs a strategic cooperation agreement in Guiyang, Guizhou Province. June 15, 2012, the Anhui Chamber of Commerce in Guizhou launches the "harmony, sincerity, development and win-win" philosophy, aiming to strengthen the exchange and cooperation between the Anhui businesspersons working in Guizhou Province.

Anhui-Hainan

[Quick Facts] Average distance = 2448 km; Geographical adjacency = 0; Index of ethnic linkages = 0.8283 (2000) and 0.8380 (2010); Freight exchange via national railway = 0 k ton (2000) and 10 k tons (2010). ★ October 18, 2005, in order to improve their traffic environments, Anqing City of Anhui Province and the Hainan Airlines Group sign a strategic cooperative agreement concerning the organizational restructuring and the opening of new routes in Hainan's airports. May 12, 2006, in order to serve the common development of Anhui-funded enterprises in Hainan, the Anhui Chamber of Commerce in Hainan is established in Haikou City. September 6, 2010, the Anhui Chamber of Commerce in Hainan convenes an academic conference on the theme entitled "Anhui Merchants' Culture, Spirit of Entrepreneurs and Construction of the International Tourism Island". April 26–27, 2012, organized by the Office of Cooperation and Exchange of Anhui Province and the Anhui Chamber of Commerce in Hainan, the "2012 National Conference of the Joint Chairpersons of Offsite Chambers of Commerce" is held in Haikou City, Hainan Province. June 15, 2012, the Anhui Chamber of Commerce in Hainan is invited to develop a large real-estate project in Haikou City. The project, which includes 134,770 mu of land, aims to speed up the construction of international tourist sites in Hainan and to promote the development of Hainan's tourist resources.

Anhui-Hebei

[Quick Facts] Average distance = 914 km; Geographical adjacency = 0; Index of ethnic linkages = 0.9631 (2000) and 0.9647 (2010); Freight exchange via national railway = 920 k tons (2000) and 1650 k tons (2010). ★ January 16, 2008, in order to serve the common development of Anhui-funded enterprises in Hebei, the Anhui Chamber of Commerce in Hebei in established in Shijiazhuang City. January 27, 2011, the AQTSs of Anhui and Hebei Provinces sign a "Memorandum of Understanding Concerning the Cooperation in Quality and Technical Supervision" in Shijiazhuang City, Hebei Province. October 27, 2011, the Huainan Mining Group of Anhui Province signs a strategic cooperation agreement with the Hebei Ports (Group) Company, which is intended to strengthen bilateral cooperation in coal transportation, personnel exchange and other technological management. December 2, 2011, the Hebei Chamber of Commerce in Anhui, which is initiated by nearly 300 Hebei-funded enterprises in Anhui, starts to run in Hefei City, Anhui Province. The establishment of the chamber will help Hebei's entrepreneurs working in Anhui to build a wide platform for economic cooperation between Anhui and Hebei. April 11, 2012, the Seed Company of Anhui and the Cotton Research Institute of Hebei Academy of Agricultural Sciences sign, in Shijiazhuang City, Hebei Province, an agreement on bilateral technological cooperation.

Anhui-Heilongjiang

[Quick Facts] Average distance = 2227 km; Geographical adjacency = 0; Index of ethnic linkages = 0.9554 (2000) and 0.9673 (2010); Freight exchange via national railway = 590 k tons (2000) and 1620 k tons (2010). ★ September 13, 2005, Anhui and Heilongjiang Provinces sign a tourist cooperation agreement, which aims to strengthen the bilateral cooperation and further promote the development of tourism of the two provinces. September 16, 2005, a key activity of Anhui's landscape and cultural tourist promotion, entitled "Experiencing Anhui in 2005", is successfully conducted in Harbin City, capital of Heilongjiang Province. This activity aims to promote exchange and cooperation between Anhui and Heilongjiang Provinces, as well as to show Anhui's beautiful landscapes and rich cultural heritages and to attract more tourists from Heilongjiang to spend holidays in Anhui. April 17, 2008, the No. 1 Construction and Engineering Company of Heilongjiang Province creates a sub-company in Hefei City, capital of Anhui Province. November 8, 2008, the BeiDaHuang Company of Heilongjiang Province decides to develop projects in Hefei City. The Hefei municipal government and the Land Reclamation Administration of Heilongjiang Province reach a preliminary agreement on the cooperation between the two sides. March 21, 2012, a 271-entrepreneur delegation, led by the President of the Anhui Chamber of Commerce in Jiangsu, visits Heilongjiang to participate in the "Project Cooperation and Exchange Promotion for Heilongjiang and Other Provinces' Entrepreneurs" held in Harbin City. The Heilongjiang provincial government and its local governments offer nearly 400 projects, covering food, raw materials, consumers' goods, petro-chemistry, electronics, pharmaceutics, etc., with a total value of 161 billion yuan.

Anhui-Henan

[Quick Facts] Average distance = 645 km; Geographical adjacency = 1; Index of ethnic linkages = 0.9940 (2000) and 0.9942 (2010); Freight exchange via national railway = 3660 k tons (2000) and 6540 k tons (2010). ★ March 6, 2008, the Anhui Chamber of Commerce in Henan is established in Zhengzhou City. October 25–28, 2010, the "2010 Annual Academic Conference" is jointly organized by the Association of Libraries of Henan Province and Anhui Province in Zhengzhou City, Henan Province. This conference is intended to develop the interprovincial cooperation and exchange of libraries. April 16, 2011, the Henan Chamber of Commerce in Anhui is established in Hefei City. Henan's enterprises in Anhui involve real estate, construction, electricity, clothing, medicine, communication, investment, and financial services. June 8, 2011, the second session of the "Joint Conference of the Security Cooperation between the Five Central Provinces" is held in Changsha; Anhui, Henan and other three provinces reach multilateral commitments to cross-provincial security cooperation. July 4, 2011, Luyi County of Henan Province carries out exchange and cooperation with Yingshang County of Anhui Province, in the hopes that all the local tourist resources can be spatially optimized and that the joint development of tourism can result in common prosperity for the two inter-provincial counties. November 26, 2011, Zhoukou City of Henan Province and Fuyang City of Anhui Province sign a "Tourist Cooperation Agreement", which aims to strengthen the bilateral tourist cooperation between and to promote the win-win tourist development of the two provinces. May 29, 2012, the Population and Family Planning Commission (PFPC) of Tanghe County of Henan Province visits Dingyuan County of Anhui Province and discusses with the PFPC of Dingyuan County concerning the comprehensive gender management of births, and signs an agreement of cooperation.

Anhui-Hubei

[Quick Facts] Average distance = 1181 km; Geographical adjacency = 1; Index of ethnic linkages = 0.9585 (2000) and 0.9591 (2010); Freight exchange via national railway = 820 k tons (2000) and 4360 k tons (2010). ★ November 25, 2009, the first "Directors' Meeting of the Union of Anhui Enterprises in Hubei Province" is held in Wuhan City. June 8, 2011, the second session of the "Joint Conference of the Security Cooperation between the Five Central Provinces" is held in Changsha;

Anhui, Hubei, and other three provinces reach multilateral commitments to cross-provincial security cooperation. February 4, 2012, the Communication Departments of Anhui, Hubei and other provinces in the middle reaches of the Yangtze River jointly sign an agreement concerning the joint construction of cross-provincial transport network. March 30, 2012, the Tiantangzhai (paradise castle) Scenic Areas of Anhui and Hubei Provinces sign the "one ticket for two places" agreement. This is the first cross-border cooperation between Anhui and Hubei Provinces after the "Tiantangzhai" trademark dispute occurred eight years ago. April 12–13, 2012, the CCP and government delegation of Anhui Province pays an inspection to Hubei Province and holds a "Conference of the Anhui-Hubei Economic and Social Exchange and Development" in Hubei, pledging to promote a wider and higher level interprovincial cooperation in order to achieve the economic rising of the two central provinces.

Anhui-Hunan

[Quick Facts] Average distance = 1222 km; Geographical adjacency = 0; Index of ethnic linkages = 0.9012 (2000) and 0.9028 (2010); Freight exchange via national railway = 480 k tons (2000) and 3080 k tons (2010). ★ August 21, 2008, the Hunan Chamber of Commerce in Anhui is established in Hefei city. The Chamber has more than 160 member enterprises, involving construction, real estate, dining, etc., with a total asset of over 10 billion yuan. May 9–17, 2011, Anhui's provincial inspectors visit Hunan Province, aiming to exchange experiences in (i) the enforcement and supervision of administrative law; (ii) the management of certification and documentation; (iii) the standardization of execution and the improvement of legislative work; and (iv) others. June 8, 2011, the second session of the "Joint Conference of the Security Cooperation between the Five Central Provinces" is held in Changsha; Anhui, Hunan, and three other provinces reach multilateral commitments to cross-provincial security cooperation. February 4, 2012, the Communication Departments of Anhui, Hunan and other provinces in the middle reaches of the Yangtze River jointly sign an agreement concerning the joint construction of cross-provincial transport network. May 16, 2012, the Anhui Chamber of Commerce in Hunan is established in Changsha City. The Chamber has 58 members, mainly engaged in real estate, clothing design and manufacturing, IT industry, media, petro-chemistry, machinery manufacturing, tourism, food processing, building materials, logistics, catering service, and biological medicine. May 19, 2012, Anhui and Hunan Provinces discuss the cultural tourist cooperation plan, in the hope that Anhui and Hunan can work together to build a higher level of partnerships in the development of cultural and tourist industries. May 21, 2012, Anhui and Hunan Provinces sign a framework agreement on cultural cooperation and jointly establish a regular conference system by which to strengthen their interprovincial cultural exchange.

Anhui-Inner Mongolia

[Quick Facts] Average distance = 1777 km; Geographical adjacency = 0; Index of ethnic linkages = 0.7984 (2000) and 0.8018 (2010); Freight exchange via national railway = 470 k tons (2000) and 910 k tons (2010). ★ November 28, 2004, the Anhui Chamber of Commerce in Inner Mongolia is established in Hohhot City. September 23, 2011, leaders of the AQTS of Inner Mongolia Autonomous Region are invited to attend a signing ceremony in Hefei City, Anhui Province. The QSBs of Inner Mongolia and Anhui sign the cooperation agreement of the quality and technical supervision. October 16–20, 2011, the People's Governments of the Inner Mongolia Autonomous Region and Anhui Province hold a meeting in Ordos City, Inner Mongolia. The two sides hope to strengthen exchange and deepen cooperation between the two provincial economies. November 1, 2011, the Tongling Non-ferrous Metals Group of Anhui Province and Xingan Meng (or League—a prefecture level administration established in China's ethnic minority areas) of and the Non-ferrous Geological Exploration Bureau of Inner Mongolia sign a trilateral cooperation agreement in Tongling City of Anhui Province. November 9, 2011, the leaders of the Zhungeer Qi (or Banner—a county-level administration established in China's ethnic minority areas) of Inner Mongolia pay an inspection to the Huainan Chemical Group of Anhui Province. The two sides pledge to cooperate in the joint R&D of coal-chemical and other high-end, coal-related products.

Anhui-Jiangsu

[Quick Facts] Average distance = 312 km; Geographical adjacency = 1; Index of ethnic linkages = 0.9960 (2000) and 0.9961 (2010); Freight exchange via national railway = 20,210 k tons (2000) and 25,910 k tons (2010). ★ December 18, 2006, the People's Governments of Anhui and Jiangsu Provinces sign, in Nanjing City, an agreement concerning the further strengthening of interprovincial cooperation in the developments of regional communication and transportation infrastructures. December 2006, the Anhui Chamber of Commerce in Wuxi of Jiangsu is established. The Chamber has more than 150 member enterprises. According to statistic, there are more than 100,000 Anhui people invest in Wuxi City, of which about 500 are large-scale enterprises. December 20, 2008, the Jiangsu Chamber of Commerce in Anhui Province is established in Hefei, aiming to strengthen the development of the trans-Yangtze River delta and of the surrounding areas. March 30, 2009, the Anhui Chamber of Commerce in Suzhou City is established. The Chamber has 359 member enterprises, with an annual output value of more than 10 billion yuan. December 15, 2009, the Anhui Chamber of Commerce in Zhenjiang City is established. November 2, 2010, the public security departments of Anhui, Jiangsu, Zhejiang and Shanghai sign an agreement in Shanghai, which aims to coordinate the four provinces' security affairs. January 10, 2011, the Anhui Chamber of

Commerce in Jiangsu is established in Nanjing City. August 31, 2011, the first meeting of social security cooperation and development in the trans-Yangtze River delta opens in Nanjing, in which Anhui, Shanghai, Zhejiang and Jiangsu jointly establish an expert team to deal with social security cooperation. April 22, 2012, the No. 1 Engineering Company of the China Energy Construction (Anhui) and the State Power Solar (Jiangsu) Co., Ltd. sign a strategic cooperation agreement in Hefei City, Anhui Province.

Anhui-Jiangxi

[Quick Facts] Average distance = 478 km; Geographical adjacency = 1; Index of ethnic linkages = 0.9944 (2000) and 0.9945 (2010); Freight exchange via national railway = 2510 k tons (2000) and 8350 k tons (2010). ★ August 2008, the Anhui Chamber of Commerce in Jiangxi is established in Nanchang City. The Chamber has more than 300 member enterprises, involving textile, printing, building materials real estate, car, education, financial services, advertising, landscaping, etc., with a total investment of about 26 billion yuan. May 9–17, 2011, Anhui's provincial inspectors visit Jiangxi Province, aiming to exchange experiences in (i) the enforcement and supervision of administrative law; (ii) the management of certification and documentation; (iii) the standardization of execution and the improvement of legislative work; and (iv) others. May 22, 2011, the Jiangxi Chamber of Commerce in Anhui Province is established in Hefei, aiming to strengthen the cooperation between Jiangxi's entrepreneurs working in Anhui Province. June 8, 2011, the second session of the "Joint Conference of the Security Cooperation between the Five Central Provinces" is held in Changsha; Anhui, Jiangxi and other three provinces reach multilateral commitments to cross-provincial security cooperation. February 4, 2012, the Communication Departments Anhui, Jiangxi and other provinces in the middle reaches of the Yangtze River jointly sign an agreement concerning the joint construction of cross-provincial transport network.

Anhui-Jilin

[Quick Facts] Average distance = 1985 km; Geographical adjacency = 0; Index of ethnic linkages = 0.9140 (2000) and 0.9253 (2010); Freight exchange via national railway = 510 k tons (2000) and 1010 k tons (2010). ★ April 10, 2011, the Jilin Chemical Fiber Company and the Somet Chemical Fiber Company of Anhui Province sign a cooperation agreement in Jilin Province. May 9, 2011, the Anhui Chamber of Commerce in Jilin is established in Changchun City. The member enterprises involve hotel, decoration, building materials, real estate, food processing and others. September 16, 2011, the representatives from the Times Publishing

Group of Anhui Province and from the Publishing Group of Jilin Province meet in Beijing and sign a strategic cooperation agreement. January 7, 2012, Mayor of Shuangliao City of Jilin Province visits the Tongcheng City of Anhui Province and pays a field inspection to the land transfer and agricultural industrialization of the New World Agricultural Materials Co., Ltd. of Anhui Province. April 14, 2012, Anhui College of Electrical Engineering and Jilin College of Information Technology hold a meeting in Anhui and reach a preliminary agreement on the cooperation between the two colleges. August 17, 2012, the Forest Industry Group of Jilin and several forestry companies of Anhui sign, in Changchun City, agreements on the establishment of a number of joint and cooperative ventures.

Anhui-Liaoning

[Quick Facts] Average distance = 1650 km; Geographical adjacency = 0; Index of ethnic linkages = 0.8459 (2000) and 0.8544 (2010); Freight exchange via national railway = 990 k tons (2000) and 780 k tons (2010). ★ July 29, 2007, in order to serve the common development of Anhui-funded enterprises in Dalian City of Liaoning Province, the Anhui Chamber of Commerce in Dalian is established. February 28, 2009, the Anhui Chamber of Commerce in Shenyang, under the Federation of Industry and Commerce of Liaoning Province, is established. Now, there are more than 100,000 Anhui people working in Liaoning Province, with more than 10 billion yuan of gross assets and an annual 100 million yuan of taxation to the local governments. September 19, 2011, the Huainan Mining (Group) Co., Ltd. of Anhui Province signs a strategic cooperation framework agreement with the Xinfeng Mining and Power Group of Liaoning Province. October 31, 2011, the Northern (Panjin) Base of the Heli Industrial Vehicles Co., Ltd. of Anhui and the Administrative Committee of the Liaobin Coastal Economic Zone of Panjin City (Liaoning Province) sign an agreement according to which the Northern (Panjin) Base will be located at the Zone. December 14, 2011, a nationwide electronic "trinity" network aiming to serve rural labors, which is sponsored by four provinces including Anhui and Liaoning, opens in Beijing. July 13, 2012, the Anhui New Century Pharmaceutical Co., Ltd. and the Liaoning Tianyi Company form a joint venture to produce capsule-filling machines.

Anhui-Ningxia

[Quick Facts] Average distance = 2002 km; Geographical adjacency = 0; Index of ethnic linkages = 0.6610 (2000) and 0.6550 (2010); Freight exchange via national railway = 70 k tons (2000) and 180 k tons (2010). ★ May 9, 2006, the Anhui

Chamber of Commerce in Ningxia Hui Autonomous Region is established in Yinchuan, with more than 160 enterprise members. March 7, 2008, the Tourism Bureaux of Anhui and Ningxia sign a cooperation agreement in Hefei, Anhui Province. April 16, 2011, the Anhui Huainan Chemical Group Co., Ltd. and Zhongwei City of Ningxia Hui Autonomous Region sign an investment and cooperation agreement on coal chemical industry. This agreement includes an investment of 15 billion yuan in the projects of nitric acid, compound chemical fertilizer and coal-related glycol. September 22, 2011, a joint delegation being composed of the Anhui Farm Group Co. and Xuancheng City of Anhui Province inspects the land reclamation area of Ningxia, in order to further deepen interprovincial cooperation in land reclamation and agricultural production. November 14, 2011, teachers and students of Anhui University of Technology visit the Ningxia Coal Mining Group of the Shenhua; and the University and the Group reach a consensus on the maintenance of a long-term, stable and friendly cooperation in the fields of scientific research, personnel training, etc. December 1, 2011, the signing ceremony of friendship between the Guyuan Prison of Ningxia Hui Autonomous Region and the Ma'anshan Prison of Anhui Province is held in Ma'anshan City, Anhui Province.

Anhui-Qinghai

[Quick Facts] Average distance = 2048 km; Geographical adjacency = 0; Index of ethnic linkages = 0.5470 (2000) and 0.5367 (2010); Freight exchange via national railway = 120 k tons (2000) and 530 k tons (2010). ★ July 26, 2009, the Anhui Chamber of Commerce in Qinghai Province is established in Xining City, Qinghai Province; in their first meeting, representatives elect the chamber's leadership. June 11, 2010, the representatives of the Xining Special Steel Share-holding Company (Qinghai Province), the Qinghai Company of the Aluminum Corporation of China (Chalco) and Anhui University hold a meeting concerning energy-saving, new energy development and technological cooperation with the enterprises of Qinghai Province. July 13, 2011, the government of Qinghai Province holds a discussion with the delegation headed by the officials of Anhui Province, which is aimed at interprovincial cooperation on the exploration and exploitation of mineral resources. July 15, 2011, the Anhui Airport (Group) Co. and the Qinghai Airport Corporation sign a cooperation framework agreement and hold the first-flight ceremony in Hefei City. May 4, 2012, the government of Qinghai Province pays an inspection to Anhui Province and participates in the "Anhui-Qinghai Meeting on Economic and Social Development and Cooperation" held in Hefei City of Anhui Province. June 10, 2012, the "Anhui's Famous Products" fair is successfully held in the International Exhibition Center, Xining City, Qinghai Province.

Anhui-Shaanxi

[Quick Facts] Average distance = 1156 km; Geographical adjacency = 0; Index of ethnic linkages = 0.9979 (2000) and 0.9978 (2010); Freight exchange via national railway = 990 k tons (2000) and 2060 k tons (2010). ★ April 7, 2007, the Anhui Chamber of Commerce in Shaanxi, under the Federation of Industry and Commerce of Shaanxi Province, is established. The members have reached more than 200, and invested more than ten billion yuan in Shaanxi Province. April 16, 2010, a delegation led by the Governor of Anhui Province visits Xi'an and meets members of the Anhui Chamber of Commerce in Shaanxi; the Governor hopes that all Anhui businesspersons working in Shaanxi make contributions to the economic development of Anhui Province. August 10–12, 2010, the Personnel Exchange Service Center of Shaanxi Province and the Human Resources and Social Security Bureau of Wuhu City of Anhui Province jointly organize the "School-Enterprise Cooperation Meeting of Shaanxi Province and Wuhu City, Anhui Province, 2010", which is held in Wuhu City, Anhui Province. November 8, 2011, the Supply and Marketing Cooperatives of Shaanxi Province and Anhui Agricultural University sign a strategic cooperation agreement. December 31, 2011, the Wanbei Coal and Electricity Group of Anhui Province and the Jinyuan Group of Shaanxi Province sign an agreement concerning the joint development of the Zhaoxian coal mine project of the Jinyuan Group. The signing ceremony is held in Anhui Province.

Anhui-Shandong

[Quick Facts] Average distance = 613 km; Geographical adjacency = 1; Index of ethnic linkages = 0.9993 (2000) and 0.9987 (2010); Freight exchange via national railway = 5270 k tons (2000) and 8900 k tons (2010). ★ October 31, 2010, the AQTSs of Shandong and Anhui Provinces sign an agreement concerning the "Mutual Recognition of Quality and Technical Supervision" in Hefei City, Anhui Province. November 1, 2010, the "Meeting of International Contracted Engineering Projects", sponsored by Commercial Department of Anhui Province, co-sponsored by the Chambers of International Economic Cooperation of Shandong Province and of International Contracted Labor Service of Shandong Province, is held in Hefei. June 19, 2011, the Shandong Chamber of Commerce in Anhui is established in Hefei City. According to statistics, there are about 1400 Shandong people invest in Anhui, investment involving finance, real estate, transportation, catering services, science and technology, mining machinery, etc. The members have reached more than 200. September 7, 2011, Anhui University of Finance and the Supply and Marketing Cooperatives of Shandong Province sign a strategic cooperation agreement aiming to strengthen the interprovincial exchange. April 16, 2012, Zaozhuang City of Shandong Province and Liuan City of Anhui Province sign, in Liuan City, an agreement concerning the interprovincial tourism cooperation. At the signing ceremony, the sponsors also show the "Two-Day Tourism in Zaozhuang" product.

Anhui-Shanghai

[Quick Facts] Average distance = 615 km; Geographical adjacency = 0; Index of ethnic linkages = 0.9978 (2000) and 0.9926 (2010); Freight exchange via national railway = 2620 k tons (2000) and 2180 k tons (2010). ★ July 17, 2004, the Anhui Chamber of Commerce in Shanghai is established. There are more than 4000 Anhui's enterprises in Shanghai, with a total registered capital over 6 billion yuan, of which private enterprises account for more than 80 %. August 18, 2007, the Fuyang Chamber of Commerce in Shanghai Municipality is established. October 14, 2009, the Shanghai Chamber of Commerce in Anhui is established. The first batch of member enterprises of the Chamber have more than 30, involving real estate, finance, manufacturing industry, new materials, logistics, cultural industry, new energy, new technology, etc. November 4, 2009, the "Anhui-Shanghai Enterprise Partnership Meeting" is held by Anhui Province in the China International Industrial Exhibition in Shanghai, in which Anhui and Shanghai sign 89 contracts of joint ventures, totaling in 20.8 billion yuan. May 7–8, 2010, Anhui Province and the Shanghai Guangming Group sign, in Shanghai, an exchange and cooperation framework agreement in agricultural industrialization. August 31, 2011, the first meeting of social security cooperation and development in the trans-Yangtze River delta opens in Nanjing, in which Anhui, Shanghai, Zhejiang and Jiangsu jointly form a professional team of social security cooperation. November 2, 2010, the public security departments of Anhui, Jiangsu, Zhejiang and Shanghai sign an agreement in Shanghai, which aims to coordinate the four provinces' security affairs. March 25, 2012, the Cultural Assets and Equity Exchange of Shanghai and the Anhui Yangtze Assets Equity Exchange sign a strategic cooperation agreement in Shanghai, aiming to establish a cultural property trading platform for the Yangtze Basin and Anhui Province in particular.

Anhui-Shanxi

[Quick Facts] Average distance = 1145 km; Geographical adjacency = 0; Index of ethnic linkages = 0.9960 (2000) and 0.9957 (2010); Freight exchange via national railway = 4040 k tons (2000) and 7830 k tons (2010). ★ April 13, 2008, the Anhui Chamber of Commerce in Shanxi, under the Federation of Industry and Commerce of Shanxi Province, is established. The number of the chamber's members reaches more than 360, involving all major sectors. September 26, 2010, the "Symposium of Utilization of Coal Resources and Tourist Cooperation", sponsored by the Anhui provincial government, is held in Taiyuan City of Shanxi Province, which is intended to promote the complementary development of coal mining and the cooperation of tourist development. October 29, 2010, the officials of Lan County of Shanxi Province and the Wanbei Coal and Electricity Group (WCEG) of Anhui Province sign a strategic cooperation agreement, which opens a new chapter in the development of the WCEG in Shanxi. January 13, 2011, the government of Linxian County of Shanxi Province meets the delegation of the WCEG, and discuss the joint construction of coal chemical base in the county and other related matters. September 27, 2011, Anhui and Shanxi Provinces sign a cooperation framework agreement, aiming to expand areas of bilateral cooperation.

Anhui-Sichuan

[Quick Facts] Average distance = 1998 km; Geographical adjacency = 0; Index of ethnic linkages = 0.9523 (2000) and 0.9414 (2010); Freight exchange via national railway = 530 k tons (2000) and 1300 k tons (2010). ★ April 20, 2009, the Anhui Chamber of Commerce in Sichuan is established in Chengdu City, Sichuan Province. The chamber's members, which are still growing in number, have reached 170. March 5, 2010, Susong County of Anhui Province and Shuangliu County of Sichuan Province sign a "Memorandum of Understanding Concerning Educational Promotion and Development" and an "Agreement of Educational Cooperation and Development". October 19, 2010, the delegations of Huangshan City (of Anhui Province) and Huanglong City (of Sichuan Province) sign a strategic cooperation agreement in the Huanglong scenic area of Sichuan Province; In the meantime, the construction of a highway in Huanglong City, which is financially supported by Anhui Province, is completed. October 23, 2010, Anhui Province and Songpan County of Sichuan Province sign a framework agreement in Chengdu, in order to enhance the pairing aid to Songpan County and to establish a long-term, effective mechanism of cooperation between the two sides. April 13, 2011, the leaders of Sichuan and Anhui Provinces hold the Economic and Social Development Meeting in Hefei City, Anhui Province. December 31, 2011, the Anhui Chamber of Commerce in Sichuan and the Bank of China Sichuan branch sign a cooperation agreement in Chengdu City, Sichuan Province. April 19, 2012, the Anhui Chamber of Commerce is Mianyang City (Sichuan) is established.

Anhui-Tianjin

[Quick Facts] Average distance = 973 km; Geographical adjacency = 0; Index of ethnic linkages = 0.9796 (2000) and 0.9810 (2010); Freight exchange via national railway = 250 k tons (2000) and 270 k tons (2010). ★ January 20, 2007, the Anhui Chamber of Commerce in Tianjin Municipality is established in Tianjin, with enterprise members reaching more than 200, and individual members more than 1000. June 28, 2011, the Tianjin Chamber of Commerce in Anhui is established in Hefei City. The Chamber has more than 100 member enterprises, involving construction, advertising, real estate, environmental protection, electronics, communication, trade, culture media, hotels, etc. September 16, 2011, the Family Planning Commission of Beichen District, Tianjin Municipality pays an inspection in Fuyang City of Anhui Province, which aims to strengthen the coordination of floating population between Anhui and Tianjin. September 18, 2011, the Tourism Bureaux of Tianjin Municipality and of Anhui Province jointly sign a cooperation agreement in Hefei, aiming to strengthen the tourist developments of Anhui and Tianjin. October 20, 2011, the Culture Exchange of Anhui Province and Tianjin Municipality sign a strategic cooperation agreement of intangible cultural heritage items. December 23, 2011, the Tianjin Chamber of Commerce in Anhui Province participates in the "Symposium of External Capital Utilization and Anhui's Chambers of Commerce", which is organized by the Exchange and Cooperation Office of Anhui Province.

Anhui-Tibet

[Quick Facts] Average distance = 3863 km; Geographical adjacency = 0; Index of ethnic linkages = 0.0649 (2000) and 0.0868 (2010); Freight exchange via national railway = 0 k ton (2000) and 100 k tons (2010). ★ August 19, 2005, the "Anhui-Tibet Forum for Trade and Economic Cooperation" is held in Lhasa, Tibet Autonomous Region. The delegations of the two provincial governments sign an agreement which is aimed at the strengthening economic and technological cooperation between Anhui and Tibet. September 19, 2008, a delegation of the Bureau of Foreign Experts, Anhui Province visits Tibet Autonomous Region, which aims to strengthen exchange and cooperation in the attraction of foreign intellectuals. May 11, 2011, the "Shannan (southern Tibet) Tourist Investment Promotion" is held in Hefei City, Anhui Province. September 15, 2011, the Anhui Forestry Vocational and Technical College receives the Tibetan teachers from the Vocational and Technical School of the Shannan Prefecture of Tibet Autonomous Region. May 27, 2012, the project promotion of the "Tibetan Culture Festival" is held in Hefei City, Anhui Province, aiming to expand the visibility and influence of Tibetan culture in Anhui Province, to promote the exchange and cooperation between Anhui and Tibet, and to strengthen the Han-Tibetan unity.

Anhui-Xinjiang

[Quick Facts] Average distance = 3724 km; Geographical adjacency = 0; Index of ethnic linkages = 0.4125 (2000) and 0.4114 (2010); Freight exchange via national railway = 200 k tons (2000) and 500 k tons (2010). ★ May 12, 2006, the Anhui

Enterprises Association in Xinjiang is established in Urumqi City of Xinjiang. August 29, 2006, the Anhui Federation of Enterprises in Xinjiang Uygur Autonomous Region is established in Urumqi—Capital of Xinjiang Autonomous Region—with the registered members reaching more than 330. September 3, 2010, during the "Urumqi Foreign Economic and Trade Fair", the delegations of Anhui Province and Xinjiang Uygur Autonomous Region hold a "cooperation-enhancing meeting". June 7, 2011, the Tourism Bureaux of Xinjiang Uygur Autonomous Region and Anhui Province hold the "Meeting of Assisting Xinjiang" in Hefei, Anhui Province, and sign a "Tourist Cooperation Agreement". June 16–19, 2011, the "Meeting of Strategic Cooperation of Construction Sector between Anhui Province and Xinjiang Autonomous Region" is held in Urumqi, Xinjiang Uygur Autonomous Region, aiming to deepen the strategic cooperation of construction industry in Anhui and Xinjiang. October 27, 2011, the Anhui provincial officials meet, in Hefei, Xinjiang's prefectural level officials enrolled in the Party School of the CCPCC, aims to further strengthen the exchange and cooperation between and to promote the economic and social development of Anhui and Xinjiang. June 16, 2012, the Anhui Chamber of Commerce in Kashi Prefecture is established in Kashi of Xinjiang.

Anhui-Yunnan

[Quick Facts] Average distance = 3098 km; Geographical adjacency = 0; Index of ethnic linkages = 0.6725 (2000) and 0.6728 (2010); Freight exchange via national railway = 210 k tons (2000) and 800 k tons (2010). ★ September 8, 2007, the opening ceremony of the Anhui Chamber of Commerce in Yunnan is held in Kunming City of Yunnan Province; the chamber has more than 130 members. Since the reform and opening up, especially since the implementation of western development strategy, a large number of Anhui entrepreneurs and business people have set up their company in Yunnan Province. Now, there are nearly 100,000 Anhui People working and doing business in Yunnan, of which 20,000 are entrepreneurs or property owners. April 18, 2009, the Anhui Chamber of Commerce in Qujing City is established. October 22, 2010, the tourist inspection delegations of Anhui and Yunnan Provinces hold a meeting in Hefei City, Anhui Province, and propose a cooperative mechanism of tourism of the two provinces. March 10, 2011, the Tobacco Monopoly Administration (Company) of Yunnan Province and Anhui's officials in charge of tobacco administration meet in Kunming, Yunnan Province, and sign an agreement to promote bilateral cooperation in tobacco processing. February 15, 2012, the Merchant and Cooperation Bureau of Yunnan Province and its Enterprise Service Department conduct an inspection and research in the Anhui Chamber of Commerce in Yunnan Province.

Anhui-Zhejiang

[Quick Facts] Average distance = 451 km; Geographical adjacency = 1; Index of ethnic linkages = 0.9926 (2000) and 0.9797 (2010); Freight exchange via national railway = 6000 k tons (2000) and 8610 k tons (2010). ★ August 8, 2002, the Zhejiang Chamber of Commerce in Anhui is established in Hefei City, Anhui Province. It has 168 members investing in more than 130 projects, with a total value of more than 200 billion yuan. August 19, 2006, the Anhui Chamber of Commerce in Hangzhou is established. The Chamber has more than 120 enterprise members. September 14, 2009, the Anhui Chamber of Commerce in Jiaxing City is established. November 2, 2010, the public security departments of Anhui and Shanghai sign an agreement in Shanghai, which aims to coordinate interprovincial security affairs. December 1–3, 2010, a Zhejiang delegation visits Anhui Province to explore interprovincial energy cooperation. December 11, 2010, the Anhui Chamber of Commerce in Zhejiang is established in Hangzhou City. December 28, 2010, the Xinhua Distribution Group of Anhui and the Zhejiang Publishing Group sign a strategic cooperation agreement. April 14, 2011, the "5th Conference of 6 Provinces plus 1 City in East China Concerning the Regional Transport Development and Coordination" is held in Suzhou City, Jiangsu Province. Through friendly consultations, the Departments of Transportation of Anhui and Zhejiang Provinces sign a protocol concerning the cross-provincial connection of two expressways (i.e., the one running from Lake Shenjia to Ningguo; and the one running from Huangshan to Lake Qiandao). October 14, 2011, Anhui and Zhejiang Provinces decide to, for the first time, establish a cross-provincial healthcare cooperation scheme from which about 30,000 migrant workers will benefit. April 12, 2012, the "Anhui-Zhejiang Economic and Social Development Exchange Meeting" is held in Hangzhou City, Zhejiang Province, aiming to strengthen the interprovincial economic cooperation and to speed up the economic development of the two provinces.

Beijing-Chongqing

[Quick Facts] Average distance = 2087 km; Geographical adjacency = 0; Index of ethnic linkages = 0.9377 (2000) and 0.9366 (2010); Freight exchange via national railway = 140 k tons (2000) and 220 k tons (2010). ★ April 29, 2006, the Chongqing Chamber of Commerce in Beijing is established. The Chamber has 87 member enterprises, involving real estate, culture, food, construction, law, etc. February 13, 2009, the Intellectual Property Departments of Beijing and Chongqing Municipalities sign, in Shanghai, a framework agreement and pledge to cooperate in the fields of law enforcement, exchange of intellectual property information, data bank of intellectual property experts, and public services. December 29, 2010, police forces of Beijing and Chongqing Municipalities conduct an interregional cooperation through the “micro blog”, aiming to enhance the exchange and sharing of information between the two regions through internet technology. January 2011, the Beijing Chamber of Commerce in Chongqing is established. According to statistics, there are more than 260 Beijing enterprises in Chongqing, involving software development, investment and finance, real estate, biological technologies, education, etc. May 25, 2011, the delegations of Chongqing University and Peking University sign a cooperation agreement in Beijing, aiming to strengthen the personnel exchange and cooperation. November 12, 2011, the Chongqing municipal government and Peking University agree to jointly establish the “Cooperative R&D Center”. The center will serve as a platform for the extensive cooperation in science and technology, policy advisory services, construction of major projects, exchange of personnel training and cultural development. May 10, 2012, the Chongqing Real-Estate Professional College and the Beijing Institute of Technology Press sign a strategic cooperation agreement. The two sides will integrate their respective strengths to jointly development high-quality publications of China’s real-estate education.

Beijing-Fujian

[Quick Facts] Average distance = 2334 km; Geographical adjacency = 0; Index of ethnic linkages = 0.9624 (2000) and 0.9668 (2010); Freight exchange via national railway = 290 k tons (2000) and 130 k tons (2010). ★ September 22, 2001, the Fujian Association of Enterprises in Beijing is established. August 2005, the Fujian Association of Enterprises in Beijing changes its name to the Fujian Chamber of Commerce in Beijing. September 12, 2008, leadership of the Xiamen Electric Power Bureau visits Beijing, and exchanges views with leaders of the Fengtai Electric Supply Company of Beijing; both sides agree to build a friendly cooperative relationship. June 2009, as a result of the emergence of many Fujian chambers at regional or local level, the Fujian Chamber of Commerce in Beijing changes its name to the Fujian General Chamber of Commerce in Beijing; now, the total of number of companies registered in the Chamber has exceeded 10,000. January 21, 2011, the Fujian Chamber of Tea Commerce in Beijing and the Bank of Beijing hold a financial cooperation meeting. May 2–3, 2012, the Dazhun Investment Management Co., Ltd. of Beijing signs project cooperation agreements with the Fujian Children’s Publishing House and the Fujian Strait Publishing House, respectively. June 2012, Wuyishan City of Fujian Province, and the Fujian Tea Association in Beijing sign a strategic cooperation agreement, aiming to promote tea trade between Beijing Municipality and northern Fujian Province. December 2012, in the “Cooperation Fair of State-owned Enterprises (SOEs)”, which is held in Beijing, the private enterprises of Pingtan City (Fujian Province) secure 123 industrial projects of integrative cooperation with the SOEs—most of which are based in Beijing, with a total investment of 846.4 billion yuan.

Beijing-Gansu

[Quick Facts] Average distance = 1811 km; Geographical adjacency = 0; Index of ethnic linkages = 0.9320 (2000) and 0.9204 (2010); Freight exchange via national railway = 250 k tons (2000) and 260 k tons (2010). ★ October 11, 2008, Beijing Forestry University and the Forestry Experimental Bureau of Xiaolong Mountain of Gansu Province sign an agreement of teaching and research cooperation in Gansu Province. December 29, 2009, Gansu Province and Tsinghua University sign a strategic cooperative framework agreement in Beijing, in order to establish a long-term cooperation mechanism in personnel training, R&D and others. April 6, 2011, the Gansu Chamber of Commerce in Beijing is established. More than 300 people (including the Deputy CCP Secretary of and the Vice Governor of Gansu Province) attend the celebrating ceremony of the Chamber. July 27, 2011, the "Symposium of China International Chamber of Commerce Concerning the Investment and Cooperation Projects of Gansu Province" is jointly organized by the Secretariat Bureau of China International Chamber of Commerce and the Gansu Association of Trade Promotion in Beijing. March 7, 2012, the Gansu provincial government and the China Everbright Group sign a strategic cooperative agreement in Beijing, aiming to establish comprehensive, multi-level strategic partnerships in financial investment. March 19, 2012, the Gansu provincial government and the Chinese Academy of Sciences (CAS) sign a technological cooperation agreement in Beijing, aiming to jointly support the construction of Gansu Academy of Sciences.

Beijing-Guangdong

[Quick Facts] Average distance = 2289 km; Geographical adjacency = 0; Index of ethnic linkages = 0.9601 (2000) and 0.9644 (2010); Freight exchange via national railway = 1030 k tons (2000) and 210 k tons (2010). ★ January 11, 2008, the Guangdong Chamber of Commerce in Beijing is established. The Chamber has more than 1000 members and has 9 subordinate branches, such as Chaoshan, Meizhou, Zengcheng, Yangjiang, Dongguan, Maoming, Huizhou, Heyuan and Wuchuan. The chamber's members mainly cover real estate, catering, finance, construction, logistics, trade and investment, science and technology, aviation, clothing and household appliances. January 2009, the Guangdong provincial government and the Chinese Academy of Sciences (CAS) in Beijing sign a comprehensive strategic cooperative agreement; more than 400 scientific and technological projects of the CAS will be transferred to Guangdong, with the newly increased output value of more than 13 billion yuan and the newly increased taxes of more than 2 billion yuan. March 14, 2011, a meeting on the strategic cooperation between Guangdong provincial government and the large SOEs is held in Beijing, in which a strategic cooperative agreement is signed. February 23, 2012, the Keyuan Xinhai Pharmaceutical Co., Ltd. of Beijing, the Center of Disease Control and Prevention of Guangdong Province and the Biological and the Drug Research Institute of Guangzhou City (Guangdong Province) sign a strategic cooperative framework agreement. March 4, 2012, the Guangdong provincial government and Peking University sign a strategic cooperative framework agreement in Beijing, aiming to attract the IT professionals and import the advanced technologies from Peking University to Guangdong. June 28, 2012, the Beijing Capital International Airport and the Guangzhou Baiyun International Airport sign a "Framework Agreement Concerning the Exchange and Cooperation of Airports Service and Management" in Beijing, aiming to strengthen the coordination and development of Chinese airports service.

Beijing-Guangxi

[Quick Facts] Average distance = 2561 km; Geographical adjacency = 0; Index of ethnic linkages = 0.6192 (2000) and 0.6321 (2010); Freight exchange via national railway = 210 k tons (2000) and 150 k tons (2010). ★ October 29, 2006, the Guangxi Chamber of Commerce in Beijing is established. The Chamber has more than 160 member enterprises, covering real estate, biotechnology, financial capital, modern electronics, machinery and equipment, tourism and culture, modern logistics, deep processing of agricultural products, etc. March 13, 2011, Guangxi Zhuang Autonomous Region holds a meeting on the strategic cooperation with the large SOEs in Beijing. March 16, 2011, Nanning City of Guangxi Zhuang Autonomous Region and Xicheng District of Beijing Municipality sign, in Beijing, a framework agreement concerning the cooperation between the two places. July 18, 2011, Guangxi Zhuang Autonomous Region and Peking University sign a cooperative agreement in Nanning City, Guangxi Province, to strengthen the economic and social development of Guangxi Province. December 29, 2011, the Commercial Departments of Guangxi and Beijing sign a cooperative agreement, aiming to establish a long-term cooperative mechanism concerning the supply of vegetables and other agricultural products from Guangxi to Beijing. April 7, 2012, the No. 8 Middle School of Beijing and the No. 2 Middle School of Beihai City of Guangxi sign a framework agreement concerning the establishment of a joint venture in Beihai City (namely: the Beihai Campus of the No. 8 Middle School of Beijing); now, there are nearly 20 cases of inter-school cooperation between Beijing and Guangxi. May 15, 2012, the Land Reclamation Group of Guangxi signs a strategic cooperation agreement with the No. 2 Commerce (Group) Co., Ltd. of Beijing Municipality. May 23, 2012, senior officials from Guangxi Zhuang Autonomous Region and Beijing University of Aeronautics and Astronautics meet in Beijing and agree to deepen their bilateral cooperation.

Beijing-Guizhou

[Quick Facts] Average distance = 2539 km; Geographical adjacency = 0; Index of ethnic linkages = 0.6309 (2000) and 0.6661 (2010); Freight exchange via national railway = 120 k tons (2000) and 190 k tons (2010). ★ November 13, 2007, the Science and Technology Department of Guizhou Province and the General Research Institute of Mining and Metallurgy of Beijing sign an agreement concerning the bilateral cooperation of science and technology. December 24, 2007, the Tourism Bureaux of Guizhou Province and Beijing Municipality, and the Xinxin Yixiang (Beijing) Tourism Agency and the China Youth Travel (Guizhou) sign a cooperative agreement concerning the Beijing Olympic tourism, respectively. June 27, 2008, the Guizhou Chamber of Commerce in Beijing is established. December 9, 2010, the State Development Bank and Guizhou provincial government sign a "Memorandum of Financial Cooperation between State Development Bank and Guizhou Province" in Beijing. March 12, 2011, the China National Petroleum Corporation (PetroChina) and the Guizhou provincial government sign a strategic cooperative framework agreement in Beijing. October 17–18, 2011, in an investment promotion meeting held in Beijing, the Guizhou provincial government invites Beijing's privately-owned enterprises to invest in Guizhou. June 1, 2012, the Educational Commissions of Haidian District (Beijing Municipality) and of Zunyi City (Guizhou Province) sign a "Memorandum of Education Cooperation" in Zunyi City, aiming to expand exchange and cooperation between the two sides.

Beijing-Hainan

[Quick Facts] Average distance = 3088 km; Geographical adjacency = 0; Index of ethnic linkages = 0.8210 (2000) and 0.8409 (2010); Freight exchange via national railway = 0 k ton (2000) and 0 k ton (2010). ★ November 24, 2004, Hainan Province and Beijing Municipality sign a memorandum of cooperation concerning the production of agricultural and sideline products in Hainan and their supply to Beijing. October 14, 2011, the Tourist Committees of Hainan Province and Beijing Municipality sign the "Agreement of Strategic Cooperation on Tourism and the Construction of Hainan International Tourist Island", and hold a special promotion meeting in Beijing. November 14, 2011, the Communications Committee of Beijing Municipality and the Department of Communications and Transportation of Hainan Province sign a strategic cooperative framework agreement; the two sides will cooperate in the fields of construction and management of communication infrastructure, technological innovation, and personnel training. November 27, 2011, the Affiliated Middle School of Hainan Normal University and the No. 4 Middle School of Beijing establish a cooperative relationship, and hold an opening ceremony of "Distance Education of the No. 4 Middle School of Beijing" in Hainan Province.

Beijing-Hebei

[Quick Facts] Average distance = 277 km; Geographical adjacency = 1; Index of ethnic linkages = 0.9867 (2000) and 0.9870 (2010); Freight exchange via national railway = 19,900 k tons (2000) and 17,330 k tons (2010). ★ March 28, 2006, the Hebei Chamber of Commerce in Beijing is established. April 17, 2009, the "Hebei-Beijing Human Resources Exchange Meeting" is held in the Beijing National Agricultural Exhibition Center. In the Meeting, the Bureaux of Human Resources and Social Security of Hebei Province and Beijing Municipality sign an agreement concerning the cooperation of human resources. July 15, 2010, Beijing Municipality and Hebei Province sign a cooperative framework agreement, aiming to encourage their enterprises to cooperate in the establishment of industrial chains; the two sides have also an agenda concerning the construction of the rail system in the Hebei areas around Beijing. January 10, 2011, Jizhou (a county-level city in Hengshui City) of Hebei Province and Beijing Municipality sign the "Agreement Concerning Cooperation on the Economic and Technological Projects", which attracts 14.9 billion yuan of investments. July 2, 2011, the Administrative Committee of Zhongguancun Science Park of Beijing Municipality and the Langfang municipal government of Hebei Province sign a regional strategic cooperative framework agreement, aiming to establish comprehensive strategic partnerships. October 21, 2011, the Banking Bureaux of Hebei Province and of Beijing Municipality sign an agreement concerning the strengthening and deepening of financial cooperation between the two sides. April 5–6, 2012, a senior delegation of the Hebei provincial government pays an inspection and research tour to Beijing, hoping to promote the social and economic development of Hebei Province.

Beijing-Heilongjiang

[Quick Facts] Average distance = 1288 km; Geographical adjacency = 0; Index of ethnic linkages = 0.9779 (2000) and 0.9847 (2010); Freight exchange via national railway = 2040 k tons (2000) and 1340 k tons (2010). ★ March 10, 2007, the Heilongjiang Chamber of Commerce in Beijing is established. March 3, 2011, Jixi City, Heilongjiang Province, and the Beijing Automotive Group sign an agreement on the cooperation in graphite industry. September 23, 2011, Heilongjiang Province and Beijing Municipality establish a strategic cooperative relationship in grain production and marketing; the signing ceremony is held in Harbin City, Heilongjiang Province. November 29, 2011, the No. 2 Commercial Group of Beijing and the Land Reclamation Bureau of Heilongjiang Province (also namely: the Beidahuang Group) sign a strategic cooperative agreement concerning the construction of a food production chain. May 30, 2012, the SASACs of Xicheng District (Beijing Municipality) and of Harbin City (Heilongjiang Province) sign a strategic cooperative framework agreement. July 3, 2012, a delegation of the Heilongjiang Chamber of Commerce in Beijing, which is composed of over 90 members, participates in the "23rd China (Harbin) International Economic and Trade Fair", which is held in Harbin City. The delegation inspects the high-tech products, building materials, medicine, organic and green food, pollution-free agricultural products and comprehensive processing of agricultural products, hoping to strengthen the economic and trade development of Heilongjiang Province.

Beijing-Henan

[Quick Facts] Average distance = 689 km; Geographical adjacency = 0; Index of ethnic linkages = 0.9694 (2000) and 0.9711 (2010); Freight exchange via national railway = 1070 k tons (2000) and 750 k tons (2010). ★ June 21, 2001, a large group of enterprises from Henan Province and the Beijing Institute of Technology jointly hold an exchange and cooperation fair in Beijing. March 3, 2008, Henan Province and Beijing Municipality sign the "Agreement on the Bilateral Cooperation in Tourism"; the two sides pledge to keep in close contact and to enhance bilateral cooperation in tourism. October 29, 2008, Beijing University of Chemistry and Technology and the Zhongyuan Coal Chemical Industry Group of Henan sign an agreement concerning personnel training, and science and technology cooperation, aiming to integrate the production and research capacities in coal and chemical sectors. August 25, 2009, the Yixing Group of Henan Province and the Xinfadi Company of Beijing Municipality sign a strategic cooperative agreement, which aims to enhance the supply chains of agricultural products from Henan to Beijing. November 9, 2009, the Beijing Branch of the Import-Export Bank signs three agreements of comprehensive strategic cooperation with Henan Railway Investment Co., Ltd., the ICBC Henan Branch, and the China Construction Bank Henan Branch, respectively. September 22, 2011, Henan provincial government and Beijing municipal government sign a strategic cooperative framework agreement in Zhengzhou, Henan Province.

Beijing-Hubei

[Quick Facts] Average distance = 1225 km; Geographical adjacency = 0; Index of ethnic linkages = 0.9598 (2000) and 0.9614 (2010); Freight exchange via national railway = 490 k tons (2000) and 520 k tons (2010). ★ June 2008, the Hubei Chamber of Commerce is established in Beijing. As of March 2009, the chamber has a total of more than 150 member companies, covering such sectors as real estate, catering, construction, medical, investment, media, technology, IT, logistics, commerce, finance, insurance, accounting, legal, food, tourism, pharmaceutics, etc. July 2, 2008, the Educational Commission of Chaoyang District, Beijing Municipality and Huanggang Middle School of Hubei Province sign an agreement on cooperation. September 23, 2011, a delegation of Beijing municipal government pays an inspection and research tour to Hubei Province; Beijing and Hubei, to take the opportunities of the construction of South-North Water Diversion Project and of the latter-stage development of Three Gorges reservoir area, hope to deepen their extensive exchange and cooperation. March 6, 2012, the Shennongjia Forest of Hubei Province and Beijing Municipality sign a strategic cooperative agreement of tourism, aiming to bring the Shennongjia Scenic Area into the tourist development strategic plan of Beijing, and to promote the tourist development of the two places. June 19, 2012, Danjiangkou City, Hubei Province, and the South-North Water Diversion Office of Beijing sign a strategic cooperative framework agreement, aimed at strengthening the wide-ranging cooperation in the field of ecological and environmental protection of water sources.

Beijing-Hunan

[Quick Facts] Average distance = 1583 km; Geographical adjacency = 0; Index of ethnic linkages = 0.9028 (2000) and 0.9053 (2010); Freight exchange via national railway = 400 k tons (2000) and 310 k tons (2010). ★ December 30, 2003, the Hunan Chamber of Commerce in Beijing, under the Federation of Industry and Commerce of Beijing Municipality, is established, with a total number of 48 members. December 8, 2006, the "Hunan Provincial Status and Key Cooperation Project Promotion" is held in Beijing. July 27, 2007, a delegation of more than 20 IT entrepreneurs from Beijing pays an inspection tour to Hunan Province; the delegation has in-depth exchange with the government officials in charge of information industry and business leaders of Hunan, and discusses opportunities for cooperation with Hunan Province. August 16, 2009, the Hunan provincial government signs a cooperative agreement with Peking University, aiming to further promote their bilateral exchange and cooperation and to speed up the process of regional economic and social development and the creation of a world-class university. January 15, 2011, the R&D Center of Beijing University of Chemistry and Technology and of the Hunan Jufa Technology and New Materials Company is established, marking the start of the 30,000 tons of Mixed Metal Oxide Pigment (MMO) project. April 17, 2011, the Hunan provincial government and Peking University sign the "Agreement of Extensive Cooperation on the IT Industry" in Beijing. June 18, 2012, the "2012 Hunan Agricultural and Manufactured Products (Beijing) Marketing Cooperation Fair" is held in Beijing.

Beijing-Inner Mongolia

[Quick Facts] Average distance = 667 km; Geographical adjacency = 0; Index of ethnic linkages = 0.8237 (2000) and 0.8273 (2010); Freight exchange via national railway = 4300 k tons (2000) and 6340 k tons (2010). ★ July 18, 2007, the Inner Mongolia Chamber of Commerce in Beijing is established. The Chamber has 260 enterprise members, mainly engaged in energy, real estate, catering and logistics. March 24, 2011, the Pairing Aid Office of and the Department of Finance of Beijing Municipality and the DRC of and the Department of Finance of Inner Mongolia Autonomous Region sign the "Agreement of Regional Financial Cooperation between Beijing and Inner Mongolia". September 14, 2011, the Department of Science and Technology of Inner Mongolia and the Zhongguancun Administrative Committee sign a strategic cooperative framework agreement in Beijing, aiming to strengthen the regional cooperation between Beijing and Inner Mongolia. September 27, 2011, Inner Mongolia Autonomous Region, China's richest place in coal resources, and the China University of Mining and Technology (Beijing) sign a strategic cooperative agreement; both sides pledge to establish long-term, comprehensive and close partnerships in talent and economic cooperation. December 24, 2011, the "Beijing-Inner Mongolia Meeting on Interregional Cooperation and Pairing Aid" is held in Hohhot City, Inner Mongolia. March 16, 2012, the Economic and Information Technology Commission of Beijing and the Xilin Gol League of Inner Mongolia Autonomous Region sign a cooperative agreement, aiming to build a new strategic industrial system for both sides. March 19, 2012, the Publications Bureau of Inner Mongolia Autonomous Region and the Beijing Institute of Graphic Communication sign a strategic cooperative agreement; both sides pledge to take their respective advantages in the implementation of bilateral cooperation.

Beijing-Jiangsu

[Quick Facts] Average distance = 1160 km; Geographical adjacency = 0; Index of ethnic linkages = 0.9603 (2000) and 0.9638 (2010); Freight exchange via national railway = 910 k tons (2000) and 490 k tons (2010). ★ April 4–10, 2000, during the "China East-West Cooperation, Investment and Trade Fair" in Xi'an City, Shaanxi Province, the Science and Technology Commission of Beijing Municipality participates in the meeting of science, technology and economic cooperation, and signs a framework agreement of strengthening the scientific and technological cooperation between Beijing and Jiangsu. August 6, 2000, Fengxian (Xuzhou City of Jiangsu Province) Chamber of Commerce in Beijing is established. March 9, 2004, the Jiangsu provincial government and Peking University sign a cooperative agreement. April 26, 2007, the Jiangsu Chamber of Commerce, under the Federation of Industry and Commerce of Beijing Municipality, is established in Beijing. April 26, 2009, the Jiangsu People's Publishing House and the Gonghe Liandong Books Co., Ltd. of

Beijing form a joint venture, aiming to enhance strategic cooperation. March 11, 2011, the Jiangsu provincial government and Tsinghua University sign a strategic cooperative agreement in Beijing. June 18–19, 2012, a delegation of Beijing municipal government pays an inspection on the South-North Water Diversion Project in Jiangsu Province, aiming to form strategic partnerships with Jiangsu Province concerning the construction of the Minyu Reservoir Storage Project. October 15, 2012, the signing ceremony of the strategic cooperation agreement between the Heilongjiang Chamber of Commerce in Beijing and the Jiangsu Chamber of Commerce in Beijing is held in Changping District, Beijing.

Beijing-Jiangxi

[Quick Facts] Average distance = 1449 km; Geographical adjacency = 0; Index of ethnic linkages = 0.9581 (2000) and 0.9606 (2010); Freight exchange via national railway = 230 k tons (2000) and 180 k tons (2010). ★ November 25, 2008, the Jiangxi Chamber of Commerce is established in Beijing. March 1, 2008, Jiangxi Province and Beijing Municipality sign a cooperative framework agreement concerning the strengthening of the agricultural products circulation, aiming to promote the agricultural cooperation between two sides. March 11, 2009, the Water Resources Research Institute of and the Soil and Water Conservation Scientific Research of Jiangxi Province sign a cooperative framework agreement with the China Institute of Water Resources and Hydropower and the Ecological Engineering Technology Research Center of the Water Conservancy Ministry, respectively. August 5, 2010, the Xinyu Company, Jiangxi Province, and the Qingshan Energy Company, Beijing Municipality sign a strategic cooperative agreement. The cooperation will accelerate the development of Beijing's power and energy storage battery industry, and add a strong support for the development of the China New Energy and Technology Zone. March 30, 2011, the Bank of Beijing and the Jiangxi provincial government sign a strategic cooperative agreement, in which a branch of the Bank of Beijing is established in Nanchang City, Jiangxi Province. May 19, 2011, the Beijing Research Institute of Mining and Metallurgy signs a contract with the Copper Industry Group of Jiangxi Province, aiming to take the technological advantages of the Research Institute, on the one hand, and the resource advantages of the Group, on the other hand.

Beijing-Jilin

[Quick Facts] Average distance = 1046 km; Geographical adjacency = 0; Index of ethnic linkages = 0.9365 (2000) and 0.9482 (2010); Freight exchange via national railway = 1240 k tons (2000) and 870 k tons (2010). ★ September 28, 2010, Jilin Province and Beijing Municipality hold a meeting of regional tourist cooperation and sign the "Beijing-Jilin Agreement on the Cooperation of Tourism and Education" and other strategic cooperative agreements. November 2, 2010, Beijing University of Aeronautics and Astronautics and Jilin University sign, in Beijing, an agreement concerning the joint training of undergraduate students. November 9, 2010, the presidents of Jilin University and Peking University sign an inter-school cooperative agreement. In accordance with the principles of comparative advantages and of resource sharing, the two sides will strengthen the cooperation of joint training of students, academic exchange and joint research in major subjects. May 6, 2011, the Deer Breeding Base of the Beijing Jiulu Company and the Jilin Institute of Agricultural Science and Technology become cooperative partnerships. September 26, 2011, the Propaganda Department of Jilin Provincial Committee of the CCP and the Jilin Bureau of Economic and Technological Cooperation hold in Beijing a meeting concerning the Jilin-Beijing cooperation on scientific, technological and cultural industries. Jilin Province expects to strengthen cooperation with Beijing's technological and cultural enterprises. October 17, 2011, Jilin University and the Beijing Zhongchuang Information Measuring Technology Co., Ltd. sign a cooperative agreement in the South Lake Campus of Jilin University, aiming to jointly explore a new way of university-enterprises cooperation.

Beijing-Liaoning

[Quick Facts] Average distance = 741 km; Geographical adjacency = 0; Index of ethnic linkages = 0.8691 (2000) and 0.8775 (2010); Freight exchange via national railway = 3080 k tons (2000) and 2330 k tons (2010). ★ October 19, 2001, the president of Peking University and the governor of Liaoning Province sign the "Comprehensive Cooperation Agreement between Peking University and Liaoning provincial government" in Beijing. December 22, 2008, the municipal government of Huludao of Liaoning Province, the Beijing Zhongguancun Administrative Committee, and the Qidi Holdings Limited of the Tsinghua Science Park Group sign a regional strategic cooperative framework agreement in Beijing. May 2010, the Liaoning Chamber of Commerce in Beijing (preparatory) is established. January 22, 2011, the Liaoning provincial government and the Beijing University of Aeronautics and Astronautics sign a strategic cooperative framework agreement in Liaoning, aiming to promote the transferring of scientific and technological products and the local economic and social development. June 17, 2011, Beijing Institute of Technology and the Liaoning provincial government sign a strategic cooperative framework agreement, in order to take the opportunity of the province-school strategic cooperation and deepen the cooperation in technological innovation, personnel training and other fields. June 27, 2012, Beijing Forestry University and the Forestry Department of Liaoning Province sign an agreement concerning the integration of teaching, research and production; in the agreement Liaoning Province will give priority for the graduates from Beijing Forestry University to be employed in the forestry sector of Liaoning.

Beijing-Ningxia

[Quick Facts] Average distance = 1343 km; Geographical adjacency = 0; Index of ethnic linkages = 0.6775 (2000) and 0.6675 (2010); Freight exchange via national railway = 410 k tons (2000) and 270 k tons (2010). ★ July 26, 2008, the Ningxia Chamber of Commerce in Beijing is established, hoping to contribute to the social and economic developments of Ningxia Hui Autonomous Region and Beijing Municipality. April 23, 2011, the "Promotion Conference of Economic and Trade Cooperation between Ningxia and Beijing" is held in Beijing, in which all the Ningxia's 15 projects have secured investors, with a total amount of 18.565 billion yuan. The cooperative fields cover new energy, energy saving and environmental protection, high technology, trade and logistics and so on. January 19, 2012, the Ningxia Land Reclamation Group and the Beijing ZhongKun Investment Group Co., Ltd. sign a cooperative framework agreement in Yinchuan City, Ningxia Hui Autonomous Region. The two sides pledge to construct a business and leisure resort in Ningxia Hui Autonomous Region. March 7, 2012, government of Ningxia Hui Autonomous Region and the Aluminum Corporation of China (Chalco) sign a strategic cooperative framework agreement in Beijing. In April 2012, the Department of Commerce of Ningxia Hui Autonomous Region and the Bureau of Commerce of Beijing Municipality sign a friendly cooperative framework agreement, in which the two sides establish a mechanism of cooperation and exchange in order to promote the agricultural specialties of Ningxia to enter the Beijing market. June 27, 2012, the Department of Commerce of Ningxia Hui Autonomous Region and the Association of Import and Export Enterprises of Beijing Municipality sign a memorandum of cooperation, aiming to further expand the areas and channels of foreign trade and economic cooperation, to accelerate and promote the inland model of economic opening and development in Ningxia Hui Autonomous Region.

Beijing-Qinghai

[Quick Facts] Average distance = 2092 km; Geographical adjacency = 0; Index of ethnic linkages = 0.5633 (2000) and 0.5499 (2010); Freight exchange via national railway = 60 k tons (2000) and 220 k tons (2010). ★ August 24, 2009, the signing ceremony of the "Agreement of Beijing Municipal Government and Qinghai Provincial Government Concerning the Extensive Cooperation of Science, Technology and Education" is held in the conference center in Xining City, Qinghai Province; Beijing Municipality donates 10 million yuan to Qinghai Province. November 13, 2009, the Educational Commission of Beijing Municipality and the Educational Department of Qinghai Province sign the "Memorandum of Understanding to Further Strengthen Educational Exchange and Cooperation"; within three years, Beijing will strengthen the exchange and cooperation between Beijing and Qinghai in eight areas (including teacher training, high school building, etc.) and support the development of education in Qinghai province. April 9, 2010, Qinghai Ethnic University and Beijing University of Technology pledge to carry out extensive exchange and cooperation. July 22, 2010, the agreement of cooperation between Beijing Municipality and Qinghai Province is signed, aiming to strengthen the exchange of experience, policy, regulation, civil information and other related documents between the two places. July 6, 2010, the meeting of education cooperation between Beijing and Qinghai is held in Xining City, Qinghai Province. The educational departments and universities of Beijing Municipality and Qinghai Province sign framework agreements of bilateral exchange and cooperation. August 24, 2010, the opening ceremony of the first-term training class of the police officers from Qinghai is held in Beijing. November 29, 2010, the Qinghai Chamber of Commerce in Beijing is established. The Chamber has 55 corporate members and over 100 individual members. March 5, 2012, the ceremony of the first-flight from Beijing to Xining, Qinghai Province, is held by the China Eastern Airlines in Beijing.

Beijing-Shaanxi

[Quick Facts] Average distance = 1159 km; Geographical adjacency = 0; Index of ethnic linkages = 0.9618 (2000) and 0.9642 (2010); Freight exchange via national railway = 580 k tons (2000) and 730 k tons (2010). ★ April 4–10, 2000, a delegation of the Beijing municipal government attends the "China East-West Cooperation, Investment and Trade Fair" in Xi'an City, Shaanxi Province. The Science and Technology Commission of Beijing Municipality signs an agreement concerning the strengthening of scientific and technological cooperation between Beijing and Shaanxi. In January 2007, the Shaanxi Chamber of Commerce is established in Beijing. May 19, 2007, the Wendela Group of Beijing and the Longgang Group of Shaanxi create a new joint venture, which is named as the Shaanxi Longmen Iron and Steel Co., Ltd., with a registered capital of 500 million yuan. December 14, 2010, the Beijing Jinwen World IT Co., Ltd. signs a cooperative agreement with Shaanxi University of Science and Technology; the company donates a suit of logistics system software to Engineering College of the University. April 27, 2011, the Bank of Beijing and the Department of Science and Technology of Shaanxi Province sign a strategic cooperative agreement in Xi'an. Under the agreement, the Bank of Beijing will provide 30 billion yuan of credit limits to Shaanxi Province within the next three years. August 2, 2011, the Shaanxi Panlong Pharmaceutical Group and the Beijing Jiuding Investment Company sign a strategic cooperation agreement concerning the joint actions to apply to the stock market. October 15, 2011, the Shaanxi Beiren Printing Machinery Co., Ltd. and Beijing Institute of Graphic Communications sign a strategic cooperative agreement. November 21, 2011, the Shaanxi Chamber of Commerce in Beijing and the Guangdong Development Bank (Beijing Branch) sign a strategic cooperative agreement in Beijing. According to the agreement, the Guangdong Development Bank (Beijing Branch) will give Shaanxi Chamber of Commerce in Beijing 1 billion yuan of credit limits.

Beijing-Shandong

[Quick Facts] Average distance = 497 km; Geographical adjacency = 0; Index of ethnic linkages = 0.9638 (2000) and 0.9667 (2010); Freight exchange via national railway = 3150 k tons (2000) and 1180 k tons (2010). ★ December 23, 2005, the Shandong Chamber of Commerce in Beijing, under the Federation of Industry and Commerce of Beijing Municipality, is established. The chamber has more than 300 member companies, with two branches (including Tai'an the Zibo) and four preparatory branches (including Liaocheng, Jining, Dezhou and Dongying). June 20, 2011, the signing ceremony of the strategic cooperative agreement between the Shandong Changlin Group and Beijing Institute of Technology is held in Shandong Province. October 20, 2010, the Jinghai Group of Beijing decides to establish long-term strategic cooperative partnerships with the Jinkai Petro-Chemical Equipments Group of Shandong. October 27, 2011, the Datang (Shandong) Power Generation Company and the Beijing Coal Group sign a cooperative framework agreement concerning the development of the new energy projects. This includes a preliminary demonstration of 50,000 kilowatts of wind power projects and solar photovoltaic power construction in wasteland. February 29, 2012, the Shandong provincial government and the Capital Agriculture Group of Beijing sign a strategic cooperative framework agreement. The agreement mainly includes the construction of healthy agricultural production bases in Shandong Province and the secured supply of agriculture products to Beijing Municipality.

Beijing-Shanghai

[Quick Facts] Average distance = 1463 km; Geographical adjacency = 0; Index of ethnic linkages = 0.9631 (2000) and 0.9696 (2010); Freight exchange via national railway = 660 k tons (2000) and 330 k tons (2010). ★ April 4–10, 2000, during the "China East-West Cooperation, Investment and Trade Fair" in Xi'an City, Shaanxi Province, the Science and Technology Commission of Beijing Municipality participates in the meeting of science, technology and economic cooperation, and sign a framework agreement of strengthening the scientific and technological cooperation between Beijing and Shanghai. December 24, 2003, the Beijing Communications Company of China Unicom and the Shanghai Bell Alcatel Co., Ltd. sign a joint venture agreement, with a total value of 20 million US dollars. The first phase of the project is to build an entire capacity of about 5000 equivalent

155 M circuits (equaling to 300,000 equivalent 2 M circuits), which is about 1.5 times of existing transmission network. February 13, 2009, the Intellectual Property Departments of the four municipalities of Beijing, Tianjin, Shanghai, Chongqing sign, in Shanghai, a cooperative framework agreement "Joint Conference of Beijing, Tianjin, Shanghai and Chongqing Intellectual Property—2009 Project Cooperation Framework Agreement" and pledge to comprehensively cooperate in the collaboration of law enforcement, exchange of intellectual property information, data bank of intellectual property experts, and public services. February 17, 2012, the Beijing Xinwei Telecom Technology Co., Ltd. and the Shanghai Xinchan Communications Services Co., Ltd. sign a memorandum of strategic cooperation in Beijing. June 28, 2012, the Beijing Capital International Airport, the Shanghai Pudong International Airport and the Shanghai Hongqiao International Airport sign, in Beijing, the framework agreement of exchange and cooperation in the airport services management, which is the first such kind of agreement in China.

Beijing-Shanxi

[Quick Facts] Average distance = 514 km; Geographical adjacency = 0; Index of ethnic linkages = 0.9600 (2000) and 0.9618 (2010); Freight exchange via national railway = 14,850 k tons (2000) and 10,040 k tons (2010). ★ April 19, 2007, the Shanxi Chamber of Commerce in Beijing is established, with a total number of 200 member enterprises. January 11, 2009, School of Engineering of Peking University and Changzhi City of Shanxi Province sign an agreement concerning the joint establishment of the New Energy and New Industrialization Center at Peking University. April 10, 2011, the Rongxinheng Technology Co., Ltd. of Shanxi and the Jigao Construction Co. Ltd. of Beijing sign a cooperative agreement in Pingyuan City, Shanxi Province. April 11, 2012, Peking University and the Shanxi Province sign the "Comprehensive Cooperation Framework Agreement between Peking University and Shanxi Provincial Government", aiming to further strengthen the cooperation in the fields of science, technology, human resources, education and decision-making and consulting. May 30, 2012, The Beijing Development Corporation (BDC), the Shanxi International Energy Group (SIEG), the Beijing Beikong (Group) Company (BBC) and the Shanxi Environmental Protection Fund (SEPF) jointly sign the "Investment and Cooperation Framework Agreement Concerning the Power Generation by the Incineration of Organic Solid Wastes in Shanxi". In this cooperative project, the SIEG, the BBC, the BDC and the SEPF, with shares of 34, 18, 33 and 15 %, respectively, will jointly develop a power generation using the organic solid waste incineration in Shanxi Province. June 29, 2012, the Property and Equity Exchange of both Shanxi Province and Beijing Municipality sign a strategic cooperative framework agreement.

Beijing-Sichuan

[Quick Facts] Average distance = 2042 km; Geographical adjacency = 0; Index of ethnic linkages = 0.9537 (2000) and 0.9437 (2010); Freight exchange via national railway = 610 k tons (2000) and 660 k tons (2010). ★ October 8, 2008, the Sichuan Chamber of Commerce is established in Beijing. As of 2009, the chamber has nearly 100 member enterprises covering such fields as real estate, catering, construction, green technology, legal consultation, IT, automotive, electronics, etc. October 8, 2008, a delegation of Sichuan Province pays an inspection and study tour to Beijing, and holds a meeting of economic cooperation with Beijing Municipality. January 9, 2010, the Zigong (Sichuan) Chamber of Commerce in Beijing is established. According to incomplete statistics, there are 60 Zigong enterprises in Beijing, involving construction, decoration, building materials, lawyer, assets assessment, etc. August 4, 2010, the Sichuan Petrochemical Group and Beijing University of Chemistry and Technology sign a comprehensive strategic cooperative agreement in Chengdu City, Sichuan Province. November 15, 2010, Neijiang City, Sichuan Province signs a cooperation framework agreement with the Beijing Hualian Supermarket. April 15, 2011, the Sichuan Museum and the Art and Design School of Beijing University of Technology hold a signing ceremony of the strategic cooperation between the two sides in Chengdu City, Sichuan Province. March 19, 2012, the scenic area of Yibin, Sichuan Province, and the Tourism Agency of Beijing sign a strategic cooperative agreement, aiming to strengthen the exchange and cooperation between Yibin and Beijing, and to promote the coordination of the two sides' tourist industries. April 4–10, 2000, during the "China East-West Cooperation, Investment and Trade Fair" in Xi'an City, Shaanxi Province and the Science and Technology Commission of Beijing Municipality sign a framework agreement concerning the strengthening of scientific and technological cooperation.

Beijing-Tianjin

[Quick Facts] Average distance = 137 km; Geographical adjacency = 1; Index of ethnic linkages = 0.9838 (2000) and 0.9837 (2010); Freight exchange via national railway = 8360 k tons (2000) and 6730 k tons (2010). ★ April 4–10, 2000, during the "China East-West Cooperation, Investment and Trade Fair" in Xi'an City, Shaanxi Province, the Science and Technology Commission of Beijing Municipality participates in the meeting of science, technology and economic cooperation, and sign a framework agreement of strengthening the scientific and technological cooperation between Beijing and Tianjin. January 13, 2008, Tianjin Municipality and Peking University sign a cooperative framework agreement in

Tianjin; Human Resources Bureau, Healthcare Bureau and Tanggu District of Tianjin also sign, respectively, agreements with Peking University. February 13, 2009, the Intellectual Property Departments of the four municipalities of Beijing, Tianjin, Shanghai, Chongqing sign, in Shanghai, a cooperative framework agreement and pledge to cooperate in the collaboration of law enforcement, the exchange of intellectual property information, data bank of intellectual property experts, and public services. October 16, 2009, the Jingbin Industrial Park of Tianjin Municipality and the Economic and Technological Development Zone of Beijing Municipality sign, in Tianjin, a strategic cooperative agreement. April 2, 2011, Haidian District of Beijing Municipality and Heping District of Tianjin Municipality sign an agreement in Tianjin; the two sides pledge to carry out comprehensive cooperation in science, technology, commerce, education, culture, tourism, and human resources. June 20, 2011, the CAS Beijing Branch and Science and Technology Commission of Tianjin Municipality agree to establish a joint cooperative team in Tianjin. October 25, 2011, the Development Zone of Tianjin Municipality signs a strategic cooperative agreement with the Zhongguancun Association of Committees of Beijing Municipality. The base of the Zhongguancun high-tech enterprises settles down in the Tianjin Development Zone.

Beijing-Tibet

[Quick Facts] Average distance = 4064 km; Geographical adjacency = 0; Index of ethnic linkages = 0.0657 (2000) and 0.0877 (2010); Freight exchange via national railway = 0 k ton (2000) and 10 k tons (2010). ★ April 24, 2009, the meeting of the "Beijing-Lhasa Pairing Aid" is held; and the "Framework Agreement of Beijing Municipality and Lhasa City Concerning Pairing Aid, 2009—2012" is signed. According to the agreement, Beijing Municipality will arrange a pairing aid for four years with a total amount of 240 million yuan mainly in the fields of the social and economic development, personnel training and industrial cooperation. June 28, 2009, the leaderships of Beijing Municipality and Tibet Autonomous Region hold a discussion meeting, aiming to understand the economic and social development of Lhasa City, and the pairing aid of Beijing to Tibet. So far, Beijing has completed more than 20 pairing aid projects in Tibet. September 3, 2009, the CCP Standing Committee of Tibet Autonomous Region signs a cooperative agreement with Beijing Normal University. August 31, 2011, the Women and Child Development Fund of, and the Women's Federation of Beijing Municipality and the Women's Federation of Tibet autonomous region hold the forum of cooperation and development in Lhasa City, Tibet Autonomous Region. In the Forum, the Beijing side donates a 300,000 yuan fund to Tibet, to be used in the Tibet's poor women and children.

Beijing-Xinjiang

[Quick Facts] Average distance = 3768 km; Geographical adjacency = 0; Index of ethnic linkages = 0.4294 (2000) and 0.4253 (2010); Freight exchange via national railway = 320 k tons (2000) and 650 k tons (2010). ★ In 2005, the Beijing Aoxinnong Agrochemicals Co., Ltd. visits the Xinjiang Production and Construction Crops (XPCC); both sides sign an agreement to build a pesticide plant in No. 16 division of the XPCC, with a total investment of a million yuan and a daily production capacity of 10 tons of pesticide. July 10, 2010, the Xinjiang Chamber of Commerce in Beijing is established. July 20, 2010, the Deputy Secretary-General of Beijing municipal government, the Commander of the Hotan Headquarters of the Beijing-Xinjiang Pairing Aid Department, the Economic Cooperation Team of Beijing Pairing Aid Department and the Leaders of the 14th Division of the XPCC hold the ceremony of the establishment of the Headquarters in Hotan. July 20, 2010, the Beijing Productivity Promotion Service Alliance and the Xinjiang Productivity Promotion Center hold a meeting in Beijing; more than 25 members (of which 5 from Xinjiang) participate in the meeting. September 8, 2010, the Associations of Science and technology of Beijing Municipality and of Hotan City of Xinjiang Uygur Autonomous Region sign an agreement of pairing aid. 2011, the Beijing provincial government offers a total of 33 industrial projects to Xinjiang; 16 well-known enterprises such as Beijing Jinyu Building Materials, Beijing Gas Group have investments in Hotan, whose projects cover energy, trade and logistics industry. May 8, 2012, Beijing Normal University and Xinjiang Normal University build a cooperative relationship, aiming to expand the pairing aid work. May 14, 2012, the Xinjiang Forestry Department and the Beijing Gardening and Greening Bureau sign a pairing aid agreement. July 2, 2012, the signing ceremony of the "2012 Beijing-Xinjiang Industrial Assistance Cooperation Agreement" is held in Xinjiang, in which Beijing will invest 16 projects (with a total amount of 6 billion yuan) in Xinjiang.

Beijing-Yunnan

[Quick Facts] Average distance = 3178 km; Geographical adjacency = 0; Index of ethnic linkages = 0.6839 (2000) and 0.6828 (2010); Freight exchange via national railway = 260 k tons (2000) and 200 k tons (2010). ★ September 20, 2009, the Yunnan Chamber of Commerce in Beijing is established. The Chamber has more than 80 members (corporate and individual). The Central United Front Department, Government Offices Administration of the State Council, the National Defense University, Minzu University of China, the Cadres Training College of the Ministry of Civil Affairs, the Management Bureau of the Diaoyutai State Guesthouse, the

Beijing Bureau of Civil Affairs, Beijing Management Office of Social Organization, and the Liaison Office of Yunnan Government attend the general assembly. March 9, 2011, the Yunnan provincial government and the China Datang Corporation sign a strategic cooperative framework agreement in Beijing. May 11, 2011, Beijing Institute of Technology and the Yunnan provincial government sign, in Kunming City of Yunnan Province, a comprehensive agreement on scientific and technological cooperation and development. June 27, 2011, the deputy governor of Chuxiong Yi Autonomous Prefecture of Yunnan Province and the delegation of Museum of Chuxiong Yi Autonomous Prefecture visit the Beijing Natural History Museum, and sign a cooperative agreement in Beijing. March 30, 2012, Beijing Institute of Graphic Communications and Yunnan Open University sign a cooperative framework agreement concerning professional printing. April 21, 2012, the Jindu Law Office of Beijing and the Department of Finance of Yunnan province sign a comprehensive strategic cooperative agreement in the Diaoyutai Hotel, Beijing, aiming to provide extensive law services for Yunnan's financial sector.

Beijing-Zhejiang

[Quick Facts] Average distance = 1589 km; Geographical adjacency = 0; Index of ethnic linkages = 0.9596 (2000) and 0.9646 (2010); Freight exchange via national railway = 420 k tons (2000) and 370 k tons (2010). ★ March 11, 2001, in order to serve the common development of Zhejiang-funded enterprises in Beijing, the Zhejiang Chamber of Commerce is established in Beijing. The Chamber has a total number of 3500 enterprise members, covering the fields of real estate, wholesale market, clothing, food and beverage, jewelry, department stores, construction, steel, energy, culture, industry, mining and others. January 11, 2003, the Ningbo Chamber of Commerce in Beijing is established, which is a member of the Zhejiang Chamber of Commerce; it is the first chamber that Ningbo has established in China. October 28, 2006, the Taizhou Branch Chamber of Zhejiang Chamber of Commerce is established in Beijing. May 24, 2007, an exchange meeting for scientific and technological cooperation between Zhejiang Province and Beijing's universities is held in the Science Park of Tsinghua University; more than 150 enterprises from Zhejiang and 200 experts and professors from 36 universities (including Tsinghua University and Peking University) participate in the meeting. July 23, 2008, the Zhejiang Chamber of Commerce in Beijing and the Alumnus Association of Zhejiang University carry out a strategic cooperation in Beijing. July 13, 2008, the signing ceremony of cooperation between Zhejiang Institute of Education and Beijing Foreign Studies University is held in Hangzhou City, Zhejiang Province. March 10, 2010, the Beijing Technological Exchange Center visits Jiaxing City of Zhejiang Province in order to implement the pairing aid activity entitled "Beijing Action Plan of Science and Technology".

Chongqing-Fujian

[Quick Facts] Average distance = 2196 km; Geographical adjacency = 0; Index of ethnic linkages = 0.9380 (2000) and 0.9394 (2010); Freight exchange via national railway = 280 k tons (2000) and 570 k tons (2010). ★ November 11, 1999, a Fujian provincial delegation pays an inspection to Chongqing Municipality, and the two provincial governments pledge to carry out comprehensive cooperation. Fujian's companies in Chongqing have now reached over 500 in number, with a total investment of 1.1 billion yuan, of which 150 million yuan is invested in the construction of Three Gorges Reservoir. August 2001, the Fujian Chamber of Commerce in Chongqing is established; it has a branch office and more than 400 members. Up to now, Fujian has invested more than 30 billion yuan and provides over 100,000 jobs in Chongqing, playing a positive role for market prosperity and economic development. November 2, 2004, the "Meeting of Economic Development and Cooperation between Fujian and Chongqing", which is organized by the Science and Technology Department of Fujian Province, is held in Fuzhou City, Fujian Province. The meeting focuses on cooperation in high-tech fields and industrial connection and so on. December 20, 2008, the Chongqing Chamber of Commerce in Fujian is established in Xiamen City of Fujian. From 2008 to 2011, the Chamber's members have increased from 40 to more than 200. March 7, 2010, the Communication and Transportation Commission of Chongqing Municipality and the Fujian Provincial Department of Communication and Transportation sign a "Memorandum of Comprehensive Transportation Corridor Construction from Meizhou Bay (Fujian) to Chongqing Municipality". Meanwhile, both sides will have an extensive cooperation in the planning of expressway network and of the transport connection between Chongqing and Fujian. November 5, 2010, Nanan District of Chongqing Municipality and Nanan City of Fujian Province hold, in Nanping City, a jobs offering meeting, with more than 1000 job opportunities from 30 enterprises. December 12, 2010, the Xianyou (Fujian) Chamber of Commerce in Chongqing is established.

Chongqing-Gansu

[Quick Facts] Average distance = 1466 km; Geographical adjacency = 0; Index of ethnic linkages = 0.9137 (2000) and 0.9070 (2010); Freight exchange via national railway = 580 k tons (2000) and 850 k tons (2010). ★ October 2007, Gansu Chamber of Commerce in Chongqing is established. The chamber sets out to assist relevant cities and counties of Gansu Province to attract investment. Now, Chongqing's entrepreneurs have invested 2 billion yuan in Gansu Province. October 18, 2010, Dingxi City of Gansu Province and the Chongqing Taiji Group sign, in Chengdu City, a strategic cooperation agreement in pharmaceutical sector.

September 15, 2010, the Dazu (Chongqing Municipality) Chamber of Commerce in Lanzhou (Gansu Province) is established. May 2011, the Sichuan-Chongqing Chamber of Commerce in Gansu is established. May 27, 2012, the Tourism Bureau of Zhangye City, Gansu Province and the Tourism Bureaux of Yuzhong District, Yubei District, Wulong County, Beibei District and Wushan County (all of Chongqing Municipality) sign an interregional cooperative agreement on tourism. The Zhangye Travel Agency and the local travel agencies of Chongqing Municipality also sign an agreement on group tourism, aiming to further strengthen the tourist cooperation between Zhangye City and Chongqing Municipality, and to promote the interaction between the two tourist markets.

Chongqing-Guangdong

[Quick Facts] Average distance = 1670 km; Geographical adjacency = 0; Index of ethnic linkages = 0.9396 (2000) and 0.9391 (2010); Freight exchange via national railway = 2190 k tons (2000) and 3810 k tons (2010). ★ October 2004, the Chongqing Chamber of Commerce in Guangdong is established. The Chamber has 1000 member enterprises, involving real estate, petroleum and chemical industry, electric light source, electronic components, building materials and sanitary ware, with a total asset of 80 billion yuan. The Chamber has established offices in Shenzhen City, Dongguan City and Foshan City of Guangdong. April 5, 2005, Guangdong Chamber of Commerce in Chongqing is established. The Chamber's members come from building materials, home appliances and daily necessities, real estate, construction, decoration, commerce, electrical machinery, food and beverage, finance, training intermediaries, and others. November 19, 2010, Guangdong Institute of Design and Chongqing University of Posts and Telecommunications sign a strategic cooperative agreement, aiming to expand the bilateral exchange and research cooperation. September 26, 2011, Chongqing and Guangdong sign, in Chongqing, over 200 trade and economic cooperation projects, with a total investment of more than 100 billion yuan. The largest project is the International Convention Center of Yanweii Mountain which is joint venture between Meidi Investment Co., Guangzhou City and the government of Jiangjin District, Chongqing Municipality. March 6, 2012, Chongqing Jiaotong University and the Guangdong JinDongHai Group hold an opening ceremony of research cooperation base, aiming to strengthen the regional economic and social development of Chongqing. March 12–15, 2011, a delegation of Chongqing Municipal League of Supply and Marketing Cooperatives and a delegation of Guangdong Provincial Supply and Marketing Cooperative hold a work exchange meeting in Guangzhou City. December 12, 2011, Guangdong and Chongqing sign, in Beijing, a strategic cooperative framework agreement, aiming to expand the field of cooperation, and create a new pattern of cooperation and joint development.

Chongqing-Guangxi

[Quick Facts] Average distance = 1338 km; Geographical adjacency = 0; Index of ethnic linkages = 0.6282 (2000) and 0.6404 (2010); Freight exchange via national railway = 1840 k tons (2000) and 3880 k tons (2010). ★ March 30, 2006, the Chongqing Chamber of commerce in Guangxi is established. The Chamber has more than 1100 members. December 3, 2006, Chongqing and Guangxi sign an economic and trade cooperation agreement; both sides will, in accordance with the principles of complementary advantages, mutual benefit and common development, carry out cooperation from five aspects of industry, natural resources, modern logistics, trade and property rights. December 3, 2006, the Communication Committee of Chongqing Municipality and the Traffic Department of Guangxi Autonomous Region sign a "Cooperation Agreement of Passage Traffic and Logistics", aiming to promote the joint cooperation in logistics in domestic and overseas channels. April 24, 2009, the CCP and Government Delegation of Guangxi Zhuang Autonomous Region visits Chongqing Municipality, the leaders of both sides hold a forum and sign a framework agreement in terms of deepening cooperation between the two places. March 2010, the Guangxi Chamber of Commerce in Chongqing is established. The Chamber's member enterprises are mainly engaged in bio-pharmaceutics, real estate and construction, and engineering development and construction. June 1, 2010, the Housing Exchange of Nanning City (Guangxi) and the Chongqing Gangyun Real Estate Company hold a opening ceremony of the development of real estate in Nanning City. March 18, 2011, Chongqing Municipality and Guangxi Zhuang Autonomous Region sign, in Chongqing, a cooperation framework agreement in order to promote the common development of news and publishing industries. June 16, 2011, the IQBs of Guangxi and Chongqing sign a memorandum of cooperation concerning the direct custom passing of imported and exported goods. March 19, 2012, the Chongqing Traffic and Transportation Group and the Guangxi Wantong Logistics Group become strategic partnerships in the construction of highways, main roads and international logistics, as well as expanding of Guangxi market.

Chongqing-Guizhou

[Quick Facts] Average distance = 463 km; Geographical adjacency = 1; Index of ethnic linkages = 0.6801 (2000) and 0.7152 (2010); Freight exchange via national railway = 2460 k tons (2000) and 5150 k tons (2010). ★ April 21, 2007, the Chongqing Chamber of Commerce in Guizhou is established. According to incomplete statistics, there are more than 100 Chongqing-funded enterprises in Guiyang City of Guizhou, involving real estate, metallurgy, energy, logistics, finance, food processing, and others. March 1, 2011, Zunyi City of Guizhou

Province and Chongqing Municipality sign a strategic cooperation framework agreement, aiming to strengthen the cooperation between Chongqing and Guizhou in the fields of electronic information, equipment manufacturing, automobile and motorcycle as well as energy, human resource, market expansion, etc. August 17, 2011, the delegations of Chongqing Municipality and Guizhou Province sign, in Guiyang City, a comprehensive strategic cooperation agreement and five specific annexes, aiming to strengthen the regional cooperation and to establish long-term strategic partnerships. April 23, 2012, the Guizhou Chamber of Commerce in Chongqing conducts a commercial trip to Anshun City, Guizhou Province, in order to evaluate the business environment and seek investment opportunities there. May 19, 2012, the Qiannan Prefectural Government of Guizhou Province and the Economic Information Commission of Chongqing Municipality jointly organize the "Promotion Meeting of Qiannan (Guizhou)-Chongqing Economic Cooperation" in Chongqing. The promotion results in 22 cooperative projects, with a total investment of 4.225 billion yuan, covering new materials, building materials, metallurgy, tourism, infrastructure, real estate, etc. June 18, 2012, the Geology and Mineral Bureau of Guizhou Province and Chongqing Wujiang Industry Group sign a cooperation agreement concerning the exploration and exploitation of manganese resources in Songtao Autonomous County, Guizhou Province. September 7, 2012, Chongqing and Gansu sign a strategic cooperation agreement on Inter-city tourism. The two sides will launch the "hundred tourist groups of Chongqing to Gansu" and the "hundred tourist groups of Gansu to Chongqing".

Chongqing-Hainan

[Quick Facts] Average distance = 1837 km; Geographical adjacency = 0; Index of ethnic linkages = 0.8361 (2000) and 0.8463 (2010); Freight exchange via national railway = 0 k ton (2000) and 70 k tons (2010). ★ September 5, 2010, the first member meeting of the Chongqing Chamber of Commerce in Hainan, under the Federation of Industry and Commerce of Hainan Province, is held in Haikou City, Hainan Province. According to incomplete statistics, the number of Chongqing's enterprises registered in Hainan Province reaches more than 1200, covering real estate, catering, construction and others, with a total accumulative investment of more than 60 billion yuan. November 28, 2010, the Chongqing Chamber of Commerce in Hainan Province holds the opening ceremony in Haikou City; the Chamber's members pledge to unite all the Chongqing's enterprises in Hainan and further promote the economic and cultural exchange and development of the Hainan international tourist island. July 9, 2012, in order to raise Chongqing's agricultural productivity, the Chongqing Academy of Agriculture constructs, with a total investment of 6.2 million yuan, a breeding base in Jiusuo Town, Ledong County, Hainan Province. This project, including 2000 m^2 of buildings and 95 mu of arable land, is expected to provide over 15 new categories of vegetable and maize seeds for Chongqing's farmers. August 8, 2011, Bank of China Hainan Branch and the Chongqing Chamber of Commerce in Hainan sign an agreement concerning 4 billion yuan credit limits provided to the Chamber.

Chongqing-Hebei

[Quick Facts] Average distance = 1810 km; Geographical adjacency = 0; Index of ethnic linkages = 0.9367 (2000) and 0.9343 (2010); Freight exchange via national railway = 580 k tons (2000) and 1320 k tons (2010). ★ September 26, 2004, the Hebei Chamber of Commerce in Chongqing is established. There are more than 300 members which come from real estate, construction, labor contracting, catering, commerce and trade and so on. June 23, 2006, the signing ceremony of the long-term agreement of cooperation between the Shijiazhuang Iron and Steel Co., Ltd. and the Chongqing Automobile Research Institute is held in Chongqing. The agreement will combine the production and research from both sides. June 10, 2010, Dingzhou City of Heibei Province and Chongqing Chang'an Automobile Co., Ltd. sign a strategic investment and cooperation agreement concerning the construction of the Chang'an Automobile Hebei base, with a total amount of 30–35 billion yuan to be invested in Dingzhou City by the end of 2015. December 30, 2010, the Chongqing Jiulong Electronic Power Co., Ltd. and the Hebei provincial government sign a strategic cooperative framework agreement, according to which the China Power Investment Group (Hebei Branch) is created in Shijiazhuang City, Hebei Province. May 17, 2012, the Hebei Jidong Technological Development Co., Ltd. signs a technological cooperation agreement with the Chongqing Lifan Automobile Company.

Chongqing-Heilongjiang

[Quick Facts] Average distance = 3431 km; Geographical adjacency = 0; Index of ethnic linkages = 0.9365 (2000) and 0.9339 (2010); Freight exchange via national railway = 270 k tons (2000) and 600 k tons (2010). ★ September 24–27, 2005, a delegation led by the Deputy Governor of Heilongjiang Province visits Wanzhou District of Chongqing Municipality to attend the "2005 Pairing Aid to the Three Gorges Reservoir Area (Chongqing) and the Economic and Trade Fair". The Heilongjiang provincial government donates one million yuan for the construction of a ecological village of Wanzhou District. October 28, 2010, a forum concerning the pairing aid of Heilongjiang Province to Wanzhou District (of Chongqing Municipality) and the interregional cooperation in trade and tourism is held in Wanzhou, Chongqing. The government officials from the two sides exchange the past experiences in the fields of pairing aid, mutual cooperation and the social security of immigrants from Chongqing to Heilongjiang (as result of the construction of the Three Gorges Reservoir in Chongqing). June 24, 2011, Heilongjiang University of Chinese Medicine and the Healthcare Department of Jiulongpo District (Chongqing Municipality) sign a "Postgraduate Refresher Course Agreement". March 28, 2012, the Sichuan-Chongqing Chamber of Commerce in Heilongjiang is established in Harbin City and has 107 members, covering construction, medicine and healthcare, catering, and so on.

Chongqing-Henan

[Quick Facts] Average distance = 1598 km; Geographical adjacency = 0; Index of ethnic linkages = 0.9365 (2000) and 0.9339 (2010); Freight exchange via national railway = 770 k tons (2000) and 1730 k tons (2010). ★ July 3, 2008, the Henan Chamber of Commerce in Chongqing is established. October 20, 2009, Chongqing University and Henan Electric Power Company establish long-term strategic partnerships. May 21, 2010, Henan Polytechnic University and Chongqing Energy Investment Corporation hold, in Henan, an opening ceremony of joint postgraduate-training base and of the master of engineering class. September 1, 2010, Henan Institute of Electric Power Test and Research and Chongqing University of Electrical Engineering sign a strategic cooperative framework agreement, aiming to promote the exchange and cooperation in science and technology. December 30, 2011, the Chongqing Tobacco Monopoly Bureau (Company) and the China Tobacco (Henan) Industrial Co., Ltd. hold the "Chongqing-Henan Business Forum", aiming to further promote technological cooperation in tobacco industry. November 11, 2011, the signing ceremony of the strategic cooperation agreement between the Coal Bed Methane Development and Utilization Co. of Henan Province and the government of Liangjiang New Zone (Yubei District) of Chongqing and the opening ceremony of the Chongqing Yushun New Energy Development Co., Ltd. are held in Chongqing.

Chongqing-Hube

[Quick Facts] Average distance = 1220 km; Geographical adjacency = 1; Index of ethnic linkages = 0.9766 (2000) and 0.9740 (2010); Freight exchange via national railway = 960 k tons (2000) and 1030 k tons (2010). ★ November 2004, the Hubei Chamber of Commerce in Chongqing is established. May 5, 2008, the Lichuan Municipal Government of Hubei Province and the Minsheng Energy Co., Ltd. of Chongqing sign an investment agreement concerning the double-track project of gas pipeline from Jiannan County to Lichuan City, with a total investment of 98 million yuan. November 27, 2009, Hubei and Chongqing governments issue the "Declaration on Tourist Cooperation of the Three Gorges Region". The two sides will open a new chapter of tourist cooperation through the organizing of the "Three Gorges International Tourist Festival". December 8, 2009, the Chongqing Chamber of Commerce in Jingzhou (Hubei) is established. May 17, 2010, the Dali Company of Hubei Province and Fuling District of Chongqing sign a strategic cooperation agreement concerning the asphalt transport, with a total investment of 40 million yuan. October 15, 2010, Chongqing University and the Hubei Yangfeng Group establish a production and research cooperative relationship; the signing ceremony of cooperation agreement is held in Chongqing University. March 29, 2011, the Chongqing Institute of Socialism and Hubei Institute of Socialism establish a comprehensive cooperative relationship; the two institutes hold, in Hubei Institute of socialism, the listing ceremony of teaching base. August 5, 2011, the signing ceremony of joint development agreement of the Yangdong River hydropower project is held in Wanzhou City, which opens the hydropower cooperation between Chongqing and Hubei.

Chongqing-Hunan

[Quick Facts] Average distance = 1094 km; Geographical adjacency = 1; Index of ethnic linkages = 0.9581 (2000) and 0.9583 (2010); Freight exchange via national railway = 530 k tons (2000) and 1360 k tons (2010). ★ August 5, 2007, the Hunan Chamber of Commerce in Chongqing, under the Federation of Industry and Commerce of Chongqing Municipality, is established; the chamber has 85 enterprise members. April 22–24, 2009, the Hunan delegation which led by the Standing Committee of Hunan Province and the United Front Work Department pays an inspection to Chongqing Municipality, aiming to deepen the exchange and cooperation, and jointly promote the development of the two places. November 6, 2010, the Sichuan-Chongqing Chamber of Commerce in Hunan is established. The Chamber has more than 90 member companies, involving catering, entertainment, technology, investment and finance, etc. August 25, 2011, the China Tobacco (Hunan) Industrial Co., Ltd. and Chongqing Tobacco Monopoly Bureau (company) sign, in Chongqing, a strategic cooperation agreement concerning the base building during 2011–2015. June 6, 2012, Chongqing Municipality sponsors a Hunan tourist promotion meeting. The Tourism Bureaux of Chongqing Municipality and Hunan Province sign a tourist cooperation agreement; the Tourism Bureaux of Jiangbei District of Chongqing and of Changde City of Hunan sign a cooperation agreement.

Chongqing-Inner Mongolia

[Quick Facts] Average distance = 2081 km; Geographical adjacency = 0; Index of ethnic linkages = 0.7930 (2000) and 0.7969 (2010); Freight exchange via national railway = 100 k tons (2000) and 500 k tons (2010). ★ 2009, the Chongqing

Zhonglian Information Industry Co. Ltd. sets up a sub-company in Chifeng City, Inner Mongolia. December 28, 2007, the Chongqing Maoge Food Development Co., Ltd. signs a strategic cooperation agreement with the Inner Mongolia Sai Feiya Corporation. June 26, 2008, the Chongqing Construction and Engineering Group and Alashan League of Inner Mongolia hold a cooperation forum in Chongqing; the two sides reach a strategic framework agreement on a package of bilateral economic cooperation and development. April 25–30, 2012, a multi-party cooperation seminar is held in the Chongqing Institute of Socialism; 19 personages with democratic-party memberships or without party affiliation from Chifeng City of Inner Mongolia participate in the seminar. July 2, 2012, Wengniute Banner of Inner Mongolia and the Chongqing Hengdu Agricultural Development Co., Ltd. sign the "Agreement of Beef Industry Development Cooperation". The Hengdu will invest 1 billion yuan in the development of a beef manufacturing project in Wengniute Banner, with the breeding stocks of 80,000 heads per year.

Chongqing-Jiangsu

[Quick Facts] Average distance = 1828 km; Geographical adjacency = 0; Index of ethnic linkages = 0.9371 (2000) and 0.9357 (2010); Freight exchange via national railway = 420 k tons (2000) and 700 k tons (2010). ★ May 10, 2006, the director of Chongqing Municipal Construction Commission and Jiangsu Bureau of Construction sign, in Nanjing City, a cooperative framework agreement concerning the strengthening of construction industry of Jiangsu and Chongqing. January 2008, the Jiangsu Chamber of Commerce in Chongqing City is established. The Chamber has nearly 200 enterprises members, mainly engaged in real estate development, building materials, hardware equipment, auto parts, medical equipment, municipal engineering, media, machinery manufacturing, electrical and mechanical hardware manufacturing, retail chain, tourism, etc. July 30, 2009, nearly 100 representatives of the well-known enterprises in Kunshan City, Jiangsu Province, visit Chongqing to carry out the exchange and cooperation in production and research. August 27, 2009, the polysilicon project which is jointly operated by the Jiangsu Daquan Group and Wanzhou district, Chongqing Municipality, is invested, with a total amount of 500 million US dollars. August 12–14, 2010, a delegation led by the CCP Secretary of and the Mayor of Chongqing Municipality visits Jiangsu Province, and has an in-depth exchange with Jiangsu counterparts. September 3, 2010, the Symposium of Jiangsu Province pairing aid to the Three Gorges Reservoir and the signing ceremony of cooperation project are held in Nanjing City. Jiangsu Province and Chongqing Municipality sign 13 cooperative project agreements, with a total investment of 24.99 billion yuan. September 6, 2010, Chongqing Municipality and Jiangsu Province establish a cooperative relationship concerning the construction of the Shuangfu International Agricultural and Trade City.

Chongqing-Jiangxi

[Quick Facts] Average distance = 1579 km; Geographical adjacency = 0; Index of ethnic linkages = 0.9365 (2000) and 0.9341 (2010); Freight exchange via national railway = 190 k tons (2000) and 620 k tons (2010). ★ March 24, 2008, Jiangxi Tungsten Industry Group Co., Ltd. visits Chongqing University to seek scientific and technological cooperation. March 20, 2009, Jiangxi Chamber of Commerce in Chongqing is established. It has over 300 member companies covering the fields of medical equipment, office stationery, hotel, ceramics, warehousing and logistics, engineering machinery, construction materials, real estate, electronic communications, food processing, catering and entertainment, and others. June 6, 2009, the Jiangxi Chamber of Commerce in Chongqing is established. The Chamber has more than 500 enterprises members, involving real estate, electron, catering, entertainment and others. January 15, 2010, the Chongqing Silian Measurement and Control Technology Company and the Jiangxi Southern Cement Company sign a strategic cooperation agreement for a period of two years, and sign a project agreement concerning the construction of the six cement production lines, with the production ability of up to 2500 tons per day. January 18, 2010, the Network Education College of Chongqing University strengthens exchange and cooperation with the Chinese Communist Party School of Jiangxi Province. December 20, 2011, the Jiangxi Provincial Highway Investment Group and the Jiangxi Guiyu Engineering Company visit Chongqing Jiaotong University to seek cooperation opportunities.

Chongqing-Jilin

[Quick Facts] Average distance = 3185 km; Geographical adjacency = 0; Index of ethnic linkages = 0.9096 (2000) and 0.9215 (2010); Freight exchange via national railway = 140 k tons (2000) and 380 k tons (2010). ★ August 26, 2008, the Jilin provincial government and Chongqing municipal government sign an agreement concerning the establishment of long-term partnerships in grain supply and marketing. According to the agreement, the Chongqing Grain Group and other Chongqing-based food enterprises will annually purchase, at the market prices, 300,000 tons of corn, 50,000 tons of rice, 50,000 tons of soybean oil from Jilin Province. September 26, 2008, the Sichuan-Chongqing Chamber of Commerce in Jilin is established and the celebration meeting of the Chamber is held in Changchun City of Jilin Province. The relevant leaders of two places attend the meeting. The Chamber has more than 60 enterprise members, covering real estate development, building materials decoration, catering services, electronic information, product sales and other industries. According the statistic, from 2008 to 2012, the number of the Chamber's members is increase from 30 (earliest) to more than 160; these member companies have a total investment of 20 billion yuan. January 28, 2011, the Chuangchun Railway Vehicles Co., Ltd. (the China North Vehicle Group Corporation) sign an agreement with the Chongqing Municipal Government, aiming to build the largest rail transportation equipment development and maintenance base in the Southwest area. February 15, 2012, the Census Research Office of Chongqing Municipality, the Chongqing Bureau of Statistics and Jilin University jointly hold a census research symposium to strengthen the connection between research and application. April 9, 2012, Jilin Province holds a tourist promotion meeting in Chongqing, and the Tourism Bureaux of the two places sign a cooperation agreement. May 22, 2012, the "10th China (Chongqing) High-tech Fair", jointly organized by the Ministry of Science and Technology, the Ministry of Industry and Information, the CAS, and the Chongqing municipal government, is held in the Chongqing International Convention and Exhibition Center. Jilin Province presents 42 innovative, high-tech products at the fair.

Chongqing-Liaoning

[Quick Facts] Average distance = 2827 km; Geographical adjacency = 0; Index of ethnic linkages = 0.8406 (2000) and 0.8495 (2010); Freight exchange via national railway = 300 k tons (2000) and 300 k tons (2010). ★ December, 2009, the total number of businesspersons and other personnel coming from the three Northeast provinces of Jilin, Heilongjiang and Liaoning has reached 50,000. July 13, 2010, the Liaoning Chamber of Commerce in Chongqing (also namely: "Union of Entrepreneurs from Northeast China"), under the Federation of Industry and Commerce of Chongqing Municipality, is established in Yubei District, Chongqing Municipality. The Chamber's members come from the fields of medical science, healthcare, petro-chemistry, building materials, finance, insurance and investment, catering, legal service, logistics, real estate, commerce, construction and others, with a total economic size of more than 12 billion yuan and an annual output value of more than 10 billion yuan. November 8, 2011, the Chongqing Youth Vocational and Technical College and the Liaoning Tianye Aviation Training School sign, in Chongqing, an employment agreement, aiming to strengthen the school-enterprise cooperation. August 13, 2012, Chongqing Normal University and the Jintong Aviation Service and Training Co. Ltd. of Liaoning sign a university-enterprise cooperation agreement. October 9, 2012, the Grain Group of Chongqing signs a cooperation agreement with Dawa County of Panjin City (Liaoning Province) concerning the construction of a agricultural production base in Dawa County. The Group will invest two billion yuan in the base.

Chongqing-Ningxia

[Quick Facts] Average distance = 1596 km; Geographical adjacency = 0; Index of ethnic linkages = 0.6557 (2000) and 0.6503 (2010); Freight exchange via national railway = 60 k tons (2000) and 190 k tons (2010). ★ March 4, 2009, the Ningxia Tourist Promotion Meeting is held in Chongqing, and the travel agencies from the two places sign several cooperation agreements. August 2, 2011, Zhongning County of Ningxia, the Agricultural Investment Group Co. Ltd. of Chongqing and an Israeli company hold, in Yinchuan City of Ningxia, an agreement signing ceremony concerning the cooperative construction of a pasture farming (with of a total 10,000 heads of dairy cattle) demonstration zone. September 16, 2011, Ningxia Hui Autonomous Region and Chongqing Municipality hold, in Yinchuan City, an energy cooperation forum in which the two places exchange ideas about their cooperation in the fields of coal, electricity and other energy items. April 6, 2012, an eight-people delegation, led by the Deputy Chief of the Department of Agriculture and Animal Husbandry of Ningxia, pays an inspection to the work of new rural shareholding cooperatives in Yongchuan District of Chongqing. May 17, 2012, the "Investment Conference of the Pairing Aid of Dadukou District of Chongqing Municipality to Ningxia Hui Autonomous Region" is held in Chongqing; and representatives from the two sides sign agreements on eight cooperative projects (with a total investment of 14.3 billion yuan), of which six (worthy of 9.34 billion yuan) are contracted and two (worthy of 5.03 billion yuan) are intended for further finalization. The cooperative projects mainly involve tourism, trade and logistics, specialty agriculture, manufacturing, and others.

Chongqing-Qinghai

[Quick Facts] Average distance = 1682 km; Geographical adjacency = 0; Index of ethnic linkages = 0.5418 (2000) and 0.5321 (2010); Freight exchange via national railway = 80 k tons (2000) and 460 k tons (2010). ★ October 12 to 14, 2009, a non-CCP delegation of cadres, led by the Chief of the United Front Work Department (also the member of the CCP Standing Committee) of Qinghai Province visits Chongqing. On March 29, 2011, the Qinghai provincial government holds, in Chongqing, the "Qinghai Investment and Project Promotion". May 4, 2012, the Communications Department of Qinghai Province visits Chongqing Jiaotong University to conduct exchange and cooperation in production and research; both sides pledge to further strengthen exchange, and promote the cooperation between the two sides. June 7, 2012, Qinghai Normal University visits the Huxi Campus of Chongqing University. The two sides conduct in-depth exchange in school construction and academic cooperation. August 15, 2012, a delegation led by the Chairman of the Chongqing United Assets and Equity Exchange inspects the Property Rights Trading Market of Qinghai Province. September 7, 2012, Chongqing and Qinghai sign a strategic cooperation agreement on inter-city tourism. According to the agreement, the two sides will launch the "one hundred tourist groups from Chongqing to Qinghai" and the "one hundred tourist groups from Qinghai to Chongqing", respectively.

Chongqing-Shaanxi

[Quick Facts] Average distance = 747 km; Geographical adjacency = 1; Index of ethnic linkages = 0.9363 (2000) and 0.9342 (2010); Freight exchange via national railway = 460 k tons (2000) and 1000 k tons (2010). ★ April 6, 2005, the Sichuan-Chongqing Chamber of Commerce in Shaanxi is established. The Chamber has more than 300 members, mainly engaged in real estate development, building services, hospitality, mechanical and electrical hardware, decoration, landscaping, shoe manufacturing sales, etc. April 14, 2008, the Chongqing Mayor and the Governor of Shaanxi Province sign, in Chongqing Municipality, the "Agreement between the People's Government of Chongqing Municipality and Shaanxi Province Concerning the Strengthening of Economic Cooperation and Social Development between Chongqing and Shaanxi". The agreement covers the six areas of agriculture, industry, tourism, science, education, transport and energy. May 5, 2008, the Shaanxi provincial government and the Chongqing municipal government sign a cooperative agreement between the two places, which includes the transportation of 5 million tons of coal from Shaanxi to Chongqing and others. July 13, 2008, the Shaanxi Chamber of Commerce in Chongqing is established. October 23, 2008, the Education Department of Shaanxi Province and Chongqing City Board of Education sign the "Shaanxi-Chongqing Education Cooperation Agreement", aiming to promote the sharing of educational resources and exchange of educational information, and to the coordinated development of regional education. June 19, 2009, the "Shaanxi Tourist Promotion—Red Tourism of the Yan'an Line", which is organized by the Shaanxi provincial government, is held in Chongqing, aiming to strengthen the all-round cooperation of tourism between Shaanxi and Chongqing, and to build the Western Golden Triangle Zone of tourist cooperation. June 24, 2011, the signing ceremony of strategic cooperation agreement of Shaanxi provincial government and the Bank of Chongqing and the opening ceremony of the Bank of Chongqing Xi'an Branch are held in Xi'an City.

Chongqing-Shandong

[Quick Facts] Average distance = 1956 km; Geographical adjacency = 0; Index of ethnic linkages = 0.9366 (2000) and 0.9341 (2010); Freight exchange via national railway = 440 k tons (2000) and 1030 k tons (2010). ★ November 2007, Shandong Chamber of Commerce in Chongqing is established. Up to now, the chamber has more than 90 members. August 2009, the Sichuan-Chongqing Chamber of Commerce in Shandong (prepared team) is established. The Chamber has 35 enterprise members. April 6, 2010, the "Chongqing-Shandong Trade and Economic Cooperation Week" starts, aiming to promote bilateral trade and economic cooperation and pairing aid work between Shandong and Chongqing. June 8, 2011, the Tourism Bureau of Weifang City (Shandong Province) and the Wefang Department of Civil Aviation jointly sponsor the "Discussion Meeting of Tourist Interaction between Weifang and Chongqing", aiming to further reinforce cooperation between the two places. May 17, 2012, a delegation headed by the Rizhao Municipal Committee and the Deputy Mayor pays an inspection to Qianjiang City, Chongqing Municipality and hold a forum there. May 17, 2012, the symposium of pairing aid of Shandong to Chongqing and the signing ceremony of economic and trade cooperation are held in Shandong Province, and 67 cooperative projects are signed, with a total amount of 31.7 billion yuan. May 29, 2012, the Shandong provincial government delegation pays an inspection to Chongqing Municipality, and signs an economic and trade cooperation agreement with a total of 45.3 billion yuan.

Chongqing-Shanghai

[Quick Facts] Average distance = 2167 km; Geographical adjacency = 0; Index of ethnic linkages = 0.9373 (2000) and 0.9376 (2010); Freight exchange via national railway = 220 k tons (2000) and 280 k tons (2010). ★ February 27, 2006, the state-owned enterprises of Shanghai and Chongqing seek cross-city cooperation, and sign an agreement concerning the state-owned enterprises cooperation between the two places. August 28, 2007, the Chongqing Chamber of Commerce in Shanghai is established. November 2, 2008, the Shanghai Chamber of Commerce in Chongqing City is established. February 13, 2009, the Intellectual Property Departments of Shanghai and Chongqing Municipalities sign, in Shanghai, a cooperation framework agreement concerning the intellectual cooperation between Shanghai and Chongqing. November 3, 2009, the opening ceremony of the "Chongqing Culture Week", part of the Shanghai International Arts Festival, is held in Shanghai. The governments of Chongqing and Shanghai sign six cultural exchange and cooperation agreements, which include personnel training, interlibrary cooperation and academic exchange, and others. May 27, 2010, the Customs of Shanghai and Chongqing sign, in Shanghai, a "Memorandum Concerning the Building of an Intensive Mechanism of Coordination and Cooperation". December 8, 2011, the Shipping Exchange of

Chongqing and Shanghai Municipalities sign, in Shanghai, a strategic cooperation agreement, under which the two sides will work together to build a modern shipping service system and to promote the constructions of the Shanghai international shipping center and the shipping center in the upper reaches of the Yangtze River in Chongqing.

Chongqing-Shanxi

[Quick Facts] Average distance = 1441 km; Geographical adjacency = 0; Index of ethnic linkages = 0.9365 (2000) and 0.9339 (2010); Freight exchange via national railway = 120 k tons (2000) and 770 k tons (2010). ★ October 11, 2007, the Chongqing Chuanyi Instrument Company and the Shanxi Coking Company decide to form strategic cooperation partnerships. January 8, 2009, Shanxi Chamber of Commerce in Chongqing Municipality is established, and the member companies cover the fields of chemistry, pharmaceutical industry, building material, real estate and others. May 18, 2011, the Sichuan-Chongqing Chamber of Commerce in Shanxi is established. According to incomplete statistics, there are hundreds of registered Chongqing enterprises in and thousands of Chongqing employees in Shanxi, involving coal, metallurgy, estate, commerce and trade, etc. December 31, 2011, the trade and investment delegation of Jiangbei District, Chongqing Municipality pays an inspection to Dingxiang County, Shaanxi Province. The two places' companies sign nine cooperative projects covering foundry industry, animal husbandry, agriculture, logistics, tourism, real estate, etc., with a total investment of 1.5 billion yuan. February 24, 2012, the Huozhou Coal and Electricity Company of the Shanxi Coking (Group) Company and the Chongqing Institute of the China Coal Science and Engineering Group hold a signing ceremony of the strategic cooperative agreement concerning the safety of coal mining.

Chongqing-Sichuan

[Quick Facts] Average distance = 338 km; Geographical adjacency = 1; Index of ethnic linkages = 0.9389 (2000) and 0.9372 (2010); Freight exchange via national railway = 6470 k tons (2000) and 12,290 k tons (2010). ★ February 3, 2004, Chongqing Municipality and Sichuan Province carry out a comprehensive cooperation; the two sides sign a framework agreement concerning the strengthening of economic cooperation and social development between Sichuan and Chongqing, and both sides sign a cooperative agreement in the fields of transport and energy infrastructure, tourism, agriculture, broadcasting, culture, and police's joint action. August 20, 2006, the Chongqing Chamber of Commerce in Sichuan is established in Chengdu City. April 2007, Sichuan and Chongqing sign the "Agreement

Concerning the Joint Construction of the Chengdu-Chongqing Economic Zone". April 6, 2007, the Sichuan Chamber of Commerce in Chongqing is established. The Chamber has 1400 members. June 2007, Chongqing Municipality and Chengdu, Sichuan Province, establish a National Urban and Rural Comprehensive Reform Pilot Area. May 6, 2008, Ziyang City of Sichuan Province and Chongqing Municipality sign thirty-six cooperative projects, with a total investment of 6.6 billion yuan. October 17, 2008, the Sichuan provincial delegation led by the CCP Committee and PCSC of Sichuan Province pays an inspection to Chongqing, and hold a forum with Chongqing municipal leaders, aiming to deepen the cooperation between and development of the two places. October 31, 2008, a symposium of regional cooperation between Chongqing Municipality and Guang'an City of Sichuan Province is held in Chongqing.

Chongqing-Tianjin

[Quick Facts] Average distance = 2091 km; Geographical adjacency = 0; Index of ethnic linkages = 0.9371 (2000) and 0.9353 (2010); Freight exchange via national railway = 140 k tons (2000) and 350 k tons (2010). ★ September 12, 2007, the Customs of Tianjin and Chongqing sign a memorandum of cooperation of the regional customs. March 18, 2008, Wanzhou District of Chongqing Municipality and the Binhai New Area of Tianjin Municipality carry out exchange and cooperation; the two sides pledge to fully cooperate in the following four aspects: the exchange of cadre training, industrial gradient transfer, investment promotion and inter-enterprise exchange and cooperation. May 28, 2011, the Chongqing Chamber of Commerce in Tianjin is established. July 5, 2011, Chongqing University and the Tianjin Baili Group sign, in Chongqing, a cooperative agreement on research and development (R&D); the two sides will carry out a comprehensive package of cooperation in science and technology, human resources, information exchange, and others. December 12, 2011, Chongqing Municipality and Tianjin Municipality sign, in Chongqing, a strategic cooperation framework agreement of healthcare. According to the agreement, both sides will fully explore their respective advantages and features to further strengthen bilateral exchange and cooperation in the fields of medical treatment and healthcare.

Chongqing-Tibet

[Quick Facts] Average distance = 3654 km; Geographical adjacency = 0; Index of ethnic linkages = 0.0621 (2000) and 0.0833 (2010); Freight exchange via national railway = 0 k ton (2000) and 5 k tons (2010). ★ November 15, 2006, the Tibetan delegation and Chongqing University sign an agreement concerning the bilateral cooperation in technical exchange, personnel training and economic development.

September 23, 2008, the Tibetan Medical College and Chongqing University discuss about their bilateral cooperation. August 7, 2008, Officials from the Department of Commerce of and the Federation of Industry and Commerce of Tibet Autonomous Region and the Lhasa municipal government officials and other relevant officials meet with the delegation of the Chongqing Association of Building Materials to Tibet; both sides also hold a symposium in Lhasa City. The Chongqing Association of Building Materials, the Kaixin Home Company and the Tibet Nanya International Trade Center sign a strategic cooperation agreement. December 29, 2008, Chongqing University and the University of Tibet sign an inter-school cooperation agreement. August 16–20, 2009, the CCP Secretary of Chongqing University pays an inspection to Tibet and signs a "Letter of Intention Concerning the Government Cooperation Project between Chongqing University and Tibet Autonomous Region". August 10, 2011, Chongqing Academy of Animal Science and Agriculture and the Animal Husbandry Academy of Sciences of Tibet Autonomous Region sign a technological cooperation agreement.

Chongqing-Xinjiang

[Quick Facts] Average distance = 3358 km; Geographical adjacency = 0; Index of ethnic linkages = 0.4082 (2000) and 0.4074 (2010); Freight exchange via national railway = 330 k tons (2000) and 640 k tons (2010). ★ April 22, 2006, the Xinjiang Chamber of Commerce in Chongqing is established. September 1, 2010, the Bureaux of Human Resource and Social Security of Chongqing and of Xinjiang Uygur Autonomous Region and the Bureau of Labor and Social Security of the Xinjiang Production and Construction Corps (XPCC) meet in Urumqi, Xinjiang Autonomous Region to carry out labor cooperation; and Chongqing and Xinjiang sign a long-term cooperative framework agreement, aiming to further strengthen the labor cooperation between two places. October 31, 2010, the Chongqing Municipal Transportation Commission and Xinjiang Department of Transportation sign a strategic cooperation agreement, aiming to accelerate the strategic cooperation between Chongqing and Xinjiang. December 18, 2010, the Government of the Xinjiang Autonomous Region sign, in Chongqing, a strategic energy cooperation agreement between Xinjiang and Chongqing. The Chongqing Energy Group will construct a coal mine, with the total production capacity of 50 million tons per year, in Hami during the "12th Five-Year" period. October 25, 2011, a delegation of Karamay City (Xinjiang Autonomous Region) holds an investment promotion meeting in Chongqing Municipality. The delegation brings 15 investment projects, with a total amount of more than 6 billion yuan, involving petroleum and petrochemicals, new materials, equipment manufacturing, tourism and other fields. September 15, 2012, the Chongqing Chamber of Commerce in the Hetian Prefecture of Xinjiang Autonomous Region is established.

Chongqing-Yunnan

[Quick Facts] Average distance = 1101 km; Geographical adjacency = 0; Index of ethnic linkages = 0.6838 (2000) and 0.6849 (2010); Freight exchange via national railway = 780 k tons (2000) and 2080 k tons (2010). ★ September 30, 2009, Chongqing Chamber of Commerce in Yunnan is established, and has 1200 members. March 16, 2010, the strategic cooperation and technological exchange meeting of Yunnan Power Grid Electric Power Company and Chongqing University is held in the Research Institute of Yunnan Power Grid Electric Power at the Kunming Science and Technology Park, Yunnan Province. September 28, 2010, the Kunming Chamber of Commerce in Chongqing is established. July 29, 2011, the Yunnan Provincial Department of Education and Chongqing Municipal Education Commission sign, in Kunming City, a strategic cooperation framework agreement of vocational education; both sides pledge to carry out comprehensive cooperation in the fields of teaching resources, personnel exchange, etc., aiming to promote the common development of vocational educations of the two places. January 4, 2012, the Commerce Commission of Chongqing Municipality and the Baoshan Municipal Government of Yunnan Province sign a framework agreement of the production and marketing of important agricultural production, aiming to strengthening the cooperation of agricultural production between the two places. February 9, 2012, a government delegation led by the CCP Secretary of Chongqing pays an inspection to Yunnan, aiming to make better use of the latter's advantage as well as to enhance cooperation between the two places. February 10, 2012, the Chongqing Municipal Transportation Commission and the Yunnan Provincial Communication Department sign a cooperation agreement, aiming to effectively strengthen the construction of the transport and logistics channels between Chongqing and Yunnan. August 6, 2012, the Ba'nan (Chongqing) Chamber of Commerce in Kunming (Yunnan) is established in Kunming City.

Chongqing-Zhejiang

[Quick Facts] Average distance = 2312 km; Geographical adjacency = 0; Index of ethnic linkages = 0.9389 (2000) and 0.9445 (2010); Freight exchange via national railway = 410 k tons (2000) and 620 k tons (2010). ★ May 19, 2000, the Zhejiang Association of Enterprises in Chongqing is established and, in 2007, changes its name to "Zhejiang Chamber of Commerce in Chongqing". The chamber now has more than 400 members. April 19, 2008, Chongqing Municipality and Zhejiang Province hold an economic and social development conference, aiming to promote mutual beneficial cooperation and common development. June 29, 2008, the Zhejiang Weikang Pharmaceutical Co., Ltd. and the Chongqing Heping Pharmaceutical Co., Ltd. sign, in Chongqing, a strategic cooperative development agreement, aiming to establish long-term partnerships. September 27, 2008, the Trade and Industry Bureaux of Chongqing and Zhejiang sign a strategic cooperation agreement, aiming to utilize the advantages of two place's resources to promote the private economic development of the two places. November 10, 2008, the CCP Secretary of Chongqing Municipality and the Association of Entrepreneurs Zhejiang Province hold a forum in Chongqing. August 25, 2009, Qijiang County of Chongqing Municipality and Zhejiang University sign a strategic cooperation agreement. Both sides pledge to cooperate in the fields of scientific research, consulting services, personnel training, agricultural technology, technological transfer, etc. September 11, 2010, the Symposium of pairing aid of Zhejiang Province to the Three Gorges Reservoir area, and the signing ceremony of cooperation projects are held in Hangzhou City, Zhejiang Province. The 12 pairing cooperative projects amount to a total investment of 18.15 billion yuan. October 26, 2011, the Zhejiang Academy of Forestry and Fuling District of Chongqing Municipality carry out a comprehensive cooperation in science and technology.

Fujian-Gansu

[Quick Facts] Average distance = 3065 km; Geographical adjacency = 0; Index of ethnic linkages = 0.9166 (2000) and 0.9099 (2010); Freight exchange via national railway = 330 k tons (2000) and 510 k tons (2010). ★ June 25, 2000, the Gansu Longhai Ceramics Co., Ltd. and the ceramic companies from Fujian Province sign an agreement, aiming to give a full play of the "Go West Policy", which is promoted by the Chinese government. August 7, 2001, the Zhejiang Enterprise Association in Gansu is established. The association's members involve the construction and building materials, real estate, commerce and trade circulation, water, electricity, chemicals, food and beverage, entertainment and other fields. May 9, 2008, the Zhejiang Enterprise Association of Gansu attends the "Investment Attraction Meeting and the Information Announcement on Major Projects" in Lanzhou City, which is sponsored by the Provincial Investment and Trade Promotion Bureau of Gansu Province. May 13, 2011, Nanan City of Fujian Province and Wushan County of Gansu Province build an exchange and cooperation relationship, aiming to jointly promote the local economic development. June 11, 2010, the Entry-Exit Inspection and Quarantine Technology Centers of Fujian and Gansu sign, in Fuzhou, a memorandum of cooperation. Both sides will further deepen bilateral exchange and cooperation. April 27, 2012, the Fujian provincial government, the Gansu provincial government Liaison Office in Beijing, the Fujian General Chamber of Commerce in Beijing and the Gansu Chamber of Commerce in Beijing jointly organize a business research and pairing investment meeting in Beijing.

Fujian-Guangdong

[Quick Facts] Average distance = 1588 km; Geographical adjacency = 1; Index of ethnic linkages = 0.9864 (2000) and 0.9872 (2010); Freight exchange via national railway = 460 k tons (2000) and 2880 k tons (2010). ★ February 21, 2009, the Federations of Returned Overseas of Guangdong and Fujian sign a cooperation agreement; this marks that the federations of the two provinces will carry out an extensive cooperation in the fields of policy making, cadre training, institute exchange, and others. May 31, 2009, a delegation of the Guangdong Institute of Standardization carries out the standardization research in Fujian Province; and holds a forum with the Fujian Institute of Information Technology and Supervision. April 21, 2010, Fujian and Guangdong Provinces hold an exchange and cooperative symposium, aiming to strengthen their economic and trade relations, and to promote exchange and cooperation; the tourism bureaux of the two places sign an agreement on tourist cooperation. April 21, 2010, Guangdong and Fujian sign a cooperative agreement concerning education of technical workers, aiming to exchange the human resources and to share the market information between the two places. December 15, 2010, the CCP Secretary, Governor, PCSC Chairman and PPCC Chairman of Guangdong Province hold, in Guangzhou City, a symposium with the government delegation of Fujian Province. December 16, 2010, the Fujian Chamber of Commerce in Guangdong is established. December 28, 2011, Fujian and Guangdong provinces hold, in Xiamen City, a forum concerning the technological exchange and cooperation in tea industry; this conference is jointly organized by the Science and Technology Department of Guangdong Province, the Fujian Provincial Department of Science and Technology, the Science and Technology Bureau of Xiamen City and the Technology Bureau of Shantou City, Guangdong Province. September 22, 2012, the Anxi (Fujian) Chamber of Commerce in Guangdong is established in Guangzhou City.

Fujian-Guangxi

[Quick Facts] Average distance = 1860 km; Geographical adjacency = 0; Index of ethnic linkages = 0.6191 (2000) and 0.6345 (2010); Freight exchange via national railway = 420 k tons (2000) and 480 k tons (2010). ★ April 27, 2005, the Agriculture Departments of Fujian Province and Guangxi Zhuang Autonomous Region sign a framework agreement concerning the strengthening of the two places' cooperation in mushroom production. August 27, 2010, the "Sixth Pan-Pearl River Delta Regional Cooperation and Development Forum and the Trade Fair" opens in Fuzhou City, Fujian Province; in the fair the governments of Guangxi and Fujian sign a framework agreement concerning the further deepening of cooperation between Fujian and Guangxi. October 8, 2010, the signing ceremony of agricultural development and cooperation between Fujian University of Agriculture and Forestry and Guangxi Zhuang Autonomous Region is held in Fuzhou City, aiming to implement the cooperation between the two places. June 17, 2011, the "Fujian-Guangxi Agricultural Cooperation Fair", which is jointly sponsored by Fujian Academy of Agricultural Science and the Department Agriculture of Guangxi is held in Fuzhou City. December 5, 2011, the Liugong Group of Guangxi and the Fujian Cement Group sign a strategic cooperation agreement in Fuzhou City. May 15, 2012, a symposium which is co-sponsored by Fujian Province and Guangxi Zhuang Autonomous Region is held in Fuzhou City, and the two sides sign a strategic agreement on bilateral cooperation.

Fujian-Guizhou

[Quick Facts] Average distance = 1838 km; Geographical adjacency = 0; Index of ethnic linkages = 0.6290 (2000) and 0.6671 (2010); Freight exchange via national railway = 460 k tons (2000) and 1220 k tons (2010). ★ December 25, 2001, the Fujian General Chamber of Commerce in Guizhou, under the Guizhou Provincial Federation of Industry and Commerce, is established in Guiyang City, Guizhou Province. It is the first such kind of chamber set up in Guizhou Province. Now, the Fujian's businesspersons working in Guizhou have offered a total employment of 100,000 people. May 24, 2006, Fujian Radio and Television University and Guizhou Radio and Television University sign an agreement on cooperation and joint construction. December 31, 2010, the entrepreneurs of Fujian General Chamber of Commerce in Guizhou pay an investment inspection to Weng'an County, Guizhou Province, and sign a strategic framework cooperation agreement with the County. Both sides plan to attract 1 billion yuan of investment within five years. May 20, 2011, the General Chamber of Commerce of Fujian Province and the Guizhou Chamber of Commerce sign, in Fuzhou City of Fujian Province, a strategic cooperation agreement between the two sides. May 31, 2011, the Fujian Chamber of Commerce in Tongren (Guizhou) is established. September 26, 2011, the Zhangping (Fujian) Chamber of Commerce in Guiyang (Guizhou) is established. June 30, 2012, officials of the Department of Commerce of Guizhou Province visit Fujian Province; the two provinces decide to establish a joint venture of methanol gasoline project.

Fujian-Hainan

[Quick Facts] Average distance = 2374 km; Geographical adjacency = 0; Index of ethnic linkages = 0.8298 (2000) and 0.8423 (2010); Freight exchange via national railway = 0 k ton (2000) and 10 k tons (2010). ★ June 8, 2002, the Fujian Chamber of Commerce in Hainan is established in Haikou City. The chamber (including individual members) has nearly 1000 members, involving the fields of construction and installation, real estate, agriculture planting plant, aquatic processing, building materials, high-tech, education, healthcare and others, with a total investment of nearly 50 billion yuan. August 27, 2010, the Hainan provincial government signs a strategic cooperative framework agreement with the Fujian provincial government, aiming to promote the construction of the West Coast Economic Zone and of the Hainan International Tourist Island. August 29, 2010, the tourist sectors of Hainan and Fujian Provinces sign a tourist cooperative framework agreement during the Conference of Pan-Pearl River Delta, aiming to carry out a comprehensive cooperation in the fields of tourist marketing, product development, management, intellectual development, etc. May 26, 2011, Sanming Municipal Government and the Fujian Chamber of Commerce in Hainan jointly hold a promotion forum of private enterprises in Hainan. The two sides emphasize the development of the projects included in the "12th Five-Year Plan". The projects involve eight key industries and modern service industry, etc., with a total number of 50 and a total of 20 billion yuan. In the conference, Sanming Municipal Government also holds a Sanming entrepreneurs meeting and sign 10 intended agreements, with a total investment of 2 billion yuan.

Fujian-Hebei

[Quick Facts] Average distance = 1915 km; Geographical adjacency = 0; Index of ethnic linkages = 0.9610 (2000) and 0.9628 (2010); Freight exchange via national railway = 910 k tons (2000) and 410 k tons (2010). ★ November 29, 2003, the Fujian Chamber of Commerce in Hebei Province, under the Hebei Provincial Federation of Industry and Commerce, is established in Shijiazhuang City, Hebei Province. Fujian's enterprises in Hebei Province have more than 3300, and involve more than 20 fields of real estate, mining, pharmaceutics, chemistry, tea industry and others, with a total output value of over a 100 billion per year. October 16, 2008, a delegation composed by the Fujian Institute of Electric Power Survey and Design, the Hebei Institute of Electric Power Survey and Design and the Inner Mongolia Institute of Electric Power Survey and Design sign an agreement concerning the engineering design consultancy and the technological transfer of the 1000 MW level ultra-supercritical unit power plant with the Sargent and Lundy Company of the US. April 26, 2009, the Fujian Chamber of Commerce in Hebei and the Hengshui Municipal Federation of Industry and Commerce hold a business and trade promotion symposium. November 17, 2010, the Hebei Logistics (Group) Co., Ltd. confers with the Fujian Material (Group) Co., Ltd. on the matter of closer cooperative partnerships. Both sides sign a strategic cooperative agreement and pledge to carry out cooperation in steel, iron ore, coal, building material, international trade and others. September 15, 2011, the Fujian Xirui Energy Co., Ltd. and the Hebei Zhongfu Coal and Gas Development Co., Ltd. sign an agreement, aiming to carry out regional economic and technological cooperation.

Fujian-Heilongjiang

[Quick Facts] Average distance = 3451 km; Geographical adjacency = 0; Index of ethnic linkages = 0.9552 (2000) and 0.9675 (2010); Freight exchange via national railway = 680 k tons (2000) and 420 k tons (2010). ★ September 13, 2004, some food enterprises of Fujian Province and of Heilongjiang Province sign an agreement concerning the purchase and sale of 56 million tons of grain. December 28, 2004, the Fujian Chamber of Commerce in Heilongjiang is established. October 13, 2009, the IQBs of Fujian and Heilongjiang Provinces sign, in Fuzhou City, a "Memorandum Concerning the Joint Promotion of Agricultural Products Exports to Russia". January 4, 2010, the Fujian Provincial Commission of Foreign Trade and Economic Cooperation and the Heilongjiang Provincial Department of Commerce sign a "Memorandum of Foreign Trade and Economic Cooperation between Fujian and Heilongjiang Provinces". December 26, 2011, the Agricultural Department of Fujian Province and the Agricultural Commission of Heilongjiang Province organize, in Fuzhou City, a meeting on the cooperation of potato production and marketing between Fujian and Heilongjiang. The two sides sign the "Agreement Concerning the Potato Cooperation between the Heilongjiang Agricultural Commission and the Fujian Department of Agriculture" and other 19 agreements of enterprise cooperation, with a total amount of 50,000 tons of potatoes. July 15, 2012, the Harbin Institute of Technology and various enterprises from Fujian sign an agreement of bilateral cooperation on R&D.

Fujian-Henan

[Quick Facts] Average distance = 1549 km; Geographical adjacency = 0; Index of ethnic linkages = 0.9869 (2000) and 0.9825 (2010); Freight exchange via national railway = 2280 k tons (2000) and 2480 k tons (2010). ★ September 23, 2010, the Human Resource Departments of Fujian and Henan Provinces sign a cooperation framework agreement concerning the exchange and sharing of human resources (HR) information between the two provinces. February 12, 2011, the Xinyang Wuyun Tea Group of Henan Province signs a strategic partnership cooperation agreement with the Anxi Tieguanyin Group of Fujian Province. September 28, 2011, the Fujian Bafang Logistics Company and the Guolong Logistics Co., Ltd., a branch of Henan Coal Chemical Industry Group, sign a memorandum of strategic cooperation. November 21, 2011, during the 3rd Ancestor Seeking and Cultural Festival which is held in Zhengzhou City of Henan Province, the Federation of Returned Overseas of Henan and Fujian Provinces sign a cooperation framework agreement, aiming to build a new platform for exchange and cooperation between the two federations. April 9, 2012, Zhumadian City (Henan Province) and the Fujian Chamber of Commerce in Henan sign, in Zhengzhou City of Henan Province, a strategic cooperation agreement. The Chamber will invest, as the first step, 20–30 million yuan in Zhumadian City. April 28, 2012, the Fujian Chamber of Commerce in Henan is established. August 11, 2012, the Fujian Chamber of Commerce in Hebi (Henan) is established.

Fujian-Hubei

[Quick Facts] Average distance = 1013 km; Geographical adjacency = 0; Index of ethnic linkages = 0.9602 (2000) and 0.9645 (2010); Freight exchange via national railway = 1840 k tons (2000) and 1660 k tons (2010). ★ March 5, 2004, the Hubei Chemical Fiber Group and the Fujian Jingwei Group sign an agreement in Hubei Province, aiming to strengthen their bilateral economic cooperation. November 8, 2008, the Hubei Chamber of Commerce in Fujian is established in Fuzhou City. By the end of 2007, there are 100,000 Hubei people working or running companies in Fujian, involving the fields of electronics, science and technology, building material, real estate, dining and entertainment, healthcare, financial security, culture, education, legal consultancy, transportation and logistics and others. In Fujian there have been about 1000 Hubei-funded enterprises which are the average size of a half million yuan or more fixed capital and over ten Hubei-funded enterprises which are the average size of one billion yuan more of fixed capital and of 10 billion yuan or more annual sales. January 13, 2010, the Fujian Chamber of Commerce in Hubei is established. January 28, 2011, Hubei and Fujian Provinces sign a cooperation framework agreement on construction industry, aiming to further strengthen cooperation, to build a bilateral exchange and coordination system, to promote the comprehensive cooperation on construction industry; and to jointly safeguard the market order of the two places. October 14–17, 2011, a delegation led by the Fujian Renjian Group and the Xinnengda Optoelectronics Technology Company pays an inspection to Hubei University to seek cooperation opportunities.

Fujian-Hunan

[Quick Facts] Average distance = 984 km; Geographical adjacency = 0; Index of ethnic linkages = 0.9029 (2000) and 0.9084 (2010); Freight exchange via national railway = 2610 k tons (2000) and 1750 k tons (2010). ★ August 25, 2009, Changting County of Fujian Province and Xinhua County of Hunan Province sign a labor exchange and cooperation agreement. April 18, 2010, the Fujian Chamber of Commerce in Hunan is established. According to incomplete statistics, the numbers of the Fujian people living in Hunan has been of nearly 20 million, with a total investment of 16 billion or more. August 26, 2010, the Hunan Chamber of Commerce in Fujian is established in Xiamen City. November 4, 2010, in the Second Conference of Ports Cooperation in the Pan-Pearl River Delta, held in Changsha City, the departments in charge of port, custom, inspection and quarantine, commercial sector, maritime, rail, electronic port of Hunan Province and their Fujian counterparts sign the "Memorandum of the Full Implementation of the Non-stop Import and Export Passing and Regional Collaboration between Hunan and Fujian Provinces". December 4, 2011, the symposium of cultural system reform and cultural industry development of Hunan and Fujian Provinces is held in Changsha City, Hunan Province. The two sides pledge to carry out an in-depth bilateral exchange and cooperation to promote common development. February 10, 2012, the Bank of Changsha and the Fujian Chamber of Commerce in Hunan hold a bank-enterprise cooperation forum in Changsha City; during the meeting, the bank and the chamber sign a strategic cooperative agreement.

Fujian-Inner Mongolia

[Quick Facts] Average distance = 3303 km; Geographical adjacency = 0; Index of ethnic linkages = 0.7959 (2000) and 0.7998 (2010); Freight exchange via national railway = 270 k tons (2000) and 270 k tons (2010). ★ September 26, 2003, the Fujian Chamber of Commerce in Inner Mongolia is established, aiming to strengthen the multilateral economic cooperation between Inner Mongolia and Fujian and to promote the economic, technological and trade development of the two places. October 16, 2008, a delegation composed by the Fujian Institute of Electric Power Survey and Design, the Hebei Institute of Electric Power Survey and Design and the Inner Mongolia Institute of Electric Power Survey and Design sign an agreement concerning the engineering design consultancy and technological transfer of the 1000 MW level ultra-supercritical unit power plant with the Sargent and Lundy Company of the United States. May 14, 2011, the Fujian Energy Group and the Zhalute Banner government of Inner Mongolia hold, in Fuzhou City, a cooperation and development meeting concerning the project of wind farm, discussing about how to accelerate the first phase construction of the 200,000 capacity of wind farm in Zhalute. September 16, 2011, the Fujian Chamber of Commerce in Chifeng (Inner Mongolia) is established. October 13–16, 2011, a 6-people delegation, led by the Director of the Editorial Committee of Local Historical Records of Fujian Province, visits Inner Mongolia to conduct inspection and exchange.

Fujian-Jiangsu

[Quick Facts] Average distance = 1174 km; Geographical adjacency = 0; Index of ethnic linkages = 0.9862 (2000) and 0.9831 (2010); Freight exchange via national railway = 1890 k tons (2000) and 820 k tons (2010). ★ April 22, 2009, the Jiangsu Chamber of Commerce in Gutian County (Fujian) is established. May 23, 2009, the Jiangsu Chamber of Commerce in Fujian is established in Quanzhou City. October 31, 2009, the "2nd Conference of 6 Provinces plus 1 City in East China Concerning the Regional Transport Development and Coordination" is held in Wuyishan City, Fujian Province. A delegation from Jiangsu Province also participates in this conference. January 5, 2011, the Jiangsu Zhongyan Tobacco Industrial Co., Ltd. and the Tobacco Monopoly Bureau (Co.) of Fujian Province sign, in Fuzhou City, a cooperation framework agreement concerning the construction of tobacco base. April 14, 2011, the "5th Conference of 6 Provinces plus 1 City in East China Concerning the Regional Transport Development and Coordination" is held in Suzhou, Jiangsu Province. A delegation from Fujian Province also participates in this conference. August 27, 2011, the Minnan (Fujian) Chamber of Commerce in Taizhou City (Jiangsu) is established. August 18, 2011, the Fu'an Electric Equipment Co., Ltd. and the Research Center of Fluid Mechanical Engineering and Technology of Jiangsu University sign a strategic cooperation agreement on production and research, and both pledge to build a cooperative mechanism in the fields of scientific and technological research, personnel training and research transferring September 19, 2011, the Forum of Economic and Social Development of Jiangsu and Fujian is held in Nanjing City, Jiangsu Province, aiming to take the opportunity of the development of the western Taiwan Strait Area (which is supported by the Chinese Government) and to promote the exchange and cooperation between the two provinces. December 22, 2011, Xuyi City of Jiangsu Province and Fuqing City of Fujian Province reach a consensus on the cooperative development of lobster industry.

Fujian-Jiangxi

[Quick Facts] Average distance = 622 km; Geographical adjacency = 1; Index of ethnic linkages = 0.9859 (2000) and 0.9819 (2010); Freight exchange via national railway = 4500 k tons (2000) and 14,000 k tons (2010). ★ December 21, 2002, the Fujian Chamber of Commerce in Jiangxi is established in Nanchang City. April 22, 2006, the Jiangxi Chamber of Commerce in Fujian is established in Fuzhou City. December 22, 2006, the vice governor of Fujian Province, the relevant departments of Fujian and the leaders of coastal port cities hold a cross-strait promotion meeting in Nanchang City. In the meeting, the Fujian and Jiangxi official in charge of inspection and quarantine, ports, customs and transportation management sign memorandum of cooperation. December 3, 2008, the Fujian provincial government and the Jiangxi provincial government sign a "Framework Agreement Concerning the Strengthening of Cooperation in the West Coastal Ports and the Promotion of Common Development of Fujian and Jiangxi Provinces". According to this agreement, Fujian will support Jiangxi to construct several large infrastructure projects (including a port of 150,000–300,000 ton berth). July 8, 2009, Ningde City of Fujian Province and Shangrao City of Jiangxi Province sign the "Cooperation Framework Agreement Concerning the Construction of Sailing Access and the "Framework Agreement Concerning the Exchange and Cooperation of Tourism". July 10, 2009, the Trade Promotion Commissions of Jiangxi and Fujian Provinces sign, in Nanchang City of Jiangxi Province, the "Strategic Cooperation Agreement Concerning the Strengthening of Bilateral Cooperation and the Promotion of West Coastal Economic Zone's Development". October 31, 2009, the Transportation Departments of Fujian and Jiangxi Provinces sign, in Wuyishan City, Fujian Province, a transportation cooperation agreement. December 17, 2010, a delegation composed by the CCP Secretary, the PCSC Chairman and the Governor of Fujian Province pays an inspection to Jiangxi Province, and the two sides hold, in Nanchang City of Jiangxi Province, an exchange and cooperation meeting. September 21, 2011, the "Symposium of the West Taiwan Strait Ports Cooperation between Jiangxi and Fujian and the Signing Ceremony of Cooperation Agreements" are held in Nanchang City. These agreements include the "Framework Agreement Concerning the Construction of the Bulk Materials Export and Import Base"; the "Cooperative Agreement on the Ruijing Railway Development Co., Ltd."; etc. November 19, 2011, the Fuzhou (Fujian) Chamber of Commerce in Nanchang (Jiangxi) is established.

Fujian-Jilin

[Quick Facts] Average distance = 3209 km; Geographical adjacency = 0; Index of ethnic linkages = 0.9125 (2000) and 0.9244 (2010); Freight exchange via national railway = 330 k tons (2000) and 430 k tons (2010). ★ October 24, 2000, the signing ceremony of the "Economic and Technological Cooperation Project between Fujian and Jilin Provinces" is held in Fuzhou City, Fujian Province. July 18, 2001, the Vice Governor of Fujian Province and the Vice Governor of Jilin Province, on behalf of their provincial governments, sign, in Fuzhou, a cooperation agreement concerning the establishment of long-term agricultural purchase and sale cooperative relationship. May 12, 2006, a delegation led by the CCP Secretary and the Governor of Jilin Province sign, in Fuzhou City, an "Agreement of the Strengthening of Economic and Technological Exchange and Cooperation" with the delegation led by the CCP Secretary and the Governor of Fujian Province. February 1, 2007, the Fujian Chamber of Commerce in Jilin Province is established. The chamber involves the fields of real estate, metallurgy, light industry, electronics, clothing, architecture, landscape design, farming, healthcare, catering, cultural entertainment, hotels, gold and silver jewelry, department stores and others, with a total investment of more than 60 billion. April 23, 2007, the agricultural cooperation meeting between Fujian and Jilin and the signing ceremony are held in Fuzhou City, Fujian Province. June 13, 2007, the Fujian Chamber of Commerce in Jilin is established. April 26, 2011, a delegation led by the CCP Secretary and the Governor of Jilin Province pays an inspection to Fujian province, and the two sides hold a cooperation symposium in Fuzhou, aiming to promote the bilateral trade and to strengthen the cooperation between the two places.

Fujian-Liaoning

[Quick Facts] Average distance = 2904 km; Geographical adjacency = 0; Index of ethnic linkages = 0.8435 (2000) and 0.8524 (2010); Freight exchange via national railway = 450 k tons (2000) and 100 k tons (2010). ★ April 22, 2004, the Fujian Frontier Corps and the Fuzhou Public Security Frontier Detachment visit the Frontier Departments of Dalian City, Liaoning Province, to discuss the cooperative matters of fight against illegal immigration. The two sides reach a preliminary agreement concerning the establishing of an anti-illegal immigration linkage mechanism and of the long-term cooperative partnerships. 2005, the Putian City (Fujian) Chamber of Commerce in Liaoning is established. April 28, 2007, the Tobacco Monopoly Bureau of Liaoning Province and the Zhongyan Company of Fujian Province reach a strategic cooperative agreement. Under the agreement, both sides will give full play to their brand and market advantages to achieve resource sharing, and will strengthen the comprehensive cooperation in industrial production, commercial marketing. January 12, 2008, the Fujian Chamber of Commerce in Liaoning is established in Shenyang City, which mainly involves real estate, stone, timber sales, ceramic production and sale, engineering, chemicals, clothing (shoes and hats), transportation, gas station, tea and seafood products, etc. January 26, 2010, the Fujian provincial government meets the delegation of the Anshan Iron and Steel Group of Liaoning Province in Fuzhou City, Fujian Province; both sides sign a cooperation agreement concerning the strengthening of cooperation in the fields of coastal steel industry, industrial restructuring, elimination of backward production capacity, development of steel industry and steel deep processing. April 20–22, 2010, the Foreign Economic and Trade Department of and the Association of Returned Overseas of Chaoyan City (Liaoning Province) pay a study visit to Ningde City, Fujian Province to seek investment and bilateral cooperation opportunities.

Fujian-Ningxia

[Quick Facts] Average distance = 3235 km; Geographical adjacency = 0; Index of ethnic linkages = 0.6587 (2000) and 0.6532 (2010); Freight exchange via national railway = 110 k tons (2000) and 140 k tons (2010). ★ August 4, 2010, the Agriculture and Husbandry Department of Ningxia Hui Autonomous Region and the Oceanic and Fishery Department of Fujian Province sign an aquatic development agreement; the two sides pledge to strengthen the cooperation in technology and information exchange, product processing, utilization and development of natural resources, etc. November 29, 2010, the government of Ningxia Hui Autonomous Region holds a promotion meeting of economic and trade cooperation between Ningxia and Fujian in Xiamen City, Fujian Province. The two sides sign a total number of 21 projects, with a total investment of 17.78 billion yuan. The cooperation involves the fields of new energy, new material, processing of agricultural products, business service and others. August 31, 2011, the Education Departments of Fujian and Ningxia sign the "Cooperation Agreement Concerning the Educational Pairing Aid from 2011 to 2012" in Yinchuan City. October 24, 2011, the "Promotion Meeting of Economic and Trade Cooperation between Ningxia and Fujian and the Signing Ceremony," organized by the Government of Ningxia Hui Autonomous Region, are held in Fuzhou City, Fujian Province. The two sides sign 17 projects (involving new energy, new building materials, agricultural product processing and others), with a total investment of 9 billion yuan.

Fujian-Qinghai

[Quick Facts] Average distance = 3281 km; Geographical adjacency = 0; Index of ethnic linkages = 0.5447 (2000) and 0.5351 (2010); Freight exchange via national railway = 130 k tons (2000) and 210 k tons (2010). ★ September 6, 2008, the Chairman of the Zijin Mining (Group) Shareholding Co. Ltd. of Fujian Province and the Vice Governor of Qinghai Province sign a strategic cooperation agreement. The Zijin and Qinghai's mining enterprises will form a joint venture (with a total investment of 8 billion yuan) in the Ganhe Industrial Park of Qinghai, aiming to produce 100,000 tons of copper, 1.2 million tons of sulphur, 650,000 tons of potassium sulfate, 400,000 tons of PVC and 5 million tons of cobalt annually. December 26, 2009, the Fujian Chamber of Commerce in Qinghai, under the Federation of Industry and Commerce of Qinghai Province is established. The chamber has nearly 200 members coming from Putian, Fuzhou, Zhangzhou, Quanzhou, etc., involving the fields of real estate, mining, healthcare, tea and others. September 7–11, 2011, the Qinghai government delegation pays an inspection to Fujian Province, aiming to deepen exchange and cooperation and to promote the cooperative development of the two places. September 7, 2011, the Tourism Bureaux of Fujian and Qinghai Provinces sign a "Framework Agreement of Cooperation on Regional Tourist Development between Fujian and Qinghai Provinces". September 8, 2011, the Port Management Offices of Qinghai and Fujian Provinces sign, in the Xiamen International Conference and Exhibition Center, the "Agreement of Cooperation on Port Passing between Fujian and Qinghai".

Fujian-Shaanxi

[Quick Facts] Average distance = 2389 km; Geographical adjacency = 0; Index of ethnic linkages = 0.9868 (2000) and 0.9826 (2010); Freight exchange via national railway = 660 k tons (2000) and 740 k tons (2010). ★ May 2003, the Fujian Chamber of Commerce in Shanaxi is established. By the end of 2010, the chamber has more than 1000 members, with a total investment of more than 100 billion yuan, which help the two provinces to achieve a multilateral, comprehensive and rapid development. April 5, 2008, the promotion meeting of science and technology project between Shaanxi and Fujian Provinces is held in Xi'an City, Shaanxi Province. More than 40 enterprises from Fujian and 26 research institutes from Shaanxi carry out exchange and docking; the two sides pledge to play their respective advantages and to achieve a win-win development. During the meeting, the two sides reach more than 20 preliminary cooperation projects, including four signed cooperation agreements. August 27, 2008, the "Xiamen Economic and Trade cooperation Forum of Shaanxi and Fujian Provinces", which is organized by Shaanxi Provincial DRC, is held in Xiamen City. The forum invites a hundred representatives of the Fujian Chamber of Commerce and of the entrepreneurs of Shaanxi, aiming to promote the investment in Shaanxi Province. September 9, 2008, the Shaanxi Chamber of Commerce in Fujian is established in Xiamen City. December 27, 2010, several companies of Ankang City of Shaanxi Province and the Zhongyan Company of Fujian Province sign a strategic cooperation agreement. March 11, 2012, the trade delegations of Shaanxi and Fujian Provinces hold a promotion meeting, aiming to promote the transferring of scientific and technological achievements and to strengthen the in-depth cooperation between the eastern and western provinces.

Fujian-Shandong

[Quick Facts] Average distance = 1837 km; Geographical adjacency = 0; Index of ethnic linkages = 0.9869 (2000) and 0.9827 (2010); Freight exchange via national railway = 1600 k tons (2000) and 900 k tons (2010). ★ July 10, 2006, the Zijin Mining Group of Fujian Province and the Guoda Gold Co., Ltd. of Zhaoyuan City (Shandong Province), both of which are the largest gold enterprises in China, sign a strategic cooperation agreement. August 14, 2008, the Fujian Chamber of Commerce in Shandong is established. The chamber has more than fifty branches, covering more than 20 industries (real estate, mining, steel, coking, petrochemical, building materials, auto parts, telecommunications equipment, jewelry, tea, aquatic products, food processing, fitness equipment and the financial sector, banks and securities, etc.), with a total investment in Shandong has over 100 billion yuan and more than one hundred thousand jobs opportunities per year in Shandong; It has become one of the major Organizations contributing to the economic development of Shandong and Fujian Provinces. June 19, 2009, the Transportation Group of Fujian Province and the Weidong Shipping Co., Ltd. of Weihai City (Shandong Province) sign a cooperation agreement concerning the construction of the none-stop sea route of passenger and freight from Fuzhou (Fujian Province) to Keelung (Taiwan). January 15, 2010, the Shandong Institute of Electric Power Engineering Consulting signs, with the Fujian Institute of Electric Power Survey and Design and the Fujian Yongfu Company, a comprehensive cooperation agreement in Jinan City. April 20, 2010, the Shandong Guoxin Group visits Yongding County, Fujian

Province and the Zhaobao Ecological Farm to seek cooperation opportunities. August 30, 2011, the Shandong Chamber of Commerce in Fujian is established. The first session of the members' congress of the chamber is held in Fuzhou.

Fujian-Shanghai

[Quick Facts] Average distance = 1173 km; Geographical adjacency = 0; Index of ethnic linkages = 0.9878 (2000) and 0.9875 (2010); Freight exchange via national railway = 940 k tons (2000) and 640 k tons (2010). ★ April 14, 2000, the Fujian and Shanghai forum is held in Shanghai. November 14, 2002, the Fujian Chamber of Commerce in Shanghai is established. The chamber has more than 800 enterprise members and more than 8000 group unit members; it is one of the largest chambers in Shanghai. March 19, 2004, the agricultural cooperation project between Shanghai and Fujian is started. April 12, 2009, the Meteorological Bureaux of Shanghai and Fujian sign a cooperation agreement concerning the construction of the "Test Base of Regional Typhoon Observation". March 25, 2010, the Fujian Huaqiao Industrial (Group) Co., Ltd. and the Shanghai Pharmaceutical (Group) Co., Ltd. sign, in Fuzhou City of Fujian Province, a comprehensive strategic cooperation framework agreement. August 19, 2011, the Shanghai Maritime Safety Administration and the Fujian Provincial Office of Marine Fisheries sign a cooperative construction agreement of water safety management work, aiming to carry out a comprehensive cooperation on the work. November 21, 2011, the Consumers Committees of Fujian Province and of Wuyishan City and the Shanghai Consumers Protection Committee sign an agreement to jointly set up a cooperative mechanism to protect the interests of consumers. January 11, 2012, the meeting of cooperation project matchmaking of Fujian and Shanghai and the signing ceremony are held in Fuzhou City, Fujian Province. The two sides sign 13 industrial cooperation projects, with a total investment of 5.13 billion yuan.

Fujian-Shanxi

[Quick Facts] Average distance = 2521 km; Geographical adjacency = 0; Index of ethnic linkages = 0.9857 (2000) and 0.9810 (2010); Freight exchange via national railway = 1280 k tons (2000) and 1120 k tons (2010). ★ January 29, 2000, the Fujian Chamber of Commerce in Shanxi Province is established. The chamber engages in more than 30 fields of valves, auto parts, decoration, tea, fruit, food, pharmaceutics, hotel, wood, stone, ceramic, steel rolling, communications equipment, plumbing fittings, construction, environment protection, go-green equipment, culture and entertainment, alcoholic drinks, health materials, fresh and dried aquatic products, computers, mining, gold processing, clothing and shoes. November 6, 2011, the Shanxi Chamber of Commerce in Fujian is established. The first session representative conference is held in Fuzhou City, Fujian Province. December 9, 2011, the Women Entrepreneurs Symposium of Shanxi and Fujian is held in Taiyuan City, Shanxi Province. The two sides sign a cooperation framework agreement. February 27–29, 2012, a delegation of Fujian investors visits Taiyuan City of Shanxi Province, and signs a purchase and sales contracts of a total weight of one million tons and half million tons of coal with the Shanmei International Energy Group and the Yangmei Guoxin Coal Sales Co., Ltd. of Shanxi Province, respectively. May 10, 2012, the "Promotion Meeting of Economic and Trade Cooperation between Fujian and Shanxi Provinces in 2012" is held in Fuzhou City, Fujian Province. The two sides reach a total of 24 agreements, involving new materials, logistics, education, medicine, tourism, culture, real estate, building materials, electricity, coal and others, with a total contracted investment of nearly 50 billion yuan and intended investment of 24 billion yuan.

Fujian-Sichuan

[Quick Facts] Average distance = 2805 km; Geographical adjacency = 0; Index of ethnic linkages = 0.9533 (2000) and 0.9445 (2010); Freight exchange via national railway = 690 k tons (2000) and 1430 k tons (2010). ★ January 15, 2005, the Fujian Chamber of Commerce in Sichuan is established. The chamber has more than 2000 members. May 23, 2008, the Sichuan Chamber of Commerce in Fujian is established in Xiamen City, Fujian Province. The chamber has 138 members, with a registered capital of 50,000 yuan. August 28, 2010, the matchmaking and cooperation meeting between Sichuan and Fujian and the signing ceremony of economic cooperation projects are held in Fuzhou City, Fujian Province. 94 projects are signed at the meeting, with a total investment of 16.48 billion yuan, involving high technology, resource utilization, modern agriculture, infrastructure, services and others. October 29, 2010, the symposium between Sichuan and Fujian Provinces and the signing ceremony of economic and social strategic cooperation agreement are held in Chengdu City, Sichuan Province. The two provinces sign five projects, including the Fujian Photoelectric Industry Zone in Suining (with investment of 2.5 billion yuan), with a total investment of 3.67 billion yuan. April 20, 2011, the Zhangzhou Municipal Government of Fujian Province and Sichuan University sign a cooperation agreement. November 24, 2011, the "Forum of Exchange and Cooperation of Fujian and Sichuan" is held in Fuzhou City, Fujian Province, aiming to implement and promote the exchange and cooperation between Fujian and Sichuan Provinces. May 14, 2012, the Hengbong Group of Sichuan Province and the Qiushi Corporation of Fujian Province carry out a discussion and cooperation meeting. April 16, 2012, Bazhong City of Sichuan Province and Quanzhou City of Fujian Province become sister cities, and the signing ceremony is held in Quanzhou. April 16, 2012, Zhangzhou City of Fujian Province and Ya'an City of Sichuan Province become sister cities; the mayors of two cities sign a strategic cooperation framework agreement.

Fujian-Tianjin

[Quick Facts] Average distance = 2197 km; Geographical adjacency = 0; Index of ethnic linkages = 0.9778 (2000) and 0.9801 (2010); Freight exchange via national railway = 210 k tons (2000) and 30 k tons (2010). ★ January 1, 2003, the Fujian Chamber of Commerce in Tianjin is established. The chamber has 404 members, mainly involving the five fields of plumbing valves, ceramic, stone, wood, tea, real estate, printing, steel, substation equipment, engineering, decoration, plastic products, food processing and others. June 30, 2007, the meeting of exchange and cooperation between Tianjin and Fujian enterprises is held in Tianjin. June 11, 2009, the Tianjin municipal delegation pays an inspection to Fujian Province, and attends a series of exchange and cooperation activities. The two sides' enterprises reach a preliminary agreement in the fields of trade, logistics, real estate, industrial, science and technology, etc., aiming to strengthen the regional cooperation between Tianjin and Fujian. July 19, 2010, the forum concerning the exchange and cooperation of Tianjin between Fujian Provinces is held in Tianjin. October 13, 2010, the Fu'an (Fujian) Chamber of Commerce in Tianjin is established. December 17, 2011, the signing ceremony of the strategic cooperation between the Binhai Development Co., Ltd. of Tianjin Municipality and the Huilong Investment (Group) Co., Ltd. of Quanzhou City (of Fujian Province) and the Forum of the Hongshu Bay Eco-Habitat are held in Quanzhou. June 21, 2012, Tianjin University of Science and Technology and the Fujian Guonong Agricultural Development Co., Ltd. sign a cooperation agreement concerning the innovation and operation of honey grapefruit processing. July 10, 2012, Fujian Institute of Architectural Design and Tianjin Municipal Institute of Engineering Design and Research sign a comprehensive strategic cooperation agreement. September 9, 2012, the Tianjin Chamber of Commerce in Fujian is established in Fuzhou City.

Fujian-Tibet

[Quick Facts] Average distance = 4887 km; Geographical adjacency = 0; Index of ethnic linkages = 0.0648 (2000) and 0.0863 (2010); Freight exchange via national railway = 0 k ton (2000) and 2 k tons (2010). ★ July 25, 2011, the Fujian Agricultural University and Linzhi Prefecture of Tibet Autonomous Region sign a strategic cooperation agreement. The cooperation projects involve mushroom and grass promoting, bee products processing, wild flowers breeding and the design of the Linzhi Natural History Museum. August 9 to 10, 2011, the dean of Fujian Academy of Agricultural Sciences visits Lhasa City, Tibet Autonomous Region, to participate in the Symposium of Agricultural Science and Technology Cooperation during the "12th Five-Year Plan", and sign an agreement on cooperation with the Tibet Academy of Agricultural Sciences. October 2011, the Fujian Chamber of Commerce in Tibet Autonomous Region, which is the first chamber of commerce in

Tibet, is established in Lhasa City. As of March 2012, the chamber has a total of over 50 member companies. November 18, 2011, Fujian and Linzhi Prefecture sign a framework agreement concerning the cooperation between Fujian Agriculture and Forestry University and Linzhi Prefecture of Tibet. December 4, 2011, a delegation of Linzhi Prefecture of Tibet Autonomous Region visits Fujian Province. Representatives from the two places hold the "Symposium of the Cooperation between Longyan of Fujian and Linzhi Prefecture of Tibet". May 4, 2012, the China People's Political Consultative Committees of Zhangzhou City (Fujian Province) and Motuo County (Linzhi Prefecture, Tibet Autonomous) sign a strategic cooperation agreement. Under the agreement, the two sides will establish a long-term strategic cooperative relationship in the fields of economic, cultural, scientific research and social studies.

Fujian-Xinjiang

[Quick Facts] Average distance = 4957 km; Geographical adjacency = 0; Index of ethnic linkages = 0.4113 (2000) and 0.4105 (2010); Freight exchange via national railway = 410 k tons (2000) and 820 k tons (2010). ★ October 8, 2002, the Fujian Chamber of Commerce in Xinjiang Uygur Autonomous Region is established. The chamber has over 210 member companies, involving finance investment, petroleum, communications, building materials, engineering and electrical machinery, transportation, grain, clothing, medicine, lighting and auto parts, etc. August 8, 2003, the Xinjiang Chamber of Commerce in Putian City of Fujian Province is established. September 28, 2003, the Bureaux of Township Enterprises of Xinjiang Autonomous Region and of Fujian Province sign an agreement concerning the establishment of their long-term relations. Some cooperative projects between the two provinces' enterprises have also been signed, with a total investment of more than 3.5 billion yuan, mainly involving mineral and energy developments. August 1, 2010, a delegation of Fujian's officials in charge of tourism visits Changji Hui Autonomous Prefecture of Xinjiang Uygur Autonomous Region and participates in the forum of tourist development and cooperation. February 4, 2010, the Changji Prefecture Government of Xinjiang Autonomous Region and the Fujian Provincial Tourism Bureau reach an agreement on pairing aid in seven fields, aiming to accelerate the tourist development of the two places. September 10, 2010, the "Promotion Meeting Concerning the Economic and Trade Cooperation between Xinjiang and Fujian" is held in Xiamen City, Fujian Province. June 3, 2011, the "Tourist Promotion of Beautiful Xinjiang" is held in Fujian Province. The Tourism Bureaux of the Fujian and Xinjiang sign a strategic cooperation agreement, and sign an agreement on the arrangements of special trains and chartered flights between the two places.

Fujian-Yunnan

[Quick Facts] Average distance = 2477 km; Geographical adjacency = 0; Index of ethnic linkages = 0.6710 (2000) and 0.6750 (2010); Freight exchange via national railway = 540 k tons (2000) and 1030 k tons (2010). ★ December 28, 1996, the Fujian Chamber of Commerce in Yunnan Province is established. May 17, 2010, Shuangjiang County of Yunnan Province and the relevant companies of Fujian Province reach an agreement on industrial integration and cooperation in tilapia production and processing. February 21, 2011, the Tobacco Monopoly Bureau (Company) of Yunnan Province and the Fujian Zhongyan Tobacco Industrial Corporation take a discussion about the long-term development of tobacco industry. March 19, 2011, the Yunnan Institute of Tobacco Science, the Kunming Yiliang Tobacco Company and the Fujian Tobacco Group hold a forum, aiming to carry out the multilateral cooperation and to promote the regional development in tobacco industry. February 1, 2012, the Departments of Human Research and Social Security of Fujian and Yunnan Provinces convene a labor cooperation forum at the Nanba Market in Kunming City, Yunnan Province. September 23, 2012, the Fujian Chamber of Commerce in Xishuangbanna Prefecture (Yunnan) is established. The Chamber has more than 300 members, mainly engaged in real estate, hotel, metal minerals, chemical building materials, jade jewelry, electronic machinery, clothing footwear, medical, construction and decoration of the tea, non-staple food, electrical appliances, integrated business, and cross border trade. The Xishuangbanna Rural Credit Cooperatives and the Chamber sign an agreement on one billion yuan of credit limit.

Fujian-Zhejiang

[Quick Facts] Average distance = 972 km; Geographical adjacency = 1; Index of ethnic linkages = 0.9896 (2000) and 0.9900 (2010); Freight exchange via national railway = 3410 k tons (2000) and 2940 k tons (2010). ★ February 6, 2007, the Zhejiang Chamber of Commerce in Fujian is established in Fuzhou City. May 12, 2008, the Tobacco Monopoly Bureau (Company) of Fujian Province pays an inspection to the Zhejiang Tobacco Industrial Co., Ltd.; and the two sides exchange views on further cooperation. October 31, 2009, the Departments of Transportation of Fujian and Zhejiang sign a cooperation agreement, aiming to speed up the highway construction, and to promote the construction of an integrated transport network. January 21, 2010, the Fujian Chamber of Commerce in Hangzhou (Zhejiang) is established. August 3, 2010, the Maritime Bureaux of Zhejiang and Fujian sign, in Hangzhou City of Fujian Province, the "Memorandum of Regional Cooperation Concerning the Shipping Security Management and Supervision", aiming to create an interprovincial security mechanism. December 10, 2010, the Fujian Institute of Metrology and the Zhejiang Institute of Metrology sign a "Letter of Intention on Strategic Cooperation." The two sides pledge to strengthen the technological and academic exchange, the cooperation of measuring, testing and scientific research and the exchange of middle-level cadres. September 16, 2011, a Fujian provincial government delegation pays an inspection to Zhejiang Province. The two provinces hold a meeting of economic and social development, aiming to strengthen the cooperation in the fields of marine science and technology, construction of resource development platform, etc., and to promote the development of their marine economies. March 24, 2012, the Zhejiang Chamber of Commerce in Xiamen (Fujian) is established. The Chamber has more than 160 member companies, involving cloud computing, science and technology, environmental protection, energy, real estate, service and others.

Gansu-Guangdong

[Quick Facts] Average distance = 2787 km; Geographical adjacency = 0; Index of ethnic linkages = 0.9138 (2000) and 0.9073 (2010); Freight exchange via national railway = 1140 k tons (2000) and 2160 k tons (2010). ★ July 1, 2006, the Gansu Chamber of Commerce in Guangdong is established. The Chamber has nearly 100 members. April 30, 2008, the Guangdong Chamber of Commerce in Gansu Province is established. The chamber currently has 381 members, covering the fields of construction, real estate, high technology, decoration, trade and logistics, hotels and catering, etc. September 23, 2011, the Dongxing Aluminum Co., Ltd. of Gansu Province and the Guangdong Materials Group sign a strategic cooperation agreement in the Longxi City, Gansu Province. May 19, 2012, the Gansu Chamber of Commerce in Dongguan City of Guangdong is established. July 5, 2012, the Forum of the Federations of Returned Overseas Chinese of Guangdong and Gansu Provinces and the Project Matchmaking Symposium are held in Lanzhou City of Gansu Province, aiming to promote economic and social development, implement the strategic plan of the "Western Development" and to achieve a mutual benefit. August 5, 2012, a senior delegation led by the CCP Secretary, PCSC Chairman and Governor of Gansu Province pays an inspection to Guangdong Province. Gansu Province will carry out an in-depth study of Guangdong's experiences in order to further strengthen and to speed up the economic transition and development of Gansu Province. August 9, 2012, the second congress of the Guangdong Chamber of Commerce in Gansu Province is held in Lanzhou City. The representatives of Gansu Province and the chamber pledge to promote the development of Gansu and to strengthen the cooperation and exchange between Gansu and Guangdong Provinces. August 10, 2012, a senior delegation led by the CCP Secretary, the PCSC Chairman and the Governor of Gansu Province pays an inspection to the China Energy Construction Guangdong Branch. The two sides hope to hold the opportunity of the "Western Development Policy" and broaden areas of cooperation.

Gansu-Guangxi

[Quick Facts] Average distance = 3059 km; Geographical adjacency = 0; Index of ethnic linkages = 0.6179 (2000) and 0.6298 (2010); Freight exchange via national railway = 170 k tons (2000) and 520 k tons (2010). ★ August 6, 2009, Gansu and Guangxi sign, in Lanzhou City, a cooperation agreement concerning the purchase and sale of seed potatoes, the agreement also includes the joint construction of the Science and Technology Park of Potatoes in Dingxi City, Gansu Province. March 4, 2011, leaders of Guangxi and Gansu hold a meeting in Beijing. The two sides pledge to further deepen the comprehensive cooperation between the two provinces in order to explore comparative advantages and to achieve common development. May 2011, the Wuchan Group of Gansu Province and the Guangxi Materials Group hold an exchange and cooperation meeting; Guangxi shows willingness of cooperation in the exploitation of Gansu's unique material resources of nickel, copper, and chemical products. October 23, 2011, the Investment Group Co., Ltd. of Guangxi visits Jiayuguan City, Gansu Province; both sides also convene a cooperation forum. April 10, 2012, a delegation of the Guangxi Grid Corporation visits the Power Corporation of Gansu. Both sides exchange ideas about the operations of wind power. August 16, 2012, the "Gansu Investment Environment Description" and a wine tasting event, sponsored by the Gansu provincial government, are held in Nanning City, Guangxi. September 12, 2012, the Gansu Academy of China Energy Engineering Group Co., Ltd. successfully accomplishes its first interprovincial project—the design of the power supply system for the Jinchuan Nonferrous Metal Processing Park of Guangxi.

Gansu-Guizhou

[Quick Facts] Average distance = 2139 km; Geographical adjacency = 0; Index of ethnic linkages = 0.6283 (2000) and 0.6616 (2010); Freight exchange via national railway = 170 k tons (2000) and 1310 k tons (2010). ★ September 6, 2007, the Guizhou Television (TV) Station and the General Radio, Film and TV Station of Gansu Province sign a cooperative development agreement, which creates the first interprovincial TV cooperation mode in China in terms of resource sharing and joint marketing. December 25, 2008, the "Media Cooperation Forum of Guizhou and Gansu Provinces", sponsored by the two provincial propaganda departments, is held in Guiyang City. The two sides hope to maintain the increasing momentum of earnings, to improve the shortage of talent and to expand cooperation areas. November 16–20, 2009, the project promotion meeting of traditional Chinese medicine industry of Dingxi of Gansu and a trade fair are held in Guiyang City, Guizhou Province. Dingxi of Gansu Province and the Bailing Pharmaceutical Company and other companies of Guizhou sign an agreement, with a total value of 280 million yuan. The agreement includes the Longxi Medicine Development Base

Project (with 100 million yuan) and the R&D Project of Longxi Medicine (with 80 million yuan). August 21, 2012, a delegation of the Trade and Industry Bureau of Guizhou Province visits Gansu Province to study and observe the operations of food security information network and of food safety monitoring platform.

Gansu-Hainan

[Quick Facts] Average distance = 3596 km; Geographical adjacency = 0; Index of ethnic linkages = 0.8284 (2000) and 0.8384 (2010); Freight exchange via national railway = 0 k ton (2000) and 10 k tons (2010). ★ April 8, 1994, the Gansu Association of Enterprises in Hainan (Hainan and Gansu Chamber of Commerce) is established. May 25, 2006, the Gansu provincial government and the Hainan Airlines Group sign, in Lanzhou City of Gansu Province, an agreement concerning the cooperation on air transportation and airport management. May 25, 2009, the signing ceremonies of strategic cooperation between Gansu provincial government and the Hainan Airlines Group and of airport property reconstruction between the SASAC of Gansu Province and the Haikou Meilan International Airport are held in Lanzhou City, Gansu Province. July 8, 2011, the 17th session of the "China Lanzhou Investment and Trade Fair" is held in Lanzhou City. Lanzhou and Hainan sign an agreement on the projects of "Ma Dahuzi Duo Disi Resort" and "the China Lanzhou Beef Noodle Shops Key Shop", with investment of 200 million yuan. November 28, 2011, the Tourist Management Department of Hainan Economic and Trade College visits Gansu Vocational School of Technology. The two sides pledge to carry out bilateral cooperation, professional exchange and others. July 11, 2012, the "Promotion Meeting of Hainan International Tourist Island Concerning Tourism, Real Estate and Agricultural Products" is held in Lanzhou City. Hainan and Lanzhou pledge to carry out a strategic cooperation in tourist development.

Gansu-Hebei

[Quick Facts] Average distance = 1599 km; Geographical adjacency = 0; Index of ethnic linkages = 0.9224 (2000) and 0.9151 (2010); Freight exchange via national railway = 810 k tons (2000) and 2060 k tons (2010). ★ June 19, 2009, the Industry and Commerce Bureaux of, the Fire Fighting Commissions of and the Express Associations of Hebei and Gansu Provinces establish a "12,305"/"12,315" calling platform, aiming to establish an information exchange and coordination mechanism and to strengthen the bilateral cooperation in the protection of consumers. March 26, 2010, the Department of Industry and Information Technology of and the Civil Blasting Bureau of Hebei Province and the Shijiazhuang Chenggong Engineering and Electronic Company pay an inspection to the Jiulian Group (Co.) of Gansu Province. June 20, 2011, the Hebei Chamber of Commerce in Tianshui City of

Gansu Province is established. The chamber has 64 enterprise members and 120 individual members, including the fields of aquaculture, cultural industries, mineral development, e-commerce, transport and logistics, building materials, IT, hotel and catering, manufacturing, engineering, machinery and others. The chamber has also 12 member companies whose average asset scale reaches 10 million yuan. December 2010, the Preparatory Committee of the Hebei Chamber of Commerce in Tianshui City of Gansu Province holds it first congress of representatives. July 2011, the Hebei Chamber of Commerce in Gansu is established. The Chamber has 115 member enterprises, covering mining, wire and cable, real estate, electrical and mechanical equipments, building materials, automobile sales, clothing and shoes, food and beverage, entertainment, etc.

Gansu-Heilongjiang

[Quick Facts] Average distance = 3099 km; Geographical adjacency = 0; Index of ethnic linkages = 0.9177 (2000) and 0.9097 (2010); Freight exchange via national railway = 270 k tons (2000) and 530 k tons (2010). ★ June 11, 2002, Gansu and Heilongjiang Provinces sign a trade and economic cooperation framework agreement, including four contracted projects, with a total value of 290 million yuan. July 10, 2006, Gansu and Heilongjiang Provinces reach an agreement on grain production and marketing cooperation, in which Gansu will purchase 100 million kg of gains annually from Heilongjiang. In addition, Heilongjiang will also help Gansu to solve its imbalanced structure grain supply (that is, rice supply heavily relies on other provinces), to promote of reform of rice production enterprises, and to improve their industrial competitiveness. December 17, 2007, the "Gansu Radio & TV Week" is officially launched in Heilongjiang. September 2, 2008, the IQBs of Heilongjiang and Gansu Provinces sign the "Memorandum of Cooperation Concerning the Joint Promotion of Gansu's Fruits Export to Russia". March 2012, Heilongjiang Chamber of Commerce in Gansu is established in Lanzhou City, Gansu Province. According to incomplete statistics, the number of Heilongjiang's entrepreneurs in Gansu reaches 200,000–300,000, involving construction, real estate, building materials, furniture, electronics, audio-visual, media, clothing, food, machinery, trade, logistics, catering and entertainment and others.

Gansu-Henan

[Quick Facts] Average distance = 1187 km; Geographical adjacency = 0; Index of ethnic linkages = 0.9247 (2000) and 0.9173 (2010); Freight exchange via national railway = 2170 k tons (2000) and 6020 k tons (2010). ★ December 16, 2008, the

Henan Chamber of Commerce in Gansu Province is established; the opening ceremony is held in Lanzhou City, Gansu Province. August 27, 2009, the "Grain Production and Distribution Fair of Gansu and Henan" is held in Lanzhou City; the two sides sign a strategic cooperation agreement; the Grain Storage and Transportation Company of and the Grain Purchasing and Selling Company of Gansu Province sign a half million ton grain purchase agreement with the grain bureaux of relevant counties of and the enterprises of Henan Province. June 9, 2010, the Coalfield Geology Bureaux of Henan and Gansu Provinces hold an exchange and cooperation forum, aiming to seek a new strategy of reform and development. May 26, 2012, the Henan Chamber of Commerce in Jiayuguan City of Gansu Province is established. According incomplete statistics, nearly 1000 Henan entrepreneurs have invested in Jiayuguan City, covering all types of industries, employing more than 50,000 people. The chamber has become an important vehicle to promote the interprovincial cooperation and exchange with Henan Province. June 25, 2012, the "Cooperation Agreement Concerning the Protection of Qinzhou's Ancient Dwellings" is signed by the Qinzhou District Government of Gansu Province and the Ancient Building Protection Institute of Henan Province.

Gansu-Hubei

[Quick Facts] Average distance = 1723 km; Geographical adjacency = 0; Index of ethnic linkages = 0.9146 (2000) and 0.9079 (2010); Freight exchange via national railway = 610 k tons (2000) and 3440 k tons (2010). ★ May 31, 2002, Gansu and Hubei Provinces sign a trade and economic cooperation framework agreement and hold the signing ceremony in Wuhan City. According to the agreement, the enterprises of Gansu and Hubei provinces will jointly develop five projects, with a total investment of 208.6 million yuan. December 20, 2007, the Hubei Chamber of Commerce in Gansu is established. The chamber involves real estate development, healthcare, energy, chemistry, architectural decoration, road construction, culture, education, tourist development, landscaping, transport supplies, catering, entertainment, jewelry, clothing and footwear as well as water and electricity, hardware, machinery, department stores, building materials, communications, tea, herbs, and planting, with a total investment of nearly 100 billion yuan. The chamber pays 100 million yuan of taxes to local governments and creates more than 10,000 jobs in Gansu. May 23–26, 2010, the Gansu's relevant municipal governments, the Yintao Company of and the Lintao County Government of Gansu Province visit the Plastic & Electric Appliance Co., Ltd. of Hubei Province, and sign an agreement on the constructions of the Lintao Economic Zone and of the Gudi Plastic Project, with a total investment of 200 million yuan.

Gansu-Hunan

[Quick Facts] Average distance = 2081 km; Geographical adjacency = 0; Index of ethnic linkages = 0.9011 (2000) and 0.9025 (2010); Freight exchange via national railway = 470 k tons (2000) and 990 k tons (2010). ★ January 18, 2010, the Hunan Chamber of Commerce in Gansu is established. April 11, 2011, the government delegation of Gansu Province pays a 4-day inspection to Hunan Province. The leaders of the two provinces hold an exchange meeting and sign a framework agreement concerning the power transmission from Gansu to Hunan Province. September 13, 2011, the official delegation led by the deputy secretary of Hunan Province pays an inspection to Gansu Province. Gansu and Hunan provincial delegations hold an economic cooperation and matchmaking symposium in Lanzhou City. The two sides contract 46 projects, with a total investment of 4.723 billion yuan, and 25 cooperative projects, with an investment of 1.7 billion yuan. September 14, 2011, Lanzhou University and the Hunan provincial government sign, in Lanzhou, a cooperation agreement. Under the agreement, the two sides will share each other's resource advantages and carry out an in-depth cooperation in personnel exchange, scientific and technological innovation, teacher training and academic construction within five years. July 26, 2012, the "Forum of Industrial Cooperation Matchmaking between Gansu and Hunan Provinces" is held in Changsha City; in the forum, the two provinces agree to become closer partnerships and to develop 67 cooperative projects, with a total amount of 10.33 billion yuan.

Gansu-Inner Mongolia

[Quick Facts] Average distance = 1144 km; Geographical adjacency = 1; Index of ethnic linkages = 0.8026 (2000) and 0.8059 (2010); Freight exchange via national railway = 1600 k tons (2000) and 2970 k tons (2010). ★ August 20–21, 2009, "the First Yellow River Shipping Development Forum" is opened. According to the "Framework Agreement Concerning the Regional Cooperation in the Yellow River Development", the Shipping Management Departments of Gansu and Inner Mongolia start the developing and constructing of the "Yellow River Shipping Transportation System". June 29, 2011, the tourist administrations and companies of Jinchang City visit Inner Mongolia Autonomous Region to promote tourist products. The two sides pledge to work together to build a high quality ecological tourist scene in desert. October 14, 2011, the signing ceremony of the agreement of friendly cooperation between the Trade and Industry Bureaux of Alashan League of Inner Mongolia Autonomous Region and Baiyin City of Gansu Province is held in Inner Mongolia, aiming to promote a comprehensive bilateral cooperation and to accelerate the two sides' economic development. March 19, 2012, the CCP

Secretaries of Inner Mongolia Autonomous Region and of Gansu Province attend the signing ceremony of strategic cooperation framework agreement concerning the economic and social development of Gansu and Inner Mongolia. August 3, 2012, Inner Mongolia and Gansu sign a "Declaration on Regional Tourist Cooperation", aiming to jointly promote tourism and cultural exchange, business cooperation and regional linkage.

Gansu-Jiangsu

[Quick Facts] Average distance = 1182 km; Geographical adjacency = 0; Index of ethnic linkages = 0.9151 (2000) and 0.9083 (2010); Freight exchange via national railway = 1750 k tons (2000) and 4010 k tons (2010). ★ April 8, 2004, the Gansu government delegation visits Jiangsu Province. The two sides sign nine economic and trade cooperation project agreements in Nanjing, with a total investment of 1.05 billion yuan, which opens a new round of economic and trade cooperation between the provinces. 2007, the Jiangsu Chamber of Commerce in Jinchang (Gansu) Province is established. The Chamber has 50 member enterprises and 120 individual members. April 25, 2007, the signing ceremony of cooperation agreement between Rudong of Jiangsu Province and Huining of Gansu Province and the ceremony of donation are held in Gansu Province. May 19, 2007, the Jiangsu Chamber of Commerce in Gansu is established. May 14, 2010, Lianyungang City of Jiangsu Province signs the "Land Bridge Logistics Alliance Agreement" with Gansu Province, aiming to work together to build the transport line between Gansu and Jiangsu, and to promote the cooperation and docking of the cities along the land bridge. June 17, 2010, more than 100 researchers and entrepreneurs of Gansu and Jiangsu provinces visit the Lanzhou Institute of Chemical Physics of the Chinese Academy of Sciences, and jointly discuss the application and development of the "Natural Nanostructures Fibrous Silicate Minerals". February 13, 2012, the Agriculture and Animal Husbandry Department of Gansu Province, the Lanzhou municipal government and the Yurun Holding Group Co., Ltd. of Jiangsu province sign, in Lanzhou City, a cooperation agreement. According the agreement, the Yurun Group will invest 3 billion yuan in agriculture-related industries of Gansu Province within five years March 8, 2012, the Federations of Returned Overseas Chinese of Gansu and Jiangsu Provinces sign a friendly and cooperative agreement. March 16, 2012, the labor matchmaking symposium between Jiangsu and Gansu Provinces is held in Nanjing City, Jiangsu Province, aiming to strengthen the rural labor exchange, promote the cooperation between the rural labors and urban employers. June 4, 2012, the press conference of the national eastern-central-western regional cooperation demonstration zone is held in Lanzhou. Gansu and Jiangsu Provinces pledge to jointly build a first national-level cross-region economic cooperation demonstration zone.

Gansu-Jiangxi

[Quick Facts] Average distance = 2088 km; Geographical adjacency = 0; Index of ethnic linkages = 0.9135 (2000) and 0.9066 (2010); Freight exchange via national railway = 130 k tons (2000) and 520 k tons (2010). ★ November 7, 2008, the Jiangxi Chamber of Commerce in Gansu is established in Lanzhou City. April 22–23, 2010, the Tourism Bureau of Jiujiang City (Jiangxi Province) visits Jiuquan City of Gansu Province to promote tourist products. The two sides sign the "Agreement Concerning the Building Friendly Tourist Cities". March 23, 2011, Gansu United University pays an inspection to the Jiangxi College of Ceramic and Arts. Both sides pledge to strengthen exchange and cooperation, and to promote their common development. April 16, 2011, a Gansu government delegation pays an inspection to Jiangxi Province; the two provinces' leaders hold a symposium in Nanchang City, Jiangxi Province, and exchange each other's views on bilateral cooperation and development. July 13, 2011, the signing ceremony of the building of the friendly relationship between Federations of Returned Overseas Chinese of Gansu and Jiangxi Provinces is held in Lanzhou City, Gansu Province. February 2, 2012, the Electric Power Investment Corporation (Group) of Gansu Province and the Saiwei LDK Solar Co., Ltd. of Jiangxi Province meet in Lanzhou City and reach a consensus on cooperation. The two sides pledge to carry out the cooperation in the solar photovoltaic industry and the scaled application of photovoltaic power in Gansu.

Gansu-Jilin

[Quick Facts] Average distance = 2952 km; Geographical adjacency = 0; Index of ethnic linkages = 0.9150 (2000) and 0.9115 (2010); Freight exchange via national railway = 130 k tons (2000) and 300 k tons (2010). ★ August 24, 2003, the provincial government leaders from Gansu and Jilin hold a meeting in Lanzhou City; the two sides discuss their economic and technological cooperation and reach an agreement on 66 projects, with a total investment of 7.29 billion yuan. July 2010, Lanzhou University and Jilin University implement an exchange program of undergraduate students. November 14, 2010, the Nongken Group of Gansu and Jilin Province carry out an inter-provincial cooperation. The two sides will build the first modern agriculture demonstration zone in Qianguo County of Jilin Province (the former Guo'erluosi Mongolian Autonomous County), aiming to improve the efficiency of agricultural production by introducing advanced irrigation technology. The demonstration zone, which occupies 2.25 million mu of land, is formally launched on April 24, 2011. September 29, 2012, the IQBs of Gansu and Jilin Provinces sign a scientific and technological cooperation agreement, aiming to promote the construction of technological inspection and quarantine and to raise the technological capacities of inspection and quarantine of both provinces.

Gansu-Liaoning

[Quick Facts] Average distance = 2552 km; Geographical adjacency = 0; Index of ethnic linkages = 0.8475 (2000) and 0.8552 (2010); Freight exchange via national railway = 620 k tons (2000) and 720 k tons (2010). ★ October 12, 2002, the "Gansu-Liaoning Economic Development Forum", which is chaired by the CCP Secretary of Gansu Province, is held in Lanzhou City of Gansu Province. The Signing Ceremony of Cooperation Projects is also held. June 11, 2008, vice governor of Gansu Province meets the delegation of the Fangda Group of Liaoning Province; both sides exchange ideas about bilateral cooperation. The Fangda donates 2 million yuan to the disaster area in Southern Gansu Province. The Gansu hopes that the Fangda broaden cooperation with the enterprises of Gansu Province. 2009, the Gansu Chamber of Commerce in Dalian (Liaoning) is established. January 5, 2012, Liangzhou government of Gansu Province and the Hefong Livestock Co., Ltd. of Liaoning Province hold a project signing ceremony. The Hefeng company will invest 100 million yuan in Wunan town of Liangzhou, with annual productions of 200,000 tons of swine and poultry feeds and 150,000 tons of ruminant feeds. June 28, 2012, Ning County of Gansu Province and Gaizhou City of Liaoning Province sign a cooperation agreement on the development of sheep industry. The two sides will, in accordance with the principles of mutual benefit, mutual support and common development, promote the sheep industry development of the two provinces.

Gansu-Ningxia

[Quick Facts] Average distance = 468 km; Geographical adjacency = 1; Index of ethnic linkages = 0.7039 (2000) and 0.6996 (2010); Freight exchange via national railway = 5110 k tons (2000) and 8760 k tons (2010). ★ January 26, 2008, the Gansu Chamber of Commerce in Ningxia is established. August 4, 2008, the Economic and Trade Commissions of Ningxia Hui Autonomous Region and Gansu Province agree to build long-term strategic partnerships in coal industry; according to the agreement signed, Gansu will purchase seven million tons of coal from Ningxia. August 20–21, 2009, "the First Yellow River Shipping Development Forum" opens. According to the "Framework Agreement Concerning the Regional Cooperation in the Yellow River Development", the Shipping Management Departments of Gansu and Ningxia start the developing and constructing of the "Yellow River Shipping Transportation System". July 5, 2010, Ningxia holds the "Investment Explanation and Project Promotion Meeting" in Lanzhou City; the promotion mainly shows Ningxia's investment environment and industrial policies and introduces the mainstay industries such as energy, chemicals, food, medicine, and tourism. July 6–9, 2010, the "16th China Lanzhou Investment and Trade Fair" is held in Lanzhou City, Gansu Province. The delegations of Gansu and Ningxia provinces sign agreements relating to energy, chemicals, metallurgy, building materials, food and many other fields. May 15, 2012, the Lanzhou College of Commerce delegation visits Zhongwei City of Ningxia Hui Autonomous Region and signs a cooperation agreement with the Intermediate People's Court of Zhongwei City, aiming to build a cooperative relationship in resource sharing and advantage complementing. March 6, 2012, the school-enterprise cooperation conference between Gansu College of Industry and Technology and the Ningxia Institute of Nuclear Industry and Geological Exploration (formerly: the No. 217 Geological Exploration Brigade of the Ministry of Nuclear Industry) is held in Gansu Province.

Gansu-Qinghai

[Quick Facts] Average distance = 215 km; Geographical adjacency = 1; Index of ethnic linkages = 0.6094 (2000) and 0.6031 (2010); Freight exchange via national railway = 3140 k tons (2000) and 3440 k tons (2010). ★ March 26, 2003, Qinghai and Gansu provinces carry out regional tourist cooperation. March 24, 2004, Gansu and Qinghai provinces decide to carry out tourist cooperation and to jointly explore green tourism. July 10, 2004, the "Lanzhou Investment and Trade Fair" is held in Xining City, Qinghai Province. Qinghai and Gansu Provinces sign six economic and trade cooperation agreements; these projects mainly involve the development of hydropower resources, processing of agricultural and livestock products. August 31, 2006, the Marketing Information Office of Qinghai Agriculture and Animal Husbandry Department and the Qinghai Agricultural and Livestock Marketing Information Center pay an inspection to Gansu Province, aiming to exchange ideas about bilateral agricultural cooperation. June 19–20, 2007, the provincial government leaders of Gansu and Qinghai hold a discussion meeting, aiming to strengthen bilateral cooperation and exchange and to promote the common development of the two provinces. July 3, 2007, the Insurance Regulatory Bureaux of Qinghai and Gansu Provinces carry out interprovincial cooperation. January 22, 2010, the Lake Qinghai delegation visits Lanzhou City of Gansu Province to carry out a tourist promotion meeting. The delegation signs, with more than 160 travel agencies of Gansu Province, the "Tourist Cooperation Agreement in 2010". July 30, 2010, the leaders of Gansu and Qinghai Provinces hold a symposium in Lanzhou City, Gansu Province; the two sides exchange ideas about bilateral cooperation and common development. The two sides pledge to strengthen the bilateral cooperation to achieve a mutual benefit and win-win solution. September 2, 2011, the Gansu Chamber of Commerce in Qinghai is established. November 19, 2011, Gansu and Qinghai provinces carry out the first scientific and technological cooperation to jointly control the ecological environment of the Qilian Mountain region.

Gansu-Shaanxi

[Quick Facts] Average distance = 676 km; Geographical adjacency = 1; Index of ethnic linkages = 0.9174 (2000) and 0.9107 (2010); Freight exchange via national railway = 2930 k tons (2000) and 8930 k tons (2010). ★ January 16, 2008, the Shaanxi Chamber of Commerce in Gansu is established in Lanzhou City. November 24, 2009, the Gansu Chamber of Commerce in Shaanxi is established. July 30, 2010, the government officials of Gansu and Shaanxi provinces hold a conference in Lanzhou City of Gansu Province, and jointly discuss the bilateral cooperation and the method to achieve common development. August 14, 2011, the Federations of Returned Overseas Chinese of Gansu and Shaanxi provinces sign a cooperation agreement; both sides pledge to carry out extensive contacts. June 13, 2011, the Science and Technology Departments of Gansu and Shaanxi Provinces reach a preliminary agreement on bilateral scientific and technological cooperation. July 16, 2011, the Agriculture and Animal Husbandry Departments of Gansu and Shaanxi Provinces sign the framework agreement concerning the agricultural cooperation and development in the Guanzhong-Tianshui (a cross-border region, belong to Shaanxi and Gansu, respectively) Economic Zone. August 26, 2011, Gansu and Shaanxi provinces sign, in Xi'an City, a cooperation agreement concerning the family planning service management of the Guanzhong-Tianshui Economic Zone. October 26, 2011, Gansu and Shaanxi Provinces sign a comprehensive cooperation agreement; both sides pledge to carry out an in-depth cooperation in new product development and application, technological transfer, etc., aiming to jointly promote the regional integration of research and production and to establish a strategic alliance relationship. November 21, 2011, the discussion conference of the Guanzhong-Tianshui Economic Zone and the first joint meeting of Shaanxi and Gansu Provinces are held in Xi'an City of Shaanxi Province; both sides sign the "Strategic Cooperation Framework Agreement Concerning the Implementation of the Development Plan of the Guanzhong-Tianshui Economic Zone", and four other special agreements involving environment, business, tourism and finance. December 26, 2011, Gansu and Shaanxi carry out cooperation in tourism; the companies from two sides sign the "Strategic Cooperative Framework Agreement on Cultural Tourist Industry" and the "Strategic Cooperative Framework Agreement on Investment and Financing of Cultural Tourism".

Gansu-Shandong

[Quick Facts] Average distance = 1853 km; Geographical adjacency = 0; Index of ethnic linkages = 0.9191 (2000) and 0.9125 (2010); Freight exchange via national railway = 800 k tons (2000) and 3780 k tons (2010). ★ July 1, 2010, the Jiuquan municipal government of Gansu and the Luneng Corporation of Shandong sign a framework agreement on the cooperation of development and construction of thermo-power and clean-energy projects. After consultations and negotiations, both sides also reach a consensus on the development of the new energy industry. April 21, 2011, the Tourism Bureaux of Gansu and Shandong Provinces sign, in Lanzhou City, a tourist cooperation agreement, aiming to build a new mechanism of bilateral tourist cooperation and of resource sharing. September 22–26, 2011, the government delegation of Gansu Province pays an inspection to Shandong Province. December 18, 2011, the Shandong Gold (Group) Co., Ltd. and Xihe County (Longnan City of Gansu Province) sign a strategic cooperative framework agreement. The agreement includes the establishment of a joint venture in Dingxi County by the Shandong gold-producing giant and the Tianlong Mining Company of Gansu Province. June 7, 2012, the Seismological Bureaux of Weifang City (Shandong Province) and of Jiuquan City (Gansu Province) become a friendly cooperative pair. July 26, 2012, the Dingxi municipal government of Gansu Province and the Zhaojin Group Co., Ltd. of Shandong Province sign a strategic cooperation framework agreement in Dingxi.

Gansu-Shanghai

[Quick Facts] Average distance = 2185 km; Geographical adjacency = 0; Index of ethnic linkages = 0.9176 (2000) and 0.9108 (2010); Freight exchange via national railway = 460 k tons (2000) and 1220 k tons (2010). ★ August 21, 2000, Gansu Province and Shanghai Municipality hold a forum of economic and technological cooperation. The signing ceremony of the cooperation between Gansu and Shanghai is held in Lanzhou City; there are a total number of 63 cooperative projects, wealthy of 8.45 billion yuan. April 10–12, 2007, Shanghai Institute of Organic and Gansu Province sign a strategic cooperation agreement. The two sides will jointly promote the development of potato processing, and carry out the R&D of biomass, lactic acid, polylactic acid, 1.3-propylene glycol and other non-petrochemical products. April 22, 2007, the Personnel Exchange Centers of Gansu and Shanghai sign an "Agreement of Personnel Exchange and Cooperation between Gansu and Shanghai". January 11, 2011, the signing ceremony of the cooperation framework agreement concerning the police joint action between Shanghai Public Security Bureau and Gansu Public Security Bureau and the opening ceremony of the first police training course are held in Shanghai Public Security College. October 24, 2011, the Public Security Bureaux of Shanghai and Gansu sign the "East-West Cooperation Agreement". December 6, 2011, the Shanghai Chamber of Commerce in Lanzhou (Gansu) is established.

Gansu-Shanxi

[Quick Facts] Average distance = 1327 km; Geographical adjacency = 0; Index of ethnic linkages = 0.9156 (2000) and 0.9083 (2010); Freight exchange via national railway = 880 k tons (2000) and 2170 k tons (2010). ★ March 31, 2007, the Shanxi

Chamber of Commerce in Gansu is established, with more than 200 enterprise members. The Federation covers real estate, mining industry, machining, auto sales, catering services, pharmaceutics, medical devices, general merchandise, biotechnology, electrical equipment, and others, with more than 1 billion yuan of fixed assets. April 15, 2011, a delegation from the Department of Science and Technology of Gansu Province and the Chinese Academy of Sciences Lanzhou Branch visits the Institute of Coal Chemistry of Shanxi Province in Taiyuan City; both sides discuss technological cooperation in the R&D of high-end, coal-related products. April 20–25, 2011, Tianshui Institute of Agricultural Sciences (Tianshui City of Gansu Province) pays an inspection to the Shanxi Academy of Agricultural Sciences; the two sides pledge to carry out regular exchange, to strengthen bilateral cooperation and to promote joint R&D activities. August 22, 2011, Taiyuan, Yangquan, and Linfen Cities of Shanxi Province and Tianshui City of Gansu Province officially launch a cross-provincial tourism cooperation activity. Tourists from these provinces will enjoy half- or free-entrance fees, valid for one year. March 15, 2012, the Wanwei Company of Gansu Province and the Telecom Company of Shanxi Province sign a cooperation agreement on technological cooperation.

Gansu-Sichuan

[Quick Facts] Average distance = 1172 km; Geographical adjacency = 1; Index of ethnic linkages = 0.9303 (2000) and 0.9267 (2010); Freight exchange via national railway = 3690 k tons (2000) and 4030 k tons (2010). ★ June 6, 2007, the Gansu Chamber of Commerce in Sichuan Province is established. May 2011, the Sichuan-Chongqing Chamber of Commerce in Gansu is established. June 17, 2011, Gansu and Sichuan Provinces sign, in Dingxi City of Gansu Province, the "Framework Agreement Concerning Human Resource Utilization and Labor Service Cooperation". July 5, 2011, the industrial cooperation forum of Sichuan and Gansu is held in Lanzhou City, aiming to promote the development of derivative products in petrochemical industry, and to deepen cooperation between Sichuan and Gansu in the fields of equipment manufacturing industry, cultural tourism and others. October 20, 2011, the Forest Public Security Bureaux of Ruoergai County of Aba Prefecture (Sichuan Province) and of Luqu County (Gansu Province) sign the "Agreement of Cross-Regional Police Cooperation in Forestry Area". October 26, 2011, the Traffic Police Departments of Gannan Prefecture (Gansu Province), Linxia Prefecture (Gansu Province) and Aba Prefecture (Sichuan Province) hold a police cooperation meeting in Gannan Prefecture. The three sides pledge to jointly punish illegal vehicles. November 7, 2011, the eighth annual meeting of regional tourist cooperation between Sichuan, Shaanxi and Gansu is held in Tianshui City of Gansu Province. The municipal representatives from Sichuan and Gansu jointly sign the "Tianshui Declaration", aiming to further strengthen the multilateral cooperation in tourism.

Gansu-Tianjin

[Quick Facts] Average distance = 1948 km; Geographical adjacency = 0; Index of ethnic linkages = 0.9320 (2000) and 0.9212 (2010); Freight exchange via national railway = 760 k tons (2000) and 1940 k tons (2010). ★ April 26–28, 2009, a delegation led by the Secretary of the CCP Gansu Provincial Committee and Governor of Gansu Province pays an inspection to Tianjin, and reaches a comprehensive strategic cooperation framework agreement with Tianjin Municipality. The delegation also holds a tourist promotion meeting, introducing the variety cultural of tourist resources of Gansu Province, aiming to strengthen the comprehensive cooperation in the fields of travel agencies, hotels, restaurants, transportation, etc. between the two places. April 28, 2009, the signing ceremony of labor transfer cooperation between Tianjin Municipality and Gansu Province is held in Tianjin. 12 enterprises and 10 technical schools of Tianjin sign the "Cooperation Agreement of Labor Transferring and Personnel Training" with the representatives of 12 prefectures and cities and of Vocational Schools of Gansu; the agreement covers the cooperation between local governments and enterprises, schools and local governments, schools and schools, schools and enterprises. June 8, 2009, Gansu Province and Tianjin Municipality sign the "Memorandum Concerning the Further Strengthening of Pairing Aid in Healthcare and the Promotion of Health Development between Tianjin Municipality Public Health Bureau and Gansu Provincial Public Health Department". March 12, 2010, the matchmaking symposium of labor cooperation and vocational training of Gansu and Tianjin is held in Lanzhou City of Gansu Province. March 15, 2010, the Gansu Provincial Government Labor Office and the Tianjin Economic and Technological Development Zone sign the "Labor Cooperation Agreements". Gansu sets a target of 5 million labor exports. August 6, 2012, the symposium concerning coordination and cooperation between the Eastern and Western areas is held in Tianjin; in which Gansu Province involves.

Gansu-Tibet

[Quick Facts] Average distance = 2188 km; Geographical adjacency = 0; Index of ethnic linkages = 0.0827 (2000) and 0.1067 (2010); Freight exchange via national railway = 0 k ton (2000) and 250 k tons (2010). ★ June 23, 2005, Gansu Province and Tibet Autonomous Region sign the "Cooperation Framework Agreement" in which Gansu will become the major partnership of Tibet's mineral processing. August 5, 2005, an economic and trade delegation of Gansu Province and relevant departments and enterprises of Tibet sign, in Lhasa city of Tibet autonomous region, several cooperation agreements, including: the "Agreement of Economic and Trade Cooperation" (signed by Gansu Provincial Department of Commerce and the Tibet Autonomous Region's Department of Commerce); the "Lhasa—Dunhuang

Regional Tourist Cooperation Agreement" (signed by Dunhuang Municipal Government and Lhasa Municipal Tourism Bureau); the "Agreement of Reconstruction and Expansion Project of the Xiang Bala Tibetan Culture Theme Hotel" (signed by the Xiang Bala Industrial Group Corporation of Gansu and the People's Government of Chengguan District, Lhasa); and the "Agreement of Construction of New Energy Materials Base and the Expansion Project of 2-Million-Ton Lithium Carbonate" (signed by the Baiyin High-Tech Industrial Park of the Chinese Academy of Sciences Gansu Province and the Tibet Mineral Development Co., Ltd). August 29, 2006, the Gansu Department of Labor and Social Security signs a cooperation framework agreement with the Tibet Labor Department; the two sides will, according to the principles of mutual benefit, long-term cooperation and common prosperity, strengthen the labor cooperation of the two provinces. June 15–16, 2007, Lanzhou and Lhasa open a non-stop flight route. The Tourism Bureaux of Gansu province and Lanzhou city, the Hainan Airlines, the Northwest Authority of China's Civil Aviation and other units hold, in Lhasa city, the "Gansu-Tibet Travel Forum". July 30, 2012, the Mining Company of Tibet and the Jinchuan Group Limited of Gansu sign a comprehensive strategic cooperation agreement. August 17, 2011, the Gansu Electric Power Company and the Tibet Power Co., Ltd. hold a meeting concerning the operation of the 750/±400 kV DC Qinghai-Tibet interconnection project; the two sides also reach consensus on other cooperative projects.

Gansu-Xinjiang

[Quick Facts] Average distance = 1892 km; Geographical adjacency = 0; Index of ethnic linkages = 0.4570 (2000) and 0.455 (2010); Freight exchange via national railway = 10,840 k tons (2000) and 22,290 k tons (2010). ★ September 20, 2010, the Gansu Chamber of Commerce in Xinjiang is established in Urumqi; it has had more than 120 member companies whose business activities are mainly concentrated in food service, real estate development, commerce, construction and building materials, and furniture manufacturing. June 23, 2011, the CCP Secretary of Xinjiang Uygur Autonomous Region holds a meeting with the delegation of Gansu Province. Both sides pledge to enhance comprehensive cooperation in coal mining, labor export, oil pipeline maintenance, etc. January 11–13, 2012, the Director of the DRC of and the Director of the Western Development Office of Gansu Province visit Urumqi to discuss matters relating to the bilateral cooperation between the two sides. December 18, 2011, the Gansu Chamber of Commerce in Kashi (Xinjiang) is established. June 9–11, 2012, the CCP Secretary, the PCSC and the Governor of Gansu Province meet the CCP Secretary and the Chairman of Xinjiang Uygur Autonomous Region. Both sides agree: (1) to enhance economic and technological cooperation; (2) to deepen cultural and tourist cooperation; and (3) to strengthen cooperation and exchange in the fields of non-ferrous metals, petrochemicals, coal and other traditional industries as well as wind power, solar power, new energy equipment manufacturing. June 18, 2012, Xinjiang and Gansu begin to develop the largest copper mine in Xinjiang (namely: the Hudehe Copper Mine), with an annual output of 6 million tons of copper minerals. The proven reserves of copper metal content are 362,500 tons (vision reserves are 1 million ton) with a total investment of 1.466 billion yuan. This project has yielded 800 million yuan of revenue per year and provided nearly 1000 jobs.

Gansu-Yunnan

[Quick Facts] Average distance = 2272 km; Geographical adjacency = 0; Index of ethnic linkages = 0.6854 (2000) and 0.6857 (2010); Freight exchange via national railway = 920 k tons (2000) and 1150 k tons (2010). ★ February 5, 2010, the AIDS Associations of Gansu Province visits Yunnan Province to exchange AIDS prevention work. May 25, 2010, a delegation led by the CCP Secretary of the PCSC of Gansu Province pays an inspection to Yunnan Province and holds a discussion meeting with Yunnan's provincial officials. Both sides pledge to further build an effective mechanism of cooperation, promote the complementary advantages, and expand the areas of development. The deputy secretary of Gansu Province and the vice Gansu governor also visit Kunming City, Wenshan Zhuang and Miao Autonomous Prefecture, Xishuangbanna Dai Autonomous Prefecture, Lijiang City, and Tengchong County of Baoshan City to inspect Chinese medicine industry and tourist development. The delegation also pays an inspection the Shanqi Technology Demonstration Park of Wenshan. July 5–10, 2012, a delegation composed of Yunnan's provincial leaders attends, for the first time, the "18th Gansu (Lanzhou) Investment and Trade Fair"; provincial leaders from Gansu and Yunnan hold productive discussions about bilateral economic and trade cooperation.

Gansu-Zhejiang

[Quick Facts] Average distance = 2311 km; Geographical adjacency = 0; Index of ethnic linkages = 0.9135 (2000) and 0.9074 (2010); Freight exchange via national railway = 550 k tons (2000) and 1830 k tons (2010). ★ August 9, 2009, Qin'an prefectural government of Gansu province and Zhejiang Enterprise Association in Gansu sign the "Friendly Cooperation Agreement", aiming to strengthen the cooperation in the field of fruits. July 29, 2001, the government delegation led by the CCP Secretary of Zhejiang province pays an inspection to Gansu and other provinces, reaching agreements on about 163 economic and technological cooperation projects, with a total investment of 6.3 billion yuan. August 7, 2001, the Zhejiang Association of Enterprises (Chamber of Commerce) in Gansu is established. Now, Zhejiang's enterprises in Gansu have reached ten billion yuan of annual sales, with nearly 300 million yuan of gross profits and taxes and more than 250 thousand jobs. The Association members involve construction and building materials, real estate, trade flows, utilities, chemicals, food, beverage and entertainment and other fields. April 29, 2010, the Department of Information Engineering of Gansu Traffic Vocational and Technical School discusses the matters of school-enterprise cooperation with the Dahua Technology Co., Ltd. of Zhejiang Province. February 13, 2011, Jiaxing City of Zhejiang Province and Xi'he County of Gansu Province hold the "Symposium of Human Resources Management and Cooperation" in Xi'he County. Both sides have an in-depth exchange in the matters of complementary advantages and long-term cooperation. September 26, 2011, the Science and Technology Departments of Zhejiang and Gansu Provinces hold a symposium of scientific and technological cooperation. The Department of Science and Technology of Zhejiang Province discusses the possibilities of cooperation with the Chinese Academy of Sciences Lanzhou Branch, Lanzhou Institute of Modern Physics, Lanzhou Institute of Chemical Physics, Lanzhou University, and Lanzhou University of Science and Technology, respectively. May 16, 2012, the Zhejiang Chamber of Commerce in Longnan City of Gansu is established.

Guangdong-Guangxi

[Quick Facts] Average distance = 1334 km; Geographical adjacency = 1; Index of ethnic linkages = 0.6290 (2000) and 0.6449 (2010); Freight exchange via national railway = 7510 k tons (2000) and 16,220 k tons (2010). ★ February 22, 2004, the governments of Guangdong Province and Guangxi Autonomous Region sign the "Agreement Concerning Comprehensive Strengthening the Cooperation of the Province and the Region". The Guangxi Chamber of Commerce in Guangdong and the Guangdong Chamber of Commerce in Guangxi are established in Guangzhou and Nanning, respectively. June 14, 2008, the Tourism Bureau of Wuzhou City of Guangxi Autonomous Region and the Association of Self Organized Tourism of Guangdong Province sign a regional cooperation framework agreement of non-stop self organized tourism, aiming to further promote the in-depth cooperation in the field tourism. August 20, 2008, the Economic and Trade Commissions of Guangxi and of Guangdong sign, in Nanning City of Guangxi, the "Agreement Concerning the Further Deepening of the Cooperation of Guangxi and Guangdong", aiming to develop the Beibu Bay Economic Area of Guangxi, to encourage and guide Guangdong's enterprises to invest in the sea-related industries of the Economic Area, including petro-chemistry, electric power, iron-steel, paper making, ship making and maintenance and IT. December, 2011, Guangdong and Guangxi sign a strategic cooperation framework agreement. Both sides pledge to set up a special cooperation demonstration zone in their border area. The zone runs across the Xijiang River, and the two governments will each develop a 50 km^2 area for carrying out the cooperation. July 16, 2012, Guangdong and Guangxi start the cooperation mechanism of the Red Tourism. Guangdong's financial aid to Guangxi reaches 35 million in that year. The supported projects involve the promotion of an integrated demonstration village, economic and trade cooperation, labor cooperation and tourism. This kind of cooperation dates back to 1996; till now, Guangdong has supported 1.2809 billion yuan to Guangxi.

Guangdong-Guizhou

[Quick Facts] Average distance = 1560 km; Geographical adjacency = 0; Index of ethnic linkages = 0.6300 (2000) and 0.6657 (2010); Freight exchange via national railway = 7050 k tons (2000) and 12,440 k tons (2010). ★ April 23, 2004, the Guangdong Chamber of Commerce in Guizhou is established. There are 1200 Guangzhou-fund enterprises in Guizhou, with a total investment of more than 130 billion yuan, covering power, mining, metallurgy, pharmaceuticals, tourism, real estate, etc. June 9, 2005, the provincial governments of Guangdong and Guizhou Provinces and the Southern China Grid Company sign, in Guiyang City of Guizhou, the "Framework Agreement Concerning the Electric Power Transformation from Guizhou Province to Guangzhou City of Guangdong". The pairing sectors of the two provinces also sign other eight framework agreements, aiming to implement the two provinces' cooperation in agriculture, science and technology, labor, bilateral economic and trade, transportation, and tourism. January 1, 2006, the Guizhou Chamber of Commerce in Dongguan (Guangdong) is established. January 6, 2008, the Guizhou Chamber of Commerce in Guangdong is established in Shenzhen City. April 22–23, 2011, a delegation led by the CCP Secretary of Guangdong (also the Member of Politburo of the CCPCC) and the Governor of Guangdong pays an inspection to Guizhou; both sides attend the "Symposium of Exchange and Cooperation between Guizhou and Guangdong Provinces" and contract 162 cooperative projects, with a total value of 131.39 billion yuan. July, 20, 2011, a delegation of Guizhou Province pays an inspection to Guangdong Province. The signing ceremony of economic and trade cooperation between the two provinces is held in Guangzhou City of Guangdong; both sides contract 30 projects, with a total investment of 60.48 billion yuan (of which 59.98 billion yuan is provided by Guangdong Province). October 27, 2012, the Suiyang County (Guizhou) Chamber of Commerce in Guangdong is established.

Guangdong-Hainan

[Quick Facts] Average distance = 794 km; Geographical adjacency = 0; Index of ethnic linkages = 0.8374 (2000) and 0.8469 (2010); Freight exchange via national railway = 0 k ton (2000) and 260 k tons (2010). ★ October 18, 2006, a delegation composed of the Fishing Administrations of 14 coast cities and led by the Department of Ocean and Fishing Industry of Guangdong Province pays an inspection to "the Deep Sea Fishing Projects" of Lingao County of Hainan

Province. Both sides discuss the fishing cooperation in deep sea areas. July 2010, Guangdong and Hainan Provinces sign the "Strategic Cooperative Framework Agreement of Guangdong and Hainan", the agreement involves all fields of economic and social development. July 8, 2010, the health departments of Guangdong and Hainan Provinces sign, in Haikou City of Hainan, the "Cooperation Framework Agreement of Medical Treatment", and the Guangdong Provincial People's Hospital reaches the "Bilateral Cooperation Agreement" with four Hainan Hospitals. December 30, 2010, the cooperation and exchange meeting of Guangdong and Hainan Provinces and the signing ceremony of the cooperative framework agreement is held in Haikou City of Hainan. According to the incomplete statistics, from 2005 to 2009, the investment between Guangdong and Hainan has reached more than 50 billion yuan; and the cooperation on tourism and infrastructure construction between the two provinces becomes closer, with a total investment exceeding 20 billion yuan. October 8, 2011, the Hainan Chamber of Commerce in Guangdong is established. May 22, 2012, the promotion meeting entitled "Cool Summer, Cool Hainan Holiday", which is organized by the Tourism Development Commission of Hainan, is held in Guangzhou City. June 16, 2012, the Chaozhou-Shantou (Guangdong) Chamber of Commerce in Hainan is established in Haikou City.

Guangdong-Hebei

[Quick Facts] Average distance = 2012 km; Geographical adjacency = 0; Index of ethnic linkages = 0.9582 (2000) and 0.9602 (2010); Freight exchange via national railway = 2750 k tons (2000) and 1060 k tons (2010). ★ July 7, 2007, the signing ceremony of the cooperation agreement between Guangdong, Hebei and other provinces is held in Hohhot City of Inner Mongolia. Jun 23, 2010, the Hebei Chamber of Commerce in Guangdong is established in Guangzhou City. 500 representatives, being composed of Hebei entrepreneurs working in Guangdong province, participate in the celebration ceremony. The Chamber pledges to play an active role in the Hebei-Guangdong economic cooperation. March 13, 2012, the Materials Group of Guangdong and the Hebei Iron and Steel Group sign, in Beijing, the "Strategic Cooperation Agreement Concerning the Sales in 2011". April 22, 2012, the Secretary of the CCP Guangdong Provincial Committee (also the Member of Politburo of the CCPCC) and the Governor of Guangdong (also the Vice Secretary of the CCP of Guangdong Provincial Committee) hold a discussion meeting with the Hebei government delegation which is led by the Secretary of the CCP of Hebei Provincial Committee. June 19, 2012, the Haida Group of Guangdong Province and the People's Government of Qingyuan County of Hebei Province reach an agreement concerning the construction of a production, storage and transfer base in Qingyuan County, with a processing capacity of 0.3 million ton fodders and grains per year.

Guangdong-Heilongjiang

[Quick Facts] Average distance = 2928 km; Geographical adjacency = 0; Index of ethnic linkages = 0.9524 (2000) and 0.9655 (2010); Freight exchange via national railway = 1540 k tons (2000) and 260 k tons (2010). ★ December 18, 2008, the Guangdong Chamber of Commerce in Heilongjiang is established. The chamber has 100 enterprise members, involving more than 20 industries such as the large shopping malls of furniture and decoration and of dining and entertainment, business services, leasing, jewelry, mechanical and electrical engineering, medicine, decoration materials, medical equipment, furniture, real estate, business and trade investment, air transport, hotel and catering, tourism and ceramics. August 1, 2009, the Heilongjiang Chamber of Commerce in Guangdong is established. The Heilongjiang companies in Guangdong Province primarily involve real estate development, machinery, electronics, light industry, footwear industry, logistics, wood products, advertising, printing, food service, sporting goods, economic and trade. March 28, 2012, Heilongjiang and Guangdong Provinces sign 33 cooperative project agreements, with a total amount of 47.45 billion yuan. These projects focus on the "ten key industries" in the northeast area of China, including new energy equipment manufacturing, new materials, modern service industry, biotechnology and green food. March 29, 2012, the Land Reclamation Bureaux of Heilongjiang and Guangdong Provinces sign, in Guangzhou City, a strategic cooperation framework agreement. This marks that the two sides have entered into a comprehensive stage of strategic cooperation. March 28–30, 2012, Heilongjiang, Guangdong and other provinces hold an exchange meeting of interprovincial trade and economic cooperation, aiming to strengthen the complementary cooperation.

Guangdong-Henan

[Quick Facts] Average distance = 1600 km; Geographical adjacency = 0; Index of ethnic linkages = 0.9863 (2000) and 0.9815 (2010); Freight exchange via national railway = 7300 k tons (2000) and 6540 k tons (2010). ★ November 18, 2006, the Henan Chamber of Commerce in Guangdong is established. August 16, 2009, the Henan Chamber of Commerce in Guangzhou (Guangdong) is established. August 20, 2011, the Henan Chamber of Commerce in Zhanjiang (Guangdong) is established. August 26, 2011, the meeting of trade and economic cooperation between Henan and Guangdong is held in the Zhengzhou International Convention and Exhibition Center, the Eastern Zhengzhou New District. The business representatives of the two provinces hold the "Exchange and Cooperation Fair Concerning the Industrial Undertaking and Technological Transferring". July 30, 2012, the Economic and Trade Cooperation Fair of Xinyang (of Henan Province) and Guangzhou Cities and the project signing ceremony are held in Guangzhou City of Guangdong. The Xinyang delegation signs 28 cooperative agreements with the enterprises from Hong Kong, Guangzhou, and Shenzhen, with a total investment of 4.552 billion yuan. April 11, 2012, Henan and Guangdong Provinces (the largest provinces in terms of labor outflow and inflow, respectively) sign, in Zhengzhou City, the "Cooperation Agreement of Human Resources and Social Security Work". The two sides pledge to strengthen employment services and interprovincial human resources cooperation. The "Symposium of Cooperation between Henan and Guangdong Provinces" is held in Zhengzhou City. The Guangdong government delegation visits the Eastern Zhengzhou New District, the Yutong Bus Co., Ltd. of Zhengzhou and the Henan Museum. The two sides hold, in the Eastern Zhengzhou New District, the opening ceremony of "Guangdong's Products in Henan" fair and the signing ceremony of cooperation. The Guangdong delegation, which is composed of 38 special groups, offers 236 cooperation projects, with a total amount of 70.562 billion yuan, of which a total of 18 projects are secured, with a total investment of 43.407 billion yuan. November 9, 2012, the Kaifeng (Henan) Chamber of Commerce in Shenzhen (Guangdong) is established.

Guangdong-Hubei

[Quick Facts] Average distance = 1064 km; Geographical adjacency = 0; Index of ethnic linkages = 0.9612 (2000) and 0.9638 (2010); Freight exchange via national railway = 6170 k tons (2000) and 5610 k tons (2010). ★ June 2006, the Hubei Chamber of Commerce in Guangdong is established in Guangzhou City. The Chamber has 16 local branches (including Guangzhou, Shenzhen, Zhuhai, Foshan, Dongguan, Huizhou, Zhanjiang, Shaoguan, Heyuan, Zengcheng, Jingzhou, Xianning, Tianmen mountain pass, Xishui and Yunmeng). June 18, 2006, the Guangdong Chamber of Commerce in Hubei is established in Wuhan City. The chamber's members involve electronic technology, building materials, real estate, clothing and shoes, dining and entertainment, furniture, appliances, medicine, environmental protection, machinery and equipment, finance and securities, media education, legal counseling, transportation and logistics, business travel, equity investments and others. According to incomplete statistics, the capital scale of the member companies registered in Hubei Province exceeds 50 billion yuan (with the annual output value of about 450 billion yuan and the annual taxes of more than 40 billion yuan), providing about 2.8 million jobs per year. March 25, 2011, Hubei Chamber of Commerce in Shenzhen (Guangdong) is established. April 9, 2012, the "Guangdong's Products in Hubei" and the signing ceremony of trade and economic cooperation between the two provinces are held in Wuhan City of Hubei. The two sides reach agreements on 219 projects, with a total investment of 118.89 billion yuan (of which industrial and trade projects account for the major portion and 12 cultural tourism projects are also signed, with a total investment of 17.118 billion yuan). The Human Resources and Social Security Departments of Guangdong and Hubei Provinces start the information network docking of labor market. The representatives of the two sides sign four agreements concerning the technical education cooperation, the school-enterprise cooperation and employment service cooperation, marking a new stage for the labor cooperation between the two sides.

Guangdong-Hunan

[Quick Facts] Average distance = 706 km; Geographical adjacency = 1; Index of ethnic linkages = 0.9062 (2000) and 0.9100 (2010); Freight exchange via national railway = 21,120 k tons (2000) and 25,920 k tons (2010). ★ September 2005, the Hunan Chamber of Commerce in Guangdong is established. June 9, 2007, the Guangdong Chamber of Commerce in Hunan is established in Changsha City. According to incomplete statistics, from 2000 to the end of 2006, Guangdong has 5088 projects in Hunan, with a total investment of 88 billion yuan. January 4, 2009, the People's Governments of Hunan and Guangdong Provinces sign the "Cooperation Framework Agreement Concerning the Strengthening of Economic and Social Development of Xiangxi Autonomous Prefecture and Guangzhou City". May 22, 2009, the signing ceremony of the projects relating to trade and economic cooperation between Guangdong and Hunan Provinces and the starting ceremony of the "Guangdong's Products in Hunan" fair are held in Changsha City of Hunan. January 9, 2012, the Changde (Hunan) Chamber of Commerce in Guangdong is established. June 18, 2012, the Zhanjiang municipal government of Guangdong Province signs a framework agreement with Yongzhou municipal government of Hunan Province, aiming to jointly build "dry port" in Yongzhou City. The port is the logistics center which has the functions of customs declaration, inspection issuing, bills of lading and other port services in inland areas.

Guangdong-Inner Mongolia

[Quick Facts] Average distance = 2962 km; Geographical adjacency = 0; Index of ethnic linkages = 0.7932 (2000) and 0.7972 (2010); Freight exchange via national railway = 850 k tons (2000) and 490 k tons (2010). ★ March 27, 2006, the signing ceremony of economic cooperation between Guangzhou and Inner Mongolia is held in Guangzhou City. A total of 25 cooperation projects are signed, with a total investment of 38.1 billion. April 16–18, 2007, a delegation of Inner Mongolia Autonomous Region, led by the vice chairman of the Region, visits Guangdong Province to carry out bilateral exchange and cooperation. August 4, 2007, the China Guangdong Nuclear Power Group Co. inspects Inner Mongolia, discussing issues such as the joint development of wind power and others. August 5, 2008, the groundbreaking ceremony of the gold and silver smelting project of the Huixin Gold and Silver Smelting Co., Ltd. of Inner Mongolia is held in the Wuchuan Economic Development Zone. The project is jointly invested by the Huixin Co., Ltd. of Inner Mongolia and the Dakuaijin Co., Ltd. of Guangdong, with a total investment of 446.53 million yuan. According to the planned standards, the smelting capacity of gold ore powder is 60,000 tons per year, with 10 and 100 tons of gold and silver bullions, respectively. July 8, 2009, the promotion meeting entitled "Yellow River, Desert and Grassland: Let's Walk into Wuhai, Alxa and Erdos of China", jointly organized by the Tourism Bureaux of Wuhai City, Alxa League and Ordos City and the Tourism Bureau of Guangdong, is held in Guangzhou City, Guangdong Province. November 1, 2009, the Inner Mongolia Chamber of Commerce in Guangdong is established in the Shenzhen Special Economic Zone of Guangdong Province. June 11, 2012, the China (Guangdong) International Tourism Expo 2012 is held in Hohhot, Inner Mongolia. August 8, 2011 the Xinhua Publishing Group of Inner Mongolia and the Guangdong Publishing Group sign, in Hohhot City of Inner Mongolia, a "Strategic Cooperation Framework Agreement". Both sides pledge to carry out an extensive cooperation in the fields of supplementary books, digital publishing, tourism, foreign trade and others.

Guangdong-Jiangsu

[Quick Facts] Average distance = 1804 km; Geographical adjacency = 0; Index of ethnic linkages = 0.9871 (2000) and 0.9837 (2010); Freight exchange via national railway = 2300 k tons (2000) and 710 k tons (2010). ★ May 27, 2006, the Jiangsu Chamber of Commerce in Guangdong is established in Guangzhou City. April 17, 2009, a delegation led by the Director and Deputy Director of the Department of Foreign Trade and Economic Cooperation of Jiangsu Province pays an inspection to Guangdong Province. Both sides pledge to further enhance bilateral economic cooperation and to jointly promote the stable development of foreign trade. August 19, 2010, the Entry-Exit IQBs of Jiangsu and Guangdong Provinces sign, in Nanjing City of Jiangsu, the "Memorandum Concerning the Establishment of Closer Cooperation Mechanism in Inspection and Quarantine". May 31, 2011, the CCP Secretary (also the member of the Political Bureau of the CCPCC) of and the Governor of Guangdong Province meet, in Guangzhou City of Guangdong, a Jiangsu delegation led by the CCP Secretary and the Governor of Jiangsu Province. Both sides pledge to further strengthen the bilateral cooperation, to promote the adjustment of their economic structures, and to accelerate the transformation of the pattern of economic development.

Guangdong-Jiangxi

[Quick Facts] Average distance = 1022 km; Geographical adjacency = 1; Index of ethnic linkages = 0.9866 (2000) and 0.9818 (2010); Freight exchange via national railway = 4180 k tons (2000) and 5560 k tons (2010). ★ March 3, 2009, the

Guangdong Chamber of Commerce in Jiangxi is established. May 17, 2009, the Jiangxi Chamber of Commerce in Guangdong is established in Guangzhou City. The chamber, with nearly 500 member companies, has liaison offices in Dongguan, Zhngshan, Huizhou, Foshan, Shunde, and Shunde Cities. May 25, 2009, a promotion meeting of agricultural products, co-sponsored by Guangdong and Jiangxi Provinces, are held in Guangzhou City. The agricultural enterprises from the two provinces contract 36 agricultural cooperation projects, with a total investment of 4.2 billion yuan. Both sides pledge to utilize their complementary advantages in agricultural sector, and to jointly seek new development opportunities. April 19–20, 2011, a delegation led by the CCP Secretary of Guangdong (also the member of the Political Bureau of the CCPCC) and Governor of Guangdong pays an inspection to Jiangxi Province, and attends the starting ceremony of "Guangdong's Products in Jiangxi" and the signing ceremony of Economic and trade cooperation projects of Guangdong and Jiangxi. August 25–26, 2011, the Jiangxi Provincial Science and Technology Department, the Jiangxi Institute of Computing Technology and the representatives of the Department of Science and Technology of Guangdong Province hold a forum to discuss issues of the rural information management, among others. September 21, 2011, Jiangxi and Guangdong Provinces hold a meeting, aiming to integrate the special tourist resources and to create a barrier-free tourism zone. According to statistics, in 2010, Guangdong Province has received a total of 6.2 million of passengers from Jiangxi, and Jiangxi Province has received about 900 million of tourists from Guangdong. June 12, 2012, Guangdong and Jiangxi hold a symposium in Guangzhou City of Guangdong. Both sides pledge to cooperate in the fields of the facility building of interprovincial transportation, industrial docking, the development and utilization of tourist resources and others.

Guangdong-Jilin

[Quick Facts] Average distance = 3341 km; Geographical adjacency = 0; Index of ethnic linkages = 0.9098 (2000) and 0.9218 (2010); Freight exchange via national railway = 870 k tons (2000) and 130 k tons (2010). ★ April 25, 2007, the Guangdong Chamber of Commerce in Jilin is established in Changchun City. The chamber has nearly 200 member enterprises, involving more than 20 industries such as real estate development, modern logistics, and machining, with a total investment of nearly 60 billion yuan, and more than 20,000 employment opportunities in Jilin Province. May 6, 2008, the "2008 Symposium of Exchange and Cooperation between Guangdong and Jilin" is held in Guangzhou City. The governors of the two provinces sign 27 cooperative projects, with a total investment of 9.1 billion yuan; the Small and Medium Enterprise Bureaux of Guangdong and Jilin Provinces sign the cooperation agreement. August-September, 2009, three Guangzhou delegations, which are organized by the Liaison Office of Jilin Province in Guangzhou, visit 19 counties (or districts) of eight cities (or prefectures) of Jilin Province. These visits help to reach cooperation agreements in 19 areas of nine sectors (agricultural products, medicine, food, real estate, tourism, finance, commerce and others), with a total investment of about 18 billion yuan. April 2, 2010, the provincial governments of Jilin and Guangdong sign the "Agreement Concerning the Establishment of Long-term Cooperative Relationship in Bilateral Food Production and Marketing". According to the agreement, Guangdong Province will purchase more than 2 million tons of grain from Jilin. The Jilin and Guangzhou Branches of the China Grain Reserves, Jilin Grain Reserve Management Co., Ltd., the Grain Reserves Corporation of Guangdong Province, and the other relevant enterprises sign a grain purchase and sale agreement, with a total amount of 2.16 million tons and a transaction amount of 43 billion yuan. September 6, 2011, the "Industrial Cooperation Matchmaking Meeting of Jilin and Guangdong Provinces" is held in the Exhibition Center of Changchun City of Jilin Province.

Guangdong-Liaoning

[Quick Facts] Average distance = 3036 km; Geographical adjacency = 0; Index of ethnic linkages = 0.8408 (2000) and 0.8498 (2010); Freight exchange via national railway = 1470 k tons (2000) and 110 k tons (2010). ★ June 7, 2002, the "Guangdong-Liaoning Economic and Trade Cooperation Fair" opens. The two provinces contract nine industrial projects, with a total investment of 1.54 billion yuan (of which 1.387 billion yuan will be invested by Guangdong Province). According to incomplete statistics, the total value of transactions in the fair will reach 15 billion yuan. November 22, 2005, the Guangdong Chamber of Commerce in Liaoning is established in Shenyang City. December 1–4, 2008, a delegation led by the Governor of Liaoning carries out a promotion of regional economic cooperation projects in Guangdong Province, aiming to learn the advanced experience of the economic construction and social development of Guangdong, to further promote the cooperation and exchange in the fields of economy and trade, science and technology, personnel and other aspects between the two provinces. June 12, 2009, the Liaoning Chamber of Commerce in Guangzhou (Guangdong) is established. July 7–15, 2011, a delegation of 12 overseas Chinese enterprises in Liaoning Province organized by the Foshan Bureau of Foreign Affairs and Overseas Chinese pays an inspection to Liaoning Province. The business representatives of two sides sign a cooperation agreement.

Guangdong-Ningxia

[Quick Facts] Average distance = 2957 km; Geographical adjacency = 0; Index of ethnic linkages = 0.6559 (2000) and 0.6505 (2010); Freight exchange via national railway = 280 k tons (2000) and 530 k tons (2010). ★ July 4, 2004, the government delegations of Guangdong Province and Ningxia Autonomous Region hold a forum; both sides exchange their experiences of economic reform and social development, aiming to strengthen the economic and trade cooperation between the two places. April 29, 2008, the Director of the DRC of Ningxia visits Guangdong to inspect the situation of the transferring of the high-tech industries. December 13, 2011, the "Guangdong-Ningxia Tourist Cooperation Forum" is held in Guangzhou. The "Agreement of Further Deepening Strategic Tourist Cooperation between Ningxia and Guangdong" is signed, aiming to jointly develop the tourist markets of the two places. January 17, 2012, the municipal government of Yinchuan City of Ningxia and the Hydropower Group of Guangdong sign a strategic cooperation framework agreement, at the same time, the Yinchuan municipal government and the Taiyangdao Photovoltaic Technology Corporation of Guangdong sign a strategic cooperative framework agreement concerning the projects of low carbon buildings and the Sunshine Industry Base in Yinchuan City. July 16, 2012, the Federations of Returned Overseas Chinese of Ningxia and Guangdong sign a friendly cooperative agreement. Under the agreement, Guangdong and Ningxia will give full play to their respective advantages, and cooperate in the fields of economy, trade, science and technology, culture and education.

Guangdong-Qinghai

[Quick Facts] Average distance = 3003 km; Geographical adjacency = 0; Index of ethnic linkages = 0.5420 (2000) and 0.5324 (2010); Freight exchange via national railway = 300 k tons (2000) and 580 k tons (2010). ★ April 14–17, 2006, a delegation led by the Governor (also the Vice CCP Secretary of Qinghai Province) pays an inspection to Guangdong, and takes an in-depth exchange with the Guangdong government delegation. Both sides pledge to strengthen cooperation in the development of minerals, water, agriculture and animal husbandry. March 24, 2009, more than 50 travel agencies of Guangdong Province attend the promotion meeting of Guangdong and Qinghai. The Guangdong Nanhu International Travel and the Guangdong CITS travel agents and 10 travel agencies of Qinghai contract cooperative agreements. April 13, 2009 to 20, the CCP Secretary (also the PCSC Chairman) of Qinghai Province, the Qinghai provincial governor and the relevant departments and bureaus of Qinghai Province visit Guangdong Province. September 25, 2009, the Salt Lake Industrial Group of Qinghai Province signs a cooperation agreement with the Foshan Lighting Company of Guangdong Province. Both sides will carry out extensive cooperation in the fields of the comprehensive utilization of salt lake resources, the battery product development, marketing and after-sales service, etc. May 2011, the Qinghai Chamber of Commerce in Guangdong Province is established in Guangzhou. The chamber has 171 member units. April 17, 2012, the "2012 China (Qinghai) Green Investment and Trade Promotion Meeting" is held in Guangzhou, aiming to open Qinghai to the outside world, to deepen cooperation with Guangdong and to promote the green economy of Qinghai. The promotion offers a total number of 258 projects of 16 categories and a total investment of 40 billion yuan, mainly focusing on new energy, new materials, equipment manufacturing, chemical industry, electron and information, culture, and tourism. August 1, 2012, the Coal Geology Bureaux of Qinghai and Guangdong sign a cooperation agreement concerning the project of "Golmud Metal Ore of Qinghai".

Guangdong-Shaanxi

[Quick Facts] Average distance = 2111 km; Geographical adjacency = 0; Index of ethnic linkages = 0.9862 (2000) and 0.9817 (2010); Freight exchange via national railway = 1950 k tons (2000) and 1720 k tons (2010). ★ October 26, 2002, the Guangdong Chamber of Commerce in Shaanxi is established. The chamber has a total of 275 members, involving real estate, restaurant, entertainment, construction, electronics, medicine, commerce, chemicals, clothing, and accumulative investment of about 600 billion in Shaanxi. September 23, 2007, the Shaanxi Chamber of Commerce in Guangdong is established. September 24, 2008, the "Shaanxi-Guangdong Trade and Economic Cooperation Forum" is held in Guangzhou. Baishui County of Shaanxi and the Hongmao Organic Fertilizer Co., Ltd. of Guangzhou sign an agreement concerning the construction of the Baishui Organic Eco-cycle Industrial Park, with a total investment of 100 million yuan. Pingli County of Shaanxi Province and the Changle Investment Co., Ltd. of Qingyuan City of Guangdong Province agree to build a potato production line which has a capacity of 10,000 tons per year, with a total investment of 70 million yuan. September 26, 2008, the "Shaanxi-Guangdong (Foshan City) Ceramics Industrial Cooperation Forum" is held in Foshan City. More than 60 business leaders and investors of Guangdong Province participate in the conference; the enterprises of Guangdong Province and Shaanxi Province contract four ceramics projects, with a total investment of 193 million yuan. April 23–26, 2009, a delegation led by the CCP Secretary of and the PCSC Chairman of Shaanxi Province pays a study tour to Guangdong Province. April 6, 2012, the "Shaanxi-Guangdong Symposium of Equipment Manufacturing Cooperation" is held in Xi'an City. Both sides sign 59 contracts of projects, with a total investment of 73.821 billion yuan. August 2, 2012, a promotion meeting for cooperation between the private enterprises from both Shaanxi and Guangdong Provinces is held in Guangzhou City.

Guangdong-Shandong

[Quick Facts] Average distance = 2151 km; Geographical adjacency = 0; Index of ethnic linkages = 0.9864 (2000) and 0.9819 (2010); Freight exchange via national railway = 2310 k tons (2000) and 520 k tons (2010). ★ September 14, 2004, the

Economic Cooperation of Liaocheng (Shandong) and Dongguan (Guangdong) and the Investment Fair are held in Dongguan City. Both sides reach 13 agreements, with a total investment of 4.732 billion yuan. June 10–12, 2005, a government delegation of Shandong Province pays a study tour to Guangdong. Both sides have an in-depth exchange in the fields of economy, trade, education, science and technology. January 8, 2007, Guangdong and Shandong Provinces sign a labor cooperation agreement titled "100,000 Shandong Elder Sisters Going to Guangdong". The agreement aims to solve the shortage of nannies in Guangdong and Shenzhen Cities. July 9, 2009, Shandong Province and the Nuclear Power Group of Guangdong Province sign a strategic framework agreement on energy cooperation March 27, 2010, the Guangdong Chamber of Commerce in Shandong is established in Jinan City of Shandong Province. April 27, 2010, Shandong Chamber of Commerce in Guangdong is established in Guangdong. The chamber has a membership of nearly 200. June 2012, the Niuanji Energy Company of Guangdong and the Quanxing Group of Shandong agree for a strategic cooperation. The Niuanji Company and the Zhaozhuang Biological Company of (a sub-company of the Quanxing) hold the starting ceremony of a new energy production base in the East China region. August 20–24, 2012, a delegation led by the CCP Secretary of Changle County, Shandong Province, visits Guangzhou, Foshan and other places to strengthen economic and trade cooperation.

Guangdong-Shanghai

[Quick Facts] Average distance = 1803 km; Geographical adjacency = 0; Index of ethnic linkages = 0.9874 (2000) and 0.9868 (2010); Freight exchange via national railway = 860 k tons (2000) and 380 k tons (2010). ★ May 27, 2006, the China Nuclear Power Group Co., Ltd. of Guangdong Province signs a cooperation framework agreement with the DRC of Shanghai and the Shanghai Electric Group Co., Ltd. in the Daya Bay Nuclear Power Base, Longgang District of Shenzhen City. December 2006, after over ten years of the establishment of the Guangdong Chamber of Commerce in Shanghai, the chamber has promoted to reach 107 cooperative projects, with a total investment of 12.5 billion yuan. June 9, 2011, the exchange and cooperation meeting of Guangdong Province and the world's top 500 enterprises is held in the Pudong New Area of Shanghai Municipality. Nearly 200 representatives of Guangdong and Shanghai attend this meeting. June 14, 2011, the Dahua Farmers Co., Ltd. of Guangdong and the Veterinary Research Institute of Shanghai sign a strategic cooperation agreement. December 23, 2011, the China Tobacco Groups of Guangdong and Shanghai sign a Framework Agreement of Brand Cooperation and Development. According to the agreement, the Shuangxi Tobacco Company of Guangdong and the Hong Shuangxi Tobacco Company of Shanghai, which are the two major tobacco companies, will be merged into one brand. The new company will become China's largest and the world's second cigarette makers. October 8, 2011, the Yueda Industrial Group Co., Ltd. of

Shanghai and the Yinda Guarantee Investment Group Co., Ltd. of Guangdong sign a letter of intention on the establishment of a financial guarantee company.

Guangdong-Shanxi

[Quick Facts] Average distance = 2243 km; Geographical adjacency = 0; Index of ethnic linkages = 0.9864 (2000) and 0.9815 (2010); Freight exchange via national railway = 2560 k tons (2000) and 1970 k tons (2010). ★ November 18, 2006, the Guangdong Chamber of Commerce in Shanxi is established. October 21, 2011, the Shanxi Chamber of Commerce in Guangdong is established. The chamber has a total of 113 member enterprises. April 16, 2012, the government delegations of Guangdong and Shanxi hold a symposium in Guangzhou City. Shanxi hopes that Guangdong selects Shanxi as the priority option for its industrial transfer, and that both provinces enhance cooperation in advanced equipment manufacturing, new energy, new materials, electronic information, automobile manufacturing, modern logistics and other aspects. Guangdong hopes to work with Shanxi in energy exploitation, marketing, cooperation between enterprises, culture, tourism and other fields. April 17, 2012, the Broadcasting and Television Station of Shanxi and the Southern Media Group of Guangdong sign, in Guangzhou City, a strategic cooperation framework agreement. Both sides pledge to strengthen exchange and cooperation in production, advertising, new media, personnel exchange and others. June 15, 2012, the "Promotion Meeting of Economic Cooperation and Investment of Shanxi and Guangdong" is held in Guangzhou City. The People's Governments of Yuncheng City of Shanxi Province and the Liaison Office of Shanxi in Guangdong sign a strategic cooperation framework agreement. The relevant enterprises reach 18 cooperation agreements (including 11 contracted projects, with a total investment of 6.6 billion yuan), with a total investment of 17.05 billion yuan.

Guangdong-Sichuan

[Quick Facts] Average distance = 2527 km; Geographical adjacency = 0; Index of ethnic linkages = 0.9532 (2000) and 0.9437 (2010); Freight exchange via national railway = 4420 k tons (2000) and 9810 k tons (2010). ★ March 28, 2003, the Sichuan Chamber of Commerce in Guangdong is established. The chamber has more than 3000 members. November 2004, the Guangdong Chamber of Commerce in Sichuan is established. The chamber's member involves industry, agriculture, trade and service industries, real estate, health care, building materials and others. July 7, 2008, after the earthquake in Sichuan, Guangdong and Sichuan provinces have decided to carry out cooperation in tourism, aiming to resume the tourist market. A number of travel agencies of Guangdong and the Sichuan provincial government sign the "Guangdong-Sichuan Tourist Cooperation Agreement". July

16, 2008, the pairing reconstruction work forum of Guangdong and Sichuan, the economic and trade cooperation meeting of the two provinces and the signing ceremony of tourist cooperation between the two provinces are held in Chengdu City, Sichuan Province. The Iron and Steel Group Co., Ltd. of Shaoguan of Guangdong and the Electric Metallurgical Company of the Aba Prefecture of Huaxi City sign an agreement concerning the cooperation on silicon iron exploitation. September 28, 2008, the Sichuan government delegation visits Guangdong Province, and holds a discussion meeting with the leaders of Guangdong government, aiming to express the gratitude of Guangdong's support during the Sichuan earthquake period, and to promote bilateral cooperation. April 29, 2010, the Guangdong and Sichuan provincial governments sign, in Guangzhou City, the "Economic and Social Cooperation Agreement". Guangdong Province and Wenchuan County of Sichuan Province also sign the "Long-term Cooperation Framework Agreement between Guangdong and Wenchuan". The enterprises of the two provinces sign a total of 104 cooperative projects, with a total investment of 32.673 billion yuan. April 30, 2010, the industrial cooperation matchmaking between Sichuan and Guangdong Provinces is held in Guangzhou City. 600 enterprises from Guangdong are invited to the meeting to negotiate cooperation with the Sichuan counterparts.

Guangdong-Tianjin

[Quick Facts] Average distance = 2431 km; Geographical adjacency = 0; Index of ethnic linkages = 0.9752 (2000) and 0.9775 (2010); Freight exchange via national railway = 500 k tons (2000) and 40 k tons (2010). ★ June 6, 2007, the Guangdong Chamber of Commerce in Tianjin is established. July 26, 2009, the "Guangdong's Products in Tianjin" fair opens. The event aims to promote the bilateral trade and economic cooperation between Guangdong and Tianjin. August 12, 2010, the Propaganda Department, Nankai District and the Zhongxin Eco-City Administrative Committee of Tianjin Municipality and the Huaqiang Group Co., Ltd. of Shenzhen sign a cooperation agreement, aiming to develop the emerging industries such as e-commerce, IT, as well as Internet, digital culture and information serves. December 9, 2010, the Guangdong Development Bank and Tianjin Bohai Commodity Exchange become strategic partnerships. March 28, 2011, the Tianjin Municipal Development Zone and Haomei Aluminum Co., Ltd. of Guangdong sign a strategic cooperation agreement. June 8, 2012, the municipal governments of Guangzhou and Tianjin sign a strategic cooperation framework agreement. Under the agreement, the two cities will strengthen bilateral cooperation in the fields of industry, regional innovation, finance, tourism, environmental protection, and energy security. Contracts of 52 joint/cooperative projects are signed, with the total amount of investment reaching 63.36 billion yuan.

Guangdong-Tibet

[Quick Facts] Average distance = 4980 km; Geographical adjacency = 0; Index of ethnic linkages = 0.0622 (2000) and 0.0837 (2010); Freight exchange via national railway = 0 k ton (2000) and 20 k tons (2010). ★ August 2, 2005, officials in charge of the publishing industry of Guangdong visit Tibet to implement the pairing aid activities and to strengthen the two places' cooperation. August 8–12, 2010, the "Guangdong-Tibet Cooperation Forum" is held in Lhasa City, Tibet. The Guangdong delegation inspects the Modern Agricultural Demonstration Zone of Tibet Academy of Agricultural Sciences. For the past 15 years, Guangdong Province has dispatched six batches of 218 cadres to work in Tibet, and provided 1.737 billion yuan of aid (in more than 720 projects) to Tibet Autonomous Region. October 21, 2010, Nyingchi Prefecture of Tibet and Shaoguan City of Guangdong sign a regional tourist cooperation agreement. August 2, 2011, a team led by the Science and Technology Department of Guangdong Province visits Nyingchi Prefecture of Tibet to inspect the pairing aid work. Guangdong Academy of Agricultural Sciences and the Science and Technology Bureau of Nyingchi Prefecture sign a cooperation agreement. April 28, 2012, the "Nyingchi Investment and Trade Fair" opens. The Bomi County of Tibet and the Pharmaceutical Group of Guangzhou sign a framework agreement concerning the development of Tibetan medicine and pharmacology; the Nyingchi County and the China Travel Service (Group) Co., Ltd. of Guangdong Province sign a strategic cooperation framework agreement concerning the planning and development of the small town of Lulang International tourism in Nyingchi County.

Guangdong-Xinjiang

[Quick Facts] Average distance = 4679 km; Geographical adjacency = 0; Index of ethnic linkages = 0.4086 (2000) and 0.4078 (2010); Freight exchange via national railway = 1300 k tons (2000) and 2120 k tons (2010). ★ August 21–26, 2006, the Guangdong delegation pays an inspection to Xinjiang, and signs an exchange and cooperation agreement with Xinjiang tourist sectors. April 2, 2008, the China Nuclear Power Group of Guangdong and Xinjiang Uygur Autonomous Region sign a strategic cooperation framework agreement concerning the exploitation of uranium resource and the construction of power projects. June 28, 2010, the "Sixth Kashi Commodity Fair" opens. Guangdong and Xinjiang (Kashgar) sign a total of 42 trade and economic cooperation projects, with a total investment of 10.2 billion yuan. August 10, 2010, the Bureaux of Overseas Chinese of Huizhou (Guangdong) and of Hami (Xinjiang) become a friendly pairing. October 25, 2010, the Electric Power Design Institute of Xinjiang and the Electric Power Design Institute of Guangdong sign a cooperation agreement in Urumqi, Xinjiang Autonomous Region. December 1, 2010, the Intellectual Property Office of Guangdong and

Kashgar Prefecture of Xinjiang sign the "Agreement of Intellectual Property Pairing Cooperation". April 28, 2011, Guangdong Province and the Xinjiang Uygur Autonomous Region hold a cooperation symposium in Guangzhou City, aiming to jointly promote the in-depth pairing aid work. September 1, 2011, the Xinjiang Chamber of Commerce in Guangdong is established. June 27, 2012, the Cotton Industry Group Co., Ltd. of Xinjiang signs a strategic cooperation agreement with the Guangdong Materials Corporation, hoping to deepen the cooperation in the fields of cotton circulation and deep processing, modern logistics, the development of mineral resources, and the trade of bulk production materials (trucks, coal, iron and steel, petrochemical products, etc.). August 22, 2012, the promotion meeting of the "New Guangzhou, New Opportunities" organized by the government of Guangzhou is held in Urumqi City of Xinjiang Autonomous Region. 40 cooperative projects are secured in this meeting, with a total investment of 25.76 billion yuan.

Guangdong-Yunnan

[Quick Facts] Average distance = 2199 km; Geographical adjacency = 0; Index of ethnic linkages = 0.6780 (2000) and 0.6825 (2010); Freight exchange via national railway = 5890 k tons (2000) and 10,160 k tons (2010). ★ September 28, 2005, the Guangdong Chamber of Commerce in Yunnan Province is established. The Chamber has more than 100 member companies involving metallurgy, electric power, real estate, bio-pharmaceutics, electronics groom suffering, building materials, chemical industry, light industry, coal, commerce, tourism services and others. December 5, 2006, the project promotion meeting concerning the cooperation in labor-intensive industry is organized by Yunnan and Guangdong Provinces and held in Guangzhou City. The meeting aims to take advantage of Yunnan's rich natural resources and low-cost labor to solve the bottleneck problem of sustainable development, and to promote the transferring of some labor-intensive industries from Guangdong to Yunnan to speed up the economic development of Yunnan. April 20, 2010, the Yunnan Chamber of Commerce in Guangdong is established in Shenzhen City. April 20, 2011, a delegation led by the CCP Secretary (also the member of the Political Bureau of the CCPCC) of Guangdong Province visits Yunnan Province. The two provinces hold, in Kunming City of Yunnan Province, the "Yunan-Guangdong Cooperation Forum". March 2, 2012, the Zhaotong (Yunnan) Chamber of Commerce in Guangdong is established in in Shenzhen City. May 10, 2012, the Power Group of Guangdong and the Energy Investment Group Co., Ltd. of Yunnan sign, in Kunming of Yunnan Province, a strategic cooperation framework agreement, aiming to build all-round strategic partnerships and to create favorable conditions for the Guangdong Group to invest in Yunnan. July 13, 2012, the "Yunnan-Guangdong Industrial Cooperation Promotion" meeting and the signing ceremony are held in Guangzhou City. The representatives of the two sides sign the strategic cooperation framework agreement. Both sides secure 77 cooperative projects, with a total investment of over 132.19 billion yuan.

Guangdong-Zhejiang

[Quick Facts] Average distance = 1602 km; Geographical adjacency = 0; Index of ethnic linkages = 0.9899 (2000) and 0.9878 (2010); Freight exchange via national railway = 1440 k tons (2000) and 570 k tons (2010). ★ June 18, 2005, the Zhejiang Chamber of Commerce in Guangdong is established in Guangzhou City. The chamber involves leather, leather goods, services, jewelry, printing, fine chemicals, machinery manufacturing, real estate, hotels and restaurants, and other industries. September 24–30, 2005, a delegation of Chenghai District of Guangdong Province pays an inspection to Zhejiang to carry out interprovincial medical care cooperation. December 20, 2010 the Taizhou (Zhejiang) Chamber of Commerce in Guangdong is established in Guangzhou City. According to incomplete statistics, there are 120,000 Taizhou businesspersons in Guangdong. April 11, 2011, Guangdong and Zhejiang Provinces jointly hold a symposium, aiming to exchange each other's successful experiences in economic and social development, and to fully complete the objectives and tasks of the "12th Five-Year Plan". May 9, 2011, the Huzhou (Zhejiang) Chamber of Commerce in Guangdong is established. July 28, 2012, Yuexiu Foreign Languages College of Zhejiang and Guangdong University of Foreign Studies start cooperation. August 1, 2012, the Bureaux of Coal Geology of Guangdong and Zhejiang Provinces reach a cooperative agreement concerning the construction of a metal ore development project in the Golmud area of Qinghai Province. May 19, 2014, Zhejiang Daxin Commodity Company of the No.36 member of the Zhejiang-Xinhua Bulk Commodity Exchange Center establishes a branch named Xinhua Daxin in Shenzhen of Guangdong Province.

Guangxi-Guizhou

[Quick Facts] Average distance = 865 km; Geographical adjacency = 1; Index of ethnic linkages = 0.6408 (2000) and 0.6522 (2010); Freight exchange via national railway = 12,930 k tons (2000) and 36,350 k tons (2010). ★ July 28, 2011, the Commercial Departments of Guizhou Province and Guangxi Zhuang Autonomous Region hold a meeting to improve the cooperation of border passing. August 4, 2011, a delegation of Guangxi pays an inspection to Guizhou Province. The two sides pledge to strengthen cooperation in the construction of transport infrastructure, energy, tourism, and trade of the Beibu (Tonkin) Gulf area. September 20, 2011, The People's Governments of Guangxi Zhuang Autonomous Region and Guizhou Province sign the "12th Five-Year Plan Strategic Cooperation Framework Agreement". The agreement focuses on the solution of traffic problems. September

28, 2011, the "Third Joint Conference of Pan-Pearl Delta Regional Port Cooperation" is held in Guiyang, Guizhou Province. Guizhou signs the "Cooperation Agreement of Port Customs Clearance" with Guangxi. December 16, 2011, the Yelang Culture Research Institute of Guizhou, under the guidance of the Department of Culture of Guizhou Province, and the Guangxi Gulf Think-Tank Group sign an agreement concerning the construction of the Yelang cultural tourist circle. Both sides pledge to promote market development, expansion and integration of business and trade, tourism and finance.

Guangxi-Hainan

[Quick Facts] Average distance = 739 km; Geographical adjacency = 0; Index of ethnic linkages = 0.6340 (2000) and 0.6453 (2010); Freight exchange via national railway = 0 k ton (2000) and 400 k tons (2010). ★ June 9, 2009, Hainan and the Guangxi sign, in Nanning, the "Cooperation Agreement Concerning the Off-Site Medical Billing". Under the agreement, both sides will establish three systems of mutual recognition of basic medical insurance. July 24, 2010, a forum of Guangxi and Hainan is held in Nanning City. Both sides reach a high degree of consensus on bilateral cooperation. August 27, 2010, the Maritime Safety Administrations of Hainan and Guangxi sign, in Haikou City, the "Maritime Management and Cooperation Agreement", aiming to promote the overall improvement of water traffic safety and create a safe, smooth, efficient, clean maritime traffic environment. September 15, 2010, under the "Framework of the Pan-Pearl River Delta Regional Cooperation", Hainan and Guangxi sign an agricultural cooperation agreement, aiming to jointly promote the development of agricultural industry and to build national tropical agricultural base. August 19, 2011, the Tourism Commission of Hainan Province and the Tourism Bureau of Guangxi Zhuang Autonomous Region sign the "Cooperation Agreement of Tourist Quality Supervision and Law Enforcement" in the sixth Pan-Beibu Gulf Economic Cooperation Forum. November 7, 2011, the Hainan Provincial Department of Agriculture visits Guangxi, aiming to strengthen bilateral agriculture cooperation. April 29, 2012, the Guangxi Chamber of Commerce in Hainan is established.

Guangxi-Hebei

[Quick Facts] Average distance = 2262 km; Geographical adjacency = 0; Index of ethnic linkages = 0.6183 (2000) and 0.6302 (2010); Freight exchange via national railway = 1350 k tons (2000) and 1040 k tons (2010). ★ December 21, 2006, Shijiazhuang City of Hebei Province decides to offer favorable policies for its local enterprises to invest in Nanning City of Guangxi. 2009, the Hebei Chamber of Commerce in Guangxi is established. The chamber involves IT, electronics, electrical appliances, communications, trade, building materials, chemicals, hotels, car repairs and other industries. March 15, 2011, a Guangxi delegation participates in the "Hebei-Guangxi Exchange and Cooperation Forum" in Shijiazhuang City, Hebei Province. The delegation investigates the Tangshan Railway Vehicle Co., Ltd. of Beiche Group in Tangshang City of Hebei, the Huifeng Lake Park, the eco-tourism area of Tangjin Canal (between Tangshan and Tianjin), Nanhu Eco-City and Caofeidian Industrial Zone, as well as the City Planning Exhibition Hall in Shijiazhuang City, and the comprehensive project of Hutuo river. November 4, 2011, Guangxi and Hebei sign a memorandum of cooperation in the inspection and quarantine of Hebei's fruits and vegetables exported to the ASEAN countries, aiming to strengthen port security and bio-invasion prevention. September 25, 2012, a delegation of the Department of Commerce of Guangxi visits Shijiazhuang City of Hebei Province, aiming to look for buyers for its bananas.

Guangxi-Heilongjiang

[Quick Facts] Average distance = 3855 km; Geographical adjacency = 0; Index of ethnic linkages = 0.6179 (2000) and 0.6297 (2010); Freight exchange via national railway = 450 k tons (2000) and 400 k tons (2010). ★ May 7, 2009, the Heilongjiang Chamber of Commerce in Beihai City (Guangxi) is established. March 23 to 25, 2010, a delegation led by the Executive Deputy Governor (also the CCP Secretary) of Heilongjiang Province pays a study tour to Guangxi Zhuang Autonomous Region. The delegation also visits Pingxiang and Guilin Cities of Guangxi to learn their experiences in promoting cross-border trade and tourism, the development of free trade zone, etc., aiming to seek new opportunities for cooperation. June 19–25, 2011, an investigation team in charge of border regional development, which is composed of 16 people and led by the deputy director of Guangxi's Department of Commerce, visits the Heihe river, the Suifen river and other areas of Heilongjiang Province to carry out in-depth exchange in the promotion of border trade, the speeding up of border economic cooperation zone, the construction of cross-border economic development zone, etc. September 2, 2012, the Guangxi, Heilongjiang and other relevant provinces hold, for the first time, an exchange and cooperation meeting in Chengdu City.

Guangxi-Henan

[Quick Facts] Average distance = 1870 km; Geographical adjacency = 0; Index of ethnic linkages = 0.6179 (2000) and 0.6298 (2010); Freight exchange via national railway = 3330 k tons (2000) and 4420 k tons (2010). ★ June 28, 2009, the Henan Chamber of Commerce in Guangxi is established. January 27, 2011, the Press and Publication Bureaux of Henan Province and the Guangxi Zhuang Autonomous

Region sign the "Cooperation Framework Agreement Concerning to the Promotion of Common Development of News and Publishing Industry". Under the agreement, both sides pledge to strengthen strategic cooperation; the two bureaux also establish a mechanism of mutual learning and exchange. October 19, 2011, the "Sixth China-ASEAN Expo" opens in Nanning City of Guangxi Zhuang Autonomous Region. Henan and Guangxi sign a strategic cooperation framework agreement; the Coal and Chemical Group of Henan Province and the Guangxi Materials Group sign an agreement of coal supply and marketing cooperation. May 7–11, 2012, 15 representatives from Henan's tourist agencies and media visit Bama, Fengshan, Lingyun and other counties of Guangxi, and sign, in Nanning City, a tourist cooperation agreement with the local relevant agencies of Guangxi.

Guangxi-Hubei

[Quick Facts] Average distance = 1336 km; Geographical adjacency = 0; Index of ethnic linkages = 0.6227 (2000) and 0.6342 (2010); Freight exchange via national railway = 2100 k tons (2000) and 3890 k tons (2010). ★ May 22, 2007 the Hubei Chamber of Commerce in Guangxi is established. Nearly 400 chamber members come from various regions of Guangxi, involving electronic technology, decorative and building materials, construction, real estate and hotel properties, dining and entertainment, health care, food and beverage, hardware, electronics, network communications, management consulting, commerce, advertising planning, transport and logistics, mineral development, and others. September 27, 2011, Hubei Provincial CCP Secretary meets, in Wuhan City, the chairman of Guangxi who is paying a visit to Hubei. Both sides agree to strengthen their bilateral cooperation by using their complementary advantages. May 11, 2012, the "Hubei-Guangxi Economic and Social Development Meeting" is held in Wuhan City. Guangxi hopes to deepen the cooperation in auto-making, steel, petrochemical, equipment manufacturing, non-ferrous metals, information software, etc.; Hubei hopes to strengthen cooperation in agriculture, forestry and water, including strengthening the cooperation in agriculture, hydropower plant construction, and sea-route transportation. According to incomplete statistics, from 2004 to 2012, Hubei's enterprises have 415 investment projects in Guangxi, with a total value of 42.03 billion yuan. August 8, 2012, a 10 people delegation of Huangshi City of Hubei pays an inspection to Liuzhou City of Guangxi.

Guangxi-Hunan

[Quick Facts] Average distance = 978 km; Geographical adjacency = 1; Index of ethnic linkages = 0.6468 (2000) and 0.6581 (2010); Freight exchange via national railway = 4800 k tons (2000) and 14,220 k tons (2010). ★ March 18, 2007, the

Hunan Chamber of Commerce in Guangxi is established in Nanning City. The chamber comprises more than 500 member companies, involving real estate, construction, building materials, electronics, chemical industry, commerce, restaurants, light industrial, communications equipment, sales of automobiles, clothing, decoration, household goods and others. According to statistics, the chamber's members have invested more than 35 billion yuan in Guangxi, with the annual output value of over 33 billion yuan, the annual revenues of over 30 billion yuan, and more than 60,000 job opportunities. October 27, 2007, Hunan Province and Guangxi Zhuang Autonomous Region sign a cooperation framework agreement in Nanning City of Guangxi. Both sides pledge to strengthen cooperation in transportation, economic cooperation and trade, etc. November 4, 2008, the "Economic and Social Development Meeting of Hunan and Guangxi" is held in Changsha City of Hunan Province. The two sides sign a framework agreement concerning the deepening of bilateral cooperation. The cooperation focuses on real estate, construction, building materials, chemicals, electronics, light industry, communications equipment, clothing and logistics.

Guangxi-Inner Mongolia

[Quick Facts] Average distance = 3234 km; Geographical adjacency = 0; Index of ethnic linkages = 0.6180 (2000) and 0.6301 (2010); Freight exchange via national railway = 230 k tons (2000) and 610 k tons (2010). ★ November 14, 2006, Manzhouli City of Inner Mongolia Autonomous Region and Pingxiang City of Guangxi Zhuang Autonomous Region become a friendly cooperative pair. According the agreement signed, the two sides will learn from each other and jointly promote cooperation in the development of border and port cities. In addition, the two northern and southern border cities pledge to establish a mechanism of bilateral exchange. October 8–14, 2010, led by the Commercial Department of Baise City, a 15 people delegation of Baise border economic cooperation zone, which is compose of the DRC, the Longbang IQB, the Longbang border check station, as well as the Napo County government and relevant unites, pays an inspection to Manzhouli City and other places of Inner Mongolia. The inspection is focused on the understanding of the planning and construction of border economic cooperation zone, and of the experiences of cross-border trade management, aiming to speed up the development of the Baise border economic cooperation zone. July 12, 2012, a delegation, led by the General Manager of the Guangxi Company of the China Gain Reserve Corporation (Sinograin) and composed of managers of the Nanning and Wuzhou Reserves Companies of the Sinograin, pays an inspection to Chifeng and Tongliao Cities of Inner Mongolia and discusses with the General Manager of the Inner Mongolia Company of the Sinograin.

Guangxi-Jiangsu

[Quick Facts] Average distance = 2076 km; Geographical adjacency = 0; Index of ethnic linkages = 0.6185 (2000) and 0.6316 (2010); Freight exchange via national railway = 950 k tons (2000) and 880 k tons (2010). ★ October 20, 2005, the Departments of Science and Technology of Guangxi Zhuang Autonomous Region and Jiangsu Province sign a framework agreement on the projects of "high-yield and high-quality hybrid mulberry" and of "new hybrid rice varieties and the demonstration application in ASEAN". May 8, 2007, the Kunshan Export Processing Zone of Jiangsu Province, which is the largest zone of its kind in China, signs a strategic partnership agreement with the Export Processing Zone of Beihai of Guangxi, which is the fastest developing zone in Western China, aiming to build an industrial shift base in Beihai City. May 27–30, 2007, an economic and trade delegation of Jiangsu's overseas Chinese entrepreneurs, which is jointly organized by the Overseas Chinese Affairs Office of State Council and the Overseas Chinese Affairs Office of Jiangsu Province, pays an inspection to Guangxi. The activity aims to promote economic cooperation between Guangxi and the Yangtze River Delta region and the industrial transfer from the eastern to the western areas. November 16, 2009, a Guangxi government delegation visits Jiangsu; the two sides hold an economic and social development forum. November 23, 2009, the signing ceremony of the cooperative project of the Guangxi Forestry Group and the Jiangsu Sunshine Group is held in Nanning City of Guangxi. The first phrase investment of the project is 600 million yuan, and the project will achieve the annual output value of 5–8 billion yuan. April 23, 2011, the People's Government of Guangxi and the Yurun Holding Group of Jiangsu sign an investment cooperation framework agreement.

Guangxi-Jiangxi

[Quick Facts] Average distance = 1294 km; Geographical adjacency = 0; Index of ethnic linkages = 0.6174 (2000) and 0.6296 (2010); Freight exchange via national railway = 1080 k tons (2000) and 2190 k tons (2010). ★ October 9, 2006, Guangxi University of Science and Technology and the Hechi municipal government of Jiangxi Province jointly establish a nonferrous metal R&D base, aiming to enhance bilateral technological cooperation. November 13, 2009, the exchange meeting of economic and social development is jointly sponsored by Jiangxi Province and Guangxi Zhuang Autonomous Region in Nanchang City of Jiangxi Province. The two sides discuss various areas of cooperation. December 12, 2009, the "Xingguo County (Jiangxi) Oranges Promotion" is held in Nanning City of Guangxi. September 20, 2011, Guangxi and Jiangxi hold, in Nanchang City, the "Promotion and Cooperation Conference of the Beibu Gulf Economic Zone of Guangxi". Guangxi, Jiangxi and other places of the Pan-Pearl Delta Region agree to cooperate on 9 projects, with a total investment of 3.45 billion yuan. The investment projects involve manufacturing, trade and logistics industry, industrial manufacturing, agriculture, forestry, fishery, animal husbandry, leasing and commercial services, etc. December 5, 2011, officials from the Federations of Overseas Chinese Affairs of Yulin City (Guangxi) and of Ganzhou City (Jiangxi) meet to seek opportunities for friendly cooperation.

Guangxi-Jilin

[Quick Facts] Average distance = 6313 km; Geographical adjacency = 0; Index of ethnic linkages = 0.6179 (2000) and 0.6297 (2010); Freight exchange via national railway = 220 k tons (2000) and 710 k tons (2010). ★ August 19, 2010, a strategic cooperation agreement concerning the production and research is signed by Jilin University and the Liugong Machinery Co., Ltd. of Guangxi. January 24, 2011 the Jilin Chamber of Commerce in Guangxi is established in Nanning. March 7, 2012, the Forestry Department of Guangxi Zhuang Autonomous Region and the China Jilin Forestry Group hold a strategic cooperation conference, aiming to gradually carry out the development of wood flooring, solid wood doors and other projects in Guangxi, and to expand the particleboard market share of the Group in Guangxi. May 20, 2012, the "Changchun-Nanjing–Nanning" air route opens. The new route will fill the air blank from Jilin to the Guangxi. The opening of the Changchun-Nanning route will further improve the distribution of Jilin regional routes, making the Jilin and Guangxi links be more closely. All this will play a more active role in the Jilin-Guangxi cooperation of trade, tourism, culture and others. June 28, 2012, a delegation led by the Deputy Chief of the Investment Promotion Bureau of Guangxi visits Jilin Province and has a meeting with officials of the Economic and Technological Bureau of Jilin.

Guangxi-Liaoning

[Quick Facts] Average distance = 3411 km; Geographical adjacency = 0; Index of ethnic linkages = 0.6180 (2000) and 0.6300 (2010); Freight exchange via national railway = 490 k tons (2000) and 250 k tons (2010). ★ April 25–27, 2006, the "Liaoning-Guangxi Commodity Exhibition and the Economic Cooperation Fair", sponsored by the People's Government of Liaoning Province, is held in the Guangxi Exhibition Center. The economic cooperation and project promotion meeting of Liaoning and Guangxi is also held; entrepreneurs from Guangxi and Liaoning participate in the meeting. August 21, 2008, a forum is sponsored by Guangxi and Liaoning in Nanning City, Guangxi. The two sides exchange their views of cooperation in five areas such as processing and manufacturing, aiming to promote common development. August 22, 2008, a government delegation led by the governor of Liaoning Province arrives in Beihai City, Guangxi Autonomous Region for an inspection of the situation of the city's economic and social development. March 8, 2012, the Dalian Port Group of Liaoning visits the Beibu Gulf International Port Group of Guangxi. Both sides carry out in-depth discussions on the logistics operations, port construction and utilization of complementary resources, and sign the "Strategic Cooperation Agreement of the Beibu Gulf Port and the Dalian Port".

Guangxi-Ningxia

[Quick Facts] Average distance = 3229 km; Geographical adjacency = 0; Index of ethnic linkages = 0.6180 (2000) and 0.6304 (2010); Freight exchange via national railway = 50 k tons (2000) and 100 k tons (2010). ★ February 28, 2008, Ningxia and Guangxi sign a tourist cooperation agreement. The Ningxia Youth Journeys and the Nanning Railway International Travel Service also sign a cooperation agreement by which to set three direct tourist trains from Guangxi to Ningxia during July to September. October 22, 2009, an investment description and tourist promotion meeting is held by Ningxia Hui Autonomous Region in Nanning City of Guangxi. In the meeting, Ningxia introduces its investment environment and policies and offers several key projects in agriculture, mining and tourism. 15 interprovincial cooperation projects are agreed between Ningxia and Guangxi, including the opening of tourist chartered flights which are jointly proposed by the Tourism Bureaux of Ningxia and Guangxi. May 29, 2010, the Liaison Office of the Yucai Shareholding Co. Ltd. of Guangxi in Ningxia is established in Yinchuan City. November 10, 2011, a delegation led by vice chairman of the China Federation of the Overseas Chinese, the Overseas Chinese Federation of Ningxia Hui Autonomous Region and chairman of the Yindi Group pays an inspection to Guangxi Zhuang Autonomous Region. September 23, 2012, the Investment Bureau of Ningxia and the Zhongmei Tianyuan Investment Group of Guangxi sign a strategic cooperation framework agreement.

Guangxi-Qinghai

[Quick Facts] Average distance = 3275 km; Geographical adjacency = 0; Index of ethnic linkages = 0.5422 (2000) and 0.5324 (2010); Freight exchange via national railway = 90 k tons (2000) and 200 k tons (2010). ★ November 20, 2010, the "Guangxi-Qinghai Cooperation Forum" is held in Nanning City of Guangxi Zhuang Autonomous Region. Officials from Guangxi and Qinghai pledge to grasp the opportunities of Qinghai's implementation of "founding the province by ecology" so as to promote Guangxi's construction of ecological and green development demonstration zone and to strengthen their bilateral cooperation in environmental protection. May 31, 2011, the Yucai Corporation of Guangxi and the Yucai Company of Qinghai sign a strategic cooperation agreement. May 8–9, 2012, a delegation composed of officials from Agriculture and Animal Husbandry Department of Qinghai Province visits Guangxi Zhuang Autonomous Region to carry out bilateral cooperation in agricultural sector. The delegation also participates in the "Qinghai-Guangxi Forum for Cooperation in the Industrialization of Agricultural Projects" in Nanning City. In the forum, many joint and cooperative projects to be invested in either Guangxi or Qinghai are secured by both sides.

Guangxi-Shaanxi

[Quick Facts] Average distance = 2383 km; Geographical adjacency = 0; Index of ethnic linkages = 0.6178 (2000) and 0.6299 (2010); Freight exchange via national railway = 900 k tons (2000) and 880 k tons (2010). ★ August 24, 2005, the Guangxi Chamber of Commerce in Shaanxi is established in Xi'an City. August 26, 2008, the Customs of the People's Government of Shaanxi Province and Guangxi Zhuang Autonomous Region sign, in Nanning of Guangxi, an agreement of cross-regional port cooperation. October 21, 2010, a tourist delegation led by the vice governor of Shaanxi Province visits Nanning City. In the promotion meeting, the tourism bureaux of the two provinces sign a tourist cooperation agreement. May 25, 2011, Chongzuo City of Guangxi and Hanzhong City of Shaanxi sign, in Hanzhong City, a friendly cooperation framework agreement; both cities will work together to broaden the areas of cooperation and seek common development and to promote their economic and social development. July 18, 2011, the signing ceremony of cooperation between the Nonferrous Metals Holding Group of Shaanxi and the municipal government of Yulin of Guangxi is held in Xi'an. The Group will build a nonferrous and electronics industrial park in the Industrial Park of Yulin City, with an investment of 21 billion yuan and an annual output of 24,000 tons polysilicon. The project covers an area of 2300 acres, and will, after completion, yield 10.2 billion yuan of revenues per year. November 12, 2011, the IQBs of Shaanxi and Guangxi sign the "Memorandum of Cooperation Concerning the Joint Promotion of Fruit and Vegetable Production and Trade in Shaanxi", aiming to establish a safe and fast channel for Shaanxi's fruits and vegetables to export via Guangxi's ports.

Guangxi-Shandong

[Quick Facts] Average distance = 2538 km; Geographical adjacency = 0; Index of ethnic linkages = 0.6179 (2000) and 0.6299 (2010); Freight exchange via national railway = 880 k tons (2000) and 820 k tons (2010). ★ July 9 and 12, 2009, the Jincheng Gold Mine of Laizhou City (Shandong Province) and the Guangxi Gold Company set up, in Nanning, the Guangxi Fengshan Tiancheng Gold Industry Co.,

Ltd., aiming to jointly develop the Jinya gold mine in Fengshan County of Guangxi Zhuang Autonomous Region. May 8, 2010, the opening ceremony of the Shandong Chamber of Commerce in Guangxi is held in Nanning City of Guangxi. According to incomplete statistics, there are more than 40,000 Shandong investors (of which over 280 hold large enterprises) in Guangxi. Shandong's business activities in Guangxi focus on the areas of marketing service, manufacturing and electrical appliances, real estate development, environmental protection and high-tech industries, mining, investment and financing, machining, logistics, trade, furniture and clothing, food and beverage services, etc. October 27, 2011, chairman of the Guangxi Federation of Returned Overseas Chinese meets a delegation of private enterprises from Shandong Province. The two sides hope to strengthen cooperation in the exchange of Chinese and foreigners. August 30, 2012, a group of Overseas Chinese businessmen from Weifang City (Shandong Province) visit Guangxi, and reaches a number of bilateral cooperation agreements in fields of mechanics and electronics, water, farming, meat processing and real estate.

Guangxi-Shanghai

[Quick Facts] Average distance = 2075 km; Geographical adjacency = 0; Index of ethnic linkages = 0.6185 (2000) and 0.6331 (2010); Freight exchange via national railway = 570 k tons (2000) and 860 k tons (2010). ★ April 15, 2008, the Guangxi Chamber of Commerce in Shanghai Municipality is established. April 8, 2010, a delegation led by chairman of Guangxi Zhuang Autonomous Region pays an inspection and study tour to Shanghai Municipality. The delegation participates in a cooperation forum and signs the "Framework Agreement Concerning the Further Deepening of the Cooperation between Guangxi and Shanghai." Since 2001, Shanghai's enterprises have invested a total of 328 projects in Guangxi, with a total value of 40.2 billion yuan. March 23, 2011, the Beibu Gulf Economic Zone of Guangxi and the Pudong New District of Shanghai sign a cooperation framework agreement, and reach a consensus in four fields including the overall cooperation between the two government agencies, industrial park construction, port logistics and enterprise cooperation. October 21, 2011, the "Well-Known Enterprises of Shanghai Visiting Guangxi", sponsored by Shanghai Jiaotong University, the CCP Committee of Guangxi Zhuang Autonomous Region, and the Investment Promotion Bureau of Guangxi, is held in Nanning. The Guangxi government and Shanghai Jiaotong University sign a strategic cooperation agreement. 10 projects are contracted, including cross-border M&As, production of auto parts, goods information connection, industrial park building and so on, with a total investment of 8.53 billion yuan. February 8, 2012, Shanghai Jiaotong University visits Guangxi's coastal areas, aiming to strengthen cooperation in the fields of electronic information, shipping and marine industries, talent training, etc.

Guangxi-Shanxi

[Quick Facts] Average distance = 2515 km; Geographical adjacency = 0; Index of ethnic linkages = 0.6179 (2000) and 0.6298 (2010); Freight exchange via national railway = 1200 k tons (2000) and 1170 k tons (2010). ★ August 10, 2009, a delegation of the Political Management College of Guangxi Province visits the Law School of Shanxi Province. October 21–27, 2010, a delegation led by the Agricultural International Cooperation and Exchange Work Station of Shanxi visits Guangxi. November 4, 2011, the Bureaux of Meteorology of Jincheng City (Shanxi Province) and of Hezhou City (Guangxi Zhuang Autonomous Region) sign, in Hezhou City, a pairing exchange and cooperation agreement. The IQBs of Guangxi and Shanxi sign a memorandum of cooperation. As the port-based and the production-based authorities, respectively, the Guangxi and Shanxi Bureaux will strengthen the supervision of the quality and safety of the import and export of fruit and vegetable products. November 9, 2011, Shanxi and Guangxi form a cultural tourist alliance and sign a cooperation framework agreement. Members of the alliance include the Jinci Museum, the Chang Family Courtyard, the China Coal Museum, etc. The two sides will make full use of each other's brand and resource advantages to expand their visibility and influence and to promote their common development of the tourist industry. July 31, 2012, Shanxi Jiaotong Vocational and Technical College and the Guangxi Liugong Machinery Co., Ltd. sign a school-enterprise cooperation agreement. September 7, 2012, a nine-people delegation, led by the President of the Guangxi Academy of Communications, pays an inspection to the Shanxi Academy of Communications.

Guangxi-Sichuan

[Quick Facts] Average distance = 1832 km; Geographical adjacency = 0; Index of ethnic linkages = 0.6199 (2000) and 0.6323 (2010); Freight exchange via national railway = 4140 k tons (2000) and 8510 k tons (2010). ★ April 19, 2010, a Guangxi government delegation visits Chengdu to participate in the "Sichuan-Guangxi Exchange Meeting for Economic and Social Development". The two sides decide to promote 12 cooperative projects, with a total investment of 9.505 billion yuan. October 11, 2010, a delegation of the Federation of Labor Union of Guangxi Zhuang Autonomous Region, led by the vice chairman of the Guangxi People's Political Consultative Congress and the president of Guangxi Federation of Labor Union, visits Sichuan. The two sides sign an interprovincial agreement concerning the protection of migrant workers. The delegation also visits the quake-hit Beichuan County, and donates 1 million yuan of facilities and equipments to Beichuan County. December 12–14, 2011, the Sichuan Chamber of Commerce in Guangxi and a delegation of the Sichuan Commission of Economic and Information Technology visit Guangxi's Fangcheng Port, Qinzhou City, Beihai City, etc.

July 16, 2012, a government delegation of Guangxi Zhuang Autonomous Region pays an inspection to the FAW Volkswagen Chengdu Branch in Longquanyi District of Chengdu, Sichuan Province. August 2, 2012, a government delegation of Sichuan Province visits Guangxi. Both sides pledge to jointly promote the construction of Sichuan's industrial park in the Beibu Gulf Economic Zone of Guangxi.

Guangxi-Tianjin

[Quick Facts] Average distance = 2703 km; Geographical adjacency = 0; Index of ethnic linkages = 0.6185 (2000) and 0.6310 (2010); Freight exchange via national railway = 180 k tons (2000) and 120 k tons (2010). ★ November 28, 2001, Guangxi and Tianjin sign an agreement on the development of the western region; the two sides will strengthen cooperation in 24 key projects (covering 7 fields including industry, agriculture, business and trade, infrastructure and science and technology), with a total investment of 1.122 billion yuan. In addition, Nankai University, Tianjin University, Tianjin Agricultural University, and the Science and Technology Commission of Tianjin Municipality also sign, with Guangxi's relevant sectors and enterprises, cooperation agreements concerning the transfer of technological achievements, resource exploitation, tourism, etc. November 19, 2007, the Liugong Machinery Co., Ltd. of Guangxi and the Tianjin Municipal Economic Commission sign a memorandum of investment cooperation. The Liugong intends to invest 2 billion yuan to build an R&D and export base in Tianjin. May 31, 2011, the Land Departments of Guangxi and Tianjin sign a strategic cooperation framework agreement under which the two sides will establish a long-term exchange mechanism, and organize relevant institutions of mining, financial and others to participate in the "China-ASEAN Mining Cooperation Forum" and the "China International Mining Conference". November 7, 2011, the Mining Rights Exchange of Tianjin and the Land Resources Trading Center of Guangxi sign a cooperation agreement in the transfer of mining rights.

Guangxi-Tibet

[Quick Facts] Average distance = 4992 km; Geographical adjacency = 0; Index of ethnic linkages = 0.0624 (2000) and 0.0837 (2010); Freight exchange via national railway = 0 k ton (2000) and 30 k tons (2010). ★ August 2005, the governments of Tibet and Gansu sign a cooperative framework agreement; one important element of this agreement is to strengthen the labor cooperation between the two sides. Now Tibet has hosted more than 60,000 workers from Linxia and more than 25,000 workers from Nanzhou. October 18, 2005, a Tibetan delegation visits Nandan of Guangxi Zhuang Autonomous Region; the two sides reach a cooperation agreement on the joint exploitation of the mineral resources in Tibet Autonomous Region.

August 31, 2006, the Labor and Social Security Department of Tibet Autonomous Region signs a cooperation framework agreement with Gansu Province. May 29, 2010, the Liaison Office of the Yucai Shareholding Co., Ltd. of Guangxi in Tibet is established in Lhasa City. September 16, 2011, the IQBs of Guangxi Zhuang Autonomous Region and Tibet Autonomous Region sign, in Lhasa, an agreement concerning the strengthening of pairing aid and exchange and the promotion of common prosperity and stability of their respective frontier regions. The two bureaux will implement the national arrangement of the pairing aid to Tibet, which is assigned by the General Administration of Quality Supervision, Inspection and Quarantine Bureau of the PRC. All this will strengthen the exchange and cooperation between, and to promote the common development of, Guangxi and Tibet. November 2, 2011, officials of the Federation of Industry and Commerce of Gansu Province visit Tibet Autonomous Region.

Guangxi-Xinjiang

[Quick Facts] Average distance = 4951 km; Geographical adjacency = 0; Index of ethnic linkages = 0.4082 (2000) and 0.4072 (2010); Freight exchange via national railway = 110 k tons (2000) and 350 k tons (2010). ★ March 31, 2011 the Tianye Group of Xinjiang Uygur Autonomous Region and the Agriculture Department of Guangxi sign, in Nanning City of Guangxi, a cooperation framework agreement concerning the promotion of drip irrigation technology in Xinjiang. July 20, 2011, the Poverty Alleviation Offices of Xinjiang and Guangxi sign, in Urumqi, a friendly cooperation agreement, aiming to strengthen the exchange and cooperation in interprovincial anti-poverty work. August 3, 2011 the IQBs of Guangxi and Xinjiang sign, in Urumqi, an agreement concerning the strengthening of pairing aid and exchange and the promotion of common prosperity and stability of their respective frontier regions. The two bureaux will implement the national arrangement of the pairing aid to Xinjiang, which is assigned by the General Administration of Quality Supervision, Inspection and Quarantine of the PRC. November 20, 2011, the Entry-Exit IQBs of Xinjiang and Guangxi sign a memorandum of cooperation to strengthen the collaborative supervision of and the joint promotion of fruit and vegetable trade via the Pingxiang and Dongxing ports of Guangxi to Southeast Asia. According to incomplete statistics, the annual exports of Xinjiang's cantaloupes exceed 20,000 tons.

Guangxi-Yunnan

[Quick Facts] Average distance = 1504 km; Geographical adjacency = 1; Index of ethnic linkages = 0.6610 (2000) and 0.6724 (2010); Freight exchange via national railway = 4900 k tons (2000) and 17,060 k tons (2010). ★ September 28, 2008, the Guangxi Chamber of Commerce in Yunnan is established. According to incomplete statistics, more than 100,000 Guangxi investors have established their companies in Yunnan, mainly in Kunming, Qujing, Chuxiong, Yuxi, Honghe, Wenshan, Banna, Diqing, Pu'er Cities. The chamber members involve steel, tourism, real estate, mining, pharmaceutics, tea, logistics and others (of which the tourist and iron and steel companies have the largest market shares in Yunnan). July 20, 2010, Wenshan City of Yunnan Province and Baise City of Guangxi hold, in Qiubei of Yunan, a meeting of forest pest control and quarantine collaboration. September 1, 2011, a government delegation of Lincang City of Yunnan Province and the Nanhua Sugar Group of Guangxi sign a cooperation agreement. September 20, 2011, a Guangxi government delegation and a Yunnan government delegation sign, in Nanchang of Jiangxi, the framework agreement concerning the establishment of the Yunnan Industrial Park in the Beibu Gulf Economic Zone of Guangxi. March 8, 2012, Yunnan and Guangxi sign, in Guilin of Guangxi, a cooperation agreement concerning cooperation in tourism. Both sides decide to set the Lijiang-Guilin tourist route as a key product. July 9, 2012, the Guangxi Investment Group and the Yunnan Coal Chemical Group sign a strategic cooperation framework agreement. Both sides pledge to work together to build a large aluminum smelting and processing base in Yunnan Province, with the production capacity of 200 million tons per year.

Guangxi-Zhejiang

[Quick Facts] Average distance = 1874 km; Geographical adjacency = 0; Index of ethnic linkages = 0.6199 (2000) and 0.6397 (2010); Freight exchange via national railway = 1200 k tons (2000) and 1170 k tons (2010). ★ December 18, 2003, the "Beihai-Zhejiang Investment Promotion Fair", sponsored by the Beihai Municipal Government of Guangxi, Guangxi Provincial CCP Committee and the Zhejiang Association of Industry and Trade, is held in Hangzhou City. Beihai City offers 66 investment projects, involving infrastructure, industrial, aquatic products processing and marine industries, modern agriculture, commerce and others; 80 private enterprises from Zhejiang agree to invest in various projects, with a total value of 30 billion yuan. January 8, 2005, the "Guangxi-Zhejiang Project Cooperation Promotion Meeting and the Project Signing Ceremony" are held Zhejiang Province. The two sides have a total of 60 cooperative projects, with a total investment of 10.53 billion yuan. April 28, 2005, the Zhejiang Chamber of Commerce in Guangxi is established in Nanning. The chamber has 1228 member companies. According to preliminary statistics, the number of Zhejiang's investors in Guangxi has reached 30 million, with a total number of 510 projects, involving almost all sectors. August 24, 2006, the first joint meeting of the Agricultural Departments of Guangxi and Zhejiang is held in Nanning City; both sides pledge to strengthen agricultural cooperation and to jointly promote the development in silkworm industry. 2007, the Guangxi Chamber of Commerce in Zhejiang is established in Hangzhou City.

The chamber has 500 enterprise members involving more than 20 industries such as IT, electronics, electrical appliances, communications, trade, building materials, chemical industry, and agriculture. May 9, 2011, the Labor and Social Security Departments of Guigang of Guangxi and Fenghua of Zhejiang sign a cooperation agreement.

Guizhou-Hainan

[Quick Facts] Average distance = 1374 km; Geographical adjacency = 0; Index of ethnic linkages = 0.6366 (2000) and 0.6731 (2010); Freight exchange via national railway = 0 k ton (2000) and 120 k tons (2010). ★ June 12, 2009, the Bureaux of Exploration and Exploitation of Geology and Mineral Resources of Guizhou and Hainan Provinces sign a strategic cooperation agreement which includes: (1) mining rights cooperation; (2) information sharing; (3) cooperative development of foreign mining; (4) the joint investment of the domestic and foreign mining resources; (5) technology research and development cooperation; (6) undertaking of construction projects; (7) technology consulting cooperation. The two sides will mainly take the ways of investment, share, equity participation and labor contracting to carry out cooperation. December 11, 2009, the Guizhou Chamber of Commerce in Hainan is established in Haikou City. There are 102 chamber members. August 15, 2011, Hainan and Guizhou Provinces hold, in Guiyang City, an exchange forum of economic and social development and sign a cooperation framework agreement. The agreement includes cooperation in 12 fields such as tourism, industry, IT, forestry and transportation. September 9–13, 2012, a Hainan delegation led by the Hainan provincial government visits Guiyang City of Guizhou Province to participate in the "Second China (Guizhou) International Wine & Spirits Fair".

Guizhou-Hebei

[Quick Facts] Average distance = 2262 km; Geographical adjacency = 0; Index of ethnic linkages = 0.6293 (2000) and 0.6627 (2010); Freight exchange via national railway = 690 k tons (2000) and 900 k tons (2010). ★ August 1, 2008, the Kailin Fertilizers Company of Guizhou Province visits the Hebei Agricultural Production Resources Co. Ltd., aiming to further integrate the two provinces' agricultural production and marketing. March 2011, the Hebei Chamber of commerce in Guizhou is established. There are over 200 Hebei-owned enterprises in Guizhou, covering electric cable, real estate, pharmaceutics, coal, agriculture, building materials, dinning and entrainment, electronics, etc. April 11, 2011, Liping County of Guizhou Province visits Beijing to promote investment, and sign the cooperation framework agreement concerning the project of forest board integrated production with the Xinxin Wood Co., Ltd. of Gaocheng City of Hebei Province. The project is expected to reach a total investment of 280 million yuan. The Xinxin Wood Co., Ltd. is a leading timber enterprise in Hebei Province and North China. After completion of the project, it is expected to yield an annual output value of 240 million yuan. November 11, 2011, the signing ceremony of interprovincial pairing aid to Guizhou universities, held by the Guizhou Provincial Department of Education, opens in Guizhou Province. Guizhou Industrial and Technical College and Hebei Industrial Vocational and Technical College sign a corresponding assistance agreement. May 19, 2012, The Hebei Chamber of Commerce in Guiyang City (Guizhou) is established.

Guizhou-Heilongjiang

[Quick Facts] Average distance = 3833 km; Geographical adjacency = 0; Index of ethnic linkages = 0.6275 (2000) and 0.6595 (2010); Freight exchange via national railway = 200 k tons (2000) and 690 k tons (2010). ★ July 2008, the Weikang Biotechnological Group of Heilongjiang, after friendly negotiations, acquires the Tianfang Pharmaceutical Co. Ltd. of Guizhou. October 28, 2011, the CCP Secretary and the PCSC Chairman of Guizhou Province meet the PCSC Deputy Chairman of the Heilongjiang Province. The Guizhou side hopes to strengthen bilateral exchange and cooperation and learn from each other; the Heilongjiang side hopes to make a positive contribution to promote the exchange and cooperation between Heilongjiang and Guizhou. August 26, 2012, the Moutai Distillery of Guizhou plans to recruit the city and county agents and dealers in Heilongjiang Province. August 31, 2012, the Sunshine Property Exchange of Guizhou Province and the Property Rights Trading Center of Heilongjiang Province discuss the opportunity for bilateral cooperation. September 23, 2012, the Chamber of Overseas Commerce of Guizhou Province and the Chamber of Chinese Businesspersons of Heilongjiang Province signed a strategic cooperation agreement. October 5, 2012, the Jiusheng Wine Co., Ltd. of Guizhou, founded in 2006 as a strategic partner of the Moutai Distillery of Guizhou, establishes a branch in Heilongjiang Province.

Guizhou-Henan

[Quick Facts] Average distance = 1850 km; Geographical adjacency = 0; Index of ethnic linkages = 0.6284 (2000) and 0.6617 (2010); Freight exchange via national railway = 860 k tons (2000) and 1930 k tons (2010). ★ November 25, 2007, the Henan Chamber of Commerce in Guizhou is established. The first chamber member congress is held in Guiyang City of Guizhou Province. According to incomplete statistics, the chamber has more than 200 enterprise members, and invested about

80 billion yuan in Guizhou, mainly involving commerce and trade, building materials, pharmaceutics, real estate, species aquaculture, dining and entertainment, tea industry, science and technology and minerals. July 23–25, 2008, a tourist and cultural promotion group of Guizhou Province visits Henan Province. The two sides sign an agreement on tourist development and cooperation, which includes the sharing of tourist resources and the joint development of tourist market. July 19, 2010, Henan Agricultural University pays an inspection to the Jinsha County Branch (Bijie Prefecture of Guizhou Province) of the Guizhou Tobacco Company. The two sides sign a strategic cooperation framework agreement. May 30, 2012, the Yonggui Energy Company of the Henan Coal and Chemical Group decides to cooperate with the Coalfield Geology Bureau of Guizhou Province; both sides sign a strategic cooperation framework agreement with the Environmental Engineering Assessment Center of Guizhou Province.

Guizhou-Hubei

[Quick Facts] Average distance = 1314 km; Geographical adjacency = 0; Index of ethnic linkages = 0.6653 (2000) and 0.6976 (2010); Freight exchange via national railway = 980 k tons (2000) and 2220 k tons (2010). ★ June 20, 2002, the agricultural sectors of Guizhou and Hubei Provinces sign a cooperation agreement by which Hubei will supply one billion kilograms of grains to Guizhou annually. August 2–5, 2004, relevant provincial departments, led by the vice governor of Hubei Province, visit Guizhou Province. In a forum held in Guiyang City, the two sides address the serious shortage problem of electricity and coal supplies and strengthen cooperation in the areas of coal mining, coal supply and marketing mechanisms and tobacco planting. April 29, 2009, the Grain Bureaux of Xiangfan City (Hubei Province) and Zunyi City (Guizhou Province) sign a cooperation agreement concerning the food production and marketing. Under the agreement, the two sides will share market information and offer the assessment of local grains' supply and demand. September 19, 2009, the Hubei Chamber of Commerce in Guizhou is established in Guiyang. Now the registered enterprises of Hubei investors in Guizhou have reached more than 10,000, with about 200,000 entrepreneurs and relevant staff. The establishment of the chamber will further promote the economic and trade relations between the two regions.

Guizhou-Hunan

[Quick Facts] Average distance = 956 km; Geographical adjacency = 1; Index of ethnic linkages = 0.7118 (2000) and 0.7445 (2010); Freight exchange via national railway = 2520 k tons (2000) and 9020 k tons (2010). ★ 2001, the Hunan Chamber of Commerce in Guizhou (formerly the Association of Private Enterprises in

Guizhou Province, founded in 1999) is established in Guiyang City. The chamber members have more than 4000. According to statistics, Hunan's businesspersons in Guizhou have more than 600,000 of which over 20,000 are business holders in Guizhou, with cumulative investment of nearly 70 billion. February 16, 2011, the Weather Modification Offices of Guizhou and Hunan Provinces hold a cooperation meeting. April 11, 2012, the "Guizhou-Hunan Economic and Social Development Exchange Meeting" is held in Guiyang City. The two provinces' governors sign a strategic cooperation framework agreement. Under the agreement, the two sides will strengthen cooperation in the fields of energy development, non-ferrous metal processing, the construction of interprovincial transportation system, and the poverty alleviation work in Wuling mountain area. From 2011 to 2012, the number of two provinces' economic cooperation projects reaches 382, with a total investment of 26.28 billion yuan. May 22, 2012, Xinhuang County and Wanshan District, which are located on the border area of Hunan and Guizhou, jointly organize a gathering of tourist cooperation. Hunan and Guizhou will use this opportunity to deepen exchange and cooperation of cultural tourism between Xinhuang of Hunan and Wanshan of Guizhou.

Guizhou-Inner Mongolia

[Quick Facts] Average distance = 3100 km; Geographical adjacency = 0; Index of ethnic linkages = 0.6290 (2000) and 0.6627 (2010); Freight exchange via national railway = 100 k tons (2000) and 370 k tons (2010). ★ October 13–16, 2011, a 3-people delegation, led by the Director of the Editorial Committee of Local Historical Records of Guizhou Province, visits Inner Mongolia to conduct inspection and exchange. December 8, 2011, a delegation of the Inner Mongolia Federation of Returned Overseas Chinese visits Guizhou Province to exchange with the Guizhou Federation of Returned Overseas Chinese, aiming to strengthen resource and information sharing. May 15, 2012, a delegation of the Radio and Television Bureau of Inner Mongolia Autonomous Region visits the Radio and Television Bureau of Guizhou Province. The two sides discuss the problem of rural television coverage. June 19, 2012, Siziwang Qi (County) of Inner Mongolia and the Grassland Husbandry Center of Qinglong County (Guizhou Province) sign a cooperation agreement concerning sheep embryo transferring and feeding standardization. According to the agreement, the Center will purchase the "Dumu sheep" from Siziwang Qi at the price of 15,000 yuan per head. This agreement aims to promote China's new rural development policies and to strengthen agricultural innovation and development. October 25, 2012, a 25-people delegation, led by the Discipline and Inspection Chief of the Department of Communication and Transportation of Inner Mongolia, pays an inspection to the Department of Communication and Transportation of Guizhou. December 12, 2012, a symposium entitled the "Developments in Optical Communication Techniques", sponsored by the Societies of Communication Engineering of Guizhou and Inner Mongolia, is held in Guiyang City.

Guizhou-Jiangsu

[Quick Facts] Average distance = 2054 km; Geographical adjacency = 0; Index of ethnic linkages = 0.6251 (2000) and 0.6593 (2010); Freight exchange via national railway = 680 k tons (2000) and 1160 k tons (2010). ★ December 16, 2010, the Jiangsu China Tobacco Industry Co., Ltd. and Guizhou Provincial Tobacco Monopoly Bureau (Company) sign a strategic cooperation framework agreement concerning the joint establishment of an industrial and commercial tobacco base in Nanjing. April 9, 2012, Guizhou and Jiangsu Provinces hold, in Guiyang City, the signing ceremony of the agreements of strategic cooperation in the IT industry and of cooperation in the Guizhou-Jiangsu Huigu Industrial Park. Under the agreements, Jiangsu will transfer a number of technologically-advanced enterprises to Guizhou. June 9, 2012, the Guizhou Chamber of Commerce in Jiangsu is established in Nanjing City. The number of chamber members is 73, involving smart grid construction, heavy machinery casting, urban water treatment, media, mechanical processing, real estate development and others. August 17, 2012, the Labor Union of the Jiangsu Chamber of Commerce is established in Nanjing City. September 7–9, 2012, a delegation led by the Vice Governor of Jiangsu Province visits Guizhou to participate in the second session of the China Wine Expo. Jiangsu and Guizhou hold an industrial cooperation forum, in which 34 enterprises of Jiangsu decide to cooperate with Guizhou in 22 projects.

Guizhou-Jiangxi

[Quick Facts] Average distance = 1272 km; Geographical adjacency = 0; Index of ethnic linkages = 0.6241 (2000) and 0.6570 (2010); Freight exchange via national railway = 590 k tons (2000) and 3320 k tons (2010). ★ November 18, 2006, the Jiangxi Chamber of Commerce in Guizhou is established in Guiyang. The chamber has more than 130 enterprise members, which mainly involve the fields of gold and coal mining and non-ferrous metal ore exploitation and processing, with the total assets of about 30 billion yuan. April 7–8, 2011, the Guizhou China Tobacco Industry Co., Ltd. and Jiangxi Provincial Tobacco Monopoly Bureau (Company) jointly organize a number of activities on bilateral technological cooperation. July 10–12, 2011, a Jiangxi delegation pays an inspection to Guizhou Province to exchange the experience of development in tea industry. The delegation also visits a tea production base in Meitan County, the Chaqing Tea Market and some tea producing enterprises. October 31, 2011, Guizhou and Jiangxi provinces establish a regular mechanism of interregional cooperation in local taxation. October 30. 2012, the President of Nanchang University of Aviation of Jiangxi Province visits Guizhou Province and signs five research projects as well as other bilateral (university-enterprise) cooperation agreements with the SOEs in Guizhou.

Guizhou-Jilin

[Quick Facts] Average distance = 3591 km; Geographical adjacency = 0; Index of ethnic linkages = 0.6288 (2000) and 0.6612 (2010); Freight exchange via national railway = 80 k tons (2000) and 690 k tons (2010). ★ March 3, 2008, a large-scale cooperative project—the Asphalt Mixing Plant, which is jointly developed by the Highway Machinery Co., Ltd. of Jilin Province and the Highway Machinery Plant of Guizhou Province—starts to operate. May 17, 2012, the Sales and Marketing Departments of China Southern Airlines Guizhou Branch and Jilin Branch hold, in Guiyang City, a ceremony of the new domestic air route (i.e., from Guiyang City to Changchun City via Qingdao City), which adds a new productive factor into the acceleration of the economic exchange and cooperation between Guizhou and Jilin Provinces. May 20, 2011, the Federations of Returned Overseas Chinese of Qiannan Buyi and Miao Autonomous Prefecture (Guizhou Province) and of Yanbian Korean Autonomous Prefecture (Jilin Province) sign a friendly agreement. Under the agreement, the two sides will share each other's intelligence data and strengthen bilateral exchange and cooperation. October 31, 2012, an 18-people delegation, led by the Deputy Chief of the Bureau of Public Health of Tongren City (Guizhou Province), visits the Bureau of Public Health of Longtan District of Jilin City (Jilin Province). Both sides discuss issues relating to the management of cooperative medical care scheme in rural areas.

Guizhou-Liaoning

[Quick Facts] Average distance = 3286 km; Geographical adjacency = 0; Index of ethnic linkages = 0.6290 (2000) and 0.6625 (2010); Freight exchange via national railway = 390 k tons (2000) and 380 k tons (2010). ★ December 18, 2007, the signing ceremony of a strategic alliance agreement between the Liaoning Tobacco and the China Tobacco of Guizhou and the industrial and commercial cooperative marketing seminar are held in Shenyang City of Liaoning Province. May 27, 2010, the Academies of Security Sciences of Liaoning and Guizhou Provinces hold a discussion meeting on special steel projects. December 21, 2010, Weng'an County of Guizhou Province and the Liaoning Communication Construction Group sign two agreements, with a total investment of 12.2 billion yuan. The agreements include the construction of four projects: (1) a highway from Guiyang to Weng'an County; (2) an expressway from Yinzhan of Weng'an County to Mulaoping; (3) a ring road of Weng'an County; and (4) a terminal infrastructure of Jiangjie River in

Weng'an. June 26, 2011, the Human Resources and Social Security Department of Liaoning Province and the Guizhou provincial government sign a memorandum concerning the joint promotion of the reform and development of human resources and social security in Guizhou.

Guizhou-Ningxia

[Quick Facts] Average distance = 2309 km; Geographical adjacency = 0; Index of ethnic linkages = 0.6286 (2000) and 0.6567 (2010); Freight exchange via national railway = 60 k tons (2000) and 240 k tons (2010). ★ February 28, 2008, the Tourism Bureaux of Ningxia and Guizhou sign a tourist cooperation agreement and hold a Guizhou tourist promotion in Ningxia. Under the agreement, the two sides will become each other's tourist market and jointly promote tourist development. August 20–26, 2012, a Guizhou delegation, composed of 20 scientific and technological specialists and managerial cadres from the Bijie Demonstration Area, Qiandongnan and Qiannan Prefectures and Wudang District of Guiyang City and organized by the Science and Technology Department of Guizhou Province, visits Ningxia Hui Autonomous. The two sides reach a substantive intention on the strengthening of bilateral cooperation in three areas including (1) livestock breeding and fodder production; (2) high-quality fruit cultivation and fruit wine brewing; and (3) industrialized breeding and vegetable cultivation. September 9, 2012, the "Ningxia-Guizhou Forum for Entrepreneurs" is held during the Second Wine Expo; the two sides' entrepreneurs discuss key investment areas of and possible cooperation between Ningxia and Guizhou.

Guizhou-Qinghai

[Quick Facts] Average distance = 2355 km; Geographical adjacency = 0; Index of ethnic linkages = 0.5480 (2000) and 0.5389 (2010); Freight exchange via national railway = 20 k tons (2000) and 90 k tons (2010). ★ November 20, 2010, a delegation of Qinghai Provincial government visits Guizhou province; the two sides hold an exchange meeting, aiming to consolidate the bilateral relations and to implement the western development policy. December 6, 2011, the Bureau of Geology and Mineral Resources of Guizhou Province and the Land Provincial Department of Qinghai sign a strategic cooperation agreement; both sides will jointly exploit the mineral resources of Qinghai Province for a period of five years. The cooperation between the two sides includes regional geology, mineral geology, geophysical exploration and hydro-geological, engineering and environmental geological surveys. June 5, 2012, a delegation of the Investment Corporation of Qinghai Province visits Wenxiu County of Guizhou Province and pays an inspection to the Huafei Corporation of Guizhou Province. Both Corporations agree to jointly invest in Wenxian County. July 7, 2012, the Wenzhou Chambers of Commerce in Guizhou and Qinghai carry out cooperation. July 10–13, 2012, the Federation of Industry and Commerce of Guizhou Province visits Xining City of Qinghai Province to participate in the 2012 China (Qinghai) International Halal Food and Commodity Exhibition.

Guizhou-Shaanxi

[Quick Facts] Average distance = 1809 km; Geographical adjacency = 0; Index of ethnic linkages = 0.6266 (2000) and 0.6595 (2010); Freight exchange via national railway = 240 k tons (2000) and 700 k tons (2010). ★ April 17–21, 2009, a Shaanxi research group led by the vice governor and composed of the Science and Technology Department, universities and research institutions, visits Guizhou Province and attends the signing ceremony of bilateral cooperation. April 21, 2009, the signing ceremony of the scientific and technological cooperation between Guizhou and Shaanxi is held in Guizhou; the two sides reach an agreement on the utilization of phosphorus chemical solid waste resources, the new technical production line of phosphorylation and the titanium ingot processing. April 8, 2010, the Guizhou Chamber of Commerce in Shaanxi is established in Xi'an. The Chamber has more than 100 enterprise members, involving petroleum, chemistry, pharmaceutics, liquor, building materials, food and beverage and entertainment industry, with nearly 20 billion investment values in Shaanxi. April 29, 2011, Guizhou and Shaanxi Provinces pledge to promote labor cooperation. September 9, 2011, a commodity promotion meeting, organized by the People's Government of Shaanxi Province, Shaanxi Provincial Department of Commerce and Guizhou Provincial Department of Commerce, is held in Guiyang City, aiming to deepen cooperation in three areas (expansion of domestic demand, the strengthening of trade and economic cooperation and mutual development). November 10, 2011, a delegation of the Guizhou Chamber of Commerce in Shaanxi Province pays an investment inspection to Fuping County of Shaanxi Province.

Guizhou-Shandong

[Quick Facts] Average distance = 2516 km; Geographical adjacency = 0; Index of ethnic linkages = 0.6276 (2000) and 0.6612 (2010); Freight exchange via national railway = 700 k tons (2000) and 2160 k tons (2010). ★ April 25, 2009, the Shandong Chamber of Commerce in Guizhou is established in Guiyang City. The Chamber has 78 enterprise members, and more than 250 individual members. May 27, 2011, the signing ceremonies of technological and strategic cooperation between the Guizhou provincial government and Shangdong University and between Guizhou University and Shandong University are held in Guiyang City.

August 17–20, 2011, a Shandong provincial government delegation, led by the deputy secretary and the Governor of Shandong, participates in the "2011 China (Guizhou) International Wine & Spirits Fair and the China (Guiyang) Investment and Trade Fair". The two sides agree to cooperate in eight projects involving processing and manufacturing, wine manufacturing, services and others, with a total investment of 7.795 billion yuan. December 18, 2011, the Yanzhou Mining Group of Shandong Province and the Guizhou provincial government sign a strategic cooperation framework agreement. Under the agreement, the two sides will strive to produce 25 million tons of coal in Guizhou by 2015.

Guizhou-Shanghai

[Quick Facts] Average distance = 2053 km; Geographical adjacency = 0; Index of ethnic linkages = 0.6275 (2000) and 0.6646 (2010); Freight exchange via national railway = 410 k tons (2000) and 530 k tons (2010). ★ June 30, 2008, the Guizhou Chamber of Commerce in Shanghai is established. July 29, 2011, the signing ceremony of economic and trade cooperation between Guizhou and Shanghai is held in Shanghai; 29 projects are included, with a total investment of 164.975 billion yuan. The two sides sign the "Agreement Concerning the Strengthening of Cooperation and Exchange of Science and Technology". February 28, 2011, the signing ceremony of strategic cooperation between the Yunfeng Group of Shanghai and the Shuanglong Industrial Group of Guizhou is held in Guizhou. The two sides will jointly invest nearly 2 billion yuan to establish a new enterprise to participate in the new round of integration of coal mining in Guizhou, aiming to raise the coal production capacity to more than 10 million tons, with the output value of over 10 billion yuan during the 12th Five Years Plan. April 13, 2012, Shanghai Jiaotong University and the Guizhou Provincial People's Government sign a strategic cooperation framework agreement. April 23, 2012, Shanghai Customs College and the Guizhou Provincial Department of Commerce sign a cooperation agreement.

Guizhou-Shanxi

[Quick Facts] Average distance = 2450 km; Geographical adjacency = 0; Index of ethnic linkages = 0.6248 (2000) and 0.6572 (2010); Freight exchange via national railway = 220 k tons (2000) and 500 k tons (2010). ★ July 23–25, 2008, the Tourist Culture Promotion Group of Guizhou visits Shanxi to promote tourist products. The Provincial Tourism Bureaux of Guizhou and Shanxi reach a cooperative development agreement, aiming to exchange tourists between the two places and to jointly develop the tourism market. Both sides strive to maintain the tourists' growth of more than 15–20 % in the next five years and to open direct flights between Guiyang and Taiyuan at an earliest date. July 26, 2008, chief leaders of Guizhou and Shanxi meet in Guiyang City to discuss bilateral tourism cooperation. The Guizhou side pledges that, in the following five years, it will not raise the prices of its scenic spots and hotels to grouped tourists from Shanxi Province. October 21–27, 2010, a delegation composed of leaders of the cities and counties of Shanxi Province, which is organized by the International Agricultural Exchange and Cooperation Workstation of Shanxi Province, visits Guizhou Province to inspect international cooperation projects, aiming to share the experiences of comprehensive agricultural development projects. January 13, 2012, the North Heavy Industry Co., Ltd. of Guizhou and the Taiyuan Steel Co., Ltd. of Shanxi agree to enhance bilateral cooperation. September 19, 2012, the Shanxi Chamber of Commerce in Guizhou offers a job opportunity in Guiyang city, Guizhou Province. November 8, 2012, Pingtang County of Guizhou and the Luxin Energy Group of Shanxi sign a 1.35 billion yuan cooperative framework agreement on the projects of coal mining and exploration, limestone exploitation and processing, construction of 4-star hotels, etc.

Guizhou-Sichuan

[Quick Facts] Average distance = 967 km; Geographical adjacency = 1; Index of ethnic linkages = 0.6504 (2000) and 0.6845 (2010); Freight exchange via national railway = 3530 k tons (2000) and 7530 k tons (2010). ★ June 30, 2006, the Sichuan Chamber of Commerce in Guizhou is established in Guiyang. The chamber has about 300 members involving real estate, mining, hydropower, pharmaceutics, catering, advertising, construction, aquaculture and processing. March 28, 2011, the Production Safety Academies of Sichuan and Guizhou Provinces sign a strategic cooperation agreement. July 27, 2011, Sichuan and Guizhou provinces hold an economic and social development meeting and a project signing ceremony. There are 92 projects in the cooperation, with a total investment of 118.4 billion yuan. The two governments hope to strengthen regional cooperation, and to promote exchange and cooperation between the two place's entrepreneurs. April 20, 2012, a Sichuan government delegation visits Guizhou and signs, in Guiyang City, a strategic cooperation framework agreement with Guizhou. Both sides pledge to promote cooperation in the fields of transportation construction, personnel exchange, market building, and environmental protection. June 18, 2012, a conference is sponsored by Sichuan University and the Panjiang Investment Holdings (Group) Co., Ltd. of Guizhou Province and the agreement signing ceremony is held in the Wangjiang Campus of Sichuan University, aiming to build a comprehensive school-enterprise cooperative relation.

Guizhou-Tianjin

[Quick Facts] Average distance = 2681 km; Geographical adjacency = 0; Index of ethnic linkages = 0.6296 (2000) and 0.6639 (2010); Freight exchange via national railway = 230 k tons (2000) and 180 k tons (2010). ★ May 12, 2011, the Geological and Mineral Exploration and Exploitation Bureaux of Guizhou and Tianjin sign a strategic cooperation agreement. July 6, 2011, the Chamber of Commerce of the Tianjin Federation of Return Overseas Chinese pays an inspection to Guiyang City. The two sides will strengthen economic cooperation. November 23, 2011, Guiyang Customs and Tianjin Customs sign a cooperation memorandum of regional passing port, and the two sides reach an agreement on the port cargo passing. May 6, 2012, the Beverly Equity Investment Fund Management Co., Ltd. of Tianjin and Weng'an County of Guizhou Province sign an investment agreement concerning the integration and investment of coal industry, with a total investment of 3.5 billion yuan. July 25, 2012, Tianjin University and the Guizhou provincial government sign a comprehensive cooperation framework agreement. The cooperation is expected to play an important role in the processes of industrialization, urbanization and agricultural modernization of Guizhou and in the promotion of production and research cooperation with Tianjin University.

Guizhou-Tibet

[Quick Facts] Average distance = 4117 km; Geographical adjacency = 0; Index of ethnic linkages = 0.0656 (2000) and 0.0875 (2010); Freight exchange via national railway = 0 k ton (2000) and 0 k ton (2010). ★ October 2005, the Yibai Company of Giuzhou and the Tibetan Medicine Corporation, two of the well-known medical shareholding enterprises, reach a strategic cooperation framework agreement. November 18, 2006, Yibai Company of Giuzhou and the Tibetan Medicine Corporation decide to jointly bid for the CCTV's gold time advertisement in 2007, which is successfully done at the price of 116 million yuan. August 6–12, 2011, an oil-crops specialists' group of Guizhou Province visits Tibet. This visit intends to carry out cooperation between Guizhou and Tibet in the research of rape planting, the introduction and identification of new varieties and the innovation of new germplasm resources. July 25–27, 2012, the Vice President of the Women's Federation of Guizhou Province visits Lhasa City of Tibet to participate in the third "Women's Development and Cooperation Organization Meeting of the Five Provinces and Regions in Southwest China", aiming to strengthen the coordination in the fields of female labor transfer, ethnic embroidery, weaving and other skill training and to build a mutually beneficial cooperation mechanism in resource sharing.

Guizhou-Xinjiang

[Quick Facts] Average distance = 3993 km; Geographical adjacency = 0; Index of ethnic linkages = 0.4146 (2000) and 0.4143 (2010); Freight exchange via national railway = 180 k tons (2000) and 470 k tons (2010). ★ October 24, 2008, the People's Government of Guizhou Province and the Xinjiang Production and Construction Corps (XPCC)—a de facto sub-provincial unit which is established in the southern area of Xinjiang Uygur Autonomous Region by and directly under Chinese central government—sign a comprehensive economic and trade cooperation agreement, aiming to jointly build a demonstration base of agricultural machinery. November 9, 2010, the XPCC, the Management Committee of the Southern Xinjiang Area and Shihezi University sign a strategic cooperation framework agreement of production and research with the Shenqi Group of Guizhou Province. The Shihezi University and the Shenqi Group will carry out a comprehensive cooperation in the development of Tibetan medicine, the joint training of nursing professionals, the exploration of cooperation education mode, etc. August 3, 2012, a Guizhou Provincial government delegation visits XPCC. The two sides will strengthen cooperation in the fields of agriculture, machinery manufacturing, aiming to strengthen exchange and cooperation to benefit from mutually complementary advantages and to achieve common development.

Guizhou-Yunnan

[Quick Facts] Average distance = 639 km; Geographical adjacency = 1; Index of ethnic linkages = 0.6862 (2000) and 0.7217 (2010); Freight exchange via national railway = 2620 k tons (2000) and 5280 k tons (2010). ★ January 2007, the Guizhou Chamber of Commerce in Yunnan is established. The chamber has more than 500 enterprise members, involving more than 20 industries such as industry, commerce, mining, food and beverage, entertainment, real estate and services. July 31, 2010, Kunming, Dali, Lijiang, Zhaotong and Chuxiong of Yunnan Province and Liupanshui and Bijie of Guizhou Province establish a system of regional cooperation, and sign an agreement of cooperation in tourist development, trade and flow of commodities. September 27, 2011, the "Third Joint Conference of the Regional Port Cooperation in the Pan-Pearl Region" is held in Guiyang City; Guizhou and Yunnan sign a cooperation agreement concerning the clearance of port customs. November 3, 2011, the Sugarcane Research Institute of Yunnan Academy of Agricultural Sciences and the Jinshan Bishui Ecological Agriculture Co., Ltd. of Guizhou sign a cooperation agreement. July 5–7, 2012, a delegation of Guizhou Provincial Tobacco Monopoly Bureau (Company) visits the Yunnan Tobacco Company. September 8, 2012, a delegation led by the governor of Yunnan Province visits Guizhou to search opportunities for bilateral economic cooperation.

Guizhou-Zhejiang

[Quick Facts] Average distance = 1852 km; Geographical adjacency = 0; Index of ethnic linkages = 0.6277 (2000) and 0.6743 (2010); Freight exchange via national railway = 670 k tons (2000) and 1150 k tons (2010). ★ May 8, 2003, the Zhejiang Chamber of Commerce in Guizhou is established. The Chamber has more than 3000 members. December 2009, Guizhou and Zhejiang Provinces sign an agreement concerning the pairing aid of hospitals. March 5, 2012, the forum of cultural cooperation between Guizhou Province and Zhejiang University, organized by the Guizhou Provincial Department of Culture, opens. The forum aims to promote the understanding of the history of Anti-Japanese War and the traditional relationship between Guizhou Province and Zhejiang University. August 1, 2012, the Industrial Technology Research Institute of Zhejiang University holds, in Guiyang, a scientific and technological cooperation symposium with Guizhou Province. Both sides pledge to deepen school-enterprise cooperation. September 5, 2012, a Zhejiang provincial government delegation, led by the CCP Secretary (also the PCSC Chairman) of Zhejiang Province, visits Guiyang City and sponsors, together with his Guizhou pairing, the "Guizhou-Zhejiang Exchange Meeting for Economic and Social Development". Zhejiang Province donates 5 million yuan each to Qiandongnan and Qianxinan Prefectures of Guizhou Province. September 12, 2012, Guizhou and Zhejiang jointly launch the "Guizhou's Wines in Zhejiang" fair. Guizhou Provincial Department of Commerce, Zhejiang Provincial Department of Commerce, the wine production enterprises of Guizhou Province and the buyer's representatives of Zhejiang jointly sign a wine purchase and sale agreement, with a total value of 2 billion yuan.

Hainan-Hebei

[Quick Facts] Average distance = 2811 km; Geographical adjacency = 0; Index of ethnic linkages = 0.8288 (2000) and 0.8386 (2010); Freight exchange via national railway = 0 k ton (2000) and 10 k tons (2010). ★ July 22, 2005, the Hebei Crop Oil (Group) Co., Ltd. and the Hainan Yanlong Agricultural Co., Ltd. decide to cooperate in the development of tropical fruits and trees planting for a period of 50 years, with a total investment of 3.6 million US dollars. November 28, 2009, the Hebei Chamber of Commerce in Hainan is established in Haikou City. Now, the number of Hebei's enterprises in Hainan has exceeded 4000. November 4, 2010, a delegation of the Hainan Association of Supply and Marketing Cooperatives pays an inspection to Hebei Province. Hainan Province hopes to carry out cooperation with Hebei's agricultural companies in fertilizer sales. September 8, 2011, a delegation led by the deputy inspector of the Agriculture Department of Hainan Province visits Shijiazhuang City, Hebei Province, to investigate the marketing situation of Hainan's vegetables and fruits in winter season. December 18, 2011, the third congress of the Hebei Chamber of Commerce in Hainan is held in Haikou City of Hainan Province, with 300 participants including business consultants, invited members as well as enterprise members. On June 29, 2012, Hainan Medical College and the Hebei Shuangwei (Group) Co., Ltd. sign, in Hainan, a framework agreement of medical cooperation.

Hainan-Heilongjiang

[Quick Facts] Average distance = 4433 km; Geographical adjacency = 0; Index of ethnic linkages = 0.8284 (2000) and 0.8381 (2010); Freight exchange via national railway = 0 k ton (2000) and 0 k ton (2010). ★ March 6, 2008, the Heilongjiang Chamber of Commerce in Hainan is established in Haikou City. The number of Heilongjiang's enterprises in Hainan has exceeded 400, involving tourism, real estate, industry, agriculture and others, with a cumulative investment of over 10 billion yuan. March 21, 2010, Sanya City of Hainan Province and Mudanjiang City of Heilongjiang Province sign a tourist cooperation agreement, aiming to carry out an in-depth and wide-range cooperation in market expansion, product innovation, personnel training, information sharing, etc. April 15, 2010, the No. 1 Affiliated Hospital of Harbin Medical University of Heilongjiang Province and the No. 3 People's Hospital of Hainan Province become interprovincial partnerships. This cooperation marks that Hainan and Heilongjiang Provinces will benefit from each other's complementary medical advantages. June 16, 2010, the Hainan and Heilongjiang provincial governments sign, in the China (Harbin) International Economic and Trade Fair, a memorandum of cooperation, aiming to promote regional economic development and cooperation through the utilization of complementary advantages. March 26, 2011, the "Heilongjiang-Hainan (North and South) Cooperation Forum" and the celebration of the "Third Anniversary of the Establishment of the Heilongjiang Chamber of Commerce in Hainan" are held in Haikou City, Hainan Province. The representatives from the two provinces exchange their experiences in bilateral economic cooperation and tourist development.

Hainan-Henan

[Quick Facts] Average distance = 2399 km; Geographical adjacency = 0; Index of ethnic linkages = 0.8283 (2000) and 0.8382 (2010); Freight exchange via national railway = 0 k ton (2000) and 90 k tons (2010). ★ January 11, 2008, the Henan Chamber of Commerce in Hainan is established. The Chamber has more than 100 enterprise members. June 10, 2008, a business delegation from Henan Province visits Hainan to draft plans to constructing a meat processing plant in Hainan. June 9, 2009, the Henan provincial government and the China Hainan Airlines (Group)

Co., Ltd. sign a strategic cooperation agreement in Zhengzhou. January 21, 2010, the Tourism Bureaux of Hainan and Henan jointly initiate a tourist cooperation union, aiming to promote regional economic development through exchange and cooperation. April 28, 2011, the Henan Salt Trading Co., Ltd. (formerly: the Salt Administration of Henan Province) and the Hainan Coconut Island Group sign, in Zhengzhou City of Henan Province, a strategic cooperation agreement. This cooperation is the first attempt of the Henan Company to conduct businesses in Hainan. March 31, 2012, the Henan provincial government, the China Hainan Airlines Group and the Foxconn Group sign a trilateral strategic cooperation agreement in Haikou City of Hainan, aiming to jointly promote the construction of the Zhengzhou Aviation Economic Demonstration Area.

Hainan-Hubei

[Quick Facts] Average distance = 1883 km; Geographical adjacency = 0; Index of ethnic linkages = 0.8324 (2000) and 0.8418 (2010); Freight exchange via national railway = 0 k ton (2000) and 130 k tons (2010). ★ February 23, 2009, the Hubei Chamber of Commerce in Hainan is established. Now, Hubei Province has more than 1000 enterprises in Hainan, with a total investment of over 10 billion yuan, involving real estate, agriculture, biotechnology, telecommunications, culture, tourism and others. February 12, 2011, a delegation led by the CCP Committee of and the government of Ledong Li Autonomous County (Hainan Province) sign an agreement concerning the cooperation between the Ledong People's Hospital and the Taihe Hospital of Hubei Medical College. The cooperation aims to improve Ledong's medical treatment through Hubei's support. December 16, 2011, the Electric Power Institutes of Hainan and Hubei Provinces sign a strategic cooperation agreement in Haikou City. The two sides pledge to cooperate in talent training, R&D and resource sharing in the development the Hainan market. June 2, 2012, the signing ceremony of the educational pairing aid of Wuhan City (Hubei) to Hainan Province is held in the Ethnic Middle School of Wanning City, Hainan Province. The education departments of the two places also sign the "Exchange and Cooperation Agreement on Basic Education".

Hainan-Hunan

[Quick Facts] Average distance = 1501 km; Geographical adjacency = 0; Index of ethnic linkages = 0.8381 (2000) and 0.8482 (2010); Freight exchange via national railway = 0 k ton (2000) and 130 k tons (2010). ★ June 11, 2007, the Hainan provincial government and representatives of Hunan Province and other places sign an international flight cooperation framework agreement in Changsha City, aiming to strengthen the interprovincial economic cooperation in the Pan-Pearl River Delta

Region. September 7, 2009, the Hunan Chamber of Commerce in Hainan, also called "Hainan-Hunan Regional Cooperation Promotion Congress", is officially established in Haikou City, Hainan Province. January 21, 2010, the Tourism Bureaux of Hainan and Hunan jointly initiate a tourist cooperation union, aiming to promote regional economic development through exchange and cooperation. June 26, 2011, the Hainan Alumni Association of Hunan Engineering College is established in Hainan. August 6, 2012, the second meeting of the Hainan-Hunan Regional Cooperation Promotion Congress (i.e., the Hunan Chamber of Commerce in Hainan) is held in Haikou City. September 21, 2012, a meeting concerning the promotion of high-quality tourist products in Hainan Province is held in Changsha City of Hunan Province. The promotion focuses on Hainan's tropical-featured tourism such as seaside resort, natural oxygen bar, forest spa, and marine tourism. According to statistics, in 2011 Hainan has received 2.511 million tourists from Hunan Province, an increase of 31.05 % of those in 2010.

Hainan-Inner Mongolia

[Quick Facts] Average distance = 3747 km; Geographical adjacency = 0; Index of ethnic linkages = 0.7940 (2000) and 0.7983 (2010); Freight exchange via national railway = 0 k ton (2000) and 10 k tons (2010). ★ July 21, 2008, the IQBs of Hainan Province and Inner Mongolia Autonomous Region sign a cooperation agreement concerning the joint promotion of exports of Hainan's fruits and vegetables to Russia and Mongolia. Erenhot City of Inner Mongolia is China's main port of exporting vegetables and fruits to Mongolia, accounting for more than 95 % of Mongolia's total imports of fruits and vegetables; Manzhouli City of Inner Mongolia is the largest land port of vegetables and fruits and other agricultural products exported to Russia, accounting for more than 60 % of freight exchange between China and Russia. May 31, 2010, the Inner Mongolia Chamber of Commerce in Hainan is established. The Chamber has 200 enterprise members, involving real estate, finance and others. The "Inner Mongolia-Hainan Trade Fair" is held in Haikou City. September 6, 2011, a Hainan delegation in charge of supply and marketing of vegetables pays an inspection to Inner Mongolia, aiming to increase Hainan's supply of vegetables and fruits to Inner Mongolia in winter season. June 2, 2012, Hainan and Inner Mongolia sign an agreement on cooperation in offsite medical billing reimbursement.

Hainan-Jiangsu

[Quick Facts] Average distance = 2597 km; Geographical adjacency = 0; Index of ethnic linkages = 0.8289 (2000) and 0.8397 (2010); Freight exchange via national railway = 0 k ton (2000) and 10 k tons (2010). ★ October 20, 2006, the Jiangsu

Chamber of Commerce in Hainan is established. The chamber has more than 300 enterprise members, involving real estate, construction, agriculture, marine, pharmaceutics, financial securities and others. May 29, 2012, a joint venture entitled Hainan Phoenix Xinhua Publishing Co. Ltd. is established in Haikou City. The company's registered capital exceeds a half billion yuan, of which the Jiangsu Phoenix Publishing & Media Co., Ltd. accounts for 51 %. July 27, 2012, a forum of police cooperation between Nantong City of Jiangsu and Sansha City of Hainan is held in Nantong City, aiming to promote the economic and social development of coastal areas and the maintenance of national territorial sovereignty. September 18, 2012, the Deputy Secretary of CCP Committee (also the Governor) of Hainan Province meets, in Haikou, a delegation led by the Vice Governor of Jiangsu Province. The two sides conduct an in-depth exchange on the strengthening of construction cooperation. September 28, 2012, the Jiangsu Construction Promotion meeting is held in Boao Town, Qionghai City of Hainan Province. The Housing and Urban-Rural Construction Departments of Hainan and Jiangsu Provinces sign a framework agreement concerning the strengthening of bilateral cooperation.

Hainan-Jiangxi

[Quick Facts] Average distance = 1750 km; Geographical adjacency = 0; Index of ethnic linkages = 0.8274 (2000) and 0.8370 (2010); Freight exchange via national railway = 0 k ton (2000) and 90 k tons (2010). ★ August 3, 2006, the Jiangxi Chamber of Commerce in Hainan is established. June 11, 2007, Hainan provincial government and the representatives of Jiangxi and other two provinces sign, in Changsha City, a framework agreement on international flight cooperation, aiming to strengthen the interprovincial economic cooperation in the Pan-Pearl River Delta Region. March 2011, the Tourism Commission of Hainan Province visits Jiangxi Province and signs, with Jiangxi Provincial Tourism Bureau, a bilateral framework agreement on tourist cooperation. August 31, 2012, at the Regional Tourist Cooperation and Consultation Meeting of the 8th Pan-Pearl River Delta, the Jiangxi Co., Ltd. of China International Travel Service (CITS) and the Hainan International Travel Agency of the CITS sign a cooperative agreement. According to the agreement, Jiangxi will send 10,000 tourists to Hainan, and Hainan will send 5000 tourists to Jiangxi. September 22, 2011, at the 7th Pan-Pearl River Delta Regional Cooperation and Development Forum and Trade Fair, Jiangxi and Hainan Provinces sign a strategic cooperation framework agreement. The two provinces also sign two agreements on tourist cooperation, the cooperation between Nanchang University and Hainan University as well as a memorandum of cooperation between Hainan's Ecological and Software Park and the Jiangxi's Jinlu Software Park.

Hainan-Jilin

[Quick Facts] Average distance = 4187 km; Geographical adjacency = 0; Index of ethnic linkages = 0.8284 (2000) and 0.8382 (2010); Freight exchange via national railway = 0 k ton (2000) and 0 k ton (2010). ★ July 28, 2010, the 2010 National Seminar of Tourist Bureau Chiefs is held in Changchun City of Jilin. The Tourism Bureaux of Hainan and Jilin Provinces pledge to carry bilateral cooperation. December 10, 2010, the Jilin Chamber of Commerce in Hainan is established. The Chamber has about 100 enterprise members. The first "Hainan-Jilin Tourism Promotion" is held in Haikou City, in which the Jilin delegation highlights a special tourist route of the Changbai Mountain. September 6, 2011, in the 7th Northeast Asia Expo, the Jilin Chamber of Commerce in Hainan and Jilin provincial government contract five cooperation projects, with a total investment of more than 30 billion. These projects mainly involve food processing, tourism, real estate development, modern logistics base construction and comprehensive energy development and utilization. September 21, 2011, the Deputy Secretary of CCP Committee (also Vice President) of Jilin University and the Director General of Sanya Municipal Taxation Bureau of Hainan Province sign a cooperation agreement concerning the joint construction of a students' practice base in Sanya City. The cooperation aims to promote the healthy development of Hainan Province through the North-South cooperation. March 30, 2012, a conference concerning the health insurance and offsite medical billing is held in Haikou City; Hainan and Jilin sign an agreement on cooperation in offsite medical billing reimbursement.

Hainan-Liaoning

[Quick Facts] Average distance = 3925 km; Geographical adjacency = 0; Index of ethnic linkages = 0.8285 (2000) and 0.8384 (2010); Freight exchange via national railway = 0 k ton (2000) and 0 k ton (2010). ★ November 13, 2008, Yingkou municipal government of Liaoning Province, Hainan Airlines Group Co., Ltd. and the China Wukuang Corporation sign the "Airport Construction Cooperation Agreement" and the "Strategic Cooperation Framework Agreement" in Shenyang City of Liaoning Province. The three sides will jointly construct the Yingkou Airport and cooperate in aviation, airport, finance, logistics, ports, tourism, hotels, real estate, business and others. September 11 to 14, 2009, a delegation led by the CCP Secretary of and the PCSC Chairman of Hainan Province pays an inspection to Dalian City, Liaoning Province. The Hainan delegation also inspects the Dalian Shipbuilding Industry Group Co., Ltd. March 12, 2011, Hainan Airlines Co., Ltd. signs a cooperation agreement with Dalian University of Technology; according to the agreement, the Hainan Airlines will directly recruit crew from the University. March 30, 2012, a conference concerning the health insurance and offsite medical billing is held in Haikou City; Hainan and Liaoning sign an agreement on cooperation in offsite medical billing reimbursement. According to statistics, more than 80 % of the people who purchases Hainan houses are from inland provinces including Liaoning.

Hainan-Ningxia

[Quick Facts] Average distance = 3716 km; Geographical adjacency = 0; Index of ethnic linkages = 0.6567 (2000) and 0.6517 (2010); Freight exchange via national railway = 0 k ton (2000) and 0 k ton (2010). ★ October 20, 2009, a delegation led by the Vice Governor of Hainan pays an inspection to Pingluo County of Ningxia Hui Autonomous Region, aiming to exchange the experiences of informationization construction in rural areas. August 27, 2012, a delegation led by the Deputy Director of the Foreign Affairs Office of Hainan Province visits Ningxia Hui Autonomous Region to learn and exchange experiences in talent importation work. The two sides have in-depth exchange in the followings: (1) the experiences and practices of introducing talents into key enterprises and major projects; (2) the policies and regulations of foreign talent importation; (3) the experiences and practices of management and service of foreign experts; and (4) the features and difficulties of overseas training work. September 3, 2012, the "Focusing on Hainan" promotion and the "Hainan Tourism Trends Conference" are held in Yinchuan City of Ningxia Autonomous Region. Ningxia and Hainan, given their differences in nature and geography, will strengthen bilateral cooperation in tourism, aiming to jointly develop the southeast, east, north, northwest, and other important tourist markets.

Hainan-Qinghai

[Quick Facts] Average distance = 3802 km; Geographical adjacency = 0; Index of ethnic linkages = 0.5428 (2000) and 0.5336 (2010); Freight exchange via national railway = 0 k ton (2000) and 10 k tons (2010). ★ October 18 to 26,2008, a Qinghai delegation, composed of the provincial government, the DRC, the Agriculture and Animal Husbandry Department and the Environmental Protection Bureau and the Forestry Bureau, and led by the provincial governor, visits Hainan to exchange issues of ecological and environmental protection, green agricultural infrastructure, the comprehensive structural reform in agricultural and pastoral regions, the urban-rural integration, the coordinated economic and social development, etc. January 1, 2011, the Qinghai Chamber of Commerce in Hainan is established. After the plan of Hainan International Tourism Island is upgraded to China's national policy, some Qinghai enterprises find business opportunities which mainly relate to tourism. The establishment of the chamber aims to promote economic development through mutual, beneficial cooperation. April 23, 2011, a government delegation of

Qinghai Province visits Hainan Province and holds, together with the Hainan's provincial government officials, a forum on the economic cooperation between Qinghai and Hainan Provinces; the delegation also pays an inspection to the Hainan International Creative Harbor and the Hainan Exhibition Hall in Haikou City.

Hainan-Shaanxi

[Quick Facts] Average distance = 2887 km; Geographical adjacency = 0; Index of ethnic linkages = 0.8281 (2000) and 0.8381 (2010); Freight exchange via national railway = 0 k ton (2000) and 10 k tons (2010). ★ January 6, 2008, the Shaanxi Chamber of Commerce in Hainan is established. More than 200 enterprise representatives of the Chamber attend the inaugural ceremony. December 28, 2011, the "Shaanxi-Hainan Trade and Cooperation Forum", sponsored by the provincial governments of Shaanxi and Hainan, is held in Haikou City. The Departments of Commerce of the two provinces sign an "Agreement Concerning Further Promotion of Business Cooperation between Shaanxi and Hainan Provinces". The two sides will further promote bilateral cooperation in industry and human resources and through pairing exchange. December 29, 2011, the "Shaanxi-Hainan Tourist Cooperation Forum" is held in the Yalong Bay of Sanya City, Hainan Province. Shaanxi Province and Xi'an City sign, with Hainan Province and Sanya City, respectively, cooperation agreements on tourist cooperation. The two provinces pledge to establish a new pattern of regional tourist cooperation. April 17, 2012, the signing ceremony of the agreement on international route cooperation between the Hainan Airlines Co., Ltd. and Shaanxi Provincial People's Government is opened. July 17, 2012, an investment promotion of the Fengdong New Zone of Shaanxi Province is held, in which five Hainan companies sign an investment agreement, with a total value of more than 13 billion yuan. The investment involves business, tourism, hotel, modern agriculture, etc.

Hainan-Shandong

[Quick Facts] Average distance = 2795 km; Geographical adjacency = 0; Index of ethnic linkages = 0.8283 (2000) and 0.8382 (2010); Freight exchange via national railway = 0 k ton (2000) and 10 k tons (2010). ★ October 3, 2002, the Shandong Luneng (Group) Company and the Qiongshan municipal government of Hainan sign a cooperative intention concerning the coastal eco-tourism resort project, with an expected investment of 10 billion yuan. March 2, 2005, Linyi City of Shandong Province and the Hainan Aili (Hong Kong) Company contract four cooperation projects, with the total estimated investment of about 30 billion yuan. December 30, 2006, the Shandong Chamber of Commerce in Hainan is established in Haikou City. The Chamber has more than 130 enterprise members. According to statistics,

Shandong's nearly 50,000 people are living and working in Hainan, with a total investment of over 15 billion yuan. November 21, 2008, the Bureau of Geology and Mineral Resources of Hainan and the Shandong Gold Group Co., Ltd. sign a strategic cooperation agreement; the two sides will establish long-term strategic partnerships, aiming to jointly develop Hainan's rich mineral resources, especially gold resources. March 14, 2012, the Jianye Agricultural Machinery Cooperative Association of Heze City, Shandong Province, visits Hainan to develop interprovincial market.

Hainan-Shanghai

[Quick Facts] Average distance = 2574 km; Geographical adjacency = 0; Index of ethnic linkages = 0.8293 (2000) and 0.8416 (2010); Freight exchange via national railway = 0 k ton (2000) and 0 k ton (2010). ★ April 26, 2007, a key cultural cooperation project—Yinlong Cinema Town— starts in Haikou City. November 22, 2008, the Shanghai Chamber of Commerce in Hainan is established in Haikou City. The Chamber has nearly 100 enterprise members, involving farming, marine fisheries, real estate, travel, dining and securities. March 26, 2009, the Hainan Provincial Blood Center signs a cooperation agreement with the Shanghai Municipal Blood Center. July 14, 2010, the Hainan Airlines Group Co., Ltd. and the Shanghai Guosheng Group sign a strategic cooperation agreement. The intended cooperation mainly concentrates in the affiliated services for the construction of two centers in Shanghai. August 1, 2011, the Deputy Director of Shanghai Overseas Chinese Affairs Office meets a delegation of Hainan Overseas Chinese Affairs. September 5, 2012, a delegation of Changning District of Shanghai Municipality visits Sanya City and signs a "Memorandum Concerning the Promotion of Economic and Cultural Cooperation Cum the Yalong Bay Commercial Center Construction Projects" with the Sanya municipal government; the total investment value of the planned project is 4.5 billion yuan. The two sides also hold an educational exchange and cooperation forum.

Hainan-Shanxi

[Quick Facts] Average distance = 2976 km; Geographical adjacency = 0; Index of ethnic linkages = 0.8284 (2000) and 0.8378 (2010); Freight exchange via national railway = 0 k ton (2000) and 20 k tons (2010). ★ August 9–17, 2009, a delegation of the Federation of Industry and Commerce of Hainan Province pays an inspection to Shanxi Province. The federations of the two provinces conduct an in-depth discussion on the development of non-public ownership economies. November 8, 2009, the Deputy Directors of Personnel Labor and Social Security Offices of Hainan and Shanxi Provinces sign an "Off-Site Medical Billing Cooperation

Framework Agreement". October 28, 2010, the Federation of Shanxi Merchants in Hainan Province is established in Hainan. Now, tens of thousands of Shanxi people run their businesses in Hainan, covering aviation, real estate, construction, hotels, agriculture, culture and education, pharmaceutics, biotechnology, finance and securities, service, IT and other industries. Many of the Shanxi-funded enterprises have become industrial leaders in and big tax payers to Hainan. December 29, 2011, in the "Shaanxi-Hainan Tourism Cooperation forum", Shaanxi and Hainan Provinces, and Xi'an and Sanya Cities, in order to push the development of tourism, sign agreements on the establishment of tourist emergency handling mechanism. March 30, 2012, a conference concerning health insurance and offsite medical billing is held in Haikou City; Hainan and Jilin sign an agreement on cooperation in offsite medical billing reimbursement.

Hainan-Sichuan

[Quick Facts] Average distance = 2829 km; Geographical adjacency = 0; Index of ethnic linkages = 0.8305 (2000) and 0.8408 (2010); Freight exchange via national railway = 0 k ton (2000) and 20 k tons (2010). ★ June 2, 2005, a Sichuan delegation visits Hainan to carry out economic and trade exchange, and holds the "Sichuan-Hainan Agricultural and Sideline Products Promotion". May 25, 2007, the "Hainan-Sichuan Cooperation and Development Symposium" and the signing ceremony of the tourist cooperation framework agreement are held in Chengdu City of Sichuan Province; the two sides will strengthen exchange and cooperation in tourism and other areas. According to statistics, Hainan has received 720,000 tourists from Sichuan in 2006. June 11, 2007, Hainan provincial government and the representatives of Sichuan Province and other places sign a framework agreement on international flight cooperation in Changsha City, aiming to strengthen the interprovincial economic cooperation in the Pan-Pearl River Delta Region. January 5, 2010, the Sichuan Chamber of Commerce in Hainan is established. The number of the chamber's enterprise members reaches 136. The Chamber aims to deepen interprovincial economic and technological exchange and cooperation, to strengthen the government relation of the two places and to safeguard the rights and interests of the Sichuan enterprises. March 25, 2010, Haikou City of Hainan Province and Mianyang City of Sichuan Province sign a tourist cooperation agreement.

Hainan-Tianjin

[Quick Facts] Average distance = 3198 km; Geographical adjacency = 0; Index of ethnic linkages = 0.8293 (2000) and 0.8398 (2010); Freight exchange via national railway = 0 k ton (2000) and 0 k ton (2010). ★ June 28, 2010, the Hainan provincial government and the Tianjin municipal government sign the "Tianjin-Hainan Strategic Cooperation Framework Agreement"; the two sides will establish comprehensive strategic partnerships in tourism, agriculture, industry and high-tech, port and shipping, education, marine economy, health care, business and trade. They also attend the opening ceremony of the Northern Headquarters of the Hainan Airlines Group. June 29, 2010, Hainan and Tianjin government leaders and educators hold a forum; Hainan provincial government signs comprehensive province-school cooperation agreements with Tianjin Vocational and Technical Normal University, Education Department of Tianjin and Nankai University, aiming to strengthen Hainan's education through Tianjin's support. Jun 28–July 5, 2010, a government delegation led by the Deputy Secretary of CCP Committee (also the Governor) of Hainan Province visits Tianjin, and attend the 17th China (Tianjin) investment and Trade Fair. March 30, 2012, a conference concerning the health insurance and offsite medical billing is held in Haikou City; Hainan and Tianjin sign an agreement on cooperation in offsite medical billing reimbursement.

Hainan-Tibet

[Quick Facts] Average distance = 5774 km; Geographical adjacency = 0; Index of ethnic linkages = 0.0629 (2000) and 0.0845 (2010); Freight exchange via national railway = 0 k ton (2000) and 0 k ton (2010). ★ May 21, 2006, the Hainan Airlines Group successfully opens the Xi'an-Lhasa route. November 12, 2009, a religious delegation composed of 30 Lamas from Tibet visits Sanya City of Hainan Province and conducts cultural exchanges with the Buddhist monks of the Conglin Nanshan Temple at Haitian of Sanya City. August 30, 2010, the Sanya Power Supply Bureau of State Grid Corporation (Hainan Branch) and the Tibet Power Co., Ltd. (Qamdo Branch) hold, in Sanya City of Hainan Province, the signing ceremony of friendly relationship. The Deputy Chief of Sanya Power Supply Bureau and the CCP Committee Members (also the Deputy General Manager) of Tibet Power Company sign the "Agreement Concerning the Establishment of Friendly Business Relationship". The agreement aims to promote the enterprises' friendship and ethnic solidarity between Hainan and Tibet, to expand the technological exchange and inter-enterprise cooperation and to improve enterprise management. March 31, 2011, the Chinese Academy of Tropical Agriculture (CATA, Hainan Province) and the Tibet Academy of Agriculture and Animal Husbandry Sciences sign, in Haikou, a strategic cooperation framework agreement. Under the agreement, the CATA will carry out extensive cooperation with Tibet Academy of Agriculture and Animal Husbandry Sciences in the fields of discipline construction, talent training, scientific and technological aid to Tibet, project cooperation, scientific and technological exchange.

Hainan-Xinjiang

[Quick Facts] Average distance = 5478 km; Geographical adjacency = 0; Index of ethnic linkages = 0.4090 (2000) and 0.4087 (2010); Freight exchange via national railway = 0 k ton (2000) and 0 k ton (2010). ★ January 26, 2007, a delegation of the No. 0.1 Prison of the Xinjiang Uygur Autonomous Region pays an inspection to the Meilan Felony Prison of Hainan Province. The two sides sign a "Friendly Prison Cooperation Agreement", aiming to exchange experiences in the management of felony prisoners. December 19, 2008, the Hainan United Mining Co., Ltd. and the Xinjiang Hongshan Mining & Metals Co., Ltd. sign a joint venture agreement. According to the agreement, the Hainan Mining Company will acquire a 70 % stake in the Hongshan Mining Company. May 15, 2011, the Xinjiang Chamber of Commerce in Hainan is established in Haikou City. According to incomplete statistics, the number of Xinjiang's enterprises in Hainan is more than 300, covering the fields of clean energy, agriculture, science and technology, real estate development, trade, tourism, hotel and restaurant. December 18, 2012, Karamay Municipal People's Government of Xinjiang and the Hainan Airlines Group sign a cooperation agreement in Haikou City. Under the agreement, the Hainan Airlines will participate in the construction and management of the Karamay Airport. This cooperation will not only improve the air traffic situation in Karamay, but it will also accelerate the economic and social development and promote the economic and cultural linkages between Hainan and Xinjiang.

Hainan-Yunnan

[Quick Facts] Average distance = 1567 km; Geographical adjacency = 0; Index of ethnic linkages = 0.6839 (2000) and 0.6841 (2010); Freight exchange via national railway = 0 k ton (2000) and 90 k tons (2010). ★ June 6, 2006, the Tourism Bureaux of Hainan and Yunnan Provinces sign a cooperation agreement, aiming to reduce the travel agencies' management procedures and to provide favorable conditions for the each other side's enterprises to develop tourism. June 12, 2007, the Tourism Associations of Yunnan and Hainan hold a forum, aiming to take joint actions to resist unfair competition. The travel agencies of Kunming (Yunnan Province) and Sanya (Hainan Province) reach a consensus for Yunnan's tourists to come to Sanya during the off-season. September 2008, the Hainan Mining Co., Ltd., the Chengdu Dashi Mining Investment Consulting Co., Ltd. and Tengchong County of Yunnan Province sign a cooperation agreement concerning the "Laoxiangkeng Iron Ore Exploration" project, with the Hainan Mining Company holding 70 % share of the project. July 15, 2009, the Land Reclamation Corporations of Hainan and Yunnan Provinces hold, in Haikou City, a signing ceremony of strategic cooperation. The two sides will work together to build the natural rubbers' market. According to statistics, the annual production capacities of natural rubbers in Hainan and Yunnan are 220,000 and 118,000 tons, respectively, which account for more than 70 % of the national total. January 21, 2010, the Tourism Bureaux of Hainan and Yunnan jointly initiate a tourist cooperation union, aiming to promote regional economic development through exchange and cooperation.

Hainan-Zhejiang

[Quick Facts] Average distance = 2407 km; Geographical adjacency = 0; Index of ethnic linkages = 0.8296 (2000) and 0.8457 (2010); Freight exchange via national railway = 0 k ton (2000) and 10 k tons (2010). ★ May 17, 2000, Hainan and Zhejiang Provinces sign a cooperation agreement on joint marine economic development. According to the agreement, the two sides will develop shallow marine aquaculture, ocean fishing, seafood processing and biochemical pharmaceutical industry. The two sides also sign agreements on the development of enterprises from diverse forms ownership, the technological cooperation and personnel exchange, and the cooperation in agriculture, tourism, communications and logistics. August 9, 2004, the Zhejiang Chamber of Commerce in Hainan is established in Haikou City. The Chamber has 258 enterprise members, involving pharmaceutics, real estate, commerce, agriculture, development, aquaculture, tourism and catering industry, with a total investment of over 300 billion yuan. April 9, 2009, Hainan Institute of Political Science and Law and Zhejiang Vocational Police College sign an agreement of pairing aid and cooperative training. July 15, 2009, the Zhejiang provincial government signs a strategic cooperation framework agreement with the Hainan Airlines Group. The two sides will carry out comprehensive cooperation in three areas: (1) the development of ship building and repairing; (2) the development of modern aviation industry in Zhejiang; and (3) the construction of modern logistics bases of Zhejiang Province. Both sides will also cooperate in such fields as financial service, tourism and professional personnel training. The Hainan Airlines Group and the Zhejiang Energy Group establish a joint venture. November 20, 2011, the Maternal and Child Health Hospital of Hainan signs, in Hangzhou City, a strategic cooperation agreement with the Obstetrics and Gynecology and the Children Hospitals of Zhejiang University.

Hebei-Heilongjiang

[Quick Facts] Average distance = 1673 km; Geographical adjacency = 0; Index of ethnic linkages = 0.9863 (2000) and 0.9835 (2010); Freight exchange via national railway = 720 k tons (2000) and 4330 k tons (2010). ★ August 25, 2005, a delegation composed of nearly 20 prestigious condiment enterprises in Hebei

Province visits Heilongjiang Province to inspect condiment market. September 21–22, 2009, a delegation of the Grains and Foods Bureau of Hebei Province visits Heilongjiang to participate in the "2009 (Fall) Heilongjiang Grains and Foods Trade and Cooperation Fair", and signs an agreement of purchase and sales with its Heilongjiang pairing. April 15, 2011, the IQBs of Heilongjiang and Hebei Provinces sign, in Shijiazhuang City, a memorandum of cooperation concerning the insurance of quality and safety of Hebei's export of fruits and vegetables to Russia via Heilongjiang. This aims to strengthen the cooperation between port and production cities and to establish a long-term cooperation mechanism. June 21, 2011, a delegation led by the CCP Committee of and the government of Qinhuangdao City visits Heilongjiang Province. The delegation offers 40 investment projects, involving equipment manufacturing, tourism and modern logistics, with a total investment of 7.714 billion US dollars. August 5–6, 2012, a 10-people delegation, led by President of the Petroleum Chamber of Commerce of the Hebei Federation of Industry and Commerce, visits Heilongjiang and signs, with the Heilongjiang Association of Petroleum Industry, a friendly cooperation agreement.

Hebei-Henan

[Quick Facts] Average distance = 412 km; Geographical adjacency = 1; Index of ethnic linkages = 0.9666 (2000) and 0.9679 (2010); Freight exchange via national railway = 3730 k tons (2000) and 4940 k tons (2010). ★ December 8, 2009, the Henan Chamber of Commerce in Hebei is established in Shijiazhuang City of Hebei Province. The chamber has more than 310 enterprise members, involving real estate, construction, mining, trade, investment, etc. April 8–16, 2010, a delegation, led by the Deputy Chief of the Supply and Marketing Cooperatives of Tangshan City of Hebei, visits the Supply and Marketing Cooperatives of Nanyang City of Henan Province, aiming to form a modern chain network in rural areas, to build a farmers' cooperative economic organization, and to construct a rural social service system. October 29, 2011, the Hebei Chamber of Commerce in Henan is established in Zhengzhou City of Henan Province. The Chamber has more than 180 member companies, involving heavy machinery, real estate and building materials, wire and cable, energy, environmental protection, steel hardware, education, food, hotel, consultancy, etc. May 16, 2012, the No. 11 Middle School of Jiaozuo City of Henan Province and the Hengshui Middle School of Hebei Province become friendly partners. May 29, 2012, the Marketing Department of the Industrial and Commercial Bank of China (ICBC) Hebei Branch, and the Henan Chamber of Commerce in Hebei sign a comprehensive cooperation agreement and a financing agreement; the two sides pledge to cooperate in loan financing, fund settlement, financial management and other financial service.

Hebei-Hubei

[Quick Facts] Average distance = 948 km; Geographical adjacency = 0; Index of ethnic linkages = 0.9587 (2000) and 0.9592 (2010); Freight exchange via national railway = 260 k tons (2000) and 3870 k tons (2010). ★ April 8–16, 2010, a delegation of the General Cooperatives of Supply and Marketing of Tangshan City of Hebei Province, led by the Deputy Director of the Cooperatives, visits the Supply and Marketing Cooperatives of Suizhou City of Hubei Province, aiming to form a modern chain network in rural areas, to build a farmers' cooperative economic organization, and to construct a rural social service system. April 17, 2012, the Federations of Returned Overseas Chinese of Hebei and Hubei Provinces hold an exchange meeting, and sign a cooperation agreement, aiming to cooperate in information sharing, economic and cultural exchange and the protection of overseas Chinese working in each other's territory. August 11–12, 2012, a delegation composed of Hubei Institute of Technological Development, the Hubei Asset Management Company and the Institute of Materials Science and Engineering, led by the Deputy Secretary of Hubei University, visits Ren County of Hebei Province, and signs a strategic agreement of scientific and technological cooperation with the County. The two sides pledge to accelerate the transformation and upgrading of traditional industries of Ren County. September 17, 2012, the Hubei Chamber of Commerce in Hebei is established in Shijiazhuang City. The Chamber members come from logistics, IT, real estate, machinery manufacturing, pharmaceutics, media, tourism, steel, automotive, biotechnology, communication, food, clothing and other fields.

Hebei-Hunan

[Quick Facts] Average distance = 1306 km; Geographical adjacency = 0; Index of ethnic linkages = 0.9015 (2000) and 0.9027 (2010); Freight exchange via national railway = 1590 k tons (2000) and 170 k tons (2010). ★ March 15, 2010, the Hunan Chamber of Commerce in Hebei is established in Shijiazhuang City. Yiyang City of Hunan Province and the Hunan Chamber sign a strategic cooperation agreement on economic cooperation and exchange. Under the agreement, Yiyang City and the Chamber will establish a mechanism of government-induced and market-led cooperation. September 25, 2010, the Hebei Chamber of Commerce in Hunan is established in Changsha City, Hunan Province. Now, there are around 10,000 Hebei-funded enterprises in Hunan, involving steel, hardware, electronics, fasteners, plumbing equipment, instrumentation, gas supply, building materials, chemicals, ceramics, auto, real estate, construction, medical equipment, infrastructure, labors and other industries, with the annual sales of about 15 billion yuan. The industries with Hebei characteristics, such as construction fasteners, have account more than 60 % share of Hunan's. September 25, 2010, the Yongding (District)

People's Government of Zhangjiajie City of Hunan Province and the Hebei Chamber of Commerce in Hunan sign, in Changsha City, a strategic cooperation agreement. According to the agreement, the two sides will promote the regional economic development of Yongding District by establishing a new investment mechanism in which the Hebei Chamber can better serve Hunan's industrial and economic development.

Hebei-Inner Mongolia

[Quick Facts] Average distance = 871 km; Geographical adjacency = 1; Index of ethnic linkages = 0.8245 (2000) and 0.8250 (2010); Freight exchange via national railway = 13,240 k tons (2000) and 111,420 k tons (2010). ★ March 27–28, 2010, a study delegation of Inner Mongolia government visits Hebei. The two sides hold a forum of economic and social development cooperation. August 12, 2010, Inner Mongolia Autonomous Region, Hebei Province and the China State Grid Corporation sign a cooperation framework agreement concerning the joint construction of coal-fuelled power project. The agreement includes the projects of two 600,000 kW domestic ultra-supercritical direct air-cooled coal-fired units and of Changtan and Bulian Coal Power Companies' integration. The three sides will deliver to Hebei 50 % of the coal it needs for the power generation. November 8, 2010, the Tourism Bureaux of Inner Mongolia Autonomous Region and Hebei Province sign a framework agreement concerning the strengthening of regional cooperation in tourism. April 27, 2011, the governments of Inner Mongolia Autonomous Region and Hebei Province sign a cooperation agreement concerning the construction of the Port Industrial Park and the Harbor for Inner Mongolia. Under the agreement, the Hebei side will plan a land area of 40 km^2 in the Caofeidian New Zone to construct the Inner Mongolia Port Industrial Park, and set a port for Inner Mongolia to develop manufacturing and high-tech industries and to export coal, ores and chemicals. November 7, 2011, a delegation, led by the Deputy Secretary (also the Governor) of Hebei Province, visits Inner Mongolia Autonomous Region. The two sides sign the "Inner Mongolia-Hebei Economic and Social Development Cooperation Agreement". February 2, 2012, the Vice Governor of Hebei Province meets the delegation led by the Vice Chairman of Inner Mongolia Autonomous Region in Shijiazhuang City of Hebei, and holds a forum concerning the strengthening of transportation cooperation.

Hebei-Jiangsu

[Quick Facts] Average distance = 964 km; Geographical adjacency = 0; Index of ethnic linkages = 0.9594 (2000) and 0.9613 (2010); Freight exchange via national railway = 400 k tons (2000) and 7090 k tons (2010). ★ April 5–8, 2007, a delegation composed of the SASAC of and the DRC of Hebei Province, the Handan municipal government and the Handan Iron and Steel Group Co., Ltd., led by the CCP Secretary of (also the PCSC Chairman) of Hebei Province, visits Suzhou City of Jiangsu Province to promote economic and technological exchange and cooperation between the two provinces. April 30, 2010, the Housing and Urban-Rural Construction Departments of Hebei and Jiangsu Provinces sign, in Shijiazhuang City of Hebei, a framework agreement concerning the strengthening of construction cooperation. It is decided that, in 2010, both each side will select ten prestigious firms to practice a zero-barrier interprovincial entrance (that is, cancelling all procedures and formalities for the registration of interprovincial enterprises) and that a real market integration in construction sector will be achieved between the two provinces within three to five years. May 3, 2011, the Jiangsu Chamber of Commerce in Hebei is established in Shijiazhuang City. The Chamber has more than 500 enterprise members, covering science and technology, electronics, medical equipment, building materials, pharmaceutics, food and beverage, real estate and other industries.

Hebei-Jiangxi

[Quick Facts] Average distance = 1293 km; Geographical adjacency = 0; Index of ethnic linkages = 0.9576 (2000) and 0.9595 (2010); Freight exchange via national railway = 760 k tons (2000) and 1060 k tons (2010). ★ January 28, 2008, the Jiangxi Chamber of Commerce in Hebei is established in Shijiazhuang City. The Chamber has more than 100 enterprise members and nearly 300 individual members, engaged in real estate, electronics, stainless steel, food, stationery, medical equipment, decoration, crafts, clothing and others. December 12, 2009, the Department of Land Resources of Jiangxi Province and the People's Government of Hebei Province sign, in Shijiazhuang City of Hebei, an agreement. Under the agreement, from 2010 to 2015, the two sides will cooperate in the diggings in the East Hebei, Chengde and Handan, explore energy, copper, lead, zinc and other key mineral resources; monitor land subsidence and establish ground subsidence warning demonstration area in Cangzhou and Tanghai of Hebei. March 29, 2012, a delegation of the Hebei Federation of Returned Overseas Chinese visits Jiangxi Federation of Returned Overseas Chinese to exchange work. The two sides discuss issues relating to the protection of overseas Chinese interests and their political participation, among others. August 27, 2012, the Yineng boilers Co., Ltd. of Hebei Province and the Far East Heavy Industry Co., Ltd. of Jiangxi Province sign a contract of a joint project worth of 600 million yuan.

Hebei-Jilin

[Quick Facts] Average distance = 1431 km; Geographical adjacency = 0; Index of ethnic linkages = 0.9481 (2000) and 0.9579 (2010); Freight exchange via national railway = 4420 k tons (2000) and 220 k tons (2010). ★ August 2008, the Tianhe Wind Power Equipment Co., Ltd. of Jilin Province and the Xinneng Construction Investment Co., Ltd. of Hebei sign a strategic cooperation agreement; the two sides will jointly develop a wind power plant in Hebei and Inner Mongolia. June 30, 2010, the Iron and Steel Group of Hebei Province and the Stock and Supply Company of Jilin Coal Group hold an exchange meeting, both sides pledge to strengthen and expand cooperation. December 8, 2010, the signing ceremony of the strategic cooperation agreement between the Sengong Jinqiao Flooring Group of Jilin Province and the Hebei Construction Investment Group is held in Beijing, aiming to strengthen cooperation in the fields of commercial housing decoration and wooden housing construction. September 26, 2011, the Hebei Chamber of Commerce in Jilin is established in Changchun City of Jilin Province. The Chamber has more than 250 member companies, covering education, real estate, financial services, packaging, printing, hotel, food, media, environmental protection, investment, wire and cable, steels and others. May 11, 2012, the IQBs of Jilin and Hebei Provinces sign a memorandum of cooperation to strengthen hi-tech quality inspection. June 17–18, 2012, Jilin University and Hebei Province have an in-depth exchange, aiming to raise the science and technology level of and the independent innovation capability of Hebei Province through the cooperation in technology, patents, personnel and advanced management methods between the two sides. August 6–7, 2012, a 10-people delegation, led by President of the Petroleum Chamber of Commerce of the Hebei Federation of Industry and Commerce, visits Jilin Province and signs, with the Petroleum Chamber of Commerce of the Jilin Federation of Industry and Commerce, a friendly cooperation agreement.

Hebei-Liaoning

[Quick Facts] Average distance = 1126 km; Geographical adjacency = 1; Index of ethnic linkages = 0.8807 (2000) and 0.8872 (2010); Freight exchange via national railway = 10,520 k tons (2000) and 11,150 k tons (2010). ★ April 30, 2009, a delegation of the Foresting Company of Liaoning visits, and offers a number of high-quality, fast-growing larch seeds to, the Saihanba Forest of Hebei. The two sides reach a consensus on the promotion of the reform and development in forest areas. June 11, 2010, the Maritime Bureaux of Liaoning and Hebei Provinces sign, in Tianjin, the "Exchange and Cooperation Agreement of Beacon Mapping and Navigation Management in the Bohai Bay Areas". November 27, 2010, the "Hebei (Chongli) Tourism Promotion" is held in Dalian City, Liaoning Province. Chongli County of Hebei Province and the Municipal Tourism Bureau of Dalian sign a strategic cooperation agreement, which marks that Chongli County will strengthen the development of tourist market in Northeast China. November 20, 2011, the "Hebei (Chongli County) Tourist Promotion" is held in Shenyang City of Liaoning Province. Chongli County and the Municipal Tourism Bureau of Shenyang become strategic cooperative partners. September 12, 2012, the Taiwan Economic cooperation Center of Hebei Province is established in the Benxi Iron and Steel Company of Liaoning Province. This is to promote the two sides' trade as well as the cooperation with Taiwan.

Hebei-Ningxia

[Quick Facts] Average distance = 1547 km; Geographical adjacency = 0; Index of ethnic linkages = 0.6680 (2000) and 0.6622 (2010); Freight exchange via national railway = 690 k tons (2000) and 14,750 k tons (2010). ★ August 11, 2009, the "Ningxia-Hebei Economic and Technological Cooperation Symposium" and the inaugural meeting of the Hebei Chamber of Commerce in Ningxia are held in Yinchuan City of Ningxia. August 18, 2009, the Hebei Chamber of Commerce in Ningxia is established in Yinchuan City. The Chamber has more than 540 member companies, involving real estate construction, steel, electrical and mechanical bearings, wire and cable, water-saving irrigation, firefighting equipment, building materials, leasing, car sales, agricultural machinery and accessories, sanitary ware, chemistry, pharmaceutics, etc. October 11, 2011, Yinchuan City of Ningxia Hui Autonomous Region and Qinhuangdao City of Hebei Province sign a "Cooperation Framework Agreement Concerning the Port Resource Sharing and the Promotion of Regional Economic Development". The cooperation aims to promote the economic development in the western region and to provide superior port conditions and preferential policies for Ningxia to import and export special agricultural and chemical products. February 20, 2012, the Wuyang Company (i.e., Hebei Iron and Steel Group) signs a strategic cooperation framework agreement with the Ningxia Coal Industry Group Co., Ltd. (of Shenhua Group). Under the agreement, Hebei Iron and Steel Group will become a major steel supplier of the "No. 1 Project" of the Ningxia Coal Industry Group.

Hebei-Qinghai

[Quick Facts] Average distance = 1815 km; Geographical adjacency = 0; Index of ethnic linkages = 0.5534 (2000) and 0.5429 (2010); Freight exchange via national railway = 250 k tons (2000) and 130 k tons (2010). ★ April 18–20, 2005, at the "Cross-Regional Port Cooperation Forum", which is held in Tianjin, Ningxia, Qinghai and other provinces sign the "Tianjin Protocol Concerning Cross-Regional Port Cooperation". June 28, 2008, the Hebei provincial government and the

Qinghai provincial government hold a labor cooperation forum in Hebei and sign a cooperation agreement concerning the strengthening of labor export and skill training. Under the agreement, the two sides will establish a mechanism of human resource information sharing to promote the interprovincial labor transfer. September 2008, Qinghai Vocational and Technical Traffic College and Hebei Vocational and Technical Industry College hold, in Hebei, an opening ceremony of joint education project. April 19 to May 10, 2010, the Disaster Relief Donations Center of Hebei Province and the Red Cross organize, in Hebei Province, a ceremony for the donation to the Yushu earthquake areas of Qinghai Province. September 1, 2012, a delegation of Qinghai provincial government visits Hebei to acknowledge the latter's assistance to the Yushu (Qinghai Province) earthquake area and to expand the bilateral cooperation in education, culture and economy.

Hebei-Shaanxi

[Quick Facts] Average distance = 923 km; Geographical adjacency = 0; Index of ethnic linkages = 0.9614 (2000) and 0.9632 (2010); Freight exchange via national railway = 1290 k tons (2000) and 4330 k tons (2010). ★ January 27, 2005, the Governor of Tourism Bureaux of Shaanxi and Hebei Provinces sign, in Nanning City of Guangxi, an agreement, according to which the two sides will carry out regular exchange and cooperation in "Red Tourism". October 22, 2006, Shaanxi University of Science and Technology and Quangping County of Handan City (Hebei Province) sign an agreement on personnel, economic and technological cooperation. July 29, 2007, the Hebei Chamber of Commerce in Shaanxi is established in Xi'an City. The Chamber has 349 member companies, involving real estate, metallurgy, coal, pharmaceutics, forging, mechanical and electrical equipment, building materials, decoration, modern agriculture and others, with a total investment of 26 billion yuan. March 15, 2011, the Industry and Information Technology Departments of Shaanxi and Hebei Provinces sign an agreement concerning the establishment of joint conference system and the promotion of industrial development and informationization construction. November 4, 2011, the IQBs of Shaanxi and Hebei Provinces sign a memorandum of cooperation to strengthen the collaboration supervision of and the joint promotion of trade in fruits and vegetables. December 8, 2011, the IQBs of Shaanxi and Hebei Provinces sign, in Shijiazhuang City, a memorandum of cooperation in rapid clearance of inspection and quarantine. July 28, 2012, the Shaanxi Chamber of Commerce in Hebei is established in Shijiazhuang City. The Chamber's member companies have over 15 billion yuan of fixed assets.

Hebei-Shandong

[Quick Facts] Average distance = 301 km; Geographical adjacency = 1; Index of ethnic linkages = 0.9632 (2000) and 0.9652 (2010); Freight exchange via national railway = 8750 k tons (2000) and 32,780 k tons (2010). ★ September 21, 2009, the distribution companies (the Xinhua Bookstores) of Shandong and Hebei Provinces carry out, for the first time, interprovincial cooperation, and hold a books fair and donations activity. May 28, 2010, the Economic and Information Technology Commission of Shandong and the Port Group Co., Ltd. of Hebei hold, in Shijiazhuang, a signing ceremony of cooperation agreement on the transference consolidation of coal transportation; the two sides will establish a long-term, close and stable relationship in coal transportation. June 11, 2010, the Maritime Bureaux of Shandong and Hebei Provinces sign, in Tianjin, the "Exchange and Cooperation Agreement of Beacon Mapping and Navigation Management in the Bohai Area". February 10, 2012, a delegation of the Electric Power Survey and Design Institute of Hebei Province visits Shandong Power Construction Corporation. Both sides also sign a cooperation agreement. May 16, 2011, the Datang Power Generation Company of Shandong and Dacheng County of Hebei Province sign a cooperation framework agreement. Dacheng County is rich in geothermal resources and has the only untapped coal bed methane and coal resources in Hebei Province.

Hebei-Shanghai

[Quick Facts] Average distance = 1267 km; Geographical adjacency = 0; Index of ethnic linkages = 0.9618 (2000) and 0.9643 (2010); Freight exchange via national railway = 1750 k tons (2000) and 1640 k tons (2010). ★ November 21, 2004, Hebei holds, in Shanghai, a forum of cooperation and development in construction industry. January 22, 2008, Dingzhou City of Hebei Province organizes an investment promotion meeting in Shanghai; the representatives of Hebei, Shanghai and the other regions in the Yangtze River Delta have an in-depth exchange in industrial cooperation. December 6, 2009, Tangshan City of Hebei Province and Shanghai sign an economic and cultural cooperation agreement. February 1, 2010, the Hebei Port Group signs, in Beijing, a cooperation agreement concerning the coal supply in the period of the World Expo (held in Shanghai) with the Ministry of Railways and the Shanghai Municipal People's Government. May 15, 2010, the Shanghai Century Publishing Co., Ltd. and the Hebei Publishing & Media Group sign, in Shanghai, a strategic cooperation agreement. December 22, 2011, the Shanghai Institute of Portland Materials and the Jinli New Energy and Material Technology Co., Ltd. of Hebei sign a cooperation agreement. April 19, 2012, the IQBs of Hebei and Shanghai sign a memorandum of cooperation. August 15, 2012, the Press and Publication Bureaux of Hebei and Shanghai sign a memorandum of cooperation and development.

Hebei-Shanxi

[Quick Facts] Average distance = 231 km; Geographical adjacency = 1; Index of ethnic linkages = 0.9596 (2000) and 0.9609 (2010); Freight exchange via national railway = 10,900 k tons (2000) and 305,540 k tons (2010). ★ June 30, 2005, the Association of Coke Industry of Shanxi Province pays an emergent visit to Shijiazhuang to discuss the issue of vicious price competition and signs an agreement with the Association of Metallurgical Industry of Hebei Province. Under the agreement, the two sides will determine the price range once every three months. July 8, 2005, Shanxi Province (whose coke production ranks the first in China) and Hebei (the largest province in iron and steel production) establish a strategic cooperation relationship. September 11, 2006, the Jinneng Mining Group (Handan) of Hebei and the Jindi Coke Co., Ltd. of Shanxi sign, in Taiyuan City, a joint development agreement. The projects involve five fields of coal, coke, electricity, chemical and building materials, with a total investment of 5.08 billion yuan. September 19, 2008, Shanxi and Hebei provincial governments sign an economic and strategic cooperation framework agreement. The cooperation covers transportation, water conservancy, energy, tourism and modern agriculture. September 27, 2011, the Publishing & Media Groups of Shanxi and Hebei Provinces sign a strategic cooperation agreement. Under the agreement, both sides will cooperate in the areas of paper procurement, textbooks promotion, etc. December 8, 2011, the IQBs of Shaanxi and Hebei Provinces sign, in Shijiazhuang City, a memorandum of cooperation concerning the rapid clearance of inspection and quarantine.

Hebei-Sichuan

[Quick Facts] Average distance = 1765 km; Geographical adjacency = 0; Index of ethnic linkages = 0.9527 (2000) and 0.9417 (2010); Freight exchange via national railway = 1440 k tons (2000) and 3450 k tons (2010). ★ December 29, 2007, the Sichuan Chamber of Commerce in Hebei is established in Shijiazhuang City. January 23, 2008, at the "Seminar of Collaboration on the Protection of Interprovincial Migrant Workers' Rights", held in Chengdu of Sichuan, the Federations of Trade Unions of Hebei and Sichuan Provinces sign a cooperation agreement on the protection of migrant workers. The two sides will also establish a human rights cooperation mechanism. October 14, 2010, members of CCP Standing Committee of and vice governor of Sichuan Province meets a government delegation of Hebei Province in Chengdu City. The two sides hold a ceremony for completion of the Hebei-supported projects in the Wenchuan reconstruction area. April 28, 2011, a delegation of Pingwu government of Sichuan Province visits Baoding City of Hebei. The delegation hopes that the two sides strengthen bilateral cooperation and friendship. September 1, 2011, a delegation led by the CCP Secretary and Deputy General Manager of the Hebei Electric Power Corporation conducts a two-day research and exchange work in the Sichuan electric Power Corporation of the State Grid. September 15, 2011, the government delegation of Sichuan Province and Hebei provincial government hold, in Shijiazhuang, an economic and social development forum, aiming to strengthen exchange and cooperation.

Hebei-Tianjin

[Quick Facts] Average distance = 419 km; Geographical adjacency = 0; Index of ethnic linkages = 0.9725 (2000) and 0.9753 (2010); Freight exchange via national railway = 18,310 k tons (2000) and 48,190 k tons (2010). ★ October 27, 2002, Hebei and Tianjin hold a forum of cooperation and development and a signing ceremony of economic and trade cooperation agreement. 16 projects are agreed, with a total investment of more than one billion yuan, including the cooperation in urban gas, pipeline investment, construction of supermarket chains, transformation of old city, real estate development, construction, technical services, etc. April 5, 2006, Tianjin University of Science and Technology and Quzhou County of Hebei Province become cooperative partnerships in education. November 4–6, 2008, a delegation led by the CCP Secretary of and Director of the Science and Technology Department of Hebei Province visits Tianjin. Both sides pledge to promote cooperation in science and technology. December 2, 2008, the Hebei provincial government and the Tianjin municipal government sign a "Memorandum of Cooperation to Strengthen Economic and Social Development". July 26, 2009, the Hebei Chamber of Commerce in Tianjin is established. The Chamber has nearly 200 member companies, involving industry, commerce, construction, logistics, real estate, catering, entertainment, financial investment, etc. June 11, 2010, the Maritime Bureaux of Tianjin Municipality and Hebei Province sign, in Tianjin, the "Exchange and Cooperation Agreement of Beacon Mapping and Navigation Management in the Bohai Area". May 10, 2012, the "2012 Hebei-Tianjin and Investment Cooperation and Tourism Promotion" is held in Tianjin.

Hebei-Tibet

[Quick Facts] Average distance = 3787 km; Geographical adjacency = 0; Index of ethnic linkages = 0.0650 (2000) and 0.0869 (2010); Freight exchange via national railway = 0 k ton (2000) and 70 k tons (2010). ★ October 13, 2010, the delegation of Tibet Autonomous Region visits Hebei Province, aiming to promote the development of aviation industry in Tibet. August 11, 2011, the China Power Investment Corporation, the Hebei Power Co., Ltd. and Tibet Autonomous Region hold, in Lhasa City, an energy project development forum and sign a strategic cooperation framework agreement. According to the agreement, the former two sides will increase investment in Tibet, so as to develop Tibet's solar, wind, geothermal and other clean energies. October 9, 2011, a Hebei provincial government delegation visits Lhasa City of Tibet Autonomous Region to participate in a pairing aid forum. The Hebei provincial government presents condolatory fund and materials to Ali Prefecture. December 15, 2011, Hebei Province and Tibet Autonomous Region hold, in Shijiazhuang City of Hebei, a civil aviation forum. Both sides pledge to establish a flight route between Tibet and Hebei, to expand economic cooperation, and to promote the prosperity and stability of Tibet. February 22, 2012, the Press and Publication Bureau of Hebei Province donates 500,000 yuan to the Press and Publication Bureau of Ngari Prefecture of Tibet; the two sides establish a long-term pairing aid in personnel training and technological development. August 24, 2012, a delegation led by the Chairman of Hebei Finance and Investment Group visits Tibet Autonomous Region and holds a meeting with the vice chairman of the PPCC of Tibet and the chairman of Tibet Bank.

Hebei-Xinjiang

[Quick Facts] Average distance = 3491 km; Geographical adjacency = 0; Index of ethnic linkages = 0.4184 (2000) and 0.4170 (2010); Freight exchange via national railway = 1260 k tons (2000) and 1690 k tons (2010). ★ June 19–20, 2010, the Hebei and Xinjiang Chambers of Petroleum Commerce hold, in Urumqi of Xinjiang Uygur Autonomous Region, an exchange and cooperation seminar. September 1, 2010, the Hebei Federation of Enterprises in Xinjiang Uygur Autonomous Region is established. The Federation has 216 members, involving exhibition, foreign trade, real estate, decoration, storage and logistics, building materials, mining, coal, chemicals, iron and steel, industrial manufacturing, silicon carbide, food and beverage, pharmaceutics, agriculture and animal husbandry, etc. August 21, 2012, the agricultural sectors of Xinjiang Uygur Autonomous Region hold, in Shijiazhuang City of Hebei Province, a promotion meeting. This activity aims to increase the sales of Xinjiang's special agricultural products in Hebei. September 24, 2012, Bayingolin Mongol Autonomous Prefecture of Xinjiang and Hebei Province carry out pairing aid and cooperation. Since the start of the new round of pairing aid, Hebei and Bazhou have signed 50 cooperation agreements, with a total investment of more than 80 billion yuan in Bayingolin, of which 20 projects (with a total investment of 21.6 billion yuan) either have been completed or are under construction.

Hebei-Yunnan

[Quick Facts] Average distance = 2901 km; Geographical adjacency = 0; Index of ethnic linkages = 0.6758 (2000) and 0.6757 (2010); Freight exchange via national railway = 790 k tons (2000) and 130 k tons (2010). ★ August 16, 2007, the Copper

Industry (Group) Co., Ltd. of Yunnan Province and Baoding municipal government of Hebei Province sign, in Kunming City of Yunnan Province, a strategic cooperation agreement, both sides will build a joint project of electrolytic copper, with annual output of 200,000 tons. October 19, 2010, the Hebei Chamber of Commerce in Yunnan is established. The Chamber has 102 member enterprises, involving mining, real estate, machinery and electronic products, tourism, hotel, communications, standard parts, motor vehicles and parts, building materials, furniture, textiles, tape, wire mesh and bearings, etc. June 20–21, 2012, the SASAC of Hebei and a delegation of Pu'er City hold, in Shijiazhuang, an exchange meeting. Both sides hope to strengthen cooperation in mineral exploitation, cultural tourism, leisure, medicine, chemical industry and others. June 25, 2012, the Guokong Mining Company of Hebei Province and Pu'er City of Yunnan Province sign a strategic cooperation framework agreement. Under the agreement, the Guokong will loan out 10 billion yuan to Pu'er City for the exploitation of mineral resources, including Huisa copper, Xilang copper, Pawashan copper, Dapingzhang copper, Shidaimao copper, Waitoushan copper, Longdonghe copper, Paduanshan copper, Hejiazhai copper, Xinzhai copper and the metal ore of Jiangcheng County as well as the potash mine of Zhengdong Town.

Hebei-Zhejiang

[Quick Facts] Average distance = 1393 km; Geographical adjacency = 0; Index of ethnic linkages = 0.9580 (2000) and 0.9603 (2010); Freight exchange via national railway = 1660 k tons (2000) and 1780 k tons (2010). ★ October 28, 2002, Zhejiang and Hebei Provinces hold, in Hangzhou City, an economic and social development forum. The two sides sign an agreement on economic and technological cooperation. April 26, 2007, the Zhejiang Chamber of Commerce in Hebei is established in Shijiazhuang City. The Chamber's member companies cover more than 20 industries, such as real estate development, electronics, clothing manufacturing, jewelry, glasses, electrical and mechanical hardware, and logistics. September 19, 2007, the Zhejiang Federation of Enterprises in Hebei Province is established. July 1, 2010, the Hebei Port Group and Zhejiang Province sign, in Qinghuangdao City of Hebei Province, a cooperation agreement on the transference consolidation of coal transportation. This agreement aims to resolve the problems of coal supply and transportation via sea line, and to meet the increasing demand of coal in Zhejiang Province. July 23, 2010, the Weikang Company and the Jinnuo pharmaceutical Company of Zhejiang meet in Shenzhen City to discuss further cooperation. May 11, 2012, the IQBs of Zhejiang and Hebei Provinces sign a memorandum of cooperation to strengthen technological and quality inspection. November 5, 2012, Chief officials of Hebei Province visit Zhejiang to conduct policy research and promote cooperation projects. The "Hebei-Zhejiang Private Economic Cooperation and the Agreement Signing Ceremony" and the

"Hebei-Zhejaing Economic and Social Development and Exchange Meeting" are held in Hangzhou City.

Heilongjiang-Henan

[Quick Facts] Average distance = 2085 km; Geographical adjacency = 0; Index of ethnic linkages = 0.9565 (2000) and 0.9683 (2010); Freight exchange via national railway = 150 k tons (2000) and 1730 k tons (2010). ★ August 16, 2003, the "Henan-Heilongjiang Seal Cutting Arts Exhibition", which is sponsored by the Calligraphers Associations of Henan and Heilongjiang Provinces, is held in Zhengzhou City. July 12–21, 2010, the Chinese (national) PPCC members in Henan pay an inspection to Heilongjiang's ecological and environmental protection and tourism. April 18, 2011, the IQBs of Heilongjiang and Henan Provinces sign a memorandum of cooperation to jointly promote Henan's export of fruits and vegetables to Russia via Heilongjiang. August 9–14, 2011, a delegation composed of the Entry-Exit IQB of and Sanmenxia municipal government of Henan Province visits Ning'an and Suifenhe of Heilongjiang Province to promote trade in fruits; the export enterprises of the two provinces sign a cross-border trade cooperation agreement, which includes 16,300 tons of fruits. August 7, 2012, the Henan Chamber of Commerce in Heilongjiang is established in Harbin City. According to incomplete statistics, Henan's enterprises have invested more than 18 billion yuan in Heilongjiang Province, with the total output value of over 20 billion yuan; crane manufacturing, sanitary and waterproof building materials account for 85, 85 and 80 % of Heilongjiang's market shares, respectively. August 16, 2012, Luohe City of Henan Province and Harbin City sign a regional tourist cooperation agreement. Under the agreement, the two sides will promote integrated, barrier-less tourism and strengthen travel information exchange.

Heilongjiang-Hubei

[Quick Facts] Average distance = 2519 km; Geographical adjacency = 0; Index of ethnic linkages = 0.9533 (2000) and 0.9588 (2010); Freight exchange via national railway = 730 k tons (2000) and 1310 k tons (2010). ★ August 21, 2007, the Chiefs of the Judicial Bureaux of Harbin City (Heilongjiang Province) and Xiaogan City (Hubei Province) sign a "Protocol Concerning the Establishment of Coordinate Mechanism of the Legal Support for Migrant Workers". April 19, 2010, the IQBs of Heilongjiang and Hubei Provinces sign a memorandum of cooperation to jointly promote Hubei's export of agricultural products to Russia via Heilongjiang. June 15, 2010, the governments of Heilongjiang and Hubei Provinces hold, in Harbin City of Heilongjiang Province, a forum concerning the strengthening of economic and social development and cooperation. Heilongjiang and Hubei sign nine economic cooperation agreements, with a total investment value of 4.48 billion yuan. November 2, 2011, the Forestry Department of Hubei Province and the Forest Industry Bureau of Heilongjiang Province hold a modern forestry construction forum and sign a strategic cooperation agreement. Both sides pledge to provide favorable condition to each other. April 27, 2012, the Forestry Research Institute of Hubei visits Heilongjiang Forestry Institute. The two sides have an in-depth exchange and sign a cooperation framework agreement. Under the agreement, the two sides will cooperate in the fields of market development, project planning and human resource management. August 15, 2012, a delegation of the Federation of Returned Overseas Chinese of Hubei Province visits Heilongjiang. Both sides have an in-depth exchange in local economic and cultural constructions and inter-federation exchange among other issues.

Heilongjiang-Hunan

[Quick Facts] Average distance = 2877 km; Geographical adjacency = 0; Index of ethnic linkages = 0.9011 (2000) and 0.9022 (2010); Freight exchange via national railway = 720 k tons (2000) and 990 k tons (2010). ★ December 5, 2007, the two major grain-producing provinces of Hunan and Heilongjiang sign the "Cooperation Agreement on the Strengthening of Grain Purchase and Marketing Cooperation between Heilongjiang and Hunan Provinces". January 2, 2008, the Hunan Chamber of Commerce in Heilongjiang is established in Harbin City. The Chamber has 80 member enterprises which are located in Harbin, Daqing, Suifenhe Cities and mainly engaged in construction, environmental protection, real estate development, mechanical and electrical equipment, medical equipment and dining. More than 420 representatives participate in the opening ceremony of the Chamber. October 19, 2009, the IQBs of Heilongjiang and Hunan Provinces sign a memorandum of cooperation to jointly promote Hunan's export of agricultural products to Russia via Heilongjiang. December 26, 2010, the second council election of the Hunan Chamber of Commerce in Heilongjiang opens. September 20, 2012, Qing'an County of Heilongjiang Province and the Hunan Chamber of Commerce in Heilongjiang hold a cooperation fair. This event is bound to promote bilateral cooperation, aiming to achieve mutual benefit and common development.

Heilongjiang-Inner Mongolia

[Quick Facts] Average distance = 1955 km; Geographical adjacency = 1; Index of ethnic linkages = 0.8234 (2000) and 0.8221 (2010); Freight exchange via national railway = 1150 k tons (2000) and 43,430 k tons (2010). ★ January 16, 2010, the communication departments of Heilongjiang and Inner Mongolia sign a cooperation framework agreement. The agreement will deepen bilateral transport cooperation and promote the development of regional transport integration. April 21, 2010, the "Heilongjiang-Inner Mongolia Forum of Economic Exchange and Cooperation" is held in Harbin City. The two sides sign five agreements, including the joint development of coal and chemical industries (signed by Hulunbeier City and the DRC of Heilongjiang Province); the deep potato processing (signed by Hulunbeier City and Songtian Group); the cement-clinker production line (signed by Hulunbeier City and Heilongjiang Beijiang Group); the aluminum foil project (signed by Tongliao City of Inner Mongolia and the Tongyuaosi Company of Heilongjiang); and the project of coal-chemical-recycling economic park construction (signed by Xilin Gol League of Inner Mongolia and the Longmei Company of Heilongjiang). October 29, 2010, the Entry-Exit IQBs of Inner Mongolia and Heilongjiang sign, in Shenyang, an agreement concerning the strengthening of regional cooperation and of the facilitating of customs clearance process. August 20, 2011, the Airport Groups of Inner Mongolia and Heilongjiang sign, in Ordos of Inner Mongolia, a cooperation framework agreement of regional route development.

Heilongjiang-Jiangsu

[Quick Facts] Average distance = 2277 km; Geographical adjacency = 0; Index of ethnic linkages = 0.9538 (2000) and 0.9666 (2010); Freight exchange via national railway = 2220 k tons (2000) and 1620 k tons (2010). ★ August 23, 2005, the Employment Bureau of Heilongjiang Province and the Employment Service and Management Center of Jiangsu Province sign, in Harbin City of Heilongjiang Province, a cooperation agreement. Under the agreement, the two sides will construct a labor output and input base; the Jiangsu side will provide over 80,000 jobs, covering more than 10 industries such as textile, clothing, machinery, electronics and food. April 12–14, 2006, a delegation led by the Heilongjiang Provincial CCP Committee visits Jiangsu Province. The two sides hold the "Jiangsu-Heilongjiang Economic and Social Development Forum", aiming to achieve a common development through combining the advantages of natural resources in Heilongjiang and of technology, capital and human resource in Jiangsu Province. April 13–16, 2006, the Science and Technology Departments of Heilongjiang and Jiangsu Provinces hold, in Nanjing City, a promotion meeting of technological cooperation. The projects include: cooperation between the Center for Transfer in Scientific and Technological Achievements of Heilongjiang and the Technology Property Exchange of Jiangsu Province; cooperation concerning the reorganization of non-performing SOEs; and property rights transaction and project financing between the Keli Investment Company of Heilongjiang and the Technology Property Exchange of Jiangsu Province. April 14, 2006, Heilongjiang and Jiangsu provinces sign, in Nanjing, 12 personnel cooperative agreements such as joint training of private entrepreneurs and personnel exchange. April 15, 2007, the Bureaux of Grains and Foods of Heilongjiang and Jiangsu Provinces jointly hold a meeting concerning the interprovincial cooperation between the two places, aiming to promote joint production and marketing.

Heilongjiang-Jiangxi

[Quick Facts] Average distance = 2689 km; Geographical adjacency = 0; Index of ethnic linkages = 0.9522 (2000) and 0.9648 (2010); Freight exchange via national railway = 340 k tons (2000) and 760 k tons (2010). ★ September 13, 2007, the Jiangxi Chamber of Commerce in Heilongjiang is established. April 12, 2012, the Zhengbang Group of and the Agriculture and Animal Husbandry Industry Group of Jiangxi visit Zhaodong City of Heilongjiang Province to investigate investment project, and exchange with the CCP Secretary of Zhaodong City. The two sides pledge to promote the construction of a pig breeding base. June 13, 2012, the Zhengbang Technology Co., Ltd. of Jiangxi and the Beidahuang Investment Co., Ltd. of Heilongjiang sign a strategic cooperation agreement in Harbin City of Heilongjiang Province. The two sides will jointly set up an aquaculture development industry fund to promote the construction of a breeding base in Heilongjiang Province. In addition, the Zhengbang Technology Co., Ltd. and the Animal Husbandry and Veterinary Bureau of Heilongjiang sign, in Harbin City, a memorandum of cooperation to construct a pigs-raising base with an annual output of 600 million heads. August 6–10, 2012, the Gongqing Farm of Heilongjiang Reclamation and Gongqing City of Jiangxi Province sign a cooperation framework agreement. The Gongqing Farm and Gongqing City were established on behalf of the Chinese Communist Youth League in 1955.

Heilongjiang-Jilin

[Quick Facts] Average distance = 242 km; Geographical adjacency = 1; Index of ethnic linkages = 0.9557 (2000) and 0.9548 (2010); Freight exchange via national railway = 23,040 k tons (2000) and 29,820 k tons (2010). ★ July 9, 2005, a delegation led by the CCP Secretary (also the PCSC Chairman) of Jilin Province, visits Harbin, Suifenhe, Dongning and other places in Heilongjiang. The delegation inspects the situation of cross-border economic, trade, and technological cooperation between Heilongjiang and Russia. The leaderships of the two places pledge to strengthen exchange and to expand cooperation, and to accelerate the development of old industrial bases in Northeast China. January 16, 2010, the communication departments of Jilin and Heilongjiang Provinces sign a cooperation framework agreement. The signing of the agreement will further deepen the bilateral transport cooperation, and promote the development of regional transport integration. April 14–15, 2010, a delegation composed of Heilongjiang's provincial counselors visits Changchun City of Jilin Province; the delegation discusses with the counselors of

Jilin Province about issues relating to the construction of border-trade areas in Northeast China. October 29, 2010, the Entry-Exit IQBs of Jilin and Heilongjiang sign, in Shenyang, an agreement concerning the strengthening of regional cooperation to facilitate customs clearance process. August 20, 2011, the airport groups of Inner Mongolia and Heilongjiang sign, in Ordos of Inner Mongolia, a cooperation framework agreement of regional route development.

Heilongjiang-Liaoning

[Quick Facts] Average distance = 547 km; Geographical adjacency = 0; Index of ethnic linkages = 0.8818 (2000) and 0.8797 (2010); Freight exchange via national railway = 33,250 k tons (2000) and 52,920 k tons (2010). ★ October 31, 2007, the Investment Guarantee Corporation of Heilongjiang Province and the Credit Guarantee Center of Liaoning Province hold a signing ceremony of strategic cooperation. October 20, 2008, the IQBs of Heilongjiang and Liaoning Provinces sign a memorandum of cooperation to jointly promote Liaoning's export of fruits and vegetables to Russia via Heilongjiang. January 16, 2010, the communication departments of Liaoning and Heilongjiang Provinces sign a cooperation framework agreement, in order to promote the integrated development of regional transport networks. June 28, 2010, Heilongjiang Fisheries Research Institute signs a technological cooperation agreement with Kuandian County of Liaoning Province. Under the agreement, the County will provide 6400 m^2 of land for the project construction and Heilongjiang will provide technological guidance and service. October 29, 2010, the Entry-Exit IQBs of Liaoning and Heilongjiang sign, in Shenyang, an agreement concerning the strengthening of regional cooperation to facilitate customs clearance process. March 31, 2012, the Grains and Foods Bureau of Heilongjiang Province and the Yingkou Port Group of Liaoning Province sign a strategic cooperation framework agreement. Both sides pledge to build a convenient and efficient food logistics channel between south and north area.

Heilongjiang-Ningxia

[Quick Facts] Average distance = 2631 km; Geographical adjacency = 0; Index of ethnic linkages = 0.6633 (2000) and 0.6566 (2010); Freight exchange via national railway = 190 k tons (2000) and 170 k tons (2010). ★ August 3, 2009, the Agriculture and Animal Husbandry Departments of Ningxia Hui Autonomous Region and Heilongjiang Academy of Agricultural Science and Technology sign a cooperation agreement in Harbin. The agreement covers the construction of a science and technology demonstration zone, the transferring and introducing of new technologies, personnel training and others. June 15, 2010, the government of Ningxia Hui Autonomous Region holds, in Harbin of Heilongjiang, an investment promotion. Ningxia and a Harbin enterprise sign an agreement of joint venture, with a total investment of 1.6 billion yuan and an annual output capacity of 250,000 tons of new biodegradable bio-materials. September 26, 2010, at the "First Forum of the Trade and Economic Cooperation between China and Arab Countries", which is held in Yinchuan City of Ningxia, Heilongjiang province exhibits their cooperation projects. October 2011, the Heilongjiang Chamber of Commerce in Ningxia is established in Yinchuan. According to reports, there are more than 200 Heilongjiang-funded enterprises in Ningxia, mainly engaged in electronic products, furniture production and sales, real estate development, advertising, decoration, fire protection engineering, trade and circulation. June 14, 2012, the "Ningxia-Heilongjiang Trade and Economic Cooperation Forum" is held in Harbin City. Both sides pledge to deepen bilateral exchange and cooperation. June 20, 2012, the Suifenhe City's tourist inspection delegation of Heilongjiang pays an inspection to Yinchuan City of Ningxia.

Heilongjiang-Qinghai

[Quick Facts] Average distance = 3386 km; Geographical adjacency = 0; Index of ethnic linkages = 0.5499 (2000) and 0.5380 (2010); Freight exchange via national railway = 80 k tons (2000) and 240 k tons (2010). ★ April 15, 2010, the Charity Federation of Heilongjiang Province and the Civil Affairs Department of Qinghai Province communicate on matters relating to what are needed in the Yushu earthquake hit area in Qinghai Province. The Heilongjiang provincial government donates 5 million yuan for local disaster relief. In addition, the Warehousing Center of Heilongjiang Province sends 32,000 sets of clothing (worth of 2.4 million yaun) to the Yushu disaster area. April 19–22, 2010, the Chanting Prayers Puja is held in Daqing City of Heilongjiang Province. The Jingjue monks pray for the Sambo salvation to the souls of Yushu earthquake victims, chanting prayers for the survivors, and call for all disciples to donate for the Yushu disaster area. May 18, 2010, Qinghai Provincial CCP Secretary meets the Heilongjiang Provincial Fire Brigade. The two sides exchange firefighting and security in the post-disaster reconstruction work. October 12, 2012, Qinghai Province and the Heilongjiang Institute of China Academy of Fishery Sciences jointly conduct a demonstration project entitled "Some Key Technologies for the Cultivation of Fresh Fishery in the Heilongjiang and Other Rivers". This is China's scientific and technological support project during the 12th five-year plan period (2011–15).

Heilongjiang-Shaanxi

[Quick Facts] Average distance = 2453 km; Geographical adjacency = 0; Index of ethnic linkages = 0.9555 (2000) and 0.9678 (2010); Freight exchange via national railway = 670 k tons (2000) and 720 k tons (2010). ★ May 26–27, 2009, the Shaanxi Administration of Surveying, Mapping and Geo-information pays an inspection to Heilongjiang Province. The two sides will strengthen exchange and establish a stable cooperation mechanism. July 8, 2009, the "Heilongjiang-Shaanxi Science and Technology Cooperation Forum" and an agreement signing ceremony are held in Harbin City. The two sides sign the "Development and Cooperation Framework Agreement of Titanium Processing Industry between Northwest Institute of Nonferrous Metals and the Jiamusi Municipal Government", and the "Innovation Cooperation Agreement between the Productivity Promotion Centers of Shaanxi and Heilongjiang Provinces". September 7, 2009, the IQBs of Heilongjiang and Shaanxi Provinces sign, in Xi'an City of Shaanxi, a memorandum of cooperation to jointly promote Shaanxi's export of fruits and vegetables to Russia via Heilongjiang. September 21–22, 2009, a Shaanxi delegation participates in the Golden-Autumn Grain Trade Cooperation Fair in Heilongjiang, and signs a purchase and sale agreement of 400 million kg of paddy with the Heilongjiang Provincial Grain Bureau. May 2012, the Heilongjiang Chamber of Commerce in Shaanxi is established in Xi'an City.

Heilongjiang-Shandong

[Quick Facts] Average distance = 1614 km; Geographical adjacency = 0; Index of ethnic linkages = 0.9558 (2000) and 0.9684 (2010); Freight exchange via national railway = 6580 k tons (2000) and 4180 k tons (2010). ★ August 23–24, 2003, a delegation of the Overseas Enterprise Development Association of Shandong Province visits Harbin; the two sides' companies sign five agreements relating to steel, paper, the deep processing of special agricultural products, etc. June 14, 2004, the AQTSs of Heilongjiang and Shandong Provinces sign a cooperation agreement. The two sides decide to construct the mechanism of mutual trust and of joint prevention of false products. May 18, 2005, the Shandong Chamber of Commerce in Heilongjiang is established in Harbin City. October 29, 2008, the Women's Federations of Suihua City of Heilongjiang Province and Weifang City of Shandong Province hold a forum and sign a cooperation agreement. The two sides will expand the cooperation in female personnel training and agriculture cooperation projects. January 27, 2010, the Animation Industry Development Base of Heilongjiang and the Xinyang Technology Co., Ltd. sign the three-dimensional animation project with the Shenggongshan Tourist Development Co., Ltd. of Rizhao City of Shandong Province, with a total investment of 10 million yuan. June 22, 2010, Weifang City of Shandong Province and the Heilongjiang Fisheries

Research Institute of China Academy of Fishery Sciences become cooperative partners. July 29, 2011, the Ministry of Industry and Information Technology of Shandong Province and Heilongjiang Provincial People's Government sign, in Harbin City, the "Strategic Cooperation Framework Agreement Concerning the Acceleration of Heilongjiang Provincial Industry and Information Technology Development".

Heilongjiang-Shanghai

[Quick Facts] Average distance = 2577 km; Geographical adjacency = 0; Index of ethnic linkages = 0.9563 (2000) and 0.9697 (2010); Freight exchange via national railway = 890 k tons (2000) and 720 k tons (2010). ★ April 10, 2006, the Deputy Director of the Shanghai Municipal Economic Commission, the Chief of the Shanghai Bureau of Grains and Foods hold, with Heilongjiang Province, a forum concerning food production and marketing; the food companies of two places sign cooperation agreements. August 9, 2010, the Shanghai Pudong Development Bank, the Beidahuang Group of Heilongjiang hold, in Harbin City, a signing ceremony of strategic cooperation agreement and a launching ceremony of financial innovation cooperative project. Under the agreement, the Bank will provide 10 billion yuan credit limit to the Group. August 31, 2010, the relevant units of Shanghai and Wuchang City of Heilongjiang sign an agreement, including: a sale cooperation of 20,000 tons of the Wuchang rice; the construction of a rice processing plant with an output of 400 ton per day; the establishment of granary with a capacity of 50,000 tons, ensuring to meet the food demand of Shanghai. July 13–14, 2011, Shanghai and Heilongjiang hold a meeting and reach a consensus on food production and marketing. Heilongjiang will provide annually more than 500,000 tons of high-quality rice (produced in Hulin District) to Shanghai. April 26, 2012, the joint investment projects of Shanghai and Heilongjiang start to operate in the New Industrial Town, south of Harbin City.

Heilongjiang-Shanxi

[Quick Facts] Average distance = 1802 km; Geographical adjacency = 0; Index of ethnic linkages = 0.9542 (2000) and 0.9666 (2010); Freight exchange via national railway = 1270 k tons (2000) and 1160 k tons (2010). ★ June 6, 2006, Shanxi and Heilongjiang Provinces sign, in Taiyuan City of Shanxi, a cooperation agreement of grain purchase and marketing. Under the agreement, Shanxi Province will purchase 500 million kg rice and soybeans annually from Heilongjiang Province; Heilongjiang Province will purchase 250 million kg millet annually from Shanxi. June 24, 2008, the Longding Group of and the Rongsheng Group of Shanxi sign a school-enterprise cooperation agreement with Heilongjiang Vocational School of

Architecture and Technology. September 2009, the Shanxi Chamber of Commerce in Heilongjiang is established. According to statistics, Heilongjiang has more 500 Shanxi-funded enterprises, with 20,000 staff and 2 billion yuan registered capital. The businesses mainly cover building materials, real estate, property management, clothing sales, clothing, commerce, home appliances marketing, medicine, bioengineering, securities, education, machinery manufacturing, wine, dining, entertainment, food processing, fruits and marketing and logistics. April 14, 2011, the Guozhong Water Supply Company of Heilongjiang and the Shanxi Water Investment Group Co., Ltd. sign an agreement of strategic cooperation. April 19, 2012, the Jinshen Energy Co., Ltd. of Shanxi and Heilongjiang College of Science and Technology sign, in Xinzhou City of Shanxi Province, a school-enterprise agreement concerning the cooperation in human resources.

Heilongjiang-Sichuan

[Quick Facts] Average distance = 3336 km; Geographical adjacency = 0; Index of ethnic linkages = 0.9525 (2000) and 0.9413 (2010); Freight exchange via national railway = 1080 k tons (2000) and 2130 k tons (2010). ★ September 24, 2007, the "Sichuan-Heilongjiang Grain Production and Marketing Cooperation Forum" is held in Chengdu City of Sichuan. October 10, 2008, a delegation led by vice governor of Sichuan Province visits Heilongjiang to acknowledge the assistance of Heilongjiang Province during the period of the Wenchuan earthquake in May. The two sides hold an investment promotion; Sichuan offers 675 projects, with a total value of 509.2 billion yuan. Jiange County of Sichuan Province and Heilongjiang Province sign a memorandum of cooperation concerning Heilongjiang's support to the construction of the Jianmen Industrial Park. Jiange County and Harbin Institute of Technology also sign a memorandum of cooperation. June 23–24, 2010, a delegation led by the Deputy CCP Secretary (also the Governor) of Sichuan Province visits Heilongjiang Province and holds an interprovincial economic and social development forum in Harbin City. After the Wenchuan earthquake in May 2008, Heilongjiang Province and Jiange County of Sichuan Province become pairing aid partnerships; Heilongjiang provides 1.55 billion yuan via 146 reconstruction projects. June 19, 2012, the Kuihua Pharmaceutical Group of Heilongjiang Province and two pharmaceutical companies in Zigong of Sichuan reach a cooperation agreement. September 5, 2012, Qing'an County of Heilongjiang Province and the Federation of Industry and Commerce of Sichuan Province hold a cooperation fair; the two places' companies sign a strategic cooperation framework agreement.

Heilongjiang-Tianjin

[Quick Facts] Average distance = 1354 km; Geographical adjacency = 0; Index of ethnic linkages = 0.9631 (2000) and 0.9766 (2010); Freight exchange via national railway = 2690 k tons (2000) and 1150 k tons (2010). ★ August 18, 2009, the Grains and Foods Bureaux of Heilongjiang Province and Tianjin Municipality sign an agreement on the strengthening of production and marketing cooperation. Heilongjiang will provide 750 million kg of stuff annually to Tianjin every year and both sides decide to hold an annual meeting on grain supply and marketing cooperation. March 3, 2011, a forum of cooperation between the Tianjin Maritime Bureau and the Heilongjiang Bureau of Surveying and Mapping is held in Tianjin. May 28, 2011, Harbin City and Tianjin's universities joint hold, in Harbin, an exchange and cooperation meeting concerning the conversion of scientific and technological achievements. The experts and professors of Tianjin's universities and research institutes discuss the internet of things, R&D of chemical products, Chinese herbal medicine development, and the conversion of scientific and technological achievements to Harbin. September 1, 2011, Tianjin municipal government participates in the "2011 Heilongjiang Golden-Autumn Grain Trading Cooperation Fair"; the two places' companies sign a contract of 358,000 tons of grains. May 18, 2012, a government delegation of Yichun City of Heilongjiang visit Tianjin. The relevant departments of the two places hold a seminar and sign cooperation agreements. July 4, 2012, the Xiangshui Rice Company of Mudanjiang City of Heilongjiang and the Tianjin Port Life Services Co., Ltd. become strategic partners. The Xiangshui Company will provide 2000 tons of rice (including 40 tons of high-quality rice) for sale in Tianjin.

Heilongjiang-Tibet

[Quick Facts] Average distance = 5409 km; Geographical adjacency = 0; Index of ethnic linkages = 0.0648 (2000) and 0.0851 (2010); Freight exchange via national railway = 0 k ton (2000) and 50 k tons (2010). ★ May 3, 2011, the Rikaze Prefectural CCP Committee of Tibet, the Administrative Office and the cadres of the 4th aid work team of Heilongjiang Province visit the Heilongjiang Provincial Bureau of Geology and Mineral Resources. September 22, 2011, a signing ceremony of cooperation agreement between the Heilongjiang Fisheries Research Institute, China Academy of Fishery Sciences, and the Institute of Vegetables of Tibet Academy of Farming and Pastoral Sciences is held in the National Agricultural Science and Technology Park in Tibet. June 14, 2011, the Tibet (Rikaze Prefecture) Tourism Symposium is held in Harbin City. Heilongjiang Province and Rikaze Prefecture reach a consensus on the further strengthening of tourist exchange and cooperation. The two sides will jointly develop tourist products, and establish air routes between Rikaze and Harbin and between Harbin and Lhasa (Rikaze). July 20, 2011, the aid work team of Heilongjiang Province and Heilongjiang Provincial government visit Rikaze to attend the 60th Anniversary of the Peaceful Liberation of Tibet, the Everest Cultural Tourism Festival and other major celebrations. July 29, 2011, a delegation of the Heilongjiang provincial government visits Rikaze, and holds a pairing aid symposium with the Rikaze Prefectural CCP Committee and the Rikaze Administrative Office. June 15, 2012, in the "China (Harbin) International Economic and Trade Fair", Tibet Autonomous Region and Heilongjiang Province hold a meeting on pairing aid work, aiming to promote the friendship between the two sides and to promote bilateral economic cooperation and cultural exchange; Heilongjiang Provincial Bureau of Geology and Mineral Resources holds a symposium of mineral resource exploitation with the Rikaze Civil Administration of Tibet, and both sides sign a strategic cooperation framework agreement.

Heilongjiang-Xinjiang

[Quick Facts] Average distance = 5062 km; Geographical adjacency = 0; Index of ethnic linkages = 0.4153 (2000) and 0.4125 (2010); Freight exchange via national railway = 230 k tons (2000) and 350 k tons (2010). ★ April 14, 2009, the Reclamation Science Institute of Xinjiang and the Agricultural Machinery and Engineering Research Institute of Heilongjiang sign a cooperation framework agreement, aiming to promote agricultural development in Xinjiang. May 30, 2011, the Tourism Bureaux of Heilongjiang and Tibet hold, in Harbin City, an aid work forum. The two sides decide to jointly build an air-ticket subsidy mechanism, aiming to promote the tourism development in Xinjiang. June 1, 2011, a delegation led by the Chief of the Xinjiang Tourism Bureau visits Heilongjiang and signs five cooperation agreements with Harbin City, including four tourist cooperation agreements and one strategic cooperation agreement between the two provincial bureaux. In addition, the two sides also reach a consensus on the issues of regular bilateral cooperation and the increase of chartered trains and flights. June 15, 2011, the Heilongjiang Academy of Geographic Information and Engineering visits the Xinjiang Institute of Surveying and Mapping. May 2012, the Fisheries Research Institute of Heilongjiang and the Aquatic Bureau of Altay Prefecture, the Aquatic Bureau of Fuhai County of Altay Prefecture and the aquatic sector of the No. 10 Agriculture Division of the XPCC become cooperative partners, aiming to jointly develop the aquatic and fishery market in Northwest China. The Heilongjiang Province has invested 150 million yuan in Tibet in 2011. June 20–21, 2012, a delegation led by the Secretary of Heilongjiang Provincial CCP Committee, visits Urumqi City of Xinjiang Uygur Autonomous Region, and holds a pairing aid symposium in Altay City of Xinjiang.

Heilongjiang-Yunnan

[Quick Facts] Average distance = 4472 km; Geographical adjacency = 0; Index of ethnic linkages = 0.6706 (2000) and 0.6699 (2010); Freight exchange via national railway = 290 k tons (2000) and 960 k tons (2010). ★ September 26, 2007, a Heilongjiang delegation and the Grains and Foods Bureau of Yunnan Province hold, in Kunming City of Yunnan, a production and marketing cooperation forum. July 24, 2008, an innovated model of bilateral cooperation in food production and marketing is established between Heilongjiang and Yunnan Provinces. November 20, 2009, the "2009–2010 Yunnan-Heilongjiang Cooperation Forum" is held in Kunming City of Yunnan. May 31, 2011, the Metrology Institutes of Yunnan and Heilongjiang Provinces hold an exchange meeting and sign a cooperation framework agreement. The two sides will cooperate in research project, R&D, personnel training and others. March 8, 2012, a delegation composed of the Deputy Chief of Baoquanling Authority of Heilongjiang Bureau of Land Reclamation, the Chairman of Zhongruixin Credit Suisse Investment Guarantee Co., Ltd. and others pays an inspection to Yunnan Province, aiming to strengthen the cooperation of food production and marketing and to build a development financing platform for food enterprises. April 16, 2012, the Hegang Coal Group Company of Heilongjiang and the Huadian Yunan Generating Co., Ltd. hold, in Yunnan, a forum of cooperation in coal exploitation. July 31, 2012, the Institutes of Metrology of Yunnan and Heilongjiang Provinces sign a memorandum of cooperation.

Heilongjiang-Zhejiang

[Quick Facts] Average distance = 2706 km; Geographical adjacency = 0; Index of ethnic linkages = 0.9522 (2000) and 0.9656 (2010); Freight exchange via national railway = 1090 k tons (2000) and 1360 k tons (2010). ★ From 9 to 11, 2010, a Zhejiang government delegation visits Heilongjiang Province; the two sides sign a cooperation agreement of grain production and marketing and of forestry during the period of 12th 5-Year-Plan. The food and forestry departments of the two provinces sign an agreement concerning the improvement of the coordinative mechanism on food transportation and a cooperation framework agreement on forestry. June 15, 2011, the "Zhejiang-Heilongjiang Trade and Economic Cooperation Fair" and the agreement signing ceremony are held in Hangzhou City. The two provinces' companies agree 25 joint projects, with a total investment of 9.207 billion yuan. October 17, 2011, the Heilongjiang Chamber of Commerce in Wenzhou City of Zhejiang is established. March 30, 2012, the "2012 Heilongjiang-Zhejiang Entrepreneurs Forum" is held in Hangzhou City. The two places' enterprises agree a total of 49 joint projects. The projects, with a total investment of 32.24 billion yuan, mainly involve green food, petrochemical, mineral economy, forest products processing, new materials, biology, new energy equipment manufacturing and transportation equipment manufacturing. August 3, 2012, the Secretary of Suifenhe

Prefectural CCP Committee of Heilongjiang meets the Zhejiang Chamber of Commerce in Heilongjiang. September 20, 2012, the "9th Heilongjiang Golden-Autumn Grain Trading Cooperation Fair" is held in Harbin City. More than 100 food production, circulation and grain processing enterprises from more than 30 cities and counties of Zhejiang Province participate in the fair. Both sides sign 24 grain purchase and sale contracts, with a total transaction of about 540,000 tons.

Henan-Hubei

[Quick Facts] Average distance = 536 km; Geographical adjacency = 1; Index of ethnic linkages = 0.9585 (2000) and 0.9589 (2010); Freight exchange via national railway = 25,180 k tons (2000) and 27,270 k tons (2010). ★ June 23, 2006, the Henan Chamber of Commerce in Hubei is established in Wuhan City. The Chamber has 176 enterprise members, engaged in agriculture, forestry, construction engineering, art and design, decoration engineering, catering, real estate, furniture sales, etc. March 2007, the Hubei Chamber of Commerce in Henan is established Zhengzhou City. The Chamber has more than 500 enterprise and individual members, mainly engaged in building materials, real estate, catering, clothing, pharmaceutics, automotive and mineral. April 27, 2008, at the "3rd Central China Investment and Trade Fair", held in Wuhan City, Wuhan of Hubei and Sanmenxia of Henan hold a promotion of bilateral economic cooperation. May 12, 2008, a delegation, led by the Secretary of CCP Committee and the Governor of Hubei Province, visits Henan to inspect the regional economic development at county level. March 13, 2010, the China Datang Corporation Henan Branch and Hubei Province sign a cooperation agreement on the wind power development in Hubei Province. June 28, 2010, a delegation of the Henan Traffic and Transportation Investment Group Co., Ltd. visits the Hubei workstation of the Beijing-Zhuhai Expressway. July 8, 2010, a delegation, composed of seven professional agricultural machinery cooperatives and led by the Tianmen Agricultural Machinery Bureau of Hubei Province, pays an inspection to Henan Province. December 6, 2010, the public security organs of Henan and Hubei sign a joint conference charter on police cooperation. May 27, 2011, Xinyang City of Henan and Suizhou City of Hubei sign a regional tourist cooperation agreement. 15 travel agencies from Xinyang participate in the meeting of cooperation agreement, and sign a land access agreement with more than 20 local travel agencies.

Henan-Hunan

[Quick Facts] Average distance = 894 km; Geographical adjacency = 0; Index of ethnic linkages = 0.9011 (2000) and 0.9024 (2010); Freight exchange via national railway = 6080 k tons (2000) and 10,830 k tons (2010). ★ May 12, 2008, the Hunan provincial government and the Henan Expressway Development Co., Ltd. sign a franchised project contract of the expressway from Yueyang to Changde. The total length of the project reaches 141.27 km, with a total investment of 9.218 billion yuan. November 20, 2008, the Henan Chamber of Commerce in Hunan is established in Changsha City. The Chamber has 112 enterprise members. January 21, 2010, Hunan Province and the Tourism Bureaux of Henan jointly initiate a cooperation alliance, aiming to jointly promote regional economic development. September 12, 2010, the inaugural ceremony of the Hunan Chamber of Commerce in Henan and the "Henan-Hunan Trade and Economic Cooperation Conference" are held in Zhengzhou City. According to incomplete statistics, Henan has more than 200,000 Hunan employees and more than 1000 Hunan-funded enterprises, with the annual output value of 30 billion yuan. The Chamber signs a strategic cooperation agreement with the Henan Chamber of Commerce in Hunan, Yueyang and Shaoyang Cities of Hunan Province, and the Zhengzhou Export Processing Zone of Henan. December 6, 2010, the public security organs of Henan and Hubei sign a joint conference charter on police cooperation. May 27, 2011, the "2011 China (Suizhou) Tourism Fair" is held in the Dahongshan scenic of Suizhou City (Hunan Province). Xinyang City of Henan Province and Suizhou City sign an agreement on regional tourist cooperation.

Henan-Inner Mongolia

[Quick Facts] Average distance = 1362 km; Geographical adjacency = 0; Index of ethnic linkages = 0.8028 (2000) and 0.8060 (2010); Freight exchange via national railway = 1370 k tons (2000) and 2490 k tons (2010). ★ August 6, 2009, the Henan Chamber of Commerce in Inner Mongolia is established in Hohhot City. The Chamber has 150 enterprise members and more than 300 individual members, mainly engaged in real estate, mining, tourism, building materials, machinery, pharmaceutics and food industry. February 25, 2011, the Bureau of Coal Geology of Inner Mongolia and the Zhongyuan Oilfield Company of Henan Province sign, in Puyang City of Henan, a long-term strategic partnership agreement. Under the agreement, the two sides will carry out cooperation in geological data sharing, project contract and technological service. November 16, 2011, the Zhengzhou Coal Industry Group and the Haoqin Tiancheng Mining Industry Co., Ltd. of the West Ujimqin League of Inner Mongolia sign an agreement, according to which the two sides will jointly develop 4.237 billion tons of coal in the Haoqin coalfield. July 2012, the Highway Administration of Alashan League of Inner Mongolia Autonomous Region and the Henan Highway Maintenance Equipment Co., Ltd. decides to jointly develop road maintenance vehicles. September 5, 2012, a delegation of the Xingyang Federation of Returned Overseas Chinese of Henan Province, led by the Chief of the Federation, pays an inspection to Inner Mongolia. September 8, 2012, the shipbuilding enterprises of Henan Province and Inner

Mongolia Autonomous Region hold a strategic cooperation conference. Both sides reach a consensus on technology sharing, capital operation, etc.

Henan-Jiangsu

[Quick Facts] Average distance = 695 km; Geographical adjacency = 0; Index of ethnic linkages = 0.9901 (2000) and 0.9905 (2010); Freight exchange via national railway = 12,530 k tons (2000) and 21,090 k tons (2010). ★ September 4, 2005, the "Henan-Jiangsu Employment Exchange" fair is held in Suzhou City of Jiangsu. The two provinces sign a cooperation agreement on interprovincial exchange of workers. Huaxian and the Qingfeng Counties of Henan sign an agreement with the Suzhou New District, which includes the exchange of 15,000 labors. June 24, 2006, Yancheng City of Jiangsu and Zhumadian City of Henan sign a labor cooperation agreement. According to statistics, the gap of labor demand in Yancheng City reaches 36,500 people, while Zhumadian has a labor surplus of 2.46 million people. May 9, 2007, a delegation of the Jiangsu Yueda Group visits Shangqiu City of Henan Province. The two sides decide to carry out extensive cooperation in energy, transportation, logistics, industrial processing and capital operation, and sign a cooperation framework agreement. March 21, 2008, a delegation of the Labor and Social Security Bureau of Lankao County, Henan Province, pays an inspection to Donghai County, Jiangsu Province. April 21, 2009, the fair of Jiangsu-Henan construction industry and workers' cooperation opens. Henan and Jiangsu Provinces sign a cooperation agreement. Under the agreement, more than 50,000 Henan's workers will join the construction enterprises in Jiangsu Province. March 1, 2010, the Jiangsu Kedi Agriculture Co., Ltd. and Henan Agricultural University sign a cooperative project agreement concerning the construction of modern tobacco and agriculture research center. April 18, 2010, the Jiangsu Chamber of Commerce in Henan is established in Zhengzhou City. March 18, 2012, the Changzhou (Jiangsu Province) Chamber of Commerce in Henan is established. The sub-provincial level chamber has 66 members. June 12, 2012, the Jiangsu Yongneng Group and Henan Agricultural University sign a cooperation agreement in production and research. July 13, 2012, the "Jiangsu's Products in Zhengzhou" fair is held in Zhengzhou International Convention and Exhibition Center.

Henan-Jiangxi

[Quick Facts] Average distance = 927 km; Geographical adjacency = 0; Index of ethnic linkages = 0.9885 (2000) and 0.9889 (2010); Freight exchange via national railway = 3410 k tons (2000) and 540 k tons (2010). ★ March 19, 2009, the Jiangxi Chamber of Commerce in Henan is established in Zhengzhou City. The Chamber has nearly 500 members, involving more than 20 industries (such as real estate, technology, bridge construction, medical equipment, culture, media, mining, education, consulting, financial services, machinery manufacturing, auto sales, clothing trade, building materials, home improvement, hotel, and food), with the total assets of nearly 30 billion yuan. December 4, 2009, the Henan Chamber of Commerce in Jiangxi is established in Nanchang City. The Chamber has more than 300 member companies, engaged in garment and textile, machinery and electronics, construction and real estate, food processing, etc. December 6, 2010, the public security organs of Henan and Jiangxi sign a joint conference charter on police cooperation. July 2, 2012, Henan Agricultural University and Jiangxi Tobacco Company sign, in Zhongzhou City of Henan, a strategic partnership framework agreement. July 9, 2012, a specialty agriculture and medicine manufacturing investment team of Lushi County of Henan Province and the Weishi Industrial Co., Ltd. of Jiangxi Province reach an agreement in the production of mulberry leaves, ginkgo, forsythia and tea. Under the agreement, the Jiangxi Company plans to invest 7 million yuan to build a production base in Lushi County, Henan. September 15, 2012, the Procurators of Henan and Jiangxi Provinces sign, in Shaoshan City of Hunan, a memorandum of understanding.

Henan-Jilin

[Quick Facts] Average distance = 1843 km; Geographical adjacency = 0; Index of ethnic linkages = 0.9152 (2000) and 0.9263 (2010); Freight exchange via national railway = 890 k tons (2000) and 950 k tons (2010). ★ July 27, 2007, the CCP Secretary and Governor of Jilin Province and the Governor of Henan Province jointly hold a "Jilin-Henan Symposium". The Henan delegation visits the FAW trucks base, Jiefang assembly plant and the production lines of FAW-Volkswagen Audi and FAW-Volkswagen. October 11–12, 2007, the Express Associations of Henan and Jilin Provinces pledge to strengthen exchange and cooperation and promote stable and healthy development. March 10–11, 2008, Jilin and Henan Provinces hold, in Beijing, a seminar concerning the quality and technical supervision of regional cooperation and the protection of product quality and safety. November 1, 2010, the Haofeng Machinery Manufacturing Co., Ltd. of Henan and the Biological and Agricultural Engineering School of Jilin University sign, in Xuchang City of Henan, an agreement on science, technology and education cooperation. The two sides hope to promote China's agricultural machinery technology to the world-class level. April 8, 2011, the Henan Chamber of Commerce in Jilin is established in Changchun City. July 26, 2012, a condolatory delegation composed of the Henan Chamber of Commerce in Jilin and led by the Civil Affairs Department of Jilin Province donates 100 bags of rice, 100 bags of flour, 80 barrels of oil and 50,000 yuan to the No. 1 Rongfu Military Hospital of Jilin Province.

Henan-Liaoning

[Quick Facts] Average distance = 1538 km; Geographical adjacency = 0; Index of ethnic linkages = 0.8477 (2000) and 0.8554 (2010); Freight exchange via national railway = 2070 k tons (2000) and 4490 k tons (2010). ★ March 10–11, 2008, Henan and Liaoning Provinces hold, in Beijing, a seminar concerning the regional cooperation in quality and technical supervision and the protection of product quality and safety. November 19, 2009, the Henan Traffic and Transportation Investment Group Co., Ltd. sign a large-scale financing agreement with Liaoning's banks, with a total capital of 17.425 billion yuan. The Henan Group plans to construct, renovate and expand five projects, with a total investment of 12.1 billion yuan, accounting for 81.7 % of the total investment plan. October 18, 2010, Neihuang County of Anyang City (Henan Province) and the Shuangfa Ceramics Co., Ltd. of Liaoning Province sign a contract. Under the contract, the Shuangfa will build four production lines in Neihuang County, with a total investment of 400 million yuan, aiming to achieve a mutually beneficial and win-win goal for the enterprise and the government. September 20, 2012, a delegation led by the deputy director of the Environmental Protection Department of Liaoning Province conducts a field-investigation to the Environmental Monitoring Center of Henan Province. The delegation visits the environmental monitoring system in Henan Province. The two sides also carry out in-depth exchange in data application, on-site supervision and inspection and enforcement work.

Henan-Ningxia

[Quick Facts] Average distance = 1357 km; Geographical adjacency = 0; Index of ethnic linkages = 0.6669 (2000) and 0.6603 (2010); Freight exchange via national railway = 330 k tons (2000) and 50 k tons (2010). ★ August 16, 2007, the Post Offices of Henan and Ningxia and the Ningxia Red Group hold, in the Ningxia Hui Autonomous Region, a joint seminar. July 18, 2008, a delegation, led by the CCP Secretary and Director of Supply and Marketing Cooperatives of Ningxia Hui Autonomous Region, pays an inspection to Zhengzhou City. June 14, 2009, the Henan Chamber of Commerce in Ningxia is established in Yinchuan City. According to incomplete statistics, Henan's enterprises have provided nearly 10,000 jobs in Ningxia, and more than 500 million yuan taxes per year. March 19, 2011, the "Ningxia-Henan Trade and Economic Cooperation Promotion" is held in Zhengzhou. Ningxia and Henan sign 17 cooperation projects, with a total investment of 4.677 billion yuan, involving new materials, new building materials, equipment manufacturing, tourism and services, all of which are the pillar industries of Ningxia. April 26, 2011, a delegation composed of officials and experts of the Ningxia Academy of Electric Power Design, visits the Henan Academy of Electric Power Design and hold an exchange meeting in Zhengzhou City. November 14,

2011, a delegation of Henan Institute of Urban Construction visits Ningxia University.

Henan-Qinghai

[Quick Facts] Average distance = 1403 km; Geographical adjacency = 0; Index of ethnic linkages = 0.5528 (2000) and 0.5421 (2010); Freight exchange via national railway = 810 k tons (2000) and 2510 k tons (2010). ★ April 4, 2003, the Yi Coal Group of Henan and Haixi Mongolian and Tibetan Autonomous Prefecture of Qinghai sign a cooperative project agreement of coal power development. According to statistics, the proven coal reserves in the prefecture are 3.8 billion tons, and the production capacity reaches more than 4 million tons per year; they hope to double the production in 2005. August 26, 2007, the Gelatin Co., Ltd., of Qinghai and the Jiaozuo (Henan Province) Jinjian Industrial Corporation sign, in Xining City of Qinghai, a strategic cooperation agreement. July 30, 2010, the Henan Chamber of Commerce in Qinghai is established in Xining City. The Chamber's member enterprises involve commerce, building materials, pharmaceutics, real estate, education and others, with a total investment of 90 billion yuan. April 26, 2011, a delegation composed of officials and experts of the Qinghai Academy of Electric Power Design, visits the Henan Academy of Electric Power Design to carry out an exchange meeting in Zhengzhou City. December 5, 2011, a delegation of Geology and Mineral Resources Bureau of Qinghai Province visits the No. 1 Exploration Brigade of the Coal Geology Bureau of Henan Province. May 8–9, 2012, a Qinghai government delegation pays an inspection to Zhengzhou City. The two sides hold the "Henan-Qinghai Economic and Social Development Forum", aiming to strengthen the interprovincial exchange and cooperation. June 14, 2012, the Electric Power Design Academy of Henan visits Qinghai Province, and signs a strategic cooperation agreement with the Electric Power Design Academy of Qinghai Province.

Henan-Shaanxi

[Quick Facts] Average distance = 511 km; Geographical adjacency = 1; Index of ethnic linkages = 0.9924 (2000) and 0.9928 (2010); Freight exchange via national railway = 4050 k tons (2000) and 5730 k tons (2010). ★ May 31, 2008, the Henan Chamber of Commerce in Shaanxi is established in Xi'an. The Chamber has more than 500 member companies, involving real estate property, building materials and construction, light manufacturing, wire and cable, dining and entertainment, arts and culture, bio-pharmaceutics, mining development, corrosion engineering, energy, machinery, etc. March 17, 2010, the "Shaanxi-Henan Tourist Cooperation Forum" is held. The Tourist Bureaux of Shaanxi and Henan Provinces sign a cooperation agreement. In addition, Weinan City of Shaanxi and Zhengzhou, Luoyang and Sanmenxia Cities of Henan sign a tourist cooperation agreement; The Famen Temple Scenic, Huaqing Hot Springs and Qianling Scenic of Shaanxi Province sign a tourist cooperation agreement with the Henan Tourist Group and others. May 20, 2011, Northwest University of Agriculture, Forestry and Technology and Henan Academy of Agricultural Science and Technology sign a strategic cooperation agreement in Zhengzhou City. July 28, 2011, the Nanyang (Henan) Hongyu Special Automobile Co., Ltd. and the Shaanxi Vader Technology Co., Ltd. decide to jointly develop the coalfield sampling vehicles. September 16, 2011, the Expressway Mechanization Engineering Co., Ltd. of Shaanxi and the Wanliqiao Corporation of Henan hold, in Xi'an, a signing ceremony of strategic cooperation agreement. December 24, 2011, the signing ceremony of the cooperation agreement between the Datang Company Henan Branch and the Shaanxi Coal Chemical Industry Group Corporation is held in Zhengzhou City. December 28, 2011, the Traffic and Transportation Departments of Shaanxi and Henan Provinces sign a cooperation framework agreement concerning the joint inspection and supervision of expressways between Shaanxi and Henan. The two sides will share information in accident, road conditions and others.

Henan-Shandong

[Quick Facts] Average distance = 666 km; Geographical adjacency = 1; Index of ethnic linkages = 0.9941 (2000) and 0.9947 (2010); Freight exchange via national railway = 8070 k tons (2000) and 22,570 k tons (2010). ★ October 30, 2007, Shandong Agricultural University and the Dayong Industrial Co., Ltd. of Henan sign a cooperation agreement in agricultural science application. June 2008, the Shandong Chamber of Commerce in Henan is established in Zhengzhou City. The Chamber has 2112 corporate and individual members; it also set up branches in Shangqiu, Luoyang, Kaifeng, Sanmenxia, Jiaozuo, and Pingdingshan Cities of Henan Province. December 23, 2009, the Rizhao Port (Group) Co., Ltd. of Shandong and the Coal Chemical Industry Group Co., Ltd. of Henan sign a strategic cooperation agreement in Zhengzhou. January 29, 2010, the "2010 Anyang (Henan)-Wendeng (Shandong) Labor Service Cooperation Fair" is held in the Labor and Social Security Bureau of Anyang City. March 24, 2010, Zhumadian City of Henan and Zaozhuang City of Shandong sign a strategic cooperation agreement in tourism. May 16, 2010, the Henan Chamber of Commerce in Shandong is established in Ji' nan City. November 18, 2010, Jining City of Shandong and Puyang City of Henan sign, in Jining, an agreement concerning the construction of a highway from Liangshan County (Shandong Province) to Fanxian County (Henan Province), with a total investment of 3.6 billion yuan. March 31, 2011, the signing ceremony of a cooperation agreement between the Human Resources and Social Security Bureaux of Puyang City of Henan and Rizhao City of Shandong is held in Puyang. October 19, 2011, Henan and Shandong provincial governments sign an agreement concerning the cooperation in tourism; the two sides will carry out in-depth cooperation in information sharing, marketing, product development, etc. September 8, 2012, the shipbuilding enterprises of Henan and Shandong Provinces hold a strategic cooperation conference. Both sides reach a consensus on technology sharing, capital and operation, and sign a cooperation agreement.

Henan-Shanghai

[Quick Facts] Average distance = 998 km; Geographical adjacency = 0; Index of ethnic linkages = 0.9924 (2000) and 0.9930 (2010); Freight exchange via national railway = 1740 k tons (2000) and 1650 k tons (2010). ★ July 15, 2009, the Wangwang Group of Shanghai and the Anyang High-tech Zone of Henan sign a cooperation agreement in beverage project. July 13, 2010, the "Meeting of Henan-Shanghai Economic and Technology Cooperation and Tourist Projects Promotion" is held in Shanghai. The Henan delegation releases 1150 investment projects (with a total investment of 756 billion yuan), of which 80 projects are signed, with a total investment of 23.95 billion yuan. May 31, 2011, the "Henan-Shanghai Economic Cooperation Fair" is held in Henan. The two sides agree to cooperate in 130 projects, with a total investment of over 700 billion yuan. June 14, 2011, Henan University and Shanghai Institute of Plant Physiology and Ecology sign an agreement concerning cooperation in personnel training and part-time professor protocol. September 5, 2012, the "Henan (Shanghai) Economic Cooperation Forum", organized by the government of Henan Province, is held in the Pudong New District of Shanghai. Both sides agree to 14 joint and cooperative projects (with a total investment of 8.708 billion yuan), including nine projects in advanced manufacturing (5.798 billion yuan), one project in modern agricultural (150 million yuan), two projects in modern service (2.06 billion yuan), one project in new energy materials (500 million yuan), and one project in biomedicine (200 million yuan). September 19, 2012, Shanghai Advanced Research Institute of CAS signs a strategic cooperation agreement with Kaifeng municipal government of and the Coal Heavy Equipment Co., Ltd. of Henan Province. September 24–26, 2012, the "2012 Henan Industrial Undertaking and Technological Transfer" fair, which is organized by Henan Province, is held in Shanghai.

Henan-Shanxi

[Quick Facts] Average distance = 577 km; Geographical adjacency = 1; Index of ethnic linkages = 0.9905 (2000) and 0.9906 (2010); Freight exchange via national railway = 8880 k tons (2000) and 26,680 k tons (2010). ★ May 29, 2005, the Henan Chamber of Commerce in Shanxi is established in Taiyuan City. October 10, 2006,

Henan and Shanxi Provinces sign a cooperation agreement, aiming to strengthen exchange and cooperation. February 1, 2010, Sanmenxia City of Henan and Yuncheng City of Shanxi establish an interprovincial mechanism for joint enforcement and coordination in regional business. August 19, 2010, the signing ceremony of a coal chemical project between the Industry Group of Henan and Shanxi University is held in Zhengzhou. October 29, 2010, the Changzhi (Shanxi) Chamber of Commerce in Henan and Pingshun County of Shanxi Province sign a cooperative agreement in the development of tourist products and the processing of agricultural and sideline products. July 7, 2011, the DRC of Luoyang City of Henan Province visits Jincheng City of Shanxi to discuss the joint development and utilization of coal-bed methane. July 21, 2011, the Lantian Group of Henan, China Petroleum Sales Co., Ltd. and the Huadun Industrial Co., Ltd. of Shanxi sign a cooperation agreement. October 15–17, 2011, a delegation, led by the Secretary of Jiyuan Municipal CCP Committee of Henan Province, visits Yuncheng, Changzhi and Jincheng Cities of Shanxi Province. The delegation signs a strategic cooperation framework agreements with the three cities. April 6, 2012, the government of Shangqiu City of Henan Province and the Shanxi Institute of Coal and Chemistry of CAS, sign a strategic cooperation agreement. May 7, 2012, the "Shanxi-Henan Economic and Social Development Forum" is held in Zhengzhou City. May 8, 2012, the "2012 Shanxi-Henan Economic and Trade Cooperation Promotion" is held in Zhengzhou. June 11, 2012, the Coking Coal Group of Shanxi and the Shuanghui Group of Henan sign a cooperation agreement.

Henan-Sichuan

[Quick Facts] Average distance = 1353 km; Geographical adjacency = 0; Index of ethnic linkages = 0.9525 (2000) and 0.9414 (2010); Freight exchange via national railway = 2720 k tons (2000) and 6030 k tons (2010). ★ June 1, 2006, the State Investment Property Rights Exchange of Sichuan and the Geology and Mineral Resources Bureau of Henan sign a strategic cooperation agreement. October 19, 2008, more than 100 representatives of Henan's enterprises visit Sichuan Province to participate in the investment seminar concerning the reconstruction of the Wenchuan earthquake-hit area. June 21, 2009, the Henan Chamber of Commerce in Sichuan is established in Chengdu City. August 26, 2010, the "Sichuan-Henan Industrial Cooperation Forum" is held in Zhengzhou. 16 large enterprises from Henan have in-depth discussions and sign cooperation agreements with the Commerce Department of Sichuan Province and the Nanchong municipal government of Sichuan Province, respectively. January 7, 2011, the Henan Tobacco Company and the Tobacco Bureau of Sichuan Province sign a strategic cooperation framework agreement concerning the joint construction of a brand-oriented and high-quality tobacco base in the 12th Five-Year Plan. September 14, 2011, a delegation, led by the deputy CCP secretary of Sichuan Province, visits Henan. The delegation acknowledges Henan's supports during the period of the Wenchuan

Earthquake, and exchanges the experiences of scientific development in Henan. This activity aims to promote bilateral cooperation.

Henan-Tianjin

[Quick Facts] Average distance = 831 km; Geographical adjacency = 0; Index of ethnic linkages = 0.9854 (2000) and 0.9863 (2010); Freight exchange via national railway = 950 k tons (2000) and 1290 k tons (2010). ★ February 16, 2006, the Henan Chamber of Commerce in Tianjin is established. From the mid-1970s, Henan's workers and investors living in Tianjin have reached more than 100,000. June 26, 2009, the "Henan-Tianjin Forum for Economic and Technological Cooperation" is held in Tianjin. The Shangzhang Village reconstruction project of Weidong District (Tianjin) is taken over by the Yuji Real Estate Development Co., Ltd. of Henan. The project covers a land area of 4.8 sq km, with an investment of 500 million yuan. May 5, 2010, the IQBs of Tianjin and Henan sign a memorandum of cooperation concerning the direct passing of Henan's exported goods in the Tianjin Port. March 1, 2012, the Geology and Mineral Resources Bureau of Henan and the Shengyao Equity Investment Fund Management Co., Ltd. of Tianjin sign an agreement in Zhongmu County of Henan. Under the agreement, the Shengyao will provide 200 million yuan per year to the Yukuang Company of Henan for a period of five years. May 21–26, 2012, Tianjin and Kaifeng City of Henan hold the "Second China (Yellow River-Binhai) Economic Development and Cooperation Forum". May 26, 2012, Tianjin and Henan hold a forum in Zhengzhou City, and sign a memorandum of cooperation. The two sides decide to jointly promote the construction of the "Tianjin Logistics Center in Central China". March 30, 2012, Changge City of Henan Province and the Stock Right Exchange of Tianjin sign a cooperation framework agreement concerning the promotion of small and middle enterprises. September 13, 2012, the Human Resources and Social Security Bureaux of Binhai New Area (Tianjin) and of Anyang City sign a human resource cooperation framework agreement; the Tianjin Port Group and Yindu District Government of Anyang City (Henan) sign the "Anyang Dry Port Project Cooperation Agreement".

Henan-Tibet

[Quick Facts] Average distance = 3375 km; Geographical adjacency = 0; Index of ethnic linkages = 0.0648 (2000) and 0.0867 (2010); Freight exchange via national railway = 0 k ton (2000) and 280 k tons (2010). ★ May 14, 2004, Henan Province and Tibet Autonomous Region sign a cooperation agreement concerning the conservation of cultural heritages. September 28, 2011, the Grains and Foods Bureaux of Xinxiang City of Henan Province and Lhasa City of Tibet sign a purchase and sale agreement. September 1, 2004, a new class of Tibetan students enters the No. 4 High School of Zhengzhou City (Note: one author of this book was the honor of being their classmate). This is part of China's long-term pairing aid program in which Henan Province offers free education for Tibetan students. December 2, 2008, as part of the State Grid's task, the Power Co. Ltd. of Henan sends technical staff to serve for one and a half years in the affiliated units of the Tibet Power Co., Ltd. July 25, 2012, a delegation of Henan University of Agriculture visits the Science and Technology Department of Tibet Autonomous Region. August 8, 2011, the Henan Academy of Geological Survey conducts a joint exploration with its Tibetan pairing and finds a large-size lead-zinc mine and a medium-size silver mine in Goma of Lhari County of Tibet; the estimated reserves are 524,100 tons (lead ore), 107,000 tons (zinc ore), 710.33 tons (silver ore), and 38,600 tons (copper ore), whose average deposit grades are Pb7.48 % Zn1.53 %, Ag101.44 × 10, and Cu0.55 %, respectively.

Henan-Xinjiang

[Quick Facts] Average distance = 3079 km; Geographical adjacency = 0; Index of ethnic linkages = 0.4182 (2000) and 0.4167 (2010); Freight exchange via national railway = 3080 k tons (2000) and 5220 k tons (2010). ★ August 29, 2005, the Henan Federation of Enterprises in Xinjiang is established. The Federation has 225 enterprise and 628 individual members. August 8, 2007, the Coal Chemical Industry Corporation of Henan and the Tianfu Company of Xinjiang jointly develop a salt and coal chemical project. March 22, 2011, Erqi District of Zhengzhou City and Hami City of Xinjiang establish pairing aid partnerships. July 8, 2011, Ruoqiang County of Xinjiang and Xinzheng City of Henan sign a cooperation framework agreement concerning the establishment of a high-tech agricultural demonstration park. July 11, 2011, the CCP committee and government of Xinjiang and Henan provincial government pledge to speed up bilateral cooperation. July 11–15, 2011, a delegation, led by the governor of Henan Province, visits Urumqi City, Ili Kazak Autonomous Prefecture, and Hami City of Xinjiang and the No. 13 Division of the XPCC and sign a strategic energy cooperation agreement. April 9, 2012, the Henan Coal Chemical Group Xinjiang Branch signs a coal mining cooperation framework agreement with the government of Kizilsu Kirgiz Autonomous Prefecture of Xinjiang. July 17, 2012, the Xinjiang and Henan Branches of the Bank of China sign a strategic cooperation agreement with Henan's enterprises involved in the aid programs to Xinjiang. March 28, 2012, the tourist promotion of Xinjiang Uygur Autonomous Region is held in Zhengzhou. The Tourist Bureaux of Henan and Xinjiang sign a cooperation framework agreement on the joint launching of the "10,000 People Tour Xinjiang" activity. September 25, 2012, Henan Province and the No. 13 Division of the XPCC sign 33 cooperation agreements on coal, wind power, chemical industry and machinery manufacturing, with a total investment of 10.4 billion yuan.

Henan-Yunnan

[Quick Facts] Average distance = 2489 km; Geographical adjacency = 0; Index of ethnic linkages = 0.6776 (2000) and 0.6775 (2010); Freight exchange via national railway = 1010 k tons (2000) and 2020 k tons (2010). ★ August 25, 2007, the Henan Chamber of Commerce in Yunnan is established in Kunming City. Since the introduction of reform and opening up in the early 1980s, Yunnan has received more than 2000 large enterprises from Henan, with a total investment of more than 10 billion yuan, mainly engaged in real estate, finance, construction, heavy machinery and jewelry industry; the number of Henan people working in Yunnan reaches more than 300,000. October 8, 2008, the General Manager of the China (Henan) Tobacco Company visits the China (Yunnan) Tobacco Company. September 30, 2009, the "2009 Yunnan-Henan Ethnic Specialties (Cultural, Tourist, Agricultural Products and Food) Exhibition" is held in the Central China International Exhibition Center of Zhengzhou City. The five-day long exhibition provides, in addition to those for other provinces, 600 and 200 rooms for Yunnan and Henan's enterprises, respectively. January 21, 2010, the Tourism Bureaux of Henan and Yunnan jointly initiate a tourism cooperation alliance, aiming to promote regional economic development through bilateral cooperation. December 14–15, 2010, the Huatai Company of Henan and the No. 4 Construction Company of Yunnan sign a cooperation agreement on the joint R&D of "concreted foam bricks" technology. October 14, 2011, the China (Yunnan) Tobacco Company and the China (Henan) Tobacco Company hold a forum in Yunnan; the two sides have an in-depth exchange, aiming to increase cooperation and promote common development.

Henan-Zhejiang

[Quick Facts] Average distance = 1124 km; Geographical adjacency = 0; Index of ethnic linkages = 0.9885 (2000) and 0.9793 (2010); Freight exchange via national railway = 2840 k tons (2000) and 2580 k tons (2010). ★ May 28, 2004, the Zhejiang Chamber of Commerce in Henan is established in Zhengzhou City. The Chamber has nearly 2000 member enterprises, engaged in real estate, high-tech industries, home appliances, telecommunications, optical, chemical, textile, furniture manufacturing, commercial service, etc. December 6, 2005, the "Henan-Zhejiang Economic and Technological Cooperation Fair", hosted by the government of Henan Province, is held in Hangzhou City; agreements on 39 cooperative projects are signed, involving real estate, machinery and electronics, logistics, petrochemicals, education, agriculture, tourism and others. August 13, 2009, the "Henan-Zhejiang Trade and Economic Cooperation Fair" is held in Hangzhou. Both sides sign seven agreements, with a total investment of 4.268 billion yuan. September 16, 2009, the inaugural meeting of the Henan Chamber of Commerce in

Zhejiang is held in Hangzhou City. The Chamber has more than 200 member companies, covering textile, chemical, pharmaceutics, building, machinery and electronics, food and beverage, building materials, trade, etc. March 23, 2011, Shangqiu and Zhoukou Cities of Henan and Cixi City of Zhejiang hold a school-enterprise labor cooperation fair. 61 key enterprises from Cixi City and 66 vocational and technical schools from Shangqiu and Zhoukou sign 272 school-enterprise agreements. June 27, 2011, the Henan Investment Group and Zhejiang University sign, in Zhengzhou City, a strategic cooperation agreement. March 19, 2012, the "Kaifeng Economic and Technological Cooperation Projects" fair is held in Shaoxing City of Zhejiang. The Kaifeng municipal government of Henan and the Zhejiang Chamber of Commerce in Henan sign an investment agreement. September 26, 2012, a delegation of the Zhejiang Chamber of Commerce of Returned Overseas Chinese visits Luoyang City of Henan Province to seek cooperation opportunities.

Hubei-Hunan

[Quick Facts] Average distance = 358 km; Geographical adjacency = 1; Index of ethnic linkages = 0.9422 (2000) and 0.9431 (2010); Freight exchange via national railway = 420 k tons (2000) and 6040 k tons (2010). ★ December 6, 2010, the public security organs of Hunan and Hubei sign a joint conference charter on police cooperation, a cooperation framework and a police cooperation agreement in 2010–2011. February 10, 2012, Hunan and Hubei governments sign a strategic cooperation framework agreement concerning the construction of the city cluster in the middle reaches of the Yangtze River. May 4, 2012, the agricultural sectors of Hunan and Hubei provinces sign, in Wuhan City, an agricultural cooperation agreement. May 24, 2012, a delegation of the Supply and Marketing Cooperatives of Hunan, led by the CCP Secretary of Hunan Province, visits Hubei. May 31, 2012, Linxiang City of Hunan and Chibi City of Hubei sign a regional cooperation framework agreement. July 4, 2012, Hubei and Hunan sign, in Wuhan, a strategic framework agreement concerning the interregional cooperation in intellectual property rights. July 27, 2012, Hunan and Hubei Provincial Departments of Culture sign a strategic cooperation framework agreement of cultural development, and jointly announce the plan of cultural events during 2012 to 2013. August 22, 2012, the Educational Departments of Hunan and Hubei Provinces, on behalf of their respective provinces, sign, in Wuhan City, an education cooperation agreement, aiming to enhance innovative capabilities. September 20, 2012, Hunan and Hubei sign a strategic cooperation framework agreement in the administration of industry and commerce.

Hubei-Inner Mongolia

[Quick Facts] Average distance = 1898 km; Geographical adjacency = 0; Index of ethnic linkages = 0.7940 (2000) and 0.7977 (2010); Freight exchange via national railway = 520 k tons (2000) and 130 k tons (2010). ★ January 2012, Inner Mongolia signs an agreement with Jingzhou and Xiangyang City of Hubei. Both sides will jointly develop the Datongdao Coal Power Station, aiming to further strengthen the coal transportation from North to South China. May 2012, the governments of Inner Mongolia and Suizhou City of Hubei sign an agreement concerning the investment of coal power station which links the coal transportation between North and South China. July 2012, the Governments of Inner Mongolia and Huanggang City of Hubei sign a strategic cooperation framework agreement; the two sides will cooperate in natural gas development. August 17, 2012, a delegation, led by the Deputy CCP Secretary of and the Vice Governor of Hubei Province, visits Hohhot City of Inner Mongolia Autonomous Region. Both sides discuss issues of bilateral strategic cooperation and sign a regional energy cooperation agreement. The Energy Office of Hubei Province and the Hubei Energy Group sign a memorandum of cooperation in energy projects and the Haolaisu mine exploration framework agreement with the Energy Bureau of Inner Mongolia Autonomous Region and the Geological Prospecting Fund Center of Inner Mongolia, respectively. September 14–15, 2012, a delegation, led by the Chairman of Hubei Provincial PPCC, visits Inner Mongolia Autonomous Region. The delegation inspects the demonstration zone which is jointly developed by Wuhan and Inner Mongolia.

Hubei-Jiangsu

[Quick Facts] Average distance = 1231 km; Geographical adjacency = 0; Index of ethnic linkages = 0.9591 (2000) and 0.9604 (2010); Freight exchange via national railway = 1120 k tons (2000) and 1820 k tons (2010). ★ August 22–24, 2011, a delegation, led by the CCP Secretary, the PCSC Chairman and the Governor of Hubei Province, visits Jiangsu Province; the two sides sign an agreement concerning the strengthening of cooperation in key areas; the agreement includes: (1) establishing an extensive cooperation mechanism; (2) strengthening the exchange and cooperation between enterprises; (3) establishing an information-sharing platform; (4) deepening cooperation in the field of agriculture; (5) strengthening pairing support of the Three Gorges Reservoir Area; (6) strengthening the cooperation in science and education; (7) promoting the attaching mechanism of government cadres in different places. December 13, 2011, Wujin City of Jiangsu and the universities and colleges from Hubei Province hold a school-enterprise human resource cooperation meeting in Wuhan City. April 17, 2012, Zaoyang City of Hubei Province and Yandu District of Yancheng City (Jiangsu Province) carry out school-enterprise and school-local government cooperation. June 14–15, 2012, a delegation, led by the Supply and Marketing Cooperatives of Hubei Province and the Hubei Yinfeng Group, visits Huaxi Group Company of Jiangsu. The Yinfeng and the Huaxi sign a cooperation framework agreement; both sides will cooperate in the marketing of agricultural products. July 26, 2012, the Huaxi Group Company of Jiangsu, the Supply and Marketing Cooperatives of Hubei Province and Shiyan City of Hubei Province sign a cooperative agreement of China (Northwest Hubei) International Agricultural Mall, with a total planned investment of 50 billion.

Hubei-Jiangxi

[Quick Facts] Average distance = 391 km; Geographical adjacency = 1; Index of ethnic linkages = 0.9575 (2000) and 0.9582 (2010); Freight exchange via national railway = 2020 k tons (2000) and 350 k tons (2010). ★ September 22, 2011, the Datang Group Jiangxi Branch sign two agreements concerning the utilization and development of stone-and soft-coal and the wind power generation project with Enshi municipal government of Hubei and the Yunxi prefectural government, respectively. February 10, 2012, the Jiangxi and Hubei governments sign a strategic cooperation framework agreement concerning the construction of city cluster in the middle reaches of the Yangtze River. February 14–15, 2012, the Department of Commerce of Jiangxi Province and the Port Administration Office of Hubei Province hold, in Wuhan City, a forum concerning the joint promotion of port cooperation between the two provinces. April 18, 2012, Jiujiang City of Jiangxi Province signs a regional cooperation framework agreement with Yueyang and Xianning Cities of Hubei Province; the tourist sectors of Jiujiang also sign a regional cooperation agreement with the two cities. April 30, 2012, Wuhan University and Jiangxi provincial government sign a comprehensive cooperation agreement. May 4, 2012, the agricultural sectors of Jiangxi and Hubei Provinces sign, in Wuhan, a cooperation agreement. July 4, 2012, Hubei and Jiangxi sign, in Wuhan, a strategic framework agreement concerning the intellectual property cooperation of city cluster in middle reaches of the Yangtze River, aiming to jointly push forward the interregional cooperation of intellectual property rights. July 27, 2012, Jiangxi and Hubei Provincial Departments of Culture sign a strategic cooperation framework agreement in cultural development, and jointly announce a plan of cultural events during 2012 and 2013. August 22, 2012, Jiangxi and Hubei Provinces sign, in Wuhan City, an agreement, aiming to promote the exchange and cooperation in education. September 20, 2012, Hunan and Hubei sign a strategic cooperation framework agreement in the administration of industry and commerce.

Hubei-Jilin

[Quick Facts] Average distance = 2277 km; Geographical adjacency = 0; Index of ethnic linkages = 0.9106 (2000) and 0.9224 (2010); Freight exchange via national railway = 350 k tons (2000) and 970 k tons (2010). ★ June 10, 2006, the Police Department of Shiyan City of Hubei decides to cooperate with the Public Security Bureau of Jilin Province concerning the joint investigation into and actions against criminal activities in Jilin City of Jilin Province. September 1, 2009, in the Northeast Asia Expo, Hubei and Jilin jointly hold an investment seminar. The two sides sign three economic cooperation agreements. Shiyan and Wuhan Cities of Hubei Province establish, with Changchun and Shiping Cities of Jilin, respectively, a sister city relationship and sign cooperative agreements. June 11, 2011, the Hubei branch of Jilin University Alumni Association holds its inaugural meeting in Wuhan City. September 2, 2010, a Jilin delegation attends the 6th China (Hubei) Cooperative Project Fair. October 25, 2011, the Jointown Pharmaceutical Company of Hubei Province and the Difu Pharmaceutical Industry Co., Ltd. of Tonghua City of Jilin sign a cooperation agreement. Under the agreement, the two sides will establish a joint venture, with registered capital of 100 million yuan (of which the Jointown and Difu account for 51 and 49 %, respectively). The Jointown will set up a branch in Tonghua City.

Hubei-Liaoning

[Quick Facts] Average distance = 1972 km; Geographical adjacency = 0; Index of ethnic linkages = 0.8416 (2000) and 0.8504 (2010); Freight exchange via national railway = 750 k tons (2000) and 1090 k tons (2010). ★ December 18, 2008, the China (Liaoyang City of Liaoning) Tobacco Company and the China (Hubei) Tobacco Company hold, in Liaoyang City, a signing ceremony of marketing strategic cooperation agreement. January 23, 2010, the Hubei Chamber of Commerce in Liaoning holds, in Shenyang City, its annual meeting; the establishing ceremony of the Hubei Investment Management Ltd. of Liaoning Province is also held. July 22, 2011, the Secretary General of the Northeast China Federation of Enterprises in Hubei Province holds a forum with the Liaoning provincial government. August 12, 2011, the Northeast China Enterprise Federation in Hubei Province holds a forum for its members. September 22–24, 2012, a delegation, led by the general manager and deputy general manager of the China (Hubei) Grain Reserve Management Company, visits the China (Liaoning) Grain Reserve Management Company and discuss the matter of corn production and marketing collaboration with relevant sub-companies under the Liaoning Company. The two sides sign a corn production and marketing agreement, aiming to integrate regional resources and to promote the common development of the two places.

Hubei-Ningxia

[Quick Facts] Average distance = 1893 km; Geographical adjacency = 0; Index of ethnic linkages = 0.6567 (2000) and 0.6511 (2010); Freight exchange via national railway = 280 k tons (2000) and 420 k tons (2010). ★ September 28, 2008, in the "Ningxia Economic and Trade Fair", Hubei Province and the Ningxia Hui Autonomous Region sign an agreement on the further strengthening of economic cooperation. Under the agreement, the two provinces will create conditions for their enterprises to cooperate. The two places will also strengthen cooperation in agriculture and labor, promoting the sharing of information and new technological achievements. October 20–25, 2009, a delegation, led by the CCP Deputy Secretary and the Vice Chairman of Ningxia Hui Autonomous Region, visits Hubei to inspect the development of modern agriculture. Both sides pledge to enhance cooperation. May 9, 2011, the AQTSs of Ningxia and Hubei jointly purchase an aircraft (Model DA-40). March 1, 2012, Hubei University and Ningxia Normal College sign, in Wuhan City, a comprehensive cooperation framework agreement. August 10, 2012, the CCP Committee and Discipline Committee of Ningxia Hui Autonomous Region meet, in Yinchuan City of Ningxia, the PCSC Chairman of Hubei Province. November 7, 2012, a delegation of the Tenglong Seeds Co. Ltd. of Hubei visits the Ketai Seeds Co. Ltd. of Ningxia. Both sides sign, in Yinchuan City of Ningxia, a strategic cooperation agreement.

Hubei-Qinghai

[Quick Facts] Average distance = 1939 km; Geographical adjacency = 0; Index of ethnic linkages = 0.5428 (2000) and 0.5329 (2010); Freight exchange via national railway = 140 k tons (2000) and 1610 k tons (2010). ★ July 19, 2005, in the Qinghai Investment and Trade Fair, Hubei and Qinghai sign an agreement concerning the further strengthening of economic and technological cooperation. May 5, 2009, the signing ceremony of the Hubei-Qinghai Economic Cooperation and the inaugural meeting of the Hubei Chamber of Commerce in Qinghai are held in Xining City. The two provinces sign 40 economic cooperation agreements, involving industry, agriculture, urban construction, tourism and others, with a total investment of 3.26 billion yuan (of which Hubei and Qinghai provide 560 million and 540 million yuan, respectively). May 10, 2009, the Qinghai Huading Heavy Machine Tool Company, the Qinghai New Energy Group Company, the Western Mining Co., Ltd. and the Qinghai Geological Survey Institute, led by the Qinghai Provincial Science and Technology Department, visit Hubei to seek support and cooperation opportunities. December 27, 2009, the Hubei Chamber of Commerce in Qinghai publishes a work report. Qinghai has more than 1000 registered enterprises from Hubei, with a total registered capital of nearly 5 billion yuan and an annual output value of more than 80 billion yuan, creating more than 30,000 jobs. The Chamber's members engaged in auto and auto parts sales, real estate development, mineral resources development, construction, energy, environmental protection, telecommunications, machinery, general merchandise, building materials, etc. June 10, 2012, in the Qinghai Investment and Trade Fair, Hubei and Qinghai hold an investment cooperation forum. The two sides sign the "Agreement Concerning the Promotion of Investment Cooperation between the two Provinces".

Hubei-Shaanxi

[Quick Facts] Average distance = 1047 km; Geographical adjacency = 1; Index of ethnic linkages = 0.9584 (2000) and 0.9591 (2010); Freight exchange via national railway = 3590 k tons (2000) and 12,070 k tons (2010). ★ December 2001, the police stations of Shaanxi, Hubei and other places establish, in Shangnan County of Shaanxi, a collaborative defense mechanism, aiming to supervise and manage the disordered boundary regions including Shangnan, Shanyang and Danfeng Counties of Shaanxi Province and Yunxi and Yun Counties of Hubei Province. December 2002, the public security departments of Shaanxi and Hubei sign an agreement of collaborative action. April 5, 2008, the Hubei Chamber of Commerce in Shaanxi is established in Xi'an City. The Chamber has 371 enterprise members, mainly engaged in real estate development, construction, energy development and investment, building materials, IT industry, business logistics, catering, and garment industry. July 30, 2009, the Shaanxi Coal Chemical Group sign, in Wuhan City, a strategic cooperation agreement with the Coal Investment and Development Co., Ltd. of and the Yichang Port Group of Hubei Province. October 28, 2010, Ankang City of Shaanxi and the Shiyan Tobacco Company of Hubei Province hold a symposium concerning the strengthening of cross-border cooperation. December 10, 2010, the Hubei Energy Group signs a strategic cooperation agreement with the Shaanxi Coal Chemical Industry Group. Under the agreement, the Shaanxi Group will supply annually one to five million tons of coal to the Ezhou Power Plant of the Hubei Energy Group. March 31, 2011, the Fruits Bureau of Hubei Province and Huazhong Agricultural University sign, in Wuhan, two agreements, aiming to strengthen personnel training and technological cooperation in citrus industry. June 21–23, 2011, a delegation, led by the CCP Secretary (also the PCSC Chairman) and the Governor of Hubei Province, visits Shaanxi Province. The two sides sign a strategic cooperation framework agreement, covering tourism, energy, rail transportation, water conservancy, etc.

Hubei-Shandong

[Quick Facts] Average distance = 1202 km; Geographical adjacency = 0; Index of ethnic linkages = 0.9585 (2000) and 0.9590 (2010); Freight exchange via national railway = 2910 k tons (2000) and 6620 k tons (2010). ★ February 28 to March 6, 2003, an agricultural delegation, led by the Vice Governor of Hubei Province, visits Shandong Province. The Xinya Food Co., Ltd. of Weifang City of Shandong signs a cooperation agreement concerning the agricultural products processing with the delegation. The two sides agree to transport 2000 tons lotus root, 3000 tons carrots and an unlimited number of stalks stems to the Weifang Company to process and export. June 19, 2010, the China (Shandong) Tobacco Company and the China (Hubei) Tobacco Company hold, in Ji'nan City, a cooperation and development forum. December 3, 2010, a delegation of Hubei University of Technology signs a school-enterprise agreement concerning the cooperation in technology and personnel training with the Shengtai Pharmaceutical Co., Ltd. of Weifang City, Shandong. April 9, 2011, the Hubei Chamber of Commerce in Shandong is established in Ji'nan City. According to incomplete statistics, Shandong has nearly 300,000 people from and more than 8000 enterprises from Hubei, involving logistics, IT, real estate, machinery manufacturing, chemical industry, building materials, construction, medicine, media, trade, automotive, aquaculture, biological research, hotel, communications, food, clothing, collectibles and others, with a total investment of 15 billion yuan, total assets of over 18 billion yuan and an annual output value of over 50 billion yuan, providing 600,000 jobs and about 1.5 billion yuan taxes to Shandong. May 24, 2011, the China (Ji'nan) International Trade Promotion Committee and the Shandong Chamber of Commerce in Hubei hold a forum. March 20–21, 2012, the Chairman and General Manager of the Hubei Seed Group visit the Runfeng Seed Industry Co., Ltd. of Shandong. The two sides hold, in Jinxiang County, a forum and sign a science and technology cooperation agreement in cotton.

Hubei-Shanghai

[Quick Facts] Average distance = 1230 km; Geographical adjacency = 0; Index of ethnic linkages = 0.9593 (2000) and 0.9625 (2010); Freight exchange via national railway = 490 k tons (2000) and 430 k tons (2010). ★ May 20, 2006, the Hubei Chamber of Commerce in Shanghai is established. The Chamber has 280 member companies, involving electronic technology, building materials, real estate, catering and entertainment, health care, finance and securities, culture, education, legal advice and logistics and transportation, etc. December 25, 2007, the Shanghai Chamber of Commerce in Hubei is established in Wuhan City. March 12, 2010, a delegation of the Shanghai municipal government visits Enshi Tujia Autonomous Prefecture of Hubei to participate in a promotion meeting. Yichang and Wanzhou Counties are the pairing aid targets of Shanghai. Shanghai decides to develop the tourist opportunities in Enshi, aiming to drive the common economic development. February 14, 2011, the Hubei Coal Geological Bureau meets, in Shanghai, the General Manager of the Overseas Corporation of the Shanghai Construction Group. The two sides hope to strengthen cooperation in overseas mineral exploitation activities. August 20, 2011, Shiyan City of Hubei and the entrepreneurs from Shanghai hold a forum. Both sides agree to cooperate in energy and medicinal resources. December 15, 2011, Shanghai and Hubei hold, in Shanghai, an Economic Cooperation Project Fair. April 12, 2012, the Yan'an Pharmaceutical Company of Shanghai and the Chengtian Pharmaceutical Company of Hubei sign a cooperation agreement. The two sides will jointly invest 80 million yuan to develop a new project, with expected sales of 300 million. September 4, 2012, Yichang of Hubei and Shanghai hold, in Yichang, a signing ceremony of cooperation agreement, including four investment projects, with a total investment of 3.8 billion yuan.

Hubei-Shanxi

[Quick Facts] Average distance = 1179 km; Geographical adjacency = 0; Index of ethnic linkages = 0.9586 (2000) and 0.9589 (2010); Freight exchange via national railway = 8560 k tons (2000) and 20,630 k tons (2010). ★ April 30, 2010, the Shanxi Provincial Department of Civil Affairs formally approves the establishment of the Hubei Chamber of Commerce in Shanxi Province. September 9–11, 2008, a delegation, led by the CCP Secretary of the Hubei Province visits Taiyuan City of Shanxi Province. Both sides sign a framework agreement concerning the further strengthening of economic and technological cooperation, a higher education cooperation agreement, and a tourist cooperation agreement. The two sides hope to strengthen cooperation in energy, human resources, agriculture and tourism. September 26, 2011, the Hubei Energy Industry Cooperation Meeting is held in Taiyuan City of Shanxi. Hubei Province bring 129 major investment projects, involving electronic information, automobile parts, shipbuilding, agricultural products and other traditional pillar industrial projects, and new energy, new materials, environmental protection, software development and other emerging industrial projects, as well as long-term cooperation projects. September 7, 2012, a delegation, led by the CCP Secretary (also the Chairman) of the Shanxi Coal Group, visits the Sanning Company of Hubei. The two sides have an in-depth exchange in production and operation conditions, the construction of new projects, etc.

Hubei-Sichuan

[Quick Facts] Average distance = 1737 km; Geographical adjacency = 0; Index of ethnic linkages = 0.9543 (2000) and 0.9439 (2010); Freight exchange via national railway = 4110 k tons (2000) and 8110 k tons (2010). ★ May 18, 2006, the Sichuan Chamber of Commerce in Hubei is established in Wuhan. October 8, 2008, a delegation, led by the Vice Governor of Sichuan Province, conducts a trip to Hubei Province to express the gratitude to Hubei people's help during the 5/12 Wenchuan earthquake period. October 9, 2008, the Sichuan provincial government holds an investment seminar of reconstruction for Ya'an City of Sichuan Province. The Tourism Bureau of Hubei Province and Ya'an City sign a cooperation agreement on tourism. July 19, 2009, the Hubei Chamber of Commerce in Sichuan is established. The Chamber has more than 300 member enterprises, involving real estate, auto parts, food and beverage, decoration and services. According to statistics, the number of Hubei's investors in Sichuan reaches over 200,000. September 5–6, 2011, a delegation, led by the CCP Secretary and the PCSC Chairman of Sichuan Province, visits Hubei Province to acknowledgement the reconstruction supports provided by Hubei. Both sides also hold, in Wuhan, an economic and social development forum. November 1, 2011, the China (Hubei) Tobacco Industry Company and the Sanyi Tobacco Co., Ltd. of Sichuan sign a cooperation project agreement. March 14, 2012, the Surveying and Mapping Bureaux of Hubei and Sichuan Provinces sign a strategic cooperation agreement. July 25, 2012, the Hongda Company of Sichuan pays an inspection to Xiangyang City of Hubei. The two sides pledge to cooperate in phosphate chemistry.

Hubei-Tianjin

[Quick Facts] Average distance = 1367 km; Geographical adjacency = 0; Index of ethnic linkages = 0.9591 (2000) and 0.9601 (2010); Freight exchange via national railway = 470 k tons (2000) and 460 k tons (2010). ★ December 29, 2008, approved by the Tianjin municipal government and Hubei provincial government, the Hubei Chamber of Commerce in Tianjin is established. The Chamber has 12,796 members (personal and corporate). March 26, 2009, Jingmen City of Hubei Province visits Tianjin to find investment opportunities in the Bohai Sea Region, and holds the Jingmen-Tianjin Trade Forum and the signing ceremony of cooperative projects. December 20, 2010, the Cement Industry Design and Research Institute of Tianjin and the Jinglan Cement Group Co., Ltd. of Hubei sign a package of strategic framework agreements. The two sides will cooperate in the procurement, warehousing, distribution and production line maintenance. March 17, 2011, the IQBs of Tianjin and Hubei sign, in Wuhan City, a memorandum of cooperation to implement direct border passing, aiming to improve the efficiency of customs clearance for imported and exported goods. September 2012, the Baodi Agricultural Science and Technology Co., Ltd. of Tianjin and Anlu City of Hubei Province sign a cooperation agreement concerning the building of a food industrial park, with a total investment of 10 billion yuan. September 17, 2011, Tianjin municipal officials visits Wuhan City of Hubei to participate in the 7th China (Hubei) Cooperative Project Fair.

Hubei-Tibet

[Quick Facts] Average distance = 3911 km; Geographical adjacency = 0; Index of ethnic linkages = 0.0628 (2000) and 0.0841 (2010); Freight exchange via national railway = 0 k ton (2000) and 70 k tons (2010). ★ March 19, 2007, the Yarra Xiangbu Industrial Co., Ltd. of Shannan Prefecture holds, in Wuhan, a products promotion meeting. January 17–18, 2010, a delegation, led by the Chief of the Shannan Prefectural Civil Affairs Bureau, visits Hubei. The two sides hope to enrich the aid and cooperation. The delegation also inspects the Jingmen, Xiangfan and Shiyan of Hubei. August 29, 2010, a delegation, led by the Hubei provincial CCP Secretary, visits Tibet to participate in the aiding-Tibet work meeting. The Shannan Prefectural Administrative Office and the Daye Nonferrous Investment Co., Ltd. of Hubei sign a cooperation agreement of large-scale industrial projects. November 28, 2011, the Daohuaxiang Group of Hubei signs investment agreements with Shannan Prefecture and Jiacha County of Tibet. The Hubei Group will invest 50 million yuan to build the Wencheng Wine Project in Tibet. May 30, 2012, the "2012 China (Tibet) Yarlung Culture Festival Promotion", organized by the Shannan Prefectural CCP Committee, Shannan Prefectural Administration Department, sponsored by Cultural Bureau and Tourist Bureau of Shannan Prefecture and co-organized by the Aiding-Tibet Office of Hubei Province, is held in Wuhan. July 30, 2012, a medical team of Hubei Province, composed of the Asian Heart Hospital and relevant staff of Hubei province, visits Nanshan Prefecture of Tibet to screen congenital heart diseases and give free treatments.

Hubei-Xinjiang

[Quick Facts] Average distance = 3615 km; Geographical adjacency = 0; Index of ethnic linkages = 0.4092 (2000) and 0.4083 (2010); Freight exchange via national railway = 980 k tons (2000) and 1630 k tons (2010). ★ June 2011, the Jinbo Seed Industry Center of the Fifth Agricultural Division of the XPCC becomes a pairing aid partnership of the Jingchu Seed Industry Co., Ltd. of Hubei. July 19–26, 2011, a number of Hubei based companies, led by the Deputy Secretary of Animal Husbandry and Veterinary Bureau CCP Committee, visit Xinjiang and sign a cooperation agreement in livestock investment. July 29, 2011, the Hubei Federation of Enterprises (Chamber of Commerce) is established in Urumqi City. The Chamber has 340 individual members and 147 enterprise members (of which 15 enterprises each have registered capital of 20 million yuan), involving energy, real estate, construction and others. September 1, 2011, at the 1st China-Asia-Europe Expo, Bortala Mongol Autonomous Prefecture of Xinjiang Uygur Autonomous Region and the Front Headquarters of Aiding-Xinjiang Team of Hubei Province hold a signing ceremony of cooperation projects. The two sides sign a total of 13 projects, with a total investment of over 50 billion yuan. December 13, 2011, the Supply and Marketing Cooperatives of Hubei Province and the Fifth Agricultural Division of the XPCC sign, in Wuhan City, a cooperation agreement of cotton industrialization. May 19, 2012, Xinjiang Branch of the CAS and the Headquarter of Aiding-Xinjiang Office of Hubei Province hold, in Bole City of Xinjiang, a cooperation forum. June 13, 2012, the Energy Group of Hubei signs an investment agreement with the Power Company of Fifth Agricultural Division of the XPCC. The two sides will carry out cooperation in wind power and coal production. July 13, 2012, the Intellectual Property Offices of Hubei and Bole City of Xinjiang hold a pairing aid cooperation forum.

Hubei-Yunnan

[Quick Facts] Average distance = 1953 km; Geographical adjacency = 0; Index of ethnic linkages = 0.6718 (2000) and 0.6718 (2010); Freight exchange via national railway = 790 k tons (2000) and 1410 k tons (2010). ★ July 24, 2004, the Hubei Chamber of Commerce in Yunnan is established. The Chamber has 700 members, engaged in flowers, cars and accessories, real estate, energy, construction materials, IT, petrochemical, agricultural and sideline products, medical and health, with total annual sales of 5 billion yuan, providing nearly 60,000 jobs. March 20, 2011, the Hubei Chamber of Commerce in Yunnan holds, in Kunming, the second meeting in which nearly 100 Hubei entrepreneurs working in Yunnan participate. April 15, 2011, the Yunnan Provincial Tobacco Monopoly Bureau (Company) and the Hubei Tobacco Industry Co., Ltd. sign, in Kunming City, a strategic cooperation framework agreement concerning the construction of high-quality tobacco bases. April 20, 2011, a delegation of the Wuhan Municipal Bureau of Commerce of Hubei visits the Yunnan Provincial Department of Commerce; the two sides have in-depth exchange in the mechanism of interprovincial labor exchange and other issues. March 30, 2012, the Hubei Seed Group Co., Ltd. and the Institute of Grains and Foods of Yunnan Academy of Agricultural Sciences establish a new seed company to develop maize, rice, wheat and other crops. In addition, the two sides also cooperate in the R&D of new seed resources.

Hubei-Zhejiang

[Quick Facts] Average distance = 1029 km; Geographical adjacency = 0; Index of ethnic linkages = 0.9602 (2000) and 0.9669 (2010); Freight exchange via national railway = 880 k tons (2000) and 1190 k tons (2010). ★ March 2006, the Zhejiang Federation of Enterprises in Hubei is established. According to incomplete statistics, there are 16,500 Zhejiang-funded enterprises and 460,000 Zhejiang businesspersons in Hubei, with a total investment of 500 billion yuan, involving industry, agriculture, energy, science and technology, medicine, education, real estate, construction, commerce, etc., providing 1.3 million jobs opportunities. March 10, 2010, the Laifeng County of Hubei and Beicang District of Ningbo City (Zhejiang) hold a labor collaborative employment fair; 16 enterprises sign employment contracts with 112 workers. The two provinces decide to further strengthen interprovincial labor cooperation. November 26, 2011, the China (Hubei) Tobacco Industry Company and the Zhejiang Tobacco Monopoly Bureau (Company) meet, in Hangzhou, and decide to establish strategic cooperative partnerships. April 23–25, 2012, a delegation, led by the CCP Secretary (also the PCSC Chairman) and the Governor of Hubei Province, visits Hangzhou. The two provinces hold an exchange meeting of economic and social development and sign a strategic cooperation framework agreement. The enterprises from Zhejiang and other places of Yangtze River Delta sign agreements with Hubei on 31 projects (with a total investment of 61.7 billion yuan). The projects cover agriculture, machinery and auto parts, green energy, environmental protection, textile, chemicals and pharmaceutics, modern service industry, tourism, etc. September 16, 2012, a delegation of the Zhejiang Federation of Enterprises in Hubei visits Dawu and Xiaogan Counties of Hubei. The three sides agree to strengthen cooperation.

Hunan-Inner Mongolia

[Quick Facts] Average distance = 2256 km; Geographical adjacency = 0; Index of ethnic linkages = 0.7943 (2000) and 0.7977 (2010); Freight exchange via national railway = 50 k tons (2000) and 1430 k tons (2010). ★ August 18, 2005, Xing'an League Administrative Office of Inner Mongolia and the Jinjian Rice Industry Co., Ltd. of Hunan sign a long-term rice supply cooperation framework agreement, aiming to promote the development of quality-rice production in Xing'an League. March 30, 2009, the Hunan Chamber of Commerce in Inner Mongolia is established in Hohhot City. According to incomplete statistics, there are more than 50,000 Hunan people living in and more than 1000 Hunan-funded enterprises (of which 10 have an avenge size of over ten million yuan) registered at Inner Mongolia, involving metals, chemicals, food and beverage, electronics technology, plastic and logistics, real estate, mining, environmental protection, etc. April 26, 2012, the Xilinhot municipal government of Inner Mongolia and the Changsha

Jingpeng Holdings Group Co., Ltd. of Hunan sign an agreement under which the company will invest 150 million yuan to build an organic cattles farm in Xilinhot. October 18, 2012, the "2012–2013 Strategic Conference of Economic Situation and Coal Purchase and Sales Meeting", organized by the China Coal Network and the China Coking Network, opens in Changsha City of Hunan. The Datang Fuel Development Co., Ltd. of Hunan and the Boyuan Coal Chemical Co., Ltd. of Inner Mongolia sign a long-term strategic cooperation agreement.

Hunan-Jiangsu

[Quick Facts] Average distance = 1200 km; Geographical adjacency = 0; Index of ethnic linkages = 0.9017 (2000) and 0.9040 (2010); Freight exchange via national railway = 100 k tons (2000) and 1580 k tons (2010). ★ March 26, 2008, the Jiangsu Chamber of Commerce in Hunan is established. The Chamber has more than 100 member companies, with nearly 10 billion yuan of total assets, involving new energy, mechanical and electrical hardware, real estate, vehicle manufacturing, environmental protection, mineral development, agricultural development, light industry, textile and others. July 3, 2008, a Hengyang (Hunan) municipal delegation visits Xuzhou City of Jiangsu Province. The two sides' tourism bureaux sign a cooperation agreement. March 11, 2010, Hunan Province holds a large-scale tourism promotion activity in Jiangsu Province. November 5, 2010, Changshu City of Jiangsu and Hunan University sign a cooperation agreement on development of human resources. April 1, 2011, the Hunan Chamber of Commerce in Jiangsu is established. There are more than 1836 Jiangsu-funded enterprises registered at and nearly 100,000 Jiangsu people living in Hunan. April 19–24, 2011, a delegation, led by the CCP Secretary and Governor of Hunan Province, pays an inspection to Nanjing, Suzhou, Kunshan, Wuxi and other places of Jiangsu and holds the "Hunan-Jiangsu Economic and Social Development Forum"; the two provinces sign 10 cooperative project agreements, with a total investment of nearly 30 billion yuan, involving trade and economy, science and technology, culture, etc. August 28–29, 2011, the Hunan Chamber of Commerce in Jiangsu signs a cooperation agreement with the Yueyang New Industrial District of Hunan. April 25, 2012, Longshan County of Hunan becomes the "Human Resources Cooperative Demonstration Base" of Kunshan City of Jiangsu Province. May 10, 2012, the Grain Administrations of Hunan and Jiangsu Provinces meet in Kunming City of Yunnan Province, aiming to establish a long-term, stable and smooth purchase and sales relations.

Hunan-Jiangxi

[Quick Facts] Average distance = 418 km; Geographical adjacency = 1; Index of ethnic linkages = 0.8999 (2000) and 0.9017 (2010); Freight exchange via national railway = 360 k tons (2000) and 9480 k tons (2010). ★ January 16, 2009, the Hunan Chamber of Commerce in Jiangxi is established in Nanchang City. According to incomplete statistics, Hunan's investors have established nearly 8000 enterprises in Jiangxi, involving metallurgy, mining, real estate, electronics technology, shipbuilding, photoelectric, natural gas, municipal services, logistics, chemical, metal, plastic, etc. December 26, 2009, the Jiangxi Chamber of Commerce in Hunan is established in Changsha City. According to incomplete statistics, there are 25,000 Jiangxi people working in Hunan; Jiangxi investors have funded thousands of firms in Hunan, with a total investment of more than 40 billion yuan, involving catering, real estate, manufacturing, building materials, medicine, etc. December 6, 2010, the public security organs of Jiangxi and Hunan Provinces establish a police cooperation mechanism. February 12, 2012, the governors of Jiangxi and Hubei Provinces sign a strategic cooperation framework agreement concerning the city cluster development in the Middle Reaches of the Yangtze River. April 9, 2012, a delegation, led by the CCP Secretary (also the PCSC Chairman) and the Governor of Hunan Province, visits Jiangxi Province; the two sides hold, in Nanchang City of Jiangxi, an economic and social cooperation and development meeting. Both sides pledge to strengthen cooperate in transportation infrastructure construction, tourist resource development, science and technology, cultural exchange and talent training. July 27, 2012, Hunan and Jiangxi Provinces sign a strategic cooperation agreement on cultural development. August 21, 2012, the Provincial Education Departments of Jiangxi and Hunan sign, in Wuhan, an agreement on educational cooperation, aiming to implement the strategic cooperation framework agreement on the city cluster development in the Middle Reaches of the Yangtze River.

Hunan-Jilin

[Quick Facts] Average distance = 2635 km; Geographical adjacency = 0; Index of ethnic linkages = 0.9011 (2000) and 0.9023 (2010); Freight exchange via national railway = 330 k tons (2000) and 1230 k tons (2010). ★ September 2, 2008, the "Hunan-Jilin Economic Cooperation Fair" and the inaugural ceremony of the Hunan Chamber of Commerce in Jilin are held in Changchun City. The Chamber has 87 member companies, involving real estate development, food and beverage service, automotive accessories, hardware and building materials, wine, medicine, etc. According to incomplete statistics, there are more than 80,000 Hunan people living or working in Jilin, mainly engaged in wholesale and retail trade, real estate development, auto parts, construction materials and pharmaceutical manufacturing.

December 29, 2009, the Chengcheng Group Co., Ltd. of Jilin and the Zhongde Real Estate Development Co., Ltd. of Hunan sign a cooperation agreement. August 7, 2010, the School of Chemical Technology of Hunan Normal University and Gongzhuling municipal government of Jilin Province agree to carry out cooperation. The two sides will jointly develop research and production project in bentonite. June 6–11, 2012, a delegation, led by the Director of Yangtze River Delta Office of Jilin Provincial Economic Cooperation Bureau, visits Hunan. The two sides hold, in Changsha City of Hunan Province, the "Changsha (Hunan)-Shuangliao (Jilin) Investment and Trade Promotion"; both sides sign an agreement on cooperative projects, with a total investment of 1.75 billion yuan.

Hunan-Liaoning

[Quick Facts] Average distance = 2330 km; Geographical adjacency = 0; Index of ethnic linkages = 0.8419 (2000) and 0.8504 (2010); Freight exchange via national railway = 730 k tons (2000) and 680 k tons (2010). ★ September 31, 2005, a delegation of Hunan Provincial PCSC visits the Experimental Middle School of Liaoning Province; both sides hold a forum in Shenyang City. December 18, 2009, the Liaoning Chamber of Commerce in Hunan is established. The Chamber's members are mainly engaged in real estate, machinery, electronics, hardware, building materials, food and beverage, food, pharmaceutics, logistics and technological industries. May 21, 2010, a delegation, led by the Chairman of the Xinde Holdings Group Co., Ltd. of Liaoning, visits Yongzhou City of Hunan Province to inspect the tourism and the Rich Mineral Paper (RMP) cooperative projects. April 22, 2012, the Human Resource and Social Security Department of Liaoning and the government of Hunan Province sign, in Changsha City, a memorandum of cooperation concerning the joint development of human resources and social security in Changsha, Zhuzhou and Xiangtan Cities. June 5, 2012, Liaoning University of Traditional Chinese Medicine and the Qingguo Software Co., Ltd. of Hunan sign a strategic cooperation agreement concerning the construction of information application system. Under the agreement, the two sides will jointly promote the technological and managerial innovations in educational informationization.

Hunan-Ningxia

[Quick Facts] Average distance = 2251 km; Geographical adjacency = 0; Index of ethnic linkages = 0.6570 (2000) and 0.6512 (2010); Freight exchange via national railway = 120 k tons (2000) and 290 k tons (2010). ★ October 18, 2003, the Hunan Chamber of Commerce in Ningxia is established in Yinchuan City. October 18,

2009, the Hunan Chamber of Commerce in Ningxia holds, in Yinchuan, its third assembly. 2009, the Hunan Chamber of Commerce in Ningxia welcomes a delegation composed of the Hunan provincial government and the Xiangxiang municipal government of Hunan Province; it also helps Xiangxiang and Zhuzhou Cities of Hunan Province and Qingtongxia and Shizuishan Cities of Ningxia to establish, respectively, friendly and brotherly partnerships. 2010, organized by the Hunan Chamber of Commerce in Ningxia, the enterprises in Ningxia donate 80,000 yuan of education fund to Xiangxiang City of Hunan. April 1, 2001, the Dongfang Tantalum Industry Co., Ltd. of Ningxia signs a cooperation agreement with the Chenzhou City of Hunan Province; the company will invest 200 million yuan to develop the tantalum-niobium ores resources in the Jianfengling area of Chenzhou City. May 15, 2011, the Hunan Provincial Bureau of Township Enterprises, holds in Yinchuan City of Ningxia Hui Autonomous Region, the "Ningxia Market Cooperation Fair", aiming to expand the market of Hunan's high-quality agricultural products in Ningxia.

Hunan-Qinghai

[Quick Facts] Average distance = 2297 km; Geographical adjacency = 0; Index of ethnic linkages = 0.5431 (2000) and 0.5330 (2010); Freight exchange via national railway = 220 k tons (2000) and 630 k tons (2010). ★ January 4, 2010, the Satellite TV Stations of Hunan and Qinghai Provinces hold, in Beijing, a signing ceremony of interprovincial cooperation agreement. April 1, 2010, a delegation, led by the CCP Secretary (also the Chief) of Qinghai Provincial AQTS, conducts a trip to Hunan Province to invite the Hunan provincial government to participate in the "2010 China (Qinghai) Green Investment and Trade Fair". June 9, 2010, the Hunan Chamber of Commerce in Qinghai is established in Xining City, Qinghai. The Chamber has 128 enterprise members, mainly engaged in mining and processing, real estate, construction engineering, building materials production, culture and entertainment, hotel and restaurant. August 4, 2011, the Hunan Chamber of Commerce in Qinghai donates stationery equipments (amounting to 185,050 yuan) to the Haibei Middle School of Qinghai Province. June 9–13, 2012, a delegation, led by the Deputy Chairman of Hunan Provincial PCSC, visits Xining City to participate in the "2012 China (Qinghai) Green Investment and Trade Fair", aiming to further expand and deepen Hunan's interprovincial cooperation (especially with western provinces); the two places' companies sign a total of 344 project agreements, with a total investment of 165.25 billion yuan. July 13–16, 2012, a delegation composed of 36 enterprises from Hunan visits Xining City of Qinghai Province to participate in the "2012 China (Qinghai) International Halal Foods and Supplies Exhibition", which is organized by the Qinghai provincial government.

Hunan-Shaanxi

[Quick Facts] Average distance = 1405 km; Geographical adjacency = 0; Index of ethnic linkages = 0.9009 (2000) and 0.9025 (2010); Freight exchange via national railway = 1070 k tons (2000) and 3080 k tons (2010). ★ April 2003, the Hunan Chamber of Commerce in Shaanxi is established in Xi'an City. Shaanxi has hosted more than 100,000 people from Hunan and thousands of Hunan-funded enterprises, mainly engaged in the fields of architectural decoration, machine manufacturing, electrics and electronics, pharmaceutics and chemistry, biotechnology, alcohol and tobacco tea and food catering. March 12, 2010, the governments of Shaanxi and Hunan Provinces sign, in Beijing, a framework agreement concerning the strengthening of energy strategic cooperation. Shaanxi will promote the electricity transportation from West to East China, aiming to ease the pressure of electricity demand in Hunan. July 2, 2010, the Shaanxi Provincial Tourism Promotion is held in Changsha City of Hunan. The Tourism Bureaux of Shaanxi and Hunan Province sign a cooperation agreement. April 5, 2011, the Catering Branch of the Hunan Chamber of Commerce in Shaanxi is established in Xi'an City. December 29, 2011, the Shaanxi Chamber of Commerce in Hunan is established in Changsha. There are over 100,000 Shaanxi people living in Hunan, establishing thousands of enterprises, with total assets of about 30 billion yuan, involving high-speed rail, construction machinery, manufacturing, highways, dining, culture, real estate, logistics, automotive, pharmaceutics, insurance, legal service, etc. September 17, 2012, a Shaanxi provincial delegation visits Changsha City and participates in the "Hunan Forum of Coal Transportation Situation", which is held by the Hunan Provincial Economic and Trade Commission. The two sides will promote the exchange of electric power enterprises between Hunan and Shaanxi and strengthen bilateral economic cooperation. September 26, 2012, the Hunan Broadcasting Group signs a strategic cooperation agreement with the Shaanxi TV Station.

Hunan-Shandong

[Quick Facts] Average distance = 1560 km; Geographical adjacency = 0; Index of ethnic linkages = 0.9011 (2000) and 0.9024 (2010); Freight exchange via national railway = 1160 k tons (2000) and 2640 k tons (2010). ★ April 28–29, 2008, a delegation, led by the CCP Secretary (also the President) of Zhongnan University of Hunan, visits Shandong Province; the two sides sign a comprehensive cooperation agreement. According to the agreement, both sides will cooperate in the fields of new materials, non-ferrous metals, recycling economy, bio-pharmaceutics, etc. April 1, 2009, a Hunan cultural delegation pays an inspection to Shandong and participates in the "Shandong-Hunan Forum of Cultural System Reform and Cultural Industrial Development". The two sides sign a bilateral cooperation agreement. February 12, 2010, the Hunan Chamber of Commerce in Shandong is established. The Chamber has more than 300 enterprise members. July 15, 2010, the Shandong Changlin Group signs the mortgage cooperation agreement with the Bank of Changsha. April 23–25, 2011, a delegation of the Shandong Provincial Tourism Bureau visits Hunan Province and signs a tourist cooperation agreement with Hunan. Shandong hopes to learn the development experiences of high-speed rail tourism in Hunan. May 31, 2011, the Dongjia Group of Shandong Province and the Rare Earth Technology Development Co., Ltd. of Hunan Province sign a cooperation agreement. June 8, 2011, the Shandong Chamber of Commerce in Hunan is established. The number of Shandong people living in Hunan is more than 100,000, founding more than 13,000 enterprises, and providing more than 500,000 jobs; the Chamber's enterprises are mainly distributed in agriculture, forestry, industry, real estate, construction and decoration industry, machinery manufacturing, IT industry, pharmaceutical industry, medical equipment industry, chemical industry and automobile manufacturing.

Hunan-Shanghai

[Quick Facts] Average distance = 1189 km; Geographical adjacency = 0; Index of ethnic linkages = 0.9021 (2000) and 0.9064 (2010); Freight exchange via national railway = 1130 k tons (2000) and 1070 k tons (2010). ★ November 13, 2008, Hunan signs a port customs clearance cooperation agreement with relevant sectors of Shanghai Port. April 14, 2009, a delegation, led by the Deputy CCP Secretary (also Mayor) of Shanghai Municipality, visits Changsha to participate in the "Hunan-Shanghai Exchange Meeting". December 3, 2009, a delegation, led by the Deputy Director of the Nuclear Division of the China Power Investment Corporation and the General Manager of the Hunan Nuclear Power Co., Ltd., pays an inspection to the Nuclear Engineering Research and Design Institute of Shanghai. The two sides sign the "Framework Agreement Concerning the Technological Supports and Services for the Nuclear Power Projects in the Xiaomo Mountain of Hunan Province", aiming to promote the nuclear power plant construction located in Dongshan Town of Huarong County (Hunan Province). January 10, 2011, Hunan University of Technology and the Caiyao New Energy Investment and Development Co., Ltd. of Shanghai jointly establish a New Energy R&D Center. September 16, 2011, the Deputy Secretary-General of the Buddhist Association of China meets, in Wanshou Temple (Yongzhou City of Hunan), a delegation which is led by the Deputy Director of the Shanghai Office of Government Exchange and Cooperation. December 28, 2011, the Hunan (Hengyang City) Chamber of Commerce in Shanghai is established. May 17, 2012, the signing ceremony of the Hunan-Shanghai economic cooperation project agreements and the inaugural ceremony of Shanghai Chamber of Commerce in Hunan are held in Changsha City. The Chamber signs three agreements with the Changde municipal government of and the Yiyang municipal government of Hunan and the Hunan Chamber of Commerce in Shanghai, respectively. The two places' companies sign 13 project agreements, with a total investment of 16.06 billion yuan.

Hunan-Shanxi

[Quick Facts] Average distance = 1537 km; Geographical adjacency = 0; Index of ethnic linkages = 0.9011 (2000) and 0.9023 (2010); Freight exchange via national railway = 250 k tons (2000) and 8770 k tons (2010). ★ September 18, 2008, in the "2nd China (Taiyuan) International Coal and New Energy Industry Expo", Shanxi and Hunan Provinces sign an inter-government economic cooperation framework agreement. The two sides will focus on cooperation in culture, coal and electricity and will establish a long-term and stable cooperative mechanism in the fields of equipment manufacturing industry, coal, and electricity. March 11, 2009, Shanxi and Hunan Provinces sign, in Beijing, a framework agreement concerning the strengthening of energy cooperation. The two sides will jointly promote the electricity transmission from Shanxi to Hunan. Shanxi will transmit 10 million kw to Hunan in the next 10 years. May 16, 2011, the "Shanxi-Hunan Energy Cooperation Forum" is held in Taiyuan City of Shanxi August 2, 2011, the Hunan Chamber of Commerce in Shanxi is established in Taiyuan City. According the incomplete statistic, Shanxi hosts nearly 100,000 Hunan people and attracts more than 1500 enterprises from Hunan. The Chamber has more than 300 member companies and provides more than 120,000 jobs to Shanxi. August 9, 2011, the Shaoli Electric Co., Ltd. of Hunan and the Gaoqiao Energy Co., Ltd. of Shanxi sign a technological agreement of mine rescue capsules. December 2, 2011, a delegation of the Tobacco Monopoly Bureau (Company) of Shanxi Province visits the China (Hunan) Tobacco Industrial Co., Ltd. March 27, 2012, Hunan and Shanxi Provinces sign an economic cooperation framework agreement.

Hunan-Sichuan

[Quick Facts] Average distance = 1923 km; Geographical adjacency = 0; Index of ethnic linkages = 0.9032 (2000) and 0.9052 (2010); Freight exchange via national railway = 1360 k tons (2000) and 3620 k tons (2010). ★ April 18, 2005, the Hunan Chamber of Commerce in Sichuan is established. The Chamber has 380 members, engaged in IT, machinery and equipment manufacturing, capital operation, car decoration, auto parts sales, construction and design, health care, logistics and tourism, etc., with a total investment of nearly 300 million yuan. June 19, 2006, in the "Hunan-Sichuan Economic and Social Development Cooperation Forum", the CCP Secretaries (Governors) of Hunan and Sichuan Provinces sign a framework agreement concerning the strengthening of economic and social cooperation.

The relevant departments of the two provinces also sign four sub-agreements, covering agriculture, rural labor, commerce, investment and tourism. October 17, 2008, the investment promotion (Hunan) of post-disaster reconstruction in Sichuan Province is held in Changsha City of Hunan. Lixian, as the pairing aid target of Hunan, proposes 29 investment projects which include chemical industry, tourism, agriculture, animal husbandry, mining industry and others; more than 150 enterprises of Hunan sign 16 investment project agreements with Sichuan, with a total investment of 3.35 billion yuan. June 19–21, 2010, the Hunan provincial government signs a strategic cooperation agreement with Sichuan University, aiming to achieve the integration of Hunan's Industry and the University's technologies. The two sides will strengthen cooperation in the fields of polymer materials engineering, biological therapy, and biomedical materials, information technology, water conservancy and hydropower, environmental engineering, energy conservation and chemical industry. November 6, 2010, the Sichuan-Chongqing Chamber of Commerce in Hunan is established. The Chamber has more than 90 member companies, involving catering, entertainment, technology, investment and finance, etc. June 21, 2012, the Hunan provincial government and Sichuan University sign, in Chengdu City, a strategic cooperation agreement.

Hunan-Tianjin

[Quick Facts] Average distance = 1725 km; Geographical adjacency = 0; Index of ethnic linkages = 0.9020 (2000) and 0.9039 (2010); Freight exchange via national railway = 290 k tons (2000) and 260 k tons (2010). ★ June 9–13, 2009, a delegation, led by the Deputy CCP Secretary (Governor) of Hunan Province, visits Tianjin and signs a province-school strategic cooperation agreement with Tianjin University. The two sides will strengthen cooperate in the fields of petrochemicals, fine chemicals, clean energy, precision instruments, heavy machinery manufacturing, electronic information, automation, new materials, urban planning and others. March 30, 2010, the Tianshi Group of Zhuzhou City (Hunan) signs a strategic cooperation framework agreement with Tianjin University of Traditional Chinese Medicine; both sides will strengthen production and research cooperation. June 20, 2010, the Hunan Chamber of Commerce in Tianjin is established. The Chamber has 150 corporate and individual members. September 9, 2011, the Zhengtaixiang Glass Company of Tianjin signs a production contract with the Hunan Provincial Science and Technology Museum. October 20, 2011, the Cultural and Arts Exchange of Tianjin Municipality and Hunan Province sign a strategic cooperation agreement. Both sides pledge to use capital market forces to promote the protection of intangible cultural heritage items. March 9–10, 2012, a delegation led by the Deputy Chief of Wuqing District of Tianjin visits Changde City of Hunan for exchange in regional development. October 24, 2012, Hongqiao District of Tianjin and Jinqiao Investment Shareholdings (Group) Co. Ltd. of Hunan sign a strategic cooperation framework agreement.

Hunan-Tibet

[Quick Facts] Average distance = 4273 km; Geographical adjacency = 0; Index of ethnic linkages = 0.0635 (2000) and 0.0843 (2010); Freight exchange via national railway = 0 k ton (2000) and 30 k tons (2010). ★ March 2, 2011, the Lightning Protection Center of Hunan Province and the Tibet Autonomous Region sign, in Lhasa City, a technological cooperation agreement. October 21, 2011, the tourism sectors of Shannan, Nyingchi and Xigaze of Tibet jointly hold a promotion of Tibet's tourism resources in Changsha City. December 1, 2011, the CCP Secretary and the Governor of Hunan Province meet, in Changsha City of Hunan, a government delegation of Shannan Prefecture of Tibet. Both sides have an in-depth exchange in bilateral cooperation and aiding-Tibet works. The delegation also pays an inspection to Shaoshan, Xiangtan, Changsha, Changde, Yueyang and Zhuzhou of Hunan Province. April 27, 2012, a large economic and trade fair and the signing ceremony of project agreement, sponsored by the Hunan Provincial Department of Commerce and the Department of Commerce of Tibet Autonomous Region, are held in Changsha City of Hunan. The 5100 Tibet Glacier Mineral Water Company signs a cooperation agreement with the Shengdong Trade Co., Ltd. of and the Yiqingyuan Tea Industry Co., Ltd. of Hunan, with a total contracted value of 40 million yuan. The two sides open a new round of pairing aid cooperation. July 7, 2012, a delegation, led by the PCSC Member of and the Chief of Organization Department of Hunan Province, visits Lhasa to participate in the Hunan-Tibet Economic and Social Development Forum. September 20, 2012, Tibet College of Nationalities holds an exchange and cooperation meeting and a project agreement signing ceremony with Hunan Vocational Technical School of Mass Media. The Hunan School donates more than 400 books to the Tibetan College; the two sides also sign a pairing aid framework agreement.

Hunan-Xinjiang

[Quick Facts] Average distance = 3973 km; Geographical adjacency = 0; Index of ethnic linkages = 0.4097 (2000) and 0.4084 (2010); Freight exchange via national railway = 240 k tons (2000) and 810 k tons (2010). ★ November 26, 2011, the Nonferrous Metals Authority of Hunan and the No. 13 Division of the XPCC hold, in Changsha City, a signing ceremony of strategic cooperation. June 23–25, 2012, a delegation, led by the CCP Deputy Secretary (and Chairman) of Xinjiang Uygur Autonomous Region, pays an inspection to Hunan and holds, jointly with Changsha City, an exchange meeting of economic and social development. July 23, 2012, the Public Security Bureau of Dongkou County (Shaoyang City, Hunan Province) and the Urumqi police of Xinjiang conduct a joint action against criminal activities. September 2, 2012, in the "2nd China-Asia-Europe Expo" which is held in Urumqi City, Hunan Province and Xinjiang Uygur Autonomous Region sign two major cooperation agreements, which are the Xinjiang Hunan-Xinjiang Investment Fund Project and the project of strategic cooperation between Hengyang City of Hunan and the Xinjiang Tebian Electric Apparatus Stock Co., Ltd. September 4, 2012, the Economic and Trade Office of Hunan Province and the Xinjiang Chamber of Commerce in Hunan hold a forum with the Xinjiang Bureau of Investment and Development. Both sides reach a consensus on the strengthening of economic exchange and cooperation and of aiding-Xinjiang works. October 16, 2012, the symposium of aiding-Tibet through tourism, sponsored by the Tourism Bureaux of Hunan Province and Xinjiang Uygur Autonomous Region, is held in Urumqi City. The two sides sign a framework cooperation agreement.

Hunan-Yunnan

[Quick Facts] Average distance = 1595 km; Geographical adjacency = 0; Index of ethnic linkages = 0.6997 (2000) and 0.7016 (2010); Freight exchange via national railway = 920 k tons (2000) and 190 k tons (2010). ★ April 8, 2007, the Hunan Chamber of Commerce in Yunnan is established. The Chamber has more than 500 member companies. June 23, 2008, Yunnan and Hunan Provinces sign a cooperation agreement on food production and marketing. Hunan will supply more than 200 million kg grains to Yunnan. August 17–21, 2009, a delegation, led by the General Manager of the China (Hunan) Tobacco Industrial Co., Ltd., visits Yunnan to discuss in-depth cooperation in industry and commerce and signs an agreement. The two sides will jointly construct a high-quality tobacco planting base. December 21, 2009, the "2009–2010 Province-Level Dynamic Grain Reserves Cooperation Forum", organized by Yunnan and Hunan Provinces, opens in Kunming City. January 21, 2010, the Tourism Bureaux of Yunnan, Hunan and other provinces jointly initiate a cooperation alliance, aiming to jointly promote regional economic development. May 10, 2012, the Grain Administration of Hunan participates in the "Yunnan Provincial Dynamic Grain Reserves Cooperation Forum", held by Kunming City of Yunnan Province, aiming to establish a long-term, stable and smooth purchase and sales relations with Yunnan. September 14, 2012, Kunming City of Yunnan and Yongzhou City of Hunan sign a regional cooperation framework agreement of cultural tourist, which officially marks the establishment of the Kunming-Yongzhou partnerships. The two cities will actively carry out cooperation in the integration of tourism routes, customs facilitating, etc.

Hunan-Zhejiang

[Quick Facts] Average distance = 998 km; Geographical adjacency = 0; Index of ethnic linkages = 0.9029 (2000) and 0.9141 (2010); Freight exchange via national railway = 2630 k tons (2000) and 2250 k tons (2010). ★ September 15, 2009, the

Zhejiang Weikang Pharmaceutical Co., Ltd. and the Hunan Qianjin Pharmaceutical Co., Ltd. sign, in Changsha City of Hunan, a strategic cooperation agreement. June 19–21, 2010, the Hunan provincial government signs a strategic cooperation agreement with Zhejiang University, aiming to achieve the fusion of Hunan's industries and the core technologies of the University. The two sides will strengthen cooperation in engineering, new energy equipment, bio-medicine and other strategic and emerging industries. July 25, 2010, the establishing ceremony of the Hunan Chamber of Commerce in Zhejiang is held in Hangzhou City. The number of Hunan's entrepreneurs and workers in Zhejiang totals one million; the Hunan-funded enterprises reach more than 3000 in Zhejiang, with a total asset of over 30 billion yuan. The Chamber has established four branches in Hangzhou, Jinhua, Wenzhou and Jiaxing Cities, with a total of more than 600 member companies, covering IT, real estate, jewelry, agriculture, chemicals, transportation, securities, medicine, construction, transportation and consulting. The Chamber signs eight project agreements with Yueyang, Changde, Hengyang, Loudi Cities and the Fuyang Economic Development Zone as well as the Zhejiang Chamber of Commerce in Hunan, respectively, with a total investment of 5 billion yuan. April 19, 2011, a delegation, led by the CCP Secretary and the Governor of Hunan Province, pays an inspection to Hangzhou City and holds, jointly with Hangzhou's municipal officials, an exchange meeting of economic and social development. Both sides sign a strategic cooperation framework agreement; the two places' enterprises sign 30 project agreements, with a total investment of 43.042 billion yuan.

Inner Mongolia-Jiangsu

[Quick Facts] Average distance = 1827 km; Geographical adjacency = 0; Index of ethnic linkages = 0.7945 (2000) and 0.7983 (2010); Freight exchange via national railway = 1710 k tons (2000) and 2090 k tons (2010). ★ May 11–13, 2005, a government delegation, led by the Deputy CCP Secretary (also the Chairman) of Inner Mongolia Autonomous Region, visits Nanjing City and holds, with Jiangsu's provincial officials, a forum. The two sides sign an agreement on cooperation in energy, chemical, agricultural and livestock products, urban infrastructure construction, tourism, etc. October 28, 2009, the Jiangsu Chamber of Commerce in Inner Mongolia is established in Hohhot City. The chamber has more than 200 member companies. October 15–18, 2010, a delegation, led by the CCP Secretary of the Supply and Marketing Cooperatives of Inner Mongolia Autonomous Region, visits Jiangsu Province to carry out bilateral exchange and cooperation. September 2–3, 2011, a Jiangsu provincial government delegation pays an inspection to Inner Mongolia Autonomous Region. The two sides sign the "Strategic Framework Agreement on the Further Strengthening of Cooperation in Energy and Other Competitive Industries". March 16, 2012, Yinjinhuoluo Banner of Ordos City (Inner Mongolia) signs a cooperation agreement with the Guoxin and the Xinnan

Groups of Jiangsu Province. Both sides will jointly build a high-tech industrial park, which is focused on high-end equipment manufacturing, IT and new industries, with a total investment of 71.2 billion yuan. May 5, 2012, the Yueda Group of Jiangsu and the Simon (Ximeng) Group of Inner Mongolia sign a cooperation framework agreement. The two sides will cooperate on the Ulanqu and the Dianli Mandula coal mines in Hohhot.

Inner Mongolia-Jiangxi

[Quick Facts] Average distance = 2674 km; Geographical adjacency = 0; Index of ethnic linkages = 0.7928 (2000) and 0.7964 (2010); Freight exchange via national railway = 220 k tons (2000) and 70 k tons (2010). ★ August 10, 2007, the Jiangxi Chamber of Commerce in Inner Mongolia is established. The Chamber has more than 100 member companies, which are mainly distributed in Hohhot, Baotou and Ordos and involve real estate, health care, medical equipment, auto sales, construction and decoration, hotel, textile and porcelain. September 24, 2008, Jiangxi Province and the Mengniu Dairy Group of Inner Mongolia sign a cooperation agreement concerning the construction of a dairy production base in Jiangxi Province. November 16, 2010, the Baotou Steel Rare Earth Group of Inner Mongolia acquires three Jiangxi companies at the price of 230 million yuan. Jiangxi is rich in heavy ions of rare earth resources; Inner Mongolia has the world's most abundant Bayan Obo rare earth resources. These acquisitions will lead to the overall development of the two places. December 15, 2010, the Bayannaoer municipal government and the Maide Wind Energy Co., Ltd. of Jiangxi sign a cooperation agreement. Under the agreement, the Maide will construct wind generators in the Bayannaoer Economic Development Zone, and will install a larger one at a later stage. January 5, 2011, a delegation, led by the Executive Director and General Manager of the Western Copper Co., Ltd. of Bayannaoer City of Inner Mongolia, visits Jiangxi University of Science and Technology and signs a strategic cooperation agreement with the University. January 7, 2012, the Jiangxi Chamber of Commerce in Inner Mongolia holds its 2011 annual work conference. More than 600 members attend the meeting.

Inner Mongolia-Jilin

[Quick Facts] Average distance = 1713 km; Geographical adjacency = 1; Index of ethnic linkages = 0.8258 (2000) and 0.8246 (2010); Freight exchange via national railway = 6760 k tons (2000) and 31,390 k tons (2010). ★ January 28, 2010, Jilin Province and Inner Mongolia Autonomous Region sign a strategic cooperation agreement. According to the agreement, the government of Inner Mongolia will encourage and support the enterprises which are listed by the Jilin government to invest and develop coal resources in Inner Mongolia and promise to give policy support to the Jilin enterprises. The two sides will take this opportunity to establish a regular exchange and coordination mechanism, aiming to strengthen cooperation in transportation, machinery processing, agricultural and livestock processing. April 18–20, 2010, a delegation, led by the Deputy CCP Secretary of Inner Mongolia Autonomous Region, pays an inspection to Jilin Province. The two sides hold an economic exchange and cooperation forum and sign a strategic cooperation agreement. The two places' companies sign seven project agreements, involving coal, natural gas, coal processing, coal-to-ethanol and others, with a total investment of 28.6 billion yuan. May 19, 2011, the Inner Mongolia Chamber of Commerce in Jilin is established in Changchun City. The Chamber has more than 50 member companies, mainly engaged in construction, human resources, real estate and new energy. August 20, 2011, the airport groups of and governments of Inner Mongolia and Jilin sign, in Ordos City of Inner Mongolia, a regional air route cooperation framework agreement, aiming to jointly promote bilateral tourism.

Inner Mongolia-Liaoning

[Quick Facts] Average distance = 1408 km; Geographical adjacency = 1; Index of ethnic linkages = 0.8371 (2000) and 0.8359 (2010); Freight exchange via national railway = 15,530 k tons (2000) and 74,910 k tons (2010). ★ January 15, 2007, the Liaoning Chamber of Commerce in Inner Mongolia is established. The Chamber has more than 60 member companies, covering catering, entertainment, financial services, trade flows, mechanical and electrical equipment, software, coral jewelry, mining, generator engineering and real estate. January 16, 2010, the transportation sectors of Liaoning Province and Inner Mongolia Autonomous Region sign a transport cooperation framework agreement, aiming to further deepen the traffic and communication cooperation and to promote the integration of regional transport networks. April 16, 2010–18, a delegation, led by the CCP Secretary of Inner Mongolia Autonomous Region pays an inspection to Shenyang City; the two sides hold an economic exchange and cooperation forum. The enterprises from Liaoning's power, iron and steel, and railway equipment manufacturing sectors sign 12 specific cooperation agreements with Xilin Gol League, Chifeng, Hulun Buir and Tongliao Cities of Inner Mongolia Autonomous Region, respectively. September 23, 2011, the second joint session of the "Northeast China Public Security Coordination" is held in Changchun. Inner Mongolia and Liaoning pledge to enhance cooperation in information sharing and to form an efficient regional police cooperation mechanism. December 28, 2011, the "2011 Annual Meeting of the Inner Mongolia Chamber of Commerce in Liaoning" opens.

Inner Mongolia-Ningxia

[Quick Facts] Average distance = 676 km; Geographical adjacency = 1; Index of ethnic linkages = 0.6690 (2000) and 0.6634 (2010); Freight exchange via national railway = 1840 k tons (2000) and 2370 k tons (2010). ★ August 7, 2006, the Inner Mongolia Chamber of Commerce in Ningxia is established in Yinchuan City. May 29, 2008, Inner Mongolia and Ningxia sign a custom passing cooperation agreement. August 13, 2008, the Entry IQB of Inner Mongolia and the Exit IQB of Ningxia sign a cooperation agreement concerning the exports of Ningxia's fruits and vegetables to Russia. March 12, 2010, Inner Mongolia, Ningxia, the China National Tobacco Corporation and the Shenhua Group Co., Ltd. jointly sign, in Beijing, an agreement concerning the integrated development of the Shanghaimiao Coal Mine in Inner Mongolia. May 11, 2011, the Communication Bank Ningxia Branch agrees to provide a credit limit of 500 million yuan to the Inner Mongolia Chamber of Commerce in Ningxia. September 1, 2011, the AQTS of Ningxia and Inner Mongolia Institute of Metrology Testing and Research sign a long-term cooperation agreement. September 26, 2011, the Customs of Yinchuan and Inner Mongolia agree to jointly build a frontier port serving as a new international economic channel. March 21–22, 2012, a government delegation of Inner Mongolia visits Ningxia. The representatives of the two places sign, in Yinchuan City, a strategic framework agreement and pledge to strengthen economic and social cooperation, especially in the fields of transportation, coal, chemical and cultural education. April 10, 2012, Ningxia and Inner Mongolia agree to jointly establish, in their border area, an economic cooperation zone, aiming to carry out cross-border industrial cooperation in coal chemistry and coal-fuelled power by using their respective advantages. October 18, 2012, the relevant departments of Ningxia and Inner Mongolia agree to optimize, within 3–5 years, their passenger and freight transport networks and logistic service structure.

Inner Mongolia-Qinghai

[Quick Facts] Average distance = 1360 km; Geographical adjacency = 0; Index of ethnic linkages = 0.5696 (2000) and 0.5593 (2010); Freight exchange via national railway = 380 k tons (2000) and 2070 k tons (2010). ★ May 6, 2010, Inner Mongolia and Qinghai carry out investment reconstruction activity. According to the statistics released by the Department of Civil Affairs of Inner Mongolia, Inner Mongolia has donated 130 million yuan to the Yushu Earthquake-hit area in Qinghai. August 3, 2012, in the "Tourism Culture and Art Festival", organized by the Zhangye municipal government and held in Zhangye City of Gansu Province, Qinghai and Inner Mongolia reach a consensus and sign a regional tourist cooperation declaration. August 10, 2012, at the "Fifth Qinghai International Thangka Arts and Culture Expo", Inner Mongolia and Qinghai sign 11 cultural industrial project agreements (including three Thangka projects, one tapestry project, four ethnic crafts projects, one Tibetan furniture project, two cultural tourist projects), with a total investment of 214.8 million yuan. August 27, 2012, a delegation, led by the CCP Secretary and Governor of Qinghai Province pays an inspection to Inner Mongolia Autonomous Region. The two places hold an economic and social development and cooperation forum and sign an agreement concerning the strengthening of bilateral economic cooperation. September 11, 2012, at the "Third Joint Meeting of the Northwest Police Cooperation Zone", which is held in Xining City of Qinghai, Inner Mongolia, Qinghai and other participating authorities sign a coordination agreement.

Inner Mongolia-Shaanxi

[Quick Facts] Average distance = 1291 km; Geographical adjacency = 1; Index of ethnic linkages = 0.7967 (2000) and 0.8004 (2010); Freight exchange via national railway = 580 k tons (2000) and 1410 k tons (2010). ★ December 13, 2007, the IQBs of Shaanxi and Inner Mongolia sign, in Xi'an City, a memorandum of cooperation to ensure security and export of the Shaanxi's fruits, via Inner Mongolia, to Russia and Mongolia. March 8, 2010, Inner Mongolia University of Science and Technology and the Zhongshi Energy Group Co., Ltd. of Shaanxi sign a cooperation agreement. April 14, 2010, the Tourism Bureau of Inner Mongolia Autonomous Region visits Shaanxi to participate in the 14th China East-West Cooperation and Investment Trade Fair which is organized by the Shaanxi Tourism Bureau. November 3, 2010, the Fire Fighting Detachments of Yulin City of Shaanxi Province and Ordos City of Inner Mongolia sign an agreement concerning fire fighting and rescue. November 28, 2010, the Shaanxi Chamber of Commerce in Inner Mongolia is established. The Chamber's members involve IT, hotel, hardware, plumbing, construction materials, engineering decorative, communications, mechanical and electrical, medical technology, agricultural products and others. September 29, 2011, the government of Bayannaoer City of Inner Mongolia and the Heimao (black cat) Group of Shaanxi hold a project cooperation meeting; the two sides decide to cooperatively develop a coking project in Wulatehou Banner. October 15, 2011, the Chemical Construction Co., Ltd. of Shaanxi and the Qinghua Group Co., Ltd. of Inner Mongolia sign, in Yangling City of Shaanxi, a strategic cooperation framework agreement. March 22, 2012, a government delegation of Inner Mongolia Autonomous Region visits Shaanxi Province. The two sides hold, in Xi'an City, an exchange and cooperation forum of economic and social development. Both sides sign a strategic cooperation framework agreement. August 26, 2012, the Transportation Authorities of Shaanxi, Inner Mongolia and other places sign an agreement, aiming to establish a joint law enforcement mechanism.

Inner Mongolia-Shandong

[Quick Facts] Average distance = 1164 km; Geographical adjacency = 0; Index of ethnic linkages = 0.7986 (2000) and 0.8028 (2010); Freight exchange via national railway = 4380 k tons (2000) and 610 k tons (2010). ★ August 2005, the Shandong Chamber of Commerce in Inner Mongolia is established in Hohhot City. The Chamber's enterprises are mainly engaged in real estate, chemical products, roads and bridges, machinery, home, clothing, and food and beverage, providing nearly 10,000 jobs in Inner Mongolia. August 10, 2007, the IQBs of Inner Mongolia and Shandong sign a technological cooperation agreement. May 13–16, 2008, a delegation led by the Deputy Director of the Communication and Traffic Department of Inner Mongolia, visits Shandong to investigate road transportation and logistics. October 27, 2008, a government delegation of Inner Mongolia conducts an inspection in Shandong; both sides sign an energy strategic cooperation agreement. September 23, 2010, the Runyuan Industrial Co., Ltd. establishes an office in the Agricultural Machinery Technology Promotion Station of Inner Mongolia. August 8, 2011, the Deputy CCP Secretary of Inner Mongolia meets a government delegation led by the CCP Secretary, the Deputy Governor and the SASAC Secretary of Shandong Province. Both sides hold a forum. August 31, 2011, the Inner Mongolia Chamber of Commerce in Shandong and the ICBC Shandong Branch sign a cooperation framework agreement. December 8, 2011, Inner Mongolia Chamber of Commerce in Shandong is established in Qingdao City. March 22, 2012, the Marine Shipping Corporations of Inner Mongolia and Shandong sign a strategic cooperation framework agreement. The two sides will carry out cooperative projects in the fields of investment, operation, capacity expansion, international logistics, etc. August 19, 2012, the Shandong Chamber of Commerce in Inner Mongolia is established in Baotou City. The Chamber has more than 300 member's companies.

Inner Mongolia-Shanghai

[Quick Facts] Average distance = 2130 km; Geographical adjacency = 0; Index of ethnic linkages = 0.7971 (2000) and 0.8021 (2010); Freight exchange via national railway = 810 k tons (2000) and 1510 k tons (2010). ★ September 1–3, 1999, a delegation, led by the CCP Secretary of Inner Mongolia, visits Shanghai. The two sides sign a cooperation agreement concerning the exploitation of rare earth resources and the development of nickel hydrogen battery. December 18, 2003, the Kaimaila Media Company agrees to help the Inner Mongolia TV Station to establish a Chinese-speaking Channel. December 26, 2005, the Shanghai Huayi (Group) Company and the Yili Resources Group of Inner Mongolia agree to jointly produce 400,000 tons of PVC and 400,000 tons of caustic soda per year. The project will cost 4 billion yuan in total. August 21, 2007, Shanghai and Inner

Mongolia sign, in Hohhot, an agreement and decide to establish a multi-level cooperative mechanism in the fields of electricity, chemicals, equipment manufacturing, agriculture, infrastructure, etc. May 17, 2009, the Inner Mongolia Chamber of Commerce in Shanghai is established. The Chamber has 239 members. August 25, 2011, a delegation, composed of the PPCC Chairman of Shanghai Municipality, and Hong Kong and Macau CPPCC members, visits Inner Mongolia and donates 400,000 yuan in cash and computers and other school supplies to Horqin Banner of Xing'an League (Inner Mongolia). June 15, 2012, the Shanghai Red Cross, the Shanghai Children Hospital and Inner Mongolia sign a cooperation agreement of pairing medical aid. August 24, 2012, the Maternal and Children Health Hospital of Inner Mongolia Autonomous Region and the Shanghai Children Hospital sign an agreement on pairing aid and cooperation. October 18–20, 2005, a delegation, led by the Propaganda Chief of and the CCP Secretary of Inner Mongolia, visits Shanghai. The two sides hold a discussion meeting, aiming to further strengthen bilateral exchange and cooperation.

Inner Mongolia-Shanxi

[Quick Facts] Average distance = 640 km; Geographical adjacency = 1; Index of ethnic linkages = 0.7949 (2000) and 0.7980 (2010); Freight exchange via national railway = 400 k tons (2000) and 4030 k tons (2010). ★ October 16, 2010, the Inner Mongolia Chamber of Commerce in Shanxi is established in Taiyuan City. March 25, 2011, Shanxi Province and Inner Mongolia Autonomous Region hold, in Taiyuan City, an economic and social development cooperation forum. April 17, 2011, Baotou City of Inner Mongolia and Taiyuan City of Shanxi hold, in Taiyuan City, an economic and social development forum. The two provinces sign a cooperation agreement. March 21, 2012, the Xilingol League of Inner Mongolia and the Huatong Road and Bridge Group Co., Ltd. of Shanxi sign, in Xilinhot City, a cyclic economic cooperation agreement, with a total investment of 8 billion yuan. The agreement includes the construction projects of the 1,4-butanediol, the autoclaved bricks, the aerated blocks and the sulfur refinery, with the annual production capacities of 300,000 tons, 220 million masses, 100 million cubic meter and 4 tons, respectively, as well as the 4 × 50 MW thermal power plant circular project in Zhengxiangbai Banner. May 26, 2012, an engineering project entitled "Intellectual Property Rights and the Promotion of the Coal Chemical Industry Development in Shanxi and Inner Mongolia Areas" is signed by two coal-rich provinces of Shanxi and Inner Mongolia. August 26, 2012, the Transportation Authorities of Shanxi and Inner Mongolia sign an agreement to build a joint law enforcement mechanism.

Inner Mongolia-Sichuan

[Quick Facts] Average distance = 2133 km; Geographical adjacency = 0; Index of ethnic linkages = 0.7944 (2000) and 0.7982 (2010); Freight exchange via national railway = 70 k tons (2000) and 1960 k tons (2010). ★ August 3, 2007, the press conference of Sichuan industrial development and economic cooperation is held in the International Convention and Exhibition Center of Inner Mongolia. The investments of Inner Mongolia in Sichuan have reached 830 million yuan, involving animal husbandry, food and beverage, chemical, energy and others. September 25, 2011, Inner Mongolia and Sichuan sign a joint action program agreement, aiming to jointly monitor the light rare earth resource. March 14, 2012, the Sichuan Fire Fighting Research Institute of and the Fire Protection Department of Inner Mongolia hold a signing ceremony of scientific and technological cooperation agreement. The two sides will conduct exchange and cooperation in the fields of fire preventions and controls in high buildings and underground public buildings, in energy and chemical areas and in grassland and pasturing areas. July 4, 2012, the Science and Technology Departments of Sichuan and Inner Mongolia, hold, in Manzhouli City of Inner Mongolia, a meeting, aiming to strengthen the scientific and technological exchange and cooperation between Sichuan and Inner Mongolia. August 13, 2012, the "Inner Mongolia-Sichuan Investment Cooperation Project Promotion" is held in Chengdu City of Sichuan. Hohhot, Tongliao, Alashan, Xing'an and other 14 Leagues (Cities) of Inner Mongolia offer 105 projects, with a total value of 133.4 billion yuan, involving equipment manufacturing, bio-pharmaceutics, high-tech, electronics, metallurgy, food processing, tourism, culture, business services, logistics, chemical, energy, building materials, park construction, etc. August 16, 2012, the Hongda Group of Sichuan and the Economic and Trade Information Commission of Inner Mongolia hold a meeting; the two sides will carry out cooperation in the field of resource exploitation.

Inner Mongolia-Tianjin

[Quick Facts] Average distance = 801 km; Geographical adjacency = 0; Index of ethnic linkages = 0.8092 (2000) and 0.8141 (2010); Freight exchange via national railway = 9220 k tons (2000) and 14,890 k tons (2010). ★ May 22, 2008, Inner Mongolia and Tianjin jointly hold a cooperative education fair in Hohhot City, with participants of 40 schools from Tianjin and 55 schools from Inner Mongolia. August 26, 2008, the PCSC member of and the Deputy Mayor of Tianjin Municipality meet a delegation led by the Chairman of the First Machinery Group of Inner Mongolia; the two sides pledge to further strengthen cooperation. April 2, 2009, the Property Rights Exchange Center of Inner Mongolia signs a cooperation agreement with the Tianjin Shares Exchange. September 9, 2010, a delegation, led by the Executive President (Also the General Secretary) of the Yellow River

Regional Economic Development and Cooperation Promotion Association of Tianjin, pays an inspection to Inner Mongolia. October 21, 2010, the Endemic Prevention Research Center of Inner Mongolia and the Disease Prevention Center of Tianjin sign a cooperation agreement on the joint prevention and control of plague. December 10, 2010, Tianjin University and the Wuhai municipal government of Inner Mongolia sign a comprehensive strategic cooperation agreement. July 25, 2011, the Vice Mayor of Bayannaoer City of Inner Mongolia and the entrepreneurs of the Inner Mongolia Chambers of Commerce in Tianjin hold a forum. June 25, 2012, the PPCC and the relevant sectors of Inner Mongolia and the Yellow River Regional Economic Development and Cooperation Promotion Association of Tianjin hold the "Yellow River—Binhai Economic Development and Cooperation Forum".

Inner Mongolia-Tibet

[Quick Facts] Average distance = 3332 km; Geographical adjacency = 0; Index of ethnic linkages = 0.0650 (2000) and 0.0871 (2010); Freight exchange via national railway = 0 k ton (2000) and 20 k tons (2010). ★ December 22, 2005, Inner Mongolia and Tibet, hold in Hohhot City of Inner Mongolia, an exchange and cooperation forum. The Vice Chairmen of the two regions sign a scientific and technological cooperation agreement. October 13, 2010, the CCP Secretary of Inner Mongolia Autonomous Region meets, in Hohhot, a government delegation which is led by the Vice Chairman of Tibet Autonomous Region. The two sides have an in-depth exchange in agricultural development and industrialization of animal husbandry. September 22, 2011, the Laoniu (old ox) Foundation of Inner Mongolia joins the public project of Aiding-Tibet Development Foundation. The Foundation donates 740,000 yuan. The Aiding-Tibet Development Foundation is nation's only privately-owned foundation in Tibet. Founded in 1987, and without any political attachment, it has received capitals and supplies amounting to a total value of 200 million yuan. The Foundation has carried out 824 aid projects, involving culture, education, health, poverty and disaster relief, technology, economic and ecological and environmental protection.

Inner Mongolia-Xinjiang

[Quick Facts] Average distance = 3035 km; Geographical adjacency = 0; Index of ethnic linkages = 0.4253 (2000) and 0.4233 (2010); Freight exchange via national railway = 560 k tons (2000) and 1250 k tons (2010). ★ June 29, 2004, the Chairman of Xinjiang Uygur Autonomous Region welcomes the delegation of Inner Mongolia Autonomous Region during the celebration of the 50th anniversary of Bayingolin Mongol Autonomous Prefecture of Xinjiang; he acknowledges the support and aid from Inner Mongolia. December 27, 2008, Inner Mongolia and Tortala Mongol Autonomous Prefecture of Xinjiang establish an education pairing aid relationship; the affiliated Hospital of Inner Mongolia University and the Bortala Mongol Autonomous Prefectural Hospital also establish a pairing aid relationship. October 4, 2009, the government of Xinjiang Uygur Autonomous Region signs a strategic cooperation framework agreement with four Inner Mongolia enterprises (i.e., the Yitai Group, the Ordos Investment Holding Group, the Dongda Mongol King Group, and the Gaofeng Group). The four enterprises will invest 100 billion yuan in Ili Autonomous Prefecture of and the Turpan-Hami area of Xinjiang to exploit coal resources for a time period of six to eight years. Inner Mongolia's enterprises in Xinjiang are mainly engaged in the development of mineral resources, the deep processing of agriculture and animal husbandry products and other industrial activities. August 18, 2011, the IQBs of Inner Mongolia and Xinjiang sign a memorandum of cooperation to deepen the joint prevention and control mechanisms and to ensure the health security in the China-Russian border area.

Inner Mongolia-Yunnan

[Quick Facts] Average distance = 3233 km; Geographical adjacency = 0; Index of ethnic linkages = 0.6764 (2000) and 0.6768 (2010); Freight exchange via national railway = 160 k tons (2000) and 410 k tons (2010). ★ August 25, 2003, the China (Inner Mongolia) Tobacco Company and the Kunming Cigarette Plant of Yunnan jointly establish, in Hohhot City, the Inner Mongolia Kunming Cigarette Co., Ltd., with a registered capital of 625 million yuan. November 2, 2006, Wengniute Banner of Chifeng City (Inner Mongolia) and the Industrial Hemp Company of Yunnan agree to jointly construct a 40-mu farm to grow hemp that is widely used in the fields of medicine, health care, cooking oil, and technological materials, with high economical values. May 21, 2009, the Educational Departments of Yunnan and Inner Mongolia and Inner Mongolia Normal University hold a symposium; the two places will carry out cooperation in continuing education. November 19, 2009, the tourism sectors of Inner Mongolia holds, in Kunming City of Yunnan, a tourist promotion. March 12–13, 2010, a delegation, led by the Mayor and Vice Mayor of Bayannaoer City of Inner Mongolia pays an inspection to Dehong Dai and Jingpo Autonomous Prefecture of Yunan. The two sides exchange experiences in the planning of cross-border economic cooperative zones. August 25, 2012, formally approved by the Yunnan Provincial Civil Affairs Department, the Inner Mongolia Chamber of Commerce in Yunnan is established. The Chamber has more than 140 members.

Inner Mongolia-Zhejiang

[Quick Facts] Average distance = 2256 km; Geographical adjacency = 0; Index of ethnic linkages = 0.7929 (2000) and 0.7974 (2010); Freight exchange via national railway = 920 k tons (2000) and 1720 k tons (2010). ★ September 12, 2006, the Zhejiang Chamber of Commerce in Inner Mongolia is established in Hangzhou City. April 1, 2009, the Industrial and Agricultural Development Corporation of Anren Town of Longquan City (Zhejiang) and the Inner Mongolia agree to construct a black fungus demonstration base. June 17, 2011 the "Inner Mongolia (Xing'an League)-Zhejiang Economic Cooperation Forum" is held in Ulanhot City of Xing'an League (Inner Mongolia). The Vice Governor of Zhejiang Province, the Inspector of Tourism Bureau of Inner Mongolia and the CCP Secretary of Xing'an League of Inner Mongolia attend the meeting. July 18–22, 2011, the Zhejiang Energy Group and Ordos City of Inner Mongolia sign an agreement under which Zhejiang will construct 2 × 1000 tons/year of coal mines and 4 × 100 million kw of coal-fired power plants in Inner Mongolia, aiming to ensuring Zhejiang's demand for coal and electricity. June 14, 2012, the Changyuan Group of Zhejiang and Jining District of Ulanqab City (Inner Mongolia) sign a cooperation project agreement concerning the production base of new environment-friendly specialty film. June 21, 2012, a trade cooperation fair between Erenhot City of Inner Mongolia and Zhejiang Entrepreneurs is held in Hangzhou City. 50 companies from both sides attend this fair. July 11, 2012, a delegation, composed of hundreds of Zhejiang tourism representatives, visits Inner Mongolia. The two sides hold the "Zhejiang-Xing'an League Tourist Exchange and Cooperation Forum"; the Tourism Bureaux of Zhejiang and Inner Mongolia also sign a cooperation agreement. October 23, 2012, Inner Mongolia and Zhejiang sign an economic and social development and cooperation framework agreement; both sides also jointly establish a new "four-in-one" cooperative mode of coal mines, power plants, transmission channels and energy market, and energy, aiming to ensuring the energy demand of Zhejiang.

Jiangsu-Jiangxi

[Quick Facts] Average distance = 838 km; Geographical adjacency = 0; Index of ethnic linkages = 0.9976 (2000) and 0.9965 (2010); Freight exchange via national railway = 1290 k tons (2000) and 2940 k tons (2010). ★ July 21, 2010, the Commercial Departments of Jiangxi and Jiangsu Provinces hold a promotion meeting on foreign trade and economic cooperation. September 18, 2010, Lantian Collage of Jiangxi signs a cooperation agreement with the Human Resource Management and Service Center of Changshu City of Jiangsu and the Dongnan District Government of Changshu City. October 25–28, 2010, a delegation, organized by the Labor and Employment Management Center of Jiangsu Province, pays an inspection to Jiangxi and signs an interprovincial labor cooperation agreement. Jiangsu is a big labor inflow province and still has a large demand gap. March 30, 2011, a delegation of Jiujiang Province pays an inspection to Yutai City of Jiangsu Province. Both sides conduct a cooperation consensus on aquatic production. October 17, 2011, a delegation, led by the Chief Engineer of the Huachang Aluminum Industry Co., Ltd. of Jiangsu, visits Jiangxi Province and signs an agreement concerning cooperation in the R&D of special technologies. December 2011, the Jiangxi Chamber of Commerce in Jiangsu is established. The Chamber has over 100 enterprise members, covering optoelectronics, IT, chemistry, real estate, etc. April 9, 2012, the Modern Professional Education Group of Jiangxi and Wuxi City of Jiangsu Province establish a labor cooperative relationship. September 19, 2012, the Supply and Marketing Cooperatives of Jiangxi and Jiangsu Provinces decide to jointly construct a modern exchange center of agricultural products. November 28, 2012, the Jiangsu Chamber of Commerce in Jiangxi is established in Nanchang City. The Chamber has over 1200 enterprise members and over 400 individual members.

Jiangsu-Jilin

[Quick Facts] Average distance = 2035 km; Geographical adjacency = 0; Index of ethnic linkages = 0.9111 (2000) and 0.9229 (2010); Freight exchange via national railway = 1110 k tons (2000) and 830 k tons (2010). ★ October, 2008, the Jiangsu Chamber of Commerce in Jilin is established in Changchun City. The Chamber has 50 member enterprises, involving machinery manufacturing, food processing, real estate, health care, etc. May 4–6, 2009, the "Jilin-Jiangsu Trade and Economic Cooperation Fair" is held in Nanjing City. The vice governors and entrepreneurs of the two provinces attend the fair. The governments and agricultural sectors of Jilin and Jiangsu sign four friendly cooperation agreements and two purchase agreements (with a total amount of 0.111 billion yuan). The enterprises of the two sides sign 24 investment contracts (with a total amount of 22.595 billion yuan) in the fields of automobiles and parts, deep processing agricultural products, mineral resources, biochemical, railway transportation, modern service, engineering, etc. March 24, 2010, the "Jiangsu-Changchun Technological and Talent Exchange and Cooperation Fair" is held in Changchun City of Jilin Province. A delegation composed of industrial parks, big SOEs and private high-tech companies and led by the PCSC member of Suzhou City (Jiangsu Province) attends the fair. The two places hope to strengthen cooperation in the fields of R&D, intellectual cultivation, etc. and to establish a long-term supply and demand relationship of directional labor training in talent-lacking industries. January 2012, a preparatory team for the establishment of the Jilin Chamber of Commerce in Jiangsu is formed.

Jiangsu-Liaoning

[Quick Facts] Average distance = 1730 km; Geographical adjacency = 0; Index of ethnic linkages = 0.8421 (2000) and 0.8509 (2010); Freight exchange via national railway = 2180 k tons (2000) and 850 k tons (2010). ★ January 4, 2006, the Labor and Social Security Sectors of Liaoning and Jiangsu Provinces sign, in Nanjing City, an agreement, marking that the two sides have officially established a labor cooperative relationship. December 22, 2008, the Jiangsu Chamber of Commerce in Liaoning is established in Dalian City. The Chamber will focus on the development of Jiangsu's advantageous industries, such as electronic equipment, medicine, auto, energy and environmental protection. April 4, 2012, a symposium of economic cooperation between Jiangsu's 200 entrepreneurs and the Huludao municipal government of Liaoning is held in Nanjing City of Jiangsu. Huludao links the two major markets of Northeast and North China; Jiangsu and Liaoning will establish 13 parks in the city, involving 68 sub-projects in real estate, tourism, equipment manufacturing, shipping and ocean engineering, etc. April 28, 2012, a delegation, led by the Chairman of the Liaoning Federation of Returned Overseas Chinese, visits Benxi City of Jiangsu Province. The enterprises of the two places pledge to strengthen cooperation in biomedical, spa, tourism, real estate, etc. July 3–4, 2012, a Jiangsu government delegation visits Shenyang City of Liaoning Province to participate in the "Jiangsu-Liaoning Economic Cooperation and Social Development Forum". The delegation also visits the Beifang (northern) Heavy Industry Group of Shenyang, the Yuanda Group of Shenyang and the Machine Tool Group Co., Ltd. of Shenyang City.

Jiangsu-Ningxia

[Quick Facts] Average distance = 2052 km; Geographical adjacency = 0; Index of ethnic linkages = 0.6572 (2000) and 0.6517 (2010); Freight exchange via national railway = 290 k tons (2000) and 670 k tons (2010). ★ August 22–23, 2000, the "Ningxia-Jiangsu Project Promotion" is held in Yinchuan City of Ningxia. Both sides sign seven project agreements, with a total investment of 0.303 billion yuan. June 30, 2009, the Jiangsu Chamber of Commerce in Ningxia is established. The Chamber has 230 enterprise members. October 11, 2010, a delegation, led by the inspector of the Changzhou Federation of Returned Overseas Chinese and the Honorary Chairman of the Federation of Returned Overseas Chinese Entrepreneurs, visits the Liyang Desheng Food Co., Ltd. of Yinchuan City of Ningxia. July 23, 2011, the "Ningxia-Jiangsu Tourism Cooperation Fair" opens in Yinchuan City of Ningxia. September 12, 2011, Jiangsu and Ningxia sign, in Nanjing, a memorandum of cooperation. Jiangsu will encourage its local energy and chemical enterprises to invest in Ningxia. March 30, 2012, the No. 4 Division of the Coal and Geology Bureau of Jiangsu and the Coal Exploitation Engineering Company of

Ningxia sign a strategic cooperation agreement. April 25, 2012, the "Ningxia-Jiangsu (Nanjing) Economic Cooperation Promotion" is held in Nanjing. The two sides sign 41 project agreements (with a total amount of 38.046 billion yuan), aiming to benefit from the low-cost advantages of land and energy resources of Ningxia and the technological, talent and capital advantages of Jiangsu and to jointly promote the two places' economic development. May 9, 2012, a government delegation of Ningxia Hui Autonomous Region pays an inspection to Jiangsu. The Culture Departments of the two sides sign the "Cultural Exchange and Cooperation Framework Agreement".

Jiangsu-Qinghai

[Quick Facts] Average distance = 2095 km; Geographical adjacency = 0; Index of ethnic linkages = 0.5433 (2000) and 0.5335 (2010); Freight exchange via national railway = 80 k tons (2000) and 3760 k tons (2010). ★ 2004, Nanjing and Xining Cities sign, for the first time, a charter-flight agreement. Both sides pledge to promote Qinghai to become a site for Jiangsu's tourists in summer. January 31, 2010, the Jiangsu Chamber of Commerce in Qinghai is established in Xining City. The Chamber has 200 enterprise members. September 13, 2011, the Supply and Marketing Cooperatives of Jiangsu and Qinghai sign, in Xining City of Qinghai, a pairing aid agreement concerning Jiangsu's aid to Qinghai in the establishment of sales channel for Qinghai's specialty agricultural and livestock products. May 11, 2012, the Weiye Construction Group of Jiangsu, the Jiangsu Chamber of Commerce in Qinghai and Bank of China Qinghai Branch sign, in Xining City, a strategic cooperation agreement. June 5, 2012, the relevant sectors of the National East-Center-West Regional Cooperation Demonstration Area (located in the Lianyungang City of Jiangsu Province) hold a press conference in Xining City of Qinghai. In Lianyungang there are 260 commercial agencies from Central and Western China; 60 % of imports and exports in the Lianyungang Port are related to the Central and Western Areas. The Lianyungang Port will become the most important logistic channel for Qinghai when the demonstration area is completed. October 8, 2012, the Jiangsu Tourist Agency and Xining City carry out charter flight cooperation. Since 2004, there have been 800 fights, carrying 125,600 passengers, between Nanjing and Xining.

Jiangsu-Shaanxi

[Quick Facts] Average distance = 1205 km; Geographical adjacency = 0; Index of ethnic linkages = 0.9975 (2000) and 0.9976 (2010); Freight exchange via national railway = 3720 k tons (2000) and 9840 k tons (2010). ★ 1996, as arranged by the State Council, Shaanxi and Jiangsu Provinces establish a closer economic cooperative relationship; the two provinces will cooperate in poverty alleviation and personnel training. September 16, 2005, approved by the Economic and Information Commission of Jiangsu Province and the Shaanxi Provincial Department of Commerce, the Jiangsu Chamber of Commerce in Shaanxi is established. The Chamber has more than 600 member companies. July 18–20, 2007, a delegation, led by the Governor of Shaanxi Province, visits Jiangsu Province. The two sides sign the "Project Agreement of the Guojiahe Mine in the Northern Baoji City" (with a planning area of 61.9 km^2 and the estimated coal reserves of 675 million tons); this project is jointly funded by the Baoji municipal government, Shaanxi Provincial Coal and Geology Bureau and the Xuzhou Coal Group of Jiangsu, with a total investment of three billion yuan. April 12, 2009, the Shaanxi Coal Chemical (Group) Corporation and the Jiangsu Yueda Group sign, in Xi'an City, a strategic cooperation framework agreement; the two sides will strengthen cooperation in energy development, machinery manufacturing, modern logistics and capital operation. April 2009, at the "Western China Trade and Investment Fair", a number of enterprises from Shaanxi and Jiangsu Provinces sign cooperation agreements. June 2, 2009, the DRCs of Jiangsu and Shaanxi sign, in Nanjing, the "Framework Agreement Concerning the Further Strengthening of Cooperation in Advantageous Industries." The two sides pledge to cooperate in energy, trade, labor, infrastructure, etc. May 12, 2010, a delegation, led by the Vice Governor of Jiangsu Province, visits Xi'an and holds the "Lianyungang's (Jiangsu) Role in Midwest China Promotion Meeting"; the two sides sign the "Continental Bridge Logistics Alliance Proposal".

Jiangsu-Shandong

[Quick Facts] Average distance = 663 km; Geographical adjacency = 1; Index of ethnic linkages = 0.9957 (2000) and 0.9952 (2010); Freight exchange via national railway = 11,740 k tons (2000) and 8580 k tons (2010). ★ May 23–26, 2007, a delegation, led by the CCP Secretary of Jiangsu, pays an inspection to Shandong, and holds an exchange meeting of development situation, aiming to exchange development experiences in coastal development and agricultural industrialization. December 12–15, 2007, the CCP Secretary of Shandong Province leads a delegation to visit Jiangsu Province. The two provinces sign a cooperation framework agreement on economic and social development. April 26, 2009, the Jiangsu Chamber of Commerce in Shandong is established in Ji'nan City. The Chamber has 1500 member companies, involving construction and installation, real estate, environmental protection, petrochemical industry, vehicle manufacturing, mechanical and electrical hardware, biological medicine, etc. September 16, 2009, the Jiangsu Phoenix Publishing Media (Group) Co., Ltd. and the Shandong Publishing Group jointly hold, in the Beijing International Book Fair, the Signing Ceremony of the "Top-Ten Strategic Cooperation Projects" agreement; the cooperation involves mergers and acquisitions, equity investment funds and others. May

28, 2010, a delegation, led by the Vice Director of the Overseas Chinese Office of Jiangsu Province and the Vice Chairman of the Overseas Exchange Association of Jiangsu Province, visits Shandong and holds a symposium with its counterparts. October 24, 2011, the Shandong Vocational Animal Science and Veterinary College and the Yike Group of Jiangsu hold a strategic cooperation agreement signing ceremony. The two sides will carry out cooperation in talents docking and cultivating. February 12, 2012, the Shandong Chamber of Commerce in Jiangsu is established.

Jiangsu-Shanghai

[Quick Facts] Average distance = 303 km; Geographical adjacency = 1; Index of ethnic linkages = 0.9971 (2000) and 0.9928 (2010); Freight exchange via national railway = 2720 k tons (2000) and 880 k tons (2010). ★ May 30, 2007, the Shanghai municipal and Jiangsu provincial governments sign the "Memorandum of Cooperation to Construct the Direct Port Passing in the Yangtze River Delta", aiming to further strengthen the customs cooperation and promote the development of the Yangtze River Delta. October 20, 2009, the Jiangsu Chamber of Commerce in Shanghai is established in Pudong District. The Chamber signs a cooperation framework agreement with Huaian City of Jiangsu and Yangpu District of Shanghai. March 1, 2010, the FDAs of Jiangsu and Shanghai sign the regional cooperation agreement on the catering services and food security during the Shanghai World Expo 2010. March 16, 2010, the Maritime Bureaux of Jiangsu and Shanghai sign an agreement; both sides will jointly ensure the water security during the Shanghai World Expo. December 26, 2010, at the "Symposium of Promotion of the Yangtze City Belt Development, Industrial transferring and Demonstration Zone Construction", the Shanghai and Jiangsu governments sign a cooperation framework agreement. April 10, 2012, the Taicang municipal government of Jiangsu and the Shanghai Institute of Technological Physics jointly establish a research center (i.e., the Taicang Institute for Research on Infrared Technology). June 16, 2012, a delegation, led by Shanghai Education Commission, participates in the "Science and Technology Festival" which is held in Haimen City of Jiangsu. The two sides agree to establish a long-term and stable cooperative relationship, aiming to promote the transformation of scientific and technological achievements.

Jiangsu-Shanxi

[Quick Facts] Average distance = 1195 km; Geographical adjacency = 0; Index of ethnic linkages = 0.9992 (2000) and 0.9976 (2010); Freight exchange via national railway = 18,860 k tons (2000) and 34,440 k tons (2010). ★ June 2000, the Jiangsu Chamber of Commerce in Shanxi is established. The Chamber has more than 100 enterprise members, mainly engaged in electricity, coal, real estate development, construction, decoration, building materials, chemical, mechanical and electrical, household appliances and agricultural and sideline products. August 8, 2007, a Jiangsu provincial government delegation visits Shanxi to acknowledge Shanxi's support in coal. April 2010, Taiyuan University of Science and Technology of Shanxi Province and Hai'an County of Jiangsu Province sign a strategy cooperation agreement. September 16, 2010, the Shanxi and Jiangsu governments sign the "Framework Agreement on the Further Strengthening of Energy Cooperation"; the Xinyi Coal Gasification Project is jointly developed by the Shanxi Coal Group and the Jiangsu Guoxin Group. June 27–28, 2011, a delegation, led by the Vice Mayor of Changzhi City of Shanxi, visits the Yueda Group's headquarters in Yancheng City of Jiangsu. Changzhi City of Shanxi and the Yueda Group sign a strategic cooperation framework agreement. July 25, 2011, the "Shanxi-Jiangsu Enterprise Exchange and Cooperation Forum" is held in Nanjing City. Both sides sign 30 cooperation agreements. March 2, 2012, the Jiangsu Guoxin Group, the Shanxi Coal Import and Export Corporation, the Jiangsu Huajing Asset Management Company (affiliated to the Jiangsu provincial government) sign, in Nanjing, an agreement concerning the joint establishment of the Guoxin Jingjiang Power Co., Ltd. of Jiangsu. August 17, 2012, the Shanxi Coking Coal Materials Trade Co., Ltd. and the China Datang Corporation Jiangsu Branch sign a long-term strategic cooperation framework agreement. August 23, 2012, the Lu'an Group of Shanxi and the Xiexin Group of Jiangsu sign a coal-fired power project agreement.

Jiangsu-Sichuan

[Quick Facts] Average distance = 2048 km; Geographical adjacency = 0; Index of ethnic linkages = 0.9528 (2000) and 0.9427 (2010); Freight exchange via national railway = 2240 k tons (2000) and 2980 k tons (2010). ★ March 21, 2007, the Offices of Returned Overseas Chinese Affairs of Jiangsu and Sichuan sign, in Nanjing, a cooperation agreement. September 11, 2007, a Sichuan economic and trade delegation and Jiangsu Province sign 22 project agreements, with a total investment of 14.997 billion yuan. October 2008, the Suzhou Red Cross of Jiangsu Province donates 43.5 million yuan to the Sichuan earthquake-hit area for reconstruction. March 23, 2009, the Jiangsu Chamber of Commerce in Sichuan is established. July 27, 2009, Yizheng City of Jiangsu and Guang'an City of Sichuan sign a contract concerning the harvest of 300,000 mu of paddy in Guang'an. March 22, 2010, Hejiang County of Luzhou City (Sichuan) and Kunshan City of Jiangsu sign an agreement on human resource development and cooperation. April 20, 2010, the Sichuan Meifeng (Holdings) Co., Ltd. and the Jiangsu Institute of Chemical Engineering Research and Design sign, in Sichuan, a strategic cooperation agreement. June 25, 2010, Jinjiang District of Chengdu City (Sichuan) and Tongzhou District of Nantong City (Jiangsu) sign a friendship agreement. The two sides will hold regular meetings on investment information, economic and social development, and scientific and technological research. April 15–17, 2011, the Huaxi Hospital of Sichuan and the Henry-Hausen Group Jiangsu Company sign, in Lianyungang City of Jiangsu, a strategic cooperation framework agreement. January 9, 2012, the Sichuan Chamber of Commerce in Jiangsu is established in Nanjing City. The Chamber has 300 enterprise members. September 12–14, 2010, a Jiangsu delegation visits Chengdu City of Sichuan and holds a Sichuan-Jiangsu Symposium. Both sides agree to consolidate and expand the pairing aid to the Wenchuan earthquake-hit areas of Sichuan and promote bilateral cooperation.

Jiangsu-Tianjin

[Quick Facts] Average distance = 1023 km; Geographical adjacency = 0; Index of ethnic linkages = 0.9760 (2000) and 0.9784 (2010); Freight exchange via national railway = 70 k tons (2000) and 220 k tons (2010). ★ December 22, 2004, the Jiangsu Chamber of Commerce in Tianjin is established. May 23–26, 2007, a delegation, led by the CCP Secretary of Jiangsu Province, pays an inspection to Tianjin and holds an economic and social development meeting, aiming to exchange the experiences of coastal development and of agricultural industrialization. May 15–16, 2008, a delegation, led by the Mayor of Tianjin Municipality, visits Jiangsu Province. The two sides hold, in Suzhou City, an exchange and cooperation forum. August 2, 2008, the Tianjin Industrial Biotechnology Development and Research Center of the CAS and the Jiecheng Biological Engineering Co., Ltd. of Jiangsu sign, in Yixing City of Jiangsu, a strategic partnership agreement. The Jiangsu Company will invest 200 million yuan in Tianjin. July 27–30, 2010, a Tanjin municipal PCSC delegation visits Nanjing and pays an inspection to Nanjing University, Southeast University and Nanjing Normal University. November 3, 2011, Tianjin University visits Nanjing City to participate in the 3rd session of the China (Jiangsu) Production and Research Cooperation Achievements Exhibition Fair. April 17–21, 2012, a Tianjin municipal tourist delegation pays an inspection to Jiangsu. The Tianjin Tourism Bureau holds in, Nanjing City, a promotion entitled "Travelling to Tianjin by High-Speed Rail". Both sides sign a tourist cooperation agreement. April 28, 2012, a Tianjin University delegation visits Xinyi City of Jiangsu to carry out production and research cooperation. May 19, 2012, the Hardware Electrical and Mechanical Branch of the Jiangsu Chamber of Commerce in Tianjin is established.

Jiangsu-Tibet

[Quick Facts] Average distance = 4072 km; Geographical adjacency = 0; Index of ethnic linkages = 0.0635 (2000) and 0.0847 (2010); Freight exchange via national railway = 0 k ton (2000) and 50 k tons (2010). ★ April 3–4, 2007, a delegation, led by the Vice CCP Secretary (also the PCSC Chairman) of Tibet visits Jiangsu Province. Both sides hold, in Nanjing City, an economic and social development forum. The Jiangsu and Lhasa governments sign the "2006–2008 Pairing Aid Construction Project Agreements". August 2010, the Productivity Promotion Centers of Jiangsu and Tibet sign a cooperation agreement; the Jiangsu Center will volunteer technical supports (including personnel training, R&D, project assessment and counseling and training) to the Tibet Center. September 3–9, 2010, the Maritime Bureaux of Jiangsu and Tibet become pairing-aid partnerships during 2010–2014. May 23, 2011, the Jiangsu Jianghuai Power Co., Ltd. acquires the Tibet Zhongkai (Holdings) Co., Ltd. July 2011, a service mission of Jiangsu University to Duilong Deqing County of Tibet visits Lhasa City for social practice. September 2011, the Jiangsu Nantong Middle School and Tibet sign an agreement; The School will host 85 Tibetan students per year. September 9–22, 2011, Jiangsu Province, the Blood Center of Tibet Autonomous Region and Health Department of Tibet sign the "Agreement Concerning the Pairing-Aid Work of Blood Supply and Collection", aiming to ensure blood supply to Tibet. March 6, 2012, Jiangsu Institute of Animal and Husbandry and Tibet Collage of Professional Technology sign a cooperation agreement. August 15, 2012, the Jiangsu Chamber of Commerce in Tibet is established in Lhasa City. The Chamber has more than 200 members (enterprise and individual), involving construction, decoration, real estate, mining, agriculture, tourism, service, culture, etc. August 16, 2012, Jiangsu Province and the Audio-Visual Library of Tibet sign a cooperation agreement concerning the joint promotion of regional educational informatization.

Jiangsu-Xinjiang

[Quick Facts] Average distance = 3774 km; Geographical adjacency = 0; Index of ethnic linkages = 0.4090 (2000) and 0.4086 (2010); Freight exchange via national railway = 1270 k tons (2000) and 4260 k tons (2010). ★ February 10, 2004, the Jiangsu Association of Enterprises (Chamber of Commerce) in Xinjiang is established in Urumqi City. The association has 200 enterprise members, engaged in real estate and decoration (accounting for 40 %), manufacturing industry (20 %), business and circulation (35 %), medicine (2.5 %) and high-tech (2.5 %). December 20, 2010, the Xuzhou (Jiangsu) Chamber of Commerce in Urumqi (Xinjaing) is established. The Chamber has more than 3000 enterprise members. 2011, the Jiangsu and Xinjiang governments sign two agreements concerning the further strengthening of strategic energy cooperation and the deepening of clean energy cooperation between the two places. April 16, 2011, 100 pairing-aid projects relating to the livelihood construction and industrial development of Yili Kazakh Autonomous Prefecture (Xinjiang) are officially launched, with a total investment of 2.655 billion yuan (of which 0.96 billion yuan is voluntarily provided by

Jiangsu). The two sides also draft the pairing-aid plans from 2011 to 2015. December 3, 2011, Xinjiang and Jiangsu sign an agreement concerning the strengthening of cooperation in construction industry. December 27, 2011, the PCSC Chairmen of Jiangsu and Xinjiang sign a cooperation agreement and pledge to strengthen cooperation in economy and trade, science, education, and culture. April 9, 2012, a delegation, led by the Vice Governor of Jiangsu Province, visits Urumqi City of Xinjiang to participate in the "Jiangsu-Xinjiang Clean Energy Strategic Cooperation Project Promotion"; Jiangsu and Xinjiang sign 26 project agreements, with a total investment of 5.18 billion yuan. June 19, 2012, the Transportation and Communication Departments of Jiangsu and Xinjiang sign a framework cooperation agreement relating to highway maintenance, personnel training, technology introducing, etc. June 27, 2012, the Jiangsu Association of Enterprises (Chamber of Commerce) in Xinjiang and the Jiangsu front headquarters of pairing aid to Kizilsu Kirgiz Autonomous Prefecture of Xinjiang sign a cooperation agreement.

Jiangsu-Yunnan

[Quick Facts] Average distance = 2693 km; Geographical adjacency = 0; Index of ethnic linkages = 0.6691 (2000) and 0.6704 (2010); Freight exchange via national railway = 940 k tons (2000) and 1610 k tons (2010). ★ July 12, 2006, the Jiangsu Chamber of Commerce in Yunnan is established. The Chamber has nearly 500 member enterprises, involving mining, petrochemical, real estate development, service industry, decoration industry, high-tech industry, etc. January 12, 2012, the Yunnan (Baoshan Municipal) Tobacco Company and the Yonglu Grain and Cooking Oil Co., Ltd. of Jiangsu hold a signing ceremony of the project agreement on modern tobacco agriculture demonstration area. April 19, 2012, the Yunnan and Jiangsu Federations of Returned Overseas Chinese sign, in Tengchong County of Baoshan City (Yunnan), a memorandum of strategic cooperation. June 27, 2012, Tengchong County of Yunnan and the Yueda Group of Jiangsu sign the "Strategic Cooperation Agreement Concerning the Construction of Relevant Industrial Projects in Tengchong"; the first-phase investment is 1.5 billion yuan, covering iron ore, tractor manufacturing, textile industrial park project, etc. September 26, 2012, a delegation of Jiangsu Province visits Yunnan to participate in the "Yunnan-Jiangsu Investment Cooperation Project Promotion Meeting"; the two sides sign 37 project agreements relating to modern agriculture, education, health care, energy, manufacturing, etc., with a total value of 53.7 billion yuan. September 27, 2012, a Yunnan delegation visits Nanjing; the delegation inspects the China (Nanjing) Software Valley, Software Industry Museum, the Headquarters of Suning Company and the ZTE Computing Center Park, etc.

Jiangsu-Zhejiang

[Quick Facts] Average distance = 429 km; Geographical adjacency = 1; Index of ethnic linkages = 0.9933 (2000) and 0.9817 (2010); Freight exchange via national railway = 2930 k tons (2000) and 1860 k tons (2010). ★ December 15, 2006, the Zhejiang Chamber of Commerce in Jiangsu is established. The Chamber has more than 300 member companies, involving real estate, financial investment, culture and education, industrial manufacturing, building materials, electronic appliances, automobiles, IT, catering and entertainment, health care, logistics, textile and garment, advisory services, agriculture, etc. May 30, 2007, the Zhejiang and Jiangsu provincial governments sign a memorandum of cooperation to construct direct port passing, aiming to promote the further development of the Yangtze River Delta. July 23, 2008, Jiangsu University of Science and Technology (JUST) and Linhai City of Zhejiang sign a cooperation contract; the Zhejiang Ship and Shipping School of the JUST is established in Linhai City; the Linhai government donates one million yuan to the School. March 1, 2010, the FDAs of Jiangsu and Zhejiang Provinces sign a regional cooperation agreement on the catering services and food security during the Shanghai World Expo 2010. December 17, 2010, Zhejiang University and Jiangsu Department of Science and Technology sign a cooperation agreement. December 26, 2010, at the "Symposium of Promotion for the Yangtze City Belt Development, Industrial Transferring and Demonstration Zone Construction", the Zhejiang and Jiangsu governments sign a cooperation framework agreement. March 25–27, 2011, the "2011 Zhejiang (Jiangsu) Tourism and Trade Fair" is held in the Nanjing International Exhibition Center, aiming to deepen tourism cooperation between Zhejiang and Jiangsu. December 27, 2011, the Anchang Investment Co., Ltd. of Zhejiang and the Dongfang Construction Project Management and Consulting Co., Ltd. of Jiangsu sign, in Changzhou City of Jiangsu, a strategic framework agreement.

Jiangxi-Jilin

[Quick Facts] Average distance = 2456 km; Geographical adjacency = 0; Index of ethnic linkages = 0.9095 (2000) and 0.9212 (2010); Freight exchange via national railway = 270 k tons (2000) and 1750 k tons (2010). ★ October 14, 2008, Jiangxi Academy of Sciences and Siping City of Jilin Province sign a framework agreement on the establishment of cooperative relationship. August 28, 2009, the Department of Commerce of Jiangxi and the Economic and Technological Cooperation Bureau of Jilin hold an exchange meeting concerning the construction and management of development zones. November 30, 2011, the "Jiangxi (Shangrao) Tourism Promotion" is held in Changchun City of Jilin. The Tourism Bureaux of Shangrao and Changchun Cities sign a tourist cooperation framework agreement; the two cities will cooperate in mutual delivery of tourists, development of special tourist routes and others. July 9, 2012, the Jiangxi Chamber of Commerce in Jilin is established in Changchun City. According to statistics, the number of Jiangxi's businesspersons who invest in Jilin has been over 80,000 and founded nearly 1500 companies, involving mining, engineering machinery, medical equipment, real estate, infrastructure, light industry and textile, modern logistics and catering services, etc., with a total investment of more than 20 billion yuan. September 21–27, 2012, the "Jiangxi (Jilin) Specialty Products and Trade Fair", organized by the Department of Commerce of Jilin and Jiangxi, is held in Changchun, aiming to strengthen information exchange and the associated operations and to promote the establishment of long-term purchase and sale relations. October 9, 2012, the Jiangxi Geology and Mineral Resources Development Bureau and Jilin University hold a forum. October 11–13, 2012, the Jiangxi and Jilin Branches of the China Grain Reserves Corporation sign a cooperation agreement concerning the provision of corn rotation of central reserve grain and the purchasing and marketing of commercial grain.

Jiangxi-Liaoning

[Quick Facts] Average distance = 2151 km; Geographical adjacency = 0; Index of ethnic linkages = 0.8404 (2000) and 0.8491 (2010); Freight exchange via national railway = 430 k tons (2000) and 360 k tons (2010). ★ May 10, 2001, more than 2700 entrepreneurs and government officials participate in the economic cooperation fair which held in Nanchang, Jiangxi. Liaoning (China's old industrial base) and Jiangxi (the old revolutionary base) sign in, Nanchang City of Jiangxi, a series of interprovincial economic cooperation agreements, as the largest scale of cooperation between the two provinces so far; more than 1000 cooperation project agreements are signed (with an estimated investment of over 14 billion yuan), of which the agreement of mutual delivery of 380,000 tourists will produce an economic benefits of 760 million yuan. April 28, 2006, the Liaoning Chamber of Commerce in Jiangxi is established. May 11, 2007, the Liaoning-Jiangxi (Nanchang) Pan-Yangtze River Delta Region Economic Cooperation Fair is held in the Jiangxi Provincial Exhibition Center. The PCSC member and Vice Governor of Jiangxi, Vice Governor of Liaoning and others attend this fair. Liaoning, Jiangxi and other regions in the Pan-Yangtze River Delta sign 29 project agreements, with a total value of 6.722 billion yuan; they include the sales project between the Zhitong Automobile Sales Co., Ltd. and the Shenyang Brilliance Jinbei Automobile Co., Ltd. (with 0.3135 billion yuan), the semiconductor LED project between the Jiangxi Lianchuang Electronic Technology Co., Ltd. and the Dalian Wafangdian Municipal Industrial Park (with 100 million yuan), and the electrolytic copper production line between the Jiangxi Copper Company and the East Port Development Zone (with 800 million yuan). February 4, 2010, Jiangxi Normal University and the Track and Field Training Center of Liaoning Province sign the "Agreement on the Joint Training of High-Level Athletes".

Jiangxi-Ningxia

[Quick Facts] Average distance = 2258 km; Geographical adjacency = 0; Index of ethnic linkages = 0.6555 (2000) and 0.6497 (2010); Freight exchange via national railway = 60 k tons (2000) and 70 k tons (2010). ★ March 5, 2008, the Deputy Chief of the Ningxia Tourism Bureau and his colleagues visit Nanchang City of Jiangxi to hold the tourism promotion entitled "Amazing Ningxia: the South Yangtze in Northwest China". The Ningxia side introduces its tourist resources, tourist lines and local customs to Jiangxi's representatives. Both sides sign an agreement relating to tourist market development. October 8, 2010, the Hengli Co., Ltd. of Ningxia acquires 10 % shares of the Xinri Development Co., Ltd. of Jiangxi. July 4, 2011, the Federations of Returned Overseas Chinese of Ningxia and Jiangxi establish a friendly and cooperative relationship. March 31, 2012, the Jiangxi Chamber of Commerce in Ningxia is established, with more than 400 people attending the inaugural ceremony. According to incomplete statistics, more than 3000 Jiangxi-funded enterprises are registered at Ningxia, mainly engaged in medical equipment, real estate, infrastructure, light industry, textile, food and beverage services, modern logistics, IT, etc., with a total investment of 30 billion yuan. April 8, 2012, the Institutes of Electric Power Design of Jiangxi and Ningxia Hui Autonomous Region sign, in Nanchang, a strategic cooperation framework agreement.

Jiangxi-Qinghai

[Quick Facts] Average distance = 2304 km; Geographical adjacency = 0; Index of ethnic linkages = 0.5414 (2000) and 0.5315 (2010); Freight exchange via national railway = 30 k tons (2000) and 270 k tons (2010). ★ April 25, 2008, the Meteorological Bureau of Shangrao City of Jiangxi and Hainan Prefecture of Qinghai sign, in Xining City of Qinghai, an agreement concerning the establishment of pairing exchange and cooperation relationship. November 23, 2008, the Jiangxi Chamber of Commerce in Qinghai is established. It is reported that, there are over 20,000 Jiangxi businessperson and nearly 3000 Jiangxi-funded companies in Qinghai, involving mining, construction, real estate, metal and non-metal manufacturing, etc. July 6, 2009, the Government of Qinghai Province and the Jiangxi LDK Solar Co., Ltd. sign a cooperation framework agreement on solar photovoltaic industry. April 21, 2010, the Xining (Qinghai)-Jiujiang (Jiangxi) flight route opens, aiming to promote the development of tourism in Northwest China. March 10, 2012, Qinghai Provincial Tourism Agency holds a boutique tourist lines promotion in Jiangxi Province. The two places pledge to strengthen cooperation in tourism. April 7, 2012, the Institutes of Electric Power Design of Jiangxi and Qinghai sign, in Nanchang, a strategic cooperation framework agreement. October 25, 2012, the Haibei Tibetan Autonomous Prefecture of Qinghai visits Nanchang City of Jiangxi to promote tourism. The two places' travel agencies sign more than 80 cooperation contracts.

Jiangxi-Shaanxi

[Quick Facts] Average distance = 1412 km; Geographical adjacency = 0; Index of ethnic linkages = 0.9959 (2000) and 0.9958 (2010); Freight exchange via national railway = 620 k tons (2000) and 3580 k tons (2010). ★ March 20, 2007, the Chongyi Tungsten Products Co., Ltd. of Jiangxi and the Northern Huashan electromechanical Co., Ltd. of Xi'an agree to cooperate in the R&D and sales of tungsten products; the Jiangxi Company will invest 57.6 million yuan or 48 % of the total investment. December 6, 2008, the Jiangxi Chamber of Commerce in Shaanxi is established in Xi'an City. The Chamber member's companies involve real estate development, medical equipment, stationery, building materials, clothing materials, office furniture, food and etc. March 29, 2010, the Jiangxi Chamber of Commerce in Shaanxi visits Weinan City of Shaanxi. The two sides agree to establish six investment directions, including energy development, metallurgical mineral resources development, new energy and photovoltaic industry, advanced equipment manufacturing, agriculture-related processing and modern agricultural logistics industry as well as modern eco-tourism. August 21, 2011, New and High-Tech School of Xi'an University of Science and Technology and the Jiangxi Chamber of Commerce in Shaanxi hold an exchange and cooperation meeting. The School and the Chamber sign an agreement concerning the joint construction of an internship base. May 26, 2012, Yan'an City of Shaanxi and Ji'an City of Jiangxi sign an agreement concerning grouped tourism. Under the agreement, up to ten tourists are entitled to receive discounted air tickets. June 7, 2012, a delegation, led by the President of Jiangxi Chamber of Commerce in Shaanxi visits Baishui County of Shaanxi to review investment progress. The prefectural government and the delegation sign an agreement relating to the construction of the Zhongrui Trade Building in Baishui, with a total investment of 80 million yuan; the delegation and the local Bureau of Agriculture reach a consensus on the construction of vegetable wholesale market in Baishui.

Jiangxi-Shandong

[Quick Facts] Average distance = 1137 km; Geographical adjacency = 0; Index of ethnic linkages = 0.9940 (2000) and 0.9933 (2010); Freight exchange via national railway = 1650 k tons (2000) and 3040 k tons (2010). ★ November 8, 2009, the Jiangxi Chamber of Commerce in Shandong is established in Ji'nan City. According to incomplete statistics, there are over 10,000 Jiangxi enterprises in Shandong, involving real estate, mining and tailings management, environmental engineering, clothing, logistics, transportation, medical equipment, steel building materials, cultural goods, etc., with a total investment of nearly 40 billion yuan. April 21, 2010, the China Tobacco (Shandong) Company and the Jiangxi Provincial Tobacco Monopoly Bureau (Company) sign a strategic alliance agreement June 10, 2011, the Special Electric Machinery Co., Ltd. of Jiangxi and the Shengjian Construction Machinery Co., Ltd. of Dezhou City of Shandong sign a purchase and sales contract. June 1, 2012, the Jiangxi Liuguo Chemical Industry Co., Ltd., the Shandong Agricultural Production Materials Co., Ltd., the Economic and Trade Department of the National DRC and the Economic and Construction Department of the Ministry of Finance sign, in Beijing, the "2012 Phosphate Fertilizer Off-Season Special Reserves Agreement", according to which Jiangxi and Shandong will reserve 20,000 tons of off-season phosphate fertilizers. December 4, 2012, the Ji'nan Special (disabled) Education Center and the Qiyin School of Nanchang of Jiangxi sign a friendly cooperation agreement.

Jiangxi-Shanghai

[Quick Facts] Average distance = 837 km; Geographical adjacency = 0; Index of ethnic linkages = 0.9949 (2000) and 0.9895 (2010); Freight exchange via national railway = 1630 k tons (2000) and 1310 k tons (2010). ★ April 10, 2004, Jiangxi and Shanghai sign an agreement on the strengthening of economic and technological cooperation. Shanghai donates 50 million yuan to the old revolutionary base of Jiangxi; the two places' companies sign 31 cooperation agreements, involving transportation, manufacturing, agricultural products, tourism, agriculture and science, and education, with a total investment of 3.4358 billion yuan. November 19, 2005, the Jiangxi Chamber of Commerce in Shanghai is established. The Chamber has nearly 300 member enterprises, involving electronics, automotive, construction, building materials, real estate, catering, etc. January 5, 2009, the Jiangxi Provincial Forestry Department and the SASAC of Xuhui District (Shanghai) agree to jointly build an industrial chain of forestry and energy and promote the development of bio-diesel, tea oil and turpentine industries. December 3, 2009, the China Import and Export Bank Shanghai Branch and the Zhongding International Group of Jiangxi and other five companies sign, in Nanchang City of Jiangxi, a financial service cooperation agreement. August 15, 2010, Xingguo County of Jiangxi, the Suning Universal Company, the Bangfu Company, and the Pingyi Company (all of Shanghai) sign a cooperation agreement on the production line of gold mine. April 17, 2012, the Vocational Tourism and Commerce College of Jiangxi Province and the ZTE Software Technology (Nanchang of Jiangxi) Co., Ltd., and the Shanghai Zhuoyue Computers Co., Ltd. sign a school-enterprise cooperation agreement. April 23, 2012, the Juwang Pharmaceutical Co., Ltd. of Jiangxi and the Tianxiang Jiantai Co., Ltd. of Shanghai agree to cooperate in the production of pharmaceutical equipments. August 6, 2012, Pingxiang City of Jiangxi Province and Shanghai

University sign a strategic cooperation agreement concerning self innovative abilities and their application to regional economic development.

Jiangxi-Shanxi

[Quick Facts] Average distance = 1944 km; Geographical adjacency = 0; Index of ethnic linkages = 0.9979 (2000) and 0.9974 (2010); Freight exchange via national railway = 1910 k tons (2000) and 4650 k tons (2010). ★ March 10, 2011, the Vice CCP Secretary of Jiangxi Ceramic Arts and Crafts College visits Huairen County of Shanxi Province. Both sides reach a consensus on cooperative education, teachers' training and technological services. April 6, 2011, the Heimao Coal Co., Ltd. of Jiangxi acquires 51 % stake of the Everbright Coal Co., Ltd. of Shanxi. April 15, 2012, the Jiangxi Chamber of Commerce in Shanxi is established in Taiyuan City. The Jiangxi's investors in Shanxi have more than 80,000 and found nearly 3000 companies, involving mining, engineering machinery, medical equipment, real estate, infrastructure, light industry, textile, modern logistics and catering services, etc., with a total investment of over 20 billion yuan. June 5, 2012, the China (Jiangxi) Power Investment Group and the Shanxi Coal Sales Group hold a forum; both sides pledge to establish a long-term strategic partnership. June 8, 2012, the Lingchuan County of Shanxi and the Zhengbang Group of Jiangxi sign an investment agreement concerning the production chain of 1.5 billion heads of pigs. September 21–27, 2012, the "Shanxi (Jilin) Specialty Products Trade Fair", sponsored by the Departments of Commerce of Jiangxi and Jilin, is held in Changchun City. Both sides pledge to strengthen the exchange of information sharing and to promote the establishment of long-term purchase and sales relations.

Jiangxi-Sichuan

[Quick Facts] Average distance = 2239 km; Geographical adjacency = 0; Index of ethnic linkages = 0.9511 (2000) and 0.9402 (2010); Freight exchange via national railway = 560 k tons (2000) and 1260 k tons (2010). ★ June 2008, the Jiangxi provincial government and its Sichuan pairing hold a forum concerning the assistance to the Wenchuan earthquake-hit area. 42 project agreements are signed, with a total investment of 1.3 billion yuan, involving livelihood construction, education, health, broadcasting television, urban infrastructure, agricultural and rural infrastructure, culture, tourism, and economic and technological cooperation. October 14, 2008, at the investment briefings to the post-disaster reconstruction in Sichuan Province, more than 200 entrepreneurs from Jiangxi sign investment agreements with Sichuan. October 27, 2008, the Jiangxi Chamber of Commerce in Sichuan is established. March 22, 2009, the "Regional Cooperation Forum of the Jiangxi Chambers of Commerce in Southwest China" is held in Chengdu City of Sichuan.

The Chambers sign a cooperation agreement. May 31-June 2, 2010, a Jiangxi government delegation, led by the CCP Secretary of Jiangxi visits Xiaojin County (a Wenchuan earthquake-hit area) to inspect the post-disaster recovery status. March 28, 2011, the Kechuang Pharmaceutical (Group) Co., Ltd., of Sichuan and Jiangxi College of Traditional Chinese Medicine sign a strategic cooperation agreement. November 25, 2011, the Chengdu Electric Power Bureau of Sichuan and Nanchang Power Supply Company of Jiangxi sign an agreement on the establishment of friendly and cooperative relations. February 23, 2012, the Sichuan Provincial Institute of Cultural Relics and Archaeology and the Heritage Protection Center of Jiangxi hold, in Jingdezhen City of Jiangxi, a review meeting for the National Archaeological Park plan.

Jiangxi-Tianjin

[Quick Facts] Average distance = 1444 km; Geographical adjacency = 0; Index of ethnic linkages = 0.9741 (2000) and 0.9758 (2010); Freight exchange via national railway = 210 k tons (2000) and 130 k tons (2010). ★ December 6, 2006, the Jiangxi Chamber of Commerce in Tianjin is established. The Chamber has nearly 200 member companies, involving cultural and educational supplies, clothing, hardware, food and beverage, food processing, hotel supplies, decorative building materials, medical devices, etc. August 21–23, 2010, a 70-people delegation, led by the CCP Secretary (also the PCSC Chairman) of Jiangxi, pays an inspection to Tianjin. January 11, 2011, Tianjin University and the Xinyu municipal government of Jiangxi sign a strategic cooperation agreement. The two sides agree to jointly promote the establishment of institutions for research on steel, new energy, new materials, information technology, manufacturing, etc. in Xinyu City. July 11–13, 2011, a 100-people delegation, led by the CCPCC Member (also the CCP Secretary) of Tianjin Municipality, pays an inspection to Jiangxi Province. September 14, 2011, the Tianjin Development Zone holds a special recruitment in Shangrao City of Jiangxi. The Motorola, Samsung and other companies located in the Tianjin Zone sign a total of 500 employment contracts with the people from Jiangxi. The Tianjin Zone and the Shangrao City sign a cooperation agreement on human resource development. The Motorola and local vocational schools sign a school-enterprise cooperation framework agreement. June 19, 2012, Jiangxi's Communist Youth League Working Committee in Tianjin Municipality is established.

Jiangxi-Tibet

[Quick Facts] Average distance = 4101 km; Geographical adjacency = 0; Index of ethnic linkages = 0.0616 (2000) and 0.0828 (2010); Freight exchange via national railway = 0 k ton (2000) and 20 k tons (2010). ★ 2001, the Jiangxi Provincial

Government Office establish the leading team of Tibet pairing aid. December 21, 2009, the "Summary and Exchange Meeting of the National Education Assistance for Tibet" is held in Nanchang City of Jiangxi. According to statistics, from 2007 to 2009, Tibet has received 275 million yuan of aid via a total of 474 projects, with 136,400 m^2 of campuses and dormitories being built and nearly 2000 teachers and staff being trained. The provinces from all over China have donated 530,000 books and dispatched nearly 980 teachers and cadres to Tibet. April 26, 2012, the Jiangxi Provincial Transportation and Communication Department, the Jiangxi Vocational and Technical College and the Tianlu Co., Ltd. of Tibet hold a signing ceremony of the school-enterprise cooperation. The Jiangxi school will continue to host the Tianlu Tibetan Class July 7, 2012, a delegation, led by the Deputy Director of Tibet Department of Education and Vice President of the Tibetan Medicine College of Tibet, visits Jiangxi College of Traditional Chinese Medicine. The two sides hold a symposium concerning the joint training of marketing talents in Tibetan medicine, aiming to implement the central government's decision on pairing aid work. August 19, 2012, a delegation, led by the Vice CCP Secretary of Jiangxi College of Traditional Chinese Medicine, visits Tibet College of Tibetan Medicine. Both sides pledge to jointly establish a research center on traditional Chinese and Tibetan folk medicine resources.

Jiangxi-Xinjiang

[Quick Facts] Average distance = 4391 km; Geographical adjacency = 0; Index of ethnic linkages = 0.4069 (2000) and 0.4061 (2010); Freight exchange via national railway = 130 k tons (2000) and 440 k tons (2010). ★ September 26, 2008, the Jiangxi Association of Enterprises (Chamber of Commerce) in Xinjiang is established in Urumqi City. The Chamber's member companies involve real estate, mining development, medical equipment, stationery, steel building materials, ceramics, glasses, clocks, logistics, transportation, etc. June 3, 2011, The Tourism Bureaux of Jiangxi and Xinjiang hold a forum and sign an agreement concerning tourist cooperation and development. September 25, 2011, the Jiangxi Vocational College of Applied Technology and the Xinjiang Bureau of Geology and Mineral Resources Exploration sign a production and research cooperation agreement. December 25, 2011, the Jiangxi Provincial Higher People's Court and the Kizilsu Kirgiz Autonomous Prefecture Court of and the Artux County Court of Xinjiang sign a pairing aid agreement. April 25–27, 2011, a government delegation of Xinjiang pays an inspection to Jiangxi Province. The Xinjiang delegation hopes to strengthen cooperation with Jiangxi in energy development, modern agriculture and animal husbandry, tourism development; Jiangxi proposes Artux County as its pairing-aid target and donates 310.2 million yuan (including 16 new projects). May 28, 2012, the Workers' Union of Xinjiang and the Jiangxi Association of Enterprises in Xinjiang sign a cooperation agreement, marking that a first province-level, association-based workers' union is established in Xinjiang. The Association has more than 360 member enterprises, covering real estate, logistics, transportation, medical equipment, stationery, craft ceramics, etc. June 26–28, 2012, a delegation, led by the Vice CCP Secretary of Xinjiang, visits Jiangxi. The delegation also inspects the Nanchang High-tech Development Zone.

Jiangxi-Yunnan

[Quick Facts] Average distance = 1911 km; Geographical adjacency = 0; Index of ethnic linkages = 0.6669 (2000) and 0.6675 (2010); Freight exchange via national railway = 660 k tons (2000) and 1210 k tons (2010). ★ June 6, 2006, the Jiangxi Chamber of Commerce in Yunnan is established. According to incomplete statistics, the number of Jiangxi's investors in Yunnan is 230,000, with a total investment of 5 billion yuan, providing more than 5000 jobs to Yunnan. March 22, 2009, the "Regional Cooperation Forum of the Jiangxi Chambers of Commerce in Southwest China" is held in Chengdu City of Sichuan. The Jiangxi Chamber of Commerce in Yunnan signs a cooperation agreement with other Jiangxi Chambers. October 11, 2010, the Yunnan Copper Group and the Anyuan County of Jiangxi sign a cooperation framework agreement on the exploration, development, deep processing and integration of the molybdenum and other metal mineral refinery projects. November 7, 2011, a delegation, led by the CCP Secretary (Vice President) of the Yunnan Vocational College of Land and Resources visits the Jiangxi Vocational College of Applied Technology. December 16, 2011, a delegation, led by the Vice Governor of Jiangxi Province visits Yunnan Province and holds a forum with the relevant sectors of Yunnan. February 17, 2012, the Investment Promotion and Cooperation Bureau of Yunnan Province and the Jiangxi Chamber of Commerce in Yunnan conduct a joint research.

Jiangxi-Zhejiang

[Quick Facts] Average distance = 636 km; Geographical adjacency = 1; Index of ethnic linkages = 0.9943 (2000) and 0.9812 (2010); Freight exchange via national railway = 6490 k tons (2000) and 12,110 k tons (2010). ★ August 2, 2002, the Zhejiang Chamber of Commerce in Jiangxi is established. According to incomplete statistics, Zhejiang has 600,000 businesspersons and over 40,000 enterprises in Jiangxi, funding and employing 2.069 million people. April 3, 2006, the Mengna Hose Company of Zhejiang invests 360 million yuan in the Yingtan Industrial Park of Jiangxi, creating more than 1600 jobs. August 2008, the Jiangxi Chamber of Commerce in Zhejiang is established. The Chamber's member companies involve real estate, high-tech industry, textile, electronics, auto parts, services, etc., with a total investment of over 20 billion yuan. July 21, 2009, Yanshan County of Jiangxi and Cixi City of Zhejiang sign an agreement concerning the joint establishment of a food production and marketing base. Since 2002, Yanshan County has provided 90,000 tons of high-quality grains to Cixi City. March 9, 2010, the Jiangxi Provincial Tobacco Company and the China (Zhejiang) Tobacco Industrial Co., Ltd. sign an industrial and business strategic alliance agreement. August 18, 2010, the Coal and Geology Bureaux of Jiangxi and Zhejiang sign, in Hangzhou City, a cooperation agreement; both sides will jointly develop the construction market in Zhejiang. November 13, 2010, Zhejiang Agricultural University and Zixi County of Jiangxi sign a scientific and technological cooperation agreement. June 8, 2011, the Wannianqing Co., Ltd. of Jiangxi and the Yongli Co., Ltd. of Zhejiang agree to invest 51 million yuan and 49 million yuan, respectively, in a new company. June 9, 2011, Leping Municipal Association of Returned Overseas Chinese of Jiangxi visits Zhoushan City of Zhejiang. September 23, 2012, the Human Resource and Social Security Department of Changxing County (Zhejiang) signs a cooperation agreement with the Personnel Exchange Center of Jiangxi.

Jilin-Liaoning

[Quick Facts] Average distance = 305 km; Geographical adjacency = 1; Index of ethnic linkages = 0.8939 (2000) and 0.8953 (2010); Freight exchange via national railway = 24,790 k tons (2000) and 39,350 k tons (2010). ★ July 19, 2006, Liaoning and Jilin sign a legislative cooperation framework agreement, marking that China's first interregional, resource-sharing legislative mechanism is established. January 16, 2010, the transport sectors of Liaoning and Jilin sign a cooperation framework agreement. April 26, 2010, the Nonferrous Geological Bureau of Liaoning and the Construction and Engineering School of Jilin University sign, in Shenyang City of Liaoning, an agreement concerning research, production and application. September 10, 2010, the Public Security Chiefs of Liaoning and Jilin sign, in Shenyang, an agreement concerning intelligence information sharing, mutual emergent assistance, collaboration against cross-border crimes, social security management and the cooperation in advantageous police resources. October 29, 2010, the Entry-Exit IQBs of Liaoning and Jilin sign, in Shenyang City of Liaoning, a memorandum to strengthen regional cooperation and to promote clearance facilitation cooperation. June 17, 2011, the Liaoning provincial government and Jilin University sign, in Shenyang, a strategic cooperation framework agreement. October 29, 2011, Jianchang County of Huludao City (Liaoning Province) and the Jilin Northeast Nonferrous Metals Co., Ltd. hold a symposium on the investment and exploration of mineral resources in the Bajiazi Economic Development Zone of Jianchang County. The two sides hope to establish a long-term cooperative development relationship. The proven reserves for iron, sulfur, manganese and molybdenum ores, and limestone in the Jianchang area are 500 million tons, 14 million tons, 13.3 million tons, 5.75 million tons and over 100 million tons, respectively. May 18, 2012, Northeast Dianli University of Jilin and the Liaoning Lide Power Electronics Co., Ltd. sign, in Changchun City, a cooperation agreement. The two sides will jointly set up an engineering and technology research center.

Jilin-Ningxia

[Quick Facts] Average distance = 2389 km; Geographical adjacency = 0; Index of ethnic linkages = 0.6645 (2000) and 0.6583 (2010); Freight exchange via national railway = 40 k tons (2000) and 190 k tons (2010). ★ December 1, 2008, Ningxia Hui Autonomous Region and Jilin Province sign a purchase and marketing cooperation agreement. The two sides exchange the reform work of grains enterprises, food purchase and sales and the central grain reserves management. September 7–10, 2009, a delegation, led by the Vice President of Jilin University, pays an inspection to Ningxia. The two sides discuss how Ningxia may better attract high-level domestic and overseas talents. Jilin University and Ningxia University sign a comprehensive cooperation framework agreement concerning innovation and development. September 2, 2010, the "Ningxia-Jilin Trade and Economic Cooperation Forum" opens. The two sides pledge to strengthen cooperation in chemistry and energy, emphasizing the comprehensive development in coal, electric power, chemical products, building materials, environmental protection. September 6, 2011, on the 7th Northeast Asia Expo, Jilin and Ningxia hold a trade and economic cooperation promotion in which Ningxia proposes a package of investment projects, covering energy, chemical industry, metallurgy building materials, equipment manufacturing, light industry, food, special tourism, modern service, etc.

Jilin-Qinghai

[Quick Facts] Average distance = 3144 km; Geographical adjacency = 0; Index of ethnic linkages = 0.5536 (2000) and 0.5418 (2010); Freight exchange via national railway = 40 k tons (2000) and 170 k tons (2010). ★ September 26, 2002, an economic and trade delegation of Haibei Tibetan prefectural government of Qinghai Province visits Jilin Province and holds a promotion meeting. The Haibei government provides investment opportunities of eight coal mining projects and of a thermal power project to Jilin. With 2.5 billion ton proven reserves of coal resources, Haibei is now only producing 1.2 million tons of raw coal per year. The two sides pledge to strengthen cooperation in coal industry. April 15, 2010, the Jilin provincial government donates eight million yuan to the earthquake-hit area of Yushu County (Yushu Tibetan Autonomous Prefecture, Qinghai Province), aiming to support Yushu's post-earthquake reconstruction work. June 16, 2012, the Electric Power Co., Ltd. of Jilin and the Golmud municipal government of Qinghai Province sign a "framework agreement of cooperation in the development and construction of new energy projects". The two sides will establish joint ventures to invest in the development and construction of solar photovoltaic (PV), wind power and other new energy projects in Golmud City. The agreement includes the projects of 500 MWp solar PV and 1000 MW wind power in Golmud, all of which are invested, constructed and operated by the Jilin Company; the Golmud municipal government will provide support in project appraisal, land use, environmental assessment and system assessment.

Jilin-Shaanxi

[Quick Facts] Average distance = 2211 km; Geographical adjacency = 0; Index of ethnic linkages = 0.9134 (2000) and 0.9251 (2010); Freight exchange via national railway = 180 k tons (2000) and 360 k tons (2010). ★ September 17, 2006, Northwest University of Political Science and Law of Xi'an (Shaanxi) and Jilin University sign an agreement concerning the Jilin University's pairing aid to the pairing training of the high-level legal personnel from Northwest China and of the Northwest University of Law and Political Science from 2006 to 2010. September 3, 2010, a tourism promotion, sponsored by the Shaanxi provincial government, is held in Changchun City of Jilin. The officials in charge of tourism sectors from 10 cities in Shaanxi, 10 travel agencies (including the Qujiang Cultural Tourism Group of Xi'an City) from Shaanxi, and more than 83 travel agencies from Jilin Province participate in the promotion activity. The two provinces anticipate signing a tourism cooperation agreement in the forthcoming "6th East Asia Expo", aiming to establish a new pattern of regional cooperation. September 18, 2011, a delegation, composed of the Meihekou municipal CCP Secretary (Mayor) and other relevant officials of Jilin Province, pays an inspection to Shaanxi College of International Business and Economics. The CCP Secretary (also the President) and the Vice President of the College and the Jilin delegation hold a forum. The two sides pledge to strengthen school-enterprise cooperation and to jointly promote the education of professional personnel.

Jilin-Shandong

[Quick Facts] Average distance = 1373 km; Geographical adjacency = 0; Index of ethnic linkages = 0.9145 (2000) and 0.9264 (2010); Freight exchange via national railway = 3210 k tons (2000) and 2470 k tons (2010). ★ April 2008, the Shandong Chamber of Commerce in Jilin is established. The Chamber has more than 130 member companies, involving real estate, construction, medicine, education, food, printing, mechanical and electric equipments, etc. June 3, 2009, Jilin University and Shandong University renew its interuniversity cooperation framework agreement. The two sides pledge to cooperate in personnel training and exchange of students.

August 10, 2009, the Tourism Bureaux of Yantai City (Shandong Province) and Yanbian Korean Autonomous Prefecture (Jilin Province) sign a cooperation agreement. May 5–6, 2010, the "Jilin-Shandong Economic Cooperation Symposium" and the "Jilin-Qingdao Economic Cooperation Symposium" are held in Ji'nan and Qingdao Cities of Shandong Province, respectively. June 14, 2011, a Jilin tourism promotion is held in Ji'nan City of Shandong. The Jilin delegation presents a number of tourist routes and five featured tourism products. In 2010, Shandong becomes Jilin's third largest domestic tourist source. August 16, 2011, a delegation of Jilin Agricultural University visits the Shandong Zhongnong Company. The two sides sign an agreement concerning the construction of a students' social practice base. August 1, 2012, the Shandong Energy Group and the Huadian municipal government of Jilin sign, in Huadian City, a strategic cooperation agreement; the two sides will jointly construct the Huadian Fengtai Oil Shale Circular Economy Park. August 30, 2012, the Jilin Chamber of Commerce in Qingdao signs a strategic cooperation agreement with the Shandong Yuanda Kejian Technology Co., Ltd. The Chamber becomes the general agent in Jilin.

Jilin-Shanghai

[Quick Facts] Average distance = 2335 km; Geographical adjacency = 0; Index of ethnic linkages = 0.9137 (2000) and 0.9268 (2010); Freight exchange via national railway = 810 k tons (2000) and 490 k tons (2010). ★ December 3, 2004, the "China Green Food (Shanghai) Expo" opens. The Jiangshan Group of Jilin and the Dianshanfu Grains Supply and Marketing Co., Ltd. of Shanghai sign more than 20 sales and purchase agreements. November 1, 2007, the Liangyou (Group) Co., Ltd. of Shanghai signs food production and marketing cooperation agreements with the Reserves and Distribution Company of the Jilin Grains Group, Taonan Municipal Grains Bureau and the County Grain Bureaux of Taobei and Zhenlai. December 18, 2007, the Jilin Chamber of Commerce in Shanghai is established. The Chamber has over 100 member companies. May 5, 2008, the "Jilin-Shanghai Trade and Economic Cooperation Fair" is held in Shanghai. The two governments, relevant sectors and enterprises sign five cooperation framework agreements and 66 project contracts, with a total investment of about 35.1 billion yuan. August 21, 2008, the "Annual Jilin-Shanghai Grains Production and Marketing Fair" and the agreement signing ceremony are held in Changchun City. Jilin Province will provide Shanghai 500,000 tons of grains, including 200,000 tons of japonica rice and 300,000 tons of corn. January 4, 2010, the Management Committee of the Hi-tech Zone of Jilin signs an agreement with the Shanghai Science and Technology Development and Exchange Center. June 4, 2010, the government of Jilin Province holds the opening ceremony of the Jilin-Shanghai (Yangtze Delta Region) Cooperation Center, aiming to promote bilateral economic and cultural exchange and cooperation. June 21, 2012, Northeast Normal University of Changchun City

(Jilin) visits Dalian Foreign Languages Institute of Liaoning and participate in the symposium of the "Chinese Project of the Shanghai Cooperation Organization".

Jilin-Shanxi

[Quick Facts] Average distance = 1560 km; Geographical adjacency = 0; Index of ethnic linkages = 0.9115 (2000) and 0.9229 (2010); Freight exchange via national railway = 1110 k tons (2000) and 1740 k tons (2010). ★ February 27, 2009, the Shanxi and Jilin Committees of the Jiusan Society carry out cooperation in the application of bio-organic fertilizers in the beans-producing areas of Jilin Province; the two sides sign a preliminary agreement. September 29, 2009, the Shanxi Chamber of Commerce in Jilin is established. The Chamber has more than 40 member companies, covering real estate, building materials, decoration, auto parts, pharmaceuticals, hotels, plus industrial, commercial, communications, electronics, bio-engineering, commodity retail, new energy, lithium batteries, etc. January 11, 2010, the Changbaishan municipal government of Jilin and the Shanxi Chamber of Commerce in Jilin sign a strategic cooperation agreement; the Jilin Baishan Economic Development Zone and the Jinji (Shanxi and Jilin) lithium battery Co., Ltd. of Jilin sign an agreement concerning the construction of iron phosphate lithium battery investment and construction, with a total investment of one billion yuan. June 10, 2012, a delegation, composed of the Coalmine Safety and Supervision Bureau of and the Production Safety and Supervision Administration of Jilin Province and the Jilin Coal Group, pays an inspection to the Zhenghui Coalmine of the Shanxi Coking Coal Group Fenxi Mining Company. September 17, 2012, a 15-people delegation of the Agricultural Machinery Bureau of Shanxi Province visits the Yutian Agricultural Machinery Cooperatives and the Agricultural Machinery Management General Station of Jiutai City of Jilin Province.

Jilin-Sichuan

[Quick Facts] Average distance = 3094 km; Geographical adjacency = 0; Index of ethnic linkages = 0.9110 (2000) and 0.9227 (2010); Freight exchange via national railway = 80 k tons (2000) and 1810 k tons (2010). ★ September 26, 2008, the Sichuan-Chongqing Chamber of Commerce in Jilin is established in Changchun. The Chamber has more than 60 member companies, covering real estate, building materials, decoration, catering services, electronic information, local specialty sales, etc. September 16, 2010, a Yibin (Sichuan) municipal economic and trade delegation visits Changchun City (Jilin). Both sides sign two large project agreements, including the inorganic powder paper project (with an annual output of 360,000 tons and a total investment of 930 million yuan) and the staple fiber project (with an annual output of 60,000 tons and a total investment of 600 million yuan). December 3, 2010, at the 3rd International Science and Technology Conference of Traditional Chinese Medicine Modernization, which is held in Chengdu, the Science and Technology Departments of Jilin and Sichuan sign a strategic cooperation agreement. The two sides will jointly construct the North-South Chinese Medicine Base and jointly promote the development of Chinese medicine modernization. June 20, 2011, the "Jilin-Sichuan Cooperation Symposium" is held in Changchun City of Jilin. Jilin Province donates 1.25 billion yuan (via 200 projects) to the earthquake-hit area in Heishui County of Sichuan Province. September 8, 2011, a delegation, led by the Deputy Chief of the Sichuan Provincial Grain Bureau, visits Jilin Province to consolidate interprovincial food production and marketing relations. It is reported that a quarter of grains needed in Sichuan relies on other provinces. April 10, 2012, a Tourism Promotion entitled "Beautiful Seasons, Wonderful Jilin" is held in Chengdu City of Sichuan. The two sides sign an agreement on the mutual delivery of tourists. April 11, 2012, a delegation, led by the Vice Governor of Jilin Province, visits Chengdu City of Sichuan to participate in the Sichuan-Jilin Tourism Forum.

Jilin-Tianjin

[Quick Facts] Average distance = 1012 km; Geographical adjacency = 0; Index of ethnic linkages = 0.9217 (2000) and 0.9346 (2010); Freight exchange via national railway = 1160 k tons (2000) and 820 k tons (2010). ★ April 5, 2006, the "Jilin-Tianjin Agricultural Exchange and Matchmaking Symposium" is held in Tianjin. Jilin Province shows more than 100 kinds of green agricultural products and processed products, and proposes nearly 100 agricultural development projects. 18 counties (cities) from Jilin Province and 11 districts (counties) from Tianjin jointly sign an agreement concerning the establishment of a long-term cooperative relationship in agriculture; the two sides also reach 10 labor cooperation agreements. The enterprises of the two places sign 20 economic and trade cooperation project agreements, with a total investment of 1.376 billion yuan. September 7, 2006, Tianjin University is invited to participate in the project matchmaking and cooperation meeting held in Tonghua City of Jilin Province. November 21, 2008, the Samsung Electro-Mechanics Co., Ltd. of Tianjin and Jilin University hold a signing ceremony of school-enterprise cooperation. November 28, 2008, Jilin University and the Zhong'ao Animal Husbandry Group of Tianjin jointly establish a center for research on veterinary technologies. May 7, 2010, the "Jilin-Tianjin Economic Cooperation Symposium" is held in Tianjin; nearly 300 people from the two places attend the meeting. November 10, 2010, Jilin Province and Tianjin Municipality sign an agreement on offsite medical billing and reimbursement cooperation.

Jilin-Tibet

[Quick Facts] Average distance = 5163 km; Geographical adjacency = 0; Index of ethnic linkages = 0.0649 (2000) and 0.0867 (2010); Freight exchange via national railway = 0 k ton (2000) and 0 k ton (2010). ★ October 25, 2002, a delegation led by Vice Governor of Jilin Province visits Tibet and holds a forum with the Vice CCP Secretary of Tibet Autonomous Region. Both sides pledge to strengthen ethnic friendship and to promote economic and social development in Tibet. June 25, 2004, a second team of Jilin's aiding-Tibet cadres arrives in Xigaze, Tibet. September-October, 2004, Jilin's aiding-Tibet cadres carry out the "solar stove project" in Dinggye, Saga and Kuala of Tibet. The project costs two million yuan, and 4000 farmers and herdsmen will benefit from it. August 26–29, 2006, the Everest Cultural Tourism Festival is held in the Tibetan Folk Customs Garden of Xigaze Prefecture (Tibet). The Garden is part of the pairing-aid program provided by Jilin Province; the total investment of the program is 33 million yuan. October 13, 2008, 15 high school teachers from Xigaze of Tibet and backbone teachers from Northeast Normal University of Jilin carry out one-month training course. This is an important part of the pairing-aid cooperation between Jilin and Tibet. The Educational Science School of Northeast Normal University, the Affiliated High School of Northeast Normal University and the schools appointed by Education Department of Changchun City participate in the cooperation. November 18, 2010, the Institute of Vegetables and Flowers of Jilin and Xigaze Institute of Agricultural Research of Tibet sign a cooperation agreement on potato production technology. September 13, 2011, Jilin's pairing-aid project (entitled "Medical Care Training Course") to Xigaze Prefecture of Tibet is launched in the CCP School of Liaoyuan City, Jilin Province.

Jilin-Xinjiang

[Quick Facts] Average distance = 4820 km; Geographical adjacency = 0; Index of ethnic linkages = 0.4186 (2000) and 0.4159 (2010); Freight exchange via national railway = 180 k tons (2000) and 230 k tons (2010). ★ October 2010, the governments of Jilin Province and Xinjiang Uygur Autonomous Region sign a cooperation framework agreement concerning Jilin's pairing aid to Xinjiang through talent introduction. The two sides will base their cooperation and development strategies on Xinjiang's advantageous natural resources and economic specialties, mainly focusing the R&D and application of oatmeal cultivation, natural pig breeding, blueberry production, and white thorn cultivation. February 2011, Jilin and Xinjiang sign the "Plan of the Jilin Province Pairing Aid to the Altay Prefecture of Xinjiang". April 26–27, 2011, a delegation, led by the CCP Secretary of Xinjiang, visits Jilin. June 1, 2011, the Tourism Bureaux of Xinjiang and Jilin sign a strategic cooperation agreement. Both sides will rely on their featured tourist resources and carry out cooperation in tourist product development, marketing promotion, investment, personnel training and others; they decide to launch the "10,000 Jilin People Visit Xinjiang" and "10,000 Xinjiang People Visit Jilin" activities, and to cooperate in providing discounted air and rail tickets. June 16, 2011, the Communist Youth League Committees of Altay and Jilin sign an aid cooperation agreement. Jilin donates books to Altay. February 25, 2012, the Agricultural Bureau of Moyu County of Hotan Prefecture (Xinjiang) and the Bureau of Commerce of Changchun City (Jilin) hold a jujube fair.

Jilin-Yunnan

[Quick Facts] Average distance = 4230 km; Geographical adjacency = 0; Index of ethnic linkages = 0.6719 (2000) and 0.6717 (2010); Freight exchange via national railway = 260 k tons (2000) and 1030 k tons (2010). ★ May 29, 2008, the Grains Bureaux of Yunnan and Jilin and the Chinese Grains Reserves Co., Ltd. hold, in Kunming City of Yunnan, a marketing and production cooperation forum. The three sides sign a cooperation agreement of dynamic interprovincial grain reserves, aiming to establish a long-term and stable grains purchase and sales relationship. October 25, 2011, Baicheng City of Jilin and Yuxi City of Yunnan sign a grain production and marketing cooperation framework agreement. November 27, 2011, the Zhaotong municipal government of Jilin and the Wentou Group of Yunnan sign, in Kunming, a cooperation agreement of cultural industry development. According to the agreement, the Yunnan Group will register a new company in Zhaotong City; the Group and Zhaoyang District of Zhaotong City will jointly build a cultural landmark which occupies 4000 mu of land (including waters); the Group will restore the Zhaotong Confucian Temple ruins; Zhaotong City will provide the land surrounding the temple, mainly used for the project development. August 23, 2012, the Economic and Technological Cooperation Bureau of Jilin Province and the Investment Promotion Bureau of Yunnan Province hold a symposium concerning the drafting and enactment of the "Ordinance of Promotion External Investment in Yunnan".

Jilin-Zhejiang

[Quick Facts] Average distance = 2464 km; Geographical adjacency = 0; Index of ethnic linkages = 0.9095 (2000) and 0.9219 (2010); Freight exchange via national railway = 960 k tons (2000) and 150 k tons (2010). ★ May 15, 2008, the Zhejiang Chamber of Commerce in Jilin is established. According to statistics, there are 100,000 Zhejiang businesspersons in Jilin. September 17, 2009, the Zhejiang and Jilin provincial governments sign a memorandum of strategic cooperation concerning the production and marketing of pig and corn. March 27–30, 2010, the Jilin

University School of Law and the Zhejiang University School of Law sign a cooperation agreement. September 6–8, 2010, a delegation, led by the Vice CCP Secretary of Zhejiang Province, visits Jilin, aiming to further expand exchange and cooperation between the two provinces, to exchange Jilin's experiences in the development of modern agriculture and to establish a long-term and stable relationship in grains supply. November 15, 2011, a delegation, composed of the Jilin PCSC Chairman and the CCP Secretary of Yanbian Korean Autonomous Prefecture of Jilin Province, visits Yiwu City of Zhejiang. The two sides sign a strategic cooperation agreement, involving economic and trade exchange, industrial development, cultural exchange, tourism, etc. Zhejiang will build, for the first time, a Yiwu market in Jilin Province. February 22, 2012, the Fusong municipal government of Jilin and the Rongshi Jiye Group of Zhejiang sign a project agreement concerning the joint development of high-end furniture in the Mt. Changbai area, with a total investment of 350 million yuan. September 10, 2012, the Jilin municipal government of Jilin and the Wanfeng Auto Holding Group of Zhejiang sign an agreement concerning the production of new energy auto parts and aluminum alloy wheels, with a total investment of 3 billion yuan. November 18, 2012, Northeast Dianli University of Jilin Province and the Zhejiang Switches Co., Ltd. hold an agreement signing ceremony of the construction of the Yangtze Delta (Zhejiang) Technology Park.

Liaoning-Ningxia

[Quick Facts] Average distance = 2084 km; Geographical adjacency = 0; Index of ethnic linkages = 0.6663 (2000) and 0.6598 (2010); Freight exchange via national railway = 1050 k tons (2000) and 1610 k tons (2010). ★ August 19, 2002, the "Liaoning-Ningxia Economic Cooperation Forum" is held in Yinchuan City of Ningxia. The vice governors of two places sign an agreement. Both sides pledge to actively participate in the development of the West China region and to expand exchange and cooperation in tourism, transportation, agriculture, infrastructure construction, ecological and environmental protection, aiming to strengthen economic and technological cooperation between the two provinces. January 18, 2008, the Ningxia Rural Credit Cooperatives sets up branches in Liaoning Province, aiming to carry out cross-regional cooperation in financial service. This also aims to promote the opening up of the rural banking market and to reduce the financial costs of central government in dead accounts and bad debts of rural financial system. April 17–19, 2009, the "China Domestic Travel Fair" is held in Dalian City, Liaoning. A delegation composed of 50 travel agencies and representatives, led by the Vice Chairman of the Ningxia Hui Autonomous Region, attend the fair. The Tourism Bureaux of Ningxia and Liaoning sign an agreement of cooperation in tourism. May 1, 2009, the direct flight between Yinchuan of Ningxia and Dalian of Liaoning is officially launched. February 21, 2012, the Ningxia Wine Industry Co., Ltd.

holds, in Shenyang, a symposium with its representatives and franchisers in Liaoning. Both sides discuss the company's development plan and target for 2011.

Liaoning-Qinghai

[Quick Facts] Average distance = 2839 km; Geographical adjacency = 0; Index of ethnic linkages = 0.5650 (2000) and 0.5530 (2010); Freight exchange via national railway = 270 k tons (2000) and 280 k tons (2010). ★ May, 2010, a delegation, composed of 17 A-level hospitals and led by the Health Department of Liaoning Province, visits Qinghai to discuss pairing aid work. The Health Departments of the two provinces fix a scheme concerning Liaoning's pairing aid to Qinghai's medical institutions. August 2, 2011, the signing ceremony of the pairing aid agreement concerning blood collection and supply from Liaoning to Qinghai Province is held in the Liaoning Provincial Blood Center. The pairing aid targets include Haibei, Hainan and Huangnan Tibetan Autonomous Prefectures, Haixi Mongol and Tibetan Autonomous Prefecture and Golmud Prefecture. October 9, 2012, the "Symposium of Pairing Aid Cooperation and the Signing Ceremony of Project Cooperation between Liaoning and Qinghai Provinces" are held in Qinghai. Liaoning and Qinghai Provinces sign a new package of pairing aid cooperation agreements. They include 21 trade and economic cooperation projects, involving personnel exchange, coal resource development, economic and technological development, tourism and sports, with a total value of 1.83 billion yuan. Liaoning Province donates 33.5 million yuan aid (in cash and material) to Qinghai Province.

Liaoning-Shaanxi

[Quick Facts] Average distance = 1906 km; Geographical adjacency = 0; Index of ethnic linkages = 0.8443 (2000) and 0.8531 (2010); Freight exchange via national railway = 620 k tons (2000) and 1050 k tons (2010). ★ May 14, 2005, the Association of Shaanxi Fellows in Liaoning Province is established. The association has 41 enterprise members and 326 individual members. June 21, 2010, the Huanqiu (Liaoning) Company and the Yanchang (Shaanxi) Refinery Company sign a project contract, with an annual production capacity of 120,000 tons of styrene. September 7, 2010, Shaanxi and Liaoning Provinces sign a tourism cooperation agreement, aiming to establish a new pattern of regional tourism cooperation and to jointly promote the two provinces' tourism brands. October 9, 2010, the Dalian municipal government of and the Changxing Island Harbor Industrial Zone of Liaoning Province sign, in Shaanxi, a cooperation framework agreement with the Shaanxi Yanchang Petroleum Group. The Yanchang Group will construct a large petrochemical project in Changxing Island which has the advantage of deepwater shorelines. January 10, 2011, the Hongyun Football Club of Liaoning and the Baorong Chanba Football Club of Shaanxi sign a player-transfer agreement. June 17, 2011, the Liaoning provincial government and Xi'an Jiaotong University, sign, in Shenyang, a province-school strategic cooperation framework agreement. The two sides will cooperate in production and research, human resource training, scientific and technological transferring, etc., aiming to improve independent innovation ability and to form a long-term cooperation relationship. June 18, 2012, the "Red Tourism Cities" of Shaanxi and Liaoning sign a memorandum entitled "Yan'an Strategic Cooperation Alliance". June 19, 2012, the No. 1 Aerial Remote Sensing Institute of the National Mapping and Geographic Information Bureau of Xi'an City and the Basic Surveying and Mapping Institute of Liaoning Province sign, in Jinzhou City, a friendship and cooperation agreement. The two institutions will cooperate in large-sized mapping and visual production.

Liaoning-Shandong

[Quick Facts] Average distance = 1067 km; Geographical adjacency = 0; Index of ethnic linkages = 0.8462 (2000) and 0.8555 (2010); Freight exchange via national railway = 4670 k tons (2000) and 4370 k tons (2010). ★ April 21, 2008, the Forestry Bureaux of Liaoning and Shandong Provinces sign a memorandum of forestry pest defense. The two sides will jointly prevent and cure the biological forest pests including xylophilus (in Shandong) and fall webworm (in Liaoning). September 24, 2009, the Maritime Safety Administrations of Liaoning and Shandong hold, in Dalian City of Liaoning, a signing ceremony of the "Regional Cooperation Agreement of Maritime Search and Rescue". Both sides pledge to further strengthen cooperation in maritime emergent search and rescue. September 2010, the Shandong Chamber of Commerce in Liaoning is established. September 19, 2010, Zhangwu County of Liaoning Province and the Shandong Ao'de Gas Co., Ltd. sign a cooperation agreement on the piped gas project; the project will cost 180 million yuan. October 15, 2010, Shandong University and the Liaoning Huishan Holdings (Group) Co., Ltd. sign a school-enterprise cooperation agreement. The Liaoning Company donates 3 million yuan to Shandong University to set up a scholarship fund. March 9, 2011, Yingkou City of Liaoning and the Langchao Electronic Information Industry Co., Ltd. of Shandong sign a cooperation agreement. The Shandong Company will provide financial services to the enterprises of Yingkou City. July 6, 2011, the Liaoning (Huludao) Chamber of Commerce in Shandong is established. July 6, 2012, the Liaoning (Benxi) Chamber of Commerce in Shandong is established and holds the first congress.

Liaoning-Shanghai

[Quick Facts] Average distance = 2033 km; Geographical adjacency = 0; Index of ethnic linkages = 0.8447 (2000) and 0.8548 (2010); Freight exchange via national railway = 950 k tons (2000) and 320 k tons (2010). ★ August 30, 2008, the Liaoning Chamber of Commerce in Shanghai is established. According to incomplete statistics, more than 500 Liaoning enterprises are registered in and more than 30,000 Liaoning people are living in Shanghai, mainly engaged in real estate, construction, trade, catering, IT, investment, logistics, culture and pharmaceutics. December 29, 2010, the Liaoning provincial government and the Shanghai Greenland Group sign a cooperation agreement on the construction project of the International Conference Center in Liaoning. March 19, 2011, the Dalian Baoyuan Nuclear Equipment Co., Ltd. of the Liaoning Machinery Group Co., Ltd. and the Shanghai Nuclear Engineering Research and Design Institute sign a strategic cooperation agreement. The two sides will carry out cooperation in the technological localization of and the production independency of nuclear power generation. April 1, 2011, Liaoning Province and Shanghai Jiaotong University sign a strategic cooperation framework agreement. The two sides will promote cooperation in R&D. July 15, 2011, the Shenyang municipal government of Liaoning and the Shanghai Automotive Group Co., Ltd. sign the "Agreement of the Further Deepening of Strategic Cooperation"; the two sides will promote the expansion project of Shanghai GM in Shenyang, which has a total investment of 7 billion yuan and annual production capacity of 300,000 vehicles. July 23, 2011, the Shanghai Greenland Group and the Panjin municipal government of Liaoning sign a cooperation agreement concerning the investment project of the "Liaohe International Eco-City".

Liaoning-Shanxi

[Quick Facts] Average distance = 1255 km; Geographical adjacency = 0; Index of ethnic linkages = 0.8425 (2000) and 0.8507 (2010); Freight exchange via national railway = 12,450 k tons (2000) and 18,150 k tons (2010). ★ August 9, 2004, the "Shanxi-Liaoning Tourism Market Fair" is held in Liaoning. The two provinces sign a tourism cooperation agreement. The Shenyang Beiguo (northland) Travel Agency and the Shanxi Sijifeng (season wind) Travel Agency sign a cooperation agreement concerning charter flights during National Day holidays; the Shenyang Yuanlin (garden) International Travel Agency of Liaoning and the Jinyang Cultural Travel Agency of Shanxi sign an agreement concerning the mutual delivery of tourists. November 24, 2006, the Shanxi Chamber of Commerce in Liaoning is established. According to incomplete statistics, Liaoning has hosted 200,000 Shanxi people and more than 1000 Shanxi enterprises (with a total investment of over 10 billion yuan), involving coal, stainless steel, pig iron, machinery oil, boiler, furniture, sponge, paint, radiator, pumps, aquaculture, grain and cooking oil. November 24–27, 2006, a Shanxi delegation, composed of the DRC, the Economic and Trade Commission, the Department of Finance, the Department of Construction, the Land and Resources Department and the SASAC and led by the Vice CCP Secretary (also the Governor), visits Liaoning Province. Both sides discuss the reform of the Northeast old industrial base and the management of the shantytowns and subsidence areas in Liaoning. July 2, 2009, the Dalian Commodity Exchange of Liaoning and the Coking Industry Association of Shanxi sign, in Taiyuan of Shanxi, a cooperation agreement. The two sides will promote cooperation in futures market, spot market services, industrial development and others. November 1, 2011, the Huite Technology Co., Ltd. of Taiyuan City of Shanxi and Electrics and Control College of Huludao City of Liaoning sign a cooperation agreement. The two sides will cooperate in R&D, professional staff training, internships and employment.

Liaoning-Sichuan

[Quick Facts] Average distance = 2789 km; Geographical adjacency = 0; Index of ethnic linkages = 0.8419 (2000) and 0.8507 (2010); Freight exchange via national railway = 1260 k tons (2000) and 1160 k tons (2010). ★ December 2005, the Sichuan-Chongqing Chamber of Commerce in Liaoning is established. The Chamber has 500 individual members. According to incomplete statistics, in the Shenyang area there are 450,000 people from Sichuan (including Chongqing). The investment from Sichuan (including Chongqing) is about 30 billion yuan, involving real estate, knitting, garments, shoes, hats, wine, food and beverage, electrical appliances, electronic communications, automotive and machinery, etc. May 9, 2010, a delegation of Liaoning Province pays an inspection to Sichuan Province to review pairing reconstruction project progress and holds, jointly with its Sichuan partners in Chengdu City, the "Liaoning-Sichuan Economic and Social Cooperation and Development Forum". The two provincial governments sign an agreement concerning the economic and social strategic cooperation between Liaoning and Sichuan. October 1, 2010, Liaoning Province and Anxian County of Sichuan Province sign a pairing aid cooperation agreement. June 22, 2011, the "Liaoning–Sichuan Exchange and Cooperation Forum" is held in Shenyang City. The two provinces sign a cooperation framework agreement. March 22, 2012, the Sichuan Airlines Co., Ltd. and the Liaoning Airport Management Corporation sign a cooperation agreement. The two sides will jointly expand the Sichuan Airlines market in Liaoning.

Liaoning-Tianjin

[Quick Facts] Average distance = 707 km; Geographical adjacency = 0; Index of ethnic linkages = 0.8543 (2000) and 0.8639 (2010); Freight exchange via national railway = 3690 k tons (2000) and 3250 k tons (2010). ★ June 13, 2008, the Dalian Huaxin Computer Technologies Co., Ltd. of Liaoning and the Tianjin High-Tech Zone sign an agreement concerning the cooperative construction of the Tianjin Huaxin Software Park, with a total investment of 20 million yuan; the project will carry out worldwide businesses in software development and customer service. October 8, 2008, the Tianjin Customs and Shenyang Customs of Liaoning sign a memorandum of interregional clearance cooperation, aiming to improve clearance efficiency and reduce intermediate service costs. August 6, 2009, the Tianjin Municipal Publishing Authority and the Liaoning Northern Publishing & Media (Group) Co., Ltd. sign a strategic cooperation framework agreement. The two sides hope to overcome the regionalized economic system and to promote cross-regional and cross-industrial integration. June 17, 2011, the agreement signing ceremony of strategic cooperation between Liaoning Province and Tianjin University is held in Shenyang City. Both sides sign a province-school comprehensive strategic cooperation framework agreement. August 14, 2012, the Science and Technology Cooperation Fair of Liaoning Province and Tianjin University is held in Shenyang City, aiming to promote the development of the Northeast China old industrial base.

Liaoning-Tibet

[Quick Facts] Average distance = 4901 km; Geographical adjacency = 0; Index of ethnic linkages = 0.0649 (2000) and 0.0869 (2010); Freight exchange via national railway = 0 k ton (2000) and 10 k tons (2010). ★ November 19, 2004, a delegation, led by the CCP Secretary of the Science and Technology Bureau of Nagqu Prefecture (Tibet), pays an inspection to Liaoning Province; both sides hold a forum. April 28, 2008, the Tibet photography exhibition entitled "Love Tibet, Love China, Love Olympics", sponsored by the Communist Youth League of Liaoning University, opens in the library of Liaoning University. 50 works are selected for the American Houston International Photography Festival Exhibition. March 22, 2011, the FDA of Liaoning Province carries out pairing aid work to Tibet; Liaoning decides to provide over 200,000 yuan per year to Nagqu Prefecture, mainly used for bilateral cooperation projects and staff training. May 15, 2011, the Liaoning headquarters for the pairing aid to Nagqu visits Nagqu Prefecture to inspect the hospital relocation project and the CCP School construction project; the two projects will cost 59.09 million yuan. August 15, 2012, the comprehensive vocational training center of the aiding Nagqu (Tibet) project, invested by the Human Resource and Social Security Department of Liaoning Province, starts. This project will cost 2.3 million yuan, mainly focusing the professional trainings of automotive repair, electric and electronic, Tibetan home knitting, Tibetan painting and Tibetan sewing embroidery. September 9, 2012, a delegation, led the Director of the Economic Cooperation Office (the office of pairing aid to Tibet) of Liaoning, visits Nagqu Prefecture to inspect the progress of the Liaoning-aided projects including the "Liaoning Departments", the Tibetan Hospital and the CCP School Administration Building.

Liaoning-Xinjiang

[Quick Facts] Average distance = 4515 km; Geographical adjacency = 0; Index of ethnic linkages = 0.4238 (2000) and 0.4208 (2010); Freight exchange via national railway = 460 k tons (2000) and 730 k tons (2010). ★ April 27, 2011, the "Tacheng-Liaoning Industrial Cooperation Project Promotion" is held in Shenyang City. The two sides sign agreements in financial support, and technological and industrial cooperation, with a total value of over 14 billion yuan. May 3, 2011, the IQBs of Liaoning and Xinjiang sign, in Dalian City of Liaoning, a pairing aid cooperation agreement. May 31, 2011, the Petroleum and Chemical Planning and Design Institute of Liaoning Province establishes a branch in Wusu City of Xinjiang, mainly responsible for the design of the development of petrochemical industrial project and the special development planning of petrochemical, coal chemical and natural gas chemical projects. June 3, 2011, a Xinjiang delegation visits Shenyang. The Tourism Bureaux of Xinjiang and Liaoning sign an agreement on pairing aid by tourism. The two sides decide to promote the "10,000 People Tour Xinjiang" and the "10,000 People Tour Liaoning" activities. July 24, 2011, a delegation, led by the Forestry Department of Liaoning, visits Tacheng Prefecture of Xinjiang; both sides sign a forestry cooperation framework agreement. September 7, 2011, the Human Resource and Social Security Department of Liaoning Province and the No. 9 Division of the XPCC sign a pairing-aid framework agreement concerning the employment and social security in the No. 9 Division. November 15, 2011, the CCP School of Benxi City (Liaoning) and Tuoli County of Xinjiang sign a joint educational agreement. July 1, 2012, the FDAs of Yumin County of Xinjiang and Jinzhou City of Liaoning sign an agreement on pairing-aid work. September 1, 2012 the Liaoning Chamber of Commerce in Xinjiang is established in Urumqi City. The Chamber has 94 member companies, with a total investment of 6.48 billion yuan in Xinjiang.

Liaoning-Yunnan

[Quick Facts] Average distance = 3925 km; Geographical adjacency = 0; Index of ethnic linkages = 0.6736 (2000) and 0.6732 (2010); Freight exchange via national railway = 360 k tons (2000) and 490 k tons (2010). ★ December 22, 2003, the

Yunnan Hongta Tobacco Co. acquires the Liaoning Tobacco Co., Ltd. with 500 million yuan (accounting for 51 % of the total shares; the remaining are held by the Liaoning provincial government). As a result, a new company, which is based on the Shenyang and the Yingkou Cigarettes Plants of Liaoning and now renamed as the Hongta Liaoning Tobacco Co., Ltd., is officially established in Shenyang. April 17, 2012, the Yingke Law Firm Kunming (Yunnan Province) Branch signs a strategic cooperation agreement with the Mingwei Forestry Resources Assets Appraisal Co., Ltd. of Liaoning Province. June 8, 2012, the Yunnan Chamber of Commerce in Liaoning is established in Kunming City. September 27–28, 2012, the "China (Yunnan) Bridgehead Construction Technology Matchmaking Fair", jointly organized by the PRC Ministry of Science and Technology and Yunnan Province, is held in the Kunming International Convention and Exhibition Center; a total of 30 interprovincial cooperation projects are signed in the fair. The Kunming High-tech Zone and the Liaoning (Benxi) National Biomedicine Base sign a strategic development cooperation agreement.

Liaoning-Zhejiang

[Quick Facts] Average distance = 2159 km; Geographical adjacency = 0; Index of ethnic linkages = 0.8405 (2000) and 0.8500 (2010); Freight exchange via national railway = 1090 k tons (2000) and 480 k tons (2010). ★ September 25, 2004, a Liaoning government delegation visits Zhejiang; the two provinces sign a cooperation agreement and pledge to further promote exchange and cooperation in economy, technology, sciences and education. February 11, 2006, a large business delegation of Fushun City (Liaoning) visits Zhejiang for investment promotion, attracting nearly one billion yuan. August 15, 2007, the Zhejiang Chamber of Commerce in Liaoning is established. There are over 200,000 Zhejiang businesspersons living in Liaoning. November 6, 2008, a delegation, led by the Fushun Municipal CCP Secretary, visits Qingtian County of Zhejiang, and holds a trade and economic cooperation forum with the Zhejiang leaders and entrepreneurs. 30 people including the Deputy Magistrate of Qingtian County, the Executive Vice President of the Overseas Chinese Association in Barcelona and the President of the Peaceful Reunification Association in Spain attend the forum. December 18, 2010, the second session of the congress of the Zhejiang Chamber of Commerce in Liaoning opens. June 30, 2011, the Huafeng Spandex Co., Ltd. of Zhejiang signs an investment agreement with the Liaoyang High-tech Industrial Development Zone. The Zhejiang Company will construct the Huafeng Industrial Park in the Zone, with a total investment of about 4 billion yuan. December 30, 2011, the Agricultural Bank of China Liaoning Branch and the Zhongnan Construction Group Co., Ltd. of Zhejiang sign a financial strategic cooperation agreement. The Liaoning Branch will offer a three billion yuan credit limit to the Zhejiang Group.

Ningxia-Qinghai

[Quick Facts] Average distance = 684 km; Geographical adjacency = 0; Index of ethnic linkages = 0.7002 (2000) and 0.6824 (2010); Freight exchange via national railway = 460 k tons (2000) and 790 k tons (2010). ★ May 30, 2005, a tourism promotion group of Qinghai holds, in Yinchuan City of Ningxia, the tourism promotion called "Mysterious Qinghai Plateau". April 17, 2009, the theme promotion called "Dream of Lake Qinghai, Eco-Cultural Tour" is held in Ningxia. The A-level scenic spot of Lake Qinghai and 78 travel agencies of Ningxia sign a tourism cooperation agreement. The Ningxia travel agencies will directly deliver tourists to the Lake Qinghai scenic spot, aiming reduce the transit costs of tourists, on the one hand, and to increase the profit of tourist agency, on the other. May 5, 2009, the "2009 Qinghai Investment and Trade Fair and the Tulip Festival" is held in Xining City of Qinghai. A delegation of Ningxia Hui Autonomous Region attends the fair. Qinghai and Ningxia hold investment seminar and sign two cooperation agreements. April 19, 2010, a heavy snowfall suddenly drops in Yushu Tibetan Autonomous Prefecture of Qinghai; the Military and the Armed Police Corps of Hui Autonomous Region immediately send 1000 coal stoves, 50 prefabricated houses and 35 cotton tents to the Yushu earthquake-hit area. April 26, 2012, the delegations of the Ningxia and Qinghai Research and Design Institutes of the China Power Construction Corporation, led by the CCP Secretaries of the two institutes, carry out study and exchange activities in Henan Province.

Ningxia-Shaanxi

[Quick Facts] Average distance = 846 km; Geographical adjacency = 1; Index of ethnic linkages = 0.6594 (2000) and 0.6535 (2010); Freight exchange via national railway = 1510 k tons (2000) and 1170 k tons (2010). ★ April 25, 2004, the Shaanxi Chamber of Commerce in Ningxia is established. The Chamber has more than 1000 members (individual and corporate). The Shaanxi-owned private enterprises in Ningxia have a total asset of over 18 billion yuan, involving real estate, construction, building materials, clothing, food, medical equipment, agricultural machinery, planting, breeding, etc. April 16, 2011, at the "Domestic Tourism Fair" held in Xi'an City, Ningxia Hui Autonomous Region and Shaanxi Province sign a framework agreement of tourism cooperation. Both sides pledge to establish an annual exchange meeting mechanism, aiming to boost the cooperation between tourism enterprises and the coordination of relevant departments of civil aviation, railway, highway, etc. The two sides also decide to gradually eliminate tourism barriers and to promote the development of new tourist routes and products. November 30, 2011, the Shanxi Provincial Power (Group) Co., Ltd. and the Ningxia Electric Power Group sign, in Yinchuan City, a strategic cooperation agreement. April 3, 2012, the governments of Shaanxi and Ningxia hold, in Xi'an City, an economic and social development forum. The two sides will jointly implement the "Plan of Revitalization for the Shaanxi-Gansu-Ningxia Old Revolutionary Base Areas", the "Development Plan of Huhehaote, Baotou, Yinchuan and Yulin Economic Zone" and the "Ningxia-Hubei-Yulin Energy Triangle Plan". May, 13–15, 2012, the Hongrui Group of Shaanxi pays an inspection to the Ningdong Industrial Park of and the Desheng Industrial Park of Ningxia Autonomous Region. The two sides conduct in-depth exchange in various industrial projects.

Ningxia-Shandong

[Quick Facts] Average distance = 1840 km; Geographical adjacency = 0; Index of ethnic linkages = 0.6610 (2000) and 0.6553 (2010); Freight exchange via national railway = 310 k tons (2000) and 1430 k tons (2010). ★ April 24, 2005, the Agriculture and Animal Husbandry Departments of Ningxia and Shandong sign a technological cooperation agreement. November 20, 2005, the Shandong Chamber of Commerce in Ningxia is established. The Chamber has 468 member companies involving electronic communication, energy, transportation, building materials, agricultural machinery, hardware, plumbing, real estate development, engineering, installation, mining, agricultural and pastoral farming, catering and tourism, seafood aquatic, foodstuff, agricultural and sideline products deep processing, clothing shoes, hats and others. August 25, 2010, the "Ningxia-Shandong (Ji'nan) Trade and Economic Cooperation Promotion" is held in Ji'nan City. The two sides sign 38 project agreements, with a total investment of 53.853 billion yuan; the projects cover new energy, new materials, agricultural machinery and equipment manufacturing, wool textile, medicine, logistics, tourism and other industries. September 15, 2010, the Linyi municipal government of Shandong signs a strategic cooperation framework agreement with Yinchuan City of Ningxia. The two places' enterprises hold the "Huifengxiang International Trade City Promotion" and sign a number of cooperation agreements, involving trade, procurement, logistics, distribution, e-commerce, information, etc. July 12, 2012, a delegation, led by the CCP Secretary of and the United Front Work Chief of Ningxia Hui Autonomous Region visits Ji'nan City to participate in the "Shandong-Ningxia Trade and Economic Cooperation Forum". The two sides pledge to jointly develop energy and chemical industries, new materials, equipment manufacturing, light industrial, agriculture and sideline products processing, textile, wine, halal, high-tech products, and tourism.

Ningxia-Shanghai

[Quick Facts] Average distance = 2355 km; Geographical adjacency = 0; Index of ethnic linkages = 0.6596 (2000) and 0.6548 (2010); Freight exchange via national railway = 350 k tons (2000) and 440 k tons (2010). ★ June 3, 2002, Ningxia

University and Shanghai Jiaotong University sign a pairing exchange and cooperation agreement. September 25, 2007, the "Ningxia (Shanghai) Economic and Cultural Tourism Promotion" is held in Shanghai. A delegation, led by the CCP Secretary and the Propaganda Chief of Ningxia Autonomous Region, attends the meeting. The China (Ningxia) International Travel Service Company and the Shanghai Spring International Travel Service Company sign a tourist train cooperation agreement. November 14, 2010, the Shanghai Chamber of Commerce in Ningxia Hui Autonomous Region is established. December 21, 2010, the Kaoer Coal Electronic Trading Co., Ltd. of Shanghai and the Western Mining Association of Ningxia sign a cooperation agreement. May 3, 2012, the China Post Ningxia Company signs a cooperation agreement with the Lujiazui Wealth Management Training Center of Shanghai. July 4, 2012, the Ningxia Agricultural Cultivation Group and the Shanghai Greenland Holding Group sign a strategic cooperation agreement. The agreement includes two projects: (i) construction of the "Ningxia Vocational Education Base" and of the supplementary buildings (with 972 mu of land area) and (ii) marketing cooperation of the "Xixia King Wine". July 10, 2012, the Shanghai Aerospace Automobile Electromechanical Co., Ltd. and Merchants of Ningxia Hui Autonomous Region sign a cooperation strategy framework agreement in photovoltaic (PV) industry. The company plans to build a 600 MW PV power plant in Ningxia from 2012 to 2015, with an expected investment of 6 billion yuan.

Ningxia-Shanxi

[Quick Facts] Average distance = 1316 km; Geographical adjacency = 0; Index of ethnic linkages = 0.6575 (2000) and 0.6511 (2010); Freight exchange via national railway = 270 k tons (2000) and 520 k tons (2010). ★ September 22, 2007, the Shanxi Chamber of Commerce in Ningxia is established. The Chamber has 58 member companies and 368 individual members, mainly engaged in building materials, mechanical and electrical equipments, chemistry, smelting, real estate, decoration, and restaurants. December 1, 2010, a delegation of Ningxia participates in the "Ningxia-Shanxi (Taiyuan) Trade and Economic Cooperation Promotion" which is held in Taiyuan City of Shanxi. Both sides reach five cooperation project agreements. On July 28, 2011, the Tourism Bureau of Yinchuan and the administrative organs of the Lake Shahu, the Helan Mountain, the Western Xia Imperial Tombs, the Lake Mingcui and other scenic spots hold a tourist attraction promotion activity in Taiyuan City and sign a strategic cooperation agreement with the Taiyuan Municipal Tourism Bureau. September 14–20, 2011, the Shanxi Agriculture International Cooperation and Exchange Workstation and the officials of the Northern Shanxi Agricultural Comprehensive Development Project visit Ningxia and pay an inspection to the project of the International Fund for Agricultural Development (IFAD). The IFAD is a specialized agency of the United Nations to finance agricultural development projects primarily for food production in developing countries.

Ningxia-Sichuan

[Quick Facts] Average distance = 1342 km; Geographical adjacency = 0; Index of ethnic linkages = 0.6570 (2000) and 0.6515 (2010); Freight exchange via national railway = 960 k tons (2000) and 5690 k tons (2010). ★ January 14, 2009, the Sichuan Chamber of Commerce in Ningxia is established. The Chamber has 26 enterprise members and 76 individual members, mainly engaged in energy, chemical industry, machinery, real estate, construction, building materials, agricultural production, processing and sales, housing decoration and design, housing agency, catering, hotel, department store, car transportation, e-commerce, etc. September 17–18, 2009, a delegation, led by the Vice President of West China Medicine School of Sichuan University, visits Yinchuan City of Ningxia to participate in the Yinchuan municipal personnel cooperation symposium and holds a signing ceremony of talent introduction. October 19, 2011, the government of Ningxia Hui Autonomous Region holds, in Chengdu City, the "Ningxia-Sichuan (Chengdu) Trade and Economic Cooperation Promotion". August 17, 2012, Sichuan and Ningxia hold, in Yinchuan City, an economic and social development meeting and sign a strategic cooperation framework agreement. September 26, 2012, a 100 people delegation of Ningxia visits Chengdu to participate in the "13th Western China International Fair", which is the sixth round of Ningxia to participate in the fair. The two sides hold the "Ningxia-Sichuan (Chengdu) Economic and Trade Cooperation Meeting" with the 200 participants from both government and business circle. 12 cooperation project agreements are signed, involving equipment manufacturing, metallurgy and chemical industry, and urban construction, with a total investment of 6.78 billion yuan.

Ningxia-Tianjin

[Quick Facts] Average distance = 1480 km; Geographical adjacency = 0; Index of ethnic linkages = 0.6776 (2000) and 0.6685 (2010); Freight exchange via national railway = 1690 k tons (2000) and 2140 k tons (2010). ★ June 26, 2008, Tianjin and Ningxia begin to cooperatively build an inland port, aiming to serve the agricultural development in Ningxia. June 17, 2009, the public security organs of Tianjin and Ningxia sign an agreement of joint police actions against cross-regional crimes. September 25, 2010, the IQBs of Tianjin and Ningxia sign a memorandum of cooperation in direct port passing. 32 enterprises are listed in the memorandum; the goods in the list involve tires, clothing, ferroalloy, apple juice and wolfberry products. The cooperation aims to improve the environment of the import and export customs clearance and promote foreign trade facilitation and regional economic development. July 14, 2011, the Ningxia Tourism Bureau visits Tianjin to hold the "Magic Ningxia" tourism promotion. The China (Tianjin) International Travel Service Company and Ningxia's travel agencies sign a cooperation agreement; both sides will jointly develop the tourism market and establish a long-term cooperation mechanism. May 14, 2012, a Ningxia delegation visits Tianjin to hold the "2012 Tianjin-Ningxia Investment and Trade Cooperation Promotion Fair". Ningxia offers project cooperation in energy, coal chemical industry, new materials, equipment manufacturing, specialty agricultural products processing, high-tech and other competitive industries; both sides sign two projects, with a total investment of 280 million yuan.

Ningxia-Tibet

[Quick Facts] Average distance = 2656 km; Geographical adjacency = 0; Index of ethnic linkages = 0.0650 (2000) and 0.0874 (2010); Freight exchange via national railway = 0 k ton (2000) and 0 k ton (2010). ★ November 3, 2009, the Ningxia Electric Power Company and the Tibet Power Co., Ltd. sign a strategic cooperation framework agreement. The two sides will further consolidate bilateral linkage and promote exchange and cooperation; aiming to speed up the construction of smart grid. Before 2020, the construction of China's smart grid will cost about 200 billion yuan. July 31, 2012, the Mobile Learning Service Center is established in Lhasa of Tibet, which is jointly invested by Tibet University and Ningxia University. The center provides service in Qamdo, Nyingchi, Ali, Rikaze and Lhasa of Tibet Autonomous Region and Guyuan and Shizuishan and Yinchuan of Ningxia. The project aims to build a multi-mode and multi-channel platform of modern distant education, to transmit digitized quality education resources and to better serve the economic and social development of minority areas in Western China. May 9, 2012, from January to April, Ningxia has transmitted a total amount of 220 million kWh of electricity to Tibet, which accounts for 28 % of Tibet's total electricity need. Different from Ningxia, Tibet is abundant in hydropower resources (except for the dry season) but lacks coal and petroleum. For the 12th five-year plan period (2011–15), Ningxia will provide Tibet 4 billion kWh of electricity. This will not only completely resolve Tibet's power shortage during the dry season, but it will also reduce 3.55 million tons of greenhouse gas emissions annually.

Ningxia-Xinjiang

[Quick Facts] Average distance = 2088 km; Geographical adjacency = 0; Index of ethnic linkages = 0.4544 (2000) and 0.4533 (2010); Freight exchange via national railway = 470 k tons (2000) and 2660 k tons (2010). ★ December 1, 2010, a 2.5 MW wind turbine, which is jointly developed by the Tianjing Group of Ningxia and the Jinfeng Science & Technology Co., Ltd. of Xinjiang, is completed. The two sides decide to enhance the annual production of the 2.5 MW wind power generators to 1000 units, with a total investment of 40 million yuan. April 14–18, 2011, the Member of Drug Control Commission (also the Director of the Drug Control Office of Xinjiang) and the Deputy Director of Xinjiang Public Security Bureau visit Ningxia. Both sides have an in-depth exchange in common concerned issues, such as drug outflow investigation, viper arresting and the "Golden Crescent" drug smuggling penetration; the two sides sign a drug control cooperation agreement. April 23, 2011, at the "Ningxia-Beijing Trade and Economic Cooperation Promotion", Ningxia announces its willingness to cooperate with Xinjiang. The "Xinjiang-Ningxia Coal Cooperation" strategy is designed to use the convenient rail transport and the land and water advantages of Zhongwei City of Ningxia to develop rich coal resources in Xinjiang, with a total investment of 300 billion yuan. September 1, 2011, a delegation of Ningxia holds, in Urumqi City of Xinjiang, a trade and investment promotion. The two autonomous regions pledge to strengthen cooperation in energy, chemical industry, new materials, machinery manufacturing, agricultural and sideline products, halal products, etc. November 6, 2011, Ningxia and Xinjiang hold, in Yinchuan City, a symposium. The Xinjiang government delegation also inspects the Lingwu Power Co., Ltd. of Ningxia, the Development Exhibition Hall of the Ningdong Energy and Chemical Base, the Shenhua Ningxia Coal Group, the Yinglite Chemical Industry Company of the State Grid, etc.

Ningxia-Yunnan

[Quick Facts] Average distance = 2442 km; Geographical adjacency = 0; Index of ethnic linkages = 0.6712 (2000) and 0.6655 (2010); Freight exchange via national railway = 10 k tons (2000) and 360 k tons (2010). ★ December 8–12, 2000, a delegation of Ningxia participates in the "First National (Yunnan) Private Enterprises Fair" and shows the "wolfberry coffee" project; the Xingke Group of Yunnan and the Ningxia delegation sign a cooperation intention on this project. Wolfberry is a special product of Ningxia, while Yunnan is rich in coffee beans. March 23, 2006, the Xingke Group of Yunnan acquire, with 18 million yuan 51 %, stake of the Ningxia wolfberry coffee invention patent. Both sides pledge to promote the cultivation of 5000 mu of wolfberry in Ningxia. January 12, 2011, the government of Ningxia and the Eastern Airlines Yunnan Branch sign a memorandum of cooperation concerning the opening of the Yinchuan-Kunming-Dubai international route. March 22, 2011, the Port Office of Yunnan Province and Ningxia Hui Autonomous Region sign, in Kunming City, a memorandum of cross-regional port cooperation between Yunnan and Ningxia. June 7, 2011, the "Ningxia-Yunnan (Kunming) Trade and Economic Cooperation Promotion" is held in Kunming City. The two sides reach nine cooperative project intentions, six project contracts and three agreements, with a total investment of 9.535 billion yuan, 3.135 billion yuan and 6.4 billion yuan, respectively. October 25, 2011, on the occasion of the "13th China International Tourism Fair", a Ningxia Tourism delegation holds, in Kunming City of Yunnan, a promotion (the theme is "Magic Ningxia"). The Deputy Directors of the two Tourism Bureaux sign a strategic cooperation agreement.

Ningxia-Zhejiang

[Quick Facts] Average distance = 2481 km; Geographical adjacency = 0; Index of ethnic linkages = 0.6556 (2000) and 0.6507 (2010); Freight exchange via national railway = 120 k tons (2000) and 50 k tons (2010). ★ May 18, 2001, the Zhejiang Chamber of Commerce in Ningxia is established in Yinchuan. The Chamber has 101 enterprise members and 232 individual members. September 25, 2007, the "Ningxia (Shanghai) Economic and Cultural Tourism Promotion" is held in Shanghai. A delegation led by the PCSC member of and Propaganda Chief of Ningxia attend the meeting. The Heping Tourism Company of Ningxia and the China Youth Tourist Service Company of Zhejiang sign a charter flight agreement. April 26–27, 2012, a delegation, led by the CCP Secretary of Ningxia Hui Autonomous Region visits Hangzhou City. The two sides hold the "Zhejiang-Ningxia Economic and Social Development Forum" and the signing ceremony of industrial framework cooperation agreement. The enterprises from the two places sign 54 project contracts, with a total investment of 55.615 billion yuan. October 25, 2012, the Ningxia Branch of the China Power Group Co., Ltd. and the Zhejiang Energy Group sign, in Yinchuan City, a cooperation agreement. The cooperation project is the world's first "ultra supercritical megawatts of indirect air cooling units"; the Fangjiazhuan (Ningxia) Power Generation and the Zhejiang Group hold 51 and 49 % of the total shares, respectively. The project production capacity is 6000 MW including a 2 × 1000 MW ultra-supercritical coal-fired cooled generator set in the first phase. The two sides will continue to seek cooperation opportunities in wind power and photovoltaic power.

Qinghai-Shaanxi

[Quick Facts] Average distance = 892 km; Geographical adjacency = 0; Index of ethnic linkages = 0.5453 (2000) and 0.5353 (2010); Freight exchange via national railway = 620 k tons (2000) and 1120 k tons (2010). ★ March 28, 2006, Shaanxi and Qinghai Provinces sign, in Xining City, an agreement concerning the restructuring of the Shaanxi Airport Management Corporation and of the Qinghai Civil Airports Co., Ltd. This marks that the Shaanxi Corporation will become the largest inter-regional airport group (only behind the Beijing Capital Airports Group); the Shaanxi Corporation has eight airports, with a total asset of 4 billion yuan, possessing nearly 90 % of the Northwest aviation market. November 24–25, 2007, a delegation, led by the Chief of the Wildlife and Nature Reserve Authority of Qinghai, visits the Shaanxi Institute of Zoology and the Institute of Northwestern Endangered Animals and holds a forum. February 29, 2012, the Cultural Department of Press and Publication of Qinghai and the China Construction Bank Qinghai Branch sign, in Xining City, a comprehensive business cooperation agreement. The signing of the agreement will further enhance the financing capacity of the cultural enterprises in Qinghai and promote the comprehensive and sustainable development of cultural industry. April 16, 2012, the Rural Credit Cooperatives of Shaanxi and Qinghai hold a forum. The two sides exchange issues relating to the reform of credit cooperatives in rural areas. July 9, 2012, the Culture and Sports Bureau of Yushu Tibetan Autonomous Prefecture of Qinghai and the Shaanxi Weinan Teachers College Music School sign a cooperation agreement of inter-school talent training. August 20–21, 2012, the "Shaanxi-Qinghai SOE Strategic Cooperation Forum" is held in Xining. The two sides hold a meeting on the further strengthening of the SOEs' cooperation and the promotion of economic growth.

Qinghai-Shandong

[Quick Facts] Average distance = 2068 km; Geographical adjacency = 0; Index of ethnic linkages = 0.5470 (2000) and 0.5371 (2010); Freight exchange via national railway = 380 k tons (2000) and 2420 k tons (2010). ★ September 16, 2009, the Shandong Gold Group Co., Ltd. and the Qinghai Bureau of Nonferrous Geology and Mineral Resources Exploration sign a cooperation agreement concerning the exploration and exploitation of gold resources in Gouli Area of Dulan County, Qinghai Province. October 30, 2009, Jining City of Shandong and Haibei Tibetan Autonomous Prefecture of Qinghai establish strategic cooperative relations. March 2011, a Qinghai Tourism Delegation visits Shandong to hold a tourism promotion activity entitled "Beautiful Qinghai". April 22, 2011, the Tourism Bureaux of Qinghai and Shandong Provinces hold, in Xining City, a forum of regional cooperation in tourism. The two sides sign a tourism cooperation framework agreement, aiming to build a new type of interprovincial relations in tourist interaction and information sharing. October 8, 2011, Qinghai and Shandong Provinces sign, in Ji'nan City, a cooperative agreement of secondary vocational education during the 12th Five-Year Plan period, which includes 10,000 students and 400 teachers from Qinghai Province to pursue their further studies in Shandong Province and about 400 teachers from Shandong to teach in Qinghai. March 8, 2012, the Shandong Gold Group and the Haixi Mongol and Tibetan Autonomous Prefecture of Qinghai sign, in Ji'nan City, a framework agreement of geological exploration and development cooperation. June 14, 2012, the Environmental Monitoring Centers of Shandong and Qinghai Provinces sign, in Ji'nan City, a business training cooperation agreement. September 28, 2012, the Agricultural Bank of China Qinghai Branch signs a comprehensive strategic cooperation agreement with the Shandong Chamber of Commerce in Qinghai. According to the agreement, the Bank will give a credit limit of not less than 5 billion yuan to the Chamber in the next three years.

Qinghai-Shanghai

[Quick Facts] Average distance = 2401 km; Geographical adjacency = 0; Index of ethnic linkages = 0.5458 (2000) and 0.5366 (2010); Freight exchange via national railway = 110 k tons (2000) and 50 k tons (2010). ★ May 5, 2011, the Saiding Biotechnology Co., Ltd. of Shanghai and Qinghai Provincial Sports Bureau sign a cooperation agreement. August 18, 2011, the Communist Youth Leagues of Hongkou District (Shanghai Municipality) and of Golog Prefecture (Qinghai Province) establish a friendly, cooperative relationship. September 14, 2011, the Prairiesun Solar Energy Technology Co., Ltd. of Shanghai and the Jingneng Construction Investment Co., Ltd. of Qinghai sign, in Qinghai, an equipment purchase contract. Under the contract, the Shanghai Company will provide 5 MW solar PV modules to the Phase II project of the Golmud PV Power Plant of the Qinghai Company. October 18, 2011, the Qinghai Vocational and Technical College and the Shanghai Yawan Hotel Management Company sign a school-enterprise cooperation agreement. June 9, 2012, the Kangtai Foundry and Machinery Co. Ltd. of Qinghai and the Shanghai Electronics Group sign a cooperation agreement on the cooperative development, with a total investment of 2.2 billion yuan, aiming to improve China's aerospace, military technology and machinery and equipment manufacturing level and to promote the economic development in Qinghai Province. July 25, 2012, the Vice Mayor of Shanghai and the Shanghai Public Security Bureau, on behalf of the Public Security Bureau, donate 100 million yuan to Qinghai Provincial Public Security Department and 100 million yuan and 200 police wool shirts to the Public Security Bureau of Golog Prefecture, Qinghai.

Qinghai-Shanxi

[Quick Facts] Average distance = 1543 km; Geographical adjacency = 0; Index of ethnic linkages = 0.5435 (2000) and 0.5328 (2010); Freight exchange via national railway = 560 k tons (2000) and 170 k tons (2010). ★ December 5, 2005, the Wentong Group of Shanxi and the Salt Lake Group of Qinghai sign a cooperation agreement; the two sides will invest and construct the projects of 100,000 ton potassium nitrate, 50,000 ton potassium and 600,000 ton coking coal in the Baijinbao Chemical Industrial Park in Wenshui County of Luliang (Shanxi), with a total investment of more than one billion yuan. April 23, 2010, the Zhendong Pharmaceutical Group of Shanxi donates injectable ampicillin sulbactam, cefoperazone sodium and sulbactam sodium antibacterial anti-inflammatory drugs, with a total value of 5.08 million yuan to the Yushu earthquake-hit area, Qinghai. In addition, 3000 employees of the Shanxi Group also donate more than 900,000 yuan in cash to the area. December 1, 2010, approved by the Civil Affairs Department of Qinghai Province, the Shanxi Chamber of Commerce in Qinghai is established.

December 26–29, 2010, a delegation, led by the PCSC Vice Chairman of Qinghai, visits Changzhi City of Shanxi to make a reunion with 1300 students and teachers who were transferred from the Yushu earthquake areas of Qinghai. May 27, 2011, the Yuanjun Industrial Group Co., Ltd. of Shanxi donates 1.5 million yuan to Qinghai for the charity school construction projects in Banma County of Golog Prefecture. May 16, 2012, a 10 people delegation, led by the CCP Secretary of the Qinghai Provincial FDA pays an inspection to the pairing unit of Shaanxi. October 10, 2012, a delegation of the Lake Qinghai scenic spots holds, in Taiyuan City, a tourism promotion. 30 travel agencies of Taiyuan sign cooperation agreement with the delegation. 200 people from tourism, culture, media, religion, united front, business community and other industries attend the meeting.

Qinghai-Sichuan

[Quick Facts] Average distance = 1388 km; Geographical adjacency = 1; Index of ethnic linkages = 0.5585 (2000) and 0.5518 (2010); Freight exchange via national railway = 630 k tons (2000) and 1330 k tons (2010). ★ October 22, 2010, the Qinghai provincial government and the Sichuan Airlines Co., Ltd. sign, in Chengdu City, a strategic cooperation agreement. December 2, 2011, the Xining municipal government of Qinghai and Deyang City of Shanxi hold an agricultural cooperation and development fair; the two sides sign an agreement concerning agricultural development and cooperation during the 12th-Five Plan. December 19, 2011, the Sichuan Chamber of Commerce in Qinghai is established. April 23, 2012, a 30 people delegation, led by the CCP Secretary (also the Director) of Qinghai Land Resources Department visits Chengdu University of Technology. Both sides sign a strategic cooperation agreement, aiming to carry out cooperation in geological exploration, mineral exploitation, geological environmental protection, and land utilization and remediation. September 24, 2012, the "5th Xining (Qinghai)-Deyang (Sichuan) Agricultural and Livestock Production and Marketing Cooperation Fair", co-sponsored by the Xining and the Deyang municipal governments and hosted by the Agro-Pastoral and Poverty Alleviation and Development Bureau of Xining City and the Agricultural Bureau of Deyang, is held in Qinghai. The two Bureaux sign a framework agreement concerning the establishment of traceability system of quality and safety in agricultural products; the Food Baskets (cailanzi) Association of Xining and Deyang Agricultural Bureau sign a vegetable purchase and sales cooperation agreement; 12 companies sign 47 grain purchase and sales contracts, with a total amount of 377,000 tons and a total value of 941.7 million yuan.

Qinghai-Tianjin

[Quick Facts] Average distance = 2235 km; Geographical adjacency = 0; Index of ethnic linkages = 0.5616 (2000) and 0.5483 (2010); Freight exchange via national railway = 280 k tons (2000) and 350 k tons (2010). ★ April 18–20, 2005, the Qinghai provincial government visits Tianjin to participate in the "Cross-Regional Port Cooperation Meeting" and signs the Tianjin Protocol. August 26, 2007, the Labor and Social Security Department of Qinghai Province and Tianjin Labor and Social Security Bureau jointly organize the employment meeting of secondary technical schools. May 28, 2008, the Qinghai Provincial Department of Education and Tianjin Municipal Education Commission sign an exchange and cooperation agreement. August 31, 2009, a delegation of the Golmud municipal government of Qinghai visits Tianjin University; both sides sign a cooperation agreement in personnel training for Golmud and learning and social practice for the University, aiming to further deepen the cooperation between east and west China. August 11, 2011, a delegation, led by the CCP Secretary and Vice Manager of the State Grid Group Haibei (Qinghai) Branch visits the Power Supply Company Binhai (Tianjin) Branch; the two sides reach a consensus on issues relating to staff training, information sharing and others and sign a cooperation framework agreement. November 1, 2012, the "13th Qinghai Green Economy, Investment and Trade Fair" opens in Xining City of Qinghai. Tianjin's enterprises in new energy, cultural and nationality, special food, etc. attend the fair. Tianjin Municipality and Huangnan Tibetan Autonomous Prefecture of Qinghai sign a cooperation agreement, including the projects of pipe construction, beef and mutton deep processing and others, with a total investment of nearly 100 million yuan.

Qinghai-Tibet

[Quick Facts] Average distance = 1972 km; Geographical adjacency = 1; Index of ethnic linkages = 0.2906 (2000) and 0.3323 (2010); Freight exchange via national railway = 0 k ton (2000) and 1060 k tons (2010). ★ September 4, 2005, Qinghai Province and Tibet Autonomous Region sign, in Lhasa City, a framework cooperation agreement. Under the agreement, the two sides will make use of their comparative advantages to enhance the exchange and cooperation in economic, trade, cultural and other fields and to jointly build the Qinghai-Tibet Economic Cooperation Zone. March 18, 2008, the China Telecom Tibet Company and the China Communications Services Co., Ltd. Qinghai Company sign a strategic cooperation framework agreement. September 16, 2010, Qamdo of Tibet and Yushu of Qinghai sign a tourism strategic cooperation agreement; the two sides will implement the "General Development Plan of the China Shangri-la Ecological Tourism Zone". September 26, 2010, a delegation, led by the General Manager of the Zhabuye Lithium Technologies Co., Ltd. of Rikaze of Tibet visits the Qinghai

Institute of Salt Lake Research of the CAS. The two sides agree to carry out scientific and technological cooperation, to strengthen resource exploitation and research in the Zabuye Salt Lake and to jointly establish a research center on the comprehensive utilization of such resources as lithium, potassium, boron, rubidium, cesium, etc. October 11, 2010, the Meteorological Observatories of Tibet and Qinghai sign the "Technological Cooperation Work Framework Agreement". The two sides will carry out cooperation in data sharing, technological exchange, scientific research, weather alarm, etc. aiming to further explore the climate change and its physical mechanism in the Qinghai-Tibet Plateau. November 26, 2010, the governments of Tibet Autonomous Region and Qinghai Province sign, in Xining City, the "Agreement Concerning the Cooperative Construction of the Coordinative Leadership Mechanism in the Golmud Tibet-Qinghai Industrial Park".

Qinghai-Xinjiang

[Quick Facts] Average distance = 2108 km; Geographical adjacency = 1; Index of ethnic linkages = 0.4626 (2000) and 0.4610 (2010); Freight exchange via national railway = 480 k tons (2000) and 110 k tons (2010). ★ April 29, 2006, the Western Mining Co., Ltd. of Qinghai and the International Border Trade Mall Industries Co., Ltd. of Tacheng City of Xinjiang agree to cooperatively develop tin ore in Kyrgyz Republic. The total investment of the project is 24.64 million US dollar. The Ming Company's annual ore processing capacities reach 330,000 tons, producing 2746 tons and 920 tons of purified tin ores and purified copper ores, respectively. April 17, 2008, Qinghai Province and the XPCC reach a consensus on labor cooperation. Qinghai's emigrated labors to Xinjiang are mainly engaged in agriculture, including about 50,000 flowers-picking workers and about 5000 seasonal agricultural workers. September 2009, Xinjiang Autonomous Region and Qinghai Province sign a framework agreement on the strengthening of regional economic and technological cooperation. Both sides reach a consensus on coal resource exploitation, infrastructure and industrial park constructions. September 16, 2012, the "Xinjiang-Qinghai Exchange Forum for Economic and Social Development" is held in Xinjiang City. The two sides sign a comprehensive cooperation agreement, aiming to strengthen exchange and cooperation in the development and utilization of energy resources, traffic channel construction, and cultural tourism. October 12, 2012, the Lianglike Copper Company of Menyuan County (Qinghai) and the Xinjiang Nonferrous Materials Company sign a strategy cooperation agreement of purified copper mineral supply from 2013 to 2017.

Qinghai-Yunnan

[Quick Facts] Average distance = 2488 km; Geographical adjacency = 0; Index of ethnic linkages = 0.5603 (2000) and 0.5504 (2010); Freight exchange via national railway = 60 k tons (2000) and 540 k tons (2010). ★ March 8, 2005, the Qinghai Institute of Salt Lake Research of the CAS signs a cooperation agreement with the Yunnan Mining Group and the Jiangcheng Potash Fertilizers Plant in Simao of Yunnan. December 23, 2009, the Yunnan Vocational College of Land and Resource Management and the Qinghai Bureau of Geology and Mineral Exploration hold a forum and sign a cooperation agreement; the two sides will strengthen cooperation in personnel exchange, project cooperation and training. January 29, 2010, the Qinghai Institute of Salt Lake Research of the CAS acquires 8.47 % stake of the Zhongliao Mining Exploitation Investment Company of the Yunnan Tianhua Group. Both sides pledge to strengthen cooperation. As of 2009, the Institute and the Yunnan Mining Company have completed the supplementary exploration in Vientiane of Laos and obtained 193.07 million tons of potassium chloride resources. September 16, 2010, Diqing of Yunnan and Yushu of Qinghai sign a strategic cooperation agreement. The two sides will implement the "General Development Plan of the China Shangri-la Ecological Tourism Zone". March 30, 2011, a delegation, led by the Deputy Chief of Qinghai Department of Education, visits Yunnan Nationality High School. October 17, 2012, a research team, composed of the Public Security Departments of Yunnan and others, visits Qinghai Province to conduct research on a new round of joint police drill training.

Qinghai-Zhejiang

[Quick Facts] Average distance = 2527 km; Geographical adjacency = 0; Index of ethnic linkages = 0.5417 (2000) and 0.5326 (2010); Freight exchange via national railway = 130 k tons (2000) and 610 k tons (2010). ★ July 9–11, 2005, the FDAs of Zhejiang and Qinghai Provinces hold a forum and sign a friendly bureaux agreement; both sides exchange views on the development of food and drug companies, aiming to improve the healthcare level of farmers and herdsmen in Qinghai. April 11, 2006, the "Zhejiang-Qinghai Economic and Social Development Forum" is held in Hangzhou City. The two sides sign 17 project agreements in tourism, mineral resource and service industries, with a total investment of 3.901 billion yuan. These projects involve the salt lake chemical industry, non-ferrous metals, coal, building materials, urban infrastructure construction, real estate, commerce, tourism, culture and entertainment and others. June 26, 2007, the "Zhejaing-Qinghai Regional Economic Research and Inspection Team", composed of the Regional Economic Association of and the DRC Training Center of Zhejiang Province, pays an inspection to Qinghai. August 28, 2009, the Jinhua (Zhejiang) Chamber of Commerce in Qinghai is established. According to incomplete statistics, Qinghai has hosted more than 24,000 Jinhua-owned enterprises. December 15, 2009, a delegation of Qinghai Provincial Science and Technology Department visits the Science and Technology Department of Zhejiang Province, Zhejiang University, and several companies in Zhejiang. June 10–13, 2010, the "2012 Qinghai Green Economy, Investment and Trade Fair" is held in the International Exhibition Center of Xining City, Qinghai. Zhejiang Ocean University and Haibei Tibetan Autonomous Prefecture of and Hualong Hui Autonomous County of Qinghai sign an agreement on the establishment of long-term technological and personnel training cooperation relations. October 30, 2012, the Zhejiang Chamber of Commerce in Delingha District, Delingha City of Qaidam of Qinghai Province is established in the Zhejiang Industrial Park.

Shaanxi-Shandong

[Quick Facts] Average distance = 1177 km; Geographical adjacency = 0; Index of ethnic linkages = 0.9978 (2000) and 0.9972 (2010); Freight exchange via national railway = 1560 k tons (2000) and 1280 k tons (2010). ★ November 24, 2010, the Tourism Bureaux of Shandong and Shaanxi sign, in Ji'nan City, a tourism cooperation agreement. The two sides will establish a travel emergency handling mechanism to resolve difficulties faced by tourists and tourism enterprises in each other's province. December 26, 2010, the Shaanxi Chamber of Commerce in Shandong is established. The Chamber has 200 member enterprises involve real estate, trade, catering, logistics, media, culture, industry, financial management consulting, and legal services. December 19, 2011, the Shandong Energy Group Zibo Mining Company and the Huaneng Power Group Shaanxi Energy Company sign a cooperation agreement in Xianyang City of Shaanxi Province. The Shandong Company and the Xianyang municipal government pledge to cooperate in following projects: (i) the Industrial Park of Coal Mining Machinery and Equipment Manufacturing, (ii) the Cement Circular Economy Park, (iii) the Advanced Medical Equipments Manufacturing Project, (iv) the Purified Coal Chemical Project and (v) the Small Ecology Towns Project. April 5, 2012, a delegation of the Shandong provincial government visits Xi'an City of Shaanxi to participate in the "16th East-West China Investment and Trade Cooperation Fair". The two provinces pledge to strengthen exchange and cooperation in agriculture, energy and mineral resources, infrastructure, equipment manufacturing, modern service industry and strategic emerging industries and others. April 6, 2012, the "Shandong Promotion Meeting on Local Specialties and Industrial Matchmaking", jointly sponsored by the Department of Commerce, the DRC and Rizhao City of Shandong Province, Weinan City of Shaanxi Province, the Shandong Chamber of Commerce in Shaanxi, and the Shaanxi Chamber of Commerce in Shandong, is held in Shaanxi.

Shaanxi-Shanghai

[Quick Facts] Average distance = 1509 km; Geographical adjacency = 0; Index of ethnic linkages = 0.9982 (2000) and 0.9927 (2010); Freight exchange via national railway = 920 k tons (2000) and 940 k tons (2010). ★ March 1992, the Shanghai Smelter Technological Company and the Baoji Manganese Plant of Shaanxi agree to jointly conduct physical and chemical surveys of manganese powder in the Tiantai Mountain area of Taizhou City, Zhejiang. April 7, 2007, the Shanghai Chamber of Commerce in Shaanxi is established in Xi'an. The Chamber has 61 member companies. The Chamber and Shanghai Jiaotong University sign a "Framework Agreement Concerning the establishment of Internship (Learning) Base." December 29, 2007, the Shaanxi Chamber of Commerce in Shanghai is established. According to incomplete statistics, there are tens of thousands of Shaanxi people in Shanghai, mainly engaged in real estate, construction, trade, hotels, catering, IT industry, industry, design, investment, logistics, media, cultural industries, and bio-pharmaceutics. April 6, 2012, as part of the "16th East-West China Investment and Trade Cooperation Fair", the "16th Shaanxi-Shanghai Symposium on Industrial Transfer and Matchmaking Cooperation" is held in Shaanxi. Shaanxi and Shanghai sign 56 project agreements, with a total investment of 29.845 billion yuan. June 5, 2012, Shaanxi Vocational and Technical College and the Shanghai Zhongrui Education Group sign the "China Automobile Education Project" agreement. Under the agreement, the Shanghai Group will provide four million yuan of teaching equipments and the Shaanxi College will train automotive technical workers. June 14, 2012, the Shaanxi government and Shanghai Jiaotong University sign a memorandum of cooperation on industrial transfer. October 8, 2012, the "Shaanxi-Shanghai Cooperation Forum for Investment and Financial Institutions", sponsored by the Department of Commerce of and the Finance Office of Shaanxi Province, is held in Shanghai. Shaanxi's representatives and the financial institutions in Shanghai agree to cooperate in projects of common interests.

Shaanxi-Shanxi

[Quick Facts] Average distance = 651 km; Geographical adjacency = 1; Index of ethnic linkages = 0.9979 (2000) and 0.9975 (2010); Freight exchange via national railway = 190 k tons (2000) and 4010 k tons (2010). ★ January 11, 2008, the Shanxi Chamber of Commerce in Shaanxi is established. According to incomplete statistics, there are more than 200,000 Shanxi people living in and fund thousands of Shanxi-owned companies in Shaanxi, with a total fixed asset of nearly 20 billion yuan and more than 5 billion yuan of tax per year. September 16, 2008, a Shaanxi provincial delegation presents a tourism promotion in Shanxi Province; the tourism sectors of the two sides sign an agreement on the strengthening of interregional cooperation. April 28, 2010, the Coal and Geological Exploration Bureau of Shanxi and Shaanxi Energy Vocational and Technical College sign a cooperation agreement on employment. September 16, 2010, the "3rd China (Taiyuan) International Energy Industry Expo" opens in Taiyuan City of Shanxi. The Lvliang municipal government of Shanxi and the Shaanxi Coking Coal Group sign a strategic cooperation agreement. Under the agreement, the Lvliang government provides land, water, electricity, and other supports to the Shaanxi Groups to construct a new modern coal chemical industrial park in Shanxi. June 29, 2011 the Shaanxi Chamber of Commerce in Shanxi is established in Taiyuan City. Shanxi has hosted about 100,000 Shaanxi people and 1000 Shaanxi-owned enterprises. July 7, 2011, Taiyuan, Yangquan and Linfen Cities of Shanxi Province, Weinan and Xianyang Cities of Shaanxi Province and other two provinces jointly launch the "2011 Four-in-One Ticket Touring". July 17, 2011, the Shaanxi Industrial Vocational and Technical College and the Shanxi Huajin Textile Printing and Dyeing Co., Ltd. sign a school-enterprise cooperation agreement and hold, in Shanxi, an inaugural ceremony of students' practice base. November 4, 2011, the IQBs of Shaanxi and Shanxi sign, in Nanning City of Guangxi, a memorandum of cooperation to strengthen coordinative promotion of trade in fruits and vegetables.

Shaanxi-Sichuan

[Quick Facts] Average distance = 842 km; Geographical adjacency = 1; Index of ethnic linkages = 0.9521 (2000) and 0.9414 (2010); Freight exchange via national railway = 4250 k tons (2000) and 7490 k tons (2010). ★ October 30, 2006, the Shaanxi Chamber of Commerce in Sichuan is established. The Chamber has more than 200 member companies, involving investment, real estate, construction, culture, media, and law, with nearly ten billion yuan of total assets. May 15–16, 2007, a 20 people delegation, led by the Deputy Director of the Sichuan Tourism Bureau, visits Hanzhong City. The two sides hold a forum. April 26, 2008, Guangyuan City of Sichuan holds, in Xi'an City, a tourism promotion. Both sides hope to strengthen, in virtue of the opening of the Xi'an-Hanzhong Highway, cooperation in tourism. October 16, 2009, the "Shaanxi-Sichuan Economic Cooperation Forum" is held in Chengdu City. April 23, 2011, the signing ceremony of "Shaanxi-Sichuan Human Resource and Employment Cooperation Framework Agreement" is held in Hanzhong City of Shaanxi. The two provinces sign more than 400 labor contracts. September 28, 2011, the Chuanwei Group of Sichuan and the Leixin Mining Group of Shaanxi sign, in Xixiang County of Shaanxi, an 800 million yuan investment deal under which to jointly develop—with 51 % and 49 % of the total stakes, respectively—the mineral resources in Xixiang County. June 12, 2012, the Military Rations Supply Station of Shaanxi, the Zhonghengxin Industrial Co., Ltd. of Sichuan and the Mincheng Jianhe Industrial Co., Ltd. of Shaanxi sign a strategic cooperation framework agreement. Shaanxi Province will sell 200,000 tons of corn (worthy of more than 400 million yuan) to Sichuan Province. July 23–24, 2012, the

"Shaanxi-Sichuan Private Enterprise Cooperation Forum" is held in Chengdu City. August 1–2, 2012, Dazhou City of Sichuan and Ankang and Hangzhong Cities of Shaanxi sign a memorandum of cooperation.

Shaanxi-Tianjin

[Quick Facts] Average distance = 1301 km; Geographical adjacency = 0; Index of ethnic linkages = 0.9779 (2000) and 0.9794 (2010); Freight exchange via national railway = 650 k tons (2000) and 680 k tons (2010). ★ February 27, 2006, the Shaanxi Chamber of Commerce in Tianjin is established. September 16, 2008, a youth entrepreneur delegation, led by the CCP Secretary of Tianjin Municipality visits Hanzhong City of Shaanxi to investigate the earthquake-hit areas of Ningqiang, Lueyang and other places. The Tianjin PCSC and Shaanxi PCSC sign a framework agreement concerning the reconstruction work in the earthquake-hit areas. October 11, 2008, the Women's Federations of Tianjin and Shaanxi sign an agreement concerning the reconstruction of schools in the Shaanxi disaster areas; the two sides sign a pairing reconstruction agreement, with a total investment of over 2.73 million yuan. April 19, 2009, Shaanxi holds a tourism promotion in Tianjin, in which Shaanxi highlights the new scenic spot of the "Famen Temple". The two places sign a tourism cooperation agreement. July 21, 2010, the signing ceremony of the "Memorandum of Cooperation of Inspection and Quarantine Work between Tianjin and Shaanxi" is held in Urumqi City, Xinjiang. August 4, 2011, the Xi'an International Port Zone and the Tianjin Port Group establish, in the Binhai New Area of Tianjin, the Jin'an International Logistics Company of the Xi'an Land Port. September 21, 2011, Hanzhong City of Shaanxi and Tianjin Municipality sign a regional port cooperation agreement. April 25, 2012, the Ankang municipal government of Shaanxi and the Tianjin Economic and Technological Development Zone hold, in Tianjin, a forum of human resource cooperation. May 21–26, 2012, a delegation, led by the former Deputy Director of the Tianjin PCSC (also the Chairman of the Tianjin Yellow River Regional Economic Cooperation and Development Association) visits Shaanxi. The Port Administration Offices of Tianjin and Xi'an sign a cooperation framework agreement.

Shaanxi-Tibet

[Quick Facts] Average distance = 2964 km; Geographical adjacency = 0; Index of ethnic linkages = 0.0647 (2000) and 0.0865 (2010); Freight exchange via national railway = 0 k ton (2000) and 80 k tons (2010). ★ July 25, 2009, a delegation, led by the Director of the Shaanxi Entry-Exit IQB, visits Lhasa City and signs the "Memorandum of Shaanxi's Exports of Fruit via the Tibet Port" with the Entry-Exit

IQB of Tibet. The Shaanxi delegation also inspects the Zhangmu Port of Tibet (connecting with Nepal). April 27, 2010, the State Development Bank Shaanxi Branch and Tibet Nationalities College sign an agreement on development and cooperation of ethnic career; the two sides establish a national unity education base. October 29, 2010, the AQTSs of Tibet and Shaanxi hold, in Lhasa City, a signing ceremony of memorandum of cooperation to aid Tibet. Shaanxi will strengthen aid to Tibet in financial assistance, project support, technical guidance, and personnel training. April 12–30, 2012, Xi'an City of Shaanxi holds the "Personnel Training Courses" in Ali Prefecture of Tibet. 14 people from the Science and Technology Bureau of Ali and other counties participate in the training course. August 16, 2012, the Shaanxi Institute of Archaeology and the Tibet Institute of Cultural Relics and Archaeology sign, in Lhasa City, Tibet, a cooperation agreement on cultural relic and archaeological research, covering training and personnel exchange, equipment supply and literature exchange. The two sides will cooperate in the subjects of the "Tibet's Tibetan Buddhist Statues" and the "Archaeological Investigation and Research of Large Cemeteries in the Tubo Period". September 7, 2012, a delegation, led by the Director of Shaanxi Salt Bureau visits Tibet and donates 300,000 yuan to the Salt Industry Corporation of Tibet Autonomous Region.

Shaanxi-Xinjiang

[Quick Facts] Average distance = 2468 km; Geographical adjacency = 0; Index of ethnic linkages = 0.4107 (2000) and 0.4099 (2010); Freight exchange via national railway = 1360 k tons (2000) and 2770 k tons (2010). ★ October 18, 2008, the inaugural meeting of the Shaanxi Federation of Enterprises (Chamber of Commerce) in Xinjiang is held in the Urumqi Global Convention Center. April 9, 2011, the Xinjiang Chamber of Commerce in Shaanxi is established in Xi'an City. August 1, 2011, the No. 1 Topographic Survey Team of National Bureau of Surveying and Mapping of Shaanxi and the No. 1 Institute of Surveying and Mapping of Xinjiang sign, in Urumqi City, a bilateral cooperation framework agreement. September 7, 2011, Xi'an Jiaotong University and other ten universities which are directly under the PRC Ministry of Education hold, in Xinjiang University, the Annual Work Meeting of Pairing Aid to Xinjiang University. The Chairman and other leaders of Xinjiang Uygur Autonomous Region attend the meeting. November 4, 2011, the IQBs of Xinjiang and Shaanxi sign a memorandum of cooperation. June 5, 2012, the CAS Xinjiang Branch and others visit the Shaanxi Provincial Institute of Microbiology. August 10–13, 2011, the "Shaanxi (Urumqi) Specialties Fair and the Shaanxi-Xinjiang Industrial Cooperation Promotion" is held in Urumqi City of Xinjiang. The two sides pledge to strengthen cooperation in energy, chemical industry, equipment manufacturing, textile and clothing, energy saving and environmental protection, and the comprehensive utilization of natural resources. October 12, 2012 the Automobile Group Co., Ltd. of Shaanxi and the Guanghui Industrial Investment (Group) Co., Ltd. of Xinjiang sign a strategic cooperation framework agreement. The Shaanxi Company will provide logistical and transport solutions to specific energy projects of the Xinjiang Company.

Shaanxi-Yunnan

[Quick Facts] Average distance = 1942 km; Geographical adjacency = 0; Index of ethnic linkages = 0.6706 (2000) and 0.6710 (2010); Freight exchange via national railway = 1050 k tons (2000) and 1810 k tons (2010). ★ April 5, 2008, the Entry-Exit IQBs of Yunnan and Shaanxi Provinces sign, in Kunming City, a memorandum to promote Shaanxi's export of safe and high-quality fruits to ASEAN; Yunnan Province will provide assistance to Shaanxi. October 8–12, 2009, a delegation, led by the Governor of Shaanxi, pays an inspection to Lijiang, Diqing, Yuxi and Kunming Cities (Prefectures) of Yunnan. The delegation exchanges the development experiences of tourism, flowers, walnut, tobacco industries and the construction of urban infrastructure. The two provinces sign a tourism cooperation agreement. August 8, 2010, the Shaanxi Chamber of Commerce in Yunnan is established in Kunming City. The Chamber has more than 150 member companies, with a total investment of nearly 2 billion yuan. Now, more than 100,000 Shaanxi people are living in Yunnan, of which more than 10,000 have owned companies in automotive marketing and auto repair, road and bridge construction, culture, tourism, agriculture and animal husbandry, planting and breeding, building materials, medical equipment, electronic technology, real estate, etc. June 9, 2011, Chang'an University of Shaanxi and the Road Development and Investment Co., Ltd. of Yunnan sign a comprehensive cooperation agreement. The two sides establish cooperative relations in personnel training and employment, scientific research, and others. September 4, 2012, a delegation, led by the Deputy General Manager of the Tobacco Monopoly Bureau (Company) of Yunnan, visits the China (Shaanxi) Tobacco Company to seek bilateral commercial cooperation.

Shaanxi-Zhejiang

[Quick Facts] Average distance = 1635 km; Geographical adjacency = 0; Index of ethnic linkages = 0.9923 (2000) and 0.9795 (2010); Freight exchange via national railway = 760 k tons (2000) and 1630 k tons (2010). ★ April 10, 2003, the Wenzhou (Zhejiang) General Chamber of Commerce in Hanzhoung City of Shaanxi is established, with the first batch of 82 memberships. There are more than 5000 Wenzhou people living and running businesses in Hanzhong, covering clothing, catering, entertainment, appliances, etc. October 15, 2003, the "Shaanxi-Zhejiang Capital Management and Cooperation Meeting" is held in Xi'an City. The Shaanxi Northwest Academy of Nonferrous Metals and the Zhejiang Economic

Construction Investment Company sign a contract of 5000 tons of titanium project, with a total investment of 440 million yuan; the Hantai District of Hanzhong City (Shaanxi), the Hanzhong Film Company and the Investment and Development Co., Ltd. of the Wenzhou General Chamber of Commerce in Hanzhong sign a project agreement, with a total investment of 120 million yuan. July 21–23, 2007, the "Shaanxi-Zhejiang Economic Cooperation Promotion Meeting" is held in Hangzhou City of Zhenjiang. Shaanxi and Zhejiang's enterprises sign nearly 20 project agreements. Xianyang of Shaanxi and Hangzhou hold a cooperation project promotion; and Yan'an of Shaanxi and Hangzhou hold a "red tourism" promotion. The Developmental Chemistry and Technology Co., Ltd. of Zhejiang and the Shaanxi Economic and Technological Development Zone decide to cooperate titanium industry, with an investment of 500 million yuan; the Yanliang Air Base Co., Ltd. of Xi'an City and the Huangjia Shipping Company of Zhejiang jointly invest 18 million US dollars to develop the light amphibious aircraft project; the Binhai Auto Parts Co., Ltd. of Zhejiang and the Xi'an High-tech Zone sign a 120 million yuan project agreement, and so on. November 30, 2010, the Zhejiang Chamber of Commerce in Weinan City of Shaanxi is established. The Chamber has more than 100 enterprise members, mainly engaged in mining, real estate, engineering and construction, and food processing.

Shandong-Shanghai

[Quick Facts] Average distance = 966 km; Geographical adjacency = 0; Index of ethnic linkages = 0.9979 (2000) and 0.9934 (2010); Freight exchange via national railway = 2370 k tons (2000) and 960 k tons (2010). ★ March 10, 2004, the Fuxing Group of Shanghai signs a comprehensive cooperation agreement with the Zhaoyuan City of Shandong; the Shanghai Group (which provides 400 million yuan of investment) and the Shandong Group will jointly set up the Zhaojin Mining Co., Ltd. March 25, 2006, the Shandong Chamber of Commerce in Shanghai is established. The Chamber has nearly 200 member companies involving construction, home appliances, metallurgy, coal, petroleum, chemicals, securities, electronics, logistics, education, culture, vegetable distribution and marketing, etc. May 11, 2007, the Shandong provincial government and Tongji University of Shanghai sign, in Shanghai, a technological cooperation agreement. March 16–17, 2009, the "Weifang (Shanghai) Investment Cooperation Forum" is held in Shanghai. January 29, 2010, the Xinhua Bookstore Group of Shandong and the Shanghai Literature and Arts Publishing Group meet, in Ji'nan City, to discuss the competitiveness of cultural SOEs. April 21, 2010, the Shanghai Volkswagen Auto Company and Shandong Business Vocational and Technical College sign, in Ji'nan City, a school-enterprise cooperation agreement. June 5, 2012, the Baosteel International Economic and Trade Co., Ltd. of Shanghai and the Huaxing Rigid Steel Co., Ltd. of Shandong sign a cooperation agreement of steel production. August 24, 2012, Weifang City of Shandong Province and the Yuantong Jiaolong Investment &

Development (Group) Co., Ltd. of Shanghai hold, in Shanghai, a signing ceremony of cooperation agreement; the two sides will build an air logistical headquarters hub in Weifang. September 11, 2012, the Shandong Gold Group and the Huangpu District of Shanghai sign, in Ji'nan City, a government-enterprise strategic cooperation agreement. October 30, 2012, the "Rencheng (Shandong)-Shanghai Economic Cooperation Forum" is held in Shanghai.

Shandong-Shanxi

[Quick Facts] Average distance = 532 km; Geographical adjacency = 0; Index of ethnic linkages = 0.9960 (2000) and 0.9950 (2010); Freight exchange via national railway = 38,880 k tons (2000) and 11,9860 k tons (2010). ★ April 20, 2010, the Jinpai Cement Group of Shanxi and the Shanshui Group of Shandong sign a joint venture agreement. The two sides will construct a new cement production line, aiming to revive the Jinpai Group and the Lu'an Cement Plant. June 16, 2010, the Shandong Chamber of Commerce in Shanxi is established. Approximately a half million of Shandong people are living in Shanxi, mainly engaged in coal, electric power, petro-chemistry, real estate, building materials, clothing and shoes, food and beverage services, agricultural machinery, and transportation. September 10, 2011, the Science and Technology Departments of Shanxi and Shandong Provinces sign, in Ji'nan City, a cooperation framework agreement. The two sides hope to establish an efficient mechanism in personnel, information and project cooperation, aiming to resolve key scientific and technological problems. September 21–23, 2011, as the only technological demonstration county in Linfen City of Shanxi Province, a delegation composed of Quwo County, Yuci District and Changzi County and other Counties pays an inspection to Shouguang City of Shandong. The Science and Technology Bureaux of the five counties (districts) sign a technological cooperation agreement with the Shouguang Bureau of Science and Technology. Under the agreement, Shanxi will establish a greenhouse technology demonstration area in the southern part of Taiyuan City (Shanxi). August 11, 2012, the Shanxi Coking Coal Group, the Shandong Iron and Steel Group and the Rizhao Port Group sign a strategic cooperation framework agreement and hold the opening ceremony of the Shanxi Rizhao Coking Coal Company.

Shandong-Sichuan

[Quick Facts] Average distance = 2019 km; Geographical adjacency = 0; Index of ethnic linkages = 0.9523 (2000) and 0.9412 (2010); Freight exchange via national railway = 1620 k tons (2000) and 350 k tons (2010). ★ May 25, 2007, the Shandong Chamber of Commerce in Sichuan is established. March 25, 2010, a Sichuan government delegation pays an inspection to Shandong and acknowledges the pairing support form Shandong, and signs the "Shandong-Sichuan Strategic Cooperation Agreement". Relevant interprovincial cooperation agreements cover the fields of education, health, tourism, human resources, industry, economic development, urban and rural planning and reconstruction. March 26, 2010, Sichuan and Shandong Provinces sign, in Ji'nan City, a strategic cooperation agreement, aiming to consolidate the pairing reconstruction partnerships between Shandong and Beichuan County of Sichuan Province and to establish a long-term cooperative relationship. April 22, 2010, Sichuan and Shandong sign a cooperation agreement. The cooperation covers the exchange of cadres and scholars and the training base construction. April 24, 2010, the Shandong Xinhua Bookstore Group and the Sichuan Winshare Publishing Co., Ltd. sign, at the 10th Beijing International Book Fair, the "Sichuan-Shandong Strategic Issuance Cooperation Agreement". Both sides pledge to expand their market shares and social impacts and to accelerate the reform of publishing and distribution system. March 22, 2011 Suining City of Sichuan and the Shandong Hi-Speed Group sign a strategic cooperation framework agreement. The two sides will cooperate in the developments of road, railway, transportation and logistics, as well as of airport, city roads, municipal engineering, public venues, affordable housing, and others. October 29, 2011, the Sichuan Chamber of Commerce in Shandong is established. According to incomplete statistics, nearly 600,000 Sichuan People are found to live and/or run more than 5000 enterprises in Shandong, involving construction, building materials, hotels, real estate, logistics, machinery manufacturing, pharmaceutics, chemistry, media, trade, automotive, farming, biological research, communications, food, clothing, and cultural industry, with a total investment of about 6 billion yuan.

Shandong-Tianjin

[Quick Facts] Average distance = 360 km; Geographical adjacency = 0; Index of ethnic linkages = 0.9798 (2000) and 0.9819 (2010); Freight exchange via national railway = 1650 k tons (2000) and 1560 k tons (2010). ★ April 27, 2008, the Cement Industry Design and Research Company of Tianjin and the Shandong Conglin Group Co., Ltd. jointly design two advanced cement-clinker production lines. May 16, 2009, Led by the Tianjin Zhongchuan Investments Co., Ltd. and approved by the Tianjin government, the Sichuan Chamber of Commerce in Tianjin is established. January 1, 2010, the China International Airlines Company Tianjin Branch and the Shandong Airlines Company sign an agent service agreement on flight operations. The Tianjin Branch offers flight operation agent services for the Shandong Company in the Tianjin Binhai International Airport. April 17–21, 2010, a tourism delegation of Tianjin visits Shandong Province. The Tourism Bureaux of the two sides hold, in Ji'nan City, a tourism promotion entitled "Tour in Tianjin by High-Speed Rail" and sign a cooperation agreement. December 15, 2010, the Zibo High-Tech Industrial Development Zone and Tianjin University jointly establish the Tianjin University (Shandong) Research Institute. December 26, 2010, the

Management Committee of the Tianjin Development Zone and the Commodity Exchange of the Shouguang (Shandong) Vegetables Group sign a cooperation agreement. March 25, 2011, the Datang (Shandong) Power Generation Company and the Tianjin Desalination and Multipurpose Utilization Institute of the State Oceanic Administration sign a desalination strategic cooperation framework agreement; both sides will build a desalination plant, with a total investment of 1.197 billion yuan and the daily desalination capacity of 30 tons. October 29, 2012, Tianjin University and the Jining municipal government of Shandong sign a cooperation agreement.

Shandong-Tibet

[Quick Facts] Average distance = 3925 km; Geographical adjacency = 0; Index of ethnic linkages = 0.0648 (2000) and 0.0868 (2010); Freight exchange via national railway = 0 k ton (2000) and 60 k tons (2010). ★ July 1991, Tibet Middle School in Shandong Province is established in Ji'nan City; it, as one of the pairing aid projects of Shandong Province, is the only specialized boarding school recruiting students from Tibet. April 9, 2007, an aiding-Tibet work forum of Shandong Province is held in Ji'nan City. According to Statistics, Shandong has completed 755 pairing aid projects, with a total investment of 930 million yuan. August 20, 2010, the Writers Associations of Tibet and Shandong agree to build a friendly and cooperative relationship. January 6, 2011, Shandong University and Tibet University sign an interschool cooperation agreement. Tibet University has received aid from a number of high-level universities for more than a decade. January 7, 2011, Shandong and Tibet sign, in Ji'nan City, a cooperation agreement concerning personnel training in tourism and hotels. April 28, 2011, the scenic spots of Yarlung River, Lake Namtso, Mt. Tanggula and Nujiang Headstream of Tibet and the Taishan Mountain scenic spots of Shandong sign a pairing aid agreement. August 25, 2011, the AQTSs of Shandong Province and of Rikaze Prefecture of Tibet sign an agreement; Shandong will provide assistance in project construction and personnel training. September 8, 2012, a delegation of the China (Shandong) Science and Technology Association signs a friendship agreement with Rikaze. Both sides hope to strengthen technological cooperation in agriculture and energy. November 2, 2012, 115 Tibetans with congenital heart diseases from Namling, Nyalam and Panam Counties of Rikaze arrive in Ji'nan for free treatments.

Shandong-Xinjiang

[Quick Facts] Average distance = 3745 km; Geographical adjacency = 0; Index of ethnic linkages = 0.4124 (2000) and 0.4117 (2010); Freight exchange via national railway = 1190 k tons (2000) and 4610 k tons (2010). ★ July 27, 2010, the

Shandong Chamber of Commerce in Bayingolin Mongol Autonomous Prefecture (Xinjiang Uygur Autonomous Region) is established. Bayingolin has more than 400 Shandong-owned enterprises, involving energy, mining, chemistry, building materials, food and beverage, tourism, etc. December 28, 2010, a cement-clinker production line, which is developed by the Yingjisha Shanshui Cement Co., Ltd. of Shandong, operates in Sixian County of Kashi Prefecture (Xinjiang), offering 400 jobs. The project has a total investment of 820 million yuan, with expected annual profits of more than 80 million yuan. April 13, 2011, the Public Security Bureaux of the XPCC and Shandong sign a cooperation agreement. 20 police officers of the XPCC will be invited to Qingdao, Zaozhuang, Laiwu, Dezhou, Liaocheng and Qidu Cities for three months of training. June 2, 2011, the Tourism Bureaux of Xinjiang and the Shandong Province sign, in Ji'nan, a strategic cooperation and development agreement. The travel agencies of Shandong sign a cooperation agreement with the Tibet Travel Agency. These enterprises will carry out the "Mutual Delivery of 10,000 Tourists" activity as well as cooperation in charter trains and discounted tickets. May 19, 2012, the Yongheng Mining Co., Ltd. of Xinjiang and the Southern Shandong Geological Engineering Investigation Institute sign, in Korla City of the Bayingolin Mongol Autonomous Prefecture (Xinjiang), a strategic cooperation agreement concerning the prospecting of mineral resources. June 21, 2012, 14 enterprises from Shandong pay an inspection to the Industrial Park of Sixian County which receives aid from Shandong. September 3, 2012, the Standardization Institutes of Shandong and Xinjiang hold, in Urumqi City, a signing ceremony of strategic cooperation.

Shandong-Yunnan

[Quick Facts] Average distance = 3119 km; Geographical adjacency = 0; Index of ethnic linkages = 0.6724 (2000) and 0.6729 (2010); Freight exchange via national railway = 820 k tons (2000) and 2230 k tons (2010). ★ March 23, 2010, a delegation of the Shandong Hi-Speed Group Co., Ltd. visits Kunming City (Yunnan); both sides hold a symposium of the highway construction project (from the Suolong Temple to Mengzi) in Yunnan and reach a consensus on the resolution to the related problems during the construction process. January 26, 2011, approved by the Shandong DRC, Yunnan Merchants Cooperation Bureau and Yunnan Civil Affairs Department, the Shandong Chamber of Commerce in Yunnan is established. March 10, 2011, the Shandong Chamber of Commerce in Yunnan is established. The Chamber has more than 100 member enterprises. May 31, 2011, the Shandong Mining Machinery Group Co., Ltd. and the Yunnan Hengding Coal Industry Co., Ltd. visit Fuyuan County of Yunnan Province to discuss the project of mining machinery manufacturing. October 26, 2011, the Shandong Chamber of Commerce in Yunnan and the China Construction Bank Yunnan Branch hold a bank-enterprise forum and sign a comprehensive cooperation agreement. January 4, 2012, a delegation, led by the CCP Secretary (also the General Manager) of the China

(Shandong) Tobacco Industrial Co., Ltd., visits Yunnan and holds a forum with the Tobacco Monopoly Bureau of Yunnan; both sides jointly discuss the raw materials supply and cigarette sales in 2012.

Shandong-Zhejiang

[Quick Facts] Average distance = 1092 km; Geographical adjacency = 0; Index of ethnic linkages = 0.9925 (2000) and 0.9797 (2010); Freight exchange via national railway = 6890 k tons (2000) and 5020 k tons (2010). ★ September 12, 2003, the Zhejiang Chamber of Commerce in Shandong is established in Ji'nan City. The Chamber's member enterprises cover the construction of municipal works, real estate, machinery and electrical appliances industry, automobile manufacturing and marketing, mining (iron, coal and gold), the high-tech industry, modern logistics, development of agricultural products, medicine and chemical industry, and metal building materials. September 9, 2011, invited by the Tourism Bureaux of Zaozhuang City (Shandong), the Zhejiang Provincial Tourism Bureau visits Shandong to seek cooperation. October 17, 2011, the Renhe Pharmaceutical Co., Ltd. of Shandong signs a cooperation agreement with the Institute of Modern Chinese Medicine of Zhejiang University; both sides will establish an innovative Chinese medicine laboratory. November 26, 2011, the Shandong Chamber of Commerce in Zhejiang is established. The Chamber has 3123 members. April 24, 2012, the Shandong Chamber of Commerce in Zhejiang and the Bank of Communications Shandong Branch sign a strategic cooperation agreement, aiming to ease the financial difficulties faced by the Chamber's small and medium-sized enterprises. June 7, 2012, Yucheng City of Shandong, the Zhejiang Chamber of Commerce in Shandong and the Shandong Technological Transfer Center of Zhejiang University sign, in Ji'nan City, a cooperation agreement. They will jointly build the Zhejiang Enterprise Industrial Park in Shandong (with a total investment of 10 billion yuan) and plan to construct, within the park, more than 10 research centers for Zhejiang University. September 19, 2012, the Development Zone of Liaocheng City (Shandong) and the Zhejiang Chamber of Commerce in Shandong sign a cooperation framework agreement.

Shanghai-Shanxi

[Quick Facts] Average distance = 1498 km; Geographical adjacency = 0; Index of ethnic linkages = 0.9968 (2000) and 0.9907 (2010); Freight exchange via national railway = 2260 k tons (2000) and 2150 k tons (2010). ★ May 21, 2005, the Shanxi Propaganda Department, the Shanxi Association of Cultural Industry Promotion and the Shanghai Lvdian Technologies Group sign, in Shanghai, a cooperation agreement of cultural industry development. June 20–23, 2006, the "Shanxi

(Shanghai) Economic Cooperation Project Promotion" is held in the Shanghai International Convention Center. Shanxi proposes nearly 1400 projects, including 707 industrial projects, 58 infrastructural projects, 323 agricultural projects, 169 tourism projects and 140 property right trading projects; more than 500 business-persons from Shanghai participate in the promotion. July 16, 2011, the Federation of Modern Service Industry of Jincheng City and Shanghai Municipality hold, in Jincheng, the "Shanghai-Jincheng Modern Service Industry Cooperation Symposium". September 22, 2011, the Shanghai Entrepreneurs Association and Gaoping City of Shanxi sign, in the Shanghai Industrial Park of Energy Saving and Environmental Protection, an economic cooperation framework agreement. Gaoping City signs project agreements with Shanghai's enterprises. June 29, 2012, a delegation of Shanghai's Chinese entrepreneurs visits the first "Global (Yangcheng) Shanxi Merchants Congress". Shanghai and Yancheng County's enterprises sign seven cooperation agreements, with a total investment of 5.5 billion yuan. August 22, 2012, a delegation, led by the Chairman of the Tongye Coal and Chemical Industry Group Company of Shanghai, visits the Linfen Coke Company of the Shanxi Coal Transportation and Sales Group; the two sides agree, in principle, to set up a coal logistics company. September 19, 2012, Shanghai and Jincheng City hold an enterprise cooperation forum. The two sides reach 22 preliminary cooperation agreements, with a total investment of 330 million yuan. The Shanghai Federation of Enterprises and the Commission of Economy and Information Technology of Jincheng City of Shanxi sign a memorandum of cooperation, aiming to enhance exchange and to better serve enterprises.

Shanghai-Sichuan

[Quick Facts] Average distance = 2351 km; Geographical adjacency = 0; Index of ethnic linkages = 0.9530 (2000) and 0.9442 (2010); Freight exchange via national railway = 1060 k tons (2000) and 2010 k tons (2010). ★ September 13, 2005, the Shanghai International Commodity Auction Company (China's largest auction company) and the Sichuan Commodity Auction Center establish strategic partnerships. February 5, 2007, the Sichuan Chamber of Commerce in Shanghai is established. The Chamber has more than 350 members, mainly engaged in energy, chemistry, real estate, construction, logistics, modern agriculture, trade, and catering. September 13, 2007, a delegation, led by the CCP Secretary (also the PCSC Chairman) of Sichuan Province, visits Shanghai and holds, with the Shanghai CCP Secretary, an economic cooperation forum. The high-tech enterprises from the two sides hold an investment promotion fair. May 27, 2008, Shanghai's first emergent aid, including disinfectant, disinfection equipments and medicines, is sent to the Mianyang Airport. According to statistics, Shanghai has provided 117 aid projects for the post-quake reconstruction of Sichuan, with a total value of 8.25 billion yuan. December 1, 2008, the CCP Secretary (also the PCSC Chairman) of Sichuan Province, leads a delegation to visit Shanghai to acknowledge Shanghai's support to the Dujiangyan post-disaster reconstruction; both sides sign an agreement for the third phase of the reconstruction. September 27, 2010, the Shanghai Municipal Agricultural Commission and the Rural Work Leading Group of the Sichuan CCP Committee sign, in Shanghai, a framework agreement on the strengthening of agricultural cooperation. March 18, 2011, the IQBs of Shanghai and Sichuan sign, in Chengdu City, a memorandum of cooperation to promote clearance facilitation. June 7, 2011, the Tianqi Lithium Industry Co., Ltd. of Sichuan and the Shanghai Aerospace Industry Corporation sign the "Strategic Cooperation Agreement Concerning the Development of Lithium-Ion Battery Industry". February 28, 2012, the Shanghai Volkswagen Automotive Company and Sichuan Vocational and Technical Collage of Communication sign a school-enterprise labor cooperation agreement.

Shanghai-Tianjin

[Quick Facts] Average distance = 1326 km; Geographical adjacency = 0; Index of ethnic linkages = 0.9789 (2000) and 0.9827 (2010); Freight exchange via national railway = 450 k tons (2000) and 310 k tons (2010). ★ December 29, 2008, the Shanghai Chamber of Commerce in Tianjin is established. According to incomplete statistics, the real estate enterprises of the Chamber have invested more than 46 billion yuan in Tianjin; the architectural enterprises of the Chamber have undertaken projects with a total value of 11 billion yuan. February 13, 2009, Tianjin and Shanghai's officials in charge of the intellectual property sign, in Shanghai, a cooperation framework agreement concerning the protection of intellectual property rights. April 15, 2009, Shanghai Maritime University and the Tianjin Port (Group) Co., Ltd. sign a school-enterprise strategic cooperation agreement. Under the agreement, the two sides will build long-term strategic partnerships in strategic studies, personnel training, joint education, scientific and technological development, and resource sharing. July 7, 2009, the Tourism Bureaux of Tianjin and Shanghai sign an agreement on resource sharing and information exchange. The two sides also reach a consensus on the establishment of annual meeting mechanism. September 10, 2009, the Tianjin Customs and the Bank of Shanghai Tianjin Branch sign a cooperation agreement concerning the implementation of online tax payments and of bank guarantees. September 27, 2011, Tianjin Institute of Software Engineering and the Bank of Shanghai sign, in Tianjin, a cooperation agreement; the two sides establish comprehensive strategic partnerships and pledge to cooperate in financial service, information and consulting, etc. November 16, 2011, a delegation of the Nankai Middle School of Tianjin visits Shanghai Jiaotong University; the two sides sign a cooperation agreement.

Shanghai-Tibet

[Quick Facts] Average distance = 4373 km; Geographical adjacency = 0; Index of ethnic linkages = 0.0652 (2000) and 0.0867 (2010); Freight exchange via national railway = 0 k ton (2000) and 10 k tons (2010). ★ June 7, 2010, the Association of Industry and Commerce of Tibet, the Shanghai Media and Entertainment Group and the Shanghai Association of Newspaper Industry sign, in Shanghai, a cooperation framework agreement, aiming to support Tibet's private enterprises which have comparative advantages to enter Shanghai and other developed region in the Yangtze River Delta. September 21, 2010, the Lhasa (Shanghai) tourism promotion is held in Shanghai. The Tourism Bureaux of the two places sign a memorandum of cooperation. November 10, 2010, Shanghai and Rikaze Prefecture sign a sanitation aid agreement. Under the agreement, Shanghai will provide equipments for Xigaze health sectors. Shanghai also donates one million yuan of disease control equipments to Xigaze. January 17 2011, Tongzhou School of Shanghai and the No. 2 Primary School of Chenguan Ditrsct (Lhasa) establish friendly school relations. The two sides announce the "2011 Pando Education Fund". June 11, 2012, as the only brokerage in Tibet Autonomous Region, the Tibet Tongxin Securities, signs a comprehensive cooperation framework agreement with the Bank of Shanghai. August 29, 2012, the "Meeting of Aiding-Tibet Work of Dungkar (Doilungdêgên County of Lhasa City) Power Generation Co. Ltd.", organized by the State Grid Corporation, is held in Lhasa. The Shanghai Electric Power Company and others will provide aid to the Tibet Power Company; the two sides also sign a technological aid agreement. September 3, 2012, the Shanbao Machinery Co., Ltd. of the Jianshe Road and Bridge Machinery Co., Ltd. of Shanghai sign a contract with a Tibetan company; the Shanghai Company will provide the equipments for the 2000 tons/day cement clinker dry production line for Tibet.

Shanghai-Xinjiang

[Quick Facts] Average distance = 4077 km; Geographical adjacency = 0; Index of ethnic linkages = 0.4116 (2000) and 0.4120 (2010); Freight exchange via national railway = 570 k tons (2000) and 1130 k tons (2010). ★ February 12, 2009, the Shanghai Intellectual Property Administration and the Aksu Prefecture delegation of Xinjiang hold, in Shanghai, a pairing aid symposium and sign cooperation project agreements. Shanghai will provide 200,000 yuan to support the construction of information platform and of the personnel training of intellectual property services in Aksu. September 6, 2011, Shanghai and Xinjiang' s Federations of Trade Union, the Communist Youth Leagues and the Women's Federations sign the "12th Five-Year Plan" cooperation framework agreements. Under the agreement, the Shanghai Trade Union will establish a 50 million yuan special aid fund, the Communist Youth League of Shanghai will construct at least 1000 healthcare stations in Xinjiang, and the two Women's Federations will jointly host educational aid activities, etc. November 12, 2011, the friendly cooperation agreement between the Shanghai PPCC and the Xinjiang PPCC is held in Shanghai. The agreement includes the joint governance of public security in Xinjiang, the development of the Kashi Special Economic Zone, pairing aid work, personnel exchange, and cooperation between enterprises. December 25, 2011, the Shanghai and Xinjiang PCSCs hold, in the Shanghai, a cooperation symposium. May 11, 2012, Shanghai and Xinjiang sign, in Urumqi City of Xinjiang, three aid agreements, involving health and education. Shanghai hopes to strengthen exchange and cooperation between relevant units and to improve medical care and education in Xinjiang. May 28, 2012, the Shanghai Federation of Enterprises (Chamber of Commerce) in Xinjiang and the front headquarters of the Shanghai pairing-aid to Xinjiang sign a cooperation agreement; the two sides will establish, in Urumqi City, the Xinjiang-Shanghai Microcredit Co., Ltd.

Shanghai-Yunnan

[Quick Facts] Average distance = 3069 km; Geographical adjacency = 0; Index of ethnic linkages = 0.6711 (2000) and 0.6743 (2010); Freight exchange via national railway = 550 k tons (2000) and 1070 k tons (2010). ★ August 28, 2006, the Yunnan Chamber of Commerce in Shanghai is established. The Chamber has 60 member companies, involving mining, electricity, machinery and electronics, commerce, hotel, tourism, etc. December 19, 2009, Shanghai and Yunnan sign an agreement concerning the promotion of Derung's economic development in Dulongjiang Township of Nujiang Prefecture, Yunnan Province. Shanghai will donate 20 million yuan of special fund for rural construction in Dulongjiang Township. Derung is one of the smallest ethnic groups in China. May 1, 2010, the Shanghai Tobacco Group Company and the Yunnan Tobacco Monopoly Bureau sign a strategic cooperation agreement. February 17, 2011, the Departments of Commerce of Shanghai and Yunnan sign a cooperation agreement on the docking of e-commerce platform. December 28, 2011, Xishuangbanna Prefecture of Yunnan and the Pudong New District of Shanghai sign a cooperation framework agreement. The agreement include: (i) the Shanghai Guangming Group builds a dendrobium planting base in Yongde County (Yunnan), with an investment of 120 million yuan; (ii) the Shenyuan Chemical Trading Co., Ltd. of Shanghai invests 50 million yuan (for the natural rubber project) in Yunnan; and (iii) the No. 6 Hospital of Shanghai and Xishuangbanna Prefecture of Yunnan jointly conduct research activities. April 14, 2012, Yunnan and the Shanghai Federation of Enterprises sign a memorandum of strategic cooperation. Both sides will cooperate in four aspects of e-commerce, foreign trade, investment information platform, and local specialties. April 27, 2012, the Chaori Solar Energy Technology Co., Ltd. of Shanghai and the Yunnan Energy and Investment Group Co., Ltd. sign a strategic cooperation framework agreement. Under the agreement, the two sides will jointly construct an 800–1000 MW photovoltaic power plant in Yunnan.

Shanghai-Zhejiang

[Quick Facts] Average distance = 201 km; Geographical adjacency = 0; Index of ethnic linkages = 0.9934 (2000) and 0.9847 (2010); Freight exchange via national railway = 210 k tons (2000) and 1440 k tons (2010). ★ March 5, 1986, the Zhejiang Chamber of Commerce in Shanghai is established. The Chamber has more than 5000 member enterprises, involving industry, trade, building materials, real estate, entertainment, health care, financial investment, culture and education, etc. In October 15, 2004, Zhejiang University Life Sciences School and the Shanghai Life Sciences Institute of the CAS hold a forum concerning the establishment of research and practice base. May 30, 2007, Shanghai and Zhejiang sign a memorandum of collaboration concerning the clearance system construction in the Yangtze River Delta. October 12, 2008: the "Integration of Yangtze River Delta and County-Level Economic Development Symposium" and the "2008 Changxin-Shanghai Forum" are held in the Shanghai International Conference Center. The Caohejing Development Zone of Shanghai and the Changxin Economic Development Zone of Zhejiang sign four economic and technological cooperation agreements. March 1, 2010, the FDAs of Shanghai and Zhejiang sign a cooperation agreement concerning the interregional action to catering service and food safety during the 2010 Shanghai World Expo. September 26, 2010, Zhejiang and Shanghai public security organs sign a regional-police cooperation agreement of criminal investigation and drug control. According to the agreement, Zhejiang and Shanghai will establish a joint action and resource sharing relationships, aiming to fight against interregional criminal activities. June 10, 2011, the Forest Pests Control and Quarantine Station of Shanghai and the Forest Pests Control and Quarantine Bureau of Zhejiang hold, in Jiaxing City of Zhejiang, a symposium of law enforcement work. The two sides sign a memorandum of cooperation. December 27, 2011, the Supervision Bureau of Shanghai and the Land and Resources Department of Zhejiang establish a cooperative mechanism.

Shanxi-Sichuan

[Quick Facts] Average distance = 1493 km; Geographical adjacency = 0; Index of ethnic linkages = 0.9523 (2000) and 0.9411 (2010); Freight exchange via national railway = 1180 k tons (2000) and 3230 k tons (2010). ★ March 9, 2001, Sichuan and Shanxi's police stations cooperate to destroy a cross-provincial car-theft group. December 29, 2006, the Shanxi Chamber of Commerce in Sichuan is established in Chengdu City. September 6, 2008, a delegation, led by the governors of Aba Tibetan and Qiang Autonomous Prefecture of and Maoxian County of Sichuan, visits Shanxi to promote investment. The two sides sign a cooperation agreement, involving deep processing of sea buckthorn and wine production. December 16, 2009, the Anxian County of Mianyang City (Sichuan) holds an investment fair in Xinzhou City of Shanxi Province. The two sides sign four cooperation agreements, covering tourism development, agriculture and chemistry, with a total investment of 780 million yuan. May 18, 2011, the Sichuan Chamber of Commerce in Shanxi is established in Taiyuan City. The Chamber has more than 70 member companies. September 7, 2011, the "Shanxi-Sichuan Economic and Social Development Forum" is held in Taiyuan City of Shanxi. Sichuan, as the first western region whose total economic output value exceeds one trillion yuan, signs an agreement on equipment manufacturing and energy development with Shanxi. September 27, 2012, at the "Thirteenth West Investment Fair", Shanxi holds a special promotion; Shanxi's enterprises bring 121 investment projects, with a total investment of 599.607 billion yuan. October 22, 2012 the Seismological Bureau of Xinzhou City of Shanxi and the Earthquake Disaster Mitigation Authority of Mianyang City of Sichuan sign a cooperation agreement.

Shanxi-Tianjin

[Quick Facts] Average distance = 650 km; Geographical adjacency = 0; Index of ethnic linkages = 0.9761 (2000) and 0.9770 (2010); Freight exchange via national railway = 36,180 k tons (2000) and 31,270 k tons (2010). ★ 1998, the Shanxi Chamber of Commerce in Tianjin is establish; it is the earliest provincial-level offsite chamber of Shanxi province. The chamber has more than 660 members, mainly engaged in environmental protection, IT, agriculture, pharmaceutics, financial services, real estate, and communications, with a total investment of over 100 billion yuan. September 17, 2007, the Taiyuan Iron and Steel (Group) Co., Ltd. of Shanxi and the Tianjin Pipe (Group) Co., Ltd. sign, in Taiyuan, a strategic cooperation framework agreement. May 18, 2008, the Fanglv Bonded Logistics Center of Shanxi signs a cooperation agreement with the Tianjin Port Group. December 13–14, 2008, a delegation, composed of the representatives of Tianjin's real estate enterprises, visits Lvliang City of Shanxi to promote real estate projects, aiming to develop Shanxi's market. March 19, 2010, the Entry-Exit IQBs of Shanxi and Tianjin sign, in Taiyuan City of Shanxi, a cooperation agreement concerning non-stop passing port. June 20, 2010, the Jinzhong City (Shanxi) Chamber of Commerce in Tianjin is established in the Binhai New Area of Tianjin. March 19, 2011, approved by the Shanxi Department of Civil Affairs, the Tianjin Chamber of Commerce in Shanxi is established in Taiyuan City. July 8, 2011, the Shanxi Coke Group and the Tianjin Port (Group) Co., Ltd. agree to jointly construct a coke-storage plant, with a 1 million square meter land area. May 8, 2012, the Shanxi government and Tianjin University sign, in Taiyuan City of Shanxi, a comprehensive cooperation framework agreement. June 7, 2012, a symposium of regional agricultural cooperation between Tianjin and Shanxi is held in Tianjin. The Baodi Group of Tianjin and the Nanjiao district government of Datong City (Shanxi) sign an investment project agreement concerning the construction of pig breeding and food processing base, with a total investment of one billion yuan.

Shanxi-Tibet

[Quick Facts] Average distance = 3515 km; Geographical adjacency = 0; Index of ethnic linkages = 0.0633 (2000) and 0.0842 (2010); Freight exchange via national railway = 0 k ton (2000) and 30 k tons (2010). ★ September 1985, the first batch of 1301 Tibetan students, from seven cities (or prefectures) of Tibet, enter 17 high schools of 16 provinces (or cities) including Shanxi; this is part of the nationwide aiding-Tibet work. May 14, 2007, Pingyang County of Shanxi Province and Jiali County of Tibet hold, in Lhasa City, a pairing aid symposium. Shanxi will further implement aid work; the two sides also hold a donation ceremony. July 5, 2009, seven students of Shanxi Normal University rid bicycle from Linfen City of Shanxi to Lhasa City of Tibet. The trip is expected to spend 40 days, covering a total distance of 4000 km. December 11, 2009, the Shanxi Electric Power Corporation helps to train, in the training bases of substation simulation of and transmission lines of Datong City and Linfen City, 60 technical workers from the Tibet Power Company. This is the first time that the two companies carry out training cooperation. April 21, 2010, a delegation led by the CCP secretary of the Electric Power Corporation of Shanxi visits the Electric Power Corporation of Tibet and conveys greetings and best wishes to its technical staff who are doing aid work in Tibet. March 27, 2012, at the Affiliated High School of Shanxi University, more than 200 students and teachers of Tibetan Classes hold the "Serfs Emancipation Day".

Shanxi-Xinjiang

[Quick Facts] Average distance = 3219 km; Geographical adjacency = 0; Index of ethnic linkages = 0.4089 (2000) and 0.4075 (2010); Freight exchange via national railway = 70 k tons (2000) and 1860 k tons (2010). ★ July 28, 2007, Xinjiang and the Lu'an Mining Co., Ltd. of Shanxi sign an agreement concerning the comprehensive development of the coal resources in Xinjiang. August 28, 2008, the Shanxi Federation of Enterprises in Xinjiang is established. There are 100 Shanxi-funded enterprises in Xinjiang, involving mineral development, coal chemistry, metallurgy, building materials, real estate, fruit planting and other advantage industries, with a total annual revenue of over 10 billion yuan. October 20, 2009, the Xinjiang government and the Shanxi Coking Coal (Group) Co., Ltd. sign, in Urumqi City, a strategic cooperation agreement. Under the agreement, the Shanxi Coking Coal Group will invest 100 billion yuan to construct a large-scale coal and chemical base, with a total processing capacity of 100 million tons. June 3, 2011, the Tourism Bureaux of Xinjiang Uygur Autonomous Region and Shanxi sign a strategic cooperation agreement. The Tourism Bureaux of and relevant sectors of Changji (Xinjiang) Hui Autonomous Prefecture and Shanxi sign agreements on pairing aid, mutual delivery of tourists, charter and special train and others. December 5, 2011, Fukang City of Xinjiang and Datong City of Shanxi sign a cooperation agreement concerning the pairing aid from Datong City to Chengguan Town of Fukang City. July 19–22, 2012, a delegation, led by the Director of the Shanxi Department of Science and Technology, pays an inspection to the No. 6 Agricultural Division (Wujiaqu City) of the XPCC. The two sides' companies sign two aiding-Tibet agreements on the technological integration and industrialization of vegetable production and on the construction of a 33 MW power plant that utilizes coal and gas. November 28, 2012, the Shanxi Department of Culture and the No. 6 Agricultural Division of the XPCC sign, in Wujiaqu City of Xinjiang, the "Cooperation Framework Agreement of Cultural Development".

Shanxi-Yunnan

[Quick Facts] Average distance = 2593 km; Geographical adjacency = 0; Index of ethnic linkages = 0.6688 (2000) and 0.6687 (2010); Freight exchange via national railway = 480 k tons (2000) and 520 k tons (2010). ★ November 9, 2009, Heshun County of Shanxi and Heshun Town of Tengchong County (Yunnan) establish friendly county-level relationships. The two sides will carry out regional cooperation in cultural tourism development, investment, nonmaterial cultural heritage, thematic cultural studies, etc. August 30, 2010, the Shanxi Chamber of Commerce in Yunnan is established. The Chamber has 160 member companies, covering financial services, mining, construction, bio-technology, culture, new energy, logistics, international trade, agriculture, tourism and catering services, with a total revenues of about 12 billion yuan and annual taxes of about 800 million yuan. September 30, 2011, Licheng County of Shanxi and the Chuxiong Huitong Cultural Tourism Development Co., Ltd. of Yunan sign, in Taiyuan City, an agreement on cultural tourism development, with a total investment of 3.5 billion yuan. April 20, 2012, at the "7th China (Yunnan) Pu'er Tea Fair", Yunnan and Shanxi Provinces sign a framework agreement on tea marketing and docking. According to incomplete statistics, there are more than 2000 tea shops in Taiyuan City of Shanxi, with total annual sales of nearly one billion yuan and the growth rate of 10 %; Yunnan's tea-planting area is 5.65 million mu, with 244,900 tons of tea production capacity, with 13.439 billion yuan of gross output value. The two sides pledge to expand tea market from the southeast coastal areas to the northeast and northwest areas. September 6, 2012, Dehong Prefecture of Yunnan and a number of Shanxi's enterprises sign, in Kunming City, a cooperation agreement concerning the construction of the "Bridgehead Golden Port". The project is one of China's key demonstration zones, and it is the largest investment project, so far, in Dehong Prefecture.

Shanxi-Zhejiang

[Quick Facts] Average distance = 1624 km; Geographical adjacency = 0; Index of ethnic linkages = 0.9925 (2000) and 0.9794 (2010); Freight exchange via national railway = 4490 k tons (2000) and 3420 k tons (2010). ★ June 16, 2001, the Zhejiang Chamber of Commerce in Shanxi is established. The Chamber has more than 600 members, with an accumulative investment of 100 billion yuan, paying tax of two billion yuan annually. November 10, 2003, the "Zhejiang-Shanxi Economic and Technological Cooperation and Development Forum" is held in Taiyuan City. The two sides sign an agreement to strengthen industrial cooperation and to establish strategic partnerships in the fields of coal, electricity and other energy aspects. January 6, 2008, the Zhejiang Chamber of Commerce in Changzhi City (Shanxi) is established. June 8, 2011, the Shanxi Chamber of Commerce in Zhejiang is established. The Chamber has more than 100 member companies, mainly engaged in medicine, finance, real estate, electrical appliances, building materials, hotel, with an accumulative investment of over 20 billion yuan. July 29, 2011, the "Shanxi-Zhejiang Enterprise Cooperation Forum" is held in Hangzhou City. Both sides sign 18 cooperation agreements. The Datong Coal Industry Group and the Zhejiang Energy Group sign a cooperation agreement on the Shuonan Power Plant. August 19, 2011, the Economic Research Institute of the Zhejiang Academy of Social Sciences visits Shanxi University Graduate School. August 21, 2011, the "Shanxi-Zhejiang Economic and Social Development Forum" is held in Taiyuan City of Shanxi. Zhejiang hopes that both sides can upgrade cooperation from energy supply and demand to a higher level. The Zhejiang provincial government delegation also visits the Shanxi Provincial Museum and the Jinci Museum. October 22, 2012, a delegation of the Shanxi Bureau of Surveying and Mapping Geographic Information pays an inspection to the Zhejiang Bureau of Mapping and Geographic Information. Both sides sign a cooperation agreement concerning geographical data exchange, information sharing, digital city construction, modern mapping technologies, etc.

Sichuan-Tianjin

[Quick Facts] Average distance = 2185 km; Geographical adjacency = 0; Index of ethnic linkages = 0.9531 (2000) and 0.9426 (2010); Freight exchange via national railway = 770 k tons (2000) and 1210 k tons (2010). ★ May 27, 2006, the Tianjin Chamber of Commerce in Sichuan is established. According to statistics, the Tianjin-funded enterprises have invested more than ten billion yuan in Sichuan. May 16, 2009, the Sichuan Chamber of Commerce in Tianjin is established. December 29, 2009, the United Investing Assurance Company of Tianjin and the Sichuan Chamber of Commerce in Tianjin sign, in the Sichuan Plaza in Tianjin, a financial cooperation agreement. September 3, 2011, the "Key Sichuan Tourism

Investment and Project Promotion" is held in Tianjin. Four cities of Ganzi, Yibin, Suining and Panzhihua of Sichuan introduce their tourism resources. October 20, 2011, the Tianjin Culture and Arts Exchange and Wenchuan County of Sichuan sign, in Tianjin, a strategic cooperation agreement on nonmaterial cultural heritage projects. April 9, 2012, the No. 3 Institute of Surveying and Mapping of Sichuan and the Institute of Surveying and Mapping of Tianjin conduct an exchange on pipeline exploration and rural land property surveys. April 10, 2012, the Tianjin Materials Group and the Neijiang municipal government of Sichuan Province sign a strategic investment agreement. The Tianjin Group will carry out auto sales and repair services in Neijiang; the Neijiang government will offer preferential policies for the Group. May 29, 2012, a delegation, led by the Zhongchuan Investment Co., Ltd. of Tianjin, visits Nanxi District of Yibin City (Sichuan). The delegation inspects the constructions of the Binjiang New City and of the Luolong Industrial Center and others. The Tianjin enterprises and Nanxi District sign an investment agreement, with a total value of one billion yuan. June 27, 2012, Tianjin University and Sichuan Province sign a cooperation agreement. Tianjin University will use technological and talent advantages to promote province-school cooperation.

Sichuan-Tibet

[Quick Facts] Average distance = 3360 km; Geographical adjacency = 1; Index of ethnic linkages = 0.0786 (2000) and 0.1030 (2010); Freight exchange via national railway = 0 k ton (2000) and 290 k tons (2010). ★ July 12, 2006, the Tibet government and Sichuan University sign, in Lhasa, a comprehensive cooperation agreement. January 17, 2012, the signing ceremony of strategic cooperation framework agreement between Sichuan and Tibet is held in Chengdu City. Both sides pledge to cooperate in infrastructure construction, processing of agricultural products, exploitation of mineral resources, tourism, maintenance of social stability and others. March 14, 2012, Ya'an City of Sichuan and Lhasa City of Tibet Autonomous Region sign, in Beijing, a regional cooperation framework agreement. The two sides will jointly develop the Tibetan Tea market, aiming to transform their resource advantages to economic benefits. In 2008, the Ya'an tea production technique has been included in China's national nonmaterial cultural heritage lists. April 9, 2012, the Bureaux of Surveying and Mapping Geographic Information of Sichuan and Tibet sign, in Chengdu, a strategic cooperation agreement. May 28, 2012, the signing ceremony of cooperation framework agreement on food and drug supervision and management between Tibet and Sichuan is held in Chengdu City. Both sides will strengthen cooperation in R&D of Tibetan medicine, personnel exchange, management of emergent affair and others. June 13, 2012, the Fushun County (Sichuan) Chamber of Commerce in Tibet is established in Lhasa City. July 12, 2012, the Frontier Defense Corps of the Public Security Bureaux of Tibet and Sichuan sign, in Chengdu, an agreement concerning the joint law enforcement on illegal immigration activities. August 2, 2012, Tibet and Sichuan sign a cooperation agreement on agriculture and animal husbandry. September 30, 2012, the Commercial Departments of Tibet and Sichuan sign in, Chengdu City, a commercial cooperation agreement. Both sides will carry out cooperation in domestic trade, logistics and circulation, trade channel construction in South Asia, foreign trade, etc.

Sichuan-Xinjiang

[Quick Facts] Average distance = 3026 km; Geographical adjacency = 0; Index of ethnic linkages = 0.4094 (2000) and 0.4088 (2010); Freight exchange via national railway = 2130 k tons (2000) and 3530 k tons (2010). ★ December 10, 2005, the Sichuan Association of Enterprises (Chamber of Commerce) in Xinjiang is established. The Chamber has more than 300 enterprise members, mainly engaged in commodity sales, product processing, construction, real estate, mobile phone production, petro-chemistry, natural gas transmission, retail, furniture manufacturing, tourism, printing, coal, and wine, with a total investment of 12 billion yuan and annual taxes of about 60 million yuan. July 1, 2008, Sichuan University and Xinjiang Uygur Autonomous Region sign a comprehensive cooperation agreement, marking that the 5-year comprehensive cooperation between Xinjiang and the University starts. October 18, 2011, the Xinjiang Chamber of Commerce in Sichuan is established in Chengdu City. The Chamber has more than 100 members. September 5, 2012, at the "2nd Asia Europe Expo", Sichuan and Xinjiang sign a framework agreement to further strengthen business and trade cooperation. Both sides will also cooperate in customs, entry-exit inspection and quarantine, port and regional clearance. September 27, 2012, the Merchants Bureau of Xinjiang and the Investment Bureau of Sichuan sign, in Chengdu, an economic cooperation agreement. Both sides agree to strengthen investment cooperation and support the development of each others' key enterprises. November 11, 2012, Sichuan and Xinjiang begin to jointly construct a ± 1100 kV power line that sets out to transmit electricity from Xinjiang to Sichuan. This project is included by the State Grid in China's power network, aiming to upgrade West China's power transmission.

Sichuan-Yunnan

[Quick Facts] Average distance = 1100 km; Geographical adjacency = 1; Index of ethnic linkages = 0.6993 (2000) and 0.7074 (2010); Freight exchange via national railway = 5430 k tons (2000) and 13,070 k tons (2010). ★ October 19, 2005, the conference of industrial and commercial departments in the Pan-Pearl River Delta Region is held in Chengdu City. Sichuan, Yunnan and other provinces jointly sign an agreement concerning the strengthening of market regulation and supervision, aiming to raise food health level. June 26, 2008, the Sichuan Chamber of

Commerce in Yunnan is established. The Chamber has over 500 members. August 30, 2008, the Workers Unions of Yunnan and Sichuan sign an agreement concerning the maintenance of migrant workers' rights and interests. July 31, 2010, Yunnan and Sichuan jointly sign a cooperation agreement on tourism development and trade circulation. June 6, 2011, Yunnan and Sichuan sign, in Kunming City, a strategic cooperation framework agreement. Both sides reach consensuses on traffic construction, economic and trade cooperation, tourism, ecological and environmental protection, establishment of inter-government exchange mechanism, etc. August 22, 2011, the Procuratorates of Yongren County of Yunnan and Renhe District of Panzhihua City of Sichuan sign a cooperation agreement on interregional administration, aiming to strengthen the management and law enforcement in border areas. November 9, 2011, Liangshan Yi Prefecture and Yibin City of Sichuan Province, Zhaotong City of Yunnan Province and the Three Gorges Group sign, in Hangzhou City, a cooperation agreement concerning the economic construction of the reservoir area in the lower reaches of the Jinsha River. According to the agreement, the two provinces will cooperate, with the Group, to accelerate the development of the hydroelectric power project in the Jinsha River. April 28, 2012, the Sichuan Chamber of Commerce in Xishuangbanna Prefecture (Yunnan) is established. The Chamber has nearly 200 member enterprises, covering real estate, health, entertainment, publishing, border trade, culture and tourism, with a total asset of over 10 billion yuan and an annual output value of 3 billion yuan.

Sichuan-Zhejiang

[Quick Facts] Average distance = 2552 km; Geographical adjacency = 0; Index of ethnic linkages = 0.9529 (2000) and 0.9445 (2010); Freight exchange via national railway = 1140 k tons (2000) and 1830 k tons (2010). ★ October 15, 2002, the Zhejiang Chamber of Commerce in Sichuan is established. According to statistics, there are more than 300,000 Zhejiang merchants in Sichuan, mainly engaged in industry, agriculture, finance, trade, logistics, service industry, and textile, with annual sales value of 30 billion yuan, providing one million jobs. September 15, 2007, Sichuan and Zhejiang Provinces sign a labor cooperation agreement. 163 training institutions of Sichuan and 226 companies of Zhejiang sign 331 labor contracts, with 148,343 of skilled workers being migrated from Sichuan to Zhejiang. March 21, 2008, the Sichuan Chamber of Commerce in Zhejiang is established. November 18, 2009, the IQBs of Zhejiang and Sichuan sign, in Chengdu City, a memorandum of cooperation. September 15, 2011, the Federations of Trade Unions of Sichuan and Zhejiang sign, in Chengdu City, a cooperation agreement of the rights maintenance for migrant workers, 23 companies and about 8.7 million workers are included in the agreement. November 9, 2011, the Zhejiang Association of Small and Medium Enterprises and Liangshan Yi Prefecture of and Yibin City of Sichuan sign, in Hangzhou City, a cooperation agreement concerning the economic construction of the reservoir area in the lower reaches of the Jinsha

River. According to the agreement, Liangshan and Yibin will use the local resource advantages to attract investment from Zhejiang's enterprises. September 14, 2012, a delegation, led by the Dongyang Municipal CCP Secretary of Zhejiang, visits Lushan County of Sichuan. Both sides sign a cooperation framework agreement on cultural exchange.

Tianjin-Tibet

[Quick Facts] Average distance = 4174 km; Geographical adjacency = 0; Index of ethnic linkages = 0.0652 (2000) and 0.0874 (2010); Freight exchange via national railway = 0 k ton (2000) and 30 k tons (2010). ★ 1994, at the third round of aiding-Tibet conference sponsored by the central government, Tianjin and Changdu of Tibet establish pairing aid relationships. As of 2010, Tianjin had donated a total value of 511 million yuan, including materials and funds to Changdu; 60 aid projects were completed, including infrastructure construction, new rural reconstruction, the Jinchang Bridge, the Tianjin Square of Lancang River area, the Songda Power Station in Changdu, and the Jinchang Sport Center. June 27, 2011, Tianjin Vocational Normal University and Tibet sign a cooperation agreement on joint education. According to the agreement, the University will provide tuitions, living expenses and scholarships for the Tibetan students. September 5, 2011, a delegation, led by the CCP Secretary (also the General Director) of the AQTS of Tianjin visits Lhasa City of Tibet to participant in the aiding-Tibet work conference; Tibet and Tianjin sign an agreement, aiming to implement a new round of pairing-aid work deployed by the Tianjin municipal CCP committee, the Tianjin municipal government and the General AQTS of the PRC. August 30, 2012, the first batch of Tianjin's medical care team visits Changdu, Jiangda and Dingqing of Tibet; the team will carry out compulsory treatment for the children who have congenital heart diseases.

Tianjin-Xinjiang

[Quick Facts] Average distance = 3911 km; Geographical adjacency = 0; Index of ethnic linkages = 0.4270 (2000) and 0.4230 (2010); Freight exchange via national railway = 1710 k tons (2000) and 2270 k tons (2010). ★ July 14, 2007, the China Steel Group Xinjiang Company and the Tianjin Institute of Geological Research of the China Steel Group sign, in Tianjin, a cooperation agreement on investment and exploitation of resources. According to the agreement, the Tianjin Institute will send two geological professionals to help the Xinjiang Company to establish a technological department in Xinjiang. September 2, 2007, the Xinjiang-Tianjin Science and Technology Park (the Liaison Office of the Tianjin municipal government in Urumqi City) is established in the Xinjiang Science Building. August

11, 2010, the "Tianjin-Xinjiang Regional Trade and Economic Cooperation Forum" is held in the Urumqi Customs Conference Center. The Forum will also be held in Korla, Aletai, Tacheng, Huoerguosi, Kashi and Alashankou. The Customs Associations of Tianjin and Xinjiang sign a memorandum of cooperation. August 20, 2010, the Tianjin Chamber of Commerce in Xinjiang Uygur Autonomous Region is established. The establishment of the Chamber aims to promote the economic growth of the two places and to further implement aiding-Xinjiang work. December 9, 2010, the XPCC Chamber of Commerce in the Binhai New Area of Tianjin is established. Some members of the Chamber are from the XPCC. June 27, 2011, Tianjin Vocational Normal University and Xinjiang sign a cooperation agreement of joint education. According to the agreement, the school will provide tuitions, living expenses and scholarships for the students from Xinjiang. May 12, 2012, the Xinjiang Chamber of Commerce in Tianjin is established. The Chamber has nearly 100 enterprise members. The Chamber is the eighth offsite chamber established by Xinjiang's entrepreneurs.

Tianjin-Yunnan

[Quick Facts] Average distance = 3320 km; Geographical adjacency = 0; Index of ethnic linkages = 0.6831 (2000) and 0.6824 (2010); Freight exchange via national railway = 30 k tons (2000) and 380 k tons (2010). ★ November 30, 2008, the Yunnan and Tianjin governments hold, in Kunming City of Yunnan, a trade cooperation and economic development forum; the Tourism Bureaux of the two sides sign a cooperation agreement. Both sides pledge to further strengthen tourism cooperation through the national policies of stimulating consumption and expanding domestic demand. According to the agreement, Tianjin and Yunnan will regularly exchange in tourism development and will comprehensively cooperate in tourism product promotion, information sharing, tourist complaints and emergency treatment. March 14, 2010, a 17-people delegation of Anning High School of Yunnan visits the Tianjin No. 2 High School. Both sides sign an inter-school cooperation agreement. The teachers from the two schools conduct an in-depth exchange on issues relating to the 2010 national university entrance test. The Yunnan delegation also pays an inspection to downtown Tianjin, the Tianjin Binhai New Area, and Yangliuqing town. May 21, 2011, the Tianjin Culture and Arts Exchange, the Yunnan Institute of Quality Supervision and Inspection of Jades and Jewelries, the Yunnan Promotion Association of Jade and Jewelry Culture and the China Merchants Bank Kunming Branch sign a strategic cooperation framework agreement. The Tianjin Exchange and other three units establish a long-term cooperation mechanism, aiming to strengthen the utilization of their respective advantages and to integrate resources.

Tianjin-Zhejiang

[Quick Facts] Average distance = 1452 km; Geographical adjacency = 0; Index of ethnic linkages = 0.9749 (2000) and 0.9777 (2010); Freight exchange via national railway = 320 k tons (2000) and 10 k tons (2010). ★ 1998, the Zhejiang Chamber of Commerce in Tianjin (formerly: the Zhejiang Promotion Association of Economic Development in Tianjin) is established. As of 2011, there are 200,000 Zhejiang people and more than 5000 Zhejiang-funded enterprises in Tianjin, involving real estate, light industry, trade logistics, high-tech industry, etc., with a total investment of 73 billion yuan, providing 400,000 jobs. October 30, 2003, the Sanshi Group of Zhejiang and the Tianjin Institute of Cement Design sign, in Zhejiang, a technological cooperation agreement from 2004 to 2005; under the agreement, the cement production capacity of the Group will reach 12 million tons. June 18, 2005, the Leqing (Zhejiang) Chamber of Commerce in Tianjin is established. April 19, 2009, Tianjin University of Technology visits Hangzhou City of Zhejiang and signs an agreement of production and research with the Yinbang Co., Ltd. of Hangzhou; the two sides will jointly establish an employment and practice base for the University. November 10, 2009, the Tianjin Institute of Industrial Biotechnology of CAS and the Xianju Junye Pharmaceutical Company of Zhejiang establish, in Taizhou City of Zhejiang, strategic partnerships on the R&D of industrial biotechnology. April 1, 2010, the Tianjin Development Zone and the Dahan Automobile Company of Zhejiang sign, in the Investment Service Center, an investment project cooperation agreement; the project's total investment and the annual output capacity are 155 million yuan and two million sets of automobile parts, respectively. October 13, 2011, the Wenzhou Municipal Education Bureau of Zhejiang and Tianjin Vocational Normal University jointly establish a teachers' training base in Zhejiang.

Tibet-Xinjiang

[Quick Facts] Average distance = 4080 km; Geographical adjacency = 1; Index of ethnic linkages = 0.0659 (2000) and 0.0896 (2010); Freight exchange via national railway = 0 k ton (2000) and 30 k tons (2010). ★ August 29, 2003, the National Nature Reserve Management Office of Aerjin Mountain of Xinjiang, the National Nature Reserve Management Bureau of Qiangtang of Tibet and other two National Nature Reserve Management Bureaux (Kekexili and the water source of the three Rivers of Yangtze, Yellow and Mekong) jointly sign a memorandum of information exchange and cooperation of Tibetan antelopes protection, aiming to strengthen the protection of the Tibetan antelope, to strengthen supervision and enforcement of the crime activities, such as smuggling and sales of Tibetan antelope products, and to effectively curb illegal and criminal activities in the protected areas. April 10, 2006, the Geological Exploitation Bureaux of Tibet and Xinjiang Autonomous Regions and the China Geological Survey Bureau sign an agreement of wild workstation management, aiming to strengthen the safety of scientific investigation activities in wild areas. November 11, 2010, the Customers' Committees (or Associations) of Xinjiang and Tibet (also including those of Hong Kong, Macau, Guangzhou and Shenzhen) jointly hold a conference on the protection of consumers' rights. The six places sign an agreement. According to the agreement, the Consumers' Committee of any side (Tibet, Xinjiang, Hong Kong, Macau, Guangzhou or Shenzhen) which receives the complaints from other five sides should promptly investigate, handle, and report the treatment progress or suggestions to the complaint side as soon as possible.

Tibet-Yunnan

[Quick Facts] Average distance = 4460 km; Geographical adjacency = 1; Index of ethnic linkages = 0.0691 (2000) and 0.0910 (2010); Freight exchange via national railway = 0 k ton (2000) and 0 k ton (2010). ★ August 9, 2007, the drug supervision sectors of 12 adjacent municipalities and prefectures of four Southwest provinces (including Tibet and Yunnan) jointly hold, in Kangding City of Ganzi Prefecture of Sichuan Province, the first regional cooperation conference; they sign a cooperation agreement on food and drug supervision in border areas, aiming to ensure the safety of minority diet and medication. September 16, 2010, Diqing Tibetan Autonomous Prefecture of Yunnan, Changdu Prefecture of Tibet and other two other adjacent counties sign a strategic cooperation agreement on tourism; according to the agreement, the four (autonomous) prefectures will jointly develop tourist routes, promote their local scene spots and establish a regular exchange mechanism, all of which aim to implement the "Overall Plan of China's Eco-Tourism Development" and to eliminate the interregional barriers of policy, market, traffic and service in tourism. December 5, 2011, the Datang (Yunnan) International Hydropower Development Corporation in the upper reaches of the Nu River and the Yadong County of Rikaze Prefecture (Tibet) sign a cooperation agreement on the Yadong solar energy project. Both sides will build the solar energy generator in Pali, Duina and other towns in the northern high altitude areas of Yadong County. According to the agreement, the first phase of the photovoltaic power plant has the capacity of more than 100 MW. October 20, 2012, the Procuratorates of Nujiang Lisu Autonomous Prefecture of Yunnan Province and Linzhi Prefecture of Tibet Autonomous Region sign, in Linzhi Town, a framework agreement on attorney coordination; both sides will strengthen cooperation to prevent and combat cross-border crimes.

Tibet-Zhejiang

[Quick Facts] Average distance = 4308 km; Geographical adjacency = 0; Index of ethnic linkages = 0.0620 (2000) and 0.0839 (2010); Freight exchange via national railway = 0 k ton (2000) and 40 k tons (2010). ★ September 2, 2006, a 100-people team of the Hongwuhuan Mechanical Co. Ltd. of Zhejiang visits Naqu Prefecture of Tibet and establishes a long-term pairing-aid relationship with No. 3 Primary School of Naqu. The Company also calls for its staff to establish the one-to-one aid relations with dozens of the orphans of the School. April 8, 2007, a delegation, led by the CCP Secretary of Tibet, visits Zhejiang and holds a forum in Hangzhou City. Both sides discuss the progress of the aiding-Tibet work. September 22, 2011, the blood centers of Zhejiang and Tibet sign an agreement concerning blood collection and supply, aiming to meet the demand of clinical-used blood in Tibet. March 30, 2012, the management scheme of Zhejiang's pairing-aid projects to Naqu Prefecture (including Naqu, Biru and Jiali Counties) is enacted. June 9, 2012, at the "2012 Zhejiang Investment and Trade Fair and the Mid-West Industrial Development Seminar", Naqu of Tibet holds a project introduction and investment promotion meeting; Zhejiang and Tibet sign four cooperation agreements. August 28, 2012, Tibet's arts workers hold a series of the performances in Zhejiang, aiming to acknowledge Zhejiang's pairing-aid to Tibet. September 14, 2012, the Haining Municipal Bureau of Justice of Zhejiang and the Judicial Office of Naqu Prefecture of Tibet sign a website construction agreement; Zhejiang will help Tibet to build the first law popularization website.

Xinjiang-Yunnan

[Quick Facts] Average distance = 4126 km; Geographical adjacency = 0; Index of ethnic linkages = 0.4235 (2000) and 0.4225 (2010); Freight exchange via national railway = 60 k tons (2000) and 1610 k tons (2010). ★ June 6, 2011, Yunnan and Xinjiang sign, in Kunming City, a strategic cooperation framework agreement. Both sides reach consensuses on traffic construction, economic and trade cooperation, development of tourism, industrial cooperation, ecological construction and environmental protection, establishment of inter-government exchange mechanism, etc. December 2, 2011, at the "First Xinjiang Tea Culture Exhibition", Yunnan, as a major tea producer, promotes its black tea and Pu'er tea. The companies from Yunnan and Xinjiang pledge to jointly develop tea market in Xinjiang which is already one of the largest five Pu'er tea's market in China. From 2009 to 2011, the total number of tea enterprises and tea bars in Urumqi City of Xinjiang has increased from some 400 to more than 800. April 25, 2012, at an international seminar entitled "Sino-Pakistani Relations: Practice and Progress", which is held in

Kunming City of Yunnan, the experts from Yunnan and Xinjiang have an in-depth exchange. They conclude that Yunnan is an important gateway for China to enter into the South Asia market and that Xinjiang can help Yunnan to open the Pakistani market, thereby enhancing cross-border trade and economic cooperation. September 17, 2012, Xinjiang releases an announcement in which graduates from Yunnan's universities are invited to apply for employment opportunities. Xinjiang will employ a total number of 500 university graduates from Yunnan and other provinces and autonomous regions to work as village carders in Xinjiang.

Xinjiang-Zhejiang

[Quick Facts] Average distance = 4065 km; Geographical adjacency = 0; Index of ethnic linkages = 0.4083 (2000) and 0.4081 (2010); Freight exchange via national railway = 750 k tons (2000) and 2640 k tons (2010). ★ November 6, 2001, the Zhejiang Chamber of Commerce in Xinjiang is established. There are 300,000 Zhejiang businesspersons in Xinjiang, with a total investment of about 100 billion yuan, providing about 500,000 jobs. March 13, 2010, Xinjiang and Zhejiang sign, in Beijing, a strategic energy cooperation agreement. September 25, 2010, the Zhejiang Materials Group and Akesu Prefecture sign an agreement on the construction of the "Southern Xinjiang Logistics Park". October 12, 2010, the Civil Affairs Departments of Zhejiang and Xinjiang sign an agreement on pairing aid. November 17, 2010, the Zhejiang Construction Group and the Aksu Prefecture of Xinjiang sign a cooperation agreement concerning the construction of roads and housing in the prefecture. November 17, 2010, Zhejiang and the No. 1 Division of XPCC in Alaer City (Xinjiang) sign an agreement on cotton and rice planting, with a total value about ten billion yuan. May 28, 2011, the Zhejiang Chamber of Commerce in Aksu Prefecture of Xinjiang is established. May 7, 2012, the Jiaxing Electric Power Bureau of Zhejiang and the Bazhou Electric Power Company of Xinjiang sign a cooperation framework agreement on grid construction. June 9, 2012, Zhejiang and Kuche County of Akesu Prefecture (Xinjiang) sign 27 project agreements including the 600,000-ton PVC project (with a total investment of 2 billion yuan), the Ningbo Plaza in Guici (with a total investment of 500 million yuan) and the 300 MW solar photovoltaic power project (with a total investment of 4.5 billion yuan). August 13, 2012, the No. 6 Agricultural Division of the XPCC and the Rifa Holdings Group of Zhejiang sign a cooperation agreement on lamb industry, with a total investment of 3.06 billion yuan. October 20, 2012, the Xinjiang Basic Geographic Information Center and the Zhejiang Geographical Information Center sign a technological cooperation agreement.

Yunnan-Zhejiang

[Quick Facts] Average distance = 2868 km; Geographical adjacency = 0; Index of ethnic linkages = 0.6691 (2000) and 0.6780 (2010); Freight exchange via national railway = 940 k tons (2000) and 140 k tons (2010). ★ December 26, 2001, the Zhejiang Chamber of Commerce in Yunnan is established. The Chamber has more than 300 members and establishes sub-chambers in Zhaotong, Qujing, Lincang, Simao, Lijiang, Wenshan, Baoshan, Chuxiong and Xishuangbanna Prefectures (or Cities); according to statistics, there are more than 2000 Zhejiang enterprises in Yunnan, with a cumulative investment of over 80 billion yuan, providing about one million jobs and one billion yuan taxes. September 16, 2009, the IQBs of Yunnan and Zhejiang sign, in Kunming City, a cooperation memorandum on silk goods' inspection. September 9, 2010, the Zhejiang Chamber of Commerce in Zhaotong City of Yunnan is established. The Chamber has nearly 200 members, mainly engaged in power plant construction, energy, minerals, machinery, cement, real estate, building materials, household appliances, clothing stores, communication equipments and fire-fighting equipments. November 9, 2011, the Zhejiang Association of Small and Medium Enterprises and Zhaotong City of Yunnan sign, in Hangzhou City, a cooperation agreement concerning the economic construction of the reservoir areas in the lower reaches of the Jinsha River. April 17, 2012, the Federations of Returned Overseas Chinese of Yunnan and the Zhejiang sign a strategic cooperation agreement, aiming to promote economic and social development in Yunnan. April 24, 2012, the "Yunnan-Zhejiang Economic Cooperation Forum" is held in Hangzhou City. The PCSC Member (also the Chief of United Front of CCP Committee) of Yunnan and the PPCC Vice Chairman (also the Chief of United Front of CCP Committee) of Zhejiang attend the meeting. July 20, 2012, the Bureaux of Maritime Affair and Ship Inspection of Yunnan and Zhejiang sign the "Cooperation Agreement on Shipping Supervision and Management" and the "Pairing Cooperation Agreement of Ship Inspection".

Chapter 3
Interprovincial Statistical Data

Status of Interprovincial Liaison Offices

Without good reason, the availability and level of a province's liaison offices established in another province can demonstrate to a large extent the closeness of political and economic ties between the two provinces concerned. In Table 1, the information about China's three types of existing interprovincial liaison offices is collected and classified. Specifically, the letters "A", "B", and "C" denote interprovincial liaison offices that are established by provincial-level governments (or defined as Class-A liaison offices), by other lower-level governments or administrations (or defined as Class-B liaison offices), and by firms or business representatives (or defined as Class-C liaison offices), respectively. All data are correct as of November 2012.

While two or more Class-B or Class-C liaison offices may exist in each pair of provinces, only one Class-A liaison office, if any, can be established for the pair. In addition, the information about the Class-B liaisons offices (i.e., those that are set up by prefectural/municipal and county/district level governments) may be incomplete. Recently, especially since the Chinese central government ordered local governments to abolish *unnecessary* liaison offices (some of which might be related to official corruption), some, if not all, of the local governments' liaison offices began to run behind public scenes. Thus, we are not able to identify all these liaison offices.

Availability of Interprovincial Chambers of Commerce

A chamber of commerce is an organization of businesspersons and business representatives that promotes local commercial interests. In China, an interprovincial chamber of commerce is the one that is established by businesspersons from a guest

R. Guo et al., *Multiregional Economic Development in China*,
DOI 10.1007/978-3-662-46620-9_3

Table 1 The information about China's three types of existing interprovincial liaison offices

Province *i*-Province *j*	Status of Province *i*'s liaison office(s) in Province *j*	Status of Province *j*'s liaison office(s) in Province *i*
Anhui-Beijing	A, B, C	C
Anhui-Chongqing	B, C	C
Anhui-Fujian	A, C	C
Anhui-Gansu	C	C
Anhui-Guangdong	A, B, C	C
Anhui-Guangxi	C	C
Anhui-Guizhou	C	C
Anhui-Hainan	A, B, C	C
Anhui-Hebei	C	C
Anhui-Heilongjiang	B, C	C
Anhui-Henan	C	C
Anhui-Hubei	C	C
Anhui-Hunan	C	B, C
Anhui-Inner Mongolia	B, C	C
Anhui-Jiangsu	C	C
Anhui-Jiangxi	C	C
Anhui-Jilin	C	C
Anhui-Liaoning	C	C
Anhui-Ningxia	C	C
Anhui-Qinghai	C	C
Anhui-Shaanxi	C	C
Anhui-Shandong	C	C
Anhui-Shanghai	A, B, C	C
Anhui-Shanxi	C	C
Anhui-Sichuan	C	C
Anhui-Tianjin	A, C	C
Anhui-Tibet	C	C
Anhui-Xinjiang	C	C
Anhui-Yunnan	B, C	C
Anhui-Zhejiang	C	B, C
Beijing-Chongqing	C	A, C
Beijing-Fujian	C	A, B, C
Beijing-Gansu	C	A, B, C
Beijing-Guangdong	A, C	A, B, C
Beijing-Guangxi	C	A, B, C
Beijing-Guizhou	C	A, B, C
Beijing-Hainan	A, C	A, B, C
Beijing-Hebei	A, B, C	A, B, C

(continued)

Table 1 (continued)

Province *i*-Province *j*	Status of Province *i*'s liaison office(s) in Province *j*	Status of Province *j*'s liaison office(s) in Province *i*
Beijing-Heilongjiang	C	A, B, C
Beijing-Henan	C	A, B, C
Beijing-Hubei	C	A, B, C
Beijing-Hunan	C	A, B, C
Beijing-Inner Mongolia	C	A, B, C
Beijing-Jiangsu	C	A, B, C
Beijing-Jiangxi	C	A, B, C
Beijing-Jilin	C	A, B, C
Beijing-Liaoning	C	A, B, C
Beijing-Ningxia	C	A, B, C
Beijing-Qinghai	C	A, B, C
Beijing-Shaanxi	C	A, B, C
Beijing-Shandong	C	A, B, C
Beijing-Shanghai	A, C	A, C
Beijing-Shanxi	C	A, B, C
Beijing-Sichuan	C	A, B, C
Beijing-Tianjin	C	A, C
Beijing-Tibet	C	A, B, C
Beijing-Xinjiang	C	A, B, C
Beijing-Yunnan	C	A, B, C
Beijing-Zhejiang	C	A, B, C
Chongqing-Fujian	C	A, B, C
Chongqing-Gansu	C	C
Chongqing-Guangdong	A, B, C	B, C
Chongqing-Guangxi	C	A, C
Chongqing-Guizhou	C	A, B, C
Chongqing-Hainan	A, C	C
Chongqing-Hebei	C	C
Chongqing-Heilongjiang	C	C
Chongqing-Henan	C	C
Chongqing-Hubei	C	B, C
Chongqing-Hunan	C	B, C
Chongqing-Inner Mongolia	C	B, C
Chongqing-Jiangsu	C	B, C
Chongqing-Jiangxi	B, C	B, C
Chongqing-Jilin	C	B, C
Chongqing-Liaoning	C	A, B, C
Chongqing-Ningxia	B, C	C
Chongqing-Qinghai	C	B, C

(continued)

Table 1 (continued)

Province *i*-Province *j*	Status of Province *i*'s liaison office(s) in Province *j*	Status of Province *j*'s liaison office(s) in Province *i*
Chongqing-Shaanxi	C	C
Chongqing-Shandong	C	A, C
Chongqing-Shanghai	A, B, C	A, C
Chongqing-Shanxi	C	C
Chongqing-Sichuan	A, C	A, B, C
Chongqing-Tianjin	C	A, C
Chongqing-Tibet	B, C	B, C
Chongqing-Xinjiang	A, B, C	C
Chongqing-Yunnan	A, B, C	A, C
Chongqing-Zhejiang	C	C
Fujian-Gansu	C	C
Fujian-Guangdong	A, C	C
Fujian-Guangxi	C	C
Fujian-Guizhou	C	B, C
Fujian-Hainan	A, B, C	B, C
Fujian-Hebei	C	C
Fujian-Heilongjiang	C	A, C
Fujian-Henan	C	A, C
Fujian-Hubei	B, C	C
Fujian-Hunan	C	C
Fujian-Inner Mongolia	C	C
Fujian-Jiangsu	C	C
Fujian-Jiangxi	B, C	A, B, C
Fujian-Jilin	C	C
Fujian-Liaoning	C	B, C
Fujian-Ningxia	C	A, C
Fujian-Qinghai	C	C
Fujian-Shaanxi	C	A, C
Fujian-Shandong	A, C	A, C
Fujian-Shanghai	A, B, C	C
Fujian-Shanxi	C	A, B, C
Fujian-Sichuan	C	A, C
Fujian-Tianjin	A, B, C	C
Fujian-Tibet	C	C
Fujian-Xinjiang	B, C	C
Fujian-Yunnan	B, C	B, C
Fujian-Zhejiang	C	C
Gansu-Guangdong	A, C	C
Gansu-Guangxi	C	C

(continued)

Table 1 (continued)

Province *i*-Province *j*	Status of Province *i*'s liaison office(s) in Province *j*	Status of Province *j*'s liaison office(s) in Province *i*
Gansu-Guizhou	C	C
Gansu-Hainan	A, B, C	C
Gansu-Hebei	C	C
Gansu-Heilongjiang	C	C
Gansu-Henan	C	C
Gansu-Hubei	C	C
Gansu-Hunan	C	C
Gansu-Inner Mongolia	C	C
Gansu-Jiangsu	A, C	C
Gansu-Jiangxi	C	C
Gansu-Jilin	C	C
Gansu-Liaoning	C	C
Gansu-Ningxia	C	C
Gansu-Qinghai	B, C	C
Gansu-Shaanxi	A, B, C	C
Gansu-Shandong	C	C
Gansu-Shanghai	A, C	C
Gansu-Shanxi	C	C
Gansu-Sichuan	C	C
Gansu-Tianjin	A, B, C	C
Gansu-Tibet	A, B, C	C
Gansu-Xinjiang	A, B, C	C
Gansu-Yunnan	B, C	C
Gansu-Zhejiang	A, C	C
Guangdong-Guangxi	C	B, C
Guangdong-Guizhou	C	A, B, C
Guangdong-Hainan	B, C	A, C
Guangdong-Hebei	B, C	C
Guangdong-Heilongjiang	C	B, C
Guangdong-Henan	C	A, B, C
Guangdong-Hubei	A, C	A, C
Guangdong-Hunan	C	A, B, C
Guangdong-Inner Mongolia	C	C
Guangdong-Jiangsu	C	C
Guangdong-Jiangxi	C	A, C
Guangdong-Jilin	C	A, B, C
Guangdong-Liaoning	C	A, C
Guangdong-Ningxia	B, C	A, C
Guangdong-Qinghai	C	A, B, C

(continued)

Table 1 (continued)

Province *i*-Province *j*	Status of Province *i*'s liaison office(s) in Province *j*	Status of Province *j*'s liaison office(s) in Province *i*
Guangdong-Shaanxi	C	A, B, C
Guangdong-Shandong	C	A, B, C
Guangdong-Shanghai	A, C	C
Guangdong-Shanxi	C	A, B, C
Guangdong-Sichuan	B, C	A, B, C
Guangdong-Tianjin	B, C	A, C
Guangdong-Tibet	C	B, C
Guangdong-Xinjiang	B, C	B, C
Guangdong-Yunnan	A, C	A, C
Guangdong-Zhejiang	C	B, C
Guangxi-Guizhou	C	A, C
Guangxi-Hainan	A, B, C	C
Guangxi-Hebei	C	C
Guangxi-Heilongjiang	C	B, C
Guangxi-Henan	C	B, C
Guangxi-Hubei	C	A, C
Guangxi-Hunan	C	B, C
Guangxi-Inner Mongolia	C	C
Guangxi-Jiangsu	A, C	A, C
Guangxi-Jiangxi	C	C
Guangxi-Jilin	C	C
Guangxi-Liaoning	C	C
Guangxi-Ningxia	C	C
Guangxi-Qinghai	C	C
Guangxi-Shaanxi	C	B, C
Guangxi-Shandong	C	C
Guangxi-Shanghai	A, C	C
Guangxi-Shanxi	C	B, C
Guangxi-Sichuan	B, C	A, C
Guangxi-Tianjin	A, C	C
Guangxi-Tibet	C	B, C
Guangxi-Xinjiang	C	B, C
Guangxi-Yunnan	C	A, B, C
Guangxi-Zhejiang	C	C
Guizhou-Hainan	A, B, C	C
Guizhou-Hebei	C	C
Guizhou-Heilongjiang	C	C
Guizhou-Henan	C	C
Guizhou-Hubei	C	C

(continued)

Table 1 (continued)

Province *i*-Province *j*	Status of Province *i*'s liaison office(s) in Province *j*	Status of Province *j*'s liaison office(s) in Province *i*
Guizhou-Hunan	C	C
Guizhou-Inner Mongolia	C	C
Guizhou-Jiangsu	C	C
Guizhou-Jiangxi	C	C
Guizhou-Jilin	C	C
Guizhou-Liaoning	C	B, C
Guizhou-Ningxia	C	C
Guizhou-Qinghai	C	C
Guizhou-Shaanxi	C	C
Guizhou-Shandong	C	C
Guizhou-Shanghai	A, B, C	C
Guizhou-Shanxi	C	C
Guizhou-Sichuan	C	B, C
Guizhou-Tianjin	A, C	C
Guizhou-Tibet	C	B, C
Guizhou-Xinjiang	A, C	B, C
Guizhou-Yunnan	C	C
Guizhou-Zhejiang	A, C	C
Hainan-Hebei	C	A, B, C
Hainan-Heilongjiang	C	A, C
Hainan-Henan	C	B, C
Hainan-Hubei	C	A, C
Hainan-Hunan	C	A, B, C
Hainan-Inner Mongolia	C	B, C
Hainan-Jiangsu	C	A, B, C
Hainan-Jiangxi	C	B, C
Hainan-Jilin	C	B, C
Hainan-Liaoning	C	A, B, C
Hainan-Ningxia	C	A, C
Hainan-Qinghai	C	B, C
Hainan-Shaanxi	B, C	A, C
Hainan-Shandong	C	A, B, C
Hainan-Shanghai	A, B, C	A, C
Hainan-Shanxi	B, C	A, B, C
Hainan-Sichuan	C	A, B, C
Hainan-Tianjin	B, C	A, C
Hainan-Tibet	C	B, C
Hainan-Xinjiang	C	B, C
Hainan-Yunnan	C	A, B, C

(continued)

Table 1 (continued)

Province *i*-Province *j*	Status of Province *i*'s liaison office(s) in Province *j*	Status of Province *j*'s liaison office(s) in Province *i*
Hainan-Zhejiang	B, C	B, C
Hebei-Heilongjiang	C	B, C
Hebei-Henan	C	C
Hebei-Hubei	C	C
Hebei-Hunan	C	C
Hebei-Inner Mongolia	B, C	B, C
Hebei-Jiangsu	C	B, C
Hebei-Jiangxi	C	C
Hebei-Jilin	C	B, C
Hebei-Liaoning	B, C	B, C
Hebei-Ningxia	C	B, C
Hebei-Qinghai	C	C
Hebei-Shaanxi	C	C
Hebei-Shandong	C	C
Hebei-Shanghai	A, C	C
Hebei-Shanxi	C	B, C
Hebei-Sichuan	C	C
Hebei-Tianjin	A, B, C	B, C
Hebei-Tibet	C	C
Hebei-Xinjiang	C	C
Hebei-Yunnan	C	C
Hebei-Zhejiang	C	C
Heilongjiang-Henan	C	B, C
Heilongjiang-Hubei	C	B, C
Heilongjiang-Hunan	C	C
Heilongjiang-Inner Mongolia	B, C	B, C
Heilongjiang-Jiangsu	C	B, C
Heilongjiang-Jiangxi	C	C
Heilongjiang-Jilin	B, C	B, C
Heilongjiang-Liaoning	B, C	B, C
Heilongjiang-Ningxia	C	C
Heilongjiang-Qinghai	C	C
Heilongjiang-Shaanxi	C	C
Heilongjiang-Shandong	C	C
Heilongjiang-Shanghai	A, B, C	C
Heilongjiang-Shanxi	C	C
Heilongjiang-Sichuan	C	C
Heilongjiang-Tianjin	A, B, C	C
Heilongjiang-Tibet	C	C

(continued)

Table 1 (continued)

Province *i*-Province *j*	Status of Province *i*'s liaison office(s) in Province *j*	Status of Province *j*'s liaison office(s) in Province *i*
Heilongjiang-Xinjiang	C	C
Heilongjiang-Yunnan	C	C
Heilongjiang-Zhejiang	C	C
Henan-Hubei	B, C	C
Henan-Hunan	C	C
Henan-Inner Mongolia	B, C	C
Henan-Jiangsu	B, C	C
Henan-Jiangxi	C	C
Henan-Jilin	C	C
Henan-Liaoning	C	C
Henan-Ningxia	C	C
Henan-Qinghai	C	C
Henan-Shaanxi	B, C	C
Henan-Shandong	A, C	C
Henan-Shanghai	A, B, C	C
Henan-Shanxi	C	C
Henan-Sichuan	C	C
Henan-Tianjin	A, B, C	C
Henan-Tibet	B, C	C
Henan-Xinjiang	A, B, C	C
Henan-Yunnan	B, C	C
Henan-Zhejiang	C	C
Hubei-Hunan	C	C
Hubei-Inner Mongolia	C	C
Hubei-Jiangsu	A, C	B, C
Hubei-Jiangxi	C	C
Hubei-Jilin	B, C	C
Hubei-Liaoning	C	C
Hubei-Ningxia	C	C
Hubei-Qinghai	C	C
Hubei-Shaanxi	B, C	A, B, C
Hubei-Shandong	C	C
Hubei-Shanghai	A, B, C	C
Hubei-Shanxi	A, B, C	B, C
Hubei-Sichuan	C	B, C
Hubei-Tianjin	B, C	C
Hubei-Tibet	C	C
Hubei-Xinjiang	A, C	C
Hubei-Yunnan	C	C

(continued)

Table 1 (continued)

Province *i*-Province *j*	Status of Province *i*'s liaison office(s) in Province *j*	Status of Province *j*'s liaison office(s) in Province *i*
Hubei-Zhejiang	A, B, C	B, C
Hunan-Inner Mongolia	C	C
Hunan-Jiangsu	C	C
Hunan-Jiangxi	C	C
Hunan-Jilin	C	C
Hunan-Liaoning	C	C
Hunan-Ningxia	C	C
Hunan-Qinghai	C	C
Hunan-Shaanxi	B, C	C
Hunan-Shandong	C	C
Hunan-Shanghai	A, C	C
Hunan-Shanxi	B, C	C
Hunan-Sichuan	C	C
Hunan-Tianjin	A, C	C
Hunan-Tibet	C	C
Hunan-Xinjiang	B, C	C
Hunan-Yunnan	B, C	C
Hunan-Zhejiang	B, C	C
Inner Mongolia-Jiangsu	B, C	C
Inner Mongolia-Jiangxi	C	C
Inner Mongolia-Jilin	B, C	C
Inner Mongolia-Liaoning	A, C	C
Inner Mongolia-Ningxia	C	C
Inner Mongolia-Qinghai	C	C
Inner Mongolia-Shaanxi	A, B, C	C
Inner Mongolia-Shandong	C	C
Inner Mongolia-Shanghai	A, C	C
Inner Mongolia-Shanxi	C	C
Inner Mongolia-Sichuan	C	C
Inner Mongolia-Tianjin	A, C	B, C
Inner Mongolia-Tibet	C	C
Inner Mongolia-Xinjiang	C	C
Inner Mongolia-Yunnan	C	C
Inner Mongolia-Zhejiang	B, C	C
Jiangsu-Jiangxi	C	A, C
Jiangsu-Jilin	C	B, C
Jiangsu-Liaoning	C	A, C
Jiangsu-Ningxia	C	C
Jiangsu-Qinghai	C	C
Jiangsu-Shaanxi	B, C	C

(continued)

Table 1 (continued)

Province *i*-Province *j*	Status of Province *i*'s liaison office(s) in Province *j*	Status of Province *j*'s liaison office(s) in Province *i*
Jiangsu-Shandong	B, C	C
Jiangsu-Shanghai	A, B, C	C
Jiangsu-Shanxi	A, C	C
Jiangsu-Sichuan	C	A, B, C
Jiangsu-Tianjin	B, C	C
Jiangsu-Tibet	C	C
Jiangsu-Xinjiang	B, C	C
Jiangsu-Yunnan	B, C	C
Jiangsu-Zhejiang	C	B, C
Jiangxi-Jilin	C	C
Jiangxi-Liaoning	C	C
Jiangxi-Ningxia	C	C
Jiangxi-Qinghai	C	C
Jiangxi-Shaanxi	C	C
Jiangxi-Shandong	C	C
Jiangxi-Shanghai	A, B, C	C
Jiangxi-Shanxi	B, C	C
Jiangxi-Sichuan	C	C
Jiangxi-Tianjin	A, C	C
Jiangxi-Tibet	C	C
Jiangxi-Xinjiang	C	C
Jiangxi-Yunnan	C	C
Jiangxi-Zhejiang	A, B, C	B, C
Jilin-Liaoning	B, C	C
Jilin-Ningxia	C	C
Jilin-Qinghai	C	C
Jilin-Shaanxi	C	C
Jilin-Shandong	C	C
Jilin-Shanghai	A, C	C
Jilin-Shanxi	C	C
Jilin-Sichuan	C	B, C
Jilin-Tianjin	A, B, C	C
Jilin-Tibet	C	C
Jilin-Xinjiang	C	C
Jilin-Yunnan	C	C
Jilin-Zhejiang	C	C
Liaoning-Ningxia	C	C
Liaoning-Qinghai	B, C	B, C
Liaoning-Shaanxi	C	A, C

(continued)

Table 1 (continued)

Province *i*-Province *j*	Status of Province *i*'s liaison office(s) in Province *j*	Status of Province *j*'s liaison office(s) in Province *i*
Liaoning-Shandong	C	C
Liaoning-Shanghai	A, C	C
Liaoning-Shanxi	C	A, C
Liaoning-Sichuan	C	A, B, C
Liaoning-Tianjin	A, C	C
Liaoning-Tibet	C	C
Liaoning-Xinjiang	C	C
Liaoning-Yunnan	C	C
Liaoning-Zhejiang	B, C	A, C
Ningxia-Qinghai	C	C
Ningxia-Shaanxi	A, C	C
Ningxia-Shandong	C	C
Ningxia-Shanghai	A, C	C
Ningxia-Shanxi	C	C
Ningxia-Sichuan	C	C
Ningxia-Tianjin	A, C	C
Ningxia-Tibet	C	C
Ningxia-Xinjiang	B, C	C
Ningxia-Yunnan	C	C
Ningxia-Zhejiang	A, C	B, C
Qinghai-Shaanxi	C	A, C
Qinghai-Shandong	B, C	B, C
Qinghai-Shanghai	A, C	C
Qinghai-Shanxi	C	C
Qinghai-Sichuan	B, C	B, C
Qinghai-Tianjin	A, B, C	C
Qinghai-Tibet	A, C	A, C
Qinghai-Xinjiang	B, C	C
Qinghai-Yunnan	C	C
Qinghai-Zhejiang	B, C	C
Shaanxi-Shandong	C	A, C
Shaanxi-Shanghai	A, B, C	C
Shaanxi-Shanxi	C	C
Shaanxi-Sichuan	C	B, C
Shaanxi-Tianjin	A, B, C	C
Shaanxi-Tibet	C	A, C
Shaanxi-Xinjiang	A, C	A, B, C
Shaanxi-Yunnan	B, C	B, C
Shaanxi-Zhejiang	C	C

(continued)

Table 1 (continued)

Province *i*-Province *j*	Status of Province *i*'s liaison office(s) in Province *j*	Status of Province *j*'s liaison office(s) in Province *i*
Shandong-Shanghai	A, B, C	C
Shandong-Shanxi	C	A, C
Shandong-Sichuan	C	C
Shandong-Tianjin	B, C	A, C
Shandong-Tibet	C	C
Shandong-Xinjiang	A, C	C
Shandong-Yunnan	B, C	C
Shandong-Zhejiang	C	C
Shanghai-Shanxi	C	A, C
Shanghai-Sichuan	C	A, B, C
Shanghai-Tianjin	C	A, C
Shanghai-Tibet	C	A, B, C
Shanghai-Xinjiang	A, C	A, C
Shanghai-Yunnan	A, C	A, B, C
Shanghai-Zhejiang	C	A, B, C
Shanxi-Sichuan	C	C
Shanxi-Tianjin	A, B, C	C
Shanxi-Tibet	C	C
Shanxi-Xinjiang	A, B, C	C
Shanxi-Yunnan	A, C	C
Shanxi-Zhejiang	C	A, C
Sichuan-Tianjin	C	A, B, C
Sichuan-Tibet	C	A, C
Sichuan-Xinjiang	A, B, C	C
Sichuan-Yunnan	B, C	C
Sichuan-Zhejiang	A, B, C	A, C
Tianjin-Tibet	C	B, C
Tianjin-Xinjiang	A, C	A, B, C
Tianjin-Yunnan	A, C	A, C
Tianjin-Zhejiang	C	A, B, C
Tibet-Xinjiang	C	C
Tibet-Yunnan	C	B, C
Tibet-Zhejiang	C	C
Xinjiang-Yunnan	C	C
Xinjiang-Zhejiang	A, C	B, C
Yunnan-Zhejiang	C	C

province (i.e., the one from which they come) in a host province (i.e., the one in which they currently reside). It is approved by the bureau (or department) of civil affairs of and is administered by (or registered at) the federation of industry and commerce of the host province or any other local administrative division thereof.

As mentioned in Part II, the term "chamber of commerce" also has several alternative names, such as "federation of enterprises", "association of enterprises", and "general chamber of commerce". Table 2 shows years in which interprovincial chambers of commerce are established (note: "?" denotes that the founding date of the chamber is unknown; and blank space indicates the unavailability of interprovincial chambers or that information is unknown or not available). All data are collected by the authors and are correct as of November 2012.

Unless stated otherwise, all chambers included in the table are established to represent (or on behalf of) the whole territories of both guest and host provinces. For example, the Anhui Chamber of Commerce in Guangdong was established for all of Anhui's businesspersons working in the whole territory of Guangdong Province. In addition, those that are marked by letters "a", "b", and "c" denote that an interprovincial chamber is established to represent (or on behalf of) the whole territory of a guest province but the partial territory of a host province (for example, the Anhui Chamber of Commerce in Dalian City of Liaoning Province), the whole territory of a host province but the partial territory of a guest province (for example, the Ningbo (of Zhejiang) Chamber of Commerce in Beijing), and the partial territories of both a guest and a host provinces (for example, the Wenzhou (of Zhejiang) Chamber of Commerce in Hanzhoung City of Shaanxi Province), respectively.

Since the number of interprovincial chambers that are established at local levels in many provinces (such as Fujian, Guangdong, Jiangsu, and Zhejiang) is increasing rapidly, we have not included information on all these local chambers in the table.

Indicators of Interprovincial Geographical Proximity

In Table 3, we try to quantitatively measure China's interprovincial geographical proximity—one of the factors that could physically shape the economic gravity between provinces. Unlike those of many Western democratic economies, China's provincial capitals usually are also the economic centers of these provinces. To this end, we use the following terms to express China's interprovincial geographical proximity. "Distance between capitals" is represented by the distance (in kilometers) between two provinces' capitals via national railway. In addition to 'distance', "interprovincial adjacency" (it denotes whether or not the provinces share a common land boundary) also influences interprovincial trade and economic cooperation.

Table 2 Years in which interprovincial chambers of commerce are established

Province *i*-Province *j*	Founding year(s) of Province *i*'s chamber(s) in Province *j*	Founding year(s) of Province *j*'s chamber(s) in Province *i*
Anhui-Beijing	2006	
Anhui-Chongqing	2006	
Anhui-Fujian	2007; ?(a)	2008
Anhui-Gansu	2010	
Anhui-Guangdong	2012	2008
Anhui-Guangxi	2007	
Anhui-Guizhou	2010	
Anhui-Hainan	2006	
Anhui-Hebei	2008	2011
Anhui-Heilongjiang		
Anhui-Henan	2008	2011
Anhui-Hubei		
Anhui-Hunan	2012	2008
Anhui-Inner Mongolia	2004	
Anhui-Jiangsu	2011; 2006(a); 2009(a)	2008
Anhui-Jiangxi	2008	2011
Anhui-Jilin	2011	
Anhui-Liaoning	2007(a); 2009(a)	
Anhui-Ningxia	2006	
Anhui-Qinghai	2009	
Anhui-Shaanxi	2007	
Anhui-Shandong	2011	2011
Anhui-Shanghai	2004; 2007(b)	2009
Anhui-Shanxi	2008	
Anhui-Sichuan	2009; 2012(a)	
Anhui-Tianjin	2007	2011
Anhui-Tibet		
Anhui-Xinjiang	2006; 2012(a)	
Anhui-Yunnan	2007; 2009(a)	
Anhui-Zhejiang	2010; 2009(a); 2007(a); 2006(a)	2002
Beijing-Chongqing	2011	2006
Beijing-Fujian		2001
Beijing-Gansu		2011
Beijing-Guangdong		2008; 2006(b); 2009(b)
Beijing-Guangxi		2006
Beijing-Guizhou		2008
Beijing-Hainan		
Beijing-Hebei		2006
Beijing-Heilongjiang		2007

(continued)

Table 2 (continued)

Province *i*-Province *j*	Founding year(s) of Province *i*'s chamber(s) in Province *j*	Founding year(s) of Province *j*'s chamber(s) in Province *i*
Beijing-Henan		
Beijing-Hubei		2008
Beijing-Hunan		2003
Beijing-Inner Mongolia		2007
Beijing-Jiangsu		2007; 2000(b)
Beijing-Jiangxi		2008
Beijing-Jilin		
Beijing-Liaoning		2010
Beijing-Ningxia		2008
Beijing-Qinghai		2010
Beijing-Shaanxi		2007
Beijing-Shandong		2005
Beijing-Shanghai		
Beijing-Shanxi		2007
Beijing-Sichuan		2008; 2010(b)
Beijing-Tianjin		
Beijing-Tibet		
Beijing-Xinjiang		2010
Beijing-Yunnan		2009
Beijing-Zhejiang		2001; 2003(b); 2007(b)
Chongqing-Fujian	2008(a)	2001; 2010(b)
Chongqing-Gansu	2011; 2010(c)	2007
Chongqing-Guangdong	2004	2005
Chongqing-Guangxi	2006	2010
Chongqing-Guizhou	2007	2012
Chongqing-Hainan	2010	
Chongqing-Hebei		2004
Chongqing-Heilongjiang	2012	
Chongqing-Henan		2008
Chongqing-Hubei	2009(a)	2004
Chongqing-Hunan	2010	2007
Chongqing-Inner Mongolia		
Chongqing-Jiangsu		2008
Chongqing-Jiangxi		2009
Chongqing-Jilin	2008	2008
Chongqing-Liaoning	2005	2010
Chongqing-Ningxia		
Chongqing-Qinghai		

(continued)

Table 2 (continued)

Province *i*-Province *j*	Founding year(s) of Province *i*'s chamber(s) in Province *j*	Founding year(s) of Province *j*'s chamber(s) in Province *i*
Chongqing-Shaanxi	2005	2008
Chongqing-Shandong	2009	2007
Chongqing-Shanghai	2007	2008
Chongqing-Shanxi	2011	2009
Chongqing-Sichuan	2006	2007
Chongqing-Tianjin	2011	
Chongqing-Tibet		
Chongqing-Xinjiang	2012(a)	2006
Chongqing-Yunnan	2009; 2012(c)	2010(b)
Chongqing-Zhejiang		2000
Fujian-Gansu	2001	
Fujian-Guangdong	2010; 2012(b)	
Fujian-Guangxi		
Fujian-Guizhou	2011(a)(c)	
Fujian-Hainan	2002	
Fujian-Hebei	2003	
Fujian-Heilongjiang	2004	
Fujian-Henan	2012; 2012(a)	
Fujian-Hubei	2010	2008
Fujian-Hunan	2010	2010
Fujian-Inner Mongolia	2003; 2011(a)	
Fujian-Jiangsu	2011(c)	2009(a)
Fujian-Jiangxi	2002	2006
Fujian-Jilin	2007	
Fujian-Liaoning	2008; 2005(b)	
Fujian-Ningxia		
Fujian-Qinghai	2009	
Fujian-Shaanxi	2003	2008
Fujian-Shandong	2008	2011
Fujian-Shanghai	2002	
Fujian-Shanxi	2000	2011
Fujian-Sichuan	2005	2008
Fujian-Tianjin	2003; 2010(b)	2012
Fujian-Tibet	2011	
Fujian-Xinjiang	2002	2003(a)
Fujian-Yunnan	1996; 2012(a)	
Fujian-Zhejiang	2010(a)	2007; 2012(a)
Gansu-Guangdong	2006; 2012(a)	2008
Gansu-Guangxi		

(continued)

Table 2 (continued)

Province *i*-Province *j*	Founding year(s) of Province *i*'s chamber(s) in Province *j*	Founding year(s) of Province *j*'s chamber(s) in Province *i*
Gansu-Guizhou		
Gansu-Hainan	1994	
Gansu-Hebei		2011; 2011(a)
Gansu-Heilongjiang		2012
Gansu-Henan		2008; 2012(a)
Gansu-Hubei		2007
Gansu-Hunan		2010
Gansu-Inner Mongolia		
Gansu-Jiangsu		2007; 2007(a)
Gansu-Jiangxi		2008
Gansu-Jilin		
Gansu-Liaoning	2009(a)	
Gansu-Ningxia	2008	
Gansu-Qinghai	2011	
Gansu-Shaanxi	2009	2008
Gansu-Shandong		
Gansu-Shanghai		2011(a)
Gansu-Shanxi		2007
Gansu-Sichuan	2007	2011
Gansu-Tianjin		
Gansu-Tibet		
Gansu-Xinjiang	2010; 2011(a)	
Gansu-Yunnan		
Gansu-Zhejiang		2001; 2012(a)
Guangdong-Guangxi	2004	2004
Guangdong-Guizhou	2004	2008; 2012(b); 2006(c)
Guangdong-Hainan	2012(b)	2011
Guangdong-Hebei		2010
Guangdong-Heilongjiang	2008	2009
Guangdong-Henan		2006; 2009(a); 2011(a); 2012(c)
Guangdong-Hubei	2006	2006; 2011(a); 2010(b); 2012(b)
Guangdong-Hunan	2007	2005; 2012(b)
Guangdong-Inner Mongolia		2009
Guangdong-Jiangsu		2006
Guangdong-Jiangxi	2009	2009
Guangdong-Jilin	2007	

(continued)

Table 2 (continued)

Province *i*-Province *j*	Founding year(s) of Province *i*'s chamber(s) in Province *j*	Founding year(s) of Province *j*'s chamber(s) in Province *i*
Guangdong-Liaoning	2005	2009(a)
Guangdong-Ningxia		
Guangdong-Qinghai		2011
Guangdong-Shaanxi	2002	2007
Guangdong-Shandong	2010	2010
Guangdong-Shanghai	1996	
Guangdong-Shanxi	2006	2011
Guangdong-Sichuan	2004	2003
Guangdong-Tianjin	2007	
Guangdong-Tibet		
Guangdong-Xinjiang		2011
Guangdong-Yunnan	2005	2010; 2012(b)
Guangdong-Zhejiang		2005; 2011(b); 2010(b)
Guangxi-Guizhou		
Guangxi-Hainan	2012	
Guangxi-Hebei		2009
Guangxi-Heilongjiang		2009(a)
Guangxi-Henan		2009
Guangxi-Hubei		2007
Guangxi-Hunan		2007
Guangxi-Inner Mongolia		
Guangxi-Jiangsu		?
Guangxi-Jiangxi		
Guangxi-Jilin		2011
Guangxi-Liaoning		
Guangxi-Ningxia		
Guangxi-Qinghai		
Guangxi-Shaanxi	2005	
Guangxi-Shandong		2010
Guangxi-Shanghai	2008	
Guangxi-Shanxi		
Guangxi-Sichuan		?
Guangxi-Tianjin		
Guangxi-Tibet		
Guangxi-Xinjiang		
Guangxi-Yunnan	2008	
Guangxi-Zhejiang	2007	2005
Guizhou-Hainan	2009	

(continued)

Table 2 (continued)

Province *i*-Province *j*	Founding year(s) of Province *i*'s chamber(s) in Province *j*	Founding year(s) of Province *j*'s chamber(s) in Province *i*
Guizhou-Hebei		2011; 2012(a)
Guizhou-Heilongjiang		
Guizhou-Henan		2007
Guizhou-Hubei		2009
Guizhou-Hunan		2001
Guizhou-Inner Mongolia		
Guizhou-Jiangsu	2012	2012???
Guizhou-Jiangxi		2006
Guizhou-Jilin		
Guizhou-Liaoning		
Guizhou-Ningxia		
Guizhou-Qinghai		
Guizhou-Shaanxi	2010	
Guizhou-Shandong		2009
Guizhou-Shanghai	2008	
Guizhou-Shanxi		?
Guizhou-Sichuan		2006
Guizhou-Tianjin		
Guizhou-Tibet		
Guizhou-Xinjiang		
Guizhou-Yunnan	2007	
Guizhou-Zhejiang		2003
Hainan-Hebei		2009
Hainan-Heilongjiang		2008
Hainan-Henan		2008
Hainan-Hubei		2009
Hainan-Hunan		2009
Hainan-Inner Mongolia		2010
Hainan-Jiangsu		2006
Hainan-Jiangxi		2006
Hainan-Jilin		2010
Hainan-Liaoning		
Hainan-Ningxia		
Hainan-Qinghai		2011
Hainan-Shaanxi		2008
Hainan-Shandong		2006
Hainan-Shanghai		2008
Hainan-Shanxi		

(continued)

Table 2 (continued)

Province *i*-Province *j*	Founding year(s) of Province *i*'s chamber(s) in Province *j*	Founding year(s) of Province *j*'s chamber(s) in Province *i*
Hainan-Sichuan		2010
Hainan-Tianjin		
Hainan-Tibet		
Hainan-Xinjiang		2011
Hainan-Yunnan		
Hainan-Zhejiang		2004
Hebei-Heilongjiang		
Hebei-Henan	2011	2009
Hebei-Hubei		2012
Hebei-Hunan	2010	2010
Hebei-Inner Mongolia		
Hebei-Jiangsu		2011
Hebei-Jiangxi		2008
Hebei-Jilin	2011	
Hebei-Liaoning		
Hebei-Ningxia	2009	
Hebei-Qinghai		
Hebei-Shaanxi	2007	2012
Hebei-Shandong		
Hebei-Shanghai		
Hebei-Shanxi		
Hebei-Sichuan		2007
Hebei-Tianjin	2009	
Hebei-Tibet		
Hebei-Xinjiang		
Hebei-Yunnan	2010	
Hebei-Zhejiang		2007
Heilongjiang-Henan		2012
Heilongjiang-Hubei		
Heilongjiang-Hunan		2008
Heilongjiang-Inner Mongolia		
Heilongjiang-Jiangsu		
Heilongjiang-Jiangxi		2007
Heilongjiang-Jilin		
Heilongjiang-Liaoning		
Heilongjiang-Ningxia	2011	
Heilongjiang-Qinghai		
Heilongjiang-Shaanxi	2012	

(continued)

Table 2 (continued)

Province *i*-Province *j*	Founding year(s) of Province *i*'s chamber(s) in Province *j*	Founding year(s) of Province *j*'s chamber(s) in Province *i*
Heilongjiang-Shandong		2005
Heilongjiang-Shanghai		
Heilongjiang-Shanxi		2009
Heilongjiang-Sichuan		2012
Heilongjiang-Tianjin		
Heilongjiang-Tibet		
Heilongjiang-Xinjiang		
Heilongjiang-Yunnan		
Heilongjiang-Zhejiang	2011(a)	?
Henan-Hubei	2006	2007
Henan-Hunan	2008	2010
Henan-Inner Mongolia	2009	
Henan-Jiangsu		2010; 2012(b)
Henan-Jiangxi	2009	2009
Henan-Jilin	2011	
Henan-Liaoning		
Henan-Ningxia	2009	
Henan-Qinghai	2010	
Henan-Shaanxi	2008	
Henan-Shandong	2010	2008
Henan-Shanghai		
Henan-Shanxi	2005	2010(b)
Henan-Sichuan	2009	
Henan-Tianjin	2006	
Henan-Tibet		
Henan-Xinjiang		
Henan-Yunnan	2007	
Henan-Zhejiang	2009	2004
Hubei-Hunan		
Hubei-Inner Mongolia		
Hubei-Jiangsu		
Hubei-Jiangxi		
Hubei-Jilin		
Hubei-Liaoning	2010	
Hubei-Ningxia		
Hubei-Qinghai	2009	
Hubei-Shaanxi	2008	

(continued)

Table 2 (continued)

Province *i*-Province *j*	Founding year(s) of Province *i*'s chamber(s) in Province *j*	Founding year(s) of Province *j*'s chamber(s) in Province *i*
Hubei-Shandong	2011	
Hubei-Shanghai	2006	2007
Hubei-Shanxi	2010	
Hubei-Sichuan	2009	2006
Hubei-Tianjin	2008	
Hubei-Tibet		
Hubei-Xinjiang	2011	
Hubei-Yunnan	2004	
Hubei-Zhejiang		???
Hunan-Inner Mongolia	2009	
Hunan-Jiangsu	2011	2008
Hunan-Jiangxi	2009	2009
Hunan-Jilin	2008	
Hunan-Liaoning		2009
Hunan-Ningxia	2003	
Hunan-Qinghai	2010	
Hunan-Shaanxi	2003; 2011(b)	2011
Hunan-Shandong	2010	2011
Hunan-Shanghai	2011(b)	2012
Hunan-Shanxi	2011	
Hunan-Sichuan	2005	2010
Hunan-Tianjin	2010	
Hunan-Tibet		
Hunan-Xinjiang		?
Hunan-Yunnan	2007	
Hunan-Zhejiang	2010	?
Inner Mongolia-Jiangsu		2009
Inner Mongolia-Jiangxi		2007
Inner Mongolia-Jilin	2011	
Inner Mongolia-Liaoning	2007	
Inner Mongolia-Ningxia	2006	
Inner Mongolia-Qinghai		
Inner Mongolia-Shaanxi		2010
Inner Mongolia-Shandong	2011	2005; 2012(a)
Inner Mongolia-Shanghai	2009	
Inner Mongolia-Shanxi	2010	

(continued)

Table 2 (continued)

Province *i*-Province *j*	Founding year(s) of Province *i*'s chamber(s) in Province *j*	Founding year(s) of Province *j*'s chamber(s) in Province *i*
Inner Mongolia-Sichuan		
Inner Mongolia-Tianjin		
Inner Mongolia-Tibet		
Inner Mongolia-Xinjiang		
Inner Mongolia-Yunnan	2012	
Inner Mongolia-Zhejiang		2006
Jiangsu-Jiangxi	2012	2011
Jiangsu-Jilin	2008	?
Jiangsu-Liaoning	2008	
Jiangsu-Ningxia	2009	
Jiangsu-Qinghai	2010	
Jiangsu-Shaanxi	2005	
Jiangsu-Shandong	2009	2012
Jiangsu-Shanghai	2009	
Jiangsu-Shanxi	2000	
Jiangsu-Sichuan	2009	2012
Jiangsu-Tianjin	2012; 2012(b)	
Jiangsu-Tibet	2012	
Jiangsu-Xinjiang	2004; 2010(c)	
Jiangsu-Yunnan	2006	
Jiangsu-Zhejiang		2006
Jiangxi-Jilin	2012	
Jiangxi-Liaoning		2006
Jiangxi-Ningxia	2012	
Jiangxi-Qinghai	2008	
Jiangxi-Shaanxi	2008	
Jiangxi-Shandong	2009	
Jiangxi-Shanghai	2005	
Jiangxi-Shanxi	2012	
Jiangxi-Sichuan	2008	
Jiangxi-Tianjin	2006	
Jiangxi-Tibet		
Jiangxi-Xinjiang	2008	
Jiangxi-Yunnan	2006	
Jiangxi-Zhejiang	2008	2002
Jilin-Liaoning		
Jilin-Ningxia		

(continued)

Table 2 (continued)

Province *i*-Province *j*	Founding year(s) of Province *i*'s chamber(s) in Province *j*	Founding year(s) of Province *j*'s chamber(s) in Province *i*
Jilin-Qinghai		
Jilin-Shaanxi		
Jilin-Shandong	?(a)	2008
Jilin-Shanghai	2007	
Jilin-Shanxi		2009
Jilin-Sichuan		2008
Jilin-Tianjin		
Jilin-Tibet		
Jilin-Xinjiang		
Jilin-Yunnan		
Jilin-Zhejiang		2008
Liaoning-Ningxia		
Liaoning-Qinghai		
Liaoning-Shaanxi		
Liaoning-Shandong	2011(b); 2012(b)	2010
Liaoning-Shanghai	2008	
Liaoning-Shanxi		2006
Liaoning-Sichuan		2005
Liaoning-Tianjin		
Liaoning-Tibet		
Liaoning-Xinjiang	2012	
Liaoning-Yunnan		2012
Liaoning-Zhejiang		2007
Ningxia-Qinghai		
Ningxia-Shaanxi		2004
Ningxia-Shandong		2005
Ningxia-Shanghai		2010
Ningxia-Shanxi		2007
Ningxia-Sichuan		2009
Ningxia-Tianjin		
Ningxia-Tibet		
Ningxia-Xinjiang		
Ningxia-Yunnan		
Ningxia-Zhejiang		2001
Qinghai-Shaanxi		
Qinghai-Shandong		?
Qinghai-Shanghai		
Qinghai-Shanxi		2010

(continued)

Table 2 (continued)

Province *i*-Province *j*	Founding year(s) of Province *i*'s chamber(s) in Province *j*	Founding year(s) of Province *j*'s chamber(s) in Province *i*
Qinghai-Sichuan		2011
Qinghai-Tianjin		
Qinghai-Tibet		
Qinghai-Xinjiang		
Qinghai-Yunnan		
Qinghai-Zhejiang		2009(b); 2012(a)
Shaanxi-Shandong	2010	
Shaanxi-Shanghai	2007	2007
Shaanxi-Shanxi	2011	2008
Shaanxi-Sichuan	2006	2005
Shaanxi-Tianjin	2006	
Shaanxi-Tibet		
Shaanxi-Xinjiang	2008	2011
Shaanxi-Yunnan	2010	
Shaanxi-Zhejiang		2003(c); 2010(a)
Shandong-Shanghai	2006	
Shandong-Shanxi	2010	
Shandong-Sichuan	2007	2011
Shandong-Tianjin	2009	
Shandong-Tibet		
Shandong-Xinjiang	2010(a)	
Shandong-Yunnan	2011	
Shandong-Zhejiang	2011	2003
Shanghai-Shanxi		
Shanghai-Sichuan		2007
Shanghai-Tianjin	2008	
Shanghai-Tibet		
Shanghai-Xinjiang	2012	
Shanghai-Yunnan		2006
Shanghai-Zhejiang		1986
Shanxi-Sichuan	2006	2011
Shanxi-Tianjin	1998; 2010(b)	2011
Shanxi-Tibet		
Shanxi-Xinjiang	2008	
Shanxi-Yunnan	2010	
Shanxi-Zhejiang	2011	2001; 2008(b)
Sichuan-Tianjin	2009	2006

(continued)

Table 2 (continued)

Province *i*-Province *j*	Founding year(s) of Province *i*'s chamber(s) in Province *j*	Founding year(s) of Province *j*'s chamber(s) in Province *i*
Sichuan-Tibet	2012(b)	
Sichuan-Xinjiang	2005	2011
Sichuan-Yunnan	2008; 2012(b)	
Sichuan-Zhejiang	2008	2002
Tianjin-Tibet		
Tianjin-Xinjiang	2010	2012; 2010(c)
Tianjin-Yunnan		
Tianjin-Zhejiang		1998; 2005(b)
Tibet-Xinjiang		
Tibet-Yunnan		
Tibet-Zhejiang		
Xinjiang-Yunnan		
Xinjiang-Zhejiang		2001; 2011(a)
Yunnan-Zhejiang		2001; 2010(a)

The data on "distance between capitals" are calculated by the authors based on the data (released by the Ministry of Railways of the PRC). If there are two or more rail lines between two provinces' capitals, our calculations are based on the following rules: (i) if both freight and passenger rail lines exist, only freight lines are considered; and (ii) if two or more freight (or passenger) rail lines exist, only the shortest distance is considered. The data on "interprovincial adjacency" are set as "1" if the provinces share a common land boundary and as "0" otherwise. All data are correct as of 2012.

Index of Interprovincial Ethnic Linkages (2000 and 2010)

The data reported in Table 4 are calculated by the authors based on the data released by the Fifth and Sixth National Population Census of the PRC (conducted in 2000 and 2010, respectively). The index of interprovincial ethnic linkages ranges between 0 and 1 (the larger the index, the greater is the ethnic linkage between the two provinces). In the extreme cases, "1" denotes that the two provinces have a common ethnic structure and "0" denotes that the two provinces do not have any ethnic linkage with each other. A detailed description of the methodology used to measure the index of interprovincial ethnic linkages can be found in Appendix B.

Table 3 China's interprovincial geographical proximity

Province-Province	Distance between capitals (km)	Interprovincial adjacency
Anhui-Beijing	1074	0
Anhui-Chongqing	1562	0
Anhui-Fujian	1196	0
Anhui-Gansu	1832	0
Anhui-Guangdong	1826	0
Anhui-Guangxi	2098	0
Anhui-Guizhou	2076	0
Anhui-Hainan	2448	0
Anhui-Hebei	914	0
Anhui-Heilongjiang	2227	0
Anhui-Henan	645	1
Anhui-Hubei	1181	1
Anhui-Hunan	1222	0
Anhui-Inner Mongolia	1777	0
Anhui-Jiangsu	312	1
Anhui-Jiangxi	478	1
Anhui-Jilin	1985	0
Anhui-Liaoning	1650	0
Anhui-Ningxia	2002	0
Anhui-Qinghai	2048	0
Anhui-Shaanxi	1156	0
Anhui-Shandong	613	1
Anhui-Shanghai	615	0
Anhui-Shanxi	1145	0
Anhui-Sichuan	1998	0
Anhui-Tianjin	973	0
Anhui-Tibet	3863	0
Anhui-Xinjiang	3724	0
Anhui-Yunnan	3098	0
Anhui-Zhejiang	451	1
Beijing-Chongqing	2087	0
Beijing-Fujian	2334	0
Beijing-Gansu	1811	0
Beijing-Guangdong	2289	0
Beijing-Guangxi	2561	0
Beijing-Guizhou	2539	0
Beijing-Hainan	3088	0
Beijing-Hebei	277	1
Beijing-Heilongjiang	1288	0
Beijing-Henan	689	0

(continued)

Table 3 (continued)

Province-Province	Distance between capitals (km)	Interprovincial adjacency
Beijing-Hubei	1225	0
Beijing-Hunan	1583	0
Beijing-Inner Mongolia	667	0
Beijing-Jiangsu	1160	0
Beijing-Jiangxi	1449	0
Beijing-Jilin	1046	0
Beijing-Liaoning	741	0
Beijing-Ningxia	1343	0
Beijing-Qinghai	2092	0
Beijing-Shaanxi	1159	0
Beijing-Shandong	497	0
Beijing-Shanghai	1463	0
Beijing-Shanxi	514	0
Beijing-Sichuan	2042	0
Beijing-Tianjin	137	1
Beijing-Tibet	4064	0
Beijing-Xinjiang	3768	0
Beijing-Yunnan	3178	0
Beijing-Zhejiang	1589	0
Chongqing-Fujian	2196	0
Chongqing-Gansu	1466	0
Chongqing-Guangdong	1670	0
Chongqing-Guangxi	1338	0
Chongqing-Guizhou	463	1
Chongqing-Hainan	1837	0
Chongqing-Hebei	1810	0
Chongqing-Heilongjiang	3431	0
Chongqing-Henan	1598	0
Chongqing-Hubei	1220	1
Chongqing-Hunan	1094	1
Chongqing-Inner Mongolia	2081	0
Chongqing-Jiangsu	1828	0
Chongqing-Jiangxi	1579	0
Chongqing-Jilin	3185	0
Chongqing-Liaoning	2827	0
Chongqing-Ningxia	1596	0
Chongqing-Qinghai	1682	0
Chongqing-Shaanxi	747	1
Chongqing-Shandong	1956	0
Chongqing-Shanghai	2167	0

(continued)

Table 3 (continued)

Province-Province	Distance between capitals (km)	Interprovincial adjacency
Chongqing-Shanxi	1441	0
Chongqing-Sichuan	338	1
Chongqing-Tianjin	2091	0
Chongqing-Tibet	3654	0
Chongqing-Xinjiang	3358	0
Chongqing-Yunnan	1101	0
Chongqing-Zhejiang	2312	0
Fujian-Gansu	3065	0
Fujian-Guangdong	1588	1
Fujian-Guangxi	1860	0
Fujian-Guizhou	1838	0
Fujian-Hainan	2374	0
Fujian-Hebei	1915	0
Fujian-Heilongjiang	3451	0
Fujian-Henan	1549	0
Fujian-Hubei	1013	0
Fujian-Hunan	984	0
Fujian-Inner Mongolia	3303	0
Fujian-Jiangsu	1174	0
Fujian-Jiangxi	622	1
Fujian-Jilin	3209	0
Fujian-Liaoning	2904	0
Fujian-Ningxia	3235	0
Fujian-Qinghai	3281	0
Fujian-Shaanxi	2389	0
Fujian-Shandong	1837	0
Fujian-Shanghai	1173	0
Fujian-Shanxi	2521	0
Fujian-Sichuan	2805	0
Fujian-Tianjin	2197	0
Fujian-Tibet	4887	0
Fujian-Xinjiang	4957	0
Fujian-Yunnan	2477	0
Fujian-Zhejiang	972	1
Gansu-Guangdong	2787	0
Gansu-Guangxi	3059	0
Gansu-Guizhou	2139	0
Gansu-Hainan	3596	0
Gansu-Hebei	1599	0
Gansu-Heilongjiang	3099	0

(continued)

Table 3 (continued)

Province-Province	Distance between capitals (km)	Interprovincial adjacency
Gansu-Henan	1187	0
Gansu-Hubei	1723	0
Gansu-Hunan	2081	0
Gansu-Inner Mongolia	1144	1
Gansu-Jiangsu	1182	0
Gansu-Jiangxi	2088	0
Gansu-Jilin	2952	0
Gansu-Liaoning	2552	0
Gansu-Ningxia	468	1
Gansu-Qinghai	215	1
Gansu-Shaanxi	676	1
Gansu-Shandong	1853	0
Gansu-Shanghai	2185	0
Gansu-Shanxi	1327	0
Gansu-Sichuan	1172	1
Gansu-Tianjin	1948	0
Gansu-Tibet	2188	0
Gansu-Xinjiang	1892	0
Gansu-Yunnan	2272	0
Gansu-Zhejiang	2311	0
Guangdong-Guangxi	1334	1
Guangdong-Guizhou	1560	0
Guangdong-Hainan	794	0
Guangdong-Hebei	2012	0
Guangdong-Heilongjiang	2928	0
Guangdong-Henan	1600	0
Guangdong-Hubei	1064	0
Guangdong-Hunan	706	1
Guangdong-Inner Mongolia	2962	0
Guangdong-Jiangsu	1804	0
Guangdong-Jiangxi	1022	1
Guangdong-Jilin	3341	0
Guangdong-Liaoning	3036	0
Guangdong-Ningxia	2957	0
Guangdong-Qinghai	3003	0
Guangdong-Shaanxi	2111	0
Guangdong-Shandong	2151	0
Guangdong-Shanghai	1803	0
Guangdong-Shanxi	2243	0
Guangdong-Sichuan	2527	0

(continued)

Table 3 (continued)

Province-Province	Distance between capitals (km)	Interprovincial adjacency
Guangdong-Tianjin	2431	0
Guangdong-Tibet	4980	0
Guangdong-Xinjiang	4679	0
Guangdong-Yunnan	2199	0
Guangdong-Zhejiang	1602	0
Guangxi-Guizhou	865	1
Guangxi-Hainan	739	0
Guangxi-Hebei	2262	0
Guangxi-Heilongjiang	3855	0
Guangxi-Henan	1870	0
Guangxi-Hubei	1336	0
Guangxi-Hunan	978	1
Guangxi-Inner Mongolia	3234	0
Guangxi-Jiangsu	2076	0
Guangxi-Jiangxi	1294	0
Guangxi-Jilin	6313	0
Guangxi-Liaoning	3411	0
Guangxi-Ningxia	3229	0
Guangxi-Qinghai	3275	0
Guangxi-Shaanxi	2383	0
Guangxi-Shandong	2538	0
Guangxi-Shanghai	2075	0
Guangxi-Shanxi	2515	0
Guangxi-Sichuan	1832	0
Guangxi-Tianjin	2703	0
Guangxi-Tibet	4992	0
Guangxi-Xinjiang	4951	0
Guangxi-Yunnan	1504	1
Guangxi-Zhejiang	1874	0
Guizhou-Hainan	1374	0
Guizhou-Hebei	2262	0
Guizhou-Heilongjiang	3833	0
Guizhou-Henan	1850	0
Guizhou-Hubei	1314	0
Guizhou-Hunan	956	1
Guizhou-Inner Mongolia	3100	0
Guizhou-Jiangsu	2054	0
Guizhou-Jiangxi	1272	0
Guizhou-Jilin	3591	0
Guizhou-Liaoning	3286	0

(continued)

Table 3 (continued)

Province-Province	Distance between capitals (km)	Interprovincial adjacency
Guizhou-Ningxia	2309	0
Guizhou-Qinghai	2355	0
Guizhou-Shaanxi	1809	0
Guizhou-Shandong	2516	0
Guizhou-Shanghai	2053	0
Guizhou-Shanxi	2450	0
Guizhou-Sichuan	967	1
Guizhou-Tianjin	2681	0
Guizhou-Tibet	4117	0
Guizhou-Xinjiang	3993	0
Guizhou-Yunnan	639	1
Guizhou-Zhejiang	1852	0
Hainan-Hebei	2811	0
Hainan-Heilongjiang	4433	0
Hainan-Henan	2399	0
Hainan-Hubei	1883	0
Hainan-Hunan	1501	0
Hainan-Inner Mongolia	3747	0
Hainan-Jiangsu	2597	0
Hainan-Jiangxi	1750	0
Hainan-Jilin	4187	0
Hainan-Liaoning	3925	0
Hainan-Ningxia	3716	0
Hainan-Qinghai	3802	0
Hainan-Shaanxi	2887	0
Hainan-Shandong	2795	0
Hainan-Shanghai	2574	0
Hainan-Shanxi	2976	0
Hainan-Sichuan	2829	0
Hainan-Tianjin	3198	0
Hainan-Tibet	5774	0
Hainan-Xinjiang	5478	0
Hainan-Yunnan	1567	0
Hainan-Zhejiang	2407	0
Hebei-Heilongjiang	1673	0
Hebei-Henan	412	1
Hebei-Hubei	948	0
Hebei-Hunan	1306	0
Hebei-Inner Mongolia	871	1
Hebei-Jiangsu	964	0

(continued)

Table 3 (continued)

Province-Province	Distance between capitals (km)	Interprovincial adjacency
Hebei-Jiangxi	1293	0
Hebei-Jilin	1431	0
Hebei-Liaoning	1126	1
Hebei-Ningxia	1547	0
Hebei-Qinghai	1815	0
Hebei-Shaanxi	923	0
Hebei-Shandong	301	1
Hebei-Shanghai	1267	0
Hebei-Shanxi	231	1
Hebei-Sichuan	1765	0
Hebei-Tianjin	419	0
Hebei-Tibet	3787	0
Hebei-Xinjiang	3491	0
Hebei-Yunnan	2901	0
Hebei-Zhejiang	1393	0
Heilongjiang-Henan	2085	0
Heilongjiang-Hubei	2519	0
Heilongjiang-Hunan	2877	0
Heilongjiang-Inner Mongolia	1955	1
Heilongjiang-Jiangsu	2277	0
Heilongjiang-Jiangxi	2689	0
Heilongjiang-Jilin	242	1
Heilongjiang-Liaoning	547	0
Heilongjiang-Ningxia	2631	0
Heilongjiang-Qinghai	3386	0
Heilongjiang-Shaanxi	2453	0
Heilongjiang-Shandong	1614	0
Heilongjiang-Shanghai	2577	0
Heilongjiang-Shanxi	1802	0
Heilongjiang-Sichuan	3336	0
Heilongjiang-Tianjin	1354	0
Heilongjiang-Tibet	5409	0
Heilongjiang-Xinjiang	5062	0
Heilongjiang-Yunnan	4472	0
Heilongjiang-Zhejiang	2706	0
Henan-Hubei	536	1
Henan-Hunan	894	0
Henan-Inner Mongolia	1362	0
Henan-Jiangsu	695	0
Henan-Jiangxi	927	0

(continued)

Table 3 (continued)

Province-Province	Distance between capitals (km)	Interprovincial adjacency
Henan-Jilin	1843	0
Henan-Liaoning	1538	0
Henan-Ningxia	1357	0
Henan-Qinghai	1403	0
Henan-Shaanxi	511	1
Henan-Shandong	666	1
Henan-Shanghai	998	0
Henan-Shanxi	577	1
Henan-Sichuan	1353	0
Henan-Tianjin	831	0
Henan-Tibet	3375	0
Henan-Xinjiang	3079	0
Henan-Yunnan	2489	0
Henan-Zhejiang	1124	0
Hubei-Hunan	358	1
Hubei-Inner Mongolia	1898	0
Hubei-Jiangsu	1231	0
Hubei-Jiangxi	391	1
Hubei-Jilin	2277	0
Hubei-Liaoning	1972	0
Hubei-Ningxia	1893	0
Hubei-Qinghai	1939	0
Hubei-Shaanxi	1047	1
Hubei-Shandong	1202	0
Hubei-Shanghai	1230	0
Hubei-Shanxi	1179	0
Hubei-Sichuan	1737	0
Hubei-Tianjin	1367	0
Hubei-Tibet	3911	0
Hubei-Xinjiang	3615	0
Hubei-Yunnan	1953	0
Hubei-Zhejiang	1029	0
Hunan-Inner Mongolia	2256	0
Hunan-Jiangsu	1200	0
Hunan-Jiangxi	418	1
Hunan-Jilin	2635	0
Hunan-Liaoning	2330	0
Hunan-Ningxia	2251	0
Hunan-Qinghai	2297	0
Hunan-Shaanxi	1405	0

(continued)

Table 3 (continued)

Province-Province	Distance between capitals (km)	Interprovincial adjacency
Hunan-Shandong	1560	0
Hunan-Shanghai	1189	0
Hunan-Shanxi	1537	0
Hunan-Sichuan	1923	0
Hunan-Tianjin	1725	0
Hunan-Tibet	4273	0
Hunan-Xinjiang	3973	0
Hunan-Yunnan	1595	0
Hunan-Zhejiang	998	0
Inner Mongolia-Jiangsu	1827	0
Inner Mongolia-Jiangxi	2674	0
Inner Mongolia-Jilin	1713	1
Inner Mongolia-Liaoning	1408	1
Inner Mongolia-Ningxia	676	1
Inner Mongolia-Qinghai	1360	0
Inner Mongolia-Shaanxi	1291	1
Inner Mongolia-Shandong	1164	0
Inner Mongolia-Shanghai	2130	0
Inner Mongolia-Shanxi	640	1
Inner Mongolia-Sichuan	2133	0
Inner Mongolia-Tianjin	801	0
Inner Mongolia-Tibet	3332	0
Inner Mongolia-Xinjiang	3035	0
Inner Mongolia-Yunnan	3233	0
Inner Mongolia-Zhejiang	2256	0
Jiangsu-Jiangxi	838	0
Jiangsu-Jilin	2035	0
Jiangsu-Liaoning	1730	0
Jiangsu-Ningxia	2052	0
Jiangsu-Qinghai	2095	0
Jiangsu-Shaanxi	1205	0
Jiangsu-Shandong	663	1
Jiangsu-Shanghai	303	1
Jiangsu-Shanxi	1195	0
Jiangsu-Sichuan	2048	0
Jiangsu-Tianjin	1023	0
Jiangsu-Tibet	4072	0
Jiangsu-Xinjiang	3774	0
Jiangsu-Yunnan	2693	0
Jiangsu-Zhejiang	429	1

(continued)

Table 3 (continued)

Province-Province	Distance between capitals (km)	Interprovincial adjacency
Jiangxi-Jilin	2456	0
Jiangxi-Liaoning	2151	0
Jiangxi-Ningxia	2258	0
Jiangxi-Qinghai	2304	0
Jiangxi-Shaanxi	1412	0
Jiangxi-Shandong	1137	0
Jiangxi-Shanghai	837	0
Jiangxi-Shanxi	1944	0
Jiangxi-Sichuan	2239	0
Jiangxi-Tianjin	1444	0
Jiangxi-Tibet	4101	0
Jiangxi-Xinjiang	4391	0
Jiangxi-Yunnan	1911	0
Jiangxi-Zhejiang	636	1
Jilin-Liaoning	305	1
Jilin-Ningxia	2389	0
Jilin-Qinghai	3144	0
Jilin-Shaanxi	2211	0
Jilin-Shandong	1373	0
Jilin-Shanghai	2335	0
Jilin-Shanxi	1560	0
Jilin-Sichuan	3094	0
Jilin-Tianjin	1012	0
Jilin-Tibet	5163	0
Jilin-Xinjiang	4820	0
Jilin-Yunnan	4230	0
Jilin-Zhejiang	2464	0
Liaoning-Ningxia	2084	0
Liaoning-Qinghai	2839	0
Liaoning-Shaanxi	1906	0
Liaoning-Shandong	1067	0
Liaoning-Shanghai	2033	0
Liaoning-Shanxi	1255	0
Liaoning-Sichuan	2789	0
Liaoning-Tianjin	707	0
Liaoning-Tibet	4901	0
Liaoning-Xinjiang	4515	0
Liaoning-Yunnan	3925	0
Liaoning-Zhejiang	2159	0
Ningxia-Qinghai	684	0

(continued)

Table 3 (continued)

Province-Province	Distance between capitals (km)	Interprovincial adjacency
Ningxia-Shaanxi	846	1
Ningxia-Shandong	1840	0
Ningxia-Shanghai	2355	0
Ningxia-Shanxi	1316	0
Ningxia-Sichuan	1342	0
Ningxia-Tianjin	1480	0
Ningxia-Tibet	2656	0
Ningxia-Xinjiang	2088	0
Ningxia-Yunnan	2442	0
Ningxia-Zhejiang	2481	0
Qinghai-Shaanxi	892	0
Qinghai-Shandong	2068	0
Qinghai-Shanghai	2401	0
Qinghai-Shanxi	1543	0
Qinghai-Sichuan	1388	1
Qinghai-Tianjin	2235	0
Qinghai-Tibet	1972	1
Qinghai-Xinjiang	2108	1
Qinghai-Yunnan	2488	0
Qinghai-Zhejiang	2527	0
Shaanxi-Shandong	1177	0
Shaanxi-Shanghai	1509	0
Shaanxi-Shanxi	651	1
Shaanxi-Sichuan	842	1
Shaanxi-Tianjin	1301	0
Shaanxi-Tibet	2964	0
Shaanxi-Xinjiang	2468	0
Shaanxi-Yunnan	1942	0
Shaanxi-Zhejiang	1635	0
Shandong-Shanghai	966	0
Shandong-Shanxi	532	0
Shandong-Sichuan	2019	0
Shandong-Tianjin	360	0
Shandong-Tibet	3925	0
Shandong-Xinjiang	3745	0
Shandong-Yunnan	3119	0
Shandong-Zhejiang	1092	0
Shanghai-Shanxi	1498	0
Shanghai-Sichuan	2351	0
Shanghai-Tianjin	1326	0

(continued)

Table 3 (continued)

Province-Province	Distance between capitals (km)	Interprovincial adjacency
Shanghai-Tibet	4373	0
Shanghai-Xinjiang	4077	0
Shanghai-Yunnan	3069	0
Shanghai-Zhejiang	201	0
Shanxi-Sichuan	1493	0
Shanxi-Tianjin	650	0
Shanxi-Tibet	3515	0
Shanxi-Xinjiang	3219	0
Shanxi-Yunnan	2593	0
Shanxi-Zhejiang	1624	0
Sichuan-Tianjin	2185	0
Sichuan-Tibet	3360	1
Sichuan-Xinjiang	3026	0
Sichuan-Yunnan	1100	1
Sichuan-Zhejiang	2552	0
Tianjin-Tibet	4174	0
Tianjin-Xinjiang	3911	0
Tianjin-Yunnan	3320	0
Tianjin-Zhejiang	1452	0
Tibet-Xinjiang	4080	1
Tibet-Yunnan	4460	1
Tibet-Zhejiang	4308	0
Xinjiang-Yunnan	4126	0
Xinjiang-Zhejiang	4065	0
Yunnan-Zhejiang	2868	0

A total number of 56 ethnic groups are included in the index of interprovincial ethnic linkages. Specifically, they are Achang, Bai, Blang, Bonan, Buyi, Dai, Daur, De'ang, Derung, Dong, Dongxiang, Ewenki, Gaoshan, Gelao, Han, Hani, Hezhe, Hui, Jing, Jingpo, Jino, Kazak, Kirgiz, Korean, Lahu, Lhoba, Li, Lisu, Manchu, Maonan, Miao, Monba, Mongol, Mulao, Naxi, Nu, Oroqen, Pumi, Qiang, Russian, Salar, She, Shui, Tajik, Tatar, Tibetan, Tu, Tujia, Uygur, Uzbek, Va, Xibe, Yao, Yi, Yugur, and Zhuang. In addition to the above 56 ethnic groups, other unknown ethnic groups and foreigners with Chinese citizenship also exist in China. However, since these ethnic identities are still not known and that there are no specific statistical data on the nationalities of these foreigners for each province, our measurement of interprovincial ethnic linkages will not take into account of these populations.

Table 4 Index of interprovincial ethnic linkages (2000 and 2010)

Province-Province	2000	2010	Changes (±)
Anhui-Beijing	0.9636	0.9658	+0.0022
Anhui-Chongqing	0.9366	0.9343	−0.0023
Anhui-Fujian	0.9870	0.9828	−0.0043
Anhui-Gansu	0.9190	0.9119	−0.0071
Anhui-Guangdong	0.9864	0.9818	−0.0046
Anhui-Guangxi	0.6179	0.6301	+0.0122
Anhui-Guizhou	0.6274	0.6611	+0.0337
Anhui-Hainan	0.8283	0.8380	+0.0097
Anhui-Hebei	0.9631	0.9647	+0.0016
Anhui-Heilongjiang	0.9554	0.9673	+0.0119
Anhui-Henan	0.9940	0.9942	+0.0002
Anhui-Hubei	0.9585	0.9591	+0.0006
Anhui-Hunan	0.9012	0.9028	+0.0016
Anhui-Inner Mongolia	0.7984	0.8018	+0.0034
Anhui-Jiangsu	0.9960	0.9961	+0.0001
Anhui-Jiangxi	0.9944	0.9945	+0.0001
Anhui-Jilin	0.9140	0.9253	+0.0113
Anhui-Liaoning	0.8459	0.8544	+0.0085
Anhui-Ningxia	0.6610	0.6550	−0.0060
Anhui-Qinghai	0.5470	0.5367	−0.0102
Anhui-Shaanxi	0.9979	0.9978	−0.0001
Anhui-Shandong	0.9993	0.9987	−0.0007
Anhui-Shanghai	0.9978	0.9926	−0.0052
Anhui-Shanxi	0.9960	0.9957	−0.0004
Anhui-Sichuan	0.9523	0.9414	−0.0109
Anhui-Tianjin	0.9796	0.9810	+0.0014
Anhui-Tibet	0.0649	0.0868	+0.0219
Anhui-Xinjiang	0.4125	0.4114	−0.0011
Anhui-Yunnan	0.6725	0.6728	+0.0003
Anhui-Zhejiang	0.9926	0.9797	−0.0129
Beijing-Chongqing	0.9377	0.9366	−0.0011
Beijing-Fujian	0.9624	0.9668	+0.0045
Beijing-Gansu	0.9320	0.9204	−0.0116
Beijing-Guangdong	0.9601	0.9644	+0.0044
Beijing-Guangxi	0.6192	0.6321	+0.0130
Beijing-Guizhou	0.6309	0.6661	+0.0352
Beijing-Hainan	0.8300	0.8409	+0.0109
Beijing-Hebei	0.9867	0.9869	+0.0003
Beijing-Heilongjiang	0.9779	0.9847	+0.0069
Beijing-Henan	0.9694	0.9711	+0.0017
Beijing-Hubei	0.9598	0.9614	+0.0016
Beijing-Hunan	0.9028	0.9053	+0.0025

(continued)

Table 4 (continued)

Province-Province	2000	2010	Changes (±)
Beijing-Inner Mongolia	0.8237	0.8273	+0.0036
Beijing-Jiangsu	0.9603	0.9638	+0.0035
Beijing-Jiangxi	0.9581	0.9606	+0.0025
Beijing-Jilin	0.9365	0.9482	+0.0117
Beijing-Liaoning	0.8691	0.8775	+0.0084
Beijing-Ningxia	0.6775	0.6675	−0.0100
Beijing-Qinghai	0.5633	0.5499	−0.0134
Beijing-Shaanxi	0.9618	0.9642	+0.0024
Beijing-Shandong	0.9638	0.9667	+0.0029
Beijing-Shanghai	0.9631	0.9696	+0.0064
Beijing-Shanxi	0.9600	0.9618	+0.0018
Beijing-Sichuan	0.9537	0.9437	−0.0100
Beijing-Tianjin	0.9838	0.9837	−0.0001
Beijing-Tibet	0.0657	0.0877	+0.0221
Beijing-Xinjiang	0.4294	0.4253	−0.0041
Beijing-Yunnan	0.6839	0.6828	−0.0011
Beijing-Zhejiang	0.9596	0.9646	+0.0050
Chongqing-Fujian	0.9380	0.9394	+0.0015
Chongqing-Gansu	0.9137	0.9070	−0.0067
Chongqing-Guangdong	0.9396	0.9391	−0.0006
Chongqing-Guangxi	0.6282	0.6404	+0.0122
Chongqing-Guizhou	0.6801	0.7152	+0.0351
Chongqing-Hainan	0.8361	0.8463	+0.0103
Chongqing-Hebei	0.9367	0.9343	−0.0024
Chongqing-Heilongjiang	0.9365	0.9339	−0.0026
Chongqing-Henan	0.9365	0.9339	−0.0025
Chongqing-Hubei	0.9766	0.9740	−0.0026
Chongqing-Hunan	0.9581	0.9583	+0.0002
Chongqing-Inner Mongolia	0.7930	0.7969	+0.0039
Chongqing-Jiangsu	0.9371	0.9357	−0.0014
Chongqing-Jiangxi	0.9365	0.9341	−0.0023
Chongqing-Jilin	0.9096	0.9215	+0.0118
Chongqing-Liaoning	0.8406	0.8495	+0.0088
Chongqing-Ningxia	0.6557	0.6503	−0.0054
Chongqing-Qinghai	0.5418	0.5321	−0.0097
Chongqing-Shaanxi	0.9363	0.9342	−0.0021
Chongqing-Shandong	0.9366	0.9341	−0.0024
Chongqing-Shanghai	0.9373	0.9376	+0.0003
Chongqing-Shanxi	0.9365	0.9339	−0.0026
Chongqing-Sichuan	0.9389	0.9372	−0.0017

(continued)

Table 4 (continued)

Province-Province	2000	2010	Changes (±)
Chongqing-Tianjin	0.9371	0.9353	−0.0018
Chongqing-Tibet	0.0621	0.0833	+0.0212
Chongqing-Xinjiang	0.4082	0.4074	−0.0008
Chongqing-Yunnan	0.6838	0.6849	+0.0010
Chongqing-Zhejiang	0.9389	0.9445	+0.0056
Fujian-Gansu	0.9166	0.9099	−0.0067
Fujian-Guangdong	0.9864	0.9872	+0.0008
Fujian-Guangxi	0.6191	0.6345	+0.0154
Fujian-Guizhou	0.6290	0.6671	+0.0381
Fujian-Hainan	0.8298	0.8423	+0.0125
Fujian-Hebei	0.9610	0.9628	+0.0018
Fujian-Heilongjiang	0.9552	0.9675	+0.0123
Fujian-Henan	0.9869	0.9825	−0.0045
Fujian-Hubei	0.9602	0.9645	+0.0044
Fujian-Hunan	0.9029	0.9084	+0.0055
Fujian-Inner Mongolia	0.7959	0.7998	+0.0039
Fujian-Jiangsu	0.9862	0.9831	−0.0031
Fujian-Jiangxi	0.9859	0.9819	−0.0041
Fujian-Jilin	0.9125	0.9244	+0.0118
Fujian-Liaoning	0.8435	0.8524	+0.0088
Fujian-Ningxia	0.6587	0.6532	−0.0055
Fujian-Qinghai	0.5447	0.5351	−0.0097
Fujian-Shaanxi	0.9868	0.9826	−0.0042
Fujian-Shandong	0.9869	0.9827	−0.0043
Fujian-Shanghai	0.9878	0.9875	−0.0004
Fujian-Shanxi	0.9857	0.9810	−0.0047
Fujian-Sichuan	0.9533	0.9445	−0.0088
Fujian-Tianjin	0.9778	0.9801	+0.0023
Fujian-Tibet	0.0648	0.0863	+0.0215
Fujian-Xinjiang	0.4113	0.4105	−0.0009
Fujian-Yunnan	0.6710	0.6750	+0.0040
Fujian-Zhejiang	0.9896	0.9900	+0.0003
Gansu-Guangdong	0.9138	0.9073	−0.0065
Gansu-Guangxi	0.6179	0.6298	+0.0119
Gansu-Guizhou	0.6283	0.6616	+0.0334
Gansu-Hainan	0.8284	0.8384	+0.0100
Gansu-Hebei	0.9224	0.9151	−0.0073
Gansu-Heilongjiang	0.9177	0.9097	−0.0080
Gansu-Henan	0.9247	0.9173	−0.0074
Gansu-Hubei	0.9146	0.9079	−0.0067
Gansu-Hunan	0.9011	0.9025	+0.0013
Gansu-Inner Mongolia	0.8026	0.8059	+0.0033

(continued)

Table 4 (continued)

Province-Province	2000	2010	Changes (±)
Gansu-Jiangsu	0.9151	0.9083	−0.0068
Gansu-Jiangxi	0.9135	0.9066	−0.0069
Gansu-Jilin	0.9150	0.9115	−0.0035
Gansu-Liaoning	0.8475	0.8552	+0.0077
Gansu-Ningxia	0.7039	0.6996	−0.0043
Gansu-Qinghai	0.6094	0.6031	−0.0063
Gansu-Shaanxi	0.9174	0.9107	−0.0067
Gansu-Shandong	0.9191	0.9125	−0.0066
Gansu-Shanghai	0.9176	0.9108	−0.0067
Gansu-Shanxi	0.9156	0.9083	−0.0073
Gansu-Sichuan	0.9303	0.9267	−0.0036
Gansu-Tianjin	0.9320	0.9212	−0.0108
Gansu-Tibet	0.0827	0.1067	+0.0240
Gansu-Xinjiang	0.4570	0.4551	−0.0019
Gansu-Yunnan	0.6854	0.6857	+0.0003
Gansu-Zhejiang	0.9135	0.9074	−0.0061
Guangdong-Guangxi	0.6290	0.6449	+0.0159
Guangdong-Guizhou	0.6300	0.6657	+0.0357
Guangdong-Hainan	0.8374	0.8469	+0.0095
Guangdong-Hebei	0.9582	0.9602	+0.0020
Guangdong-Heilongjiang	0.9524	0.9655	+0.0131
Guangdong-Henan	0.9863	0.9815	−0.0048
Guangdong-Hubei	0.9612	0.9638	+0.0026
Guangdong-Hunan	0.9062	0.9100	+0.0037
Guangdong-Inner Mongolia	0.7932	0.7972	+0.0040
Guangdong-Jiangsu	0.9871	0.9837	−0.0033
Guangdong-Jiangxi	0.9866	0.9818	−0.0048
Guangdong-Jilin	0.9098	0.9218	+0.0120
Guangdong-Liaoning	0.8408	0.8498	+0.0091
Guangdong-Ningxia	0.6559	0.6505	−0.0053
Guangdong-Qinghai	0.5420	0.5324	−0.0096
Guangdong-Shaanxi	0.9862	0.9817	−0.0045
Guangdong-Shandong	0.9864	0.9819	−0.0045
Guangdong-Shanghai	0.9874	0.9868	−0.0006
Guangdong-Shanxi	0.9864	0.9815	−0.0049
Guangdong-Sichuan	0.9532	0.9437	−0.0096
Guangdong-Tianjin	0.9752	0.9775	+0.0024
Guangdong-Tibet	0.0622	0.0837	+0.0215
Guangdong-Xinjiang	0.4086	0.4078	−0.0008
Guangdong-Yunnan	0.6780	0.6825	+0.0045

(continued)

Table 4 (continued)

Province-Province	2000	2010	Changes (±)
Guangdong-Zhejiang	0.9899	0.9878	−0.0020
Guangxi-Guizhou	0.6408	0.6522	+0.0113
Guangxi-Hainan	0.6340	0.6453	+0.0113
Guangxi-Hebei	0.6183	0.6302	+0.0119
Guangxi-Heilongjiang	0.6179	0.6297	+0.0118
Guangxi-Henan	0.6179	0.6298	+0.0119
Guangxi-Hubei	0.6227	0.6342	+0.0115
Guangxi-Hunan	0.6468	0.6581	+0.0114
Guangxi-Inner Mongolia	0.6180	0.6301	+0.0121
Guangxi-Jiangsu	0.6185	0.6316	+0.0131
Guangxi-Jiangxi	0.6174	0.6296	+0.0122
Guangxi-Jilin	0.6179	0.6297	+0.0119
Guangxi-Liaoning	0.6180	0.6300	+0.0120
Guangxi-Ningxia	0.6180	0.6304	+0.0124
Guangxi-Qinghai	0.5422	0.5324	−0.0098
Guangxi-Shaanxi	0.6178	0.6299	+0.0121
Guangxi-Shandong	0.6179	0.6299	+0.0120
Guangxi-Shanghai	0.6185	0.6331	+0.0145
Guangxi-Shanxi	0.6179	0.6298	+0.0118
Guangxi-Sichuan	0.6199	0.6323	+0.0124
Guangxi-Tianjin	0.6185	0.6310	+0.0125
Guangxi-Tibet	0.0624	0.0837	+0.0212
Guangxi-Xinjiang	0.4082	0.4072	−0.0010
Guangxi-Yunnan	0.6610	0.6724	+0.0114
Guangxi-Zhejiang	0.6199	0.6397	+0.0199
Guizhou-Hainan	0.6366	0.6731	+0.0365
Guizhou-Hebei	0.6293	0.6627	+0.0334
Guizhou-Heilongjiang	0.6275	0.6595	+0.0319
Guizhou-Henan	0.6284	0.6617	+0.0333
Guizhou-Hubei	0.6653	0.6976	+0.0324
Guizhou-Hunan	0.7118	0.7445	+0.0327
Guizhou-Inner Mongolia	0.6290	0.6627	+0.0337
Guizhou-Jiangsu	0.6251	0.6593	+0.0341
Guizhou-Jiangxi	0.6241	0.6570	+0.0329
Guizhou-Jilin	0.6288	0.6612	+0.0324
Guizhou-Liaoning	0.6290	0.6625	+0.0335
Guizhou-Ningxia	0.6286	0.6567	+0.0282
Guizhou-Qinghai	0.5480	0.5389	−0.0091
Guizhou-Shaanxi	0.6266	0.6595	+0.0329
Guizhou-Shandong	0.6276	0.6612	+0.0337

(continued)

Table 4 (continued)

Province-Province	2000	2010	Changes (±)
Guizhou-Shanghai	0.6275	0.6646	+0.0371
Guizhou-Shanxi	0.6248	0.6572	+0.0324
Guizhou-Sichuan	0.6504	0.6845	+0.0341
Guizhou-Tianjin	0.6296	0.6639	+0.0343
Guizhou-Tibet	0.0656	0.0875	+0.0219
Guizhou-Xinjiang	0.4146	0.4143	−0.0003
Guizhou-Yunnan	0.6862	0.7217	+0.0355
Guizhou-Zhejiang	0.6277	0.6743	+0.0465
Hainan-Hebei	0.8288	0.8386	+0.0099
Hainan-Heilongjiang	0.8284	0.8381	+0.0098
Hainan-Henan	0.8283	0.8382	+0.0099
Hainan-Hubei	0.8324	0.8418	+0.0094
Hainan-Hunan	0.8381	0.8482	+0.0100
Hainan-Inner Mongolia	0.7940	0.7983	+0.0043
Hainan-Jiangsu	0.8289	0.8397	+0.0107
Hainan-Jiangxi	0.8274	0.8370	+0.0096
Hainan-Jilin	0.8284	0.8382	+0.0098
Hainan-Liaoning	0.8285	0.8384	+0.0100
Hainan-Ningxia	0.6567	0.6517	−0.0050
Hainan-Qinghai	0.5428	0.5336	−0.0092
Hainan-Shaanxi	0.8281	0.8381	+0.0100
Hainan-Shandong	0.8283	0.8382	+0.0098
Hainan-Shanghai	0.8293	0.8416	+0.0123
Hainan-Shanxi	0.8284	0.8378	+0.0094
Hainan-Sichuan	0.8305	0.8408	+0.0103
Hainan-Tianjin	0.8293	0.8398	+0.0105
Hainan-Tibet	0.0629	0.0845	+0.0216
Hainan-Xinjiang	0.4090	0.4087	−0.0003
Hainan-Yunnan	0.6839	0.6841	+0.0002
Hainan-Zhejiang	0.8296	0.8457	+0.0161
Hebei-Heilongjiang	0.9863	0.9835	−0.0028
Hebei-Henan	0.9666	0.9679	+0.0013
Hebei-Hubei	0.9587	0.9592	+0.0005
Hebei-Hunan	0.9015	0.9027	+0.0012
Hebei-Inner Mongolia	0.8245	0.8250	+0.0004
Hebei-Jiangsu	0.9594	0.9613	+0.0020
Hebei-Jiangxi	0.9576	0.9595	+0.0018
Hebei-Jilin	0.9481	0.9579	+0.0099
Hebei-Liaoning	0.8807	0.8872	+0.0065
Hebei-Ningxia	0.6680	0.6622	−0.0058
Hebei-Qinghai	0.5534	0.5429	−0.0105

(continued)

Table 4 (continued)

Province-Province	2000	2010	Changes (±)
Hebei-Shaanxi	0.9614	0.9632	+0.0018
Hebei-Shandong	0.9632	0.9652	+0.0020
Hebei-Shanghai	0.9618	0.9643	+0.0025
Hebei-Shanxi	0.9596	0.9609	+0.0013
Hebei-Sichuan	0.9527	0.9417	−0.0110
Hebei-Tianjin	0.9725	0.9753	+0.0028
Hebei-Tibet	0.0650	0.0869	+0.0219
Hebei-Xinjiang	0.4184	0.4170	−0.0014
Hebei-Yunnan	0.6758	0.6757	+0.0000
Hebei-Zhejiang	0.9580	0.9603	+0.0024
Heilongjiang-Henan	0.9565	0.9683	+0.0118
Heilongjiang-Hubei	0.9533	0.9588	+0.0056
Heilongjiang-Hunan	0.9011	0.9022	+0.0011
Heilongjiang-Inner Mongolia	0.8234	0.8221	−0.0014
Heilongjiang-Jiangsu	0.9538	0.9666	+0.0128
Heilongjiang-Jiangxi	0.9522	0.9648	+0.0127
Heilongjiang-Jilin	0.9557	0.9548	−0.0008
Heilongjiang-Liaoning	0.8818	0.8797	−0.0021
Heilongjiang-Ningxia	0.6633	0.6566	−0.0067
Heilongjiang-Qinghai	0.5499	0.5380	−0.0119
Heilongjiang-Shaanxi	0.9555	0.9678	+0.0123
Heilongjiang-Shandong	0.9558	0.9684	+0.0126
Heilongjiang-Shanghai	0.9563	0.9697	+0.0134
Heilongjiang-Shanxi	0.9542	0.9666	+0.0124
Heilongjiang-Sichuan	0.9525	0.9413	−0.0112
Heilongjiang-Tianjin	0.9631	0.9766	+0.0136
Heilongjiang-Tibet	0.0648	0.0851	+0.0203
Heilongjiang-Xinjiang	0.4153	0.4125	−0.0028
Heilongjiang-Yunnan	0.6706	0.6699	−0.0007
Heilongjiang-Zhejiang	0.9522	0.9656	+0.0134
Henan-Hubei	0.9585	0.9589	+0.0004
Henan-Hunan	0.9011	0.9024	+0.0013
Henan-Inner Mongolia	0.8028	0.8060	+0.0032
Henan-Jiangsu	0.9901	0.9905	+0.0004
Henan-Jiangxi	0.9885	0.9889	+0.0004
Henan-Jilin	0.9152	0.9263	+0.0112
Henan-Liaoning	0.8477	0.8554	+0.0077
Henan-Ningxia	0.6669	0.6603	−0.0065
Henan-Qinghai	0.5528	0.5421	−0.0107
Henan-Shaanxi	0.9924	0.9928	+0.0004

(continued)

Table 4 (continued)

Province-Province	2000	2010	Changes (±)
Henan-Shandong	0.9941	0.9947	+0.0006
Henan-Shanghai	0.9924	0.9930	+0.0006
Henan-Shanxi	0.9905	0.9906	+0.0000
Henan-Sichuan	0.9525	0.9414	−0.0111
Henan-Tianjin	0.9854	0.9863	+0.0009
Henan-Tibet	0.0648	0.0867	+0.0219
Henan-Xinjiang	0.4182	0.4167	−0.0015
Henan-Yunnan	0.6776	0.6775	−0.0001
Henan-Zhejiang	0.9885	0.9793	−0.0092
Hubei-Hunan	0.9422	0.9431	+0.0009
Hubei-Inner Mongolia	0.7940	0.7977	+0.0037
Hubei-Jiangsu	0.9591	0.9604	+0.0014
Hubei-Jiangxi	0.9575	0.9582	+0.0008
Hubei-Jilin	0.9106	0.9224	+0.0118
Hubei-Liaoning	0.8416	0.8504	+0.0088
Hubei-Ningxia	0.6567	0.6511	−0.0056
Hubei-Qinghai	0.5428	0.5329	−0.0099
Hubei-Shaanxi	0.9584	0.9591	+0.0006
Hubei-Shandong	0.9585	0.9590	+0.0005
Hubei-Shanghai	0.9593	0.9625	+0.0032
Hubei-Shanxi	0.9586	0.9589	+0.0003
Hubei-Sichuan	0.9543	0.9439	−0.0104
Hubei-Tianjin	0.9591	0.9601	+0.0010
Hubei-Tibet	0.0628	0.0841	+0.0213
Hubei-Xinjiang	0.4092	0.4083	−0.0009
Hubei-Yunnan	0.6718	0.6718	+0.0000
Hubei-Zhejiang	0.9602	0.9669	+0.0067
Hunan-Inner Mongolia	0.7943	0.7977	+0.0034
Hunan-Jiangsu	0.9017	0.9040	+0.0023
Hunan-Jiangxi	0.8999	0.9017	+0.0017
Hunan-Jilin	0.9011	0.9023	+0.0012
Hunan-Liaoning	0.8419	0.8504	+0.0085
Hunan-Ningxia	0.6570	0.6512	−0.0058
Hunan-Qinghai	0.5431	0.5330	−0.0102
Hunan-Shaanxi	0.9009	0.9025	+0.0016
Hunan-Shandong	0.9011	0.9024	+0.0013
Hunan-Shanghai	0.9021	0.9064	+0.0043
Hunan-Shanxi	0.9011	0.9023	+0.0012
Hunan-Sichuan	0.9032	0.9052	+0.0020
Hunan-Tianjin	0.9020	0.9039	+0.0019
Hunan-Tibet	0.0635	0.0843	+0.0209

(continued)

Table 4 (continued)

Province-Province	2000	2010	Changes (±)
Hunan-Xinjiang	0.4097	0.4084	−0.0013
Hunan-Yunnan	0.6997	0.7016	+0.0019
Hunan-Zhejiang	0.9029	0.9141	+0.0112
Inner Mongolia-Jiangsu	0.7945	0.7983	+0.0038
Inner Mongolia-Jiangxi	0.7928	0.7964	+0.0036
Inner Mongolia-Jilin	0.8258	0.8246	−0.0012
Inner Mongolia-Liaoning	0.8371	0.8359	−0.0012
Inner Mongolia-Ningxia	0.6690	0.6634	−0.0056
Inner Mongolia-Qinghai	0.5696	0.5593	−0.0103
Inner Mongolia-Shaanxi	0.7967	0.8004	+0.0037
Inner Mongolia-Shandong	0.7986	0.8028	+0.0042
Inner Mongolia-Shanghai	0.7971	0.8021	+0.0049
Inner Mongolia-Shanxi	0.7949	0.7980	+0.0031
Inner Mongolia-Sichuan	0.7944	0.7982	+0.0038
Inner Mongolia-Tianjin	0.8092	0.8141	+0.0049
Inner Mongolia-Tibet	0.0650	0.0871	+0.0221
Inner Mongolia-Xinjiang	0.4253	0.4233	−0.0020
Inner Mongolia-Yunnan	0.6764	0.6768	+0.0005
Inner Mongolia-Zhejiang	0.7929	0.7974	+0.0044
Jiangsu-Jiangxi	0.9976	0.9965	−0.0011
Jiangsu-Jilin	0.9111	0.9229	+0.0118
Jiangsu-Liaoning	0.8421	0.8509	+0.0088
Jiangsu-Ningxia	0.6572	0.6517	−0.0055
Jiangsu-Qinghai	0.5433	0.5335	−0.0098
Jiangsu-Shaanxi	0.9975	0.9976	+0.0000
Jiangsu-Shandong	0.9957	0.9952	−0.0005
Jiangsu-Shanghai	0.9971	0.9928	−0.0043
Jiangsu-Shanxi	0.9992	0.9976	−0.0015
Jiangsu-Sichuan	0.9528	0.9427	−0.0101
Jiangsu-Tianjin	0.9760	0.9784	+0.0024
Jiangsu-Tibet	0.0635	0.0847	+0.0212
Jiangsu-Xinjiang	0.4090	0.4086	−0.0004
Jiangsu-Yunnan	0.6691	0.6704	+0.0013

(continued)

Table 4 (continued)

Province-Province	2000	2010	Changes (±)
Jiangsu-Zhejiang	0.9933	0.9817	−0.0116
Jiangxi-Jilin	0.9095	0.9212	+0.0117
Jiangxi-Liaoning	0.8404	0.8491	+0.0087
Jiangxi-Ningxia	0.6555	0.6497	−0.0058
Jiangxi-Qinghai	0.5414	0.5315	−0.0100
Jiangxi-Shaanxi	0.9959	0.9958	−0.0001
Jiangxi-Shandong	0.9940	0.9933	−0.0007
Jiangxi-Shanghai	0.9949	0.9895	−0.0054
Jiangxi-Shanxi	0.9979	0.9974	−0.0005
Jiangxi-Sichuan	0.9511	0.9402	−0.0109
Jiangxi-Tianjin	0.9741	0.9758	+0.0017
Jiangxi-Tibet	0.0616	0.0828	+0.0212
Jiangxi-Xinjiang	0.4069	0.4061	−0.0008
Jiangxi-Yunnan	0.6669	0.6675	+0.0006
Jiangxi-Zhejiang	0.9943	0.9812	−0.0131
Jilin-Liaoning	0.8939	0.8953	+0.0015
Jilin-Ningxia	0.6645	0.6583	−0.0062
Jilin-Qinghai	0.5536	0.5418	−0.0119
Jilin-Shaanxi	0.9134	0.9251	+0.0117
Jilin-Shandong	0.9145	0.9264	+0.0119
Jilin-Shanghai	0.9137	0.9268	+0.0131
Jilin-Shanxi	0.9115	0.9229	+0.0113
Jilin-Sichuan	0.9110	0.9227	+0.0118
Jilin-Tianjin	0.9217	0.9346	+0.0129
Jilin-Tibet	0.0649	0.0867	+0.0218
Jilin-Xinjiang	0.4186	0.4159	−0.0027
Jilin-Yunnan	0.6719	0.6717	−0.0002
Jilin-Zhejiang	0.9095	0.9219	+0.0124
Liaoning-Ningxia	0.6663	0.6598	−0.0064
Liaoning-Qinghai	0.5650	0.5530	−0.0120
Liaoning-Shaanxi	0.8443	0.8531	+0.0088
Liaoning-Shandong	0.8462	0.8555	+0.0093
Liaoning-Shanghai	0.8447	0.8548	+0.0101
Liaoning-Shanxi	0.8425	0.8507	+0.0082
Liaoning-Sichuan	0.8419	0.8507	+0.0088
Liaoning-Tianjin	0.8543	0.8639	+0.0096
Liaoning-Tibet	0.0649	0.0869	+0.0220
Liaoning-Xinjiang	0.4238	0.4208	−0.0030
Liaoning-Yunnan	0.6736	0.6732	−0.0004
Liaoning-Zhejiang	0.8405	0.8499	+0.0094
Ningxia-Qinghai	0.7002	0.6824	−0.0178

(continued)

Table 4 (continued)

Province-Province	2000	2010	Changes (±)
Ningxia-Shaanxi	0.6594	0.6535	−0.0059
Ningxia-Shandong	0.6610	0.6553	−0.0057
Ningxia-Shanghai	0.6596	0.6548	−0.0048
Ningxia-Shanxi	0.6575	0.6511	−0.0064
Ningxia-Sichuan	0.6570	0.6515	−0.0056
Ningxia-Tianjin	0.6776	0.6685	−0.0091
Ningxia-Tibet	0.0650	0.0874	+0.0224
Ningxia-Xinjiang	0.4544	0.4533	−0.0011
Ningxia-Yunnan	0.6712	0.6655	−0.0057
Ningxia-Zhejiang	0.6556	0.6507	−0.0049
Qinghai-Shaanxi	0.5453	0.5353	−0.0100
Qinghai-Shandong	0.5470	0.5371	−0.0100
Qinghai-Shanghai	0.5458	0.5366	−0.0092
Qinghai-Shanxi	0.5435	0.5328	−0.0106
Qinghai-Sichuan	0.5585	0.5518	−0.0066
Qinghai-Tianjin	0.5616	0.5483	−0.0133
Qinghai-Tibet	0.2906	0.3323	+0.0417
Qinghai-Xinjiang	0.4626	0.4610	−0.0016
Qinghai-Yunnan	0.5603	0.5504	−0.0099
Qinghai-Zhejiang	0.5417	0.5326	−0.0092
Shaanxi-Shandong	0.9978	0.9972	−0.0005
Shaanxi-Shanghai	0.9982	0.9927	−0.0055
Shaanxi-Shanxi	0.9979	0.9975	−0.0004
Shaanxi-Sichuan	0.9521	0.9414	−0.0107
Shaanxi-Tianjin	0.9779	0.9794	+0.0016
Shaanxi-Tibet	0.0647	0.0865	+0.0218
Shaanxi-Xinjiang	0.4107	0.4099	−0.0008
Shaanxi-Yunnan	0.6706	0.6710	+0.0005
Shaanxi-Zhejiang	0.9923	0.9795	−0.0129
Shandong-Shanghai	0.9979	0.9934	−0.0045
Shandong-Shanxi	0.9960	0.9950	−0.0009
Shandong-Sichuan	0.9523	0.9412	−0.0110
Shandong-Tianjin	0.9798	0.9819	+0.0021
Shandong-Tibet	0.0648	0.0868	+0.0220
Shandong-Xinjiang	0.4124	0.4117	−0.0007
Shandong-Yunnan	0.6724	0.6729	+0.0004
Shandong-Zhejiang	0.9925	0.9797	−0.0128
Shanghai-Shanxi	0.9968	0.9907	−0.0062
Shanghai-Sichuan	0.9530	0.9442	−0.0089
Shanghai-Tianjin	0.9789	0.9827	+0.0038
Shanghai-Tibet	0.0652	0.0867	+0.0214

(continued)

Table 4 (continued)

Province-Province	2000	2010	Changes (±)
Shanghai-Xinjiang	0.4116	0.4120	+0.0003
Shanghai-Yunnan	0.6711	0.6743	+0.0032
Shanghai-Zhejiang	0.9934	0.9847	−0.0087
Shanxi-Sichuan	0.9523	0.9411	−0.0112
Shanxi-Tianjin	0.9761	0.9770	+0.0010
Shanxi-Tibet	0.0633	0.0842	+0.0209
Shanxi-Xinjiang	0.4089	0.4075	−0.0015
Shanxi-Yunnan	0.6688	0.6687	+0.0000
Shanxi-Zhejiang	0.9925	0.9794	−0.0131
Sichuan-Tianjin	0.9531	0.9426	−0.0105
Sichuan-Tibet	0.0786	0.1030	+0.0244
Sichuan-Xinjiang	0.4094	0.4088	−0.0006
Sichuan-Yunnan	0.6993	0.7074	+0.0080
Sichuan-Zhejiang	0.9529	0.9445	−0.0084
Tianjin-Tibet	0.0652	0.0874	+0.0222
Tianjin-Xinjiang	0.4270	0.4230	−0.0040
Tianjin-Yunnan	0.6831	0.6824	−0.0007
Tianjin-Zhejiang	0.9749	0.9777	+0.0028
Tibet-Xinjiang	0.0659	0.0896	+0.0237
Tibet-Yunnan	0.0691	0.0910	+0.0218
Tibet-Zhejiang	0.0620	0.0839	+0.0219
Xinjiang-Yunnan	0.4235	0.4225	−0.0010
Xinjiang-Zhejiang	0.4083	0.4081	−0.0003
Yunnan-Zhejiang	0.6691	0.6780	+0.0088

Interprovincial Freight Exchange via National Railway (2000 and 2010)

The data reported in Table 5 are cited from "China Communications Yearbook" (2000 and 2010, edited by China Association of Communications and Transportation and the National Development and Reform Commission of the PRC and published by China Communications Yearbook Press in 2001 and 2011, respectively). The data on the freight exchange via local or privately-owned railways are not considered in this table. Blank space indicates that the figure is not large enough to be measured with the smallest unit in the table, or data are unknown or are not available. It should be noted that interprovincial freight exchange via national railways only accounts a small portion of the whole interprovincial freight exchange, especially in China's nearby provinces where railway is a less economical means for transportation than highway. Along with the fast development of transprovincial highways in China, interprovincial freight transportation via highways is growing at even higher rates than that via national railways.

Table 5 Interprovincial freight exchange via national railway (2000 and 2010)

Province *i*-Province *j*	2000 (in thousand tons)		2010 (in thousand tons)	
	Export	Import	Export	Import
Anhui-Beijing	160	210	220	130
Anhui-Chongqing	60	80	210	80
Anhui-Fujian	1720	380	1720	240
Anhui-Gansu	150	230	380	700
Anhui-Guangdong	1200	220	1100	70
Anhui-Guangxi	170	310	500	510
Anhui-Guizhou	70	100	340	200
Anhui-Hainan			10	
Anhui-Hebei	320	600	1050	600
Anhui-Heilongjiang	160	430	240	1380
Anhui-Henan	600	3060	1090	5450
Anhui-Hubei	260	560	3620	740
Anhui-Hunan	330	150	2790	290
Anhui-Inner Mongolia	70	400	230	680
Anhui-Jiangsu	17,170	3040	19,550	6360
Anhui-Jiangxi	2150	360	8060	290
Anhui-Jilin	190	320	220	790
Anhui-Liaoning	320	670	320	460
Anhui-Ningxia	10	60	40	140
Anhui-Qinghai	30	90	180	350
Anhui-Shaanxi	240	750	360	1700
Anhui-Shandong	980	4290	3430	5470
Anhui-Shanghai	2040	580	1790	390
Anhui-Shanxi	150	3890	350	7480
Anhui-Sichuan	220	310	900	400
Anhui-Tianjin	110	140	200	70
Anhui-Tibet			80	20
Anhui-Xinjiang	70	130	180	320
Anhui-Yunnan	100	110	570	230
Anhui-Zhejiang	5550	450	8230	380
Beijing-Chongqing	100	40	170	50
Beijing-Fujian	120	170	50	80
Beijing-Gansu	160	90	80	180
Beijing-Guangdong	410	620	140	70
Beijing-Guangxi	70	140	90	60
Beijing-Guizhou	60	60	160	30
Beijing-Hainan				

(continued)

Table 5 (continued)

Province *i*-Province *j*	2000 (in thousand tons)		2010 (in thousand tons)	
	Export	Import	Export	Import
Beijing-Hebei	5180	14,720	4750	12,580
Beijing-Heilongjiang	330	1710	140	1200
Beijing-Henan	520	550	260	490
Beijing-Hubei	210	280	230	290
Beijing-Hunan	220	180	120	190
Beijing-Inner Mongolia	540	3760	810	5530
Beijing-Jiangsu	560	350	280	210
Beijing-Jiangxi	160	70	60	120
Beijing-Jilin	230	1010	240	630
Beijing-Liaoning	1290	1790	1030	1300
Beijing-Ningxia	70	340	30	240
Beijing-Qinghai	40	20	40	180
Beijing-Shaanxi	410	170	310	420
Beijing-Shandong	880	2270	850	330
Beijing-Shanghai	250	410	70	260
Beijing-Shanxi	820	14,030	840	9200
Beijing-Sichuan	300	310	330	330
Beijing-Tianjin	5180	3180	3230	3500
Beijing-Tibet			10	
Beijing-Xinjiang	130	190	200	450
Beijing-Yunnan	150	110	110	90
Beijing-Zhejiang	260	160	200	170
Chongqing-Fujian	80	200	180	390
Chongqing-Gansu	60	520	100	750
Chongqing-Guangdong	800	1390	1090	2720
Chongqing-Guangxi	1220	620	1610	2270
Chongqing-Guizhou	1200	1260	1490	3660
Chongqing-Hainan			40	30
Chongqing-Hebei	100	480	240	1080
Chongqing-Heilongjiang	50	220	200	400
Chongqing-Henan	140	630	320	1410
Chongqing-Hubei	390	570	340	690
Chongqing-Hunan	130	400	320	1040
Chongqing-Inner Mongolia	20	80	70	430
Chongqing-Jiangsu	160	260	340	360
Chongqing-Jiangxi	40	150	120	500
Chongqing-Jilin	20	120	50	330
Chongqing-Liaoning	70	230	90	210

(continued)

Table 5 (continued)

Province *i*-Province *j*	2000 (in thousand tons)		2010 (in thousand tons)	
	Export	Import	Export	Import
Chongqing-Ningxia	20	40	20	170
Chongqing-Qinghai	10	70	30	430
Chongqing-Shaanxi	120	340	130	870
Chongqing-Shandong	160	280	290	740
Chongqing-Shanghai	70	150	70	210
Chongqing-Shanxi	40	80	70	700
Chongqing-Sichuan	3650	2820	6050	6240
Chongqing-Tianjin	40	100	60	290
Chongqing-Tibet			20	30
Chongqing-Xinjiang	60	270	180	460
Chongqing-Yunnan	240	540	620	1460
Chongqing-Zhejiang	150	260	220	400
Fujian-Gansu	130	200	230	280
Fujian-Guangdong	380	80	2060	820
Fujian-Guangxi	60	360	120	360
Fujian-Guizhou	150	310	400	820
Fujian-Hainan				10
Fujian-Hebei	270	640	180	230
Fujian-Heilongjiang	270	410	80	340
Fujian-Henan	470	1810	460	2020
Fujian-Hubei	570	1270	490	1170
Fujian-Hunan	1170	1440	730	1020
Fujian-Inner Mongolia	90	180	70	200
Fujian-Jiangsu	770	1120	250	570
Fujian-Jiangxi	1070	3430	8500	5500
Fujian-Jilin	120	210	30	400
Fujian-Liaoning	280	170	70	30
Fujian-Ningxia	50	60	70	70
Fujian-Qinghai	60	70	70	140
Fujian-Shaanxi	300	360	620	120
Fujian-Shandong	320	1280	230	670
Fujian-Shanghai	470	470	440	200
Fujian-Shanxi	140	1140	100	1020
Fujian-Sichuan	390	300	1120	310
Fujian-Tianjin	70	140	20	10
Fujian-Tibet			20	
Fujian-Xinjiang	210	200	500	320
Fujian-Yunnan	260	280	440	590

(continued)

Table 5 (continued)

Province *i*-Province *j*	2000 (in thousand tons)		2010 (in thousand tons)	
	Export	Import	Export	Import
Fujian-Zhejiang	2620	790	1800	1140
Gansu-Guangdong	790	350	1690	470
Gansu-Guangxi	100	70	250	270
Gansu-Guizhou	130	40	320	990
Gansu-Hainan			10	
Gansu-Hebei	360	450	1590	470
Gansu-Heilongjiang	80	190	150	380
Gansu-Henan	1240	930	3090	2930
Gansu-Hubei	490	120	2490	950
Gansu-Hunan	320	150	810	180
Gansu-Inner Mongolia	330	1270	690	2280
Gansu-Jiangsu	1000	750	2520	1490
Gansu-Jiangxi	90	40	440	80
Gansu-Jilin	60	70	160	140
Gansu-Liaoning	320	300	320	400
Gansu-Ningxia	670	4440	1210	7550
Gansu-Qinghai	1570	1570	1510	1930
Gansu-Shaanxi	2210	720	6360	2570
Gansu-Shandong	360	440	2220	1560
Gansu-Shanghai	310	150	1080	140
Gansu-Shanxi	340	540	830	1340
Gansu-Sichuan	2900	790	3310	720
Gansu-Tianjin	500	260	610	1330
Gansu-Tibet			230	20
Gansu-Xinjiang	870	9970	1950	20,340
Gansu-Yunnan	400	520	490	660
Gansu-Zhejiang	380	170	1660	170
Guangdong-Guangxi	3630	3880	12,560	3660
Guangdong-Guizhou	2550	4500	5710	6730
Guangdong-Hainan			110	150
Guangdong-Hebei	810	1940	260	800
Guangdong-Heilongjiang	790	750	100	160
Guangdong-Henan	1050	6250	1060	5480
Guangdong-Hubei	1970	4200	1300	4310
Guangdong-Hunan	7170	13,950	15,380	10,540
Guangdong-Inner Mongolia	160	690	90	400
Guangdong-Jiangsu	480	1820	120	590
Guangdong-Jiangxi	1340	2840	3080	2480

(continued)

Table 5 (continued)

Province *i*-Province *j*	2000 (in thousand tons)		2010 (in thousand tons)	
	Export	Import	Export	Import
Guangdong-Jilin	310	560	20	110
Guangdong-Liaoning	890	580	10	100
Guangdong-Ningxia	130	150	110	420
Guangdong-Qinghai	90	210	170	410
Guangdong-Shaanxi	820	1130	1220	500
Guangdong-Shandong	590	1720	140	380
Guangdong-Shanghai	390	470	190	190
Guangdong-Shanxi	390	2170	290	1680
Guangdong-Sichuan	2330	2090	6540	3270
Guangdong-Tianjin	210	290	20	20
Guangdong-Tibet			20	
Guangdong-Xinjiang	650	650	970	1150
Guangdong-Yunnan	3530	2360	5950	4210
Guangdong-Zhejiang	830	610	260	310
Guangxi-Guizhou	2320	10,610	7940	28,410
Guangxi-Hainan			230	170
Guangxi-Hebei	490	860	390	650
Guangxi-Heilongjiang	100	350	50	350
Guangxi-Henan	710	2620	1260	3160
Guangxi-Hubei	690	1410	1430	2460
Guangxi-Hunan	1750	3050	8570	5650
Guangxi-Inner Mongolia	40	190	70	540
Guangxi-Jiangsu	590	360	530	350
Guangxi-Jiangxi	420	660	960	1230
Guangxi-Jilin	60	160	60	650
Guangxi-Liaoning	280	210	130	120
Guangxi-Ningxia	20	30	50	50
Guangxi-Qinghai	10	80	70	130
Guangxi-Shaanxi	120	780	450	430
Guangxi-Shandong	340	540	430	390
Guangxi-Shanghai	370	200	430	430
Guangxi-Shanxi	120	1080	220	950
Guangxi-Sichuan	2030	2110	5640	2870
Guangxi-Tianjin	80	100	60	60
Guangxi-Tibet			20	10
Guangxi-Xinjiang	40	70	160	190
Guangxi-Yunnan	2040	2860	9110	7950
Guangxi-Zhejiang	890	310	930	240

(continued)

Table 5 (continued)

Province *i*-Province *j*	2000 (in thousand tons)		2010 (in thousand tons)	
	Export	Import	Export	Import
Guizhou-Hainan			110	10
Guizhou-Hebei	480	210	490	410
Guizhou-Heilongjiang	50	150	330	360
Guizhou-Henan	330	530	760	1170
Guizhou-Hubei	250	730	940	1280
Guizhou-Hunan	1480	1040	6710	2310
Guizhou-Inner Mongolia	30	70	160	210
Guizhou-Jiangsu	400	280	710	450
Guizhou-Jiangxi	340	250	1890	1430
Guizhou-Jilin	30	50	320	370
Guizhou-Liaoning	270	120	280	100
Guizhou-Ningxia	40	20	210	30
Guizhou-Qinghai	10	10	50	40
Guizhou-Shaanxi	60	180	310	390
Guizhou-Shandong	480	220	1670	490
Guizhou-Shanghai	260	150	200	330
Guizhou-Shanxi	140	80	280	220
Guizhou-Sichuan	1710	1820	4910	2620
Guizhou-Tianjin	180	50	80	100
Guizhou-Tibet				
Guizhou-Xinjiang	40	140	280	190
Guizhou-Yunnan	940	1680	4050	1230
Guizhou-Zhejiang	440	230	730	420
Hainan-Hebei				10
Hainan-Heilongjiang				
Hainan-Henan			20	70
Hainan-Hubei			10	120
Hainan-Hunan			40	90
Hainan-Inner Mongolia				10
Hainan-Jiangsu				10
Hainan-Jiangxi			50	40
Hainan-Jilin				
Hainan-Liaoning				
Hainan-Ningxia				
Hainan-Qinghai				10
Hainan-Shaanxi				10
Hainan-Shandong				10
Hainan-Shanghai				

(continued)

Table 5 (continued)

Province *i*-Province *j*	2000 (in thousand tons)		2010 (in thousand tons)	
	Export	Import	Export	Import
Hainan-Shanxi				20
Hainan-Sichuan			60	140
Hainan-Tianjin				
Hainan-Tibet				
Hainan-Xinjiang				
Hainan-Yunnan			40	50
Hainan-Zhejiang				10
Hebei-Heilongjiang	2860	4340	1290	3040
Hebei-Henan	2770	960	3300	1640
Hebei-Hubei	1450	1150	2680	1190
Hebei-Hunan	1180	410	1370	330
Hebei-Inner Mongolia	2600	10,640	1900	109,520
Hebei-Jiangsu	3300	700	2930	4160
Hebei-Jiangxi	600	160	860	200
Hebei-Jilin	1980	2440	1170	1030
Hebei-Liaoning	5430	5090	4860	6290
Hebei-Ningxia	160	530	210	14,540
Hebei-Qinghai	150	100	60	1240
Hebei-Shaanxi	550	740	1230	3100
Hebei-Shandong	3990	4760	12,040	20,740
Hebei-Shanghai	1470	280	1430	210
Hebei-Shanxi	3910	105,090	4680	300,860
Hebei-Sichuan	770	670	2570	880
Hebei-Tianjin	14,030	4280	30,070	18,120
Hebei-Tibet			70	
Hebei-Xinjiang	360	900	750	940
Hebei-Yunnan	290	500	540	760
Hebei-Zhejiang	1340	320	1600	180
Heilongjiang-Henan	1060	440	1250	480
Heilongjiang-Hubei	410	320	720	590
Heilongjiang-Hunan	440	280	880	110
Heilongjiang-Inner Mongolia	2330	9170	3840	39,590
Heilongjiang-Jiangsu	1610	610	1060	560
Heilongjiang-Jiangxi	260	80	690	70
Heilongjiang-Jilin	18,330	4710	17,240	12,580
Heilongjiang-Liaoning	26,210	7040	40,960	11,960
Heilongjiang-Ningxia	130	60	110	60
Heilongjiang-Qinghai	50	30	140	100

(continued)

Table 5 (continued)

Province *i*-Province *j*	2000 (in thousand tons)		2010 (in thousand tons)	
	Export	Import	Export	Import
Heilongjiang-Shaanxi	490	180	560	160
Heilongjiang-Shandong	3990	2590	2030	2150
Heilongjiang-Shanghai	590	300	580	140
Heilongjiang-Shanxi	720	550	630	530
Heilongjiang-Sichuan	850	230	1920	210
Heilongjiang-Tianjin	2120	570	680	470
Heilongjiang-Tibet			50	
Heilongjiang-Xinjiang	150	80	240	110
Heilongjiang-Yunnan	210	80	650	310
Heilongjiang-Zhejiang	680	410	1230	130
Henan-Hubei	22,970	2210	24,780	2490
Henan-Hunan	5480	600	10,120	710
Henan-Inner Mongolia	450	920	380	2110
Henan-Jiangsu	9210	3320	8470	12,620
Henan-Jiangxi	3250	160	5070	330
Henan-Jilin	400	490	320	630
Henan-Liaoning	820	1250	2360	2130
Henan-Ningxia	160	170	70	430
Henan-Qinghai	410	400	1200	1310
Henan-Shaanxi	2120	1930	960	4770
Henan-Shandong	4650	3420	5160	17,410
Henan-Shanghai	1270	470	1180	470
Henan-Shanxi	1710	7170	1280	25,400
Henan-Sichuan	1760	960	5000	1030
Henan-Tianjin	410	540	200	1090
Henan-Tibet			250	30
Henan-Xinjiang	340	2740	970	4250
Henan-Yunnan	360	650	1250	770
Henan-Zhejiang	2650	190	2350	230
Hubei-Hunan	2630	1570	4690	1350
Hubei-Inner Mongolia	100	420	350	950
Hubei-Jiangsu	560	560	1070	750
Hubei-Jiangxi	1530	490	2040	1460
Hubei-Jilin	180	170	430	540
Hubei-Liaoning	340	410	480	610
Hubei-Ningxia	40	240	90	330
Hubei-Qinghai	40	100	180	1430
Hubei-Shaanxi	570	3020	1690	10,380

(continued)

Table 5 (continued)

Province *i*-Province *j*	2000 (in thousand tons)		2010 (in thousand tons)	
	Export	Import	Export	Import
Hubei-Shandong	1690	1220	2710	3910
Hubei-Shanghai	220	270	180	250
Hubei-Shanxi	610	7950	620	20,010
Hubei-Sichuan	1680	2430	4160	3950
Hubei-Tianjin	290	180	230	230
Hubei-Tibet			70	
Hubei-Xinjiang	130	850	680	950
Hubei-Yunnan	640	150	1000	410
Hubei-Zhejiang	660	220	980	210
Hunan-Inner Mongolia	70	430	70	1360
Hunan-Jiangsu	470	530	550	1030
Hunan-Jiangxi	2020	1580	3650	5830
Hunan-Jilin	160	170	50	1180
Hunan-Liaoning	360	370	160	520
Hunan-Ningxia	50	70	50	240
Hunan-Qinghai	30	190	30	600
Hunan-Shaanxi	200	870	400	2680
Hunan-Shandong	320	840	940	1700
Hunan-Shanghai	730	400	530	540
Hunan-Shanxi	180	2320	280	8490
Hunan-Sichuan	540	820	1950	1670
Hunan-Tianjin	160	130	100	160
Hunan-Tibet			10	20
Hunan-Xinjiang	120	120	230	580
Hunan-Yunnan	530	390	680	1220
Hunan-Zhejiang	1470	1160	1940	310
Inner Mongolia-Jiangsu	1490	220	1810	280
Inner Mongolia-Jiangxi	200	20	670	30
Inner Mongolia-Jilin	5280	1480	29,560	1830
Inner Mongolia-Liaoning	10,740	4790	70,060	4850
Inner Mongolia-Ningxia	1120	720	1480	890
Inner Mongolia-Qinghai	220	160	280	1790
Inner Mongolia-Shaanxi	530	50	1190	220
Inner Mongolia-Shandong	3560	820	4360	1740
Inner Mongolia-Shanghai	710	100	1330	180
Inner Mongolia-Shanxi	1610	2390	1360	2670
Inner Mongolia-Sichuan	560	140	1770	190
Inner Mongolia-Tianjin	8520	700	10,270	4620

(continued)

Table 5 (continued)

Province *i*-Province *j*	2000 (in thousand tons)		2010 (in thousand tons)	
	Export	Import	Export	Import
Inner Mongolia-Tibet			20	
Inner Mongolia-Xinjiang	160	400	530	720
Inner Mongolia-Yunnan	60	100	150	260
Inner Mongolia-Zhejiang	800	120	1640	80
Jiangsu-Jiangxi	670	620	2630	310
Jiangsu-Jilin	460	650	310	520
Jiangsu-Liaoning	760	1420	370	480
Jiangsu-Ningxia	90	200	320	350
Jiangsu-Qinghai	400	400	2000	1760
Jiangsu-Shaanxi	580	3140	3100	6740
Jiangsu-Shandong	1360	10,380	2510	6070
Jiangsu-Shanghai	2360	360	710	170
Jiangsu-Shanxi	360	18,500	6560	27,880
Jiangsu-Sichuan	1020	1220	2030	950
Jiangsu-Tianjin	320	380	130	90
Jiangsu-Tibet			50	
Jiangsu-Xinjiang	470	800	1760	2500
Jiangsu-Yunnan	500	440	810	800
Jiangsu-Zhejiang	2680	250	1560	300
Jiangxi-Jilin	60	210	60	1690
Jiangxi-Liaoning	170	260	200	160
Jiangxi-Ningxia	10	50	30	40
Jiangxi-Qinghai	10	20	20	250
Jiangxi-Shaanxi	60	560	80	3500
Jiangxi-Shandong	250	1400	440	2600
Jiangxi-Shanghai	970	660	820	490
Jiangxi-Shanxi	40	1870	100	4550
Jiangxi-Sichuan	340	220	800	460
Jiangxi-Tianjin	30	180	70	60
Jiangxi-Tibet			10	10
Jiangxi-Xinjiang	50	80	150	290
Jiangxi-Yunnan	120	540	350	860
Jiangxi-Zhejiang	4120	2370	4900	7210
Jilin-Liaoning	16,250	8540	23,800	15,550
Jilin-Ningxia	10	30	50	140
Jilin-Qinghai	30	10	70	100
Jilin-Shaanxi	130	50	270	90
Jilin-Shandong	1590	1620	930	1540

(continued)

Table 5 (continued)

Province *i*-Province *j*	2000 (in thousand tons)		2010 (in thousand tons)	
	Export	Import	Export	Import
Jilin-Shanghai	510	300	250	240
Jilin-Shanxi	280	830	300	1440
Jilin-Sichuan	650	150	1650	160
Jilin-Tianjin	780	380	410	410
Jilin-Tibet				
Jilin-Xinjiang	130	50	120	110
Jilin-Yunnan	170	90	690	340
Jilin-Zhejiang	740	220	1400	100
Liaoning-Ningxia	110	940	150	1460
Liaoning-Qinghai	180	90	130	150
Liaoning-Shaanxi	390	230	890	160
Liaoning-Shandong	2320	2350	2110	2260
Liaoning-Shanghai	540	410	190	130
Liaoning-Shanxi	830	11,620	1080	17,070
Liaoning-Sichuan	850	410	810	350
Liaoning-Tianjin	3080	610	2720	530
Liaoning-Tibet			10	
Liaoning-Xinjiang	200	260	330	400
Liaoning-Yunnan	170	190	240	250
Liaoning-Zhejiang	690	400	310	170
Ningxia-Qinghai	410	50	550	240
Ningxia-Shaanxi	1430	80	640	530
Ningxia-Shandong	120	190	630	800
Ningxia-Shanghai	300	50	370	70
Ningxia-Shanxi	80	190	240	280
Ningxia-Sichuan	740	220	5450	240
Ningxia-Tianjin	1450	240	1130	1010
Ningxia-Tibet				
Ningxia-Xinjiang	230	240	1450	1210
Ningxia-Yunnan	50	50	70	290
Ningxia-Zhejiang	70	50	480	20
Qinghai-Shaanxi	390	230	740	380
Qinghai-Shandong	220	160	1190	1230
Qinghai-Shanghai	80	30	430	70
Qinghai-Shanxi	210	350	970	730
Qinghai-Sichuan	360	270	1120	210
Qinghai-Tianjin	150	130	210	140
Qinghai-Tibet			1010	50

(continued)

Table 5 (continued)

Province *i*-Province *j*	2000 (in thousand tons)		2010 (in thousand tons)	
	Export	Import	Export	Import
Qinghai-Xinjiang	60	420	90	1010
Qinghai-Yunnan	30	30	190	350
Qinghai-Zhejiang	80	50	550	60
Shaanxi-Shandong	890	670	9480	3320
Shaanxi-Shanghai	470	450	520	420
Shaanxi-Shanxi	510	1390	1500	2510
Shaanxi-Sichuan	2650	1600	6540	950
Shaanxi-Tianjin	340	310	220	460
Shaanxi-Tibet			70	10
Shaanxi-Xinjiang	260	1100	460	2310
Shaanxi-Yunnan	430	620	1060	750
Shaanxi-Zhejiang	570	190	1480	150
Shandong-Shanghai	1980	390	670	290
Shandong-Shanxi	2850	36,030	27,790	92,070
Shandong-Sichuan	800	820	2240	1260
Shandong-Tianjin	970	680	780	780
Shandong-Tibet			60	
Shandong-Xinjiang	420	770	1840	2770
Shandong-Yunnan	320	500	830	1400
Shandong-Zhejiang	6500	390	4880	140
Shanghai-Shanxi	140	2120	140	2010
Shanghai-Sichuan	630	430	1250	760
Shanghai-Tianjin	220	230	280	30
Shanghai-Tibet			10	
Shanghai-Xinjiang	350	220	550	580
Shanghai-Yunnan	270	280	410	660
Shanghai-Zhejiang	780	1320	510	930
Shanxi-Sichuan	830	350	2930	300
Shanxi-Tianjin	34,980	1200	27,400	3870
Shanxi-Tibet			30	
Shanxi-Xinjiang	170	530	1140	720
Shanxi-Yunnan	70	410	210	310
Shanxi-Zhejiang	4370	120	3280	140
Sichuan-Tianjin	420	350	450	760
Sichuan-Tibet			190	100
Sichuan-Xinjiang	470	1660	570	2960
Sichuan-Yunnan	2730	2700	5410	7660
Sichuan-Zhejiang	700	440	1030	800

(continued)

Table 5 (continued)

Province *i*-Province *j*	2000 (in thousand tons)		2010 (in thousand tons)	
	Export	Import	Export	Import
Tianjin-Tibet			30	
Tianjin-Xinjiang	690	1020	900	1370
Tianjin-Yunnan	110	190	250	130
Tianjin-Zhejiang	210	110	40	60
Tibet-Xinjiang				30
Tibet-Yunnan				
Tibet-Zhejiang				40
Xinjiang-Yunnan	410	190	1060	550
Xinjiang-Zhejiang	430	320	1880	760
Yunnan-Zhejiang	590	350	830	570

In Table 5, the terms "export" and "import" are defined as to represent goods that are freighted from Province *i* to Province *j* and from Province *j* Province *i*, respectively. Notice that "re-exports" may exist in China's interprovincial trade. They are generated by either the unavailability of or the inconvenient access to national railways. For example, in 2000 the freight exchange between Anhui and Hainan Provinces, whose data are not reported in the "Anhui-Hainan" entry, may possibly be conducted via railway from Anhui to Guangdong and via other land/sea route from Guangdong to Hainan. In this case, the amount of the freight exchange should not be included in the "export" or the "import" of the "Anhui-Guangdong" entry for the year 2000. Unfortunately, we are not able to identify such kind of "re-exports" in the table.

Appendix A
Quantifying the Industrial Comparative Advantages by Province

In order to have a better understanding of the comparative (dis)advantages of China's provinces, let us calculate the location quotient of China's provinces.

The Location Quotient Technique is the most commonly utilized spatial economic analysis method. It was developed in part to offer a slightly more complex model to the variety of analytical tools available to economic base analysts (See, for example, Isserman 1977). A recent case study of China's provinces can be found in Guo (2013, pp. 164–165). This technique compares the local economy to a reference economy, in the process attempting to identify specializations in the local economy. Location quotient compares the regional share of economic activity in a particular industry to the national share of economic activity in the same industry. The result reveals the degree of regional specialization in each industry.

If the location quotient for a particular industry is less than one, the region is less specialized than the nation, while location quotients greater than one reveal greater specialization of the industry in the local economy than in the national economy. Also, observing location quotients over time show if an industry is becoming more or less specialized in the region.

To calculate any location quotient the following formula is applied. Note that in this formula we are comparing the regional economy (often a province) to the national economy. The location quotient (*LQ*) of region j in industry i can be calculated as:

$$LQ(i,j) = \frac{\text{Provincial employment in industry } i \big/ \text{Total provincial employment}}{\text{National employment in industry } i \big/ \text{Total national employment}}$$

Mathematically, if x_{ij} is the employment of the ith industry ($i = 1, 2, \ldots$) in the jth province ($j = 1, 2, \ldots$), the values of *LQ* can be calculated as follows:

$$LQ(i,j) = \frac{x_{ij} \big/ \sum_i x_{ij}}{\sum_j x_{ij} \big/ \sum_i \sum_j x_{ij}}$$

R. Guo et al., *Multiregional Economic Development in China*,
DOI 10.1007/978-3-662-46620-9

Interpreting the Location Quotient (LQ_{ij}) is very simple. Only three general outcomes are possible when calculating location quotients: (i.e., $LQ_{ij} < 1$, $LQ_{ij} = 1$, and $LQ_{ij} > 1$). Their implications are as follows:

- If LQ_{ij} is less than one, it suggests that province *j* is less than expected for industry *i*. Therefore, industry *j* is not even meeting local demand for a given good or service; in other words, it has comparative advantages.
- If LQ_{ij} is equal to one, it suggests that province *j* is exactly sufficient to meet the local demand for a given industry *i*. Therefore, industry *j* is meeting local demand for the given good or service; in other words, it has no comparative (dis)advantages.
- If LQ_{ij} is greater than one, it suggests that province *j* is greater than expected and it is therefore assumed that there is an "extra" part of goods and services for industry *i*. This extra economy then must export their goods and services to other areas; in other words, industry *i* has comparative disadvantages.

References

Guo R (2013) Understanding the chinese economies. Academic Press/Elsevier, Oxford and Waltham, MA (available at: http://www.elsevierdirect.com/companions/9780123978264)

Isserman AM (1977) The Location quotient approach for estimating regional economic impacts. J Am Inst Plan 43:33–41

Appendix B
Quantifying the Index of Interprovincial Ethnic Linkages

The index of interprovincial ethnic linkages can be constructed in different ways. The simplest method is to use a dummy index; i.e., using '1' for provinces to share a common ethnic group with each other, and using '0' otherwise. This method cannot precisely measure the extent to which provinces are ethnically linked each other.

In this book, a comprehensive method is used to construct ethnic linkage indexes. Suppose that the population shares of China's 56 ethnic groups are expressed by $(x_1, x_2, \ldots, x_{56})$ and $(y_1, y_2, \ldots, y_{56})$ for provinces X and Y, respectively. x_i and y_i (where, $x_i \geq 0$ and $y_i \geq 0$) belong to the same ethnic group. Mathematically, the ethnic linkage index between the provinces X and Y can be measured according to the following formula:

$$\text{Linkage} = \sum_{i=1}^{56} \min(x_i, y_i)$$

In the above equation, min (•) denotes the minimization of the variables within parentheses. The values of LINKAGE range between 0 and 1. In the extreme cases, when LINKAGE = 1, the two provinces have a common ethnic structure (i.e., for all i, $x_i = y_i$); when LINKAGE = 0, the two provinces do not have any ethnic linkage with each other (i.e., for all i, x_i (or y_i) = 0). In the other words, greater values of LINKAGE indicate greater ethnic linkage between two provinces. This formula has been used in Guo (2004, 2006, p. 123) and Noland (2005).

Several other methods can also be used (Boisso and Ferrantino (1997), for example, use $\sum x_i y_i$ as the construct of similarity index). However, the equation we use in this book can prevent the index of ethnic linkages from further reduction when the values of x_i and y_i are small.

R. Guo et al., *Multiregional Economic Development in China*,
DOI 10.1007/978-3-662-46620-9

References

Boisso D, Ferrantino M (1997) Economic distance, cultural distance and openness in international trade: empirical puzzles. J Econ Integr 12:456–484

Guo R (2004) How culture influences foreign trade—evidence from the US and China. J Socio Econ 33(6):785–812

Guo R (2006) Cultural influences on economic analysis—theory and empirical evidence. Palgrave-Macmillan, New York

Noland M (2005) Affinity and international trade. Working paper series no. WP 05-3, Institute for International Economics, Washington

Kolibri 360 GmbH
Ferdinand-Jühlke-Straße 7
99095 Erfurt, Deutschland
produktsicherheit@kolibri360.de